COMPUTING ESSENTIALS

DON CASSEL

PRENTICE HALL, Englewood Cliffs, New Jersey 07632

Library of Congress Cataloging-in-Publication Data

Cassel, Don
  Computing essentials / Don Cassel.
    p.   cm.
  Includes index.
  ISBN 0-13-179086-2
  1. Computers. 2. Electronic data processing. I. Title.
QA76.5.C3853 1994
004—dc20   93-28149
                                                        CIP

Editorial/production supervision: *bookworks*
Interior design: *Lorraine Mullaney*
Manufacturing buyer: *Patrice Fraccio*
Photo research: *Teri Stratford*
Photo editor: *Lori Morris-Nantz*

© 1994 by Prentice-Hall, Inc.
A Paramount Communications Company
Englewood Cliffs, New Jersey 07632

All rights reserved. No part of this book may be
reproduced, in any form or by any means,
without permission in writing from the publisher.

Printed in the United States of America

10 9 8 7 6 5 4 3 2 1

ISBN 0-13-179086-2

Prentice-Hall International (UK) Limited, *London*
Prentice-Hall of Australia Pty. Limited, *Sydney*
Prentice-Hall Canada Inc., *Toronto*
Prentice-Hall Hispanoamericana, S.A., *Mexico*
Prentice-Hall of India Private Limited, *New Delhi*
Prentice-Hall of Japan, Inc., *Tokyo*
Simon & Schuster Asia Pte. Ltd., *Singapore*
Editora Prentice-Hall do Brasil, Ltda., *Rio de Janeiro*

BRIEF CONTENTS

Part I INTRODUCTION TO COMPUTERS

| 1 | The World of Computers | 1 |

Part II COMPUTER HARDWARE

2	Computer Processors	35
3	Input and Output	61
4	Secondary Storage	93
5	Computers and Communication	117

Part III SYSTEMS AND SOFTWARE

6	Operating Systems and Software Platforms	149
7	Application Software	175
8	Word Processing and Desktop Publishing	205
9	Spreadsheet Software	233
10	Integrated, Graphics, and Other Software	255
11	Database Systems	275

Part IV DESIGNING AND IMPLEMENTING INFORMATION SYSTEMS

12	Programming Concepts	299
13	Systems Analysis and Design	329
14	Management Support Systems	359

Part V CURRENT ISSUES

| 15 | Issues and Trends | 383 |

APPENDICES

A	ORIGINS: A History of Computing and Information Systems	405
B	Checklist for Buying a Computer	421
C	Number Systems	433

CONTENTS

PREFACE   **xv**

Chapter 1 THE WORLD OF COMPUTERS   **1**

  A View of the Chapter Ahead   1
  Introduction   2
  Why Do We Need Computers?   4
  What Is a Computer?   6
  Information Systems   8
    Data and Information   8
    Computers and Information Systems   9
    Information Systems Departments   10
  Factors to Consider for Computer Use   12
  What Is a Computer System?   13
    Sizes of Computers   13
  Computer Components   16
    The Processor   16
    Other Components in a Computer   18
  Input and Output Devices   18
    Input   20
    Output   20
  Computer Software   20
    Systems Software   21
    Application Software   21
      Word Processing   22   Spreadsheets   22   Database Management Systems (DBMS)   24
      Graphics   25   Integrated Software   26
    Communications   27
    Multimedia Software   28
  Computers and Your World   29
  Chapter Summary   30
  Important Terms and Concepts   31
  Self-Testing Questions   31

Chapter 2 COMPUTER PROCESSORS   **35**

  A View of the Chapter Ahead   35
  Introduction   36

Processor Characteristics   36
   Bits, Bytes, and Words   36
   Bits   37
   Bytes   39
   Words   40
Components   40
   Speed   42
Computer Codes   42
ICs and Microprocessors   43
Memory   45
   RAM   45
   ROM   46
   Addressing Memory   47
RISC Microprocessors   47
Attaching Devices to the Computer   49
Compatibles   49
The Shrinking Computer   52
Mainframe Processors   53
   Speed   53
   Memory Size   53
   Software   54
   Special Needs   55
The PC's Effect on Mainframe Computers   55
Chapter Summary   57
Important Terms and Concepts   58
Self-Testing Questions   58

Chapter 3 INPUT AND OUTPUT　　　　　　　　　　　　　　　　　61

A View of the Chapter Ahead   61
Introduction   62
Input Devices   62
   Keyboards   63
     Choosing a Keyboard   63
   Mouse   64
   Voice Recognition   65
   Pen-Based Computers   66
   Scanners   66
Output Devices   67
   Display Screens   67
     Monochrome Displays   67   Color Displays   68   Display Features   71
     Text Display   71   Graphics Display   72   Full-Page Displays   73   Flat Displays   74
   Touch Screens   76
   Light Pens   78
   Printers and Printed Output   78
     Types of Printers   79   Printing Efficiency   79   Dot Matrix Printers   79
     Laser Printers   81   Ink Jet Printers   83
   Plotters   83
   Special-Purpose Devices   85
     Point-of-Sale (POS) Terminals   85   Universal Product Code (UPC)   86
     Wand Readers   86   Automated Teller Machine (ATM)   86   Optical Recognition   87
     Magnetic Ink Character Reader (MICR)   89
Chapter Summary   90
Important Terms and Concepts   91
Self-Testing Questions   91

Chapter 4 SECONDARY STORAGE 93

A View of the Chapter Ahead 93
Introduction 94
Primary and Secondary Storage 94
Why Are Disks Used? 95
Disk Characteristics 96
   Floppy Disk 97
   Hard Disk 99
   Benefits of Disk 101
Disk Backup 102
CD-ROM 103
Disk Use on Mainframe Computers 108
Magnetic Tape 110
   Using Tape to Backup Hard Disk 110
Access Methods 111
   Sequential Files 111
      Sequence Fields 112   When to Use a Sequential File 113
   Nonsequential Files 113
      Relative Files 113   Pros and Cons of Relative Files 114
Chapter Summary 114
Important Terms and Concepts 114
Self-Testing Questions 114

Chapter 5 COMPUTERS AND COMMUNICATION 117

A View of the Chapter Ahead 117
Introduction 118
Types of Data Communication 118
How Does Data Transmission Work? 121
Network Topology 123
   Star Network 124
   Ring Network 126
   Bus Network 129
Local Area Networks 129
On-line Communications Services 133
   CompuServe 135
   GEnie 135
   Prodigy 135
   Electronic Mail 136
   Bulletin Board Services 137
Micro-Mainframe Links 139
   Client/Server Computing 139
Telecommunications Hardware 140
   Modem 141
      Bit Rate 142   Types of Modems 142
Summary 143
Chapter Summary 144
Important Terms and Concepts 145
Self-Testing Questions 145

Chapter 6 OPERATING SYSTEMS AND SOFTWARE PLATFORMS 149

A View of the Chapter Ahead 149
Introduction 150

Functions of the Operating System   151
   Input/Output Management   152
   Memory Management   152
   Command Processing   152
   Utilities   153
Classes of Operating Systems   155
   Single Tasking   155
   Multitasking   155
   Multiuser   156
PC-DOS and MS-DOS   157
DOS Commands   158
   Internal and External Commands   158
   Entering DOS Commands   158
Disk Directories   159
   Directory Organization   161
Other Operating Systems   162
   OS/2   162
   UNIX   164
   Macintosh Operating System   165
Windows   165
   Windows Basics   166
   Windows and Non-Windows Applications   166
   Object Linking and Embedding (OLE)   167
   Windows Applications   169
Operating Systems Today   170
Chapter Summary   170
Important Terms and Concepts   171
Self-Testing Questions   172

Chapter 7 APPLICATION SOFTWARE   175

A View of the Chapter Ahead   175
Introduction   176
Application Software Packages   176
   Software Packages   177
   Main and Overlay Programs   179
   To Program or Use Application Software?   180
Using the Keyboard   182
   Keyboard Templates   185
Using a Mouse   185
Using Software   186
   User Interfaces   186
      Menus   186   Function Keys   189   Prompts   189   Commands   189
      Form Filling   191   Graphical User Interface (GUI)   193
   Multi-interface Programs   193
   Help Screens   194
Installing Software   198
Install Programs   198
   Device Drivers   199
   Default Settings   200
Application Software and You   200
Chapter Summary   200
Important Terms and Concepts   202
Self-Testing Questions   202

Chapter 8 WORD PROCESSING AND DESKTOP PUBLISHING   205

A View of the Chapter Ahead   205
Introduction   206
The Benefits of Word Processing   206
Stages of Word Processing   206
The Language of Word Processing   209
Choosing a Word Processor   216
Other Features   218
  Spelling Checkers   218
  Thesaurus   219
  Mail Merge   220
  Outliners   220
Windows Word Processors   224
Desktop Publishing   225
  Page Composition Software   226
  The Computer   226
  The Screen   226
  The Input   227
  Clip Art Software   227
  The Printer   228
  Is Desktop Publishing for Everyone?   228
Chapter Summary   229
Important Terms and Concepts   230
Self-Testing Questions   230

Chapter 9 SPREADSHEET SOFTWARE   233

A View of the Chapter Ahead   233
Introduction   234
Spreadsheets   235
  Typical Spreadsheet Applications   235
  "What If" Questions   236
  Spreadsheet Components   237
    Cells and Addressing   238   The Control Panel   238
  Creating a Spreadsheet   238
  Ranges   240
  Using Ranges in the Spreadsheet   240
  Formatting the Spreadsheet   240
  Addressing in Formulas   241
  Graphs   243
    Types of Graphs   244
  Macros   246
  Three-Dimensional Spreadsheets   248
Spreadsheet Presentation Features   250
Chapter Summary   252
Important Terms and Concepts   253
Self-Testing Questions   253

Chapter 10 INTEGRATED, GRAPHICS, AND OTHER SOFTWARE   255

A View of the Chapter Ahead   255
Introduction   256

Integrated Software 256
  Benefits of Using Integrated Software 256
    Reducing the Number of Packages to Learn 257   Reducing the Cost of Software 258
    Changing Environments 258   Data Transfer 258
  Problems with Integrated Packages 258
  Windows Software 259
  Presentation Software 259
Graphics Software 261
  Graphic Types 263
Other Software Packages 264
  Personal Information Managers 264
  Project Management 267
Multimedia Software 268
CAD/CAM 269
Chapter Summary 271
Important Terms and Concepts 271
Self-Testing Questions 272

Chapter 11 DATABASE SYSTEMS 275

A View of the Chapter Ahead 275
Introduction 276
  Fields and Records 277
What Is a Database? 277
File Managers and DBMS 278
Designing a Database 280
Characteristics of the Database 281
Creating a Database 282
  Defining the File 282
Sorting the Database File 284
Using an Index 285
Database Queries 286
  Menu-Driven Queries 287
  Query Languages 287
Multiple File DBMS 289
  Normalizing Files 289
  Relations 289
  Joining Files 290
DBMS Programming 291
Networks and Database Systems 293
  File Locking 293
  File Security 294
  Networks, PCs, and Mainframe Systems 294
Chapter Summary 295
Important Terms and Concepts 296
Self-Testing Questions 296

Chapter 12 PROGRAMMING CONCEPTS 299

A View of the Chapter Ahead 299
Introduction 300
What Is Programming? 300
Program Specifications 301
Input and Output 302

The Tools of Program Design 304
   Structure Charts 304
   Pseudocode 305
   Program Flowcharts 306
Structured Programming 309
   Sequence Structure 309
   Selection Structure 309
   Repetition Structure 310
Program Coding 311
Programming Languages 313
   Procedural Languages 315
      BASIC 315   COBOL 315   FORTRAN 318   Pascal 318   Modula-2 319
      C Language 319
   Fourth-Generation Languages 320
Object-Oriented Programming 322
   What Do You Mean Object-Oriented? 322
   The Benefits of OOP 324
Chapter Summary 324
Important Terms and Concepts 326
Self-Testing Questions 326

Chapter 13 SYSTEMS ANALYSIS AND DESIGN 329

A View of the Chapter Ahead 329
Introduction 330
The Importance of Information 330
To Purchase or Develop a System? 331
What Is a System? 332
Information Systems Life Cycle 332
Feasibility Study 333
   System Definition 333
   Economics 335
   Feasibility Report 335
System Analysis 336
   Data Gathering 336
      Observing Existing Procedures 337   Interviews 338   Questionnaires 338
      Data Collection 338
   Charting the System 339
      Data Flow Diagrams 339   System Flowcharts 341   Decision Tables 341
System Design 344
   Project Scheduling 344
   Output Design 344
   Input Design 345
   File and Database Design 348
   Prototyping 348
      Benefits of Prototyping 350   Tools for Prototyping 350
Program Development 350
   The Steps of Program Development 351
Implementation 351
   Training 352
   Conversion 353
   Parallel Operation 354
Maintenance 354
Chapter Summary 354

Important Terms and Concepts 356
Self-Testing Questions 356

Chapter 14 MANAGEMENT SUPPORT SYSTEMS — 359

A View of the Chapter Ahead 359
Introduction 360
Management Information Systems 360
  Defining an MIS 360
  MIS and Business Objectives 360
  Information Reporting 361
  The Organization of MIS 362
    Corporate Structure 362   Information Systems Department 364
Decision Support Systems 366
  Models 366
  "What If" Questions 367
  Goal Seeking 368
Expert Systems 370
  Introduction 370
  Expert System Applications 370
    Business 370   Medicine 371   Financial Planning 373
  Knowledge Engineering 374
  When Is an Expert System Useful? 375
  Developing an Expert System 376
    Expert System Architecture 377   Rules 378
  Languages for Expert Systems 379
Chapter Summary 379
Important Terms and Concepts 380
Self-Testing Questions 380

Chapter 15 ISSUES AND TRENDS — 383

A View of the Chapter Ahead 383
Introduction 384
Fears and Fantasies 384
  Computer Errors 384
  Unemployment 385
  Computers and the Solution to Your Problems 386
  You Need to Be Good at Math or Be a Programmer to Use a Computer 386
Software Piracy 386
Software Licensing 387
  Site Licensing 387
  Network Licensing 389
Computer Crime 389
  Unlawful Computer Entry 389
  Theft of Currency by Computer 390
  Theft of Computer Time 390
  Theft of Computer Hardware 390
Privacy and Security 390
Ethics 393
Computer Careers 394
Career Opportunities 395
  Data Entry Operator 395
  Computer Operations 395

Programmers 397
Systems Programmer 397   Applications Programmer 397
Systems Analyst 398
Business Analyst 399
Database Administrator (DBA) 399
Information Center Staff 399
Marketing 399
Chapter Summary 400
Important Terms and Concepts 401
Self-Testing Questions 402

A ORIGINS: A HISTORY OF COMPUTING AND INFORMATION SYSTEMS 405

Abacus 406
Blaise Pascal 406
George Boole 407
Charles Babbage 408
James Ritty and NCR 409
William S. Burroughs 410
Herman Hollerith 410
Thomas Watson and IBM 411
Presper Eckert, John Mauchly and ENIAC 412
John von Neumann and EDVAC 412
Computer Generations 413
  First Generation (1951–1959) 413
  Second Generation (1960–1964) 414
  Third Generation (1964–1970) 414
Computer Languages and Software 416
  First-Generation Computers 416
  Second-Generation Computers 417
  Third-Generation Computers 417
  Computers and Fourth Generation 418
The First Personal Computers 418
  The Birth of Apple and the IBM PC 419

B CHECKLIST FOR BUYING A COMPUTER 421

Getting Started 422
Basic Choices 422
Selecting Hardware 422
  System Unit 423
  The Central Processor 424
  Memory 424
  Display 424
  Color or Monochrome 425   Screen Ergonomics 426
  Keyboards 426
  Mouse 427
  Disk Drives 427
  Hard Disk 427   Floppy Disk 427
  Printers 428
  Other Devices 428

Service and Support 430
Software 431

C NUMBER SYSTEMS   433

Decimal Numbers 434
Binary Numbers 436
Hexadecimal Numbers 437
Converting Between Binary and Hexadecimal 438
Converting Decimal to Other Bases 438

GLOSSARY   441

INDEX   449

PREFACE

Computing Essentials introduces you to the exciting world of computers and their use. It is an easy reading book that primarily addresses personal computing with occasional looks into the world of mainframes. Understanding computer concepts and keeping up to date with the technology is of utmost importance to everyone entering the work force in the 1990s. No longer is the computer limited to large corporations or those with programming skills. We believe students will find this book interesting and relevant to their use of computers both in school and in the business world. Instructors will find that the text supports them with coverage of the many topics needed for an introductory course as well as with the accompanying supplement package.

THE CONTENT

Computing Essentials covers the topics needed for the introductory computer course that is oriented to personal computers. Each chapter begins with a story of how a specific company or organization uses computers as it relates to the current chapter. Then the chapter proceeds with the more objective subject matter. Included are topics on the uses of computers, hardware devices, data storage, data communications, operating systems and platforms such as Windows and OS/2, programming concepts, systems analysis and design, management information systems, and ethics. Six full chapters are devoted to application software including word processing, desktop publishing, spreadsheets, integrated packages, presentation graphics, and database management. A final chapter addresses the current issues of computer phobia, software piracy, licensing, computer crime, viruses, security, ethics, privacy, and computer careers.

CHAPTER ORGANIZATION

Computing Essentials is organized into five sections that each focus on a central theme. This structure works well for most courses but offers the flexibility needed for those who wish to follow a different route. The chapter content is summarized as follows:

PART I—INTRODUCTION TO COMPUTERS

This section introduces the reader to the world of computers beginning with most readers' current experience and building on this background. Topics include why computers are needed, what is a computer, different types of computers, and a general introduction to the types of software used on today's computer systems. This section gives the student an exposure to the concepts and terms that will be developed in greater depth throughout the book. Because ethics is an important concern today, a box is used to introduce the topic as it relates to computer users.

Complex topics are introduced briefly early in the book and then covered in depth in later chapters. For example, the subjects of computer hardware, input/output, spreadsheets, word processing, multimedia, database, integrated software, and communications are each introduced briefly in Chapter 1. Later chapters develop each topic more fully.

PART II—COMPUTER HARDWARE

The four chapters in this section cover the major topics relating to computer hardware. This ranges from a discussion on bits and bytes to notebook computers, from RAM and ROM to data communications. Included are topics such as microprocessors, PS/2, multimedia, display screens, printers, plotters, disk storage, networks, communication systems, and local area networks. Most of the material relates to PC hardware and covers the hardware in widespread use as well as newer developments such as the 80486 and Pentium-based computers, SuperVGA and Multi-sync screens, and CD ROMs.

PART III—SYSTEMS AND SOFTWARE

This section contains six chapters on software and related topics. The section begins with a discussion on operating systems, including MS-DOS, Windows, OS/2, and UNIX. Next, Chapter 7 presents an overview of application software with a discussion on the use of user interfaces, templates, help screens, and how software is installed. The last four chapters cover the major software applications: word processing, spreadsheets, graphics and other software, and database management. Related material is included on desktop publishing, three-dimensional spreadsheets, integrated software, presentation graphics, Windows application software, CAD/CAM, and project management.

PART IV—DESIGNING AND IMPLEMENTING INFORMATION SYSTEMS

This section proceeds from the micro to the macro view of systems. It begins with programming concepts and establishes why programs are necessary. Program development tools such as structured methodology are discussed, as are the major procedural languages. Fourth-generation languages are also examined and why they are so important today and recent developments in object-oriented programming. Next we cover systems analysis and design covering the life cycle from the feasibility study, through analysis, design, programming, implementation, and maintenance. The section ends with Management Support Systems including MIS, Decision Support Systems, and Expert Systems.

PART V—CURRENT ISSUES

The text is ended with a discussion of social issues that have been introduced as a result of the computer impact. These issues include computer phobia, software piracy, software licensing, computer crime, viruses, privacy, security, and ethics. The last section of Part V discusses various computer careers that are of interest to the student who wants to pursue a computer-based career.

APPENDICES

Some topics are considered optional by instructors of an introductory computer course. These have been collected into the appendices and can be used as required or left out of the mainstream of the course at the professor's discretion. Included in Appendix A are computer history, computer generations, the history of languages and software and the first PCs. Appendix B provides a checklist and a discussion on how to buy a computer. Appendix C covers number systems as they relate to the computer.

FEATURES

Writing Style. The writing style is conversational in tone and attempts to be light and interesting to retain the attention of the student and to encourage further involvement in the subject matter.

Use of Photographs and Figures. The book is highly visual in the sense that there are figures, photographs, and/or graphic art on most pages to support the textual material. These are accompanied by descriptive captions that provide further support to the related topic in the text.

Inserts. Most chapters have inserts on special topics such as "Ethics and Computers," "Estimating Hard Disk Storage Requirements," "Data Interchange at Wal-Mart," "E-Mail—The Alternate to a Postage Stamp," and so on. Inserts are also used when a particularly difficult concept is presented in order to give an alternate perspective on the topic.

Photo Essays. Photo essay inserts are also included in many chapters. These essays add spice to the chapter by presenting a visual tour of a specific topic such as WordPerfect for Windows, Multimedia, desktop publishing, expert systems, and CorelDraw, that is related to the chapter content. One of these essays is used in Chapter 1 to show a variety of fields where computers are being used. Another is used to show the benefits of desktop publishing in Chapter 8.

LEARNING AIDS IN THE BOOK

Each chapter begins with chapter objectives called "A View of the Chapter Ahead." Objectives are stated in a manner to promote "understanding" of the subject. Glossary notes are included in the margins to define new terms as they occur in the body of the text.

Each chapter ends with a series of self-testing questions with answers provided at the end of the chapter. There are fill-in and true/false questions. Each chapter also includes questions for critical thinking that require the application of the chapter content into new directions or to solve new problems.

Chapters contain boldfaced keywords with a summary of terms at the end of the chapter. A chapter summary highlights and reviews major topics at the end of each chapter, which is useful for test preparation. An extensive glossary and complete index are included at the end of the book.

SUPPLEMENTS PACKAGE

A collection of supplements is available for both students and instructors of the course.

1. This book is part of the Source 1—Computing Essentials custom publishing series. In this series, software lab manuals are available for a wide variety of application software. Currently the series offers the following manuals, with more being added on a continuing basis.

   Operating Systems: DOS 4.0, DOS 5.0, DOS 6.0, Windows

Word Processing:	WordPerfect 4.2, WordPerfect 5.1, WordPerfect 6.0
Spreadsheets:	Lotus 1-2-3 Rel. 2.2, Lotus 1-2-3 Rel. 2.3, Quattro 1.01, QuattroPro 3.0, Excel 4.0
Database:	dBASE III Plus, dBASE IV 1.1, dBASE IV 1.5, dBASE IV 2.0, Paradox
Languages:	QBASIC

2. **Instructor's Manual**—Prepared by the author of the text, this manual supports the book with chapter descriptions, learning objectives, vocabulary, teaching tips.
3. **Test Bank**—A set of test questions is included in the instructor's manual for each chapter of the text. Each section includes fill-in, matching, and multiple choice questions with answers provided.
4. **Laserdisc**—Prentice Hall is proud to announce a first in supplements for introductory computing—a laserdisc. The laserdisc makes a wide variety of source material available to you during lectures. This multimedia supplement is organized into 16 popular topic areas, such as I/O, word processing, and MIS. Each topic is supported by dynamic illustrations, summaries, colorful images, and full-motion video, all of which can be accessed directly.

OTHER SUPPLEMENTS

Prentice Hall Inc. also provides a number of supplements to support instructors of introductory computer courses. Included are transparency masters and test generation software. Ask your Prentice Hall representative for details.

ACKNOWLEDGMENTS

A book of this scope represents the efforts of many people representing a diversity of skills and backgrounds. Each has made a unique contribution which is much appreciated by the author. First are the reviewers. These professors took time out from their full schedules to read the manuscript and comment on their reaction to its content. Although it wasn't possible to include every change suggested, much of this feedback made a valuable contribution to the final revision. Thank you goes to the following who reviewed the original text, *Understanding Computers*.

- R. A. Barrett, Indiana University/Purdue University
- George P. Grill, University of North Carolina
- David Harvey, Ryerson Polytechnical Institute
- Seth A. Hock, Columbus State Community College

- Peter L. Irwin, Richland College
- Marion E. Kempe, Lampton College of Applied Arts and Technology
- Randall L. Lechlitner, Collin County Community College
- Paul E. Lecoq, Spokane Falls College
- Anthony P. Malone, Raymond Walters College
- Charles Miri, Delaware Tech
- Thomas W. Osgood, Indiana University East
- Ernest Philipp, Northern Virginia Community College
- Guy W. Pollock, Mountain View College
- Frank Relotta, DeVRY Technical Institute
- David J. Rooser, Essex County College
- Daniel Rota, Robert Morris College
- Edward Solinsky, Purdue School of Engineering and Technology
- Julia Tinsley, Indiana University at Kokomo
- Anthony L. Tiona, Broward Community College
- John P. Traynor, Northern Illinois University
- Dennis L. Varin, Southern Oregon State College
- Barbara Walters, Ashland Community College

The following professors made an additional contribution to the revised edition, *Computing Essentials*. We thank them for helping to update this material in what is a fast changing discipline.

- Jt Chirco, Rutgers University
- Richard J. Easton, Indiana State University
- Orlynn R. Evans, Stephen F. Austin State University
- Leonard Presby, William Paterson College
- Judith Scheeren, Westmoreland County Community College
- Joanne Shansky, Milwaukee Area Technical College
- Billy L. Williams, Lamson Junior College

The work and support of C.I.S. editor P. J. Boardman at Prentice Hall is much appreciated. P. J. contributed unselfishly of her time and energy to make this project work. Thanks P. J. for your constant encouragement. Other professionals at Prentice Hall also made significant contributions in the planning and production of this book. A special thank you goes to Lori Morris-Nantz for the photo research; bookworks, production editor; Lorraine Mullaney, design; and Debbie Emry and Patti Arneson in marketing. You all are a great team. Thanks for your efforts.

CHAPTER 1

THE WORLD OF COMPUTERS

A VIEW OF THE CHAPTER AHEAD

After reading this chapter you will understand

- ▶ why computers and information systems are needed in business and industry.
- ▶ when it is useful to use a computer and when purchasing a computer might not be the best solution to a business problem.
- ▶ the concept of a computer system and the basic components it contains.
- ▶ the concept of application software and you will be able to identify the main types of software used on personal computers.

INTRODUCTION

Computers have become a way of life in our society. It seems that everyone is using a computer, or planning to in the near future. Take the familiar activity of ordering a pizza from Dominos. When you dial the Dominos number, a computer intercepts the call and determines your location from your phone number. It then matches your location with a built-in map that determines the nearest Dominos store to your location. The computer then passes your call along to the store and your call is answered only a few seconds after you dialed the number.

The Dominos example is one of a computer application that is completely transparent. You are never aware of the presence of the computer and for the most part neither is the Dominos employee to whom you speak. But many computer applications require hands-on use of the computer and training to use it effectively. Whether you are a marketing expert, an accountant, a manager, a lawyer, or an engineer, the use of computer technology will be a necessary component of your career skills. Most computer users today use a personal computer and some use a mainframe terminal. The ability to use a word processor, spreadsheet, or database is becoming as common as the ability to read and write. Those without computer skills will discover that employment is increasingly difficult to find.

Do you currently own a computer or use one on a regular basis? If so, you are no doubt familiar with the terms floppy disk, hard disk, display screen, mouse, printer, and possibly many more. Even if you don't own a computer, most college students have given serious thought to its purchase. Maybe you have looked at newspaper advertisements such as the one shown in Figure 1-1. The computer terminology used also includes words

(Courtesy Domino's Pizza)

CHAPTER 1 The World of Computers

FIGURE 1-1
Major newspapers frequently contain sales on computers and related components.

such as megabytes (MB), RAM, VGA, and MHz. Even computer users are sometimes confused by the meaning of these terms.

This book will help you to understand computer terminology and prepare you to use the computer in some very practical ways. You will find that learning about computers is a delightful experience and learning to use application software is a skill that everyone can master. This book will not make you a computer expert, but you will gain a broad understanding of

---

▶ **THE PC**
WHAT'S IN A NAME

Everyone, it seems, calls a desktop computer a PC. The term has become a generic one and is used for many types of desktop computers. When the IBM personal computer was announced in 1981, the name PC became synonymous with the IBM PC. Since the release of that historic computer, millions of personal computers have been purchased by corporations, small companies, educational institutes, and individuals.

Today most desktop computers are called PCs whether produced by IBM, Compaq, Tandy, or any one of many corporations who build competing computers. Even the more advanced models, such as PS/2s, 80386s, or 80486s are usually called by the name personal computer. However, mainframe terminals that have a screen and a keyboard are not PCs, although they may look like one. In this book the names PC or personal computer are intended to refer to the complete range of personal computers whether they are the IBM PC, PS/2, or compatible computers from any number of competitors. In cases where a specific type of computer has a feature that is unique to that model, a more direct reference will be made to that computer.

computer concepts and become familiar with the use of several computer programs that are widely used in business. Doing hands-on activities with the computer using the tutorials available with the book will help you build confidence in your ability to use a computer and to apply it to real life problems.

In the remainder of this chapter you will look at why computers are used and some important concepts about their use. Some writers have called the computer "the mind tool," and so it is, because of its ability to store facts, recall them quickly, and do many types of processes with them. But while learning about the computer, you will need to apply your mind to the learning process. That means you will need to read and absorb new concepts, make notes, and do some old-fashioned studying. But in the learning process, be prepared to reap the rewards that new knowledge can bring.

WHY DO WE NEED COMPUTERS?

Personal Computer (PC). A desktop computer intended for the use of one person.

What is it that an accountant, a novelist, a restaurateur, a business executive, an electronics engineer, a sales person, and an investment counselor have in common? They all use a computer to supply, store, and process information in order to do their job or run their company more effectively (Figure 1-2).

The accountant uses a personal computer to help analyze clients' taxes, keep track of the payroll, and prepare year-end reports. A novelist, of course, uses a computer to write books, and the restaurateur uses the computer to record sales of meals, keep track of the waiters' gratuities, and tabulate the amount owed to the credit card companies. The business executive uses the computer to monitor the performance of the company and its various functions. The computer can help the executive to identify business trends, and with this knowledge he can make informed business decisions and plan new directions for the company.

The electronics engineer uses a computer to design circuits based on computer-related microelectronic principles. Computer use in electronic design saves time over manual methods and allows the engineer to try out different circuit designs without the need to wire many components together for initial testing. The salesperson uses a personal computer to keep track of her sales. Records of customers, their likes and dislikes and past spending habits can be maintained so that more time can be spent promoting the products that will satisfy customer needs. The computer can even recommend optimum intervals for meeting with a customer, ensuring that both the salesperson and the customer's time is used profitably.

Investment counselors use computers to analyze their client's investment goals and to suggest investment strategies that should be followed. The computer can also be used to track the client's investments and calculate the potential effect of choices made in the investment program.

While the personal computer is an important part of each of these job functions, there are two other important ingredients for a successful operation. One ingredient is the personnel who are involved with the task. Although the computer may have specific programs that relate to account-

CHAPTER 1 The World of Computers

FIGURE 1-2
Computer training is an essential component of most business programs in today's college courses. Employees in small to large companies are also being trained in the use of the personal computer, a skill that, if lacking, can contribute to the loss of promotion or even lack of employability. (Courtesy Nickolay Zurek, FPG International.)

ing, restaurants, or investment, it cannot begin to replace the professionals who bring their expertise to the jobs described. Knowledgeable people are needed to use the computer effectively, and without them the computer might just as well be used as a boat anchor.

The other ingredient for successful use of a computer is information (Figure 1-3). For either the professional or the computer to work effectively, relevant information is required. The kind of information used can vary greatly and how it is used can also be quite different. For the accountant, information will exist primarily as numbers that represent debits and credits in the accounts of their clients. By contrast, the novelist uses ideas and words as information. The engineer might use ideas as well, but he also uses the rules of electronics as information that determine how these ideas might be used.

All of these new directions in our society show an increased need for information and the computer is often the central tool for providing this information. This trend has resulted in a new type of employee called the

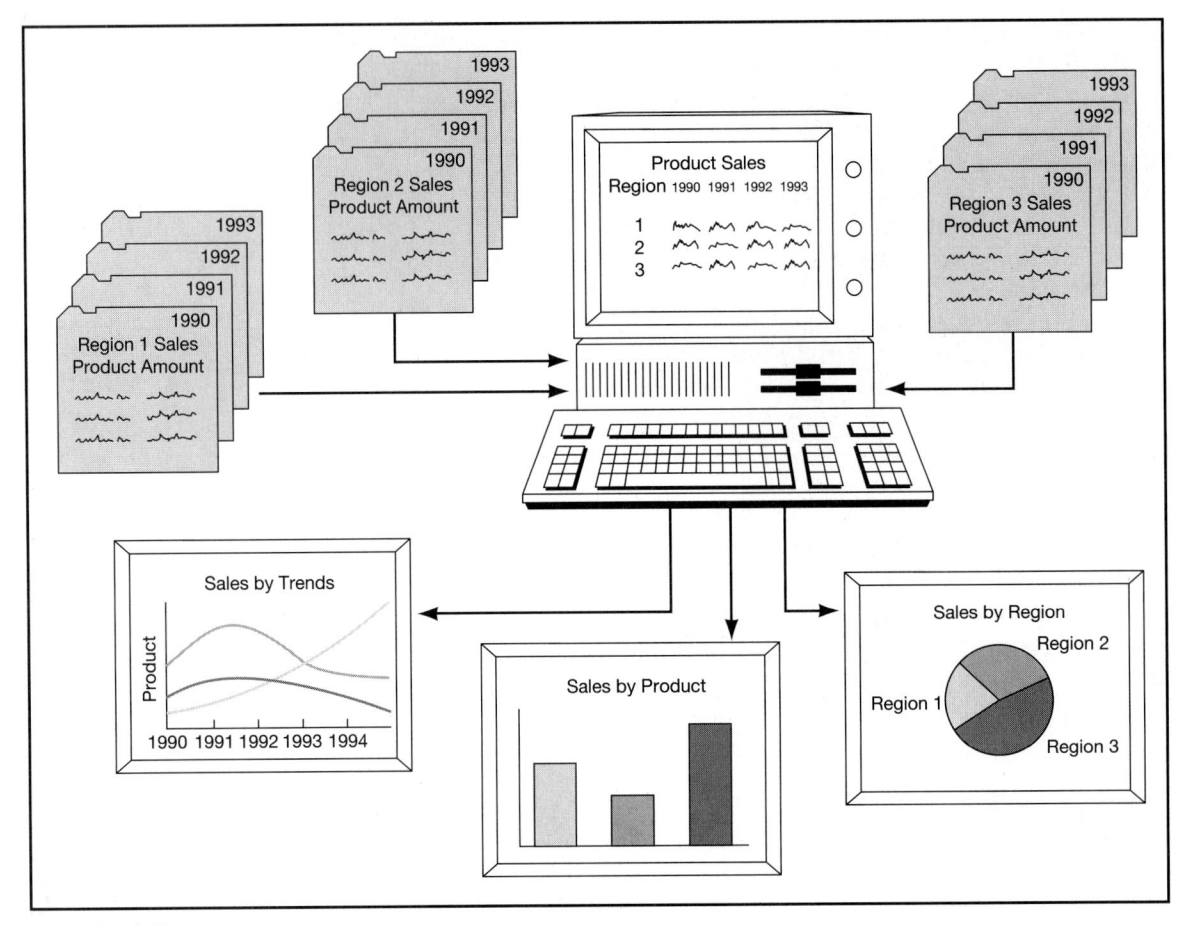

FIGURE 1-3
Sales documents are gathered from each region of the company and entered into the computer for processing. Numerous interpretations of the data are possible including both numeric and graphic displays of the results. Some of these displays show total product sales by region for each of the previous four years, a line graph showing sales trends, a percentage distribution of sales by region shown in a pie chart, and a bar graph comparing sales for each product.

Knowledge worker. Someone whose job function depends primarily on the use of knowledge or information.

knowledge worker. A **knowledge worker** is a person whose job depends largely on the use of knowledge or information. Clearly people in many different career paths are knowledge workers because they use information as a primary ingredient of their job. Now let's understand what a computer is.

WHAT IS A COMPUTER?

A lot of concepts are needed for a full understanding of the computer, and in the next few chapters you will be expanding on the basics given here. But first, let's use the analogy of a television set to draw some parallels. A television set uses an antenna or cable to capture a signal from the TV station and feed it into the electronic circuits. The electronics are then used to process the signal and convert it into a picture and sound.

In reality there are many signals, from different channels, that are captured by the antenna, and the TV set must separate these into a signal for the channel that you select. Not only that, but the signal received is extremely weak and must be amplified in order for it to produce good picture and sound quality. Part of the processing also involves identifying the various colors in the picture and displaying them on the screen to give you a pleasing color picture.

In computer language you can think of the antenna as the input that reads or captures the signal. The electronics of the TV set is the processor that processes the signal and creates the information or output that you require. And the picture and sound are outputs that are created as a result of the processing. Each of these terms—input, process, and output—have similar counterparts in the computer.

- **Input** uses a device, such as the keyboard, mouse, or disk that provides data for the computer to process or act on.
- **Process** refers to the computer's processor and related electronics that acts on the data to provide a variety of useful information needed for reports or graphs.
- **Output** is the result of processing and can be displayed on the screen,

Stock Investing by Computer. Using data communication lines and a personal computer, a financial analyst can access current stock market prices. Stock analysis programs are used to graph the price trends of a specific stock over a period of time. Some analysts use these programs to help predict future performance of the stock. The PC simplifies the recording of investment data for quick and easy access as investment decisions are required. Reports for both the analyst and the client may be produced directly from the personal computer. (Courtesy New York Stock Exchange.)

similar to the TV, or printed on paper for a permanent copy of the results. Output can also be stored on disk for later use by the computer.

Interestingly, television sets are moving closer to the computer in the way that they operate. Digital selection of channels, on-screen channel and time display, and integration with VCRs and computers are all a result of computer technology. However similar the two may be, there are still many features and concepts that are unique to the computer.

INFORMATION SYSTEMS

Data and Information

Data. A collection of facts or raw material that are gathered and used as input to the computer.

When computers are discussed, the terms data and information are often used (Figure 1-4). **Data** refers to the raw material or facts that are gathered and used for input to the computer. **Data entry** is the process of entering data into the computer, often by typing. Items such as name, description, year, age, program number, grade received, phone number, course number, and so on are all examples of data. Data is something like the signal that is received by a television antenna. By itself it is not very useful. Just as the television can only give a useful image after the signal is amplified, and

FIGURE 1-4
Data are the raw material that represents the facts, while information is a collection of the data into a meaningful pattern.

Data Items

HUDSON   933-1055   Business   Administration   1989   BA101

231-019   Communications   81   231-010   Information Systems   85

231-015   Business Math   75   231-031   Accounting   79

Information is data in an organized form.

Name	Program Description	Number
Hudson	Business Administration	BA101

Course	Name	Grade
231-010	Information Systems	85
231-015	Business Math	75
231-019	Communications	81
231-031	Accounting	79
Average Grade		**80**

CHAPTER 1 The World of Computers

processed, so can data be useful only after it has been collected and processed.

Information is data that has been processed and organized into a useful pattern. This is comparable to the TV picture that results only after the processing of the television signal. Similarly, the data items described above can be organized into a student record to provide meaningful information. The system that collects and organizes the data into a useful form is called an **Information System**. Well-designed information systems contribute to worker productivity and increase excellence in the workplace.

An information system is necessary for the business person, manager, or professional to do his or her job effectively, and most often this system requires the use of a computer. Without information, daily tasks necessary to the operation of the business could not be performed adequately, and without the computer, the time required to do many of these tasks would be excessive.

Well-designed information systems contribute to worker productivity and are an important tool for implementing excellence in the workplace. In this book you will be mainly concerned with the use of computers and information in business, but occasionally you will look at other areas that are important to understanding the use of computers.

> **Information.** Data that has been processed and organized into a useful format.
>
> **Information system (IS).** A system that collects and organizes data into a useful format.

Computers and Information Systems

With management's need for timely and accurate information, the computer has become an instrumental part of a **management information system (MIS)**. These systems use computers to collect data, process it, summarize it, and use it to generate a variety of reports that provide all levels of management with the information they need. A sales reporting system may not only provide lists of customers who have made purchases, or whose payment is outstanding, but may also identify trends in sales so that management may guide the company's efforts in the right direction.

A **decision support system (DSS)** refers to a system where information from a computer is used for decision making. The term "decision support" suggests that management relies on the computer for more than just the day-to-day operation of the company. Indeed, the computer is used for making decisions that have long-term implications in the welfare of the company and its employees.

Information systems have not always depended on the computer; some still don't. Manual systems of collecting information and analyzing it were the most common method used until the advent of the computer. These systems were called **business systems** and although some of them used electromechanical devices such as the accounting machine or the calculator, others were completely manual. Now the computer is changing all of that, resulting in a group of specialists whose work revolves around the use of the computer.

> **Management information system (MIS).** A total information system that is integrated with manual and automated methods of providing information for management decisions.
>
> **Decision support system.** A system where computer-based information is processed to support decision making.

Information Systems Departments

Large companies such as manufacturers, head offices for banks, franchise operations, retail stores, insurance companies, government, and education all depend on information and the use of computers for their operation.

FIGURE 1-5
Centralized mainframe computers or networked personal computers are typically supported by a staff of information systems professionals who in turn support the many users located throughout the company. The information systems or data processing department consists of people trained in computer programming, systems analysis, computer operations, and data entry. These professionals develop and implement computer applications, run the computers, and enter data. (Courtesy Jon Feingersh, Uniphoto; IBM; Hewlett Packard.)

CHAPTER 1 The World of Computers

Until the 1980s, these organizations used centralized computer systems with a staff of computer professionals to design, implement, and maintain the system. The **information systems (IS)** or **data processing (DP) department** was self-contained and provided the company with much of its information requirements (see Figure 1-5).

Different kinds of systems (Courtesy of NASA; Bob Daerich, Stock Boston; George Contorakes, Stock Market; Comshare.)

System		An organization of elements or things into a workable order or scheme.	Solar system, telephone system
Information System (IS)		A system that provides information for the function of an operation.	A cash register may provide information for the operation of a company.
Management Information System (MIS)		A system that collects information for management's use in making the daily decisions about the operation of the company.	Sales reports, inventory, profit, and accounts provide this information.
Decision Support System (DSS)	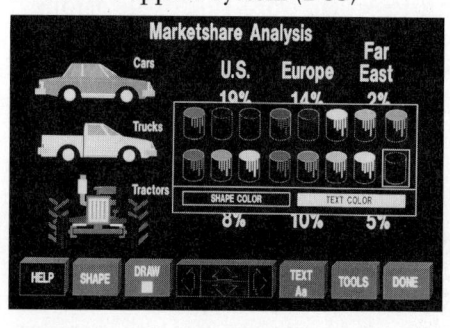	A system that helps management to make decisions regarding the future or long-term direction of the company and its products or services.	DSS may start with the same information as an MIS but goes beyond it to consider market and social trends.

These departments consisted of computer operators, programmers, systems analysts, and data entry operators who had the responsibility for running the computer, entering the data, designing, implementing, and maintaining the information system. The **users** were the accounting, payroll, personnel, and order departments who depended on the central computer system and the IS department for their support. These users concentrated on the role of accounting or payroll, etc., while the information systems department provided the technical expertise.

By the late 1970s, the personal computer came on the scene and within a few years its price, capacity, and speed made it possible for each user department to have its own computer or, if necessary, to have a computer for each person. Now in the 1990s a computer on every desk is not a dream anymore, but is becoming a reality in many organizations. However, throughout this revolution the central computer has also developed higher speeds and greater capacity for less money and is still a major force in computing. As we will see in this book, the central computer often works directly with the personal computer, sometimes supplying it with information and at other times collecting information that is available to it from the personal computer.

While most large organizations have a centralized information systems department, much of the computing is now done on the desktop of individual workers in the company. Decentralization of computing resources is now a reality within the large organization, while the personal computer also brings computing power to the smallest company where there is no information systems department but individuals in various job functions who depend on the computer to do their tasks.

FACTORS TO CONSIDER FOR COMPUTER USE

Often computers seem to be a pat solution to many problems. If operating expenses are higher than management would like, personnel are too costly, efficiency of the operation is low and not responsive enough, a frequent response is to get a computer. But often this is not the right answer or may only be part of a complete solution. The following are some considerations for using or not using a computer.

- **A job is routine and repetitive.** Computers tend to be able to handle repetitive tasks more effectively than tasks that are full of decisions and traps, which take training and skill to handle effectively. Accounting, payroll, expense accounts, budgets, are usually well-defined repetitive tasks that are easily implemented on the computer. More advanced software is placing many applications within reach of the computer. Even tasks that are often considered to be creative and not suitable for computer implementation, such as engineering or architectural design, are finding the computer to be a useful tool.
- **There is already software in existence to do the task required.** Software is generally quite expensive to develop and may require years of work before it is completed. Thus, the value saved may be more than offset by

the cost of developing the software. However, there are many software packages available for a wide variety of applications in business and industry. This software may be purchased at a fraction of the cost it would take to develop and therefore may be a cost-effective way to implement a solution on the computer.
- **Using a computer would be more expensive or unwieldy than doing the job manually.** Although the computer is capable of handling payroll, and there is software available, it would not make much sense for a company that had only a few employees. Probably a manual system would work just as well and at considerably less cost.
- **A service company will do the job at a fraction of the cost.** Just as it may not be worthwhile to use a computer to do payroll for only two or three employees, service companies also do jobs such as payroll, and because they are doing these tasks for many different companies, they can do them for less cost than an individual firm could with its own computer.

WHAT IS A COMPUTER SYSTEM?

What image comes to mind when you hear the term computer system? Do you think of a home computer that is attached to a television set and includes a joystick and a keyboard? Or do you think of an Apple Macintosh or an IBM Personal Computer or compatible with a floppy disk drive, display screen, keyboard, and printer. Maybe you have seen a large mainframe business computer with many different devices such as processors, operator consoles, disk storage devices, and printers. A computer system such as this would occupy a large room.

All of these descriptions may apply when the term computer system is used. A **computer system**, then, is an electronic device which consists of several components that together provide the capability of executing a stored program for input, output, and processing.

Computer system. An electronic device with several components that provides for input, processing, and output under the control of a stored program.

Certainly there is a great deal of difference among computers. A low-cost home computer is usually used for fun and enjoyment, whereas a large mainframe computer is serious business and may be used for significant applications such as recording and tracking reservations for a major airline. In the latter case, speed and efficiency are also important, as is the accuracy of processing data. Of course there are many sizes of computers with a wide range of capability between the two extremes.

Sizes of Computers

Computers come in all sizes. At the low end there is the microcomputer, which is better known as the **personal computer** or **desktop computer**.

The **minicomputer** is a medium size and performance computer. Some minis are desktop, but most are larger and must occupy their own floor space. Usually a mini is a multiuser system, whereas many micros are a single-user system. However, more upscale micros now boast a capability that is comparable to the minicomputer.

At the next level of speed and capacity is the **mainframe computer.** It

▶ PHOTO ESSAY

A microcomputer or personal computer is used in homes, offices, scientific labs, and even student dorms. The PC is priced to be affordable by a wide range of users, both individual and corporate. PCs are user friendly and have no unusual power or environmental considerations. Some computers, such as the IBM PS/2, can be connected with mini- and mainframe computers. (Courtesy NCR.)

The minicomputer is refrigerator-sized and usually sits on the floor. Minis can serve several users each located at separate terminals in the office. A mini is a natural step up for a company that has used a personal computer but due to the growth of the business has increased storage and processing needs, requiring more computer power. A new trend is the use of networked PCs instead of a more costly minicomputer. (Courtesy IBM.)

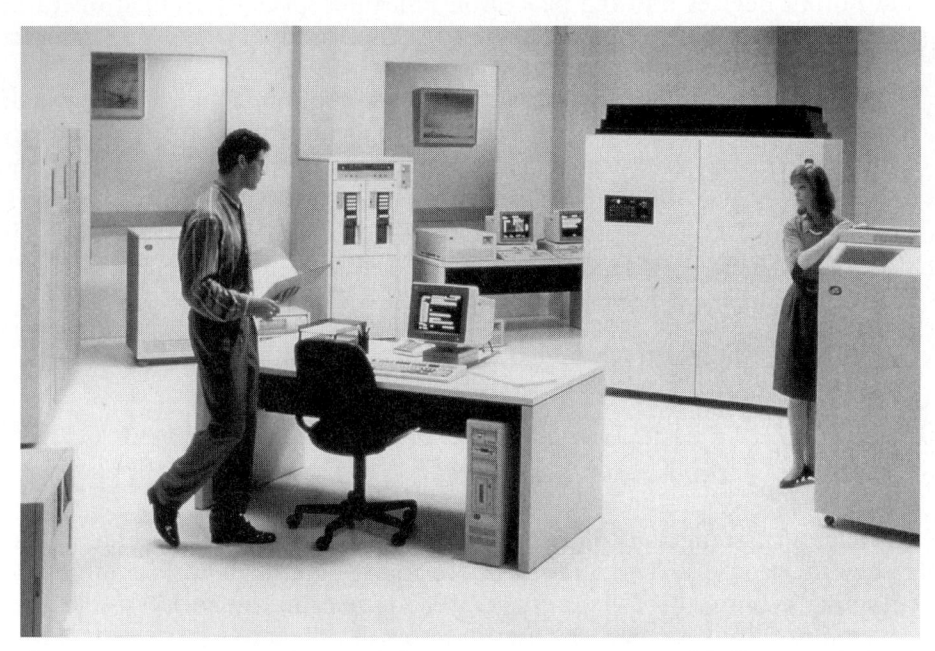

A computer center with a mainframe computer system. Medium- to large-sized businesses use the mainframe because its large storage and processing capacity simplifies the sharing of information within the company. A single mainframe computer can service hundreds of people at one time. Companies with mainframes are also using PCs for many computing needs throughout the company because the PC is inexpensive and easy to use. (Courtesy IBM.)

A supercomputer such as this Cray system is used for very specialized computing needs, for example, weather forecasting. Compared to mainframe computers, only a small number of systems such as this exist, and scientists and researchers often need to book computer time on them months in advance. (Courtesy Boeing.)

again is physically larger and may often require a specially designed room with extra air conditioning and a subfloor to run cables between the input and output devices and the processor. Full-time specially trained operators are usually required to operate these computers and a staff of programmers is needed to develop the application software.

The fourth level of computer is the **supercomputer.** This computer is designed for large-scale, complex, scientific applications such as weather forecasting, seismic activity research, and aerospace. These computers are very expensive, often costing in the millions of dollars to purchase.

While it is convenient to think of computers in these clearly defined categories, the reality is somewhat different. Many microcomputers today have comparable power to minis. And there are minis that could be classed as mainframes. The reverse is also true. So these terms are used to give a relative difference between major groupings of computers.

COMPUTER COMPONENTS

To fully understand the computer concept, it is important to recognize that a computer consists of several components (see Figure 1-6). In a large-scale computer system, these components may number in the hundreds, but usually you can think of the computer in terms of only a few parts. These components are called the **hardware** and may be broadly defined into three categories: processor, input, and output.

The Processor

System unit. Contains the central processor with memory, ALU, and control unit.

The **processor,** often called the **central processing unit** or **CPU** and sometimes called the **system unit,** is the brains of the computer system. All activity in the system originates here under the control of a program that is stored in the processor's memory. The processor is made of one or more silicon chips. A processor typically has three major components regardless of whether it is a personal or mainframe computer.

1. **Primary storage section.** The primary storage section or **random access memory (RAM)** is used for several purposes. It provides storage space for data that is arriving from an input device, such as a keyboard, or going to an output device, such as the display screen. Primary storage is also used to store the program while it is executing. Finally, primary storage acts as a temporary scratch pad for the computer to use while doing calculations and other operations required by the program.

2. **Arithmetic and Logic Unit.** The arithmetic and logic unit or **ALU** for short, is where all of the calculations take place in the computer. Calculations such as addition, subtraction, multiplication, and division are done here under control of the program. For example, a payroll program might read the number of hours and the rate of pay for an employee and give an instruction to multiply these numbers to give the gross pay earned for the week. It is the function of the arithmetic portion of the ALU to do this type of operation.

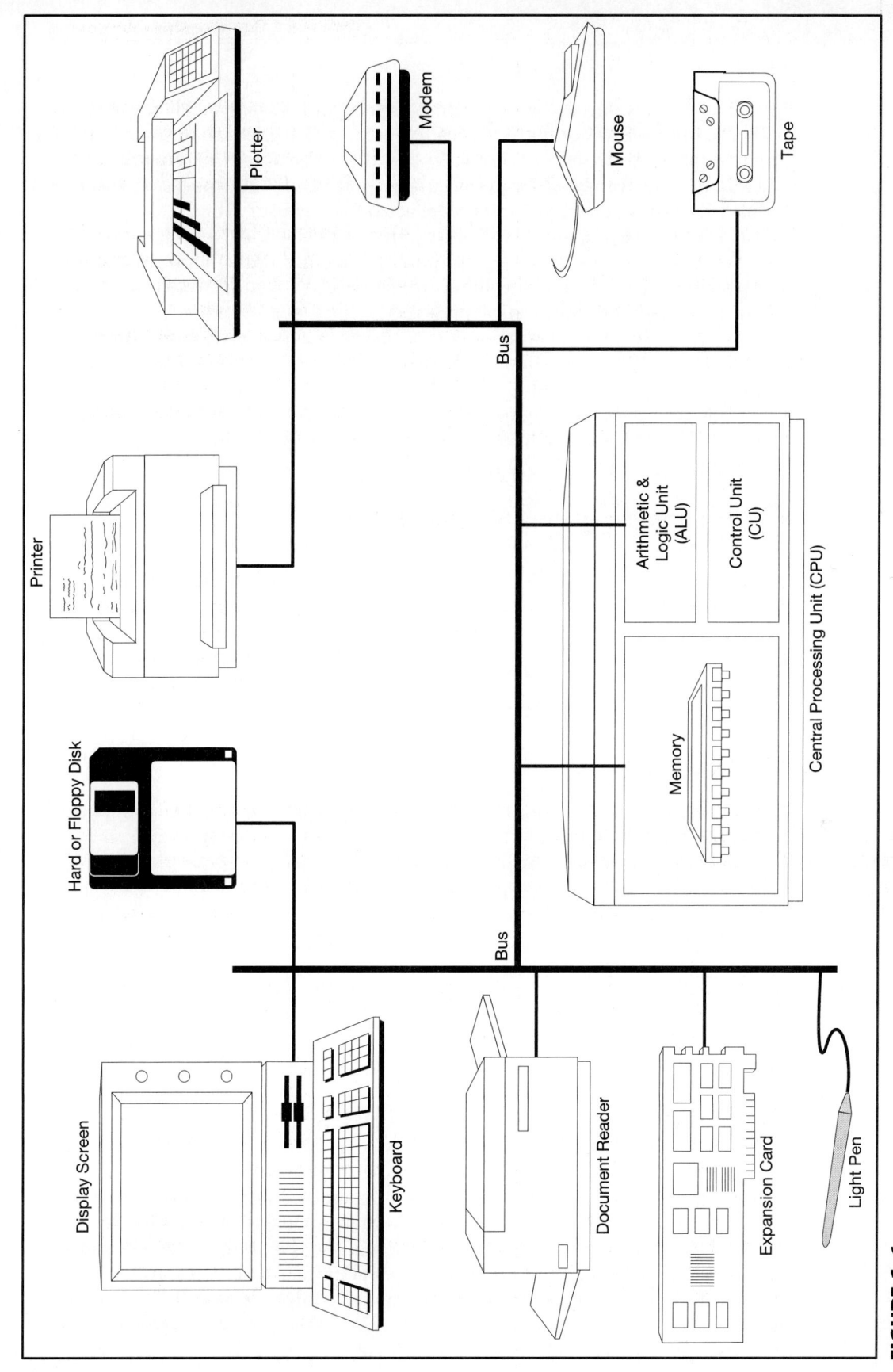

FIGURE 1-6

Personal computer components. The system unit of the computer consists of a processor, memory, and arithmetic and logic unit. Input devices include the keyboard, light pen, mouse, and document reader, while output devices include the display screen, printer, and plotter. A modem operates as both input and output. Devices such as disk and tape provide for secondary storage and provide both input and output.

The logic side of the ALU does comparisons or logical operations. These operations compare values for greater than, less than, or equal to some other value. For example, in payroll the program may instruct the logic unit to compare the gross salary to $100. If the salary is less than $100, it determines that no tax deduction is necessary. But if the gross is equal to or greater than $100, then a tax deduction is necessary.

The logic unit may also compare alphabetic data. Thus, the name Henderson is less than the name Jones because Henderson begins with an H, which alphabetically precedes J in Jones. Similarly, the name Smythe is greater than the name Smith because the letter y in Smythe is alphabetically greater than the letter i in Smith.

3. **Control Unit.** The control unit is something like the conductor of a symphony. It directs the activity of the processor and determines which component should play its part and when. It is the control unit that decides when the ALU is to do an arithmetic or logical operation or data is to be transferred from an input device to memory. The control unit decodes each instruction received from the program and acts on the instruction. By translating each instruction, it determines the action to be taken and then communicates the necessary instructions to the other components of the processor.

Other Components In a Computer

Computers also contain several components along with the processor to create a fully functioning unit. There are usually three of these features, as described here.

1. The **bus** is an electronic circuit that sends data and messages between the other components of the system.
2. **Ports** are provided to attach input and output devices, such as the screen, keyboard, printer, mouse, and modem to the computer. Usually a port is a plug or socket located on the outside of the computer's chassis.
3. Most personal computers also have **expansion slots** built internally in the computer. These allow the addition of extra features such as memory expansion, high-resolution graphics, or a Fax card.

INPUT AND OUTPUT DEVICES

Imagine a stereo system without a record player, cassette player, or CD unit. Then suppose that it had no speakers or headphones. A stereo like this would not be of much use, and certainly there would be little pleasure derived from owning one. The devices named for the stereo system are the equivalent to the input and output devices (Figure 1-6) on a computer system. Without input and output capability the computer would be no more useful than the sound system without sound.

Input devices

Keyboard (Courtesy Key Tronic Corp.)

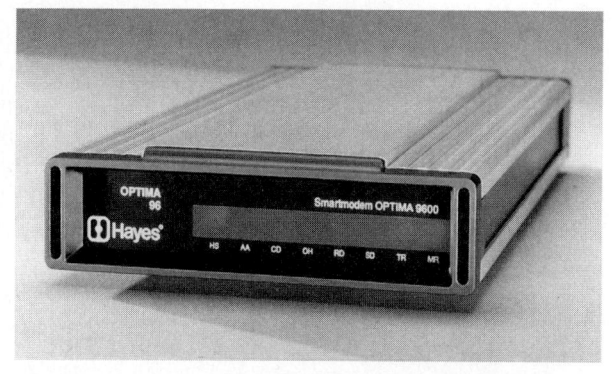

Modem (Courtesy Hayes Microcomputer Products, Inc.)

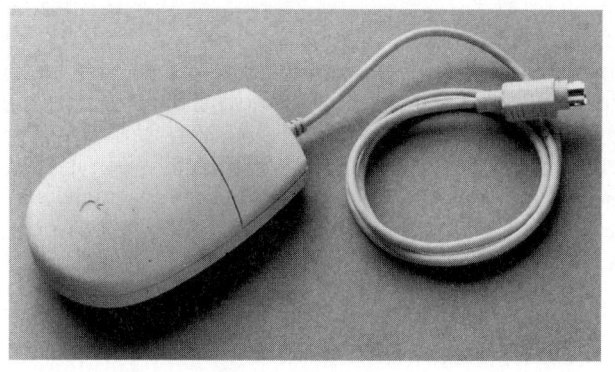

Mouse (Courtesy John Greenleigh, Apple Computer, Inc.)

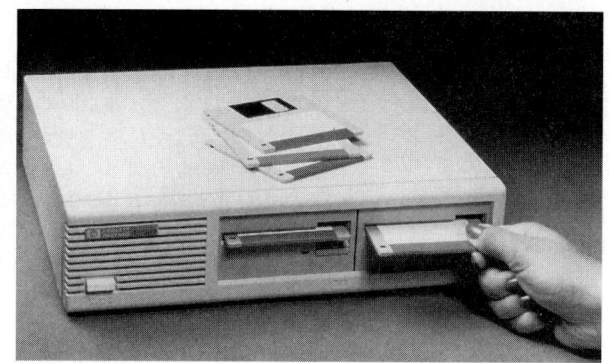

Disk drive (Courtesy Hewlett-Packard Company.)

Output devices

Display screen (Courtesy Mosgrove Photo, Apple Computer, Inc.)

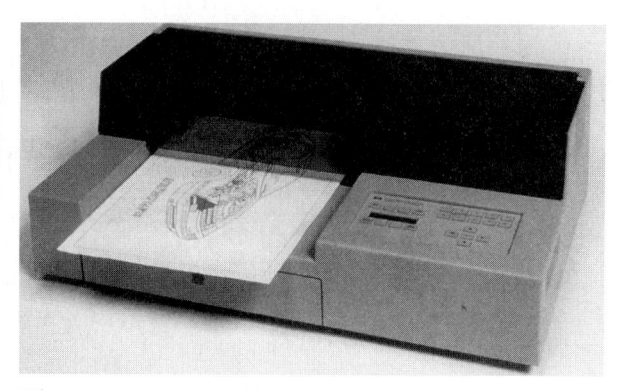

Plotter (Courtesy Hewlett-Packard Company.)

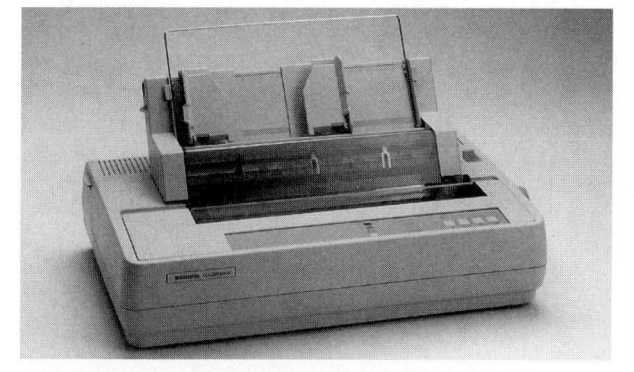

Printer (Courtesy Tektronix, Inc.)

Hard disk (Courtesy Seagate.)

Input

Input. Data provided to the computer for processing or storage.

Input devices supply data for the computer to act upon. Some devices are meant for human interaction with the computer and are usually relatively slow in speed. Others are for use by the computer and usually operate at a much higher speed. On a personal computer the keyboard is the most common input device for human use, followed by the mouse, digitizer, and light pen. Devices that provide input for use by the computer are the floppy disk drive, hard disk, and modem. Some less frequently used input devices on the PC are tape, CD ROM, and a voice reader.

Output

Output. Information created as a result of computer processing.

Output devices are like the speakers or headphones on a stereo system. They either let us see the results of the computer's operation or are used to store these results for later use. As for input, there are slower speed output devices for human use, while the outputs that the computer may use to store data are generally much faster in operation.

The display screen is the most common output device, and the printer is second in use. Displayed output, called **soft copy,** is temporary (although there is no practical limit to how long data may be displayed) while printed results, **hard copy,** are more or less permanent. Other output devices are the floppy or hard disk. These devices are both known as **secondary storage devices** because they store data for later use by the computer.

A personal computer may also use a plotter to create quality graphics, magnetic tape storage, a modem, and voice output.

COMPUTER SOFTWARE

All computers require software called a program to function. The **program** supplies the instructions for the computer to follow. Just as you may follow instructions in a recipe to prepare a soufflé, the computer follows instructions in the form of a program to complete a given task.

Software. A program that provides the instructions for the computer's operation.

Programs are called software because they are not a physical object as is the hardware. **Software** consists of commands or instructions that are placed into memory from a floppy or hard disk or some other device. The program is located in memory only during the time that the computer requires it. Because the program in memory is a copy of what was read from disk, the program is reusable and may be used by the computer over and over again.

Early computer users were technically trained programmers who knew a great deal about the inner workings of the computer. Business users simply supplied the data and received the results without a need to know how the computer accomplished its task. But today many business people use a computer directly in their jobs. If they are to use a computer effectively without the need for a lot of technical knowledge, then programs known as systems software and applications software will be essential.

> ## ▶ ETHICS AND COMPUTERS
>
> Ethics is the study of human conduct and how it relates to right and wrong. You might rightly ask what that has to do with the study of computers and whether there can be a meaningful discussion of right and wrong where computers are concerned. As with any other physical object, it is the human use of the computer and not the computer itself that comes under scrutiny and ultimately leads to questions of ethics.
>
> One of the leading ethical issues today is the copying of computer software. Unlike the book you are holding, which cannot be economically copied, a program that costs hundreds of dollars can be readily copied for the cost of a few diskettes. Although this practice is illegal it is extremely difficult for the lawmakers to monitor this practice and apprehend the practitioners.
>
> The practice ranges from individuals who copy software for their own use to companies that have copied major software packages and sold them as if they were the original. Lotus Corporation is one company whose best-selling spreadsheet Lotus 1–2–3 has been illegally copied and sold as the original product. Lotus has been extremely active in pursuing companies who follow this practice and has taken individuals and companies to court over such practices.

Systems Software

These are general-purpose programs that make the computer and other software function more effectively and apply to all computer users. The most important program classified as **systems software** is the operating system. On personal computers, this program is commonly called **DOS**, which is an acronym for **Disk Operating System.** The word disk means that this program is located on disk and that it is used to assist in any activities that use the disk or other input/output devices. DOS is used to read and write data to and from the disk, to load programs, to look at the disk contents, and for many other operations. Later in the book we will examine other systems software such as OS/2, an operating system, and Windows, a software platform.

Operating system. A program that aids in the handling of disk and other input/output operations.

Application Software

Systems software, such as DOS, is general in nature while application software tends to have more specific uses. **Application software** is designed to perform a specific function. For example, a common use of the personal computer is to do word processing and so word processing application packages are widely available for that purpose. Word processing, spreadsheets, database, and graphics programs all belong in this category.

Figure 1-7 shows that the computer requires both systems software and application software to function. While program developers could design their software with all of the features provided by the systems software, this would be like reinventing the wheel. Instead, most programs call on DOS to provide the capabilities of the system software. They will, for example, use the DOS functions for reading from disk, writing to disk, displaying information on the screen, and so on. This approach greatly simplifies program development and also makes it easier for the user of the software to understand the commonly used features.

Application software. Programs, such as spreadsheet or database, that are designed to perform a specific function.

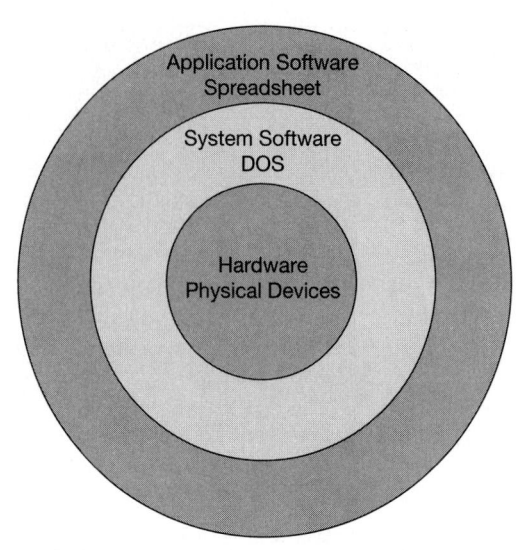

FIGURE 1-7
At the first layer in the hierarchy is the computer hardware. Next is the systems software, such as DOS, which attends to basic operations like accessing data from disk. The last level is the application software. This is the software that interacts with the user of the system.

Word processor. A program that aids in the typing, editing, and formatting of documents.

Word Processing. Anyone who has become reasonably competent at using a word processing program on a personal computer would not be easily persuaded to return to the typewriter. Gone is the need for retyping a page if too many errors have been made. There is no need to use correction fluid or special correcting ribbons. Neither is a copier needed if two or three extra copies of the document are required.

A **word processing program** aids in the typing of text ranging from short memos and letters to manuscript-length documents. Word processors provide for automatic word wrap at the end of a line, correcting typing errors, underlining, centering, and changing the location of words, sentences, or paragraphs in the text. Many can be used to create automatic headers and footers on every page, use a variety of fonts, and provide for searching and replacing of text in the document. Full-feature word processors also provide a merge capability for creating form letters; they may have a spelling checker, a thesaurus, and even line drawing and graphics ability.

Of course, a word processor must interface with a printer, and a good one will permit a variety of printers to be used with it. Another feature that is important to many users is known as **WYSIWYG,** meaning "What you see is what you get." This expression means that the document on the screen should appear the way it will be printed so that the user will know what to expect when the command to print is given.

Some widely used word processing programs for personal computers are WordPerfect (see Figure 1-8), Microsoft Word, and AmiPro. Later in the book you will look at word processors in much greater depth.

Spreadsheet. A program that stores data in rows and columns for use in numerical calculations.

Spreadsheets. Imagine a department manager a generation ago developing an annual budget. As the figures are recorded on paper there may be

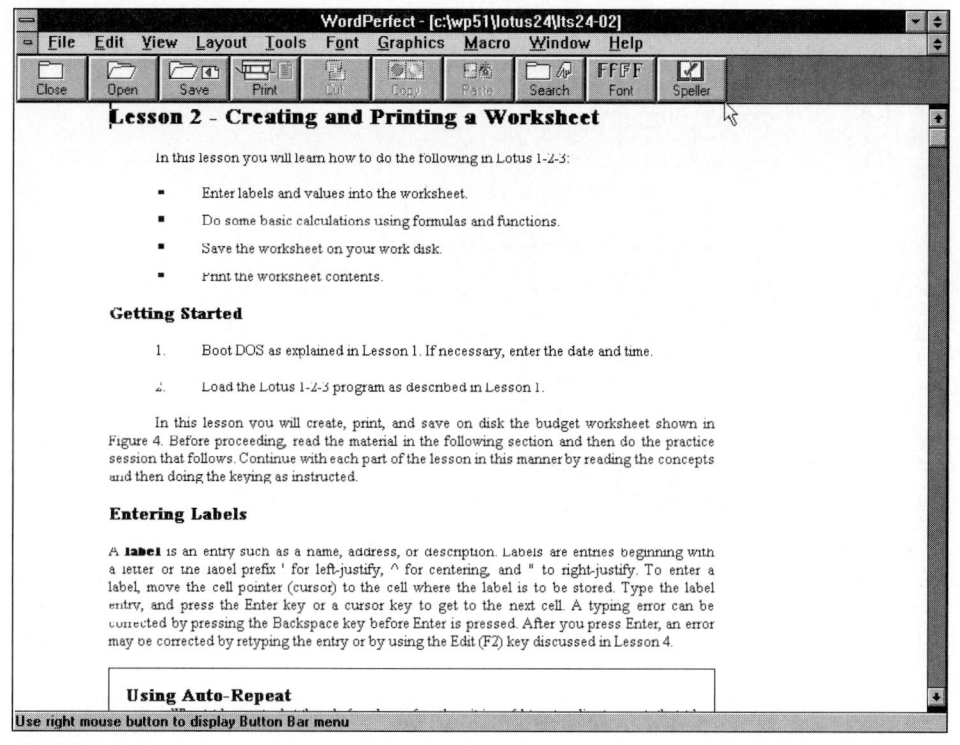

FIGURE 1-8
A word processing program improves the productivity of tasks that are typing intensive. Good word processors provide for easy correcting or updating of documents and creating form letters from a file of names and addresses. Advanced programs also have automatic spelling checkers and graphics capability.

several hundred calculations needed to develop all of the monthly and annual totals and the totals by expense item category. After spending several days at this task, the president of the company announces a change to the department's funding. Now the manager needs to redo the entire budget and all of the calculations, taking several more days and maybe a few late nights. By contrast, today's manager would use a spreadsheet on a personal computer and only the items in the budget that had changed would need to be reentered in a fraction of the time taken by yesterday's manager. All of the calculations would be done automatically by the software.

You can see why spreadsheets are among the most widely used software on personal computers. A **spreadsheet** is a program that permits the entry of data and formulas in rows and columns on the screen. As new values are entered, all formulas are automatically recalculated, and the results are shown immediately on the screen. Thus, the user may ask questions, called "what if" questions, by entering new data and observing the results.

Spreadsheet applications are developed for budget planning (Figure 1-9), financial forecasting, depreciation, loan amortization, and virtually any application that uses rows and columns of data. Lotus 1-2-3, is the leading spreadsheet package, followed by Microsoft's Excel and Borland's Quattro Pro. Current spreadsheets offer important features such as windows, graph-

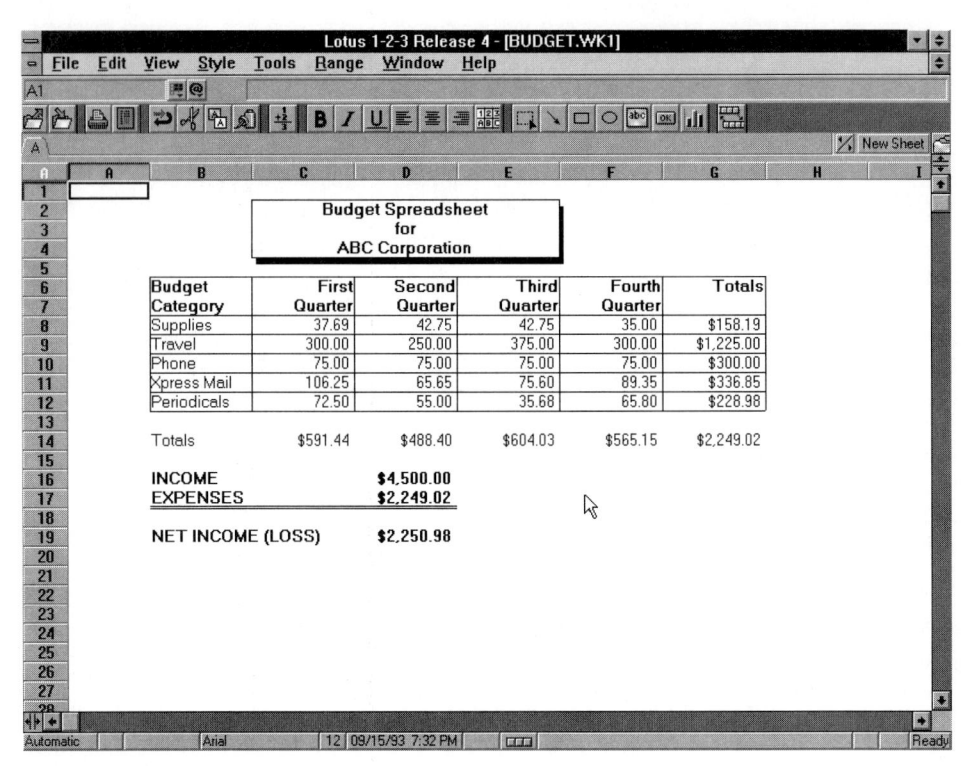

FIGURE 1-9
A spreadsheet program is used for many different applications within the company. Here, a spreadsheet is used by management to record budget amounts for each quarter of the year.

ing, database, and presentation capabilities. Later in the book you will examine spreadsheets in more detail.

Database Management Systems (DBMS). Imagine a filing cabinet with hundreds of pages of information about each of a company's customers and the orders they have placed. There is a second file that contains the current inventory of items in stock. Now, a customer calls to find out the status of the order and is required to wait several minutes while the file is manually searched for the order and then the separate inventory file checked to determine if the shipment of parts has been received.

If the company had used a database program, instead of the manual system, then the customer data, orders, and inventory could all be recorded on a hard disk on a personal computer. By entering the appropriate commands to the database program, the computer can provide the information the customer requires within a few seconds.

A **database** program permits the storing of data in a systematic way on a disk file so that it may be easily retrieved and updated as required. Database programs can easily do things that are often too time consuming in a manual system. Suppose you want to know all of the customers who have ordered a specific part. In a manual system, every customer's record would need to be examined, taking many hours of labor. However, a simple

Database. A collection of files relating to a given application with query and update capabilities.

query (Figure 1-10) on a database program could find the answer in as little time as a few minutes.

Some of the features of a database program are as follows.

1. The ability to add new records to the file as new activity occurs.
2. The ability to revise existing records as data about that record changes.
3. The ability to delete records that are no longer required.
4. A query capability that permits asking questions about the contents of the database.
5. The ability to organize or sort large amounts of data into a more usable form.
6. The ability to generate reports from the database with appropriate totals or summarizing of data.

Some commonly used database programs for personal computers are dBASE IV, Paradox, PFS File, and Microsoft Access.

Graphics. To rephrase an ancient saying, a graph is worth a thousand words. A **graph** portrays numerical data pictorially. Using graphs to communicate the relationships between numbers can be much more effective than trying to explain the same data (Figure 1-11). Graphs can also help in the analysis of the numbers when a simple mathematical formula just won't do.

Although many spreadsheet programs produce graphs, they do not have the specialized abilities of the graphics software packages. Sometimes data

Graphics program. Software that assists in the preparation, editing, and presentation of graphic images.

FIGURE 1-10
Data stored in a database management system (DBMS) may be accessed in a variety of ways. Here a query operation is used to find out which customers have ordered SVGA Screens for their computers.

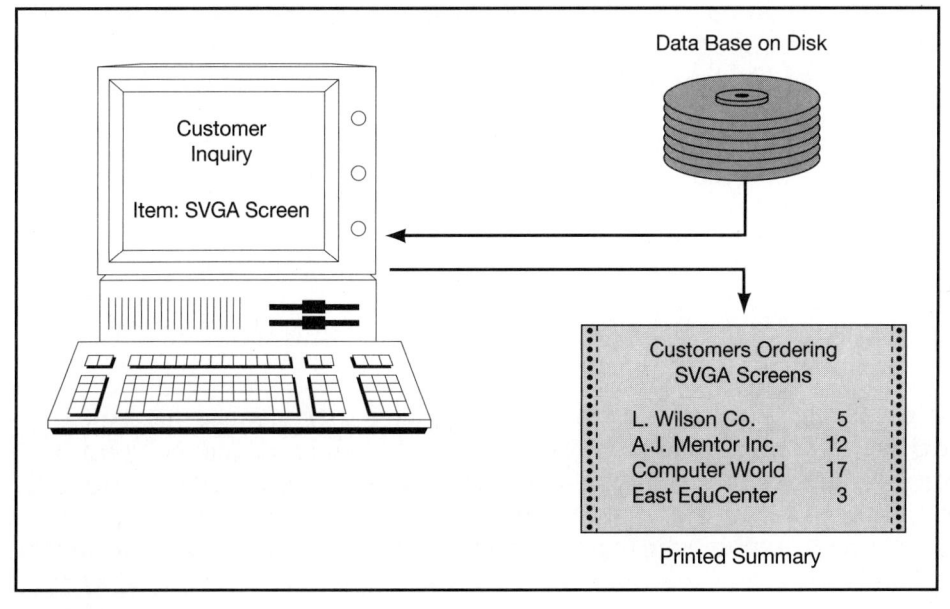

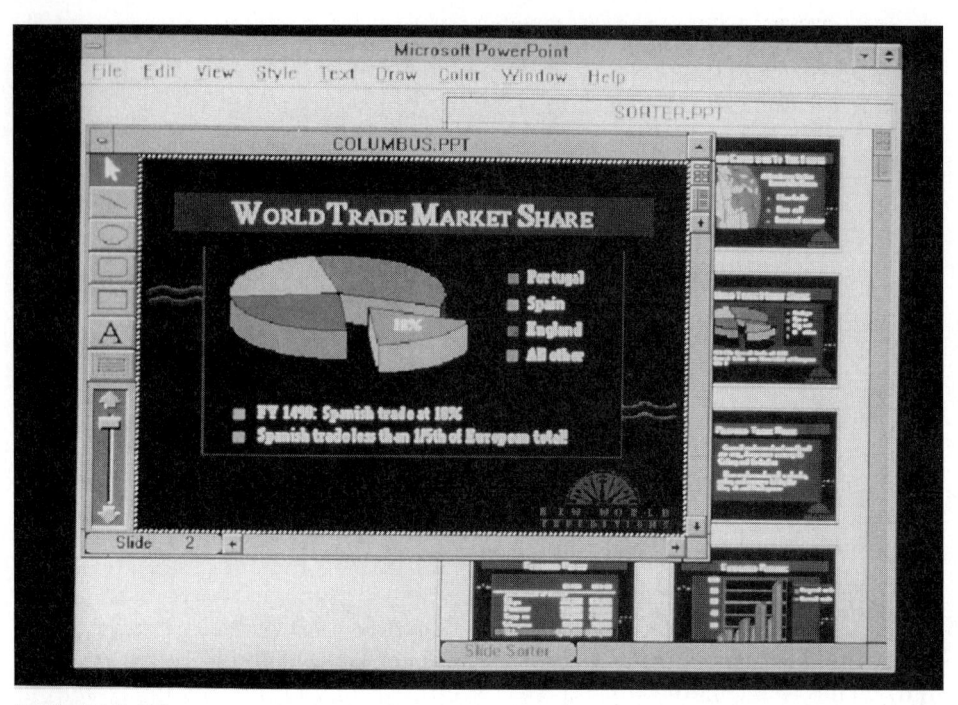

FIGURE 1-11
Graphic displays are used to enhance the presentation of numerical data. (Courtesy Microsoft.)

is organized in a spreadsheet such as Lotus 1–2–3, and a rough graph is produced by 1–2–3 to give a feel for the presentation. Then the data is sent to one of the specialized graphic programs which can produce dazzling graphs with high-quality output.

Some graphics programs are essentially charting programs that produce a variety of bar or pie charts with various type styles on a dot matrix printer, laser printer, or plotter. Others can create an animated presentation that is projected like a slide projector for use in business meetings or sales presentations.

Specialized graphic packages can be used to create flow charts, organization charts, or other analytical graphics. Many graphic programs work with specialized output devices such as a film recorder or camera that create high-quality 35mm slides of the graph. Because these devices are often more expensive than the computer, a service bureau that specializes in creating quality graphs is often used.

Some widely used graphic programs are Lotus Freelance, Harvard Presentation Graphics, and CorelDRAW.

Integrated Software. When a computer user has become skilled in the use of the major software programs including spreadsheets, word processing, and database management, the next major need usually is the ability to transfer data between each of these programs. Often a manager who is creating a report will require some data that exists on the database as

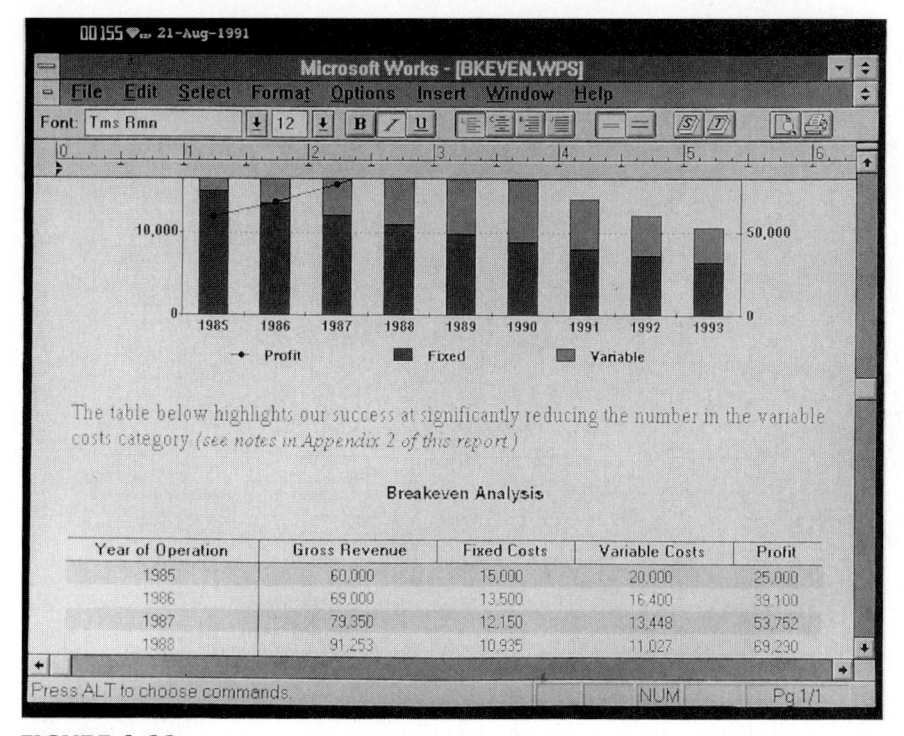

FIGURE 1-12
This integrated software provides the user with word processing, spreadsheet, database, graphics, and communications capability. (Courtesy Microsoft.)

well as some statistics and graphs provided by the spreadsheet. Pulling these together into a single report can be the task of the word processor.

Achieving the above tasks with most software is either impossible or quite complex. One solution is to use an integrated software package that provides all of the above capabilities and more in a single software solution. **Integrated software** (Figure 1-12) typically supplies five functions in the one package: word processing, spreadsheet, database, graphics, and communications. Enable and Microsoft Works are two popular integrated packages. A newer solution to the integration problem is the use of Windows and Windows applications, which permit the transfer and sharing of data between a variety of applications using **object linking and embedding (OLE)**.

Communications

Many personal computers operate as **stand-alone** machines, which means that they function independently of other computers. But, for systems like this, it is difficult or inefficient to share information between them. To solve this problem many computers are being connected together (Figure 1-13) so that they may share common software and even access the same files from a common disk drive.

Integrated software. Software that supplies word processing, spreadsheet, database, graphics, and communications in one package.

Object linking and embedding. A method of transferring and sharing data between applications.

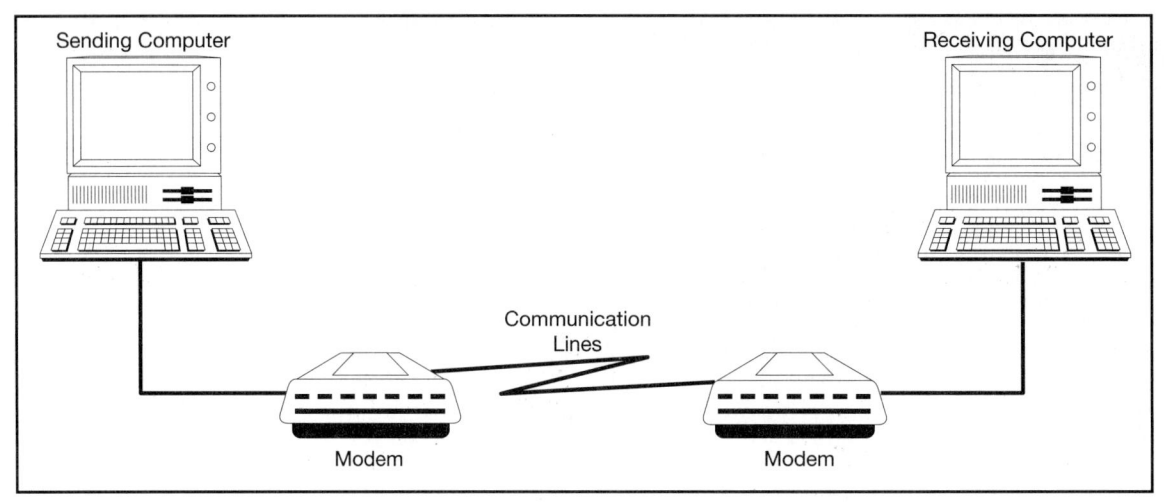

FIGURE 1-13
A modem is used to connect a computer to a communication line so that it may communicate with a remote computer that is similarly equipped.

Local area network (LAN). A communication network that connects computers for the purpose of data sharing.

Computers in close proximity to each other, such as several PCs in an office space, can be connected by electrical wires as a **local area network (LAN)**. More remote systems, such as computers located in different cities or even different countries, use established telephone systems or telecommunications networks to communicate. When computers are connected either locally or at a distance, additional hardware and software are required to make communication possible.

There are many reasons for communicating with a remote computer. One is to let the computer have access to electronic mail or electronic bulletin boards for the exchange of information of common interest. Another is to let the personal computer access a mainframe system that contains public databases such as stock market quotations, news, or travel information. Personal computers with communication capability may also act as a remote terminal for a mainframe computer to collect data that is forwarded to the mainframe system.

Many software packages recognize the need that computer users have for linking with other computers and now provide built-in features for data communications. This capability reduces the need to have separate communications software. Built-in communication capability is a common component of integrated software.

Multimedia system. A computer system that uses a mixture of audio and visual devices for sound, video, graphics, text, and animation.

Multimedia Software

Computers that are used for training or education packages, sales presentations, or special applications such as medical reference systems or encyclopedias need more than the usual mix of input and output. These **multimedia systems** (Figure 1-14) may also require a mixture of audio and visual devices such as CD-ROMs, videodisks, MIDI systems, and audio CD to operate effectively.

FIGURE 1-14
Multimedia systems provide audio and video capabilities with access to billions of characters of information to the user. (Courtesy Radio Shack, A Division of Tandy Corporation.)

Because of the increasing demand for multimedia systems such as these, multimedia authoring software is becoming more widely available to personal computer users. Multimedia authoring software supports many different hardware devices and file formats so that a production that combines sound, video, graphics, text, and animation can be created from a single software package. Some current software products for multimedia are Authorware Professional, Multimedia Toolbook, and IconAuthor. Windows 3.1 also has available a Multimedia Extension that supports this fast-developing area.

COMPUTERS AND YOUR WORLD

In the discussion and photographs of this chapter you have been given a general idea of what computers are all about. You have looked at what computers are and why they are useful. You have seen that for computers to be used effectively, both hardware and software is necessary. Hardware includes the processor and several input and output devices such as a keyboard, screen, printer, disk drive, and other possible devices. Software includes both systems software (DOS) and application software such as spreadsheets, word processing, database, graphics, and integrated systems. As you read the following chapters you will gain a fuller understanding of the computer and how it is being used in your world.

CHAPTER SUMMARY

1. Many business people use a personal computer to supply, store, and process information so that they may do their job or run their company more effectively.
2. A **knowledge worker** is a person whose job depends largely on the use of knowledge or information.
3. A **computer system** is an electronic device which consists of several components that together provide the capability of executing a stored program for input, output, arithmetic, and logical operations.
4. **Data** represents the raw facts while **information** is data that has been collected and presented in a meaningful way.
5. An **Information System** is a system that collects and organizes data into a form that has meaning for a specific business function.
6. A **management information system (MIS)** uses the computer to collect data, process it, summarize it, and use it to generate a variety of reports that provide all levels of management with the information they need.
7. A **decision support system (DSS)** refers to a system where information from a computer is used for decision making.
8. A **personal computer** is intended for use by one person. Many personal computers may be networked so that they may share the same programs and data.
9. A **mainframe computer system** is intended for centralized use by many people and requires computer professionals for its implementation and operation.
10. Computer components fall into three categories: processor, input, and output.
11. The **processor** consists of primary storage or memory, the arithmetic and logic unit (ALU), and the control unit (CU). A personal computer also has a **bus** for sending data between components in the system, **ports** to attach input/output devices, and **expansion slots** to add new features.
12. **Input** devices supply data for the computer to act on. Input devices include a keyboard, mouse, digitizer, floppy disk drive, hard disk drive, and modem.
13. **Output** devices let us see the results of the computer's operation or store the results for later use. Output devices are the display screen, printer, plotter, floppy disk drive, hard disk drive, and modem.
14. **Software** is a program that supplies the instructions for the computer to follow.
15. **Systems software** makes the computer and its applications programs function effectively. The most widely used systems software is the disk operating system (DOS).
16. **Application software** is designed to do a specific function such as word processing, database, or spreadsheet software.
17. A **spreadsheet** is a program that permits the entry of data and formulas in rows and columns on the screen. As new values are entered all formulas are automatically recalculated and the results shown immediately on the screen.
18. A **word processor** is a program that aids in the typing of text ranging from short memos to manuscript-length documents. The program aids in underlining, formatting, boldface, reorganizing, error correction, and may provide

CHAPTER 1 The World of Computers

other advanced features such as headers and footers, spelling checks, and form letters.

19. A **database management system (DBMS)** is a program that permits the storing of data in a systematic way on a disk file so that it may be easily retrieved and updated as required.
20. A **graphics** program portrays numerical data pictorially. Using graphs to communicate the relationships between numbers can be much more effective than trying to explain verbally the same data.
21. **Integrated software** usually supplies five functions in one package: word processing, spreadsheet, database, graphics, and communications.
22. Computers in a local setting may communicate with one another using a **local area network**, while other computers located at a distance may use telephone lines or communication facilities to transfer data.
23. A **multimedia system** is a computer that contains a mixture of audio and visual devices such as CD-ROMs, videodisks, MIDI systems, and audio CD in addition to the usual input and output devices.

IMPORTANT TERMS AND CONCEPTS

Application software
Arithmetic and Logic Unit (ALU)
Bus
Business system
Central Processing Unit (CPU)
Computer system
Control unit
Data
Database Management Systems (DBMS)
Decision Support System (DSS)
Desktop computer
Disk Operating System (DOS)
Expansion slots
Graphics
Information
Information system (IS)
Input device
Integrated software
Knowledge worker
Local area network (LAN)

Mainframe computer
Management Information System (MIS)
Memory
Microcomputer
Minicomputer
Multimedia
Object linking and embedding (OLE)
Output device
Personal computer (PC)
Ports
Primary storage
Processor
Query
Secondary storage
Software
Spreadsheet
Supercomputer
Systems software
Word processing

SELF-TESTING QUESTIONS

Fill-In

1. _____ uses a device, such as the keyboard to provide data for the computer to process or act upon.

2. _____ is when the computer acts upon the data to provide a variety of useful information needed for reports or graphs.
3. _____ is the result of processing and can be displayed on the screen, printed, or stored on disk.
4. The term _____ refers to the raw material or facts that are gathered for input to the computer.
5. When these facts are collected and organized in a meaningful pattern they are called _____.
6. Physical devices such as the processor, screen, printer, and disk drive are called _____.
7. Programs such as word processors and spreadsheets are called _____.
8. The term _____ means "What you see is what you get."
9. A _____ is a program that permits the entry of data and formulas in rows and columns on the screen.
10. A _____ program permits the storing of data in a systematic way on a disk file so that it may be easily retrieved and updated as required.

True/False

1. Computers come in all sizes. At the low end there is the microcomputer, which is better known as the personal computer or desktop computer.
2. Only the high-end personal computers have internal expansion slots for adding extra features such as memory expansion, high-resolution graphics, or a Fax card.
3. DOS is an acronym for Desktop Office System.
4. A word processing program aids in the typing of text ranging from short memos and letters to manuscript-length documents.
5. Integrated software typically supplies five functions in the one package: word processing, spreadsheet, database, graphics, and communications.
6. Database management systems (DBMS) are so complex that they require a mainframe computer for their implementation.
7. Computers in close proximity to each other, such as several PCs in an office space, can communicate using a local area network.
8. Multimedia systems are called by that name because they are primarily radio- and television-oriented.

ANSWERS

Fill-In: 1. Input, 2. Processing, 3. Output, 4. data, 5. information, 6. hardware, 7. software, 8. WYSIWYG, 9. spreadsheet, 10. database
True/False: 1. T, 2. F, 3. F, 4. T, 5. T, 6. F, 7. T, 8. F

Questions for Critical Thinking

1. With the release of the IBM PC, personal computers finally became best sellers. Some predicted that the PC's popularity signaled the end of the large mainframe computer system. Why do you think this prediction has failed to come true?

2. From your daily observations discuss the ways that people use computers in their daily lives.
3. Why is it that information systems are so important to a broad variety of businesses today?
4. Your friend BW offers you the loan of the disks for a major word processing program so that you can load it onto your hard disk. Risk Free Real Estate is a company that has 20 computers with users who all need a word processor. Instead of buying sufficient copies, the department manager loads the one copy on each computer. AG is an entrepreneurial individual who sees a profit to be made by selling copies of a leading word processor.

   Each of the above scenarios presents a different situation where software is being copied for personal or business use. Discuss the ethics of each of these practices.

CHAPTER 2

COMPUTER PROCESSORS

A VIEW OF THE CHAPTER AHEAD

After reading this chapter you will understand

- ▶ the major components of the system unit including the CPU, memory, and buses and the terminology used to compare them.
- ▶ that letters, digits, and other characters are represented in ASCII code.
- ▶ the characteristics of IC technology that made personal computers possible.
- ▶ the importance of computer interfaces.
- ▶ the variety of computers on the market and the features they offer to satisfy many different needs.
- ▶ some of the differences between the PC and the mainframe processor and why the mainframe is decreasingly used in business.

INTRODUCTION

When Liz Weiss saw WordPerfect for Windows demonstrated in the computer store, she immediately knew it was the word processor she was looking for. Liz runs a home and business insurance franchise and often needs to prepare insurance quotations for her clients. When she saw the Windows version of WordPerfect, she knew it would be ideal for producing letters and quotations in an attractive format and yet be an efficient tool to make fast work of a routine requirement. But when she installed the program on her 386SX computer, it ran much slower than she expected. In the store, the salesperson had shown her how commands were selected using a mouse and the response had been immediate. Now she was finding that there was always a long wait before WordPerfect responded to each command she selected.

After explaining the problem to her friend Monica, the first question Monica asked was how much memory (RAM) did Liz have on her computer? It turned out that the computer only had 2MB of RAM, which is the minimum needed to run WordPerfect for Windows. Monica explained that Windows applications generally run faster with either a faster computer or more memory or both. Because more memory costs much less than a new computer, this seemed the obvious choice and it was all that was needed to solve Liz's problem.

When the decision has been made to purchase a computer, the first question often asked is "what computer should I buy?" This may seem to be a question that is easily answered when personal computers are the objective, but even with the desktop computer there are many factors to be considered. Making the right decision about a desktop, laptop, palmtop, or notebook computer, the type of processor (do I need a 386, 486, or faster), the memory size, processing speed, display and communication capabilities, available secondary storage and printer compatibility are all determined in relation to the processor or components that are directly attached to it.

Even when the choice of computer has been made by management consensus or some other process, the knowledge of the processor components is important. By understanding the function of the various components of the processor, you will be better equipped to determine what activities can be realistically done on the computer. This knowledge will let you know if graphs can be displayed or printed, whether the memory is sufficient to handle a specific piece of software effectively, or whether data from another computer made by a different manufacturer will be able to be processed on yours.

PROCESSOR CHARACTERISTICS

Bits, Bytes, and Words

When computer designers began using electronic components back in the early 1940s, they soon realized that using decimal numbers to represent

CHAPTER 2 Computer Processors

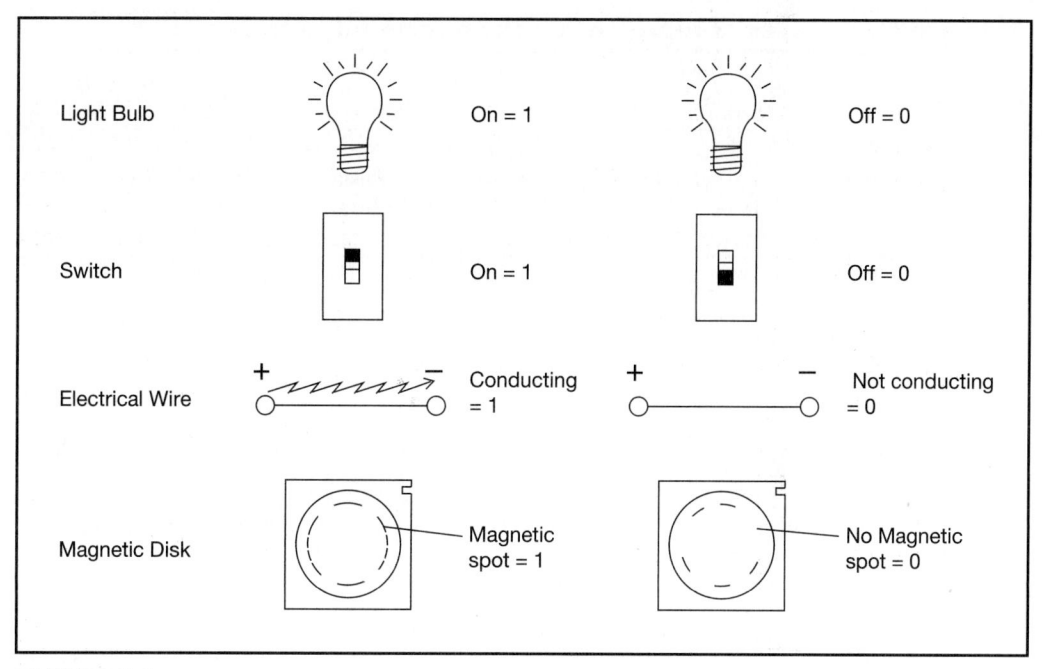

FIGURE 2-1
A binary number is formed from a combination of zeros and ones. Common devices such as a light bulb or a wall switch can be used to represent binary values. If the light bulb is on, it represents the value 1, but if it is off it represents binary zero. Such a method of coding is used with magnetic spots to record data on the surface of a disk.

data did not work very well. The reason for this problem was that electronic components were essentially switches. They could be in one of two states—on or off. As Figure 2-1 shows, an on or off state can represent only two values, zero or one, which are the fundamental properties of the binary number system.

Bits

The decision to base computer design on the binary number system turned out to be a wise choice because many of the advances in electronics and micro technology have been developed from the binary number principle. It is from the binary number that we get the term bit. The word bit is derived from **binary digit**. A **bit** is the smallest element or value that is represented in the computer and, as we have seen, it represents the value zero or one.

Bits are used in many areas in the computer. Data in memory is represented at its most basic level by bits. Data flows from the processor to other input or output devices as a stream of bits, and it is stored on secondary storage devices such as a magnetic disk in the form of magnetic bits. So you can see that the use of a bit is fundamental to most operations in the computer.

Bit. Binary digits 0 and 1 represent the smallest element in computer memory.

TABLE 2-1   Terms representing the number of bytes.

Term	Number of bytes	Prefix	Meaning	Greek	Original Meaning
Kilobyte	1,024	kilo	thousand	khilioi	thousand
Megabyte	1,048,576	mega	million	megas	great
Gigabyte	1,073,741,824	giga	billion	gigas	giant
Terabyte	1,099,511,627,776	tera	trillion	teras	monster

Source: *PC Magazine*, Nov. 25, 1986, p. 150.

TABLE 2-2   ASCII character set values.

Decimal Value	Character	Decimal Value	Character	Decimal Value	Character
32	space	65	A	97	a
33	!	66	B	98	b
34	"	67	C	99	c
35	#	68	D	100	d
36	$	69	E	101	e
37	%	70	F	102	f
38	&	71	G	103	g
39	'	72	H	104	h
40	(	73	I	105	i
41	)	74	J	106	j
42	*	75	K	107	k
43	+	76	L	108	l
44	,	77	M	109	m
45	-	78	N	110	n
46	.	79	O	111	o
47	/	80	P	112	p
48	0	81	Q	113	q
49	1	82	R	114	r
50	2	83	S	115	s
51	3	84	T	116	t
52	4	85	U	117	u
53	5	86	V	118	v
54	6	87	W	119	w
55	7	88	X	120	x
56	8	89	Y	121	y
57	9	90	Z	122	z
58	:	91	[	123	{
59	;	92	\	124		
60	<	93	]	125	}
61	=	94	^	126	~
62	>	95	_	127	⌂
63	?	96	`	128	?
64	@				

Bytes

Although bits are useful for electronic components, they need to be grouped together into bytes for a more meaningful representation of data. A **byte** is the term used to describe a group of eight bits and is the basic unit of data in the computer. A byte can be used to represent a character, such as an upper- or lowercase letter, a number, a punctuation symbol, or even a graphic symbol. Because there are eight bits in a byte and a bit can be one of two values, a byte can represent 2^8 or 256 different values, which is more than enough for most applications.

The byte is used as a measure of the computer's memory size and of disk storage capacity. Because memory is usually in the thousands of bytes, the letter K is used to represent kilo, which comes from the Greek language meaning thousand. K in computer talk, however, refers to 1024 bytes. Memory size in excess of 1 million bytes uses the letter M from the Greek mega. Thus, we have 2MB or 2 million bytes of memory and so on. Larger sizes are also represented by letters, as shown in Table 2-1. Table 2-2 shows how size in bytes is measured for both primary storage (memory) and secondary storage (disk).

Byte. Normally composed of 8 bits, a byte is the space required to store a single character.

K. A measure used to represent 1024 bytes.

▶ HOW MANY BITS IS YOUR COMPUTER?

A computer is often described as having a 16-bit or a 32-bit processor. This term is used to describe the size of the word used within the computer. The bits measurement refers to the number of bits that the computer can process in one operation. For arithmetic, a 16-bit computer may require several steps to complete the operation on a large number, while a 32-bit computer may be able to do the same operation in one step, thus completing the calculation much faster.

16-BIT COMPUTERS

This class represents by far the largest number of personal computers in use during the 1980s. The IBM Personal Computer is the best known example of a 16-bit computer, and some models of the PS/2 come in this category. Of course the many compatibles offered by companies such as Compaq, Dell, Texas Instruments, and Zeos are included in this group. Some minicomputers are also 16-bit computers. 16-bit computers are good at a variety of tasks including spreadsheets, word processing, database management, and many other business and even scientific applications. In the early 1990s, the 16-bit computer is fast becoming extinct because of the falling prices on 32-bit computers.

32-BIT COMPUTERS

In the mid-1980s a new class of personal computer became available. Although 32 bits and more were not unusual on minicomputers and mainframes, they were previously too expensive for PCs. The Apple Macintosh was the first of the 32-bit personal computers and was soon followed by others. IBM brought out a new version of the PC called the PC/AT for Advanced Technology, followed by their Personal System/2. 32-bit systems have greater memory capacity and higher speeds than 16-bit computers and are used where very large spreadsheet applications, networking, and multitasking is necessary. The 80286, 80386, 80486 are all variations on the 32-bit processor. In the 1990s a 32-bit computer has become a necessity for virtually all applications.

64-BIT COMPUTERS

In 1993, Intel announced the Pentium (a new name for the P5 or 80586) processor. Its speed is over 100 MIPS (million instructions per second, twice the performance of a 486DX-33). No doubt this high-end processor will redefine the direction of personal computing in the years to come.

A typical office computer has 2MB bytes of random access memory (RAM) and a fixed disk drive with a 100MB capacity. RAM of this size is sufficient for most applications, but can be expanded for applications such as Windows when 2M is not enough for effective operation. Computers like an 80386 can have up to 16 million bytes of main memory. By contrast, disk drives of much higher capacity (300M or more) are available, and if one is not enough, then two or more may be used on the computer. (Courtesy NCR.)

Words

A **word** is a logical unit of information consisting of a number of bits. In an 8-bit microprocessor, a word is 8 bits in length, which is the same as a byte. You might have guessed that a 16-bit processor's word is 16 bits long and therefore consists of two bytes. It is this measurement that determines the size of the machine language instruction that can be executed by the computer and indirectly the speed of processing.

CPU. The Central Processing Unit contains the arithmetic and logic unit (ALU) and a control unit to direct the computer's operations.

COMPONENTS

We have already seen in Chapter 1 how a computer system consists of several components that operate together to make up a functional computer. The main components found in a computer system are shown in Figure 2-2. These components are:

1. The **central processing unit (CPU)** or **microprocessing unit (MPU)**, as it is sometimes called, which follows the directions in the program to de-

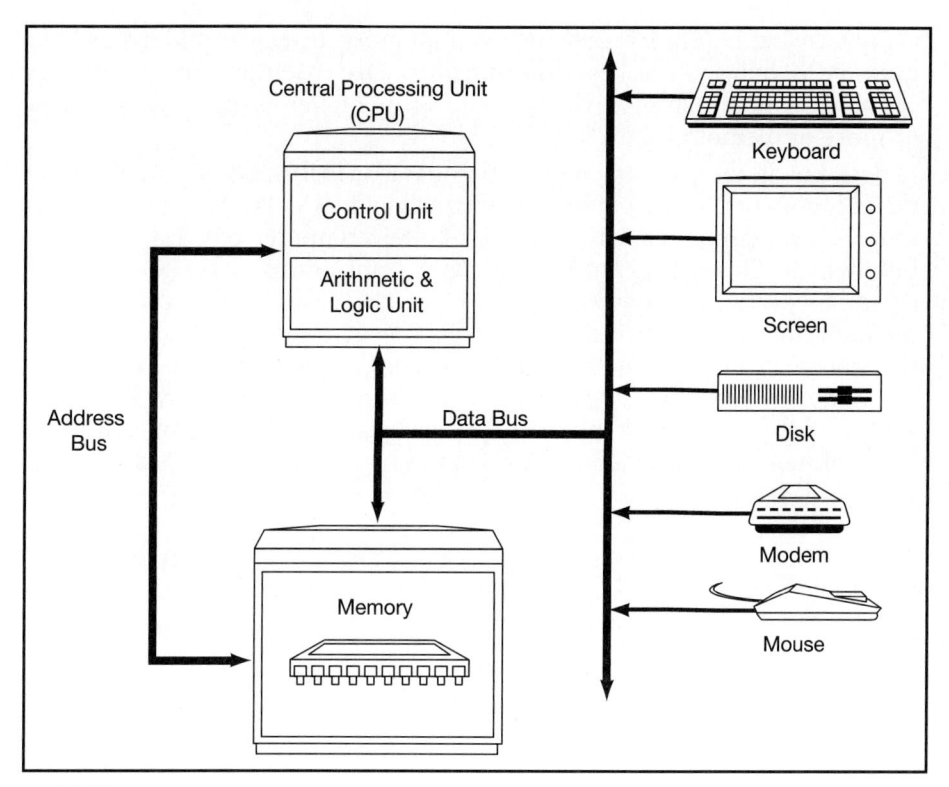

FIGURE 2-2
The primary components of the computer's processor.

termine the actions to be taken by the computer. Most processors in today's personal computers reside on a single integrated chip. A 16-bit processor can do operations on data that is 16 bits or 2 bytes in length. Larger numbers, or operations on more than two bytes, will require two or more operations for each calculation. Some computers will use a **co-processor,** which is a second processor designed for doing faster numeric processing.

2. The **memory** is the component that stores the program and the data be-

(Courtesy IBM.)

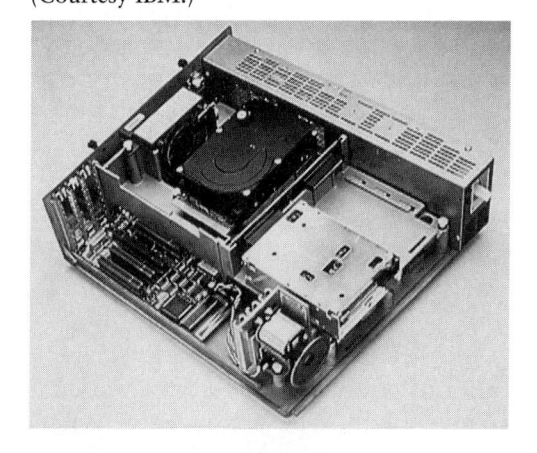

ing processed. Memory consists of a number of integrated chips. On PCs, 640K bytes is the beginning memory size. Memory above 640K is called extended memory. Most 386 level or higher computers have 2M or more of memory.

Bus. An electronic path that carries data or instructions for the computer's operation.

3. A **data bus** is the path through which data or instructions flow between the components of the computer. The original IBM PC had a 16-bit microprocessor and an 8-bit data bus. A 486 computer has a 32-bit data bus, which allows for much faster data transfer than the PC. The **address** bus carries memory addresses to all devices that are connected to the data bus. The bit size of the address bus determines the size of memory that may be addressed. Early 8-bit computers had a 16-bit address bus and could address 2^{16} (65,536) bytes of memory. The IBM PC had a 20-bit address bus, thus allowing a theoretical maximum of 1 million bytes of memory, while 486 computers use a 32-bit address bus that can address 32 megabytes.

The characteristics of these components of the computer determine to a large extent the capabilities of the system. The specifications of the processor determine the type of software that can be used on the computer and the speed at which the programs will run.

Speed

We have seen that the more bits a processor or bus can handle the faster the computer will operate. Another factor that affects the speed of the computer is the clock. Each personal computer contains an electronic clock in its circuitry that acts as a timer to ensure that all of the activity going on in the computer is coordinated. If a new activity begins before a previous one is finished, the computer will simply fail to operate accurately and so the clock controls the timing of all events.

Clock speed. A speed measured in megahertz (MHz) that identifies the speed at which the processor carries out its operations.

The speed of the clock is measured in **megahertz (MHz),** which is a term referring to the number of cycles per second at which it operates. This is something like a stop watch that measures time in thousandths of a second, except that time in a microcomputer is measured in MHz or millionths of a second.

A typical clock speed on a 386SX computer is 20MHz or more. Some high-end processors will operate at speeds of up to 50 MHz and more. Ultimately, the speed at which the computer completes a given task depends not only on clock speed, but on a variety of factors that include disk speed, the type of software used, and the way the bus is designed.

COMPUTER CODES

Although numbers in a computer are described by a number system such as binary, the actual binary digits can be used to represent all kinds of data including letters and numbers. (See Appendix C for more detail.) In addition to binary, all computers use some kind of internal code to represent characters, that is, digits, letters, and special symbols. The most widely used code

FIGURE 2-3
The integrated circuit is at the heart of all computer design and construction. A chip such as this Intel 80386 is about a square inch in size and yet contains over 100,000 circuits that the computer uses in its operation. (Courtesy Intel.)

for personal computers is the **American Standard Code for Information Interchange (ASCII)**. This is an 8-bit code meaning that characters are represented with eight bits of binary digits. In most ASCII definitions, seven of these bits are used for the character and the eighth bit is used for error checking. Using this system provides a capability for up to 128 different characters, digits, or letters in the code.

In the computer's processor and on some storage devices, such as magnetic disk, each character is represented as a binary value. For example, the number 1 is stored in ASCII as 0110001, which is equivalent to the decimal value 49. The uppercase letter A is stored as 1000001, which is decimal 65. Most operations, such as programming or other software development, use the decimal equivalent or even the character itself as it is typed at the keyboard. Figure 2-3 shows a selected number of the ASCII values for a typical character set.

Some mainframe computers also use the ASCII code, but a more widely used code on IBM and other mainframes is **EBCDIC**, which is an acronym for **Extended Binary Coded Decimal Interchange Code**. This code bears some similarity to ASCII in that is also has 8 bits per character, but the coding system used is quite different.

ASCII. American Standard Code for Information Interchange is a code used for representing data in the computer.

EBCDIC. Extended Binary Coded Decimal Interchange Code is a code used mostly for representing data in mainframe computers.

ICs AND MICROPROCESSORS

The **microprocessor** is the chip that contains the processor, arithmetic and logic unit, and control unit. **Integrated circuits (IC)** are silicon chips that contain a number of transistors on one chip. The transistor is a solid state device that was invented by John Barder, William Shockley, and Walter

Integrated circuit. A silicon chip containing circuits for microprocessors or other electronic devices.

Bratten at Bell Telephone Laboratories in 1948. The transistor revolutionized the electronics and computer industries because of its compact size, speed of operation, and durability.

Since that time, further developments in microelectronics have enabled designers to pack more transistors into a single integrated circuit (Figure 2-3). Packing more circuits into a single IC has had several effects on computer technology, a major one being to make the personal computer a reality. Here are some of the other significant effects.

1. **Size.** The computer can be much smaller in size when ICs of greater density are used.
2. **Cost.** Using ICs in computer design results in less expensive computers compared to previous technologies.
3. **Speed.** Because of the smaller size, electrons in the circuit need to travel shorter distances, resulting in higher operating speeds.
4. **Power.** Electrical power consumption is less with IC components. These components also generate less heat than previous technologies, thus requiring no special cooling.

Since IC technology appeared there has been a continual reduction in size and corresponding increase in the number of transistors packed into the IC. Several levels of design have appeared with this improving technol-

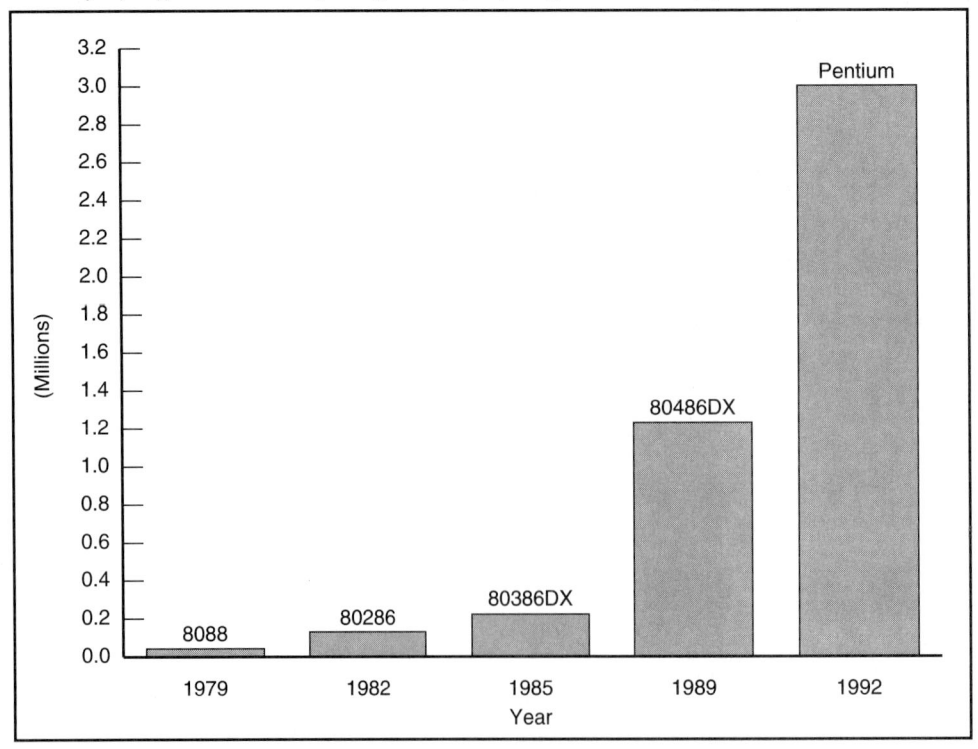

FIGURE 2-4
Density of different levels of integration for five generations of processors.

CHAPTER 2 Computer Processors

ogy. Chip densities are expressed in terms of integration of scale. Low-density chips are **SSI** (small-scale integration) and **MSI** (medium-scale integration), followed by **LSI** (large-scale integration), **VLSI** (very-large-scale-integration), and **SLSI** (super-large-scale integration). Figure 2-4 shows the relative density of processor chips in terms of the number of transistors they contain.

MEMORY

Memory, also called primary storage, is an essential component of the computer. Memory is primarily used to store programs, which are the instructions performed by the processor, and data, which are used for the arithmetic and logical operations. Memory capacity is measured in K for thousands or M for millions of bytes of storage. Memory in today's computers is made from silicon chips in a similar manner to the manufacture of processor chips. There are two main kinds of memory chips in a Personal Computer—RAM and ROM.

Memory. A part of the computer that stores data and instructions for the computer's use.

RAM

The term **RAM** means **random access memory** (Figure 2-5) and is the memory where a program, such as a word processing program or a spreadsheet program, is stored when it is presently active in the computer. When an ex-

RAM. Random access memory is memory that stores temporary data such as a spreadsheet or a program.

FIGURE 2-5
The relationship of input and output to RAM, ROM, and the processor.

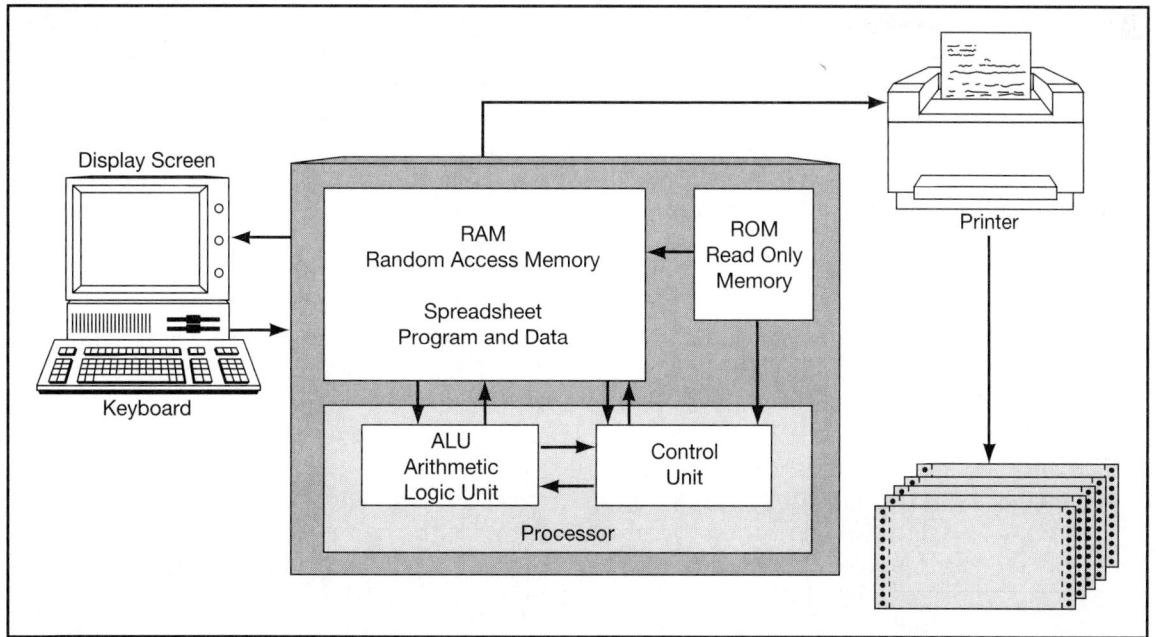

A memory chip such as this 16-MB SIMM is used in a 486 computer for random access memory. (Courtesy Motorola.)

pression like 640K or 4MB is used to describe the size of memory, it refers to the storage capacity of random access memory.

Most RAM is **volatile,** which requires the continuous application of power to retain data and programs. The practical impact of volatile RAM is that it retains the program or data only so long as the power is applied. If the computer's power is turned off, everything in RAM is lost unless it has first been stored or saved on a disk or other secondary storage device. **Nonvolatile** RAM, which is also called CMOS RAM, can retain their contents by the use of rechargeable batteries that are part of the RAM circuit.

RAM provides large memory capacity that is relatively easy and inexpensive to expand by adding more chips to the board. Because the contents of RAM is easily changed (unlike ROM), it is simple and fast to change from a word processing application to a spreadsheet and then to a database with only a few simple commands at the keyboard.

ROM

ROM. Read only memory. Stores data permanently in the computer. ROM is read only and cannot be changed.

Read only memory (ROM) is similar to RAM except that ROM chips store information permanently in the computer. The contents of ROM can be read by the processor but not written, thus the name "read only." A benefit of this property is that the contents are not lost when the power to the computer is interrupted.

Important system software is stored in ROM. One of these is a program that assists in the process of starting up the computer and doing such basic input/output operations as reading the keyboard or writing on the screen. Programs in ROM are permanent and are not normally changed during the lifetime of the computer.

Addresses						
Decimal	0	1	2	3	4	5
Hexadecimal	0	1	2	3	4	5
Decimal	16,378	16,379	16,380	16,381	16,382	16,383
Hexadecimal	3FFA	3FFB	3FFC	3FFD	3FFE	3FFF

FIGURE 2-6
Addressing 16K of memory. Each byte of memory has a unique address that is used by programs to access data at that location. Addresses begin with 0 and increase by 1 until the end of memory is reached. Addressing is done in the computer using binary values, which can be represented as decimal or hexadecimal for the convenience of computer programmers.

Addressing Memory

Memory chips form an array of locations where data and programs may be stored. As the computer is following the instructions in the program, it needs to know where to get the data to carry out the required operation. Programs also need to branch within themselves to carry out decision making or looping. All of this activity requires that the exact location or address of program instructions or data be known.

Each byte of computer memory has a unique address, as shown in Figure 2-6. To access an item of data, the program needs to know the address of that data and to supply it to the control unit, which in turn makes the data available to the program. Memory addressing begins at zero and increases to the value of the maximum address. A 16K computer would have 16,384 bytes of memory and so its addressing would be from 0 to 16,383.

Processors, such as the 80486 from Intel, use a 32-bit scheme to address up to 4GB (gigabytes) of memory. The Macintosh uses a Motorola 68000 processor which is also a 32-bit processor with addressing up to 4GB. With the appropriate operating system, these computers can also use disk space for virtual memory which in effect increases the amount of memory available to applications.

RISC MICROPROCESSORS

Computer engineers are always looking for ways to make the microprocessor operate faster and execute more program instructions. This search isn't

▶ FROM INTEL'S 80486 TO THE PENTIUM

What is 50 times faster than the original IBM PC and more powerful than an 80386 processor chip? It is the 80486 Intel microprocessor released in early 1989. Computers based on this 32-bit processor offer mainframe-like performance in a desktop computer.

The 80486 is an advance on the 386 technology, which already has become a widely accepted standard in the computing industry but is fast being replaced by the 486. One weakness of the 386 was the need for extra components to speed up mathematical and graphic functions. These components are fully integrated into the design of the 486 processor.

Intel's most successful processor contains 1,180,285 transistors and offers full compatibility with the 386. The new technology supports complex scientific calculations and financial modeling. It helps to manage local area networks, electronic messages and imaging such as those used in fax systems, and supports advanced graphics functions such as color separation for desktop publishing. For the average user this may seem like too much power, but as more intensive Windows and OS/2 applications are used, the 486 is necessary to achieve adequate performance for many applications.

In 1992 Intel released a 50-MHz 486DX/2 processor (followed closely by a 66-MHz 486DX/2). The 50-MHz 486DX/2 processor costs about the same as a 25-MHZ 486 chip did a year previously. The 50-MHz processor uses a speed doubling technology that is based on the 486/25 but with the clock running at 50-MHz for internal processing. Communication with the system bus operates at 25 MHz, which means that input and output goes at the speed of a 486/25. Applications that are process intensive will benefit from this new chip, whereas I/O-intensive operations, such as a file server computer in a network, will gain little from this new technology.

The trend of ever faster and more powerful processors continued when Intel released the Pentium processor chip in the spring of 1993. Early releases of the Pentium run at 60-MHz, but with a 64-bit data path and two 8KB caches compared to the 486's single 8KB cache the Pentium runs at approximately double the speed of a 66-MHz 486DX/2. The Pentium also has two internal pipelines for executing instructions. Using two pipelines lets the Pentium process two commands simultaneously to further enhance processing efficiency. Programs that are written specifically to take advantage of this multiprocessing will gain more from this method than existing programs. Computers that require high levels of performance for Windows/NT, OS/2, graphics, and networks will gain the most from this newest development from Intel.

just to lay claim to the faster computer but has practical results in the type of software that can be developed. Software that is used to manage a network to supply large volumes of data from a large database to hundreds of users or simply programs that do many calculations effectively can have a need for a faster processor.

One solution to this problem is the **reduced instruction set computer** (**RISC**, pronounced risk). RISC is really a processor chip that uses fewer instructions in its programming language than other chips. By reducing the number of instructions, the chip can be made to operate more efficiently and therefore faster. However, some engineers claim this is not an effective solution to the speed problem because RISC offers the programmer less flexibility. But for many specialized applications, the RISC-based computer (Figure 2-7) can be an effective solution.

FIGURE 2-7
The IBM POWERserver 970 is from the RISC System/6000 family of computers. It is a high-performance computer used for network management using AIX, IBM's version of the UNIX operating system. (Courtesy IBM.)

ATTACHING DEVICES TO THE COMPUTER

Microprocessors need a way to communicate with input or output devices that are attached to the computer. To achieve this communication link, data is sent and received over a bus or channel which forms the pathway to the device. Because each device is different, a special board, called an expansion board, is needed to provide for the link between the bus and the device. Commonly used devices, such as the display screen, printer, and keyboard, already have a built-in **port** or **interface** to which they are attached.

For other devices, the computer has a number of expansion slots into which **expansion boards** may be installed. The number of slots varies from one computer to another. A board placed in one of these slots may provide the capability for the computer to be attached to a given device or to install special devices such as a CD-ROM drive, fax board, or a sound board (Figure 2-8). Other boards may provide an interface for attaching a high-speed graphics display, while another may be used to connect a page scanner.

Interface. A connector, usually on the rear of the computer, where a device such as a printer or screen is attached.

COMPATIBLES

The original IBM PC that was introduced in 1981 became the standard against which all other personal computers were measured. Within a short time of the PC's introduction other manufacturers introduced their own

Compatible. A computer that runs all software and operates in the same manner as the IBM PC or more recent model of computer.

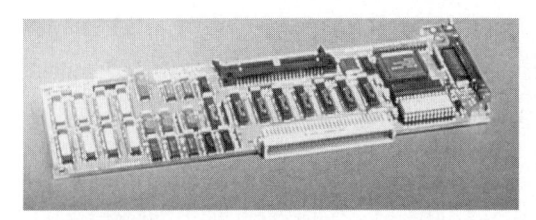

FIGURE 2-8
Expansion slots are provided in most computers for expansion boards that equip the computer with a variety of functions. A board such as this one from MicroNet Technology provides for attaching the computer to a network. (Courtesy MicroNet Technology, Inc.)

versions of the PC. These computers were known as **compatibles** or **clones** because they came close to duplicating the features of the IBM PC and could run all the same software. Early clones were not always 100 percent compatible; some software would run correctly while other programs ran into difficulty or would not run at all. So the quest for a true compatible continued.

Some of these compatibles were more successful than others because they

PC compatibles have become popular because of their competitive pricing, generally good reliability, and compatibility with other computers. Buying a compatible requires a good understanding of your computer needs because memory size, disk drives, screens, keyboards, and software may all have special options to meet your needs at a higher price than the bottom line advertised. Some computers come completely equipped, while others have an option list like a Chevrolet. (Courtesy NCR.)

▶ THE DIFFERENCE BETWEEN PARALLEL AND SERIAL INTERFACES

Different devices require either a serial or parallel port to be attached to the computer. Some devices, such as a printer, can be used as either a serial or a parallel device; the choice depends on the kind of interface available.

A serial interface is one where the data bits that form each character are sent to a device, such as a modem, one at a time. If a character is formed of eight bits, which is the case for ASCII code, then it will take eight units of time to send a character to the device. Serial interfaces operate considerably slower than parallel interfaces, which makes them practical for slow-speed devices such as the modem or mouse.

```
                     Character A in ASCII
                     ────────────────────
    A                   1 0 0 0 0 0 1  ⟩         A

                     Serial interface
Character 'A' sent   seven units of time      Character 'A'
from the computer    plus one unit of         received by
                     time for a check bit     a device
```

A parallel interface (a common one is a Centronics interface named after the company that made it popular) sends all bits for a single character simultaneously along a line. This technique requires a wire or communications path for each bit in the character plus several control paths to identify when data is starting and stopping. A parallel interface is significantly faster than a serial interface although it is more costly. Interfaces to disk drives and many printers are parallel to optimize the transmission of data.

```
                     Character A in ASCII
                     ────────────────────
                              1
                              0
                              0
    A                         0                  A
                              0
                              0
                              1
                     ────────────────────
                     Parallel interface
Character 'A' sent   one unit of time         Character 'A'
from the computer                             received by
                                              a device
```

offered closer compatibility to the PC at a lower price. Many purchasers learned to bring their own software to the store to make sure it would run on the clone before buying it. Other manufacturers offered compatibles at lower prices, faster speeds, or with free software to attract a corner of the market. Today's compatibles will run virtually all mainstream software, so buyers look for the features and price that are most attractive.

THE SHRINKING COMPUTER

Personal computers are expected to be small enough to fit on a desktop and yet leave room for notes or papers that are needed by the user. However, with the demand for greater power and capacity, the physical size of the personal computer has had a tendency to increase.

But, in 1987 a new wave of PCs began to have an impact on the market. First came the smaller footprint computers. The term **footprint** referred to the amount of desk space required for the computer. These computers were a third smaller than others of the same power and capacity. Most of the size reduction came not from using smaller chips as might be expected, but through careful reorganization of the location of components within the computer.

Another trend in downsizing personal computers is in the use of **portable computers** or **laptops,** as the smaller ones are often called. These compact computers offer all of the features of their big brothers with comparable memory capacity, speed, and disk storage. Next came the **notebook** computer (Figure 2-9), which was lighter and more compact than the laptop yet retained most of the same features. Then came the **palmtop,** which is a less

Footprint. The area of space required for a computer. Laptops, notebooks, and palmtops each have successively smaller footprints.

FIGURE 2-9

A notebook computer, such as this Compaq, is truly portable. Operating from a built-in rechargeable battery it provides the computer user with up to 2 hours of operation without a recharge. This computer comes with a standard 4MB of memory, a 120MB hard disk drive, and a 3 1/2 inch floppy disk drive. The screen is a active-matrix LCD display which provides a clear display. (Courtesy Maples & Associates, Irvine, CA.)

powerful computer than the above but, as the name implies, it almost fits into the palm of your hand.

Personal computers continue to grow in speed and capacity and to shrink in price. New developments occur frequently and demand that the aware user continually keep up-to-date with prices and features. Subscribing to a computer magazine is one of the best ways to be sure that you are informed of current developments in the industry.

MAINFRAME PROCESSORS

We have so far discussed the concepts of the processor as it relates to the personal computer. What about the mainframe? Although the PC market has sold millions of computers, the mainframe computer is still in use by most large companies and continues to be an important source of computing power. A mainframe computer is a centralized source of processing that may be accessed simultaneously by many different users, unlike the PC, which is used by one person. So the mainframe must be quite different from the micro. In some ways it is different, but in many ways it is quite similar to a microcomputer, and with the increased speed and capacity of personal computers the differences are becoming less obvious.

Mainframe processors have **primary storage** (memory), an arithmetic logic unit, and a control unit. These components are made from silicon chips with generally greater speed and capacity than a microcomputer's chips. To the user of a mainframe the differences may be rather subtle, but to the programmer there can be major differences between the two types of computers.

Speed

Because mainframes are designed to handle the processing of many users (perhaps hundreds) at the same time, the computer must function many times faster than a PC. Processors in the mainframe run at a high rate of speed often expressed in millions of instructions per second (**MIPS**). Figure 2-10 shows the units used to measure computer speed and how these relate to different generations of computers. Some mainframes may use multiple processors, each of which does a part of the processing task. By using more than one processor the operating speed of the computer is greatly increased.

Memory Size

Mainframe computers have generally greater memory capacity than personal computers. Until the PC/AT and other 80286-based systems, personal computers were generally restricted to 640K or less for the maximum memory size. Mainframes, however, have had memory sizes exceeding a million bytes for many years. But since the PC/AT, maximum memory for PCs and mainframe computers is not much different; memory is a comparison of computer size that is quickly losing significance.

Unit	Fraction of a Second	Computers
Millisecond (ms)	One-thousandth (1/1,000)	First generation
Microsecond (us)	One-millionth (1/1,000,000)	Second generation
Nanosecond (ns)	One-billionth (1/1,000,000,000)	Third generation to present time
Picosecond (ps)	One-trillionth (1/1,000,000,000,000)	

FIGURE 2-10
The units of measure for computer speed. If you are good at arithmetic you might multiply two, eight-digit numbers together in one minute. In the same amount of time a computer that requires 1 microsecond to do the operation would be able to multiply 1 million pairs of numbers in a minute. A faster computer that does 50 operations per microsecond could do 50 million multiplication operations while you do one.

Software

Because mainframe computers are much faster than PCs and memory size has exceeded a million bytes for some time, mainframe software has been designed to take advantage of these factors. Operating systems on mainframes have been multiuser-oriented for many years and have essentially solved the problems that a multitask environment creates (Figure 2-11).

FIGURE 2-11
A mainframe processor and its related components are usually installed in a specially designed computer room with unique power, air conditioning, and security controls. Large mainframes supply computing power to hundreds of users in a diversity of locations with a variety of needs. (Courtesy IBM.)

▶ THE LIMITS OF PI

For hundreds of years mathematicians have been interested in the number Pi. You remember Pi? It's the odd number expressed by the Greek symbol π used to express the ratio of the diameter to the circumference of a circle. You might remember it best in the formula where the area is equal to Pi times the radius squared.

Thousands of years ago the Ancient Hebrews thought of this ratio as being close to the value of three and a little later 3 1/7 or 22/7 which we sometimes use even today. If you're measuring the size of a pizza, that's probably close enough. But for other measurements, such as that used in astronomy, greater accuracy is essential. At first mathematicians occupied their time just trying to find out if there was any end to the sequence of digits in Pi. You might remember the first few digits as 3.14159 but it goes on and on beyond these digits.

William Shanks, a nineteenth-century English mathematician, spent the better part of 15 years of his life calculating the value of Pi. He was looking for a pattern in the sequence of numbers and calculated Pi to 707 decimal places. Unfortunately for Shanks, about a century later in 1949, someone discovered an error in the 528th decimal place, thus making the remainder of his calculations incorrect. Poor Shanks had spent many fruitless years on these last decimal places and they needed to be recalculated.

Recently a Cray-2 supercomputer at NASA devoted 28 hours to the calculation of Pi. Again there was an attempt to find some pattern in the sequence of digits. The Cray crunched out 29,360,128 digits of Pi but again no pattern was discovered. Now, a Japanese team of mathematicians plans to upstage NASA and go for 100 million or more decimal places. By now all bets are off whether Pi has a pattern.

Personal computers are just beginning to get into this area of computing technology.

Special Needs

Cost is a significant factor, with mainframe computers costing in the hundreds of thousands to millions of dollars. With this much at stake many organizations rent or lease their computer. A mainframe often requires special accommodation in the form of a custom-designed computer room. Usually this room requires extra air conditioning and a special electrical power source. In many installations sophisticated fire detection equipment and extinguishers are used. Mainframe systems are an essential component to the successful operation of most major corporations and as a result, special security provisions are needed to protect the system from unauthorized intruders (Figure 2-12).

THE PC'S EFFECT ON MAINFRAME COMPUTERS

With faster and more powerful personal computers, much of the work formerly done on the mainframe is now being assigned to the PC. This **downsizing** trend is affecting all aspects of computing with many companies finding that the PC is the only computer needed for their computing

Downsizing. The process of replacing a larger computer, such as a mainframe, with a smaller computer.

FIGURE 2-12
These computer users communicate with the mainframe processor from these terminals. A terminal, which looks much like a personal computer, does not contain its own processor but relies on the mainframe computer for its processing needs. Using a mainframe simplifies the communication of commonly used data between many hundreds of users in a single corporation. With the centralized mainframe a large storage capacity disk may store data for accounting, payroll, inventory, and sales in one central location. Each authorized user may then access and if necessary update this data so that all users have current information to do their jobs. (Courtesy IBM.)

applications. Other companies that have previously used mainframes extensively are finding that they can function effectively with personal computers and use the mainframe for only some of their major applications.

Over the years application programs for many different needs have been developed for mainframes, which reduces the need for new or original development. However, PCs are being used for many applications, which is leading to some very creative software development that in turn is impacting the mainframe environment. An example of this trend was the development of the spreadsheet and graphics on a personal computer. This software had such a large impact that it spawned other mainframe software developments that may not have occurred, at least not as soon, without the PC.

Until the PC, most mainframe software was developed by professional programmers. Users who needed a computer application had to wait until a program was developed, which sometimes required several years. Personal computer software made user-developed applications possible with the use of spreadsheet and database programs. As a result many applications moved off the mainframe to the PC because the job could be done quickly and according to the users' needs.

Mainframe software has not always been considered user-friendly either. Often it required technical knowledge and intensive training to be used. But since the advent of the personal computer with its user-friendly software, mainframe users have begun to demand the same treatment, resulting in much improved software. Many of the techniques used in PC software have appeared in mainframe software, leading to greater productivity and increased user satisfaction.

CHAPTER SUMMARY

1. The word **bit** is derived from binary digit and is the smallest element or value that is represented in the computer.
2. Personal computers can be described as 8-bit, 16-bit, or 32-bit computers.
3. A **byte** is the term used to describe a group of eight bits and is the basic unit of data in the computer. A byte can be used to represent many types of data including a character such as an upper- or lowercase letter, a number, a punctuation symbol, or a graphic symbol.
4. The **central processing unit** (CPU) or microprocessing unit (MPU) controls the actions taken by the computer. Most processors in today's personal computers reside on a single integrated chip. A 16-bit processor can do operations on data that is 16 bits or 2 bytes in length.
5. The **memory** is the device that stores the program and the data being processed.
6. A **data bus** is the path that data or instructions follow between the components of the computer. The address bus carries memory addresses to all devices that are connected to the data bus.
7. Computer speed depends on the speed of the clock, which is measured in **megahertz (MHz)**; a term referring to the number of cycles per second that it operates.
8. The most widely used code for personal computers is the **American Standard Code for Information Interchange (ASCII)**. This is an 8-bit code meaning that values are represented with seven bits plus a check bit providing a capability for up to 128 different characters, digits, or letters in the code.
9. The **microprocessor** is the chip that contains the processor, arithmetic and logic unit, and control unit. **Integrated circuits** (IC) are silicon chips that contain a number of transistors on one chip.
10. **Random access memory (RAM)** is the memory where a program such as a word processing program or a spreadsheet program is stored when it is presently active in the computer. When the expression 2M is used to describe the size of memory it refers to the storage capacity of random access memory.
11. **Read only memory (ROM)** is a memory chip similar to RAM except that the ROM chip stores information permanently in the computer. ROM usually contains a program that assists in the process of starting up the computer and doing basic input/output operations.
12. Computers contain a number of expansion slots into which **expansion boards** may be installed to provide additional features.

13. Different input/output devices require either a **serial** or **parallel** port to be attached to the computer.
14. The term **footprint** refers to the amount of desk space required for the computer.

IMPORTANT TERMS AND CONCEPTS

American Standard Code for
    Information Interchange (ASCII)
Binary
BIOS (Basic Input Output System)
Bit
Bus
Byte
Central processing unit (CPU)
Compatible
Expansion slots
Footprint
Integrated circuits (IC)
Interface
Kilobyte
Laptop
Megabyte

Megahertz (MHz)
Memory
Microprocessor
Microsecond
Millions of instructions per second
    (MIPS)
Millisecond
Notebook
Parallel
Port
Random access memory (RAM)
Read only memory (ROM)
Serial
User friendly
Word

SELF-TESTING QUESTIONS

Fill-In

1. A _____ is the smallest element or value that is represented in the computer.
2. The term _____ comes from the Greek, meaning million, and is used as a measure of storage capacity in the computer.
3. The _____ code is used in most personal computers to represent characters as binary values.
4. _____ is the area of the computer where the program and data are stored during program execution by the processor.
5. _____ are installed in the computer to provide for the attachment of I/O devices such as a CD-ROM drive or fax card.
6. A _____ interface is more likely to be used for a printer while a _____ interface would be used for a modem.
7. Computers that offer mostly the same features and performance of the IBM are called _____.
8. A _____ computer is lightweight, offers the same features as the desktop PC, and is battery powered for portable operation.

True/False

1. Binary numbers are used in the computer because they require less space.
2. A 32-bit computer is generally faster than a 16-bit computer.
3. A bit is composed of zeros and ones, while a byte requires eight bits.
4. The term megahertz refers to the speed of the computer. The lower the number the faster the computer.
5. Using large-scale integration in the processor chip design has the end result of smaller and more powerful computers.
6. A parallel interface sends one byte at a time, while a serial interface sends one bit at a time to an I/O device.
7. One difference between a mainframe computer and a PC is that the mainframe generally operates faster.
8. Although mainframes are faster than PCs they can only be used by one person at a time.

ANSWERS

Fill-In: **1.** bit, **2.** mega, **3.** ASCII, **4.** memory or RAM, **5.** expansion slots, **6.** parallel, serial, **7.** compatibles, **8.** laptop or notebook

True/False **1.** F, **2.** T, **3.** T, **4.** F, **5.** T, **6.** T, **7.** T, **8.** F

Questions for Critical Thinking

1. Why is it cost effective to buy the fastest computer that you can justify rather than the slowest or lowest price computer?
2. As computer prices fall and more power is packed into a smaller package, what effect might this have on the use of computers in education and business? Consider the history of the calculator when answering this question.
3. With smaller and more portable computers it is becoming easier to exchange data and software from one computer to another. What ethical implications does this have for computer users?

CHAPTER 3

INPUT AND OUTPUT

A VIEW OF THE CHAPTER AHEAD

After reading this chapter you will understand

- ▶ the concepts of data entry and the differences between batch and on-line.
- ▶ the role of the keyboard and display screen when interacting with the computer.
- ▶ the characteristics of a monochrome and color display screen.
- ▶ the major printer types and the advantages and disadvantages of each.
- ▶ the various special-purpose devices used for banking, retail store operations, and other special applications.

INTRODUCTION

William O. Hawley, chief of Information Resource Management Service at the Veterans Administration Medical Center in Perry Point, Maryland, manages a staff of nine technical people who service 1,500 end users of different computer systems. In the summer of 1991, users began switching to Windows using applications such as Word for Windows, Excel, CorelDraw, and DOS applications such as WordPerfect and dBASE IV. Even when the user had a new 386 computer the performance often seemed sluggish, especially when doing a spell check or importing clip art. As we saw in Chapter 2, a solution for this problem is often to add more memory and for some users this was the answer. Hawley found another solution that worked for the other users. By adding a graphics accelerator card and following a few other software installation tricks such as using a disk cache, the graphic-oriented software ran 200 to 500 percent faster.[1]

By now you understand that the computer consists of many components including the processor, RAM, and ROM and various interfaces and boards. But to use all of these components requires some external devices so that we may communicate our needs to the computer and receive results from it. If different components in the computer are not evenly matched, then performance will suffer, as Hawley discovered. In his case, graphics displays were slow because the interface card between the processor and the screen was a bottleneck. By upgrading this card, the entire computer ran faster.

In this chapter we will look at the devices that provide input and output for the computer. Input devices such as the keyboard, document reader, or mouse provide a means for supplying data or commands to the computer, or more correctly, to the program. After the computer has acted upon our instructions or processed our data, we will want to see some results. After all, that is the main reason for entering the data. The results may tell us something about the inventory or the status of a customer's account, which we then act upon to help our business operate more effectively. Output can be displayed on the screen, printed on paper by a printer, or drawn in graphic form on a plotter.

INPUT DEVICES

Almost all users of a personal computer use a keyboard and screen for their primary form of interaction with the computer. Some early computers used a **terminal,** which was made of a display screen and keyboard built into one container. Users of mainframe computers frequently use a terminal of this type to communicate with the computer, although many now use a PC that doubles as a mainframe terminal.

---

[1] *PC World*, "Can Your Hardware Handle Windows," November 1992, p. 33.

Keyboards

Computer keyboards (Figure 3-1) are the most widely used device for data entry and also to enter commands and instructions to the software you are using. Most of the work you do on the computer will require the use of the keyboard. This doesn't mean you will need to be a skilled typist, but knowing where the keys are located will make your work much easier than using the "hunt and peck" method.

Keyboards will vary from one computer to another, but the similarities are usually greater than the differences. The keyboard will be discussed in greater detail in Chapter 7.

Choosing a Keyboard. Ordinarily you get whatever keyboard is supplied with the computer and, unlike the screen, you normally do not purchase the keyboard as a separate item. However, keyboards do vary considerably from one computer to another, and, for users who must do a lot of data entry on the keyboard, choosing the right computer will ensure that the keyboard is also right. Third-party keyboards are available for separate purchase providing various features, such as separate numeric and cursor keypads, that might not be included on a standard keyboard.

The placement of the alphabetic and numeric keys will be the same on all keyboards, but other keys such as function keys, control keys, and cursor keys may vary in their location. Laptop and notebook computers will have more variation in their keyboard layout than desktop computers.

Another consideration in keyboard design is the feel of the keys as they are pressed. While this may seem to be a subjective matter, there are some factors that affect feel. One is the surface design of the key. A slightly curved surface works better than a flat one. Another factor is tactile feedback. This term refers to the pressure and click noticed when a key is pressed. Some keyboards have an indefinite feel and the user is never quite sure when the key has been completely pressed. The IBM keyboard is considered to be a standard in this area because its tactile feedback is preferred by many users. Using a quality keyboard can improve typing performance and result in less user fatigue.

FIGURE 3-1
A typical extended keyboard used on a personal computer. (Courtesy IBM.)

Mouse

Mouse. A device that moves a pointer on the screen in a direction that corresponds to the movements of the mouse on the desktop. Pressing a button on the mouse makes a selection.

Software is usually designed to use the keyboard and screen for user interaction. The screen may display the choices, which are then made by entering a character or command at the keyboard. But with software making greater use of a GUI (graphical user interface), the use of windows, movement of a pointer on the screen, or selection of an icon is frequently done by using a mouse.

A **mouse** (Figure 3-2) is a device that attaches to the computer's serial port and replaces many of the functions of the cursor and enter keys in some software. The mouse is used by rolling it on the surface of the desk. As it is moved, a pointer on the screen moves in the same direction. Small movements of the mouse in any direction make for corresponding movements of the pointer on the screen.

A mouse has at least one button; some have two or three. Pressing a button causes a selection to be made on the screen, such as selecting an icon or choosing an option from a menu. In MicroSoft Windows the choice of software to run, such as a spreadsheet, filing system, word processor, communications, and so on is made by pointing to the icon representing the option with the mouse and double clicking the left button to indicate the selection. The mouse is also used to expand or contract the size of a window by pointing to a corner of the window and then dragging it in a direction that makes the window larger or smaller.

Keyboard advocates prefer not to use a mouse because it requires removing the hands from the keyboard, thus creating inefficiencies, while mouse advocates praise the ease of use of the mouse over the use of cursor keys. However, newer software that is designed specifically for mouse use operates much more effectively with a mouse rather than using the keyboard, which is usually an alternative.

There are two basic types of mice—mechanical and optical. The main

FIGURE 3-2
A mouse is used with application software for making choices in the program. (Courtesy IBM.)

advantage of an optical mouse is that it has no moving parts and thus will not ordinarily require any maintenance. Some software, such as the DOS versions of Lotus 1–2–3, Microsoft Word, or dBASE IV requires a special software driver (usually provided with the mouse) to make the mouse active in the program.

Voice Recognition

Voice recognition systems (Figure 3-3) are slowly obtaining a following as these input devices are becoming more reliable. To use a voice system, the computer user speaks into a microphone which is attached to a compact electronic converter. The converter changes the voice impulses, which are in analog form, into digital impulses. Computer software then translates these digital impulses into meaningful words or phrases.

Most voice recognition systems require the user to train the system by speaking the required words, such as Copy, Print, Sum, Move, and so on into the microphone so the software can recognize the speaker's voice pattern. A serious limitation with these systems is that they will not recognize everyone's voice but only the person who trained the system. In some circumstances this limitation might prove to be a benefit by offering a form of system security.

In 1992, Microsoft announced the Microsoft Sound System that can be used to control a variety of Windows applications. The system includes an audio board, microphone, headphones, and software that lets you speak to Windows. In addition to giving voice commands to Windows applications, other software such as Pagemaker, 1–2–3 for Windows, and WordPerfect for Windows will also accept spoken commands.

Most current systems only accept commands and cannot be used for

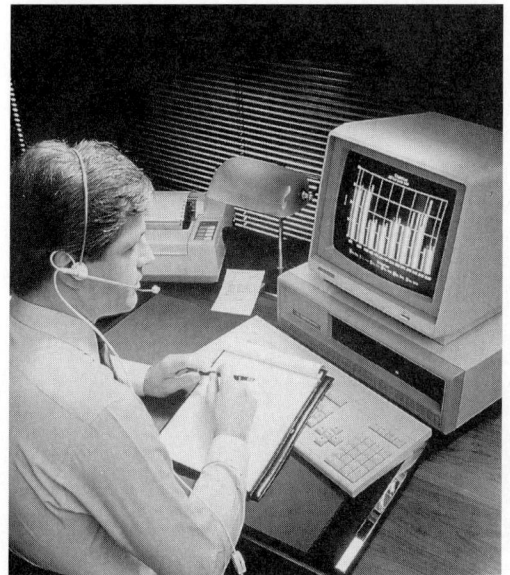

FIGURE 3-3
Using a voice recognition system. (Courtesy Texas Instruments.)

large amounts of data entry as, for example, entering a letter into a word processing program. But, as voice detection software improves, recognizing plain English may soon become an everyday reality.

Pen-Based Computers

What skill do all computer users have in common? While not everyone may be trained to type, we can all write with a pen or pencil. Some computer companies have recognized the reluctance of some potential users to learn even the rudimentaries of typing in order to use the computer effectively. While most students learn some typing skills in high school, there are still many people who find the process awkward and slow. For these customers, a computer with a penlike stylus is used for handwriting and drawing (Figure 3-4). Special software is needed, such as Windows for Pen-Based Computing, to use this equipment. While voice recognition systems need to be trained to recognize a person's commands, a pen-based system requires that the user be trained to write in a form acceptable to the computer.

Scanners

Applications that frequently use graphics, such as desktop publishing, have a need to capture images such as photographs or artwork that are on paper but not on the computer in a format that can be used by the program. By using a scanner (Figure 3-5) the image can be captured and stored on disk in a format that can be used by graphic software.

Both gray-scale and color scanners are available, with the price spread between them diminishing. With a scanner, a page containing the image to be captured is placed inside the device. Using photosensitive cells, the scanner "reads" the image and translates it into either shades of gray or color.

FIGURE 3-4
The Sharp Wizard has a scrapbook function allowing users to write or draw images on the touch screen. (Courtesy Sharp Electronics.)

FIGURE 3-5
A scanner is used for scanning graphic images and creating a disk file of the image to be used by desktop publishing or other graphics programs. (Courtesy of Hewlett-Packard Company.)

Depending on the scanner, up to 24 bits per pixel (a dot on the image) giving 16.8 million possible colors is captured. Some professional models provide up to 69 billion colors for commercial quality reproduction. But many users can do nicely with a relatively inexpensive desktop model.

Pixel. The smallest dot or point of light that appears on a display screen.

OUTPUT DEVICES

Display Screens

Display screens are the output device where computer users usually view the results of computer processing. The display screen or monitor, as it is sometimes called, shows the results of an inquiry, presents the values for a budget, displays an account's current status, or identifies options in a program.

When a program is used, its options may be displayed on the screen in the form of a menu. An option is selected by a keyboard entry and the results of that option are displayed on the screen. As the user enters data it displays on the screen and, when information from a disk file is requested, it is also displayed. It's not surprising then that the screen is one of the most important components of a computer system.

A **display screen** is a TV-like device that displays text or graphics depending on the needs of the program. Early computer users had a choice of monochrome for text display or color for graphics and lower resolution text. The early Apple computers were of this type. Today's personal computers can also use monochrome, but increasingly more users are showing a preference for color monitors, and, whether color or monochrome is selected, both text and graphics can be displayed on the screen.

Monochrome Displays. Monochrome (Figure 3-6) refers to the type of screen that displays in one color with a contrasting background. A color

Monochrome display. A display screen that displays images in different shades of a single color.

FIGURE 3-6
The monochrome display screen.

in wide use on monochrome screens is green with a black background. Text characters display in green while the surrounding area is black. White on black is also used but is thought to be harder on the eyes. European systems use amber (a shade of yellow), which is considered to be easier on the eyes than most colors. Amber is becoming more widely used in North America and several manufacturers such as Amdex and Panasonic offer amber monitors.

Monochrome displays are less expensive than color and are superior for text display such as that needed in word processing, desktop publishing, CAD/CAM, and database applications or where color graphics are not frequently needed. Although most monochrome monitors can display graphics, color usually gives superior results when graphics are needed; however, dollar for dollar, monochrome is unrivaled in clarity and sharpness of character definition.

Color display. A display screen that displays images using as many as 256 different colors.

Color Displays. A color display (Figure 3-7) can certainly be very pleasing to the eye, and experts tell us that using color communicates more information to the user, especially when graphics are used. In general there are two types of color monitors—composite and RGB.

A **composite** monitor operates on the same principle as a television set in which the screen receives a composite signal on one channel containing the display information. It is usually used for games or on some home computers. **RGB** (red, green, blue) monitors receive three different signals, one in each of the three color spectrums, leading to higher definition and better clarity of the image over a composite monitor.

The number of colors that can be displayed depends on the software and the color adaptor board used in the computer. Choosing an adaptor board

CHAPTER 3 Input and Output

FIGURE 3-7
A color display screen on a personal computer is pleasing to the eye as it uses colors to highlight important information in the graphic. (Courtesy IBM.)

is as important as choosing the right screen and one depends on the other. There are at least five levels of boards in use for personal computers, but the most widely used are VGA, SuperVGA, and Multisync. Older computers may use CGA or EGA screens.

- **VGA** (Video Graphics Adaptor). This is the basic level display for most computers. It has a 640 by 480 resolution (see the discussion on resolution) with a 16-color mode out of 262,144 colors. A mode with 320 × 200 density allows 256 of the 262,144 colors to be displayed.

A comparison of color graphics adaptors for the PC.

CGA	EGA	VGA	SuperVGA	Multisync
640 × 200 (4 colors) 320 × 200 (16 colors)	640 × 350 (16 colors)	640 × 480 (16 of 262,144 colors)	1024 × 768	1280 × 1024

- **SuperVGA.** Becoming very popular among Windows users, SuperVGA offers higher level resolution of 800 × 600 to 1024 × 768. The higher resolution can be important for improved clarity when graphics-oriented work is dominant on the computer.
- **Multisync.** This is a color graphics board that provides compatibility between several display standards. Some manufacturers provide a resolution of up to 1280 × 1024 or greater. With a multisync monitor the program can select the display resolution that is most suitable for the application.

When graphics are displayed, it is not uncommon to require a million bits or more of data for one screen display. When such is the case, faster adaptors are available to satisfy these special needs. One of these is the ATI graphics accelerator, which sends data to a graphics screen at a much faster rate than a standard SuperVGA card. Another solution is the local bus

▶ SCREEN RESOLUTION

The **resolution** of the display determines the clarity of the character displayed for text and the precision of the image for graphics. A screen with high resolution will be easier to read and less tiring on the eyes. Originally, monochrome screens offered the highest resolution, but now color is available with comparable or better images.

What determines the resolution of the screen is the screen capability and the graphic or display board used. Specifically, resolution depends on the number of dots or points of light on the display. These dots, as shown in the diagram, are called **pixels**. When more pixels are used to form a character, a clearer, sharper image is created. A resolution of 640 × 200 pixels provides for 128,000 points on the screen, while a higher resolution screen of 640 × 350 provides 224,000 or almost twice the resolution.

Another factor that affects the readability of images on the screen is the **dot pitch**. The dot pitch is the distance between the dot or pixels on the screen. The lower the pitch the easier it will be to read the screen. A pitch of .28 would be preferable to a pitch of .41 because it gives greater readability over the higher dot pitch.

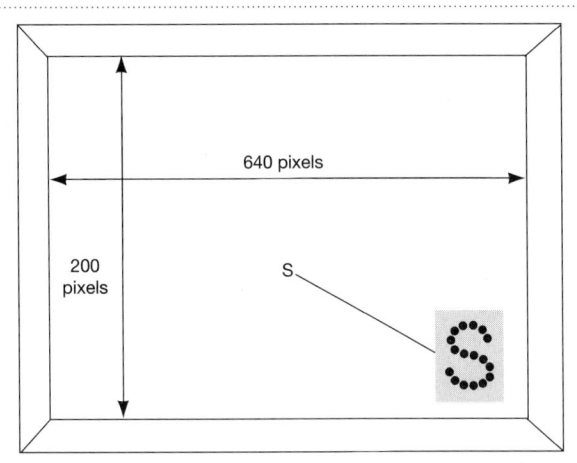

Resolution of the screen with standard text display.

Resolution	PIXELS	Line × Column
Very low	64,000	320 × 200
Low	128,000	640 × 200
Medium	224,000	640 × 350
High	307,200	640 × 480
Very high	540,000	900 × 560
Super high	1,048,576	1024 × 1024

Comparison of screen resolution in pixels as defined for business PCs. The higher the resolution the sharper the image. In some applications, notably engineering, a resolution of 1024 × 1024 would be considered moderate.

video. This is a video adaptor that uses a 32-bit instead of a more common 16-bit data path from the processor to the video. Local bus video needs to be designed into the processor board to be effective and is not usually an add-on component.

Display Features. Some features are common to all screens. Among these are the use of a blinking **cursor** on the screen to show where entries are to be made. Another is the scrolling of the screen contents when more data is to be displayed at the bottom of the screen. When the screen is full and another line needs to be displayed, all lines scroll up by one line and the top line disappears off the screen.

A similar process is moving the page up or down with the page up or page down key on the keyboard. A page refers to the amount of data the screen can display, not the amount on a printed page. If the screen is currently showing the first page of a document, say lines 1 to 23, then pressing page down would cause lines 24 to 46 to appear. Page movement is a function of the software and some programs, notably DOS, do not provide this capability even though the screen could handle it.

Figure 3-8 illustrates boldfacing, underlining, italics, and reverse video, attributes that are useful in word processing and other text-oriented programs.

Boldface characters on the screen are brighter than the surrounding characters. On a printed page, boldface is printed darker than other characters. Underlining is used for headings or other words that need to draw the reader's attention. *Italics* are ordinarily available on high-resolution displays and are only used by some software. **Reverse video** is useful to highlight program messages or blocks of text that are to be deleted or copied by the program.

Text Display. When text is displayed on the screen, the screen characteristics are described in terms of rows (or lines) and columns. A typical screen (Figure 3-9) will have 25 rows and 80 columns. For applications such as a word processor, fewer than 25 rows may be available for text because the program uses some of these lines for on-screen information. For example,

FIGURE 3-8
Use of screen features in a word processing program. (Courtesy Alexander Communications.)

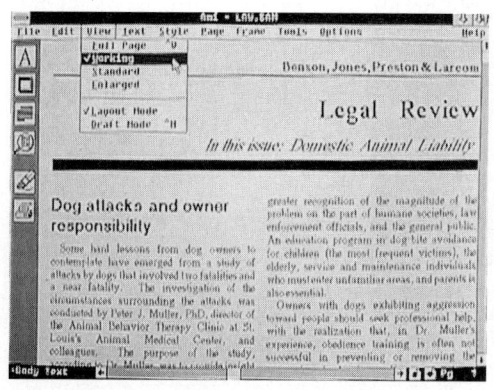

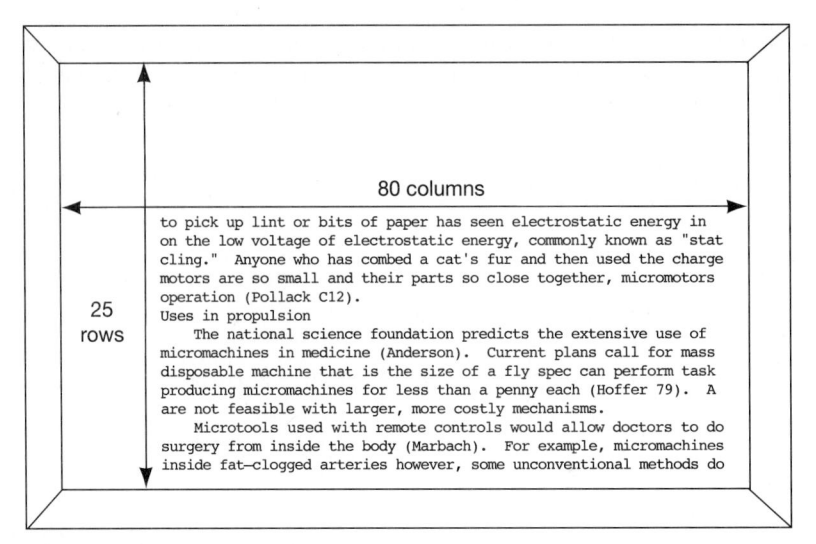

```
                    80 columns
        ┌──────────────────────────────────┐
        │ to pick up lint or bits of paper has seen electrostatic energy in
        │ on the low voltage of electrostatic energy, commonly known as "stat
        │ cling."  Anyone who has combed a cat's fur and then used the charge
        │ motors are so small and their parts so close together, micromotors
   25   │ operation (Pollack C12).
  rows  │ Uses in propulsion
        │    The national science foundation predicts the extensive use of
        │ micromachines in medicine (Anderson).  Current plans call for mass
        │ disposable machine that is the size of a fly spec can perform task
        │ producing micromachines for less than a penny each (Hoffer 79).  A
        │ are not feasible with larger, more costly mechanisms.
        │    Microtools used with remote controls would allow doctors to do
        │ surgery from inside the body (Marbach).  For example, micromachines
        │ inside fat-clogged arteries however, some unconventional methods do
```

FIGURE 3-9
Allocation of rows and columns on a display screen.

WordPerfect uses one line for status information and the remaining 24 lines may be used for text. When a VGA or SuperVGA screen is used, some programs offer a mode that will display more lines per screen. For example, Quattro Pro will display up to 50 lines of a spreadsheet in VGA mode compared to only 25 lines in the standard mode.

The Apple Macintosh II has a screen resolution of 640 × 480 pixels for impressive color graphics capabilities. The Mac is promoted as a user-friendly system because its use of graphics and icons simplifies operations for the first-time computer user. Early Macintosh systems were limited by the paucity of software available, but more major software companies, such as Lotus and Microsoft, have been adapting their software for use on the Macintosh. (Courtesy John Greenleigh, Apple Computer, Inc.)

CHAPTER 3 Input and Output

Graphics Display. Most computers display text characters based on predefined pixel formats that are part of the contents of the computer's ROM. Graphics-oriented programs such as Microsoft Windows and Windows applications use **bit mapping,** where each pixel on the screen is controlled by the program to determine the exact format of the character. These programs use graphics for displaying windows, icons, and special text fonts.

Bit mapping has both advantages and disadvantages. The main disadvantage is that it requires more memory to set up the screen contents compared to a regular character display. Programs using bit mapping also tend to run more slowly than other programs.

The advantages of bit mapping are important. First, graphics of all kinds can be displayed, even three-dimensional graphs can be produced with sophisticated software. For character or text display, more character types can be made available. For example, the popular word processor Microsoft Word is able to show italics, boldface, underlining, super and subscripts, and other special character fonts that would be impossible to display without bit mapping (Figure 3-10).

Full-Page Displays. With the expansion of word processing into desktop publishing, the demand for screens that can display the entire contents of one page has grown. The average display screen shows 25 lines and because of the software's needs for status lines or menus, this size may shrink by several lines. The end product is a display that shows only about one third of a printed page at a time. To get the complete view of the page, the user must do frequent scrolling from the keyboard.

In contrast to the line limit of standard screens, **full-page display screens**

> **Bit mapping.** A technique where the program generates each bit used to display characters on the screen.

> **Full-page display.** A display screen that shows the contents of an entire printed page for WYSIWYG results.

FIGURE 3-10
A screen display of Ami Pro using bit mapping. (Courtesy Lotus Development Corporation.)

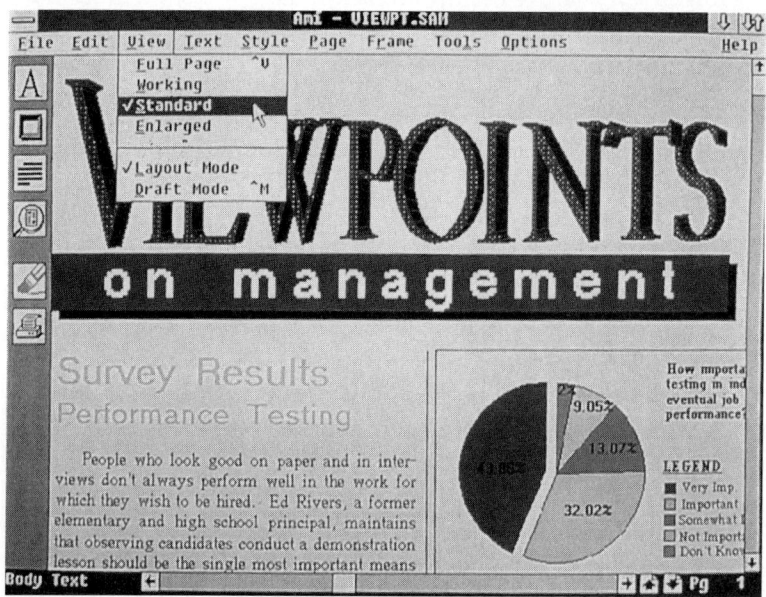

▶ GETTING THE MOST FROM A GRAPHICS DISPLAY

As higher screen resolutions and color become more widely used in computing, more information needs to be delivered to the screen to create an image. Today's SuperVGA screens use 800 by 600 pixels per screen. This is 480,000 pixels at 8 bits per byte the computer needs to send 60K of data to the screen for a black and white image. At 1024 by 768 the screen needs to receive 100K, and at 1280 by 1024 a black and white image needs 164K of data. Using color ups the ante even further. A 24-bit display with 1024 by 768 resolution needs 2.36MB for the display.

The implications of this amount of data are twofold. First, the computer needs memory to store the data before sending it the screen. Next it needs a graphics adaptor to send the data to the screen for display. The graphics adaptor used supplies the memory and then sends the image on to the screen. How effectively this is done depends on the design of the adaptor.

As you use a higher resolution display, a faster adaptor is needed. If the adaptor is too slow then there will be a noticeable delay when graphics and/or color is displayed. Windows, OS/2, graphics, CAD, or animation users may find the response to be less than desirable. For many users the solution is to add an accelerator board such as ATI Graphics Ultra Plus or Hercules Graphics Station Gold. Adding a graphics accelerator to an existing computer can significantly improve graphic performance.

Another solution is possible with the 486 level computers. These models may often be ordered with a local bus video adaptor. The local bus allows the video signal to be processed at the speed of the processor rather than the speed of the data bus, which is considerably slower. Local bus video has one negative. It cannot be added to an existing computer but must be built into the original design of the motherboard. But purchasers of a new computer may find the local bus to be a more effective solution than adding a graphics accelerator.

show all lines of the page for a true "what you see is what you get" (WYSIWYG) display. Not all software will support these large screens, but some, such as Ventura and PageMaker (Figure 3-11), are page composition packages that use the capability of these large screens.

Flat Displays. Developments in liquid crystal technology have led to the use of **flat display** screens that are as little as an inch in thickness. The **liquid crystal display (LCD)** is based on the same technology used in digital watches and calculators.

LCD flat displays are primarily used on laptop and notebook computers (Figure 3-12) where the size is an important factor. LCD systems also consume much less power than other displays so that some portable systems operate from a rechargeable battery. Flat displays also emit no radiation, which is of concern to some people who use regular monitors.

Some users also complain about the visibility of the LCD screen. In well-lighted areas the screen is usually quite readable, but in low-light situations the screen can be difficult to read. More recent developments in LCD technology, such as backlit panels and active matrix display, have produced LCDs with exceptional display quality.

CHAPTER 3 Input and Output

FIGURE 3-11
A full-screen display for use in desktop publishing. (Courtesy of Micro Display Systems, Inc.)

FIGURE 3-12
Notebook and laptop computers are the most frequent users of flat display screens. (Courtesy IBM.)

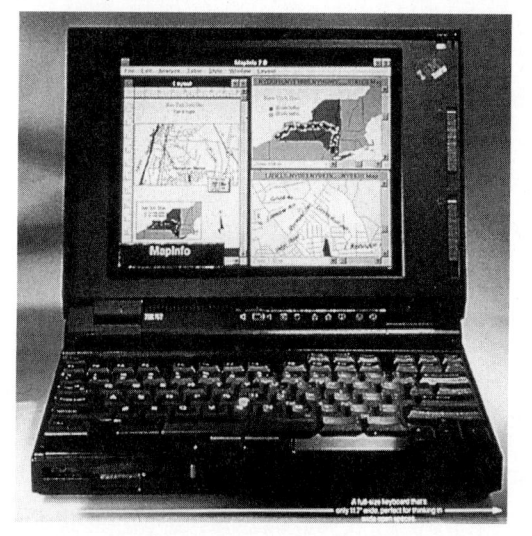

▶ CHECKLIST FOR CHOOSING A DISPLAY SCREEN

- Do you require text only display or minimal graphics? In this case monochrome may be adequate. If you are choosing a monochrome display, check the contrast and brightness controls to ensure that the two levels of black and white display distinctly. You will need to run software that uses two levels of brightness to determine this contrast. Many software packages require the display of different shades of gray when color is not used.
- Do you expect to display graphs or use software that requires color? Then choose a color display.
- If you choose color, what quality of display is needed? When choosing a color screen look for a screen that displays true colors with good distinction between them. Color tends to be a subjective matter so choose a display that looks good to you. Try adjusting the color and tint controls to see if the results are within a range that you can accept. Try scrolling the text on the screen and check to see if there is color smearing as the display contents are changed. A good screen should not show any color smearing.
- What level of resolution is needed? You can select from VGA, SuperVGA, or Multisync. The level of resolution will depend on the type of software you plan to run. If you are only doing the usual word processing or spreadsheet work, then VGA will be fine. If you are working under Windows try a Super-VGA screen and compare the difference. For work such as specialty graphics, desktop publishing, or computer-aided design, a higher resolution may be required.
- Check color displays for clarity of image, true color, and lack of smear.
- Check the glare on the screen from overhead lights and windows. Stores often position displays to minimize glare and you should too when it is placed where it will be used. However, some locations may not eliminate all glare and so a screen that reflects less light will be easier to read.
- Look for clarity of characters on the screen. Are all characters, especially at the corners and edges, clearly displayed without distortion? Compare units with different dot pitches.
- Some screens have a height and tilt adjustment, although most simply sit on the desk or on top of the processor. Some people with special needs may find an adjustable screen more suitable.
- For desktop publishing applications look for full-page screens.

Touch Screens

Touch sensitive. A screen that displays choices that are selected by pointing a finger to the option on the screen.

Some computers may use screens that are touch sensitive as an alternate to the keyboard or mouse for selecting options. Instead of pressing a key or clicking a button on a mouse, the user points with a finger to a choice or command that is displayed on the screen (see Figure 3-13). Some proponents of the touch screen predict that it will replace the mouse because it is as easy to use, but does not require another device to be attached to the computer.

Touch screens use one of three methods to function.

1. **Infrared light.** These invisible light beams criss-cross the surface of the screen and form a gridlike pattern. When a finger points to a location on the screen representing a choice from the software, the finger interrupts the beam of light that is detected by the computer's circuitry. The result-

Graphic display terminals are frequently used in computer-aided design (CAD) *and computer-aided manufacturing* (CAM) *applications.* (Courtesy IBM.)

Graphic VDT terminals have been widely used for **Computer-Aided Design** (CAD) *in the automotive, aircraft, and ship design industries. Using graphic terminals makes the development of the design and model testing much easier and less costly than manual methods. Changes to the design can be easily incorporated at anytime during the design stage. Resulting designs on the computer can be readily included in the manufacturing stage when* **Computer-Aided Manufacturing** (CAM) *is used, as for the construction of a car or aircraft.* (Courtesy Ford Motor Company.)

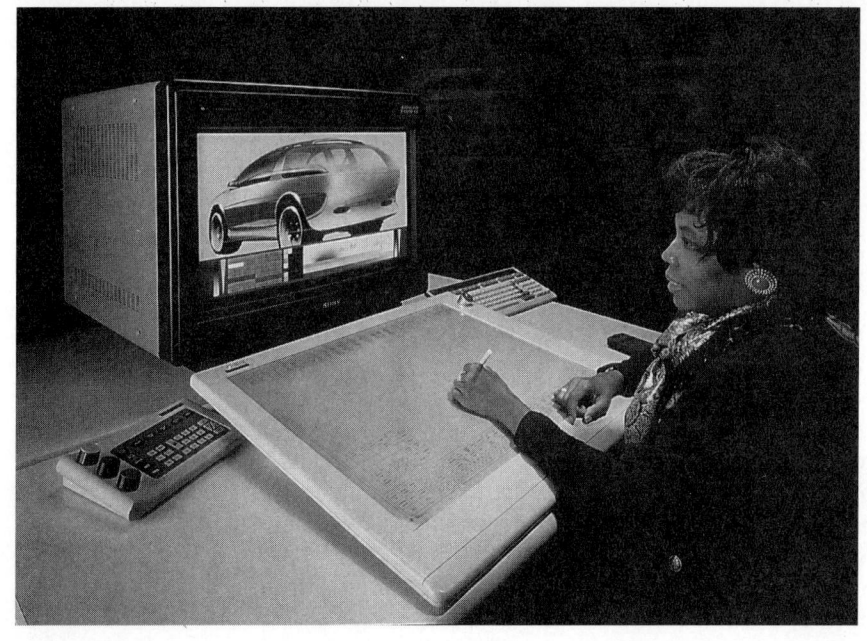

FIGURE 3-13
Using a touch-sensitive display screen. (Courtesy Microtouch Systems, Inc.)

ing signal causes the choice to be made and the computer responds accordingly.

2. **Capacitance.** This method uses a technique that can sense the change in electrical capacitance when touched by a finger. Capacitance technology used in these systems is similar to devices used for bio-feedback instruments for relaxation training.
3. **Pressure sensitive.** These screens have a built-in matrix of wires on mylar sheets. When the surface is pressed, two wires make contact, thus signaling the computer of the location that was touched on the screen.

Light Pens

Another way of touching the screen is with a light pen. This device is a pen that is attached with a cable to the screen and senses light that is emitted at certain points on the screen. Light pens had a degree of popularity on mainframe systems but have not retained a high level of usage in recent years. Light pens have never become popular on personal computers.

Printers and Printed Output

Hard copy. A report that is printed on paper as opposed to being displayed on the screen.

Printer. An output device used for creating printed reports and other hard copy results.

When display screens first came into use, many advocates suggested that a major reason for using a screen was to reduce or eliminate paper output. While the use of screens may have had the potential to reduce the quantity of printed output, or **hard copy**, as it is often called, printed reports are still a major need in information systems and some would argue that paper use is as extensive as it ever was before the display screen.

A printer is usually attached to the parallel port of the computer. Occasionally, it is attached to a serial port. Compared to some outputs, such as disk or screen displays, the printer is a slow device. Although some printers on a personal computer may print up to 700 characters per second (cps), speeds of 100 to 200 cps are more common.

Types of Printers. There are basically three printer groups and each satisfies a specific printing need, so much so that some offices will have a printer from at least two of the groups. Printer categories are:

1. **Dot matrix,** which forms its characters from a matrix of dots.
2. **Laser,** which uses laser technology to print full pages in a manner similar to that used by a copier machine.
3. **Ink jet,** which forms a character by directing a jet of ink onto the paper to produce the character. Recently, ink jet printers are having a wider following for personal computers because they have a quality comparable to a laser but at a lower price.

A few years ago the daisy wheel was the second most used type of printer behind the dot matrix. It uses a fully formed character for letter or typewriter quality printing. But, due to the laser's popularity, the daisy wheel has lost favor with users and seems to be past history where new systems are concerned.

Printing Efficiency. When a report or other output is printing, the operation ties up the computer so that no other tasks may be done until printing has finished. This is an obvious waste of the computer resource, so software companies have devised several solutions. Many full-featured word processors such as WordStar and WordPerfect permit the use of the word processor while simultaneously printing a report.

Another solution is to use print buffers that store the contents of a document in memory. Some programs, especially word processors, include this as a built-in feature. While the document is printing from memory, other software may then use the computer. A third solution is to use software that permits the simultaneous use of more than one program. Operating systems such as UNIX and OS/2 provide this capability on personal computer systems. Windows uses a similar method to print reports in the background while other work is done by the computer user.

Dot Matrix Printers. Personal computer users who want a good quality printer at low cost usually select a dot matrix printer. **Dot matrix printers** are the most widely used printer with PCs and they come with a variety of features and capabilities. A matrix printer contains a print head with a number of pins that are electrically fired against a fabric ribbon to make an impression on the paper (Figure 3-14). Pins are fired in a pattern to create different characters. Usually the better the printer the greater the number of pins and the higher the print quality. Nine- and 24-pin matrix printers are the most common types in use.

Because physical contact is necessary to create an image on the paper, the matrix printer falls into a category of printers called **impact printers.** A daisy wheel printer is also an impact printer. Matrix printers can be quite noisy and often require an acoustical printer cover when used in a quiet office environment.

Selecting a dot matrix printer can be confusing at best because of the many choices of printers and features. Printers generally come with a carriage that permits continuous form stock paper that is $9^{1}/_{2}$ inches wide in-

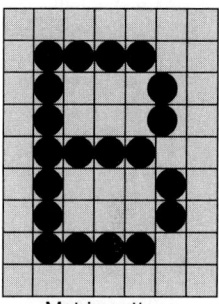

Matrix pattern
FIGURE 3-14
The print head creates a pattern of dots to form specific characters when printing.

Dot matrix printer. An impact printer that forms a character by firing a matrix of wires against an ink ribbon to create an image on the paper.

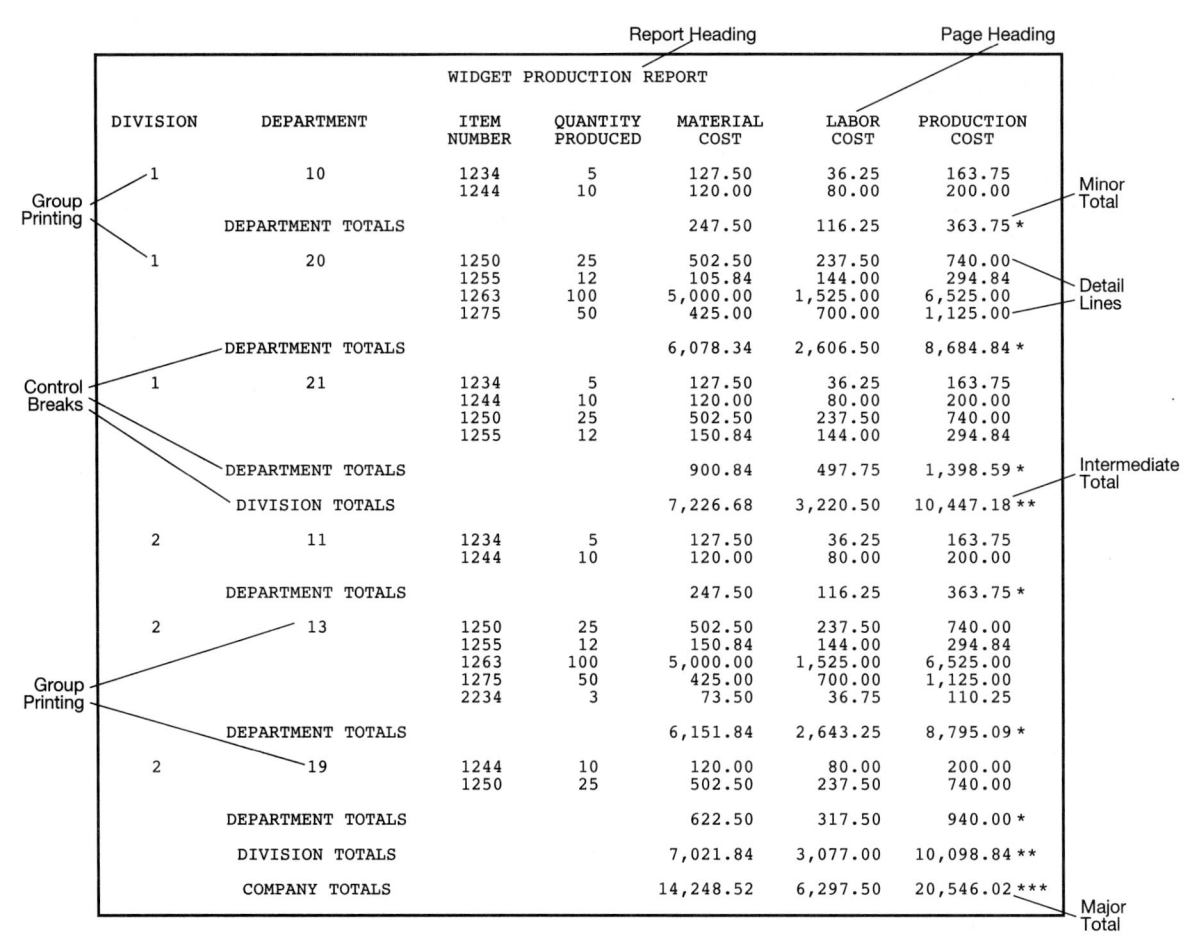

```
                           Report Heading              Page Heading
                    WIDGET PRODUCTION REPORT

       DIVISION   DEPARTMENT    ITEM    QUANTITY   MATERIAL    LABOR    PRODUCTION
                               NUMBER   PRODUCED     COST       COST       COST

          1          10         1234       5        127.50     36.25     163.75        Minor
                                1244      10        120.00     80.00     200.00        Total

                     DEPARTMENT TOTALS               247.50    116.25     363.75 *

          1          20         1250      25        502.50    237.50     740.00
                                1255      12        105.84    144.00     294.84        Detail
                                1263     100      5,000.00  1,525.00   6,525.00        Lines
                                1275      50        425.00    700.00   1,125.00

                     DEPARTMENT TOTALS             6,078.34  2,606.50   8,684.84 *

          1          21         1234       5        127.50     36.25     163.75
                                1244      10        120.00     80.00     200.00
                                1250      25        502.50    237.50     740.00
                                1255      12        150.84    144.00     294.84

                     DEPARTMENT TOTALS               900.84    497.75   1,398.59 *    Intermediate
                                                                                       Total
                     DIVISION TOTALS               7,226.68  3,220.50  10,447.18 **

          2          11         1234       5        127.50     36.25     163.75
                                1244      10        120.00     80.00     200.00

                     DEPARTMENT TOTALS               247.50    116.25     363.75 *

          2          13         1250      25        502.50    237.50     740.00
                                1255      12        150.84    144.00     294.84
                                1263     100      5,000.00  1,525.00   6,525.00
                                1275      50        425.00    700.00   1,125.00
                                2234       3         73.50     36.75     110.25

                     DEPARTMENT TOTALS             6,151.84  2,643.25   8,795.09 *

          2          19         1244      10        120.00     80.00     200.00
                                1250      25        502.50    237.50     740.00

                     DEPARTMENT TOTALS               622.50    317.50     940.00 *

                     DIVISION TOTALS               7,021.84  3,077.00  10,098.84 **

                     COMPANY TOTALS                14,248.52 6,297.50  20,546.02 ***   Major
                                                                                       Total
```

Group Printing (left annotation) · Control Breaks (left annotation)

The Anatomy of a Report. A detail report with control breaks is a common report required in business. Data for this production report is in order by division and department number. As the report is printed, subtotals are given after each department and again at the end of a division. These total lines, called control breaks, are flagged with asterisks (*) to show whether they are a minor (*), intermediate (**), or major (***) control break. Group printing is also used so that duplicate data, such as the division and department numbers, are only shown at the beginning of a common group of records.

cluding the perforated edge for the tractor feed. This width will be useful for printing 80 characters per line at a density of 10 characters per inch. This density is commonly called pica type. Wider carriages of up to 19.5 inches are available on some printer models to accept wider paper.

Speed is another factor to consider when selecting a printer and is expressed in characters per second. Many matrix printers offer several choices of speed depending on the mode in which the printer is operating. Two commonly available modes are draft and near-letter-quality (NLQ), also called correspondence quality. Draft mode is the higher speed and produces a readable but lower quality output than near-letter-quality.

Most dot matrix printers also offer a graphics mode, the possibility of condensed or expanded type, and a variety of fonts and pitches is also

Font. A set of characters of a specific design such as Roman or Italic.

> ### ▶ Printer Drivers
>
> To make use of the unique features available in a specific printer, software requires the use of a printer driver. A driver is additional software that provides the specifications needed to use the printer's features. Without a driver, only the most basic characteristics of the printer will be available.
>
> For example, MS-DOS is software that does not generally support the various features available on most printers. Because DOS does very little printing, this is not generally a problem. By contrast, WordPerfect supplies drivers for hundreds of different printers. Without a driver, WordPerfect could only print a basic 10-character per inch Courier font. By using the appropriate driver, all of the printer's fonts, speeds, special features, and graphics can be made available. However, a driver cannot supply a feature that a printer does not have built-in. Thus, the limiting factor is the printer and not the printer driver.

available. A final consideration in selecting a printer is its compatibility to certain standards. The two standards generally accepted are Epson and IBM. Most application software is designed to handle printers that conform to these standards, but if a printer is chosen that does not, the program may not be able to use all of the printer's features.

A few dot matrix printers are capable of color printing which is especially useful if graphs are printed. Table 3-1 shows several matrix printers and compares their prices and features.

Laser Printers. Until a few years ago, laser printers were available only for use with million-dollar mainframe computer systems. But now technology has made laser printing affordable for the office on almost any personal computer. Some laser printers for personal computers now cost under $1,000.

There are several reasons the laser printer is becoming popular. Price, of course, is one. Speed and print quality are also important. Laser printers are **nonimpact** because no physical impact is needed to create an image on the page. Instead they operate like a photocopier and print a full page at a time (Figure 3-15). Thus, speed is quoted in pages per minute (ppm). The

Laser printer. A nonimpact printer that uses laser technology to form characters on a page.

TABLE 3-1 A comparison of dot matrix impact printers.

Printer	Print Head Pins	Rated Speed Char. per Second	Type Pitch (Char. per inch) Selected Features*
Seikosha SL-90	24	240 draft	10, 12, 15, proportional
Star Micronics XR-1000	9	160 draft	10, 12, 15, eight NLQ fonts, color option
Epson LQ-850	24	300 draft	10, 12, 15, proportional Roman, sans serif fonts
IBM Proprinter XL	9	200 draft	5, 6, 8, 10, 12, 17
Tandy DMP-240	24	120 draft	10, 12, 15, three fonts, color option
Mannesmann Tally 490	18	400 draft	5, 6, 7, 8, 10, 12, 15, 17

* These features are for comparison only and may not be complete.

FIGURE 3-15
Using a laser printer. (Courtesy Hewlett-Packard Company.)

lower priced print at 4 pages per minute (ppm), while a few more dollars will get you 8 ppm. Print quality on a laser is substantially better than the best a dot matrix can produce in letter quality mode. Like matrix printers, lasers also have font and pitch capabilities, and are capable of graphics,

▶ POSTSCRIPT PRINTING

When printing text with a variety of fonts, most laser printers will produce the quality expected by the user. However, when the output contains graphics such as a halftone image (photographs, art from paint and draw programs, and Encapsulated PostScript files all use halftones) the amount of memory required in the printer can be excessive.

One solution is to buy a PostScript printer, which uses a page description language that converts lines and shapes into algorithms. The algorithm describes the shape of the image, which can then be quickly resized without the need for additional memory. Because a PostScript printer may be too costly for some users another approach is to add a PostScript cartridge to an existing laser printer. The cartridge contains software that improves the printer's ability to handle the graphic-oriented output. The result is improved graphics at a cost of slightly slower printing. Besides adding PostScript operation, some cartridges also add additional fonts as an added attraction.

Two other approaches to adding PostScript are to install an expansion board in the computer which then plugs into the printer. However, not all printers are able to use this option. A third approach is to use software that simulates PostScript. These programs generally operate slower than either a cartridge or a board and add fonts that are not as pleasing as the other approaches.

which makes them the prime choice for desktop publishing applications. High-end lasers are also the printer of choice because of their speed, quality of output, and networking capability.

Because laser printers are nonimpact, they are also quiet. Printing is done electronically and the only noise generated is from the movement of paper through the machine. This makes them an attractive alternative to the much noisier dot matrix in the office environment. Much software that was written prior to the availability of the laser did not provide support for this type of printer. But now, most software packages are providing printer drivers for some of the more widely used laser printers, such as the Hewlett-Packard Laserjet printer.

Ink Jet Printers. While dot matrix printers tend to be noisy, lasers are exceptionally quiet but relatively expensive. Even if you pay top dollar for a 24-pin matrix printer, the quality of the output will not match the lowest priced laser. But, for a price between the matrix and laser printer, the ink jet delivers quality and quietness of operation that is close to the laser.

Ink jet printers spray a thin jet of liquid ink through 30 to 60 nozzles to form a character. Compared to a 24-pin matrix printer, even 30 jets will result in a higher resolution. Some ink jet printers are able to emulate the 300 dot per inch resolution of a laser printer. Printers vary in size from a notebook size that can fit in a briefcase to desktop size that is comparable to a laser. Both monochrome and color are available. Different models can print on either single sheet paper like a laser or continuous form paper like the dot matrix.

Older ink jet printers had problems with the nozzles clogging with dried ink after a period of use. Newer ink jets use a replaceable ink cartridge that also replace the jet nozzles. When the ink runs out, a new cartridge replaces the ink supply and the nozzles, thus eliminating the problem. Ink is also of a fast-drying variety so that smearing is not likely after the printed page is removed from the printer. Color ink jet printers are available for users who require color printing at a reasonable cost. Although the ink jet does not quite match the quality of the laser, it is a good alternative to the dot matrix. Users that want laserlike results but find the price too steep should consider the ink jet as a competitive choice.

Ink jet printer. A nonimpact printer that forms a character by shooting a thin stream of ink at the page.

Plotters

Dot matrix printers have limited abilities to produce quality graphics that are suitable for reproduction into presentation graphic form. And lasers don't have as high a resolution as needed for some applications and most can't print in color. Plotters can take graphs generated by spreadsheet programs or specialty graphic programs and produce high-quality drawings (see Figure 3-16). Plotters can also use large sheets of paper for creating architectural drawings or other design-oriented documents.

Typical plotters have a supply of pens, similar to colored ink markers, that are selected and used to draw the images sent from the computer. Some plotters select a different color of pen automatically, while others require a manual change. Plotters draw lines rather than using dots and as a result the density of the image is significantly greater than that produced by a ma-

> ## ▶ CHECKLIST FOR CHOOSING A PRINTER
>
> - Do you require draft quality or near-letter-quality or both? Then choose a dot matrix printer.
> - Do you need letter-quality printing most of the time? Then choose a laser or ink jet printer.
> - Do you need color?
> - What is the volume of your printing? A dot matrix printer printing 400 words per page, at 100 characters per second, will produce 3 pages per minute or 180 pages an hour. At 20 characters per second (for NLQ), you get only 36 pages per hour. This is considerably slower than the slowest laser, although faster matrix printers are available.
> - If you require graphics capability, then check your software to see what printers it supports and choose from this group. Usually a laser printer is what you need.
> - Do you print extra-wide documents such as spreadsheets or other charts? A wider carriage might be the solution. Other approaches are to choose a printer with a suitable compressed mode or to use software that can print sideways on a matrix printer.
> - Is your printer to be used in a quiet environment? How about choosing a laser or ink jet printer? Or maybe an acoustical cover would be the solution.
> - Will you be using desktop publishing software? Then a laser printer, or a postscript option should be considered.

trix or even a laser printer. Plotters can draw on paper or for presentation graphics a transparency master may be inserted and the image drawn directly on it.

Like most printers, plotters must also be compatible with the software

FIGURE 3-16
A plotter used to prepare presentation-quality graphics. (Courtesy Hewlett-Packard Company.)

▶ NEW ADVANCES IN BAR CODES

Using the traditional bar code seen on grocery store items, the Gettysburg Address would require 24 feet of code. But Symbol Technologies has developed a bar code, called the PDF417, that could record Lincoln's speech in less than 2 inches.

The new code, which looks something like a tire tread, is less than three inches wide and about an inch and a quarter high. It can record enough information to store an employee's photograph, name, address, date of birth, start date with the company, social security number, age, sex, height, weight, hair and eye color, and blood type.

New uses for this bar code could be to replace paper documents used in warehousing to tell the contents of a box, special handling instructions, and where to ship it. Hazardous materials use the code to provide instructions on its care and disposition. The codes are scanned by lasers with a device similar to the ones used to read retail bar codes.

---

that drives it. Most graphic software is provided with a set of drivers that can interface with a variety of plotter devices, but it is essential before choosing either a plotter or graphic software to ensure compatibility.

Special-Purpose Devices

Point-of-Sale (POS) Terminals. You have seen the automated checkout registers used in many food and department stores (Figure 3-17).

Point of Sale (POS). These terminals are common in retail stores for recording customer purchases by reading the UPC from the item purchased.

FIGURE 3-17
A POS terminal in a supermarket. (Courtesy NCR.)

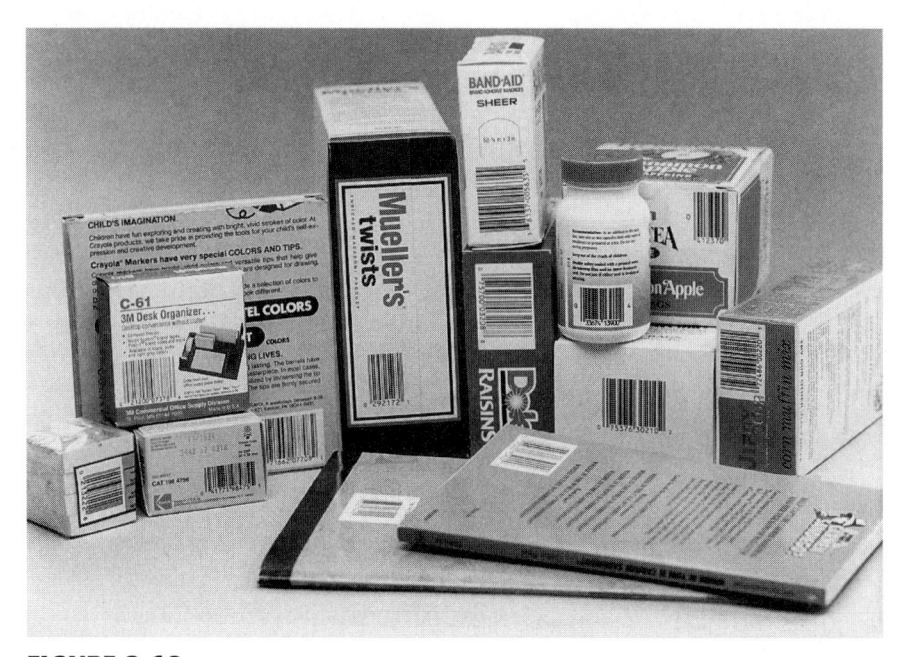

FIGURE 3-18
Grocery items with UPC bar codes from a major supermarket chain store. (Courtesy Teri Stratford.)

These cash registers are called **point-of-sale (POS)** terminals and are used to record purchases by reading the universal product code recorded on each item purchased. POS terminals are attached to a computer which stores the prices of all items in the store. Storing prices in a central location ensures consistency in the price used by the cashier and allows for fast and easy updating when price changes occur.

UPC. The universal product code is the bar code used on many retail items such as clothes and groceries to identify the item.

Universal Product Code (UPC). The Universal Product Code (UPC) is a bar code that is in widespread use by grocery chains for automatic recording of prices on checkout. The label on each item in the store is marked with the bar code (see Figure 3-18) that identifies the product. A store computer uses this data to look up the description and price of the item, which is then printed on the cash register tape, supplying the customer with a complete record of the purchase.

Wand Readers. The wand reader (Figure 3-19) is another form of point-of-sale device that is used by department stores to read the price tag on clothes, household goods, and hardware. Items in the store are identified by a magnetically encoded price tag. Product identification that has been previously recorded magnetically on the price tag is captured by the wand for automatic data entry at the cash register.

ATM. An automated teller machine is used by bank customers for financial transactions such as withdrawing funds from their account.

Automated Teller Machine (ATM). Banks across the country have been providing customers with the option of using walk-in or drive-in **automated teller machines** (Figure 3-20) to make withdrawals and deposits 24 hours a day. Customers are supplied with access cards, similar to a credit card, containing a record of the customer's account and credit limit on a

▶ PERSONAL VERSUS CORPORATE ETHICS

What would you do if you made a withdrawal of $300 from an ATM machine and received $500 instead? More than half of a survey of more than 7.4 million 7-Eleven customers said they would keep the extra money. Of course the remaining people said they would return the extra. But what if you made a withdrawal of $500 and received only $300? No doubt everyone would expect to get a correction from the bank to make up the difference.

Personal ethics relates to how each of us responds to moral dilemmas. When we are faced with an issue such as the ATM error, how do we respond? With absolute honesty, or do we muddy the waters when it is to our personal advantage? Do we react differently when the issue involves another person as compared to when it involves a corporation?

Corporate ethics by comparison often deals with business policy. These policies affect the relationship between the company and its employees, shareholders, and customers. Layoffs, perks, and promotions may be affected by corporate ethics as they relate to the employee while refunds, exchanges, and problem-solving ethics may affect the customer.

---

magnetically encoded strip on the back of the card. As financial transactions occur at the ATM, the system uses **electronic funds transfer (EFT)** to update a computer record to reflect the current balance in the customer's account.

Optical Recognition. Optical character recognition (OCR) refers to a range of optical scanning procedures for the recognition of special codes, or characters, on a document. OCR machines read characters that conform to a special font character set. Variations of these devices recognize bar codes, handwritten characters (with some limitations), and machine-printed char-

OCR. Optical character recognition is used to scan special codes or characters on a document for direct input into the computer.

FIGURE 3-19
Using a wand reader in a department store. (Courtesy NCR.)

FIGURE 3-20
A teller machine at a major bank used for making deposits and withdrawals.
(Courtesy Jonathan Taylor, Uniphoto.)

acters. OCR has been used for many applications including payment processing by utility companies, medical claim forms, hospital registration, and attendance reporting. Although these devices originally gained attention on mainframe systems, low-cost OCRs are now available for personal computers.

Mark sensing is a form of optical device that senses the presence or ab-

FIGURE 3-21
A check with the branch and account number coded in magnetic ink at the bottom.

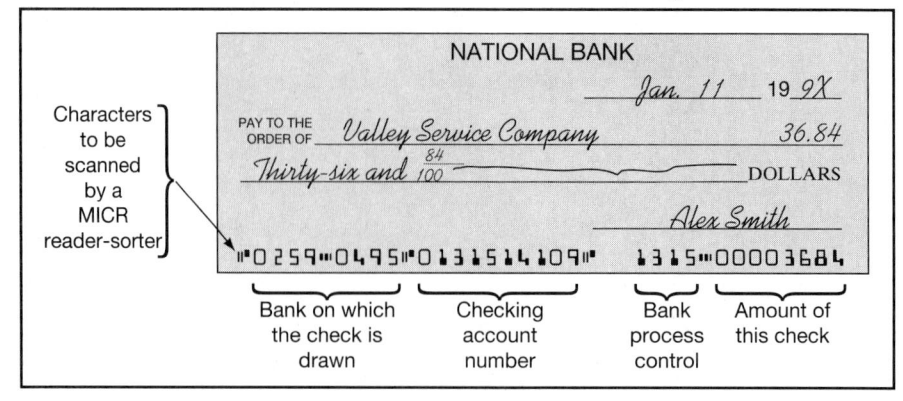

Characters to be scanned by a MICR reader-sorter:

NATIONAL BANK

Jan. 11 19 9X

PAY TO THE ORDER OF Valley Service Company   36.84

Thirty-six and 84/100 _____ DOLLARS

Alex Smith

⑈0259⑈0495⑈0131514109⑈   1315⑈00003684

- Bank on which the check is drawn
- Checking account number
- Bank process control
- Amount of this check

CHAPTER 3 Input and Output

sence of a mark on a document. You have probably written a test or filled out a questionnaire using a special marking sheet for your answers. This sheet has areas where a pencil mark is used to record an answer to a multiple choice or true/false test question. A mark sensing machine is used to read these marks on the answer sheet and converts them to digital codes to be read by the computer.

Magnetic Ink Character Reader (MICR). You have likely noticed the oddly shaped characters located at the bottom of a check (see Figure 3-21). These are magnetic ink characters that are read into the computer by a **magnetic ink character reader (MICR)**. The magnetic content and unique shape of each character are what allows it to be read by the reader and yet can also be read by humans.

MICR encoded checks are used by banks to speed the processing of financial transactions through the complex banking network. When you use a check to make a purchase, it arrives at the bank's data processing center, where the amount of the purchase is encoded on the check. Your check is then processed with thousands of other checks by the MICR device, which not only reads the amount on the check that will be deducted from your account, but also sorts the checks by account and branch so that the check can be routed back to your branch (Figure 3-22).

In this chapter we have looked at the primary devices used for input and output. On the personal computer, the keyboard, screen, and printer are the most widely used primary input and output devices. We have seen that a variety of screens and printers are available to suit many different needs.

MICR. Magnetic ink character recognition machines are used by financial institutions to read the magnetically encoded branch and account numbers recorded on checks.

FIGURE 3-22
A magnetic ink character reader (MICR) used to read and sort checks in a banking system. (Courtesy IBM.)

Other devices for interaction include the mouse and touch screens. By contrast, the mainframe uses the display terminal, which combines the keyboard and screen in a single package. Often a personal computer is used for access to a mainframe computer. Special-purpose devices are available for use in supermarkets, department stores, and the banking industry. In the next chapter we will look at devices, such as magnetic disk, for storing data in the computer to make it available for later use.

CHAPTER SUMMARY

1. Computer **keyboards** are used for data entry and to enter commands and instructions to the software you are using. Keyboards have alphabetic and numeric keys like a typewriter, as well as special-purpose keys such as cursor control, insert, delete, and function keys.
2. A **display screen** is a TV-like device that displays text or graphics depending on the needs of the program. Screens can be monochrome or color.
3. Color displays can be either **composite** or **RGB**. Composite is a TV-like display, while RGB gives significantly better results. A color display also requires a color board in the computer. Three commonly used levels of color boards are VGA, SuperVGA, and Multisync.
4. The **resolution** of the display determines the clarity of the character displayed for text and the precision of the image for graphics. Resolution depends on the number of dots or points of light, called **pixels,** on the display.
5. **Bit mapping** is a technique for displaying characters by controlling each pixel on the screen to determine the exact format of the character as needed for special fonts and graphics.
6. A **full-page display** shows the entire contents of a printed page on the screen, compared to a regular display screen, which only displays a maximum of 25 lines. The full-page display is especially useful for desktop publishing applications.
7. **Flat display screens** use liquid crystal display (LCD) technology for a compact screen as used in portable computers. LCD displays are smaller, lighter in weight, and consume much less power than other screens.
8. A **mouse** is a device that replaces some of the functions of the cursor key. It is used by rolling it on the surface of a desk, which in turn moves a pointer on the screen. By pressing a button on the mouse a software option may be selected.
9. A **touch screen** lets the user select options by pointing at them on screen with a finger. The touch screen requires a specially designed screen with either infrared light beams, capacitance-sensitive, or pressure-sensitive technology.
10. **Voice recognition** systems may be used for limited data entry or the selection of program options. Most voice systems require the system to be trained to recognize an individual user's voice.
11. **Pen-based** systems use a special stylus attached to the computer screen to allow handwritten input.
12. The three main printer groups are dot matrix, laser, and ink jet. Using a

printer ties up the computer, but by using a print buffer, the computer can be used simultaneously with printing.

13. **Dot matrix** printers are the most widely used printers on a PC and have a variety of features. Features may include a wide carriage, a range of speeds, near-letter-quality (NLQ) or draft mode, color, graphics, and condensed or expanded type. Dot matrix printers are a type of impact printer and can be quite noisy.
14. **Laser** printers are available for less than $1,000. Lasers are quiet and operate faster than many dot matrix printers with a higher print quality. Laser printers can print a variety of fonts and pitches and graphics, making them a suitable candidate for desktop publishing.
15. An **ink jet** printer is less expensive than a laser but offers many of the same quality features. It is a good choice for low cost color printing.
16. A **plotter** is used for graphic applications to produce a high-quality reproduction of a graph. Plotters are especially useful for preparing full color presentation graphics on a transparency master.
17. Special-purpose devices for computers are many and varied. Some of these in common use are the POS terminal that reads a UPC code, wand readers that read a magnetic code, ATM and MICR machines for banks, and OCR devices for special applications.

IMPORTANT TERMS AND CONCEPTS

Bit mapping
Color graphics adapter
Composite
Cursor
Cursor control keys
Display
Dot matrix
Flat display
Full-page display
Function keys
Hard copy
Impact printers
Ink jet
Keyboards

Laser printers
Light pen
Monochrome
Mouse
Near-letter-quality (NLQ)
Pixels
Plotters
Presentation graphics
Printer
Resolution
RGB
Scrolling
Touch screen
Voice recognition

SELF-TESTING QUESTIONS

Fill-In

1. Two types of display screens are VGA and _____.
2. Screen _____ is determined by the number of pixels displayed. One such measurement is 1024 × 768 pixels.

3. The flashing _____ on a screen shows where the next character to be typed will appear.
4. A dot matrix printer is a form of _____ printer.
5. The _____ is a nonimpact printer that operates quietly and offers a high-resolution output.
6. A _____ is a pointing device typically used with Windows software applications.
7. Many food and department stores use _____ terminals to read and record the universal product code from each item purchased.

True/False Questions

1. Bit mapping is used on display screens when geographic maps are displayed.
2. LCD displays are mostly used on television screens but have not advanced to a level where they can be used for computer displays.
3. Pen-based computer input is fast becoming a replacement for using the keyboard.
4. Printing reports in the background while you do other work on the computer is a feature found in Windows and OS/2.
5. Ink jet printers are a less expensive alternative to the laser printer with output quality that approaches the laser.
6. MICR is the magnetic strip found on the back of bank and credit cards.
7. The automated teller machine (ATM) is a computer terminal used by many banks for customer deposits and withdrawals.

ANSWERS

Fill-In: 1. SuperVGA, 2. resolution, 3. cursor, 4. impact, 5. laser, 6. mouse, 7. point of sale

True/False: 1. F, 2. F, 3. F, 4. T, 5. T, 6. F, 7. T

Questions for Critical Thinking

1. Most computers provide for both screen and printer output. Compare applications that benefit from either screen or printer as the primary output.
2. The most commonly used keyboard uses the QWERTY layout, which is named after the leftmost letter keys in the top row. Research an alternate keyboard called the Dvorak keyboard and discuss its advantages and disadvantages.
3. Consider a legal firm that is installing a computer. What type of printer would best serve them if it is used for applications ranging from internal memos to legal documents?
4. You are working in a retail store when an employee shows you how to access credit records of their customers. Your job does not require you to do credit checks. Although the access does no damage to the customer's record and is done merely for amusement purposes, you feel uncomfortable about it. Discuss the ethical and legal implications of this practice.

CHAPTER 4

SECONDARY STORAGE

A VIEW OF THE CHAPTER AHEAD

After reading this chapter you will understand

- ▶ the need for disk storage and how it benefits the computer user.
- ▶ how data is stored and accessed on disk.
- ▶ the purpose of tape units for backing up disk files and for off-line storage.
- ▶ how to estimate disk storage requirements.
- ▶ new technologies that are being developed for storage media.

INTRODUCTION

When employees in the dealer services departments of Ford New Holland, the Ford Motor Company's agricultural machinery division in New Holland, Pennsylvania, needed parts information, they signed on to a mainframe system terminal. Dealers from across the country used the costly on-line system for access to prices, descriptions, and other data they needed to know about the 300,000 parts from the company's product line. All of this data was stored on disk at the company headquarters and sent out over communication lines at the request of the local dealers.

Late in 1988, Carmen J. Martin began to develop a CD-ROM-based system that would replace the costly on-line system. A computer-based CD-ROM looks like an audio CD but can store 500 MB or more of data. Using CD-ROM authoring software, she was able to develop a system that provided instant cross-reference to all of the parts formerly available on the mainframe. To get information on a starter for a tractor, the parts department employee simply types in the word starter and the model of the tractor and the PC quickly searches the CD-ROM for the required information. Instead of signing on to an expensive communication system, each dealer has all of the needed information available for their immediate use.

A CD-ROM is one form of data storage that you will read about later in the chapter. Although it is only now coming into widespread use, other forms of data storage such as disk and tape have been around for decades. In this chapter you will examine the different types of storage devices in use on today's computers.

PRIMARY AND SECONDARY STORAGE

Data in a computer system often originates at the keyboard as a result of a data entry operation. Other forms of entry, such as voice or document reading, may be used but the end result is still the same. As data is entered into the computer, a place is needed for permanent storage. On most systems the storage device of choice is disk, while some special applications may use tape or other media for storage.

As data is entered, it resides in random access memory (RAM), which is also called primary storage. The problem with RAM is that it is temporary; as soon as the power to the computer is turned off, all data in RAM is lost. The solution is to have a **secondary storage** medium, such as disk, that can retain data permanently.

Figure 4-1 shows how data that is entered from the keyboard goes into RAM and from there is written, under program control, to disk storage. Writing to disk requires a separate operation by the program in addition to reading the source data from the keyboard. Often this requires the user to enter a command to save a file on disk before leaving the computer. Disk storage is nonvolatile; it does not depend on electrical power being present on the computer, and usually has much greater capacity than RAM.

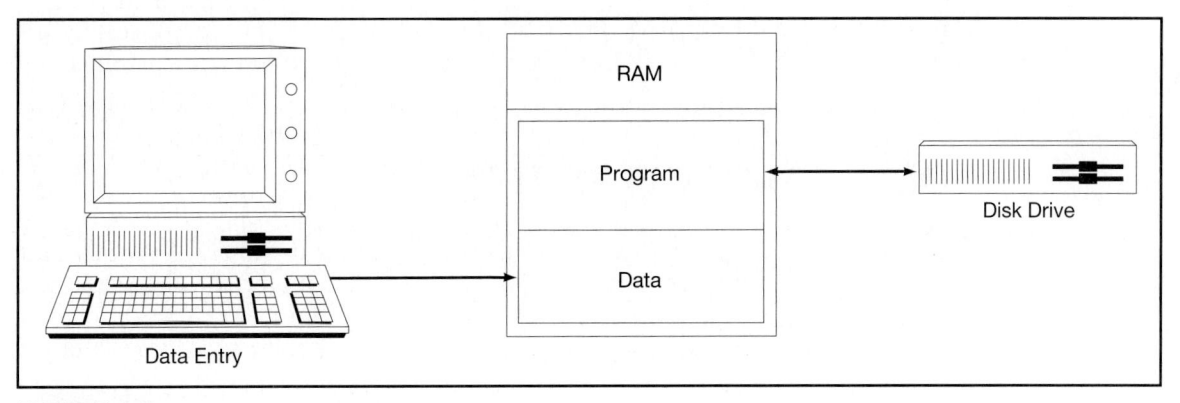

FIGURE 4-1
Data entry to a computer must also result in the saving of the data on some type of secondary storage such as a floppy disk.

WHY ARE DISKS USED?

On personal computer systems there are two basic forms of disks: **removable diskettes,** which includes floppy (5 1/4-inch) and microfloppy (3 1/2-inch) diskettes, and **fixed disk,** which is commonly called hard disk. We have already seen that disk offers a permanent medium for storage, but disk is also a much faster form of storing and accessing data than other alternatives such as tape. Disk also offers both sequential and direct access to records stored on the disk surface.

Floppy disks provide unlimited storage by using as many disks as necessary, but they must also be inserted and removed from the disk drive as new data is required. Fixed disks have large capacities ranging from 20 MB (megabytes) to over 1,000 MB and do not require any physical contact by the user. Floppy disks are easily transportable and are a popular method for

The 3 1/2-inch microfloppy disk can store a minimum of 720K bytes, giving it double the capacity of most 5 1/4-inch floppy disks. A high-density version stores 1.44 MB and some models offer 2.88 megabytes of storage capacity. (Courtesy IBM Corporation.)

transporting data or programs from one location to another. Virtually all software companies use floppy disks for providing products to customers.

DISK CHARACTERISTICS

All forms of disk use similar methods for recording data. The 5¼-inch and the 3½-inch floppy are made from a flexible mylar material, while the hard disk is made from a firm material, usually aluminum. The disk is coated with a material that can be magnetized and is the key to recording data on the surface of the disk.

The magnetic surface of the disk is organized into **tracks** as shown in Figure 4-2. Data bits are recorded magnetically, using positive and negative polarities to represent the zeros and ones of the ASCII code along these tracks. Disk surfaces are also divided into **sectors,** which aids the software in finding the data quickly and with a minimum of delay. On the 5¼-inch floppy the disk typically has 40 tracks and 9 sectors. The basic 3½-inch disk uses 80 tracks and 9 or 18 sectors.

When the disk is in operation, a disk drive motor in the computer spins the disk while, at the same time, an **access arm** positions a **read/write head** on the disk surface (Figure 4-3). Some hard disk drives (particularly those on mainframe computer systems) use compressed air to keep the head in close proximity to the disk surface. To write on disk, electrical signals from the computer flow to the head, which writes the data magnetically on the track. Reading is just the reverse. The head senses the magnetic spots on the track and sends the data these spots represent to the computer.

FIGURE 4-2
Tracks and sectors on the disk surface.

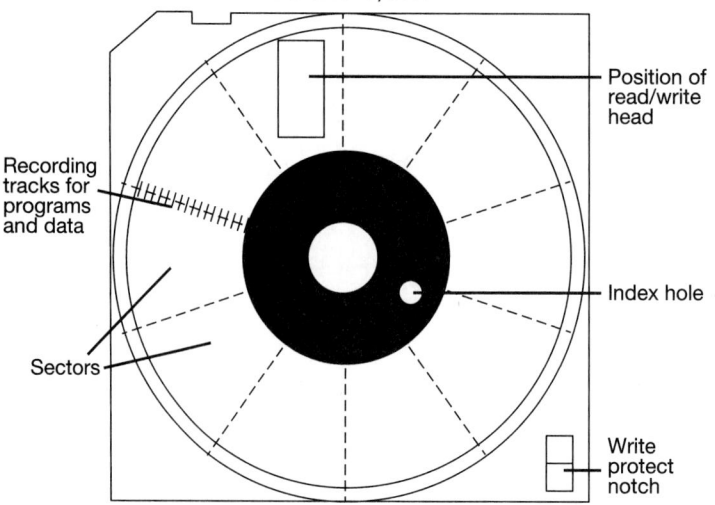

CHAPTER 4 Secondary Storage 97

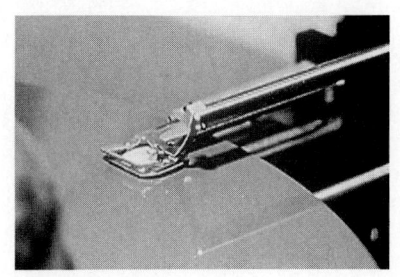

FIGURE 4-3
An access arm with a recording head is used for reading and writing data on the disk. (Courtesy BASF Systems Corporation.)

Floppy Disk

The mainstay of the disk industry has been the 5¼-inch **floppy disk** with a typical capacity of 360K bytes in double density or 1.2M bytes in high density. It consists of a flexible mylar platter enclosed in a sturdy storage envelope that protects the recording surface from scratches, fingerprints, and dust. The oval slot in the envelope is where the read/write head accesses the data and is an area of the disk that should never be touched as it is placed in the disk drive.

The central hole is called the hub and is where the disk drive grips the disk so that it may be spun during reading and writing. The smaller circular hole is the sector hole, which identifies the location of the first sector on the disk while a read or write operation is under way.

The envelope is notched on the edge near one corner. This is the write-protect notch which allows you to write data on the disk if it is open. By covering the write-protect notch with an adhesive-backed tab, writing on

Floppy disk. A low-capacity removable magnetic disk either 5¼″ or 3¼″ in size used for storing data.

The 5¼-inch floppy disk is widely used in PCs and PC compatibles for data storage.

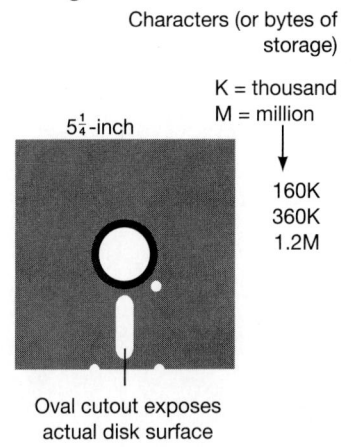

5¼-inch

Characters (or bytes of storage)

K = thousand
M = million

160K
360K
1.2M

Oval cutout exposes actual disk surface

Data Rate

Data rate is the speed in bytes per second that data is transferred to or from the disk. As a disk is being read or written, it revolves in the drive at about 300 RPM for a floppy or 3600 RPM for a hard disk. It is this speed that is a major factor in the rate at which data is transferred from the disk, the other factor being the density of the data on the track. Floppy disk is generally about one twentieth the speed of a hard disk, although this is certainly not a hard and fast rule. An average hard disk has a data transfer rate of 625,000 (625K) bytes per second (BPS) with some operating up to 1M (one million) or more BPS.

Average Access Time

Data rate is an important measure of a disk's speed but it only comes into play after the data you require from the disk has been found. Suppose a database program requires a record for a specific item in inventory. There are two aspects to determining the time required for locating this record on the disk. First, the disk drive must position the head to the track containing the record: this is called **seek time.** Then the disk drive must wait while the disk rotates until the record required is positioned under the head: this is called **rotational delay.** After both of these delays occur, the disk can read the record and transfer it to the program. Because the seek time and rotational delay can vary for each record, the average of these times is called the **average access time,** which refers to the time required to access a record. Average access times, a lower number is faster, can be on the order of 10 to 100 milliseconds (thousands of a second) depending on the type of disk drive used.

When a query is issued on a database, several factors affect the amount of time taken to access the record. The data rate, seek time, and the average rotational delay all contribute to the waiting time experienced by the user after issuing the request. (Courtesy of IBM.)

CHAPTER 4 Secondary Storage

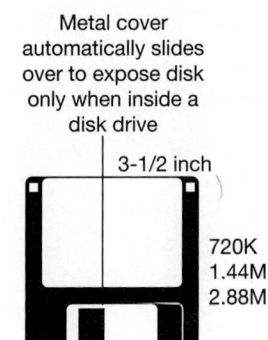

The 3¹/₂-inch microfloppy disk is widely used in 386 and 486 computers, laptops, and notebooks for data storage.

the disk is prevented and thus protects against unwanted recording or erasing of files.

To identify the disk contents, an adhesive backed label is placed on the surface of the envelope. Information about the disk's contents should be written on the label by using a felt-tipped pen, rather than a ball point pen, to avoid damaging the disk.

A floppy that is designed to be recorded on both sides is a double-sided disk. The amount of data that can be packed on the disk is determined by the number of tracks and the density. The 5¹/₄-inch floppy disk is double density and has 40 tracks for recording data. A disk labeled as DSDD means double side double density that contains 360K bytes, while high density is a 1.2M byte disk.

Floppies are inexpensive and quite durable. However, reasonable care should be taken to avoid bending or exposing the disk to foreign substances such as spilled coffee or dust. When disks are not in use, they should be placed back into their sleeve to minimize damage.

Newer PCs such as the 80386- and 80486-based computers, laptops, and notebook computers are causing the 3¹/₂-inch microfloppy disk to grow in popularity and are fast replacing the 5¹/₄-inch disk as the number one choice in disks. These microfloppies consist of a floppy disk contained in a rigid plastic enclosure. The exposed surface of the disk is covered by a metal sliding shutter which is opened only when the disk is accessed in the drive by the computer. A movable plastic tab is used to provide read only capability. 3¹/₂-inch disks can store either 720 or 1.44 megabytes, with a few models capable of 2.88M. On a Macintosh the 3¹/₂-inch disk is formatted for 800K or 1.2M for double or high density, respectively.

Hard Disk

Today's computer users consider hard disk drives a necessity for their speed, convenience, and high-capacity data storage. **Hard disks,** also known as **Winchester disks,** have from 20 to over 1,000 MB (1 gigabyte) capacity, with larger disk capacities on the way. To get this volume of storage, hard disks are manufactured with extremely close tolerances, which is

Hard disk. A high-capacity permanently mounted fixed disk that stores data for computer use.

A fixed disk resides permanently in the computer providing fast access to large amounts of data. (Courtesy Microscience International Corporation.)

why they are mounted in a fixed location in the computer and are not removable. The fixed disk is mounted in a sealed enclosure that protects the disk from environmental hazards such as dust and smoke particles, which can be damaging to the disk and its contents.

Many hard disks come as a half-height drive which permits stacking two of them in one disk slot in the computer for extra storage capacity. Hard

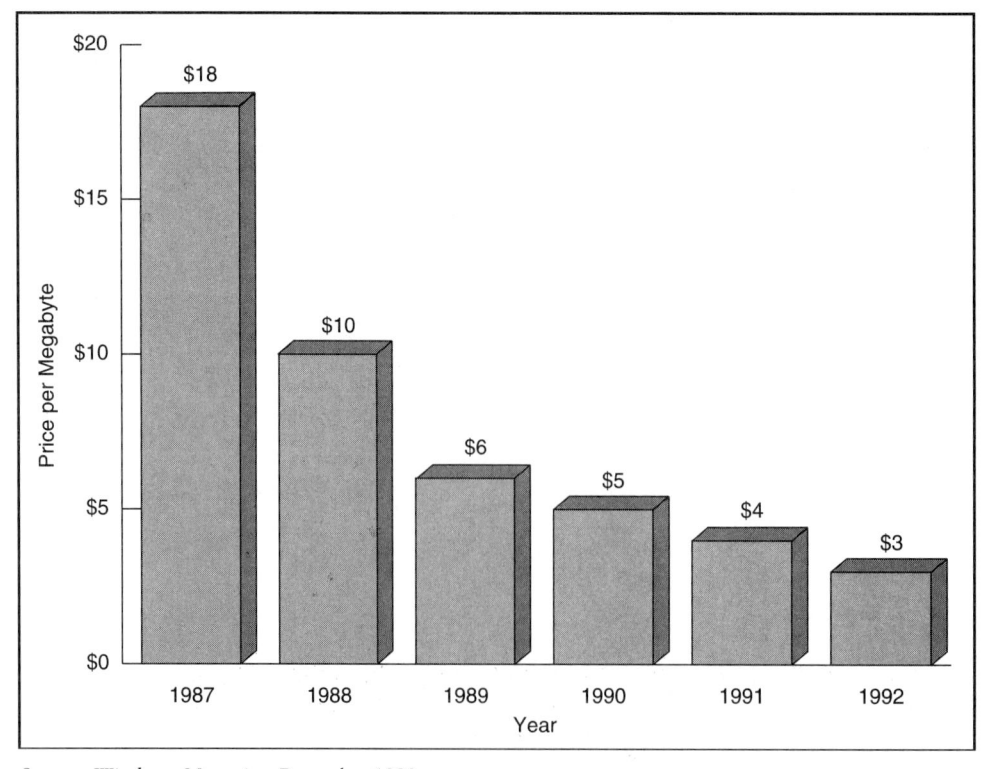

Source: *Windows Magazine*, December 1992.

▶ ESTIMATING HARD DISK STORAGE REQUIREMENTS

When purchasing a system, a wide range of storage capacity is available for the hard disk drive. How is one to know the best size that is suitable for the needs of the application? Basically, there are two considerations when choosing the disk size. One is the amount of space required for the software to be used and the other is the storage requirements for files.

Each software package has its own unique requirements, so that figure will need to come from the specific packages to be used. File space will also vary according to the application. Word processing and spreadsheet files tend to accumulate and thus grow in space requirements over time, whereas database files frequently begin with large requirements that can be computed in advance, but these calculations also need to allow for increasing requirements.

The following calculations demonstrate how disk space requirements are calculated. Consider a system that uses 3MB for DOS, 10MB for Windows, 25MB for a graphics program and related files, a 5MB word processor, a 8MB spreadsheet, and a 4MB database program. The database consists of two files: the inventory file has 5,000 records with 200 bytes per record and the customer file has 8,000 records with 2,000 bytes each. The word processing files are expected to require 10MB and the spreadsheet files 5MB after a year of use. The calculations are as follows:

DOS	3,000,000
Windows	10,000,000
Graphics Draw program	25,000,000
Windows Word Processor	15,000,000
Word Processor files	10,000,000
Windows Spreadsheet	8,000,000
Spreadsheet files	5,000,000
Database program	4,000,000
Inventory file (5000 X 200)	1,000,000
Customer file (8000 X 2000)	16,000,000
	97,000,000

Consider that this total of 97MB would almost fill a 100MB hard disk. We have not considered backup files, which will occupy some additional disk space. The database will also require some space for index files, report files, and other support files. Finally, consider that figures such as these are always estimates and should allow for some expansion. Considering these factors, it seems that a 130MB hard disk is the minimum size that should be used in this application and that a 200MB disk might be worth considering to plan for future needs.

---

disks are noted for their reliability, and laptops now have built-in hard disks owing to their compactness and reliable operation.

After-market hard disks are widely available for upgrading existing computers. So if your computer storage space is filling up, an extra hard disk can be added to the system for additional storage space.

Under ordinary conditions, the hard disk requires no special care other than using it in a clean, dust-, and smoke-free environment. To ensure the safety of the data, backing up the contents of a hard disk is an important operation that must be done at frequent intervals. See the section on disk backup for a discussion on this method.

Benefits of Disk

Both floppy and hard disk offer many benefits to the computer user. Some of these are summarized below.

Access time. The time it takes the disk drive to access data. A 16ms (millisecond) disk drive will access data faster than a 28ms drive.

- **Speed of access.** Data that is stored on a disk may be accessed quickly with a minimum of delay.
- **Access method.** Both floppy and hard disk offer sequential or direct accessing of data. With direct access only the data required by the user needs to be read, significantly improving the time needed for accessing disk records compared to tape, which must access records sequentially.
- **Large storage capacity.** This is especially true of hard disk with capacities up to a gigabyte and more, making a large amount of data available to the user at all times. Today's Windows and OS/2 users are finding that a minimum of 200MB is a requirement for hard disk capacity.
- **Storage cost.** While hard disk is more expensive than a floppy disk drive to install, the differences are not excessive. The larger storage capacity and faster speed of hard disk frequently outweigh the small difference in cost.

DISK BACKUP

Most disk users agree that storing data using magnetic disk of all forms is a reliable storage media. But what about those times when something does go wrong and a file is accidentally erased or is damaged to the point that it cannot be retrieved? Losing a file can be a minor inconvenience at best or a major catastrophe at worst. To guard against inadvertent loss, experienced computer users regularly **backup** their disk files so that an alternate source is available if data is lost.

When using floppy disk, backing up means making a copy of the disk on a second diskette. Usually the copy should be made after a file on the master disk has been changed. This file, or the entire disk, is then copied to the backup disk to create a second copy. If a problem occurs with the master, then the backup disk may be used to retrieve the data. In the business environment backup procedures should be done even more carefully. When important activities such as accounts receivable and payable are recorded on hard disk, then a single backup on a floppy may not be enough. In this situation the business also needs to guard against not only loss of data but loss of business. A single backup disk is adequate if the concern is only for losing a file, but what if the backup disk is lost or destroyed due to fire or other catastrophe? Then a third backup done at, say, weekly intervals is ideal. This third backup should be stored in another location, preferably another building for complete safety.

Figure 4-4 shows a series of backups proposed for many years in the information systems industry as being the ideal for accessing lost data. It is called the grandparent, parent, child method. The child is the most recent backup, while the parent and grandparent represent earlier backup files. When a new child backup file is created the old child becomes the parent, the parent disk becomes the grandparent, and the old grandparent disk is no longer needed and may be reused for other data.

Although the above procedure seems easy enough to follow, the large ca-

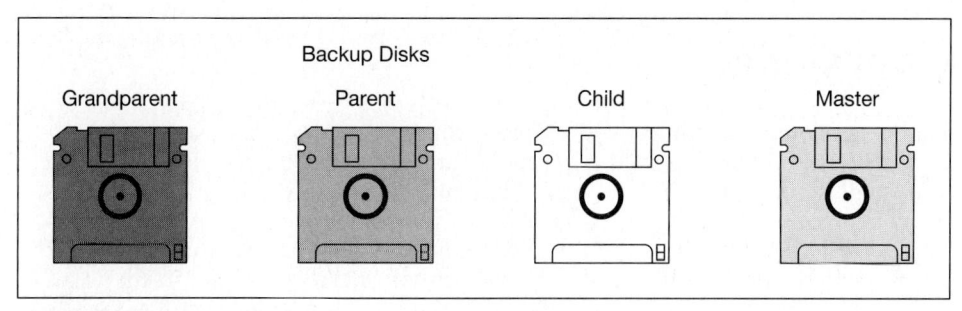

FIGURE 4-4
Three levels of disk backups for removable disks.

pacity of hard disk creates some unique problems. A 20MB hard disk requires 55 DSDD floppy disks or about 14 high-density microfloppies for all of its contents. But, if you maintain grandfather, father, and son backups, multiply that number by three. If the time comes to recreate a damaged hard disk from these floppies, the process is extremely time consuming. Loading these floppies onto the hard disk will take on the order of several hours of time. Imagine the problem for backing up a 300 megabyte disk!

While floppies are inexpensive, a better solution for most businesses is to use a specialized tape backup system which has high capacity and a speed that is many times faster than using floppy disks. These devices are discussed in the section on tape, which follows in this chapter.

CD-ROM

With compact disks (CD) becoming the latest audio craze, this technology is also beginning to impact the computer field. The attraction of CDs to the computer industry is enhanced by its extensive storage capacity. While a typical hard disk may have 200 megabytes of storage, a CD-ROM (compact disk read only memory) can store 500 megabytes to 2 gigabytes of digital data. This large storage capacity makes more information directly available to the computer user than had ever been possible with previous technologies.

One application of the CD-ROM is Microsoft's Bookshelf (Figure 4-5). It is a single CD that contains 10 commonly used reference works including a dictionary, thesaurus, the *World Almanac and Book of Facts*, the *Chicago Manual of Style*, and *Bartlett's Familiar Quotations*. Bookshelf can run with a variety of popular word processors, making this information available to the user with a few keystrokes. Data found on the CD can be printed, stored on a floppy disk, or transferred directly to a document using a paste operation.

With its large storage capacity, CD-ROM is becoming a popular format for delivering clip-art graphic images to computer-based publishers and multimedia producers. Some photo agencies are beginning to use CD-ROM to supply photographs to their business clients for in-house use. Because

CD-ROM. A compact disk characterized by its large storage capacity that contains read only data for computer use.

▶ DATA COMPRESSION

What happens when you buy a computer with a 60MB (or any size) hard disk and a year later find out that it is just too small. One solution is to replace the old drive with a new disk drive that has greater capacity. Upgrading the hardware is an expensive solution that may not be necessary.

An alternative is to use a data compression program such as Stacker or SuperStor. These disk utility programs take the data on your disk and compress it so that it requires only half or less of its original space. As you save a file or write software on disk, it is compressed so that less storage space is required. Then, when a file is needed it is automatically decompressed and read into RAM. To the computer (and to DOS) the files look normal.

Most compression programs use a compression algorithm published by two Israeli professors, Abraham Lempel and Jacob Ziv, in 1977. Using the algorithm, computer software looks for redundant data in a string and converts it into a shorter token. For example, in the word Mississippi, the second group of letters "iss" is redundant and can be replaced by a token which tells the program to use the previous three letters. Now this is an oversimplification of the method, but, by clever use of the technique most files can be stored in half the space. Graphics and database files do even better because they tend to contain more redundancies than text.

▶ CACHE MEMORY

Personal computer users are always looking for ways to speed up the operation of their software. Many programs exist on disk in parts and only the parts that are needed are brought into RAM. This method is frequently used in word processing and database software which often have extensive features. Thus, the disk contains a main program and one or more overlay programs that are brought into RAM as needed. Although this technique reduces the amount of RAM needed to run a program, it creates excessive disk activity which slows down the operation of the computer.

When data is read from disk, part of the disk sector is read to provide the record. When the next record is accessed the sector must be read again to get the record, causing a further delay. This constant activity causes a delay in processing, which can be mildly annoying to the experienced user and also results in lowered productivity. One solution is to use a faster disk but this can prove to be expensive. Another is to use a disk cache that stores an entire disk sector in memory so that when more records are needed they can often be accessed from fast RAM instead of from disk, which is slower.

For example, a 6MB computer could have 1 or 2 MB allocated as cache memory and still have enough memory available for most applications. Some of the data from disk will go into the cache even before it is needed. Then as the program requires this data, it goes to the cache to retrieve it. Using cache memory can be significantly faster than using the same amount of memory without a cache. Some software, such as Windows, provides its own caching system, while others depend on third-party software that provides for memory management options such as disk caching.

FIGURE 4-5
Microsoft's Bookshelf provides a CD-ROM for personal computer users containing 10 reference works. (Courtesy Microsoft.)

photos are CD-ROM based, they can be read into the computer and manipulated like any other graphic image, giving greater flexibility in their use.

Like disk, the CD-ROM stores data along circular tracks. But data on a CD-ROM is stored as a bubble or flat spot which represents a one or zero respectively. The bubbles are smaller than a magnetic spot and so more of them may be packed on the surface of the disk, resulting in the CD-ROM's greater storage capacity. A laser beam is used to read the data by reflecting its light off the bubble. CD-ROMs are most useful for applications where large amounts of data are needed and the data is not changing frequently.

CD-ROM's large storage capacity lends it to many uses not considered effective on magnetic disk. In addition to its capacity for huge amounts of text, CD-ROM can also store graphic images, sound, and video clips. With its random access capability, these various types of data can be organized into a format that weaves text, graphics, and video into a total presentation for use in training, education, or entertainment.

The availability of CD-ROM software is still limited, but for organizations such as school libraries, more variety is becoming available. A case in point is the Queen Anne's County High School in Centreville, Maryland. The school has 140 computers connected by four networks throughout the building. Access to CD-ROM software is available to students throughout the network. Using CDs reduces the high cost of purchasing and storing books, encyclopedias, and periodicals. By using the network, students and faculty have access to Grolier's *Academic American Electronic Encyclopedia,* Infotrac's *Magazine Index,* Wilsondisc's *Reader's Guide to Periodical Literature,* and Microsoft *Bookshelf.*

▶ PHOTO ESSAY—MULTIMEDIA

Multimedia is a term that applies both to the gathering of information and to its dissemination. Initially, multimedia hardware and software are used to collect a variety of information from diverse sources such as video, sound, graphics, and text. This information is then organized so that the user can be informed, trained, educated, and even entertained by the resulting product.

A top of the line computer with a high-resolution graphics display is central to multimedia applications. The 486 or higher level computer is essential to handling graphics, video, and sound that are process-intensive activities. A large amount of disk storage is also important as multimedia files are typically very large and occupy extensive disk space.

(Courtesy Compaq Computers.)

A CD-ROM is becoming the foremost device for multimedia applications. Its relatively low cost and the capability for using graphics, text, video, and sound make it an all-around input device for many types of multimedia applications.

(Courtesy Franz Moore, Apple Computer, Inc.)

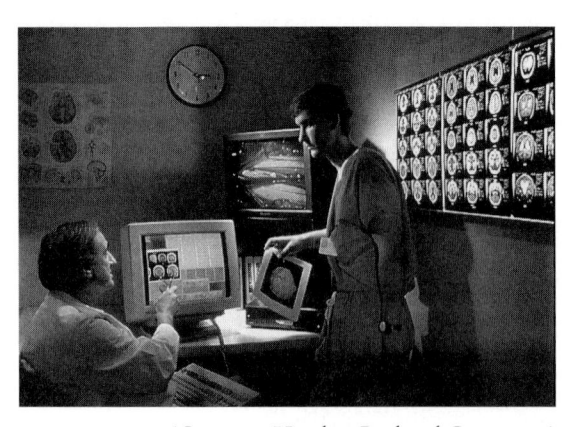

Medical training systems were one of the first to use a multimedia approach to training medical personnel. By showing real life examples captured as digitized images, the student can interact with the computer to learn to solve medical problems.

(Courtesy Hewlett-Packard Company.)

Video is an important component of some multimedia presentations. A system with appropriate multimedia software can capture video images from a VCR or television and incorporate the images into the presentations as stills or active video images.

(Courtesy Greenleigh Photo.)

Using a laser disk provides a source for video and still images that can be directly accessed. For training and educational applications, direct access to video information greatly enhances the learning process compared to watching consecutive frames from a video tape.

(Courtesy Pioneer New Media Technology, Inc.)

Multimedia software is used to develop multimedia applications. The program is used to bring together the various sources of information into a useful product. Software requires the ability to work with graphics, sound, video, and text, and to develop a script for interacting with the user of the product.

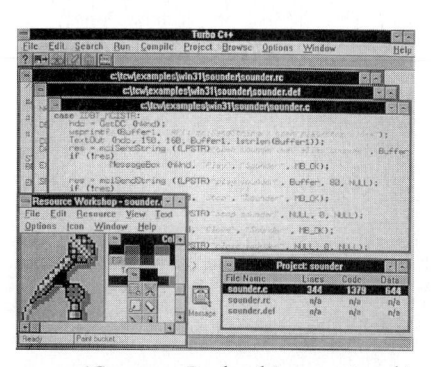

(Courtesy Borland International.)

▶ IMAGING—A DOCUMENT ALTERNATIVE

American businesses had accumulated 545 billion documents by 1992, and the number is expected to grow to 800 billion by 1994. In Alberta, Canada the Workman's Compensation Board handles an average of 65,000 claims a year. And each claim averages 32 pieces of paper per file. With so much documentation to store and manage, firms are looking for new methods that are faster and more compact.

A computer-based technology called imaging uses an image scanner to record data from forms, invoices, notes, and other documents including photographs. The data, which is stored electronically on optical disks, can be indexed for easy access, transmitted to other computers, and retrieved by any number of people at the same time.

Documents are accessed by users at a computer with a graphics display. Regardless of whether the original file contained handwritten notes, typed reports, an invoice, photographs, or newspaper clippings, they can all be viewed on the screen. Files can be marked as read only so they cannot be changed, and it is virtually impossible to lose a file. Imaging is an emerging technology, but already more than 1,700 companies in Japan are using imaging systems.

▶ OPTICAL STORAGE DRIVES

An optical disk storage system is based on a technology similar to CD (compact disk) ROMs. Of course, a CD as we know it for music systems can only play back its recordings. We cannot record on it. A rewritable optical drive can be written on just like a hard disk and the data read whenever it is needed. Optical drives are intended for use where the storage of large amounts of data is needed by the computer user.

Optical drives use a removable 3½-inch disk cartridge not unlike the 3½-inch floppy disk but somewhat thicker. To record data, a sliding shutter opens giving the magnetic-optical head in the drive access to the disk. Capacity for each disk is 128MB before formatting. Each disk is like having a 128MB hard disk and you can have as many as needed. But the optical disk operates at about half the speed of a hard disk.

Users that have very large files will find the optical disk a good alternative to other disk media. For desktop publishing, graphics, and multimedia systems, the optical disk can bring greater flexibility for storing files in these storage-intensive applications.

DISK USE ON MAINFRAME COMPUTERS

As personal computers become faster and more powerful, they move closer to the capabilities of the mainframe. Some organizations have even replaced their mainframe computer with networked PCs that are capable of doing the same tasks. However, for multiuser capability, raw computing power, and large data storage capacity it is still difficult to replace the mainframe computer system.

Disk drives on mainframe computers most closely resemble the PC's hard disk, but are usually constructed of more than one circular metal platter with a magnetic coating on both sides of the platter. The disk platter is mounted on a central hub, which is motor driven, to rotate the disk. When there is more than one platter, these are stacked one above the other on the

FIGURE 4-6
A disk drive and a drive assembly for a mainframe computer system. (Courtesy Amdake.)

central hub. Figure 4-6 shows a disk drive with several disks mounted on the central hub.

To read or write data on the surface of the disk, the entire disk is rotated on the hub. The data are read or written by the read/write heads that are mounted on access arms and positioned in close proximity to the surface of the disk. Usually there is one head per disk surface, although very high speed disks may have one head per track.

When several disks are stacked on a single drive hub, each surface will have a track and a read/write head that are accessible without head movement. If there are 10 surfaces that contain recording tracks, then each surface will have a track 0 located in a vertical column. Then when the head for one surface is positioned to track 0, all other heads will also be a track 0 on their respective surfaces. These stacked tracks form a **cylinder,** so-called because the shape of the tracks form a cylinderlike object.

To save time when reading or writing sequential files, records are stored along a track until the track is filled. Then the data are stored on the next track in the same cylinder and so on until all tracks in the cylinder contain data. If the cylinder contains 10 tracks, then all 10 tracks of sequential data may be read or written without the need to move the heads. This approach to sequential access minimizes the seek time.

Timing considerations on mainframe disks are similar to other disk drives. There is the **rotational delay** determined by the speed of the disk's rotation. There is also **seek time,** which is the time taken for the head to reach the track containing the data. And then there is the **data rate,** which is the speed at which data flows to or from the disk to the CPU.

Access time is a term that refers to the time it takes to access a record on the file. Access time considers all aspects of the functions of the disk drive including the rotational delay, seek time, and reading time (data rate). The capacity of the mainframe disk drive begins at the top end of PC disk capacity, but capacities of 1 billion or more bytes per drive is common. A typical mainframe computer will have several disk drives, which effectively multiplies the capacity by the number of drives in the system.

Speed of access and data transfer are important advantages of mainframe disks. Data transfer rates ranging from 806 KB (thousands of bytes per second) to over 3,000 KB is a significant improvement over a PC hard disk and is of particular importance on the mainframe, where many users require access to the same data on a centralized system. While the personal computer offers many benefits to the individual user, the mainframe must often serve hundreds of users with billions of bytes of data, which can only be handled by large-capacity disk drives.

MAGNETIC TAPE

Early personal computers such as the Apple and the Commodore PET used magnetic tape for storing programs and data. These tape units were basically audio cassette recorders such as you would use for the recording and playback of music. While audio tape is an inexpensive means for storing data, it is many times slower than the slowest disk unit. Tape must be read sequentially from the beginning, causing an additional delay if the data required is located nearer the end of the tape.

For these reasons tape soon lost favor with personal computer users and as disks and disk drives became less costly and more widely available, they were soon adopted in favor of tape. However, with disk came the problem of fast and efficient backup of the disk contents, as discussed earlier in this chapter. An important solution to the backup problem was the arrival of tape backup units that were designed to backup hard disk contents quickly and easily. And with recent developments in DAT (digital audio tape) capacity and speed of tape has improved considerably.

Using Tape to Backup Hard Disk

The tape used for hard disk backup is often called a streaming tape because of its high-speed continuous movement as it is recording data from the disk. Tape backup systems are specialized hardware units that come with special software to ease the task of backing up hard disk contents. These systems are much different from the tape units used on earlier computers and cannot be used for data storage other than that required to backup the disk.

Tape backup. A magnetic tape unit used to store backup copies of hard disk contents to protect the data in the event of disk failure.

Most backup units use a tape cartridge that may be replaced so that several levels of backup (grandfather, father, son) can be created. The cartridge contains a ¼-inch (0.635 cm) tape that can store up to 100 or more megabytes of data (see Figure 4-7). Some units plug into a port and so may be shared between several computers in the office rather than purchasing a separate backup system for each PC. Backup tape units are also available

FIGURE 4-7
A tape backup system and tape cartridge. (Courtesy IBM.)

with a built-in hard disk drive to offer a useful alternative to expanding disk storage as well as providing for file backup.

Some models permit backing up the disk by file so that only files that have been changed need to be copied to the tape. Other units backup the entire disk contents in one operation.

ACCESS METHODS

In any application, whether it is accounts receivable or payable, inventory or payroll, data needs to be stored on files in a manner that is easily accessible. As we have discussed earlier in the book, a file consists of a number of records, as shown by the relationship in Figure 4-8 between a field, record, a file, and a database.

A field refers to items such as an account number, item description, unit cost, quantity, or date. A record contains a single transaction such as all fields that relate to the purchase of an item. At the next level is the file that contains all records for a given application. There will be many files, including an accounts receivable file, an inventory file, a payroll file and so on, in a business system.

In general, a collection of related files in a system is called a database, but in some cases a database will be a single file composed of elements of data that might otherwise exist in several files. A more complete discussion on this concept is found in the database chapter.

Sequential Files

Sequential tape or disk files are files whose records are stored in a consecutive order. Records in a sequential file are ordered one after the other from the beginning to the end of the file. The contents of each record do not need to bear any relationship to the order of these records because the term sequential refers to the physical order of the records. But, in reality, records

Sequential file. A file of data where the records are stored in consecutive order.

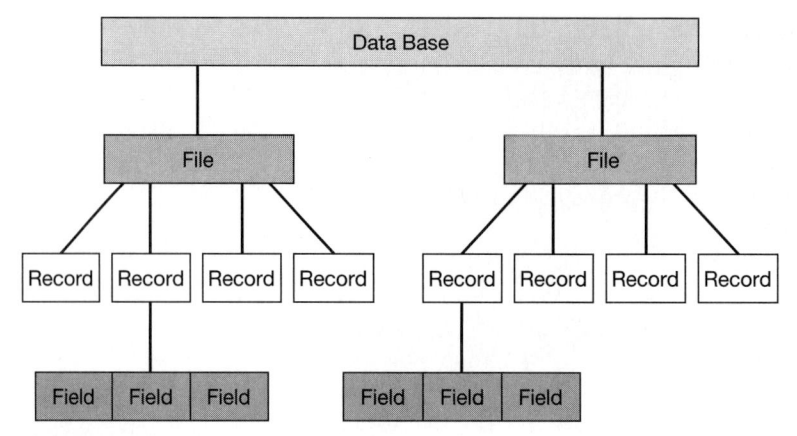

FIGURE 4-8
The relationship of items in a database. The smallest element of definition is the field. Records are composed of one or more fields that relate to a specific activity or transaction. All related records are recorded together in a file and a collection of these elements is called a database.

are often stored in some order, such as account number sequence or customer name sequence. Sequential files must always be read in this order whenever they are used by a program.

Sequence Fields. Records on a sequential file are often stored in a logical sequence. For example, accounting records would be stored in order by account number on the sequential file (Figure 4-9). The first record in the file would contain the lowest account number, the second record the next highest account and so on. The last record on the file would be the highest

FIGURE 4-9
Records stored in sequence on account number in a sequential file.

Record Number	Account Number (sequence field)	Amount	Date
1	120	145.85	04/26/92
2	122	35.86	05/19/92
3	125	145.72	09/18/92
4	126	456.82	01/14/93
5	130	143.88	06/03/93
6	137	6.45	01/09/94
7	141	195.20	04/30/92
8	143	295.90	07/19/93

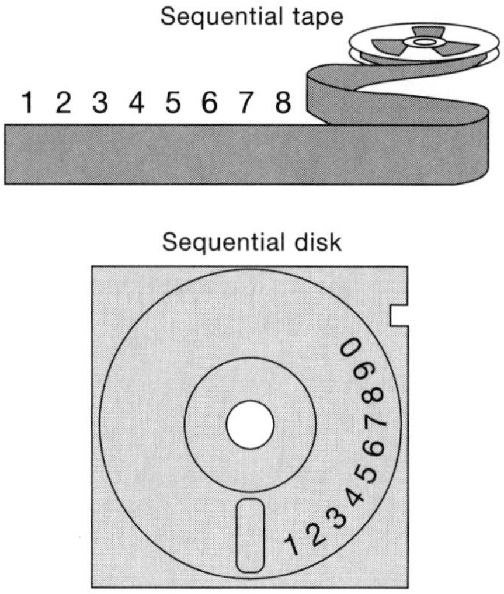

account number. The account number is called the sequence field. Notice that there are often gaps between the account numbers. Account number 120 is first but the next account on the file is account 122. This is a usual characteristic of sequential files and has some implications for programmers who write programs to handle these file types.

The previous example showed records in sequence by account number. Other files may use a customer number or an employee number. In some cases several fields may be involved in the sequence. If there are two sequence fields such as salesperson number within region, we would have a major (region) and minor (salesperson) sequence. There could be more fields involved in the sequence depending on the type of data and the characteristics of the application.

When to Use a Sequential File. A significant disadvantage of sequential files is the need to read through the file from beginning to end, even if only a few records are required for processing. Some PC applications such as word processing or spreadsheets give you very little choice and almost always use sequential files.

Other software, particularly database software, may give an option. Choosing to process a file sequentially will depend on the needs of the application. A payroll file may need to be accessed sequentially to produce paychecks and, of course, all employee records need to be read so that everyone will get paid. A high level of activity such as this would justify a sequential access method.

In other cases, using a sequential file would be inefficient and time consuming. For example, an employee personnel file may need to be accessed only occasionally to change an employee's address, or basic salary, a tax deduction, or a department. Because these changes seldom occur for most employees, in any given time period possibly less than 1 percent of the file will be affected. A low activity such as this will benefit from the use of a nonsequential file organization.

Nonsequential Files

Disks have a second form of file access known as **relative or random access files.** This access method permits the direct access to any record in the file without the need to read any of the other records. An indexed organization is also used which uses an index to access a given record. This method has some advantage over the relative file as we will see shortly. These access methods are particularly important when using high-volume storage devices such as disk or CD-ROM. With direct access to data, the time to find specific information would be prohibitive.

Relative Files. Consider an application where 1,000 employee records are to be maintained on a disk file with direct access capability. For some uses the file needs to be read sequentially, but most of the time only the record affected by the processing needs to be accessed due to a low file activity ratio. Conveniently, these employees each have a unique employee number from 0001 to 1000 which could act as a key to identify the record. In such a situation, a relative file would be an appropriate file organization method to use.

Relative files. A file where the records are stored based on a numbering method that identifies each record.

Pros and Cons of Relative Files. Other than the benefits of the access method, a relative file uses disk space efficiently. Records are stored consecutively from the beginning of the file. Each disk address contains a record so there is no space wasted between records other than what the disk drive needs for its operation. This space efficiency, however, would not apply if some of the keys were not needed. Suppose there were no employees with numbers 0500 to 0549. These 50 records would still occupy space on disk although they are not needed by the application. Thus, relative files are most useful in applications where there are few gaps in the keys.

This is clearly a limitation. Relative files are fine if the application uses consecutive numbers such as the employee file mentioned already. But many applications do not fit so neatly into this pattern.

What about the company that stocks parts from several suppliers and must record them under the supplier's number. These numbers may not be consecutive or may have many gaps between groups of numbers. Part numbers can also be alphanumeric, which creates other problems.

Even though the employee file discussed earlier looks foolproof, it could be changed over time. Employees quit, and their number is discontinued after a reasonable time period. New employees are hired and must be given new numbers. The company expands, and so on. Of course, we could suggest that employee numbers get recycled, but this may then cause excessive work to keep track of unused numbers.

Because of the inherent problems with relative files, other methods such as indexed files have become more popular and, in their own way, have resolved these problems with keys and storage efficiency.

CHAPTER SUMMARY

1. Data stored in RAM is temporary and is lost when the power is turned off, so a **secondary storage** medium, such as disk, is used to retain data permanently.
2. On personal computer systems there are two basic forms of disks: **removable disk**, which includes 5¼-inch and 3½-inch floppy disks, and **fixed disk**, which is commonly called hard disk.
3. Disk surfaces are divided into **tracks** and **sectors**, which aids the software in finding the data quickly and with a minimum of delay.
4. The mainstay of the disk industry has been the 5¼-inch **floppy disk** with a capacity of 360K bytes or 1.2MB bytes in high density. Newer PCs such as the 80386 and 80486 computers, laptops, and notebook computers are using the 3½-inch microfloppy disk with capacities of 720K, 1.44MB, or 2.88MB and are fast replacing the 5¼-inch disk as the number one choice in disks.
5. **Hard disks** (also known as Winchester disks) are used for their speed, convenience, and high storage capacity of from 20 to 1,000MB.
6. Disks in general offer high access speed, both sequential and direct accessing of data, high storage capacity, and low storage cost.
7. To guard against inadvertent loss, experienced computer users regularly **backup** their disk files so that an alternate source is available if data is lost.
8. A **backup system** in widespread use in information systems is called the grand-

parent, parent, child method. The child is the most recent backup, while the parent and grandparent are previous backups.

9. Using **cache memory** involves allocating part of memory for the use of disk data that reside there while running an application. Instead of going to disk for the data, the application can access these in the cache area, significantly improving access times.

10. **CD-ROMs** are beginning to be used in the computer industry because of their large storage capacity of from 540 million to 2 gigabytes. CD devices use a laser beam to read data that has been stored as a series of bubbles on the surface.

11. **Optical storage devices** function in a manner similar to a CD-ROM but are rewritable. Speed is about half that of hard disk, but storage capacity is 128MB before formatting and the disk is removable, giving access to extremely large amounts of data.

12. **Tape** units on personal computers are mainly used for backup of hard disk data.

13. **Sequential files** on tape or disk are files whose records are stored in a consecutive order. Records in a sequential file are ordered one after the other from the beginning to the end of the file and must be read in this order.

14. A **sequence field** is a field such as an account number that is used to determine the order of records within a file.

15. **Relative files** use an access method that permits direct access to any record in the file without the need to read any of the other records.

IMPORTANT TERMS AND CONCEPTS

Access arm
Access time
Backup
Cache memory
CD-ROM
Database
Data rate
Directory
Field
File
Fixed disk
Floppy disk
Hard disk

Microfloppy
Optical storage
Read/write head
Record
Relative file
Removable disk
Root
Secondary storage
Sector
Sequence field
Sequential file
Tape backup system
Track

SELF-TESTING QUESTIONS

Fill-In

1. A _____ disk generally has the capacity for 20MB to over 1,000MB in the larger personal computers.

2. The _____ disk drive uses removable disks that are placed in a protective sleeve when not in use.
3. The _____ _____ is positioned on the surface of the disk by the access arm in order to read or write data magnetically.
4. _____ time is a measure of disk performance. The lower the number the faster data is made available.
5. _____ memory reserves an area of RAM that helps in speeding up the frequent access of data from disk.
6. _____ is a read only form of disk that is used for applications requiring large amounts of data such as reference works or multimedia data.
7. A magnetic _____ drive is a sequential storage device that is useful for backing up disk data.
8. A _____ _____ is a field such as an account number that is used to determine the order of records within a file.

True/False

1. The floppy disk is a removable diskette, while the hard disk is fixed in the computer.
2. A floppy disk is generally faster and stores more data than a hard disk.
3. Disk backup is a procedure for going back to work done at a previous time such as a sales history.
4. A CD-ROM contains about as much data as a floppy disk.
5. An optical storage device is similar to a CD-ROM except that the optical device is rewritable.
6. Sequential files are files that are read from the beginning to the end.
7. Relative files are a form of sequential file where data can only be read in sequence.

ANSWERS

Fill-In: 1. hard, 2. floppy, 3. read/write head, 4. access, 5. cache, 6. CD-ROM, 7. tape, 8. sequence field

True/False: 1. T, 2. F, 3. F, 4. F, 5. T, 6. T, 7. F

Questions for Critical Thinking

1. Hard disks for PCs come in a variety of sizes and speeds. Develop a way to compare disks of different capacities and prices to determine the best dollar value.
2. CD-ROMs can on average store 500MB of data per disk of read only data. Discuss the implications of using data that is stored in this manner.
3. College libraries often have computerized search facilities to provide on-line access to research information. Discuss the hardware and software needs for such a system.
4. Personal computers can store as much data as a mainframe computer could only a few years ago. Assuming this trend continues, what are the implications for computing in the future?

CHAPTER 5

COMPUTERS AND COMMUNICATION

A VIEW OF THE CHAPTER AHEAD

After reading this chapter you will understand

- ▶ the use of data communication between computers and the need for local area networks.
- ▶ the various types of network topologies used for communications.
- ▶ the types of communications hardware required for transmitting and receiving data.
- ▶ the different types of on-line communications services.

INTRODUCTION

Many forms of communication have been developed to help us humans exchange information and ideas more effectively. There is the most effective one-on-one verbal conversation, but when we are farther apart, the telephone, a letter, or a fax is used. Other less intimate ways of communicating are radio and television, sometimes using satellite relay of material, and there are also books and other publications that relay information to the reader. Most of us have some familiarity with all of these systems, but what about computer communication?

Serious use of computer communication began with mainframe systems back in the 1960s. At that time, mainframe computers were centralized systems with no means of communication between them other than physically moving data, in the form of tape or disk, from one computer to the other. As the need to share data increased, communications systems were developed so that computers could, in effect, talk to each other, usually over ordinary telephone lines.

One of the best known and widespread uses of data communications is the Minitel system in France. Established in 1980, Minitel links more than 5 million computer terminals in homes and businesses across the country. Initially, Minitel provided an on-line electronic phone book, and the French took to it like wine and cheese, making more than 500 million inquiries to the database annually. Today, the network provides users with more than 12,000 different services including banking, mailorder, investing, and grocery shopping. Although the electronic phone book is the main money maker for the system, the additional services and new computer terminals with extra features were added to generate more income to keep the system financially viable.

TYPES OF DATA COMMUNICATION

Several types of needs were satisfied with the use of communications and they have not essentially changed with the advent of personal computers. Although the circumstances may be different, the requirement for data communications is the same whether a large or small computer system is used. But due to increased availability, new markets and uses of communications systems have evolved. Some of these needs are the following.

- **Data sharing.** Computers sometimes need to communicate when one computer contains data that is needed by another computer system. For example, a stock analyst needs the daily stock quotations on her computer. Rather than going to the stock exchange and copying the data to a floppy disk and then taking the disk to her computer, the data can be received over communication lines from a stock service in a manner similar to using the telephone.
- **Inquiry.** Sometimes it is the computer user who requires data that is located on a remote computer system. For example, a car dealer needs to

▶ DATA INTERCHANGE AT WAL-MART

When Wal-Mart sends an order for goods to Procter and Gamble, there is no purchase order form to send. No shipping notice is prepared to get the goods on their way, and no check to pay for the goods received. Instead, all of these activities are done by computer and electronic data interchange (EDI).

As goods are sold at Wal-Mart, the point-of-sale terminal (an electronic cash register) is connected directly to P&G's computers. Bar codes on the product tell the computer what item has been sold and how many. Using direct satellite transmission this data goes to P&G, where the computer determines when it is time to ship more supplies.

When goods are sold, Wal-Mart pays P&G for the sale. But instead of a check, Wal-Mart's computers transfer the funds electronically to P&G's account with additional data to show what they are paying for. Using this system with P&G and other suppliers, Wal-Mart is not only reducing the paperwork but is responding more effectively to customer needs.

(Courtesy George Disario, Stock Market.)

know when a car ordered for a customer will be delivered. Rather than physically going to the computer containing the data, the salesperson can make a remote inquiry and have the needed information delivered through the communication system.

- **Data entry.** An insurance agent needs to send daily sales to the company's head office computer. This data is collected during the day, and when the agent arrives at the hotel that night he can leisurely send the data over the telephone to the remote computer, where it is stored for future use.
- **Device sharing.** This is a relatively simple requirement but one that is common to many users. An office has several computers that do different

Inquiry (Courtesy Ron Chapple, FPG International.)

tasks, but each needs access to a common printer. A simple device can allow each user to access the printer without interfering with the others.

In each of the above cases, data communication via a transmission line communicates information either to the user or to the computer or other hardware device. A personal computer could be used for all of the above examples, or, in some cases, a mainframe may be used or a combination of

Data entry (Courtesy Ron Chapple, FPG International.)

Data sharing (Courtesy Charles Feil/Stock Boston.)

CHAPTER 5 Computers and Communication

the two. In the following material we will see examples of how both personal computers and mainframes use data communication.

HOW DOES DATA TRANSMISSION WORK?

When you pick up the telephone to make a call to a friend, you can take for granted that the technology will work and the only skill you need to master is dialing the number. Now that data communications is out of its infancy, using a computer on a communications line is almost as easy. But, as we will see before the end of the chapter, data communications can have its own complexities, and there are many choices of different types of networks for a variety of needs.

A simple, yet useful, communications system is shown in Figure 5-1, where a single personal computer communicates with another PC. The computers are linked together by a **communications line,** which is usually a telephone line, unless they are located in close proximity to each other, such as in the same room or in the same building, in which case a short cable can be used.

Because computers use digital transmission of data (the human voice is analog), a device called a **modem** which translates data between digital and analog is located at each computer. The modem at the sending computer translates computer talk (digital code) into an analog signal that can be sent over the communications line. The modem at the receiving computer takes this analog signal and converts it back to digital form which the receiving computer can understand.

A communications system such as this might be used when one computer

Communications line. A line that links computers together for the purpose of data communication.

FIGURE 5-1
The sending computer transmits a digital signal that is converted to analog by the local modem. This analog signal, which represents the data, is transmitted over a communications line to the remote modem. At this end the signal is converted back to digital and read by the receiving computer.

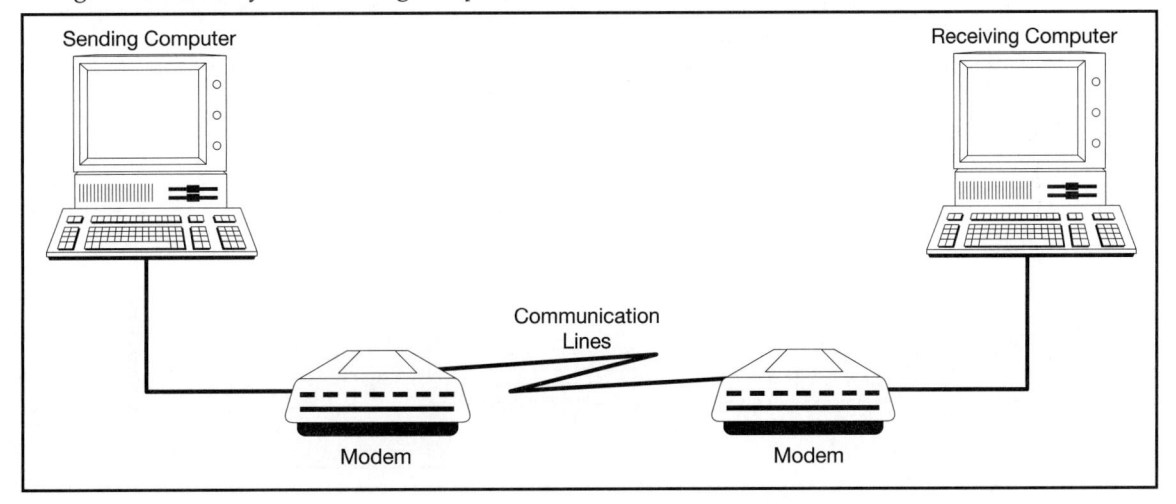

contains data on its disk that is needed by a second computer. Let's take an example of a franchise operation where the head office needs to have the sales figures sent to it each week from the branch office. The branch office computer becomes the sending computer and the head office computer is the receiving computer (see Figure 5-2). Data is transmitted over the telephone lines to the head office, where it is received and stored on disk until needed for use.

Because a franchise typically has several branches, each branch may have its own computer and send its data in a similar manner to a head office. In this example, only one branch can transmit at one time. This situation is similar to three or four friends trying to phone you at one time. Only the one who gets you first will make contact, while the others will receive a busy signal and will need to try again later. With computer communications there are networks and other devices that can get around this type of problem, but a simple communications system is not much different from a phone call.

Head office may also need to send data to the branches. Updated prices, information on new products, and other data can be transmitted to the branch from the head office computer. Then the head office becomes the sending computer and the branch the receiving.

Clearly there is extra hardware required when data communications is necessary between computers. In many instances there is a modem needed

FIGURE 5-2
A branch office for a franchise operation sends sales data weekly from its local computer to the head office computer over regular telephone lines. Each branch in the operation can send its data in a similar manner, but only one branch can send at a time.

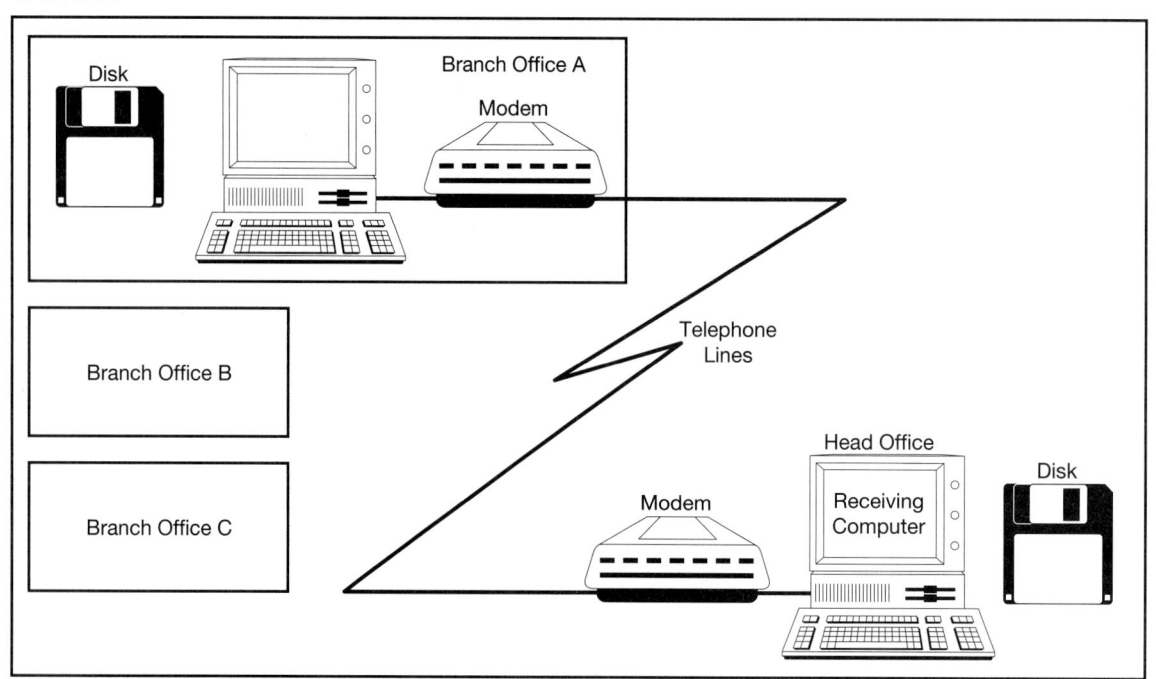

at each computer, while in other cases a special board in the computer may be required. In addition to hardware, there are software requirements. A communications program will be necessary for many applications, while in other cases an existing program may provide communications capability. Some software, such as Windows or Microsoft Works, have a built-in communications section which makes it easy to transmit spreadsheets, word processing documents, or other files to remote computers and to receive data from these computers.

NETWORK TOPOLOGY

Networks, such as Ethernet and Novell, are communications systems that provide a way for several computers to communicate with each other. Because communication needs vary there are different types of networks available to satisfy the requirements of a variety of situations. Many networks connect a variety of computers, from micros and minis, to mainframes. Some connect several terminals with a central computer, while others use a more decentralized approach with several computers on the network.

Network. A system that has various computers connected to provide for data transfer.

Whatever the type of network, and mix of computers and terminals used, there are a few basic networks that form the core of communications systems. This physical organization is called **network topology** and there are three basic types: the star, ring, and bus networks (Figure 5-3).

Network topology. The physical organization of communication lines and devices used in a network.

Networks such as these share the workload between several computers rather than having all of the load on one central computer. Messages and data can be shared between users and each user can manipulate his or her own data without the fear of destroying data needed by another operation.

Working at a local computer can be more efficient with fewer time delays than accessing a remote system. The user does not need to wait on an over-

These AT&T computers are linked together with the StarLAN network. This network uses a star topology with a central host computer that acts as a file server to all personal computers on the network. (Courtesy AT&T Archives.)

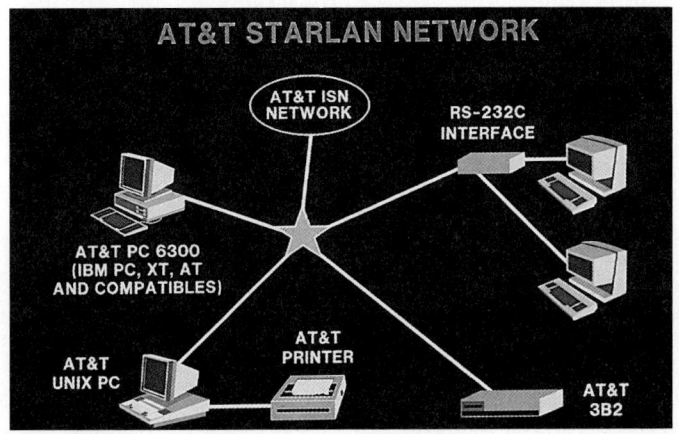

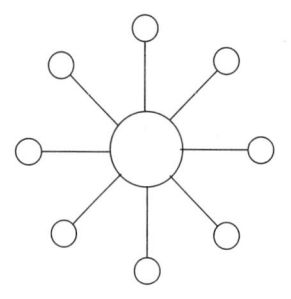

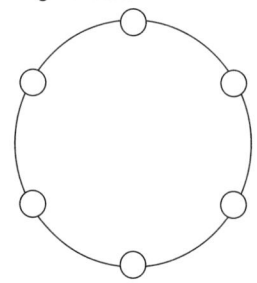

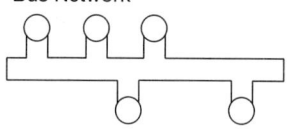

FIGURE 5-3
Network topology. A star topology uses a central computer through which all other computers operate. Ring networks connect all computers together, with each being of equal status. The bus network shares several computers or devices on the same network.

loaded mainframe to answer her request but can get speedy responses from a local PC. Working on a local computer still gives easy access to remote data and programs located on the mainframe. And there is a sense of being in control when your work is done on a local desktop computer instead of some giant computer that no one really seems to understand.

There can also be a few disadvantages of networking computers. The extra hardware and software required can cost more than a single system, and there is the need for technical support at the remote location. Having copies of databases on each computer can result in updating problems unless only a single, centralized database is maintained. Then there is less control over security with many different computers and individuals who use them. But, in the view of most people the benefits of networking computers far outweigh the disadvantages.

Star network. A network that uses a centralized computer which connects to all other computers in a starlike pattern.

Star Network

A **star network** (Figure 5-4) is configured in a starlike pattern with a computer at the center of the pattern. The central computer is the **host**

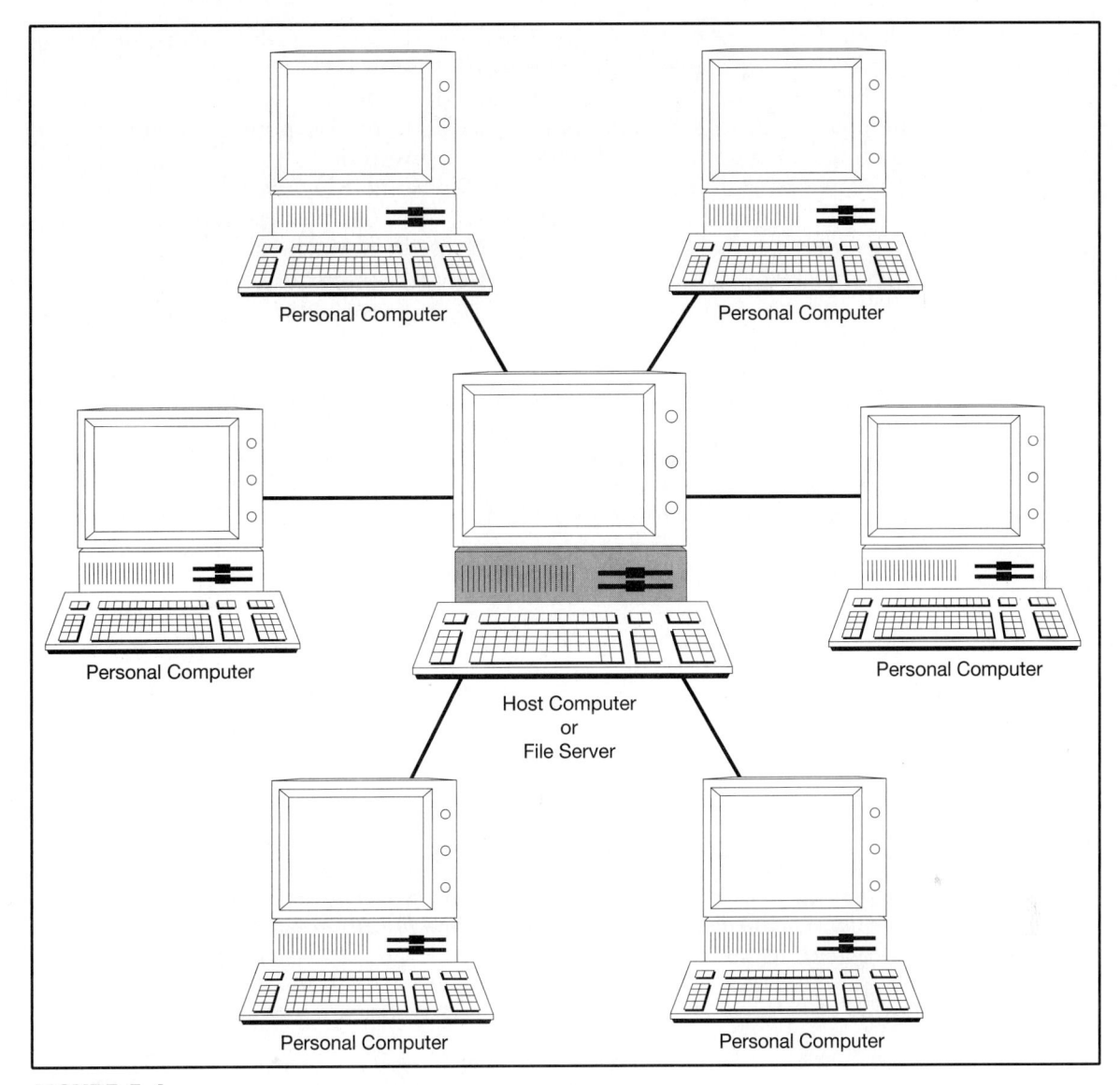

FIGURE 5-4
A star network used for a personal computing local area network. Each computer on the network shares data and software situated on the file server computer.

computer which supplies information and computer resources to the other computers in the network. When the host is a mainframe, it often provides database support to the other computers and supplies extra computing power when the node is a terminal.

A personal computer star network uses a PC as the host which is called a **file server.** The central PC contains databases and programs that are needed by the other computers, thus requiring large disk storage capacity. Rather than storing data and software on the local computer, the file server provides this service, thus eliminating duplication. Sharing programs can also reduce software cost by getting a network license rather than purchasing many separate copies of the program.

For personal computing, star networks are mainly used to connect a number of office's computers together and are also popular in educational settings for student use. The University of Waterloo's JANET Network is an example of such a configuration used by some educational institutes, while AT&T's StarLAN is a network that is used in business settings. Twisted-pair wire or shielded twisted-pair are used to attach each computer in the network, which makes movement of the computers to other locations difficult. Adding new computers to the network can also be disruptive to the existing network.

Computers on a star network cannot communicate directly with each other, which limits sharing of resources between them. Data can be passed to the central computer for subsequent sharing with other computers in the network, but this inhibits fast and efficient transmission of data where this procedure is frequently needed. A significant problem with star networks is the reliance on the host computer. If this computer fails, all other computers on the network will either become nonoperational or be seriously limited in their operation due to lack of support from the host.

Ring Network

Ring network. A network that connects all computers together on a single channel using a ring pattern.

The **ring network** (Figure 5-5), such as IBM's Token-Ring Network which is a variation of this concept, connects a number of computers to a continuous communication ring. There is no host computer, but each computer on

These personal computers are attached via IBM's Token-Ring network. This network combines the physical properties of a star network with the operational or logical qualities of a ring network. An electronic token is passed between the computers to determine who has transmission priority. (Courtesy Sperry.)

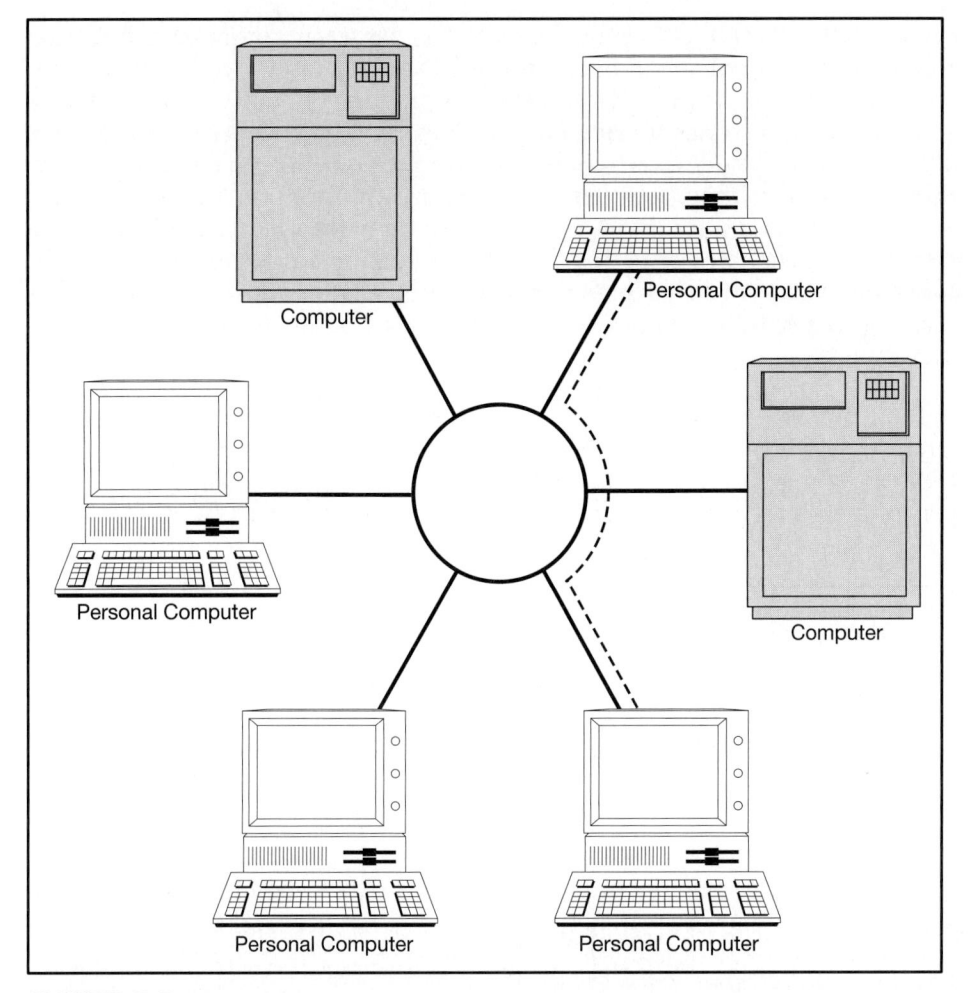

FIGURE 5-5
A ring network ties all computers together on a single communication channel. A computer in the network can communicate with any other computer on the network by passing its data along the ring. Data not meant for a given computer is passed on until it reaches the system for which it is intended.

the ring can communicate with all other computers. Data is passed along the ring from one computer to the next until it arrives at the receiving computer. All other computers simply pass the data along. In one form of ring network a non-functioning computer can cause an interruption of data traffic because it is unable to forward data.

A variation on this network permits a malfunctioning computer to be switched out of the ring, thus retaining communication with all remaining computers. This makes the ring network more reliable and not dependent on any one computer in the ring. If one goes down all of the others can continue to operate.

The cost of communication lines in a ring can also be less expensive because lines of the shortest distance between adjacent computers can be used rather than longer lines usually required in a star. Being attached to a ring network also simplifies the passing of data between computers. The two communicating computers need only talk to each other, while other computers in the system ignore their transmissions.

This benefit also has its side effects. Because all computers use the same network, special codes and communications controllers are needed to ensure that data flowing between two computers does not get confused with other transmissions going on at the same time with other computers in the system. By having access to any computer in the network, potential security problems exist, requiring passwords and other software protection to ensure that the right users have access to legitimate data.

FIGURE 5-6
A bus network connects all nodes by a common cable. Messages are sent along the cable with a unique address for each device, so only the device recognizing the address receives the data.

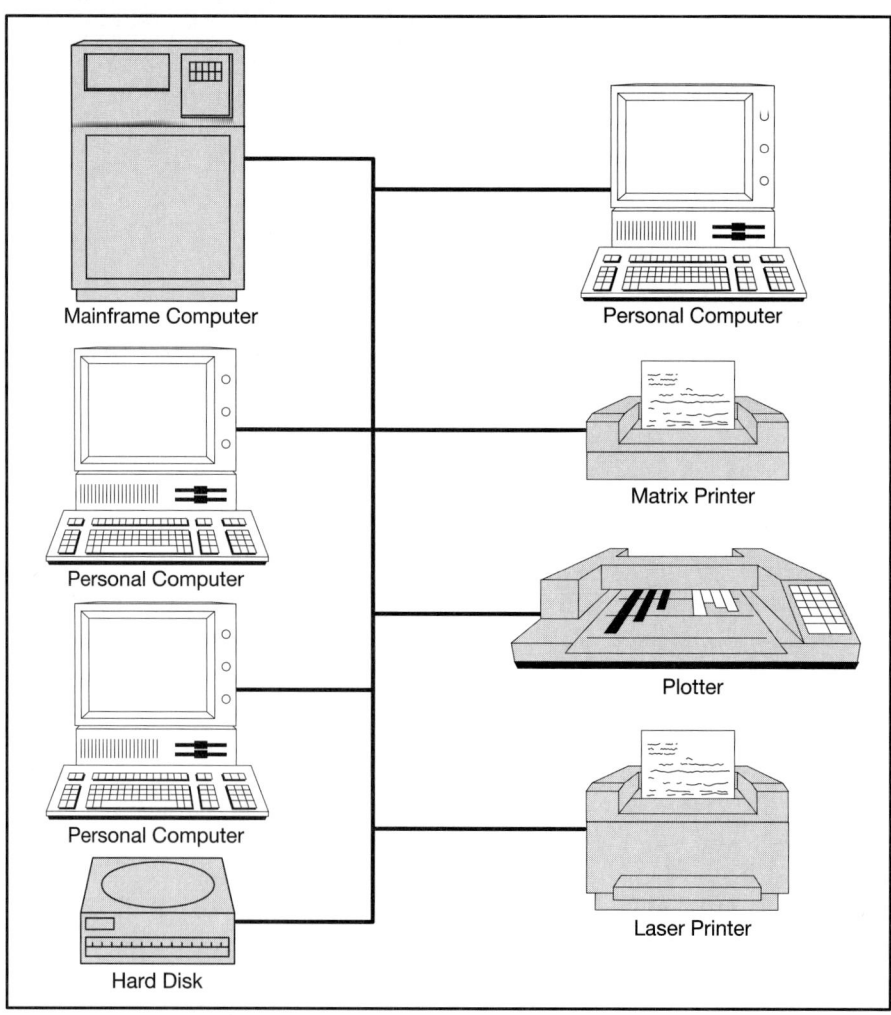

▶ THE ETHICS OF COMPUTER MONITORING

Users of networks and mainframe computer terminals have raised an important ethical question on the rights of an employer to monitor their work. By using specially designed programs, management is able to gather statistics on the performance of each employee who uses a computer on the network. Where data entry is a major component of the job, then data on the speed of data entry, the number of errors, time spent not entering data, and other statistics can be gathered for each person.

More sophisticated programs let the manager "sign on" to the employee's computer and observe the activity of the user. The user can be unaware that this is happening when the software hides the effect of computer monitoring. E-mail can even be captured as it is being transmitted and then reviewed by a manager or security person in the company.

Employers claim there are legitimate reasons for monitoring the work and activities of the employee. Employees on the other hand are sensitive about being observed at work, especially when they are not aware that observation is being used. Clearly the technology available today would permit extensive monitoring practices, but a balance is needed between the employee's right to privacy and the employer's need to maintain security and productivity.

Bus Network

Many of the problems associated with star or ring networks are resolved by using a bus network. A **bus network** is a local area network that uses a cable to interconnect a series of computers and devices together. Often the cable is a coaxial cable, but twisted-pair wire or fiber optic cable can also be used. While this may seem similar to a ring network, the devices on the bus are each independent of the other.

Transmission on a bus network consists of messages that contain a device address as part of the data. Instead of a central computer, as in a star network, each device on the bus has its own CPU which recognizes when a message is sent to it. Additional devices may be added to the bus by attaching a new node to the cable at any point, and similarly a device is as easily removed. Failure on the part of any one device has no effect on other devices in the network.

A bus network simplifies the sharing of devices as shown in Figure 5-6. Several computers may share data resources as well as use a common printer, plotter, or remote mainframe system. The bus is not without some problems. Shared cabling means that when data is being sent to one device the others must wait. So if printing is going on, disk access is not possible. A solution to this problem is to use memory buffers at the slower devices, such as a printer, to store data and thus free the channel for other messages. Many local area networks (LANs) use this type of networking.

Bus network. A network that connects all devices by a single cable.

Node. A device such as a computer, printer, or plotter that is connected to a network.

LOCAL AREA NETWORKS

A **local area network (LAN)** can be likened to having your own private telephone network, but in this case we are referring to a computer network.

Local area network. A network that connects computers for the purpose of data and program sharing.

▶ CHOOSING A LAN

Making the right choice for a local area network can be a frustrating experience. Because there are dozens of networks to choose from, these guidelines can help to pull together the various features and how they can address the needs of a specific installation.

SECURITY
There are two levels of security to consider. One is safeguarding against users getting into the wrong files either intentionally, or unintentionally, and the other is protecting the system from entry by unauthorized users. Network software provides protection for both of these concerns by requiring a password for entry to the system. Some software also permits access to data based on a user profile so that only certain parts of the system are accessible.

Tapping into a system can more easily be done if twisted-pair or coaxial cable is used. Fiber optic cable, on the other hand, is difficult to tap into and discourages would-be wiretappers.

RELIABILITY
The concern over reliability depends largely on the use of the network. Computer networks used for medical applications, or robot control in process control manufacturing, have a more critical level than a network used in an office environment. Star networks are inherently more reliable because no one node of the system depends on the others, while a ring network has greater dependencies.

Some systems offer additional factors to improve reliability. For example, Proteon has a system with redundant cabling. If one cable fails, the other is used without an interruption in the process. Novell offers a system with extra hard disks and/or processors. If one fails the other picks up without missing a beat.

COST
If wiring is already in place (usually twisted-pair telephone cable) this can be a significant cost saver. A bus or ring network can require less wiring than a star and so one of these will keep cost down. Software can be a significant part of the cost of a network. Networking software can run from a low of about $100 to several thousand dollars.

NETWORK PERFORMANCE
The performance of the network is affected by the number of stations, line speed, and the type of software used. Generally, as more stations are added to a network, the performance is degraded. Using a faster file server such as an 80386 processor or even an 80486 with a high-speed hard disk will improve performance.

Using the same kind of computer for each station is desirable for maximum performance. While other hardware can be used, mixing can require special connections and even conversion software to ensure compatibility. This problem is particularly evident when micros, minis, and mainframes are tied together in a network.

A LAN might be thought of as the third utility in a building, following the telephone and electrical utilities. The term local means that the computers and devices are located in the same vicinity. Often a local area network serves computer devices within the same office space or in several adjacent offices. In other situations, the network can serve users several miles apart. IBM's PC Net can use a maximum coaxial cable length of 6.3 miles (10 kilometers), while Corvus Systems' Omninet uses twisted-pair wire to reach 0.8 miles. Speeds range from 1 million bits per second (1Mbps) to 8 Mbps. LANs are not intended for cross-country or international communication. By contrast, a **wide area network (WAN)** covers a substantial geographical area ranging from a city to many different countries.

▶ IBM'S TOKEN-RING NETWORK

In theory, networks often seem to have simple topologies, but in practice more complexities are often found. The IBM Token-Ring Network is one of these examples. Physically, the IBM Token-Ring Network has a starlike topology with individual stations connected to a central access unit. But, inside the multistation access unit the multiconductor cables are electrically connected like a ring.

To operate, the network uses an access method called token passing. An electronic token is circulated among the stations while they are waiting idly for some activity. When a station has a message to transmit, it waits until the token arrives at its location. It then takes the token, something like a relay runner taking the baton, and then proceeds to send its message. All other stations must wait until the token becomes free again. In this way stations cannot interfere with one another's transmissions.

IBM's Token-Ring Network comes as a starter kit which includes one Multistation Access Unit, with cables and interface cards for four stations. Cables can be twisted-pair wires or fiber optic cable. Using shielded twisted-pair, the network operates at 4-Mbps with a maximum of 96 stations.

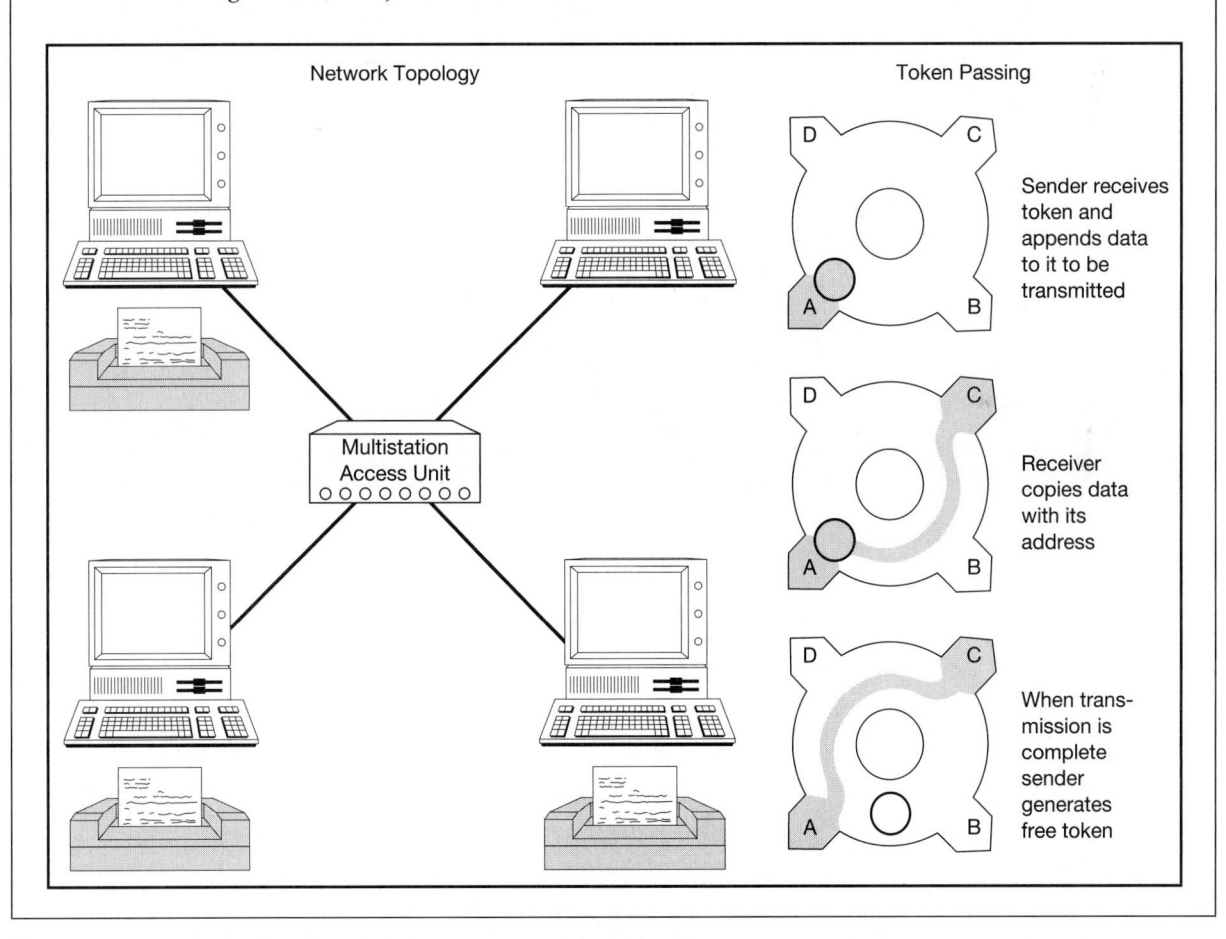

Network Topology

Token Passing

Sender receives token and appends data to it to be transmitted

Receiver copies data with its address

When transmission is complete sender generates free token

▶ A WIDE AREA NETWORK

The central computer forms the hub of the starlike pattern to which other computers or terminals in this wide area network (WAN) are attached. In complex mainframe-based systems, such as those used by the banking industry, a node on the central hub can represent a computer located in a remote city. This node may itself be the hub of another star network to which other computers and terminals in that city are attached. The node in Boston is a computer that offloads much of the processing from the central computer in New York. Similar computer nodes in other centers take on local computing tasks, freeing the central system for other major functions.

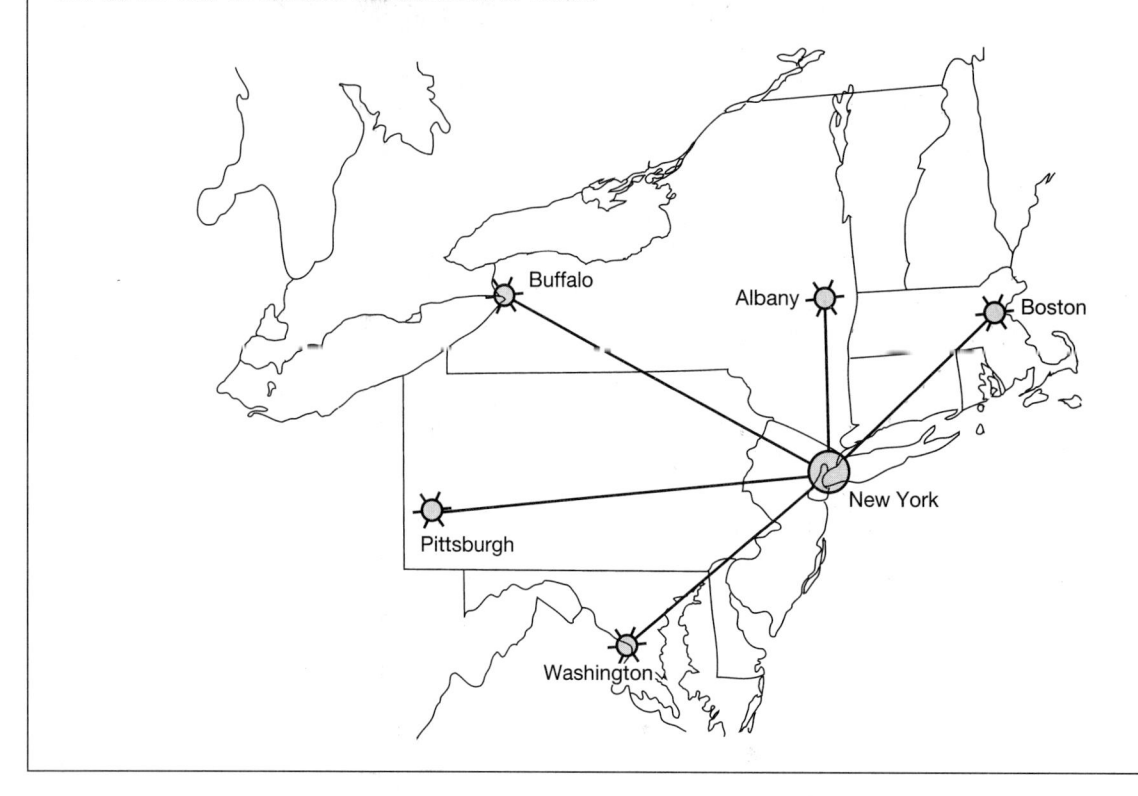

LANs use different network topologies but many have adopted the star network concept described previously. Businesses use local area networks for a variety of reasons, including many of the following.

- Sharing common data located on a central hard disk.
- Sharing a common printer to reduce hardware costs or to make several types of printers such as a high-speed dot matrix and a laser printer available to all computers on the network.
- Simplifies communicating with other computers in the business, as when electronic mail is used for internal management communication.
- Saves software costs by permitting the use of network licensing, which is less expensive than separate copies of the same program.

- Provides a backup of computer resources. If one computer in the network is down, the job can often be done by another computer on the same LAN by transferring tasks to the available computers.
- Helps to increase user productivity.

ON-LINE COMMUNICATIONS SERVICES

When was the last time you stopped by the library to look up a last-minute reference for the paper you're writing only to find that someone else beat you to the document or reference book? With many of the more than 3,000 on-line data services, you can now access a huge variety of information from your home computer. Services such as Prodigy, CompuServe, Dow Jones News/Retrieval, and Bibliographic Retrieval Service (BRS) offer access to a wide assortment of databases that accommodate many needs.

Some services offer special interest data or such features as electronic mail or an electronic bulletin board where you can advertise items for sale or purchase. Other services, such as CompuServe, provide access to many databases to address the needs of a broad variety of users. Hundreds of subjects are available through on-line databases, including topics such as airline schedules, investment, foreign news, sports, UPI news, and so on.

The cost for on-line services vary, but most charge a connect fee of from $0.08 to $2.00 per minute depending on the type of service supplied. Some have a minimum monthly charge. Some services have a reduced rate for non-prime time users, usually for use after midnight.

There are three fundamental types of on-line communications services.

- **Videotext.** These services are the most widely used and provide a broad range of services for home, education, business, and professional users. The Source, CompuServe, and Delphi are all videotext operations. Included in these services are serious applications such as databases, and communications, and more fun things like games and chat features.
- **Communications.** This type of service offers electronic mail, bulletin boards, and message services. Primarily designed for business users, this category is represented by Dialcom, EasyLink, and MCI Mail.
- **Database.** BRG, Dialog, and Infomaster are all database services. These are aimed at the business and educational research community by providing data on books in print, magazine bibliographies, census data, and stock futures.

Some on-line services provide access to fundamental types of information, while others give broad access. Some services give access to others, which can save the expense of subscribing to several different services if the needs of the user are extensive. In the following section we will look at some of the on-line services.

▶ PHOTO ESSAY COMMUNICATION SERVICES

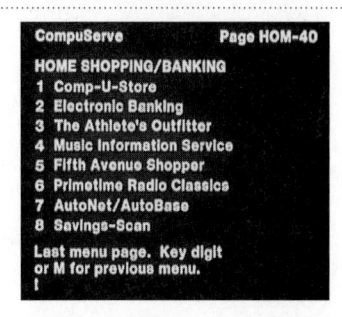

A CompuServe menu for home shopping and banking. (Courtesy CompuServe.)

CompuServe was one of the first communication services for computer users. Here the subscriber is provided with services that include shopping and banking.

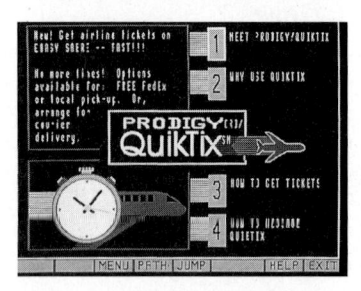

Prodigy combines graphics and text. (Courtesy Prodigy.)

Many communication services are text oriented. Prodigy is one of the few that combines graphic material with text such as used in this on-line encyclopedia.

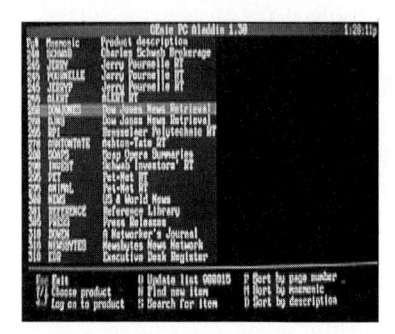

A menu of services from GEnie. (Courtesy GE Information Services.)

GEnie is a popular communication service for business and professional people. Items ranging from up-to-date news to brokerage services can be accessed by computer.

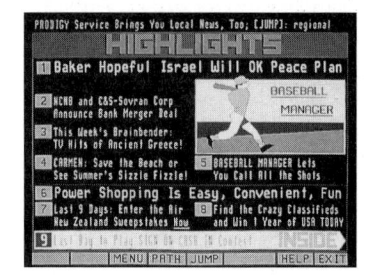

A communication service sales screen. (Courtesy Prodigy.)

Using graphics and text in an on-line communication service makes it possible to offer some unusual services. Here a shop-by-computer service is made available.

CompuServe

One of the oldest services, CompuServe was established in 1969 and now is one of the most diverse communications services. Business, professional, educational, and other users have access to electronic mail, reference works, bulletin boards, travel services, electronic conferencing, and airline reservation.

CompuServe offers a "chat" feature where subscribers have access to other users on the system so they can chat about topics of similar interest. CompuServe also offers several services where messages can be forwarded to other users of the system. Electronic mail supplies users with a mailbox where mail can be received and forwarded electronically. There are also 340 forums where messages can be posted for anyone to read. This service is used for getting help with technical problems, selling personal items, or advertising for items needed.

Communication services, such as CompuServe, generally have a fixed monthly rate for access to a full array of basic services. Extended services are available at additional cost ranging from an extra monthly charge to paying for the amount of connect time to the service.

GEnie

General Electric's on-line service is strong on its professional services that range from Dow Jones' library of databases to Advanced Research Technologies Bookshelf. Researchers can also subscribe to a clipping service for a flat monthly fee. Financial services include the ability to buy and sell stocks for those users who are investment oriented. Aladdin, GEnie's front-end program, is used to provide E-mail service that features automatic download of mail, and off-line composition of text to save line charges. GEnie is also a leader in on-line games, and a RoundTable, which is GEnie's bulletin board service. Many of the advanced features are only available at extra cost, usually an hourly rate (see Figure 5-7).

Prodigy

Prodigy's Interactive Personal Service combines a rich array of features within its basic monthly rate structure. Screens feature graphic displays which add a richness to the system that others services lack to the same degree. A variety of experts are available on numerous topics, such as Brendan Boyd from *Investment Digest* on finance and Dick Schaap on sports. A complete *Academic American Encyclopedia* is available for researchers, or current news and business reports from the Dow Jones News/Retrieval service. Active bulletin boards post over 90,000 messages a day. Other services include on-line cookbooks, travel guides, trip reservations, on-line shopping, and E-mail. As with all of the above services, Prodigy provides many more on-line activites than can be listed here. Each one has its own strengths that will appeal to a broad variety of users.

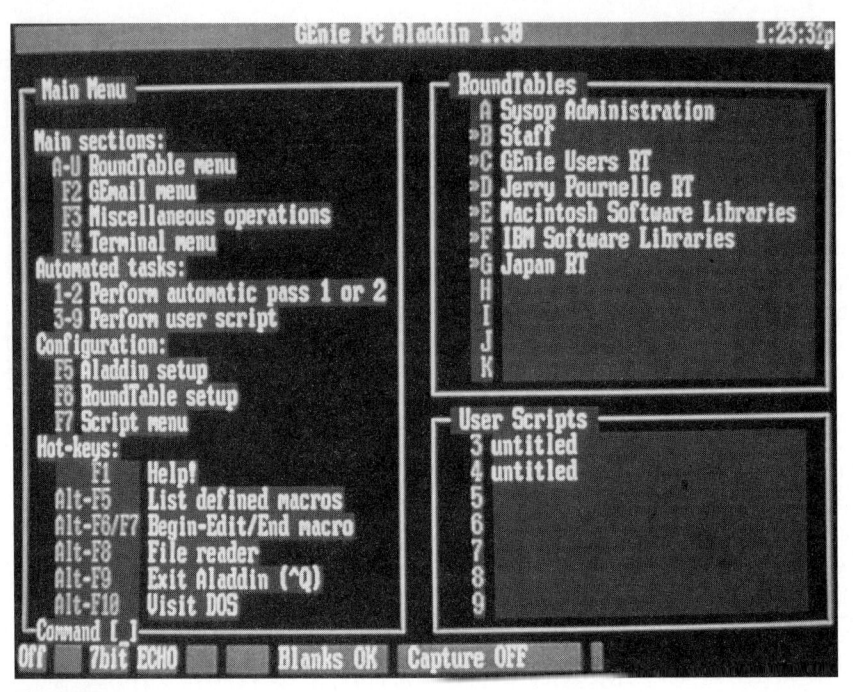

FIGURE 5-7
Using graphics and text in an on-line communication service makes it possible to offer some unusual services. Here a news and sports service is made available.
(Courtesy GE Information Services.)

Electronic Mail

E-mail. A network that provides for the transmission of mail electronically between subscribers to the service.

E-mail is a generic name for a communication system (Figure 5-8) that provides the ability to exchange mail electronically between users of the system. Special E-mail software, such as Beyond Mail, cc:Mail, or WordPerfect Office, resides in each computer to provide a standard base from which communications proceed. Electronic mail replaces public mail only if both the sender and receiver subscribe to the same service or a compatible one. Some services such as CompuServe provide E-mail links to other services such as InterNet. That way users of one service can send mail to a user on a different service. One variation of E-mail prints out the letter at the receiving end, which is then delivered by the local postal service.

A user of E-mail sends a message by logging onto the network and entering a password to gain access. Then he proceeds by typing a letter on his computer. Some systems permit the letter to be composed off-line to reduce line costs and then transmitted when the letter is complete. The letter includes a destination, which can be a name and address or a mailbox number, depending on the system. When the letter has been typed, it is stored in the central computer until the recipient logs onto her computer.

Most E-mail users will check their "mailbox" several times a day and thus get messages within a few minutes or hours after they were sent rather than days or weeks by more traditional means. Systems can be limited to a

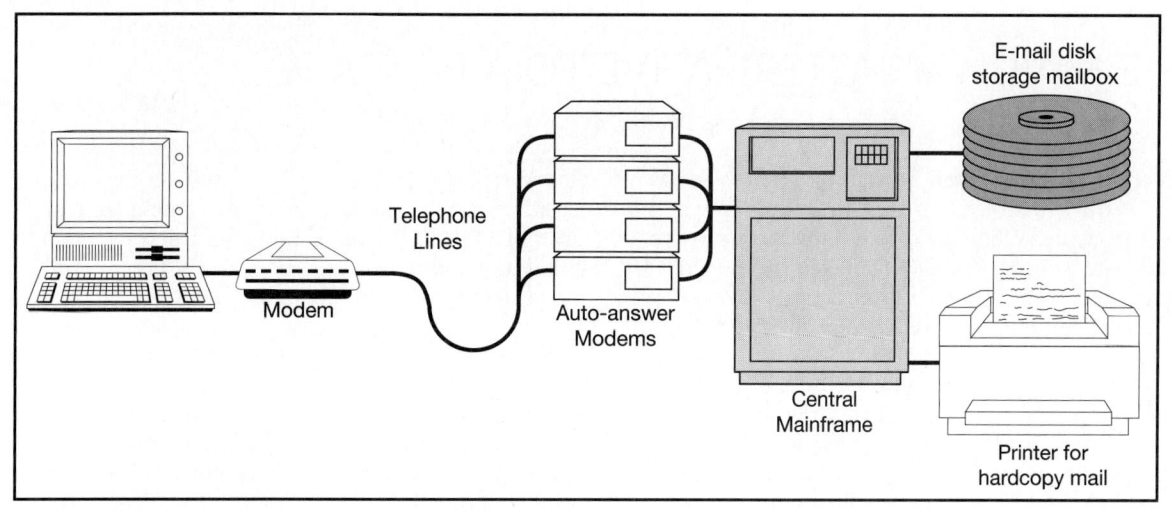

FIGURE 5-8
This E-mail system uses a central computer to collect mail. Users dial in to send or receive mail, which is stored under their box number or by name and user identification.

local area network within a single company. Other systems are worldwide and have subscribers in Canada, the United States, Europe, South America, and other remote locations. This type of system is particularly popular among universities where researchers in related disciplines can easily keep in touch with their colleagues.

Bulletin Board Services

Many organizations use a bulletin board service (BBS) because the system is easily installed with a minimum of expense. All that is required is a personal computer, a telephone line, a modem, and some software. Numerous colleges and universities have set up electronic bulletin boards for student and faculty access for the announcement of new programs, tutorial help, message passing, and even student dating services.

Students wanting to sell an old car, or some textbooks, might find a purchaser through the BBS. Some bulletin boards also provide some entertainment in the form of games or software to help with academic needs such as statistical packages. Bulletin boards can also be used by business to provide needed services to customers. For example, *PC Magazine* uses this method to provide program code from their magazine to subscribers by downloading the program to the personal computer over the telephone. Special-purpose BBSs also exist for pharmacists and doctors to check on recent drug releases.

Because of the small investment required to install a bulletin board, many of them are free while others have a minimal subscription rate.

▶ E-MAIL—AN ALTERNATIVE TO A POSTAGE STAMP

Janet Wilson has given up licking stamps in favor of an E-mail system that lets her send mail electronically. When she has a letter or report to mail, she simply sits down at her home computer and with her communications software, dials the number of MCI Mail, an E-mail service.

When MCI Mail responds to her call, Janet enters a password and a seven-digit mail ID. If there is mail waiting for her to read, MCI notifies her with an on-screen message. She then sends her mail by either typing it directly on-line or if it is a longer report Janet would have typed it earlier with her word processor and now simply transmits the report to MCI.

After Janet has finished her session and signed off, the E-mail system sends it on to the recipient. Depending on the urgency of the message, Janet could have coded it to be held until the recipient signed on to MCI and received the letter. If it was more urgent, and the recipient did not look at his mail, then the E-mail service could type a hard copy of the document and route it either overnight or by U.S. Mail to the recipient.

E-mail services are generally substantially less costly than express mail such as Federal Express. The important consideration is that the recipient also subscribe to the same service, otherwise using the overnight hard copy service can result in comparable costs. Some E-mail services also provide access to other on-line data services as discussed in the text. Business E-mail services are also available for intracorporation mail. These are potentially the most widely used systems because of the need for fast mail delivery within the many branches and offices of a large organization.

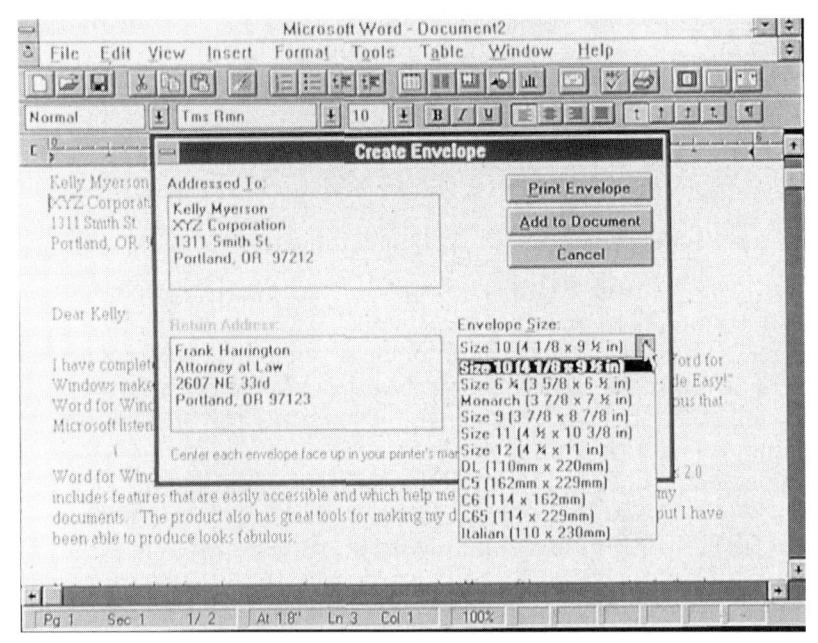

A personal computer is used to send and receive electronic mail through a communications service. (Courtesy of Microsoft.)

MICRO-MAINFRAME LINKS

Many networks and message services involve the linkage between mainframe and personal computers. In most cases the central system is the mainframe containing the database and other features, while the subscriber to the service uses a PC. These systems have a natural user interface and often the user is unaware that a mainframe computer is even being accessed.

But there are many applications where the PC user needs access to data that is located on a mainframe: data that was not designed with personal computers in mind. Large corporate systems frequently have systems that were designed before the advent of micros and as a result do not link naturally with the PC. Rather, special software often needs to be written to permit the linking of PCs with mainframe data.

One of the differences between the personal computer and mainframe is the internal coding system used. Personal computers use ASCII, while mainframes (at least IBM's) use EBCDIC. Thus, the software needs to make a conversion between these coding systems if compatibility is to occur.

PC software also stores data differently. While both PCs and mainframes use databases, the method of storing data on the two systems is vastly different. PCs frequently use spreadsheets, but data on the mainframe is not often in a format that a spreadsheet can use. Thus, extra software is needed to do the conversion from the mainframe format to the PC or vice versa. Many of these problems of data exchange are being solved by software companies who provide compatible software for both the mainframe and the PC.

Sending data from the local computer to another computer is often called **uploading**. Receiving data from another computer to your computer is called **downloading**. File transfer software is available that assists in the uploading and downloading of data.

Uploading. The process of sending data from a PC to a mainframe computer.

Downloading. The process of receiving data at the PC from a mainframe computer.

Client/Server Computing

Corporations often have many different hardware and software platforms to satisfy a variety of needs throughout the organization. Increasingly users are turning to personal computers as their number one choice for flexibility and productivity. But even with a PC there is a need to communicate with other users and to access data that is only available from a mainframe or communications network. But for users that need access to a variety of hardware and software, there often results a confusing array of sign-on procedures, commands, and operating procedures. Further data security and integrity is often compromised when data is not under the control of a central Management Information System (MIS).

To minimize these problems, a new order of software is emerging that provides a common operating platform regardless of the application and brings together information into a cohesive environment. Client/server computing offers a common interface for the user so that much of the sign-on and operating procedures become transparent. Often a graphical user interface is provided. When a user wants to access a given application, the appropriate GUI is selected. Software acts on this selection by logging on to

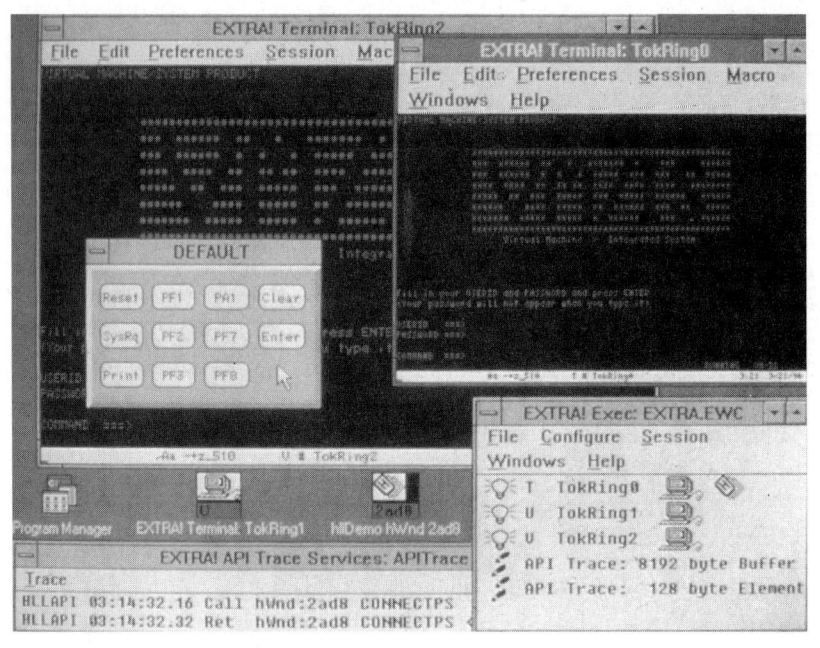

A client/server system provides access to a variety of applications ranging from personal computer to mainframe systems and communication networks. (Courtesy Microsoft.)

the appropriate hardware, software, or communication system. The user doesn't need to know the sign-on procedure or even which system is being accessed. This process can extend to the application so that commonly used procedures, such as querying a database, can be automated and reduced to selecting an icon from the client/server screen.

Client/server solutions is an emerging technology that satisfies the needs of the end users to maintain autonomy in their working environment. Yet MIS can maintain security and integrity over crucial aspects of the system and provide information resources as needed to the end users.

TELECOMMUNICATIONS HARDWARE

Connecting a personal computer to another PC or to a large mainframe requires both software and hardware. Because computers are essentially digital devices and communication lines are analog, there is a basic lack of compatibility between them. As Figure 5-9 shows, there is a big difference between an analog and a digital signal. The analog signal varies in tone something like a musician playing a tune on a flute, or if you prefer, a synthesizer. Digital signals are more like the dots and dashes of Morse code. The same tone is always used but the presence or absence of the tone and its length determines the differences in value.

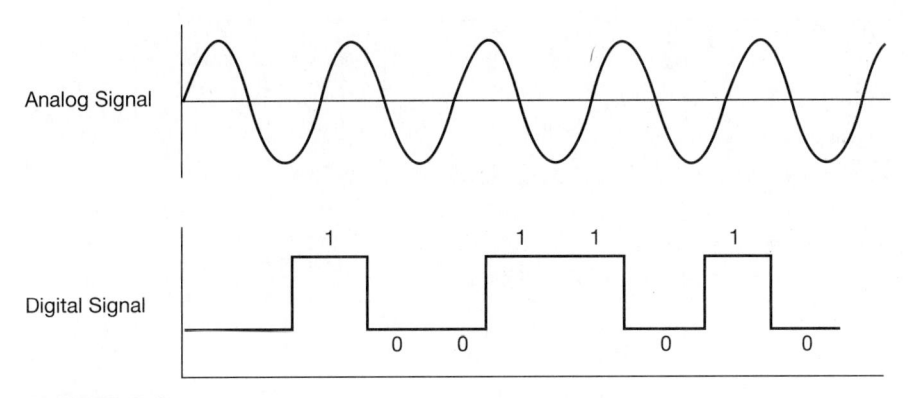

FIGURE 5-9
The difference between an analog and digital signal explains why a modem is required to convert from one form to the other.

Modem

A modem (Figure 5-10) is an electronic device that converts a computer's digital signal to its analog equivalent. When receiving an analog signal, the modem converts it to digital form before sending it on to the computer. The name modem comes from the terms modulate and demodulate. **Modulation** is the process of converting digital signals to analog form while **demodulation** is the opposite: converting an analog signal to digital.

When one PC communicates with another, each one requires a modem as shown in Figure 5-11 (see the accompanying box about exceptions to this rule). At the sending end, the computer transmits digital signals that flow as single bits into the modem. The modem converts these signals to analog form and sends them over the telephone line or other communication channel. At the receiving end, the analog signal arrives at the remote modem and is converted to a sequence of digital bits. These are sent on to the computer, which reads them as input data.

Modem. A device that converts the computer's digital data to analog or the reverse for transmission to a remote computer.

FIGURE 5-10
A modem is a device for converting digital and analog signals. This fax/modem contains a built-in microprocessor that offers auto-answer capability. This feature permits the modem to receive calls to the computer without the need for human intervention. Service organizations that provide bulletin board or other services benefit from the capabilities of the smart modem. (Courtesy Hayes.)

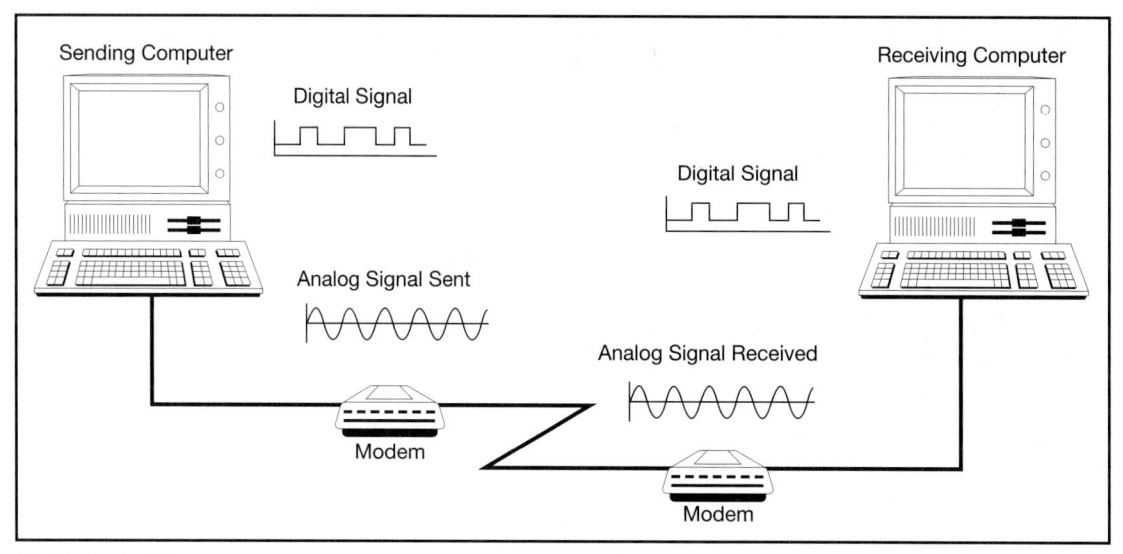

FIGURE 5-11
Transmitting data from one computer to another using a modem at each end. At the sending end the modem converts digital code to analog signals which travel over the telephone lines. The receiving modem translates the analog signal to digital, which is accepted by the receiving computer.

Bit rate. The number of bits per second (BPS) transmitted over a communication line.

Bit Rate. The rate or speed of transmission depends on the type of modem in use at each end of the communication line, the quality of the line, and the type of software used. Transmission speed is measured in **bits per second (BPS).** Speeds of 1,200, 2,400, and 9,600 BPS are in common use on personal computers, with some systems operating at up to 19,200 bits per second.

Modems are attached to the computer by an RS-232C serial connector. This is a standard connector used throughout the industry for serial data communications. The RS-232C standard is supported by the Electronic Industries of America (EIA) and is used when one bit at a time is transmitted between computer devices.

Types of Modems. Modems come in several varieties. Early models were often **acoustic couplers** which made the connection to the telephone by placing the telephone receiver on rubber cups in the modem. Signals were audibly sent and received through the coupler. The advantage of the acoustic coupler is that no direct connection to the telephone line is necessary and any standard telephone can be used to make the connection. Acoustic couplers are useful on the road for telephone connection such as in phone booths or motels rooms where a direct connection is not possible. Although acoustic couplers are still available today, most other users prefer the direct-connect modem.

Direct-connect modems are plugged directly into the telephone line. With the move by phone companies to standard wall jacks, the direct-connect modem can be attached permanently to the wall connector with the other end connected to the serial port on the computer. A variation of this type of modem is the internal modem, which is installed in an expansion slot inside

CHAPTER 5 Computers and Communication

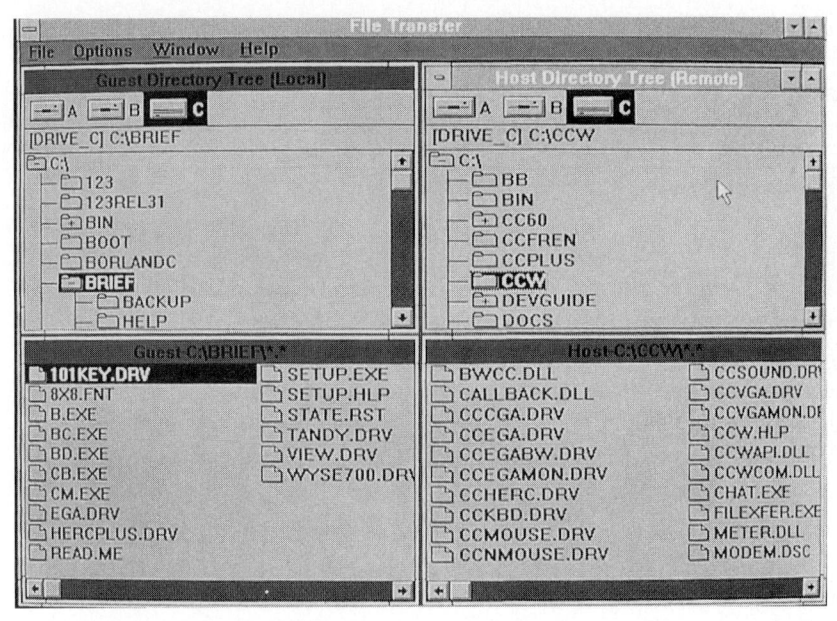

A communications program is needed with the modem to complete the link between remote computers. This Carbon Copy *screen shows some of the choices that are made when establishing computer communications over a telephone line. Communications choices are made by pointing at the options on the menu line at the top of the screen.* (Courtesy Microcom.)

the computer, thus requiring no external component. With the popular use of designer phones and other multifunction business phones, the direct-connect modem is by far the most widely used.

A **smart modem** is usually a direct-connect modem with a built-in microprocessor. The smart modem was brought to popularity by Hayes Microcomputer Products Inc., whose Smartmodem led the field in the use of these second-generation modems. A smart modem offers a number of features such as auto-answer capability where the modem will automatically, without human intervention, connect the line to the computer when a call comes over the phone. Smart modems can also dial the phone to make outgoing calls from the computer. To function fully, these modems are provided with software that gives them the calling and auto-answering capability including built-in telephone directories created by the computer user.

SUMMARY

Data communications is one of the fastest growing areas in computer technology. Much of this growth has been brought about by the widespread acceptance of the personal computer and the need to share information between users. Telecommunications systems have been struggling to keep pace with the demand that goes well beyond the local area network to include wide area networks and large-scale data communication services.

New developments in voice mail, video and teleconferencing are all factors that will keep communications at the forefront of advances in computer technology.

CHAPTER SUMMARY

1. Computers need to communicate with each other for several reasons including data sharing, inquiry into a database from a remote computer, to provide for remote data entry, and for device sharing.
2. For simple data communications, two computers are linked together by a communications line. A modem at the computer is used to convert digital to analog at the sending end, and analog to digital at the receiving end.
3. In addition to the communications line and a modem, communications software is necessary for data transfer.
4. **Networks** are communications systems that provide a means for multiple computers to communicate with each other.
5. **Network topology** refers to the three kinds of network configurations. These are the star, ring, and bus networks.
6. A **star network** is configured in a starlike pattern with a computer at the center of the pattern. If the central computer is a mainframe, it is called the host computer. If a PC is used, it is called a file server.
7. In a **hierarchical star network,** the central computer forms the hub of the starlike pattern to which other computers or terminals in the network are attached. A node can be the hub of another star to form a hierarchy.
8. The **ring network** connects a number of computers to a continuous communication ring. There is no host computer, but each computer on the ring can communicate directly with all other computers. Ring networks cost less than a star network because of the shorter lines required.
9. A **bus network** is a local area network that uses a cable to interconnect a series of computers and devices together. Transmission on a bus network consists of messages that contain a device address as part of the data that is recognized by the device to which it is sent.
10. A **local area network (LAN)** ties together several computers in a nearby area such as within an office space or between adjacent offices. A LAN is used to share computer resources such as common data or printer(s), or for electronic mail, reduces the cost of software, and provides a backup of computer resources.
11. **On-line communication services** offer special interest data or services such as electronic mail or an electronic bulletin board where you can advertise items for sale or wanted, or they provide access to many databases to address the needs of a broad variety of users. Hundreds of subjects are available through on-line databases including topics such as airline schedules, investment, foreign news, sports, UPI, and so on.
12. **E-mail** is a system based on a central computer with many PCs attached in a star network fashion. Special software in each computer provides for communicating mail electronically between users who subscribe to the same service.

CHAPTER 5 Computers and Communication

13. When micros and mainframes are linked together, special software is frequently needed to ensure compatibility. Changing data formats, converting ASCII or EBCDIC code, and the ability to **upload** and **download** files are all part of the requirements for the micro-to-mainframe link.
14. A **client/server** application provides a common interface for users of a variety of applications ranging from PCs to mainframes and communication systems.
15. A **modem** converts digital signals to analog by the process of modulation. Demodulation is the process of converting analog to digital. The modem is attached to the computer's serial port.
16. Directly connected PCs do not require a modem for data communication but are hardwired together with coaxial or other types of cable.
17. The rate at which data is transferred is expressed in **bits per second (BPS)**. Typical transmission rates are 1,200, 2,400, and 9,600 bits per second.
18. Modems come as **acoustic couplers** which use rubber cups to secure the telephone receiver, **direct-connect** which are plugged directly into the telephone jack on the wall, or as a **smart modem,** which has a built-in microprocessor and software to provide auto-answer and auto-dial features.
19. There are many types of communication lines available for data transmission, ranging from twisted-pair wire and coaxial cable, to telephone lines, microwave, satellite links, and fiber optics.

IMPORTANT TERMS AND CONCEPTS

Acoustic coupler
Bit rate
Bulletin Board Service (BBS)
Bus network
Client/server
Communication channel
Direct-connect modem
Downloading
Electronic mail (E-mail)
File server
Host computer

Local area network (LAN)
Modem
Network
Network topology
On-line data services
Ring network
Smart modem
Star network
Token passing
Uploading
Wide area network

SELF-TESTING QUESTIONS

Fill-In

1. A _____ line links two computers together for data communications.
2. _____ are communications systems that provide a means for multiple computers to communicate with each other.
3. The physical organization of a network is called the network _____.
4. The type of network that has a computer at the center of a starlike pattern is called a _____ network.

5. The central computer, called the _____ computer, supplies information and computer resources to other computers in the network.
6. A _____ _____ is another name for a computer at the center of a network that provides each computer on the network with programs and data such as a common database.
7. A _____ network may connect many different devices including computers, printers, and plotters.
8. An _____ system uses a computer to collect and distribute mail for users on a network.
9. A _____ is an electronic device that converts a computer's digital signal to its analog equivalent.
10. This is a network used over a wide geographical area that has a local network attached to a node of the main network.

True/False

1. A network is often used when common data needs to be shared among different computer users.
2. Some networks are better suited to sharing different hardware devices than others.
3. Computers can usually be connected directly to the telephone line without additional hardware to be used for data communication.
4. One problem with a ring network is that all computers on the network depend on a functional file server computer.
5. Computers in a single office environment would use a local area network that would not need to be connected to external telephone cables.
6. On-line communication services are usually available free of charge from local utility companies.
7. E-mail is available only to universities and large corporations that have a mainframe computer available to support the system.
8. A modem would be used to connect a PC to the telephone line for communication with a remote computer.

ANSWERS

Fill-In: 1. communication, 2. Local area networks, 3. topology, 4. star, 5. host, 6. file server, 7. bus, 8. E-mail, 9. modem, 10. wide area network

True/False: 1. T, 2. T, 3. F, 4. F, 5. T, 6. F, 7. F, 8. T

Questions for Critical Thinking

1. As networks become more widespread, data is no longer stored in a central mainframe computer but can be located anywhere on the network. What are the implications of this trend?
2. With E-mail in widespread use in today's corporations, what are the pros and cons of phasing out the use of paper mail?

3. Communications software is often used to download information to the local computer. Discuss why this approach is preferred to reading the information on-line.
4. With personal computers, modems, and communication lines readily available and affordable, some companies are allowing their employees to work at home using a home computer to communicate with the office computer. Do you think employees can be trusted to work unsupervised? Discuss the desirability of this practice for the employee and the employer, considering both the pros and cons.

CHAPTER 6
OPERATING SYSTEMS AND SOFTWARE PLATFORMS

A VIEW OF THE CHAPTER AHEAD

After reading this chapter you will understand

- ▶ the purpose of an operating system and how it functions in the computer.
- ▶ the three basic operating system classes of single tasking, multitasking, and multiuser.
- ▶ the basic principles and use of MS-DOS.
- ▶ other significant operating systems and where they are used.
- ▶ Windows as an operating platform for DOS.

INTRODUCTION

Bill Gates was still in his teens when he founded Microsoft with Paul Allen in 1975 to develop and sell computer languages. Like most small businesses, Microsoft struggled for a few years, but in 1981 a major coup was to set the scene for the future. The stroke of success came when IBM made the decision to use the Microsoft disk operating system (DOS) for their new personal computer, the IBM PC. By 1982, Bill Gates and company of 200 employees were selling $34 million worth of software and were on the road to becoming one of the largest and most successful PC software companies. Today Microsoft employs over 4,000 people and makes many familiar software products including Microsoft Windows, Word, Excel, and C++.

The **operating system** that Gates developed is a program that manages all activity in the computer and its components. Virtually all computers require an operating system to function. The operating system is the first program executed when the computer is turned on, and most applications depend on its presence to function. Often the operating system is described as a computerized traffic cop that directs the flow of activity in the computer.

Booting is the term used to describe when the operating system is loaded into memory from disk. When the IBM PC came on the scene, most operating systems were supplied on a floppy disk that was booted when the computer's power was turned on. Most personal computers today have a hard disk drive that contains the operating system. Booting takes place from the hard disk when the power is turned on in the system unit.

MS-DOS. The Microsoft disk operating system is the most widely used operating system on personal computers.

The **disk operating system (DOS)** that is used on IBM computers is called **PC-DOS**. A similar operating system is the **Microsoft Disk Operating System (MS-DOS)**. It was MS-DOS that IBM adopted for their computers and renamed it PC-DOS when it was marketed under their nameplate. MS-

▶ BOOTING DOS

Before using a PC it is necessary to boot DOS from either a floppy or hard disk drive. There are two ways of booting DOS on your PC: one is by turning the power on to the computer—a cold start, and the other is used when the power is already on—a warm start.

COLD START
To do a cold start, just turn on the power, making sure that no disk is located in the A: drive. After a minute or two DOS will be loaded from the hard disk into memory. The reason for the delay is that the hardware does a self-test to make sure everything in the computer is working correctly before loading DOS. DOS can also be booted from a floppy disk by inserting a DOS disk into drive A: and turning on the power.

WARM START
This method is used when the computer has already been in use and you need to reboot DOS. Pressing the Ctrl, Alt, and Del keys together causes a warm start. To press these keys, hold down Ctrl and Alt with your left hand and then press the Del key. When this is done booting takes only a few seconds, as most of the self-checking features are not done. Warm starting is useful when a program stops running due to an uncorrectable program bug or the system locks up for no reasonable explanation.

DOS has undergone many revisions since its inception and is the most widely used operating system on personal computer systems. More recently IBM has provided **Operating System/2 (OS/2),** also developed with Microsoft, for their Personal System/2 computers and compatibles, and Microsoft offers a competing **Windows NT.**

FUNCTIONS OF THE OPERATING SYSTEM

There are many activities that occur while you are engaged in a session on the computer. Keyboard entries or mouse selections are made in order to call up a program. Entries are also made when text or graphic displays are needed on the screen, data is read from disk and written back when it has been changed, or when there is a need for external communication with another computer.

While an application program will initiate most of these operations, it is the operating system that carries out its orders. To handle each of these operations, an operating system has several components that provide for a variety of functions to be executed on the computer (see Figure 6-1).

FIGURE 6-1

Operating systems perform the functions of input/output management, memory management, and command processing.

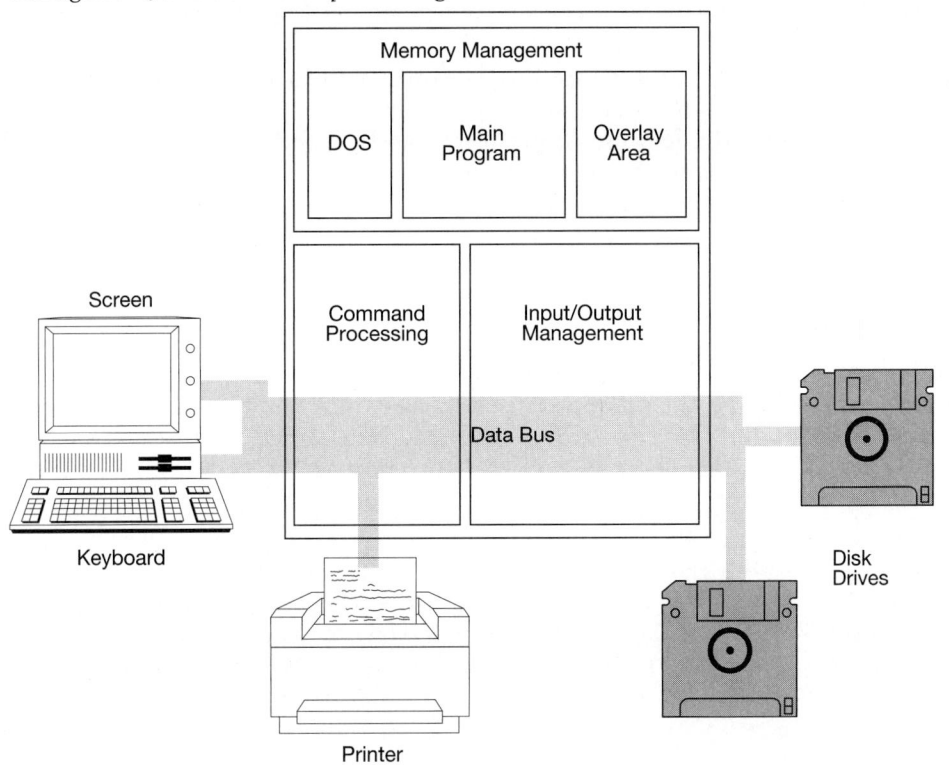

Input/Output Management

The component of the operating system for input/output (I/O) management takes care of the flow of data to and from the various devices attached to the computer. For example, when a key is pressed on the keyboard, the I/O manager interprets the code for that key and routes its signal to the appropriate part of memory. It also causes an image of the character represented by the key to appear on the screen.

Another function of the I/O manager applies when the program asks for data to be stored on disk. The I/O manager knows the right sequence of codes needed to send the data to the requested disk drive and controls the location on the disk where the data will be stored. It can also route data to the printer or accept directions from a mouse. All of this is done without mixing up signals from different devices or confusing input with output.

Memory Management

With computers containing thousands or even millions of memory locations, good management of this memory space is essential for efficient operation. Memory management is another function of the operating system.

DOS resides in a relatively small part of memory, leaving space for an application program. The memory management function of DOS must remember exactly how much memory space is available and assign it to a program when we ask it to be loaded. If the program is another resident program, such as Windows, then DOS needs to allocate its requirements and reserve the rest of memory for a word processing program or maybe a spreadsheet.

Because many programs are too large to fit into memory at one time, they are organized into main and overlay programs. Memory management also assists with the loading of program overlays and manages the link between the overlay and the main program that uses it. Eventually control is passed back to the main program, again with the assistance of the memory manager.

Command Processing

COMMAND.COM. A DOS file that contains internal DOS commands such as DIR and COPY.

Another function of the operating system is the processing of commands that are entered by the computer user (Figure 6-2). Command processing is a function of the DOS program, COMMAND.COM, that is loaded into memory as a result of booting DOS. DOS provides a wide range of commands for copying, erasing or renaming files, defining and using subdirectories on disk, and listing the contents of a directory. All of these activities begin by commands that are entered at the DOS prompt.

Until recently, the most widely used operating systems were command-driven programs that have their own language for use. DOS 4 was the beginning of operating systems that used menus rather than commands for their operation (Figure 6-3).

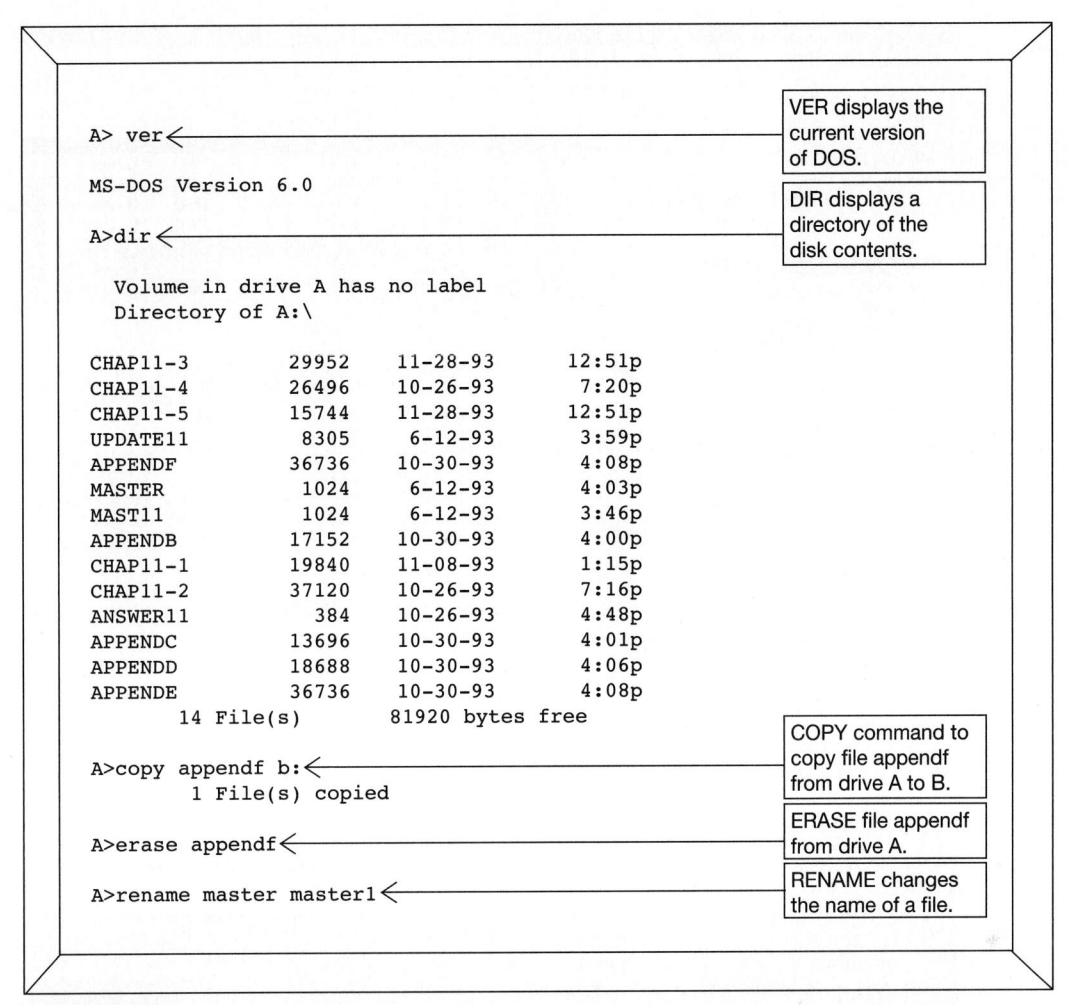

```
A> ver  ←──────────────────────────────────────

MS-DOS Version 6.0

A>dir  ←──────────────────────────────────────

   Volume in drive A has no label
   Directory of A:\

   CHAP11-3        29952    11-28-93     12:51p
   CHAP11-4        26496    10-26-93      7:20p
   CHAP11-5        15744    11-28-93     12:51p
   UPDATE11         8305     6-12-93      3:59p
   APPENDF         36736    10-30-93      4:08p
   MASTER           1024     6-12-93      4:03p
   MAST11           1024     6-12-93      3:46p
   APPENDB         17152    10-30-93      4:00p
   CHAP11-1        19840    11-08-93      1:15p
   CHAP11-2        37120    10-26-93      7:16p
   ANSWER11          384    10-26-93      4:48p
   APPENDC         13696    10-30-93      4:01p
   APPENDD         18688    10-30-93      4:06p
   APPENDE         36736    10-30-93      4:08p
         14 File(s)       81920 bytes free

A>copy appendf b:  ←──────────────────────────
        1 File(s) copied

A>erase appendf  ←───────────────────────────

A>rename master master1  ←───────────────────
```

Annotations:
- VER displays the current version of DOS.
- DIR displays a directory of the disk contents.
- COPY command to copy file appendf from drive A to B.
- ERASE file appendf from drive A.
- RENAME changes the name of a file.

FIGURE 6-2
VER, DIR, COPY, ERASE, and RENAME are all DOS commands that are acted upon when entered from the keyboard.

Utilities

Utilities are operating system programs that can be run to perform disk maintenance or other activities. One of these is the FORMAT utility (Figure 6-4) that prepares a new disk for use. Other utilities can be used to copy the entire contents of one disk to another, check a disk for errors, sort a disk directory, or organize the way the computer's memory is used. Utilities reside on the DOS disk rather than in memory but are activated in the same manner as other DOS commands.

For hands-on work with DOS, see the DOS tutorial module, which provides other examples and exercises using DOS commands.

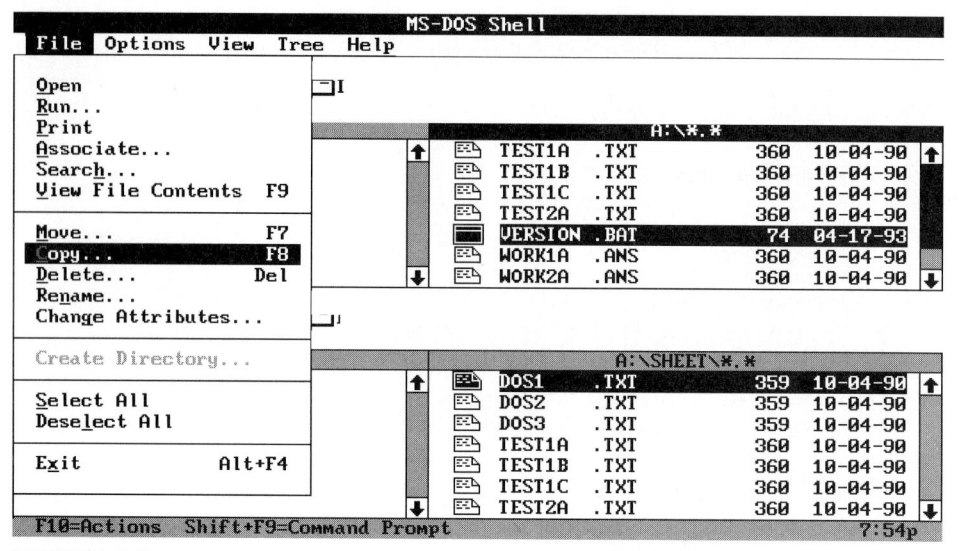

FIGURE 6-3
Using the DOS Shell provides a selection of DOS commands from a menu. In this screen the Copy command is selected from the File menu.

FIGURE 6-4
Windows file manager uses the DOS utility program FORMAT to prepare a new diskette for use.

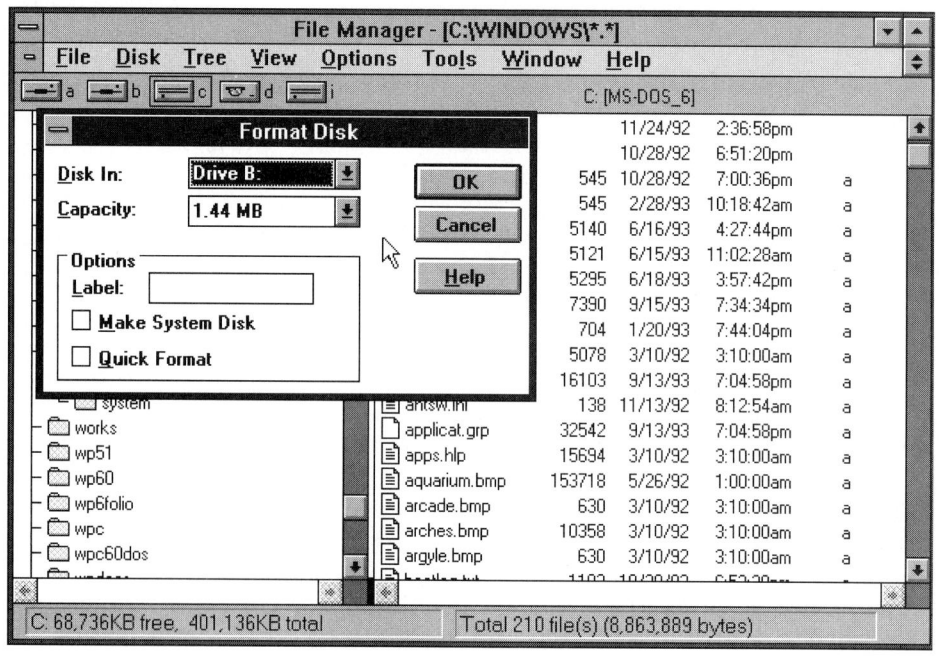

CLASSES OF OPERATING SYSTEMS

An operating system may be classified into one of three basic groups according to how it manages the user environment. These groups are single tasking, multitasking, and multiuser.

Single Tasking

Most personal computer operating systems fall into this category. A **single-tasking** operating system, as the name suggests, can work on one task at a time. The practical meaning of single tasking is that only one program can run on the computer at any one time. Thus, if a spreadsheet is being calculated, the computer is not able to receive communications from a modem or to print a report.

MS-DOS and PC-DOS are the most widely used single-tasking operating systems. Dr. DOS is also a single-tasking operating system for personal computers. For personal computing, MS-DOS has set the industry standard for single-tasking operating systems due to its vast user base.

Single tasking. An operating system that works on one activity or task at a time.

Multitasking

When two or more tasks or programs may be run simultaneously, this is called **multitasking**. In its simplest form, a multitasking operating system permits two programs to operate together on the computer, but only one instruction gets executed at a time. One program, such as a word processor, may be in direct use by the user and is therefore in the **foreground,** while a second program that may be printing a report is operating in the **background.**

UNIX is one of the most well-known multitasking operating systems that

Multitasking. An operating system that is capable of performing two or more tasks simultaneously.

Apple's Macintosh is a computer that has multitasking built into the operating system. (Courtesy Apple Computer, Inc.)

was originally developed for the minicomputer market. It is now available for personal computers under names such as Xenix and Venix. Other systems that use a multitasking-like environment are Macintosh's MultiFinder, IBM's OS/2, and Microsoft's Windows NT.

These systems permit several programs to do **concurrent processing,** which permits switching from one application to another without the need to leave the current task. For example, in Windows NT, several different applications may appear in different windows on the screen. The user may switch between them with a few keystrokes and change tasks without the need to discontinue work in any one environment.

Multiuser

Multiuser system. A system that permits many users to access a central computer system.

Mainframe computer systems and many minicomputers have multiple users accessing the same central computer. Until recently, visual display terminals (VDT) were used which have no processing capability and therefore relied on the central computer for all processing requirements. This type of computer system requires a **multiuser** operating system. The purpose of this operating system, in addition to functions already described, is to coordinate the processing needs of each terminal and ensure that each gets adequate access to the processor.

IBM's Disk Operating System/Virtual Storage (DOS/VS) and Operating System/Multiprogramming Virtual Storage (OS/MVS) are two examples of mainframe operating systems that provide multiuser capability. Digital Equipment Corporation's RSTS is one operating system used on their VAX minicomputer series of computers.

▶ MS-DOS RELEASES

MS-DOS 6
Winter 1993
  Compression, memory optimization, utilities

MS-DOS 5
June 1991
  Memory management, utilities

MS-DOS 4.01
November 1988
  Large hard disks, expanded memory, shell interface

MS-DOS 3.3
April 1987
  Multiple partitions on hard disk

MS-DOS 3.1
March 1985
  Microsoft networks

MS-DOS 3.0
August 1984
  1.2MB floppy disks

MS-DOS 2.0
March 1983
  Hierarchical files and hard disks

MS-DOS 1.0
August 1981
  DOS debuts on IBM PC

Source: Microsoft Corporation

Personal computers in a local area network (LAN) might seem to require a multiuser operating system. But this is really a special case because each user has a PC that contains its own operating system (usually single-tasking). If there is a central computer on the LAN, it is frequently a file server that provides access to programs and data but does not provide any processing power to the users on the network. Thus, a LAN may run a file serving program but it does not require a multiuser operating system.

PC-DOS AND MS-DOS

In 1981 Microsoft was mainly known for its Microsoft BASIC, which was in use on many different brands of microcomputers. But in that year, Microsoft bought an operating system from a small hardware company called Seattle Computer Products. They did some reworking of the operating system and licensed it under the name MS-DOS meaning, of course, Microsoft DOS.

One of the purchasers of MS-DOS was IBM, who released it on their Personal Computer as PC-DOS. When the IBM PC's sales took off, so did PC-DOS, to the point where it is practically considered to be a standard in the business today.

In 1991, MS-DOS Version 5 was released with a number of upgrades not included in previous releases of DOS. Two significant features of release 5 are the improved use of memory and easier installation. In addition, a graphical DOS shell has been added and a number of new DOS commands have been supplied, as well as a Help system.

The MS-DOS **Shell** is a graphical interface that provides users with menus for a variety of DOS operations. Instead of typing commands at the old DOS prompt, the user of DOS 5 selects an operation, such as directory, by using the cursor keys or a mouse from the menu. Familiar DOS operations, such as type, copy, rename, delete, and format are available. Activities such as sorting the contents of a directory can also be selected from a menu. Moving a file from one directory to another can be done in one step. The Shell also manages the activity of programs in the system and switches between them when needed.

Several new commands in MS-DOS 5 are **unformat** and **undelete.** The unformat command allows you to undo a format, which ordinarily erases all existing files from the disk. Undelete allows you to selectively undo a delete for one or more files on the disk using appropriate file names.

MS-DOS 5 also includes the QBASIC program for writing BASIC programs. QBASIC provides an extensive programming environment for writing and editing BASIC programs.

DOS 5 still permits the user to escape to the familiar DOS prompt. Experienced DOS users may be comfortable entering their own DOS commands, but new PC users will likely find the menus of the Shell to be much more user-friendly and less intimidating until they get up to speed on DOS operations.

DOS Shell. A program that provides DOS users with a graphical interface for DOS operations.

DOS COMMANDS

Internal and External Commands

When a DOS command is used, it is basically one of two types of commands: internal or external (Figure 6-5). When DOS is booted, the program COMMAND.COM is loaded into memory from the DOS disk. COMMAND.COM contains a number of frequently used DOS commands, such as DIR and COPY, called **internal commands** because they are located in memory and do not require any further disk access when they are used.

Other DOS commands, such as FORMAT and DISKCOPY, are **external** because they reside in the DOS directory and require a disk access to be used. External commands require that the DOS directory be active when the command is used, otherwise a Not Found message will be displayed. When DOS is on hard disk the external commands are essentially always present, but on floppy disk, it is not unusual for other disks to be in the drive, which then requires a swap of disks before using an external DOS command.

Entering DOS Commands

Beginning with DOS 4, commands may be entered as DOS commands at the prompt or they may be selected from a menu. Prior to DOS 4, all commands were given at the prompt.

When using DOS as a command-driven language it is necessary to know the commands you wish to use and to be familiar with their format. DOS commands are then typed at the DOS prompt, either A> for the floppy A disk, or C> for the hard disk. A command is typed immediately following the prompt and the Enter key is pressed after typing the command. For some practical exercises with the more commonly used DOS commands, refer to the DOS tutorial module.

When using DOS from the Shell, commands are selected from a menu using either the keyboard or a mouse. Generally, a menu is easier to use for the beginner because it presents the user with a list of choices. When a se-

DOS prompt. A symbol used to indicate that DOS is ready for a command. The prompt can also display the current directory.

FIGURE 6-5
Some of DOS's internal and external commands. Internal commands are brought into memory with the COMMAND.COM program when DOS is booted. Using these commands does not require the DOS directory to be active. External commands are located in the DOS directory, which must be available when the command is issued.

Internal DOS Commands			External DOS Commands	
COPY	DEL	TIME	CHKDSK	FORMAT
DATE	ERASE	TYPE	DISKCOPY	DISKCOMP
DIR	RENAME	VER	GRAPHICS	COMMAND.COM

CHAPTER 6 Operating Systems and Software Platforms

lection has been made, additional choices or a prompt is displayed. Thus, the user does not need to be intimately familiar with the language to use DOS commands.

DISK DIRECTORIES

Using a disk requires that you know the names of the files that it contains. It is not usually enough to look at the label of a floppy disk and identify it as containing budget data, but rather, we will need to know the exact file that is required. On a hard disk, with its large capacity, there can be literally hundreds of files to choose from, while a floppy may have several dozen. For this reason a **directory listing** of files may be displayed by most programs or by using a DOS command prior to running the program.

Figure 6-6 shows the way a DOS command is issued to display a disk directory. When the command is given, DOS reads the file allocation table (FAT) on the disk, which contains a record of file names. This information is then displayed on the screen as a directory listing.

Figure 6-7 shows a typical directory screen for a hard disk, displayed in this case by the word processor WordPerfect. Other software packages will display a directory using some variation of this technique, frequently with less information than shown here. The top of the directory screen shows the date and time, the directory name, and the amount of free disk space still available.

The remainder of the screen shows the names of files available on the disk, the size of the file in bytes, and the date and time they were last re-

Directory listing. A display of the files contained on disk.

▶ THE DEFAULT DRIVE CONCEPT

After booting DOS the C> prompt—A> if you are using a floppy disk—will appear on the screen. This is the default disk drive (also called the logged drive) and is the drive that will be affected by commands entered at the keyboard. For example, if you enter the DIR command you will get the directory of drive C:. If you type the name of a program, then DOS will expect to find the program on the default disk drive. The default drive can be changed by typing the name of the new drive. Typing b: will change the default disk drive to drive B: and the prompt will appear as B>. Similarly, the DOS Shell user can select the default drive from a list of drive icons on the screen that represent the drives available for the computer in use.

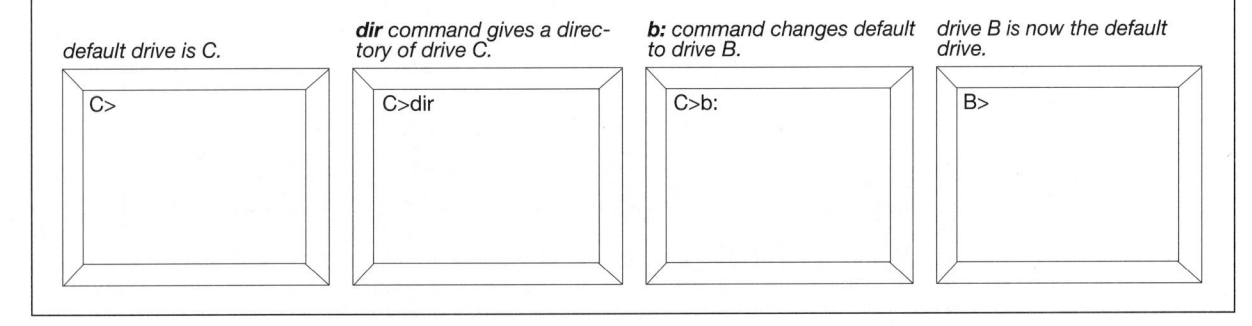

default drive is C.	**dir** command gives a directory of drive C.	**b:** command changes default to drive B.	drive B is now the default drive.
C>	C>dir	C>b:	B>

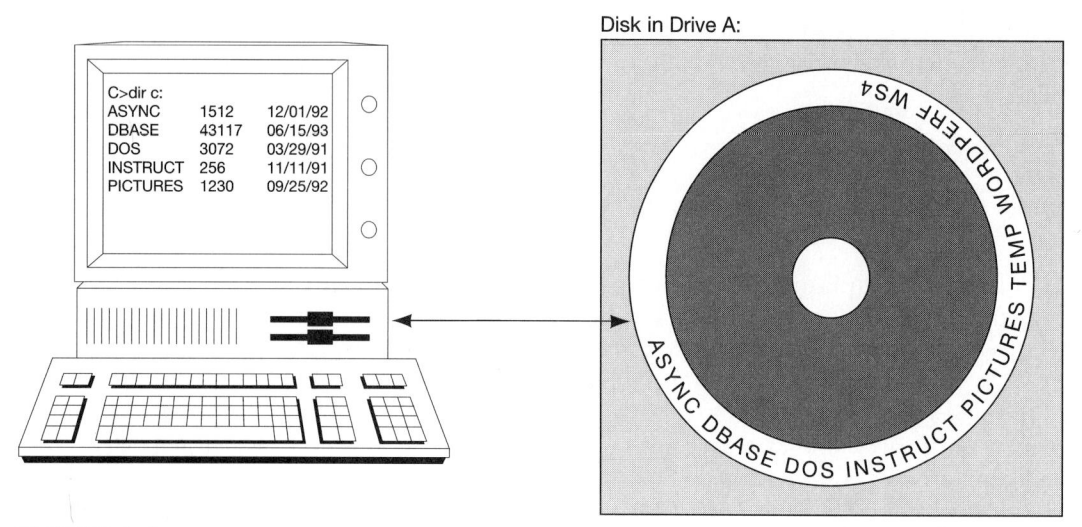

FIGURE 6-6
The DOS directory command reads the file allocation table on disk and displays the list of files on the screen.

FIGURE 6-7
A WordPerfect screen display of a hard disk directory containing both files and subdirectories.

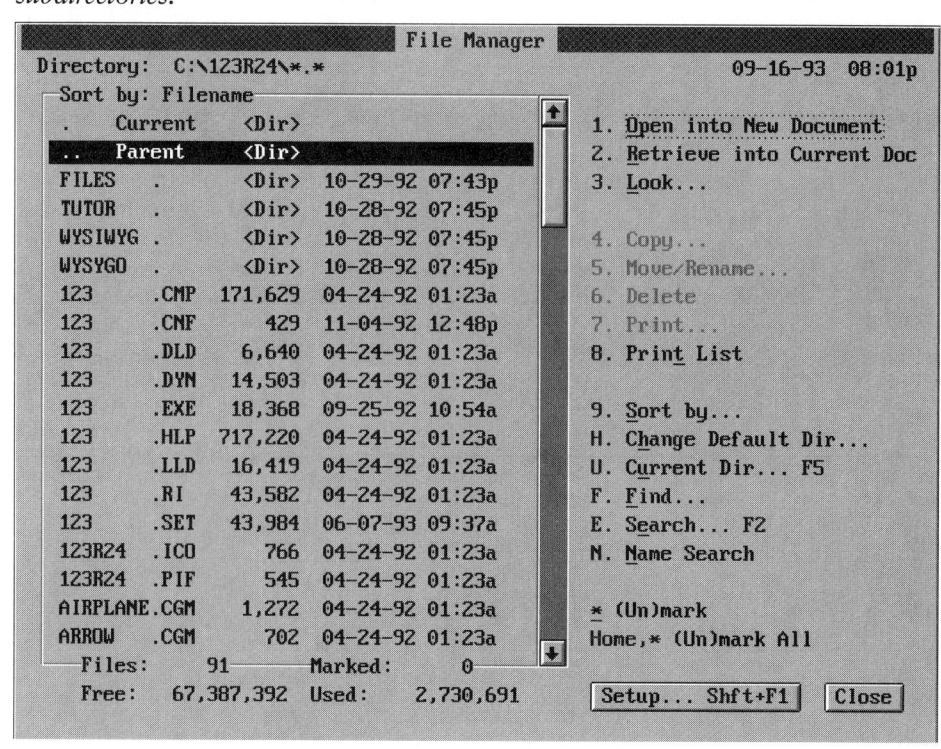

vised. Entries with the <Dir> indicator signify that these are subdirectories that may themselves contain additional files.

Directory Organization

Fixed disks have capacities of usually a minimum of 20 megabytes (MB) and up to or exceeding several hundred MB, which presents special problems when trying to find a file on the disk. Listing a directory of hundreds of files, let alone finding the specific file required, can be a challenging task. To resolve this problem, hard disks may be organized into directories with each directory acting something like a separate mini-disk. Floppy disks may also have directories, but with their relatively small capacity, there is less need for this kind of organization.

Directory organization on the hard disk can be thought of as an upside down tree structure, as shown in Figure 6-8. The trunk is the **root** or **parent** directory that contains several branches, each of which are directories. Each directory may contain a number of files or may also contain lower level subdirectories. Using this organization requires that files of a given type be located in a specific directory.

For example, word processing files may go in one directory while spreadsheets are in another. Within the word processing directory there may be

Directories. An organization of files on disk using a tree structure with a number of subdirectories.

FIGURE 6-8
Using directories on a hard disk simplifies finding the file needed for a specific application.

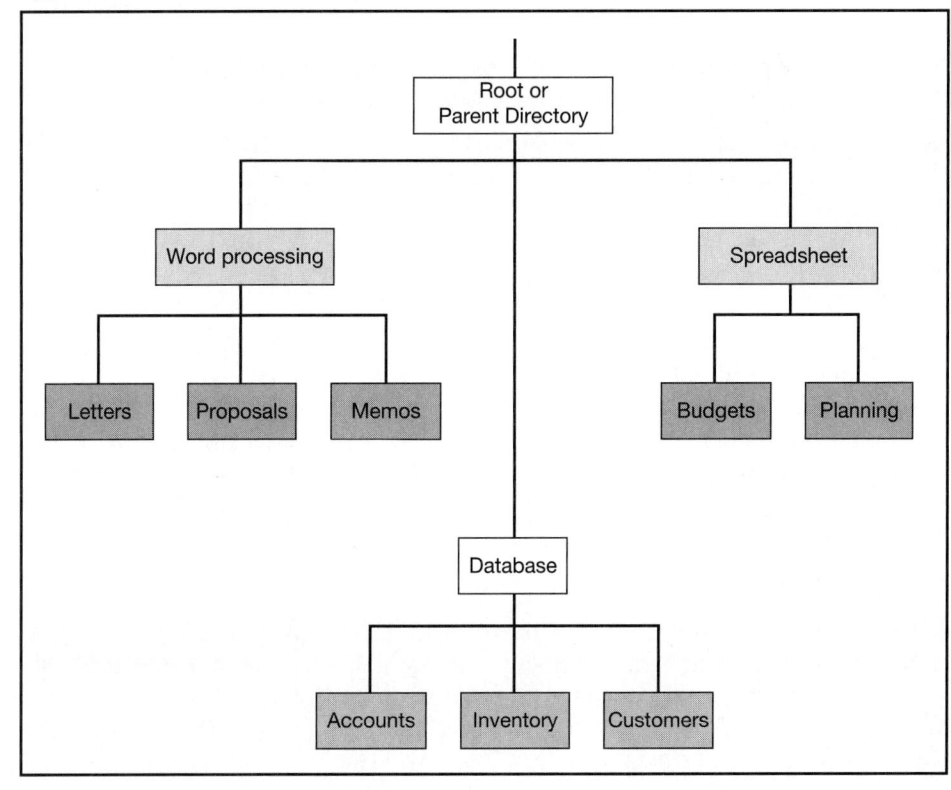

```
                            MS-DOS Shell
File  Options  View  Tree  Help
C:\
[=]A  [=]B  [C]  (CD)D  []I

         Directory Tree                          C:\*.*
[]C:\                                 []  AUTOEXEC.01      441  04-17-93
 └─[]123R24                           []  AUTOEXEC.BAK     453  06-01-93
    ├─[+] FILES                       []  AUTOEXEC.BAT     419  08-09-93
    ├─[] TUTOR                        []  AUTOEXEC.OLD     388  01-14-93
    ├─[] WYSIWYG                      []  AUTOEXEC.SYD     399  06-09-93
    └─[] WYSYGO                       []  CATALOG .CAT     439  12-09-92
 ├─[+]123R34                          []  CHKLIST .MS      135  04-02-93
 ├─[+]123R4W                          []  COMMAND .COM  52,925  03-10-93
 ├─[]3DMENU                           []  CONFIG  .BAK     328  06-02-93
 ├─[+]ALDUS                           []  CONFIG  .OLD     144  10-28-92
 ├─[+]BOOKS                           []  CONFIG  .SYD     345  09-12-93
 ├─[]BTFONTS                          []  CONFIG  .SYS     329  09-12-93
 ├─[]CCPLUS                           []  FRECOVER.DAT 122,368  10-26-92
 ├─[]CDROM                            []  LOGFILE .TXT     136  11-04-92
 ├─[+]CORELDRW                        []  LOOKUP  .PAR      22  01-11-93
 ├─[]DAZ                              []  MENU    .BAT      16  09-23-92
 ├─[+]DBASE                           []  SD      .INI   2,497  10-26-92
 └─[]DOS                              []  UNTITLED.CAT     258  12-09-92
F10=Actions  Shift+F9=Command Prompt                              8:03p
```

FIGURE 6-9
Using DOS 6 to manage and view the relationship between the root and its directories.

other subdirectories, such as one for letters, another for proposals, and a third for memos. Therefore, to find a letter to a client you would first look under word processing and then in the letters subdirectory rather than looking at all files located on the hard disk.

Some programs, such as DOS 6, PC Tools, and Norton Utilities, simplify the use of directories on the disk by showing graphically the relationship between the directories on the disk. Figure 6-9 shows how DOS 5 displays this graphic for the directory listing shown earlier.

OTHER OPERATING SYSTEMS

OS/2

OS/2. A multitasking operating system from IBM for 32-bit microprocessor-based computers.

When IBM announced the new Personal System/2 computer a parallel announcement of Operating System/2 (OS/2) was made by Microsoft. A major upgrade, OS/2 2.0 was released in early 1992 by IBM as Microsoft placed all their bets on Windows. OS/2 is an operating system that is designed to move users into the world of 32-bit microprocessors and harness the power of Intel's 80386SX processor chip and the faster but similar 80386 and 80486 or higher chips. OS/2 requires a minimum of 4 megabytes of RAM, but needs at least 6 MB to be effective, and 31 MB of hard disk space to install.

One goal in designing OS/2 was to create a system that would be suited to an automated office environment. As such, OS/2 is a multitasking, single-user operating system that incorporates windowing and a graphical Workplace Shell Desktop (Figure 6-10) that uses icons and resembles the Macintosh's user interface.

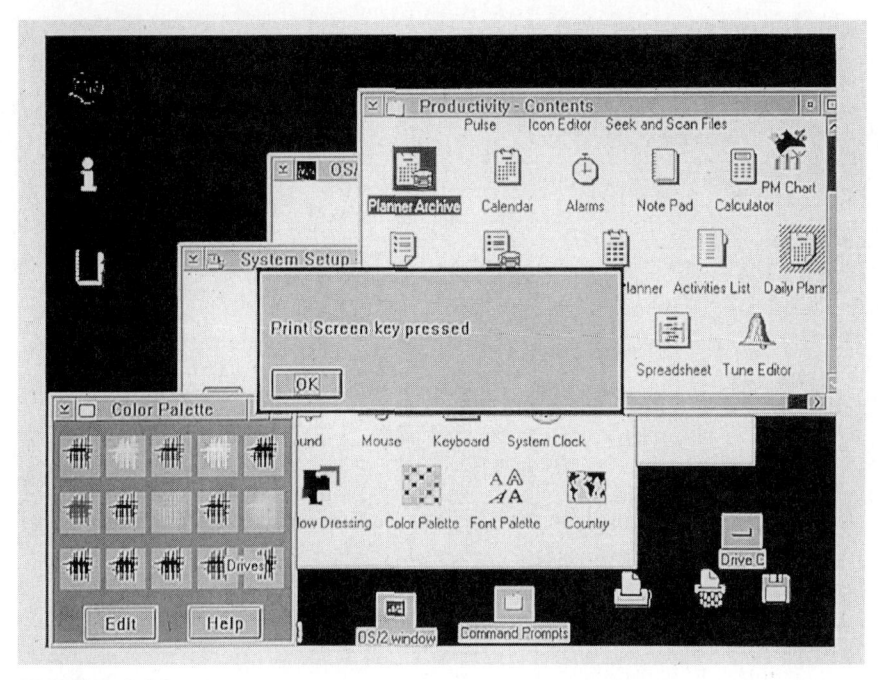

CHAPTER 6 Operating Systems and Software Platforms

FIGURE 6-10
OS/2's Workplace Shell uses icons that are selected by a mouse to begin a task.
(Courtesy IBM Corporation.)

The Workplace Shell is object-oriented. **Objects** are items such as icons, folders for system information, applications, and files. **Object-oriented** means that the user concentrates on the task to be done and not on the commands needed to do the job by using icons on the screen that represent tasks. Icons permits the left and right mouse buttons to control different functions. Double clicking on an object opens that function. Clicking the right mouse button pops up an object's system menu.

OS/2 supports several modes for multitasking: a Real mode that will run a single DOS-based application program, and a Protected mode, which uses multitasking to run a theoretically unlimited number of tasks from RAM. For example, you could format a disk in drive A, begin a database query, and print out a document all simultaneously. The number of tasks will be limited by the size of RAM and the performance of the system.

Multitasking provides features such as software protection, virtual memory management, and task management. Software protection is necessary when several programs are running together. If an error or program bug occurs in one program, it is isolated from other programs on the system to ensure that further errors are not created. Applications can use up to 16 megabytes of real memory and a gigabyte of virtual memory space on disk.

OS/2 also includes a LAN manager to manage local area networks. The assumption seems to be that LANs will become a standard feature of computers that use this operating system. Any computer in the network will be able to function as a file server as well as a work station at the same time. The LAN manager will provide for file and print sharing, user security features, and powerful network administration tools.

Object. An item such as an icon that is used to represent a task.

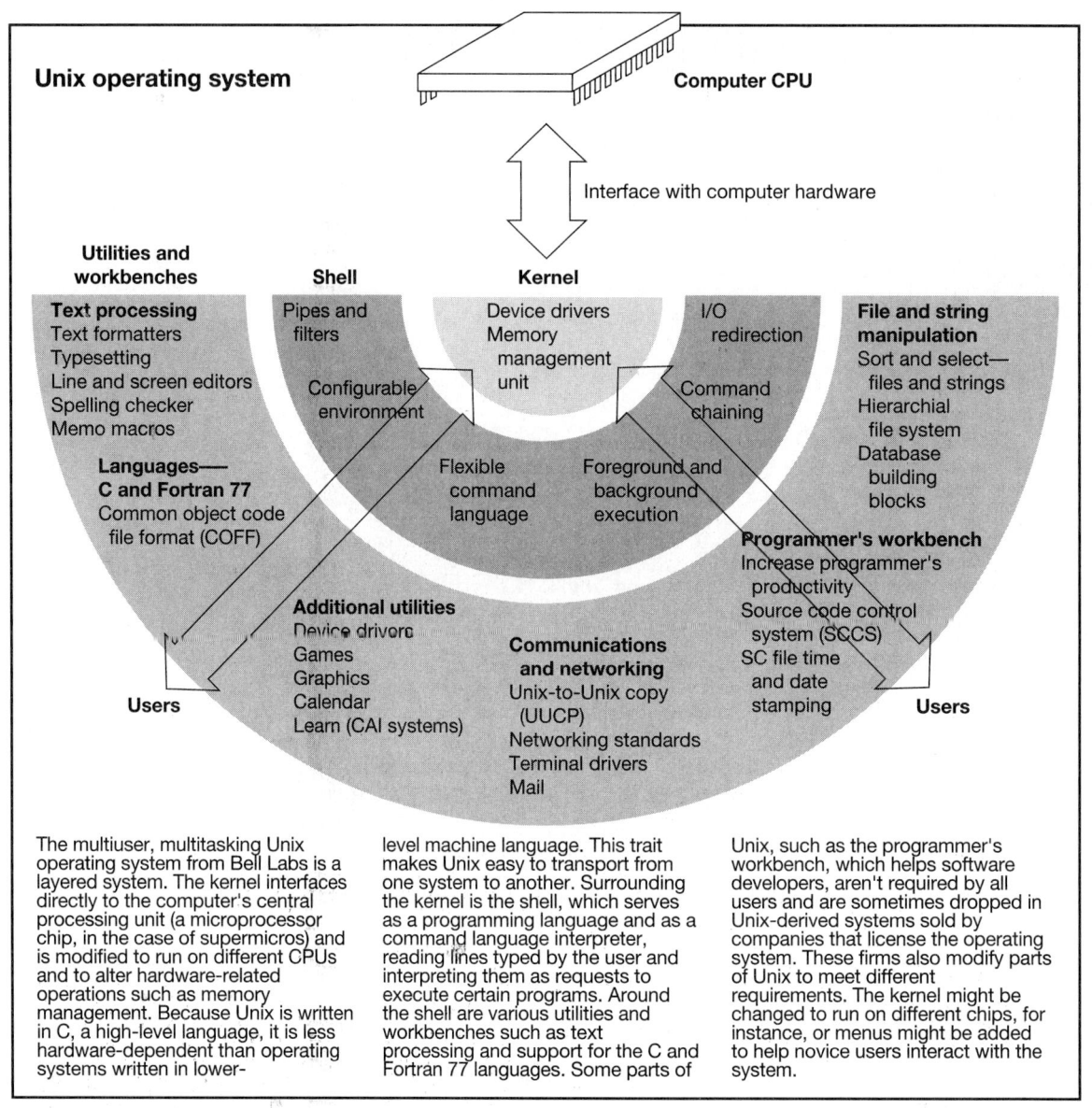

Unix operating system

Utilities and workbenches

Text processing
Text formatters
Typesetting
Line and screen editors
Spelling checker
Memo macros

Languages—C and Fortran 77
Common object code file format (COFF)

Additional utilities
Device drivers
Games
Graphics
Calendar
Learn (CAI systems)

Shell

Pipes and filters
Configurable environment
Flexible command language

Communications and networking
Unix-to-Unix copy (UUCP)
Networking standards
Terminal drivers
Mail

Kernel

Device drivers
Memory management unit
I/O redirection
Command chaining
Foreground and background execution

File and string manipulation
Sort and select—files and strings
Hierarchial file system
Database building blocks

Programmer's workbench
Increase programmer's productivity
Source code control system (SCCS)
SC file time and date stamping

Computer CPU

Interface with computer hardware

Users

The multiuser, multitasking Unix operating system from Bell Labs is a layered system. The kernel interfaces directly to the computer's central processing unit (a microprocessor chip, in the case of supermicros) and is modified to run on different CPUs and to alter hardware-related operations such as memory management. Because Unix is written in C, a high-level language, it is less hardware-dependent than operating systems written in lower-level machine language. This trait makes Unix easy to transport from one system to another. Surrounding the kernel is the shell, which serves as a programming language and as a command language interpreter, reading lines typed by the user and interpreting them as requests to execute certain programs. Around the shell are various utilities and workbenches such as text processing and support for the C and Fortran 77 languages. Some parts of Unix, such as the programmer's workbench, which helps software developers, aren't required by all users and are sometimes dropped in Unix-derived systems sold by companies that license the operating system. These firms also modify parts of Unix to meet different requirements. The kernel might be changed to run on different chips, for instance, or menus might be added to help novice users interact with the system.

FIGURE 6-11
UNIX operating system.

With the move to 32-bit processing, OS/2 is an operating system that opens the window to more sophisticated applications in the world of office computing and eases the transition to larger and more capable systems.

UNIX

UNIX is a multiuser multitasking operating system developed in the late 1960s at the Bell Laboratories that gained prominence under AT&T's leadership. It is a large and complex operating system that is loaded with fea-

CHAPTER 6 Operating Systems and Software Platforms

tures, and is used by many university computer systems. Because of its extensive nature, UNIX takes a long time to learn, but users who have made the commitment are generally enthusiastic about the software.

The part of UNIX that communicates with the user is called the **shell** (see Figure 6-11). It is distinctive from DOS in that it can be customized in any environment to meet the users' needs. By modifying the shell, UNIX can be made very user-friendly and as a result the complexities of the system can be reserved for the professionals.

Because UNIX is developed for different systems and under different names, there needed to be some consistency in its implementation. This consistency is ensured through the heart of the UNIX system called the **kernel**. This is the part of the operating system that is essentially the same on all versions of UNIX. All utilities are then developed external to the kernel and can vary from one system to another. Because AT&T continues to provide UNIX with their PCs, and because of its popularity on a variety of minicomputers, UNIX will likely be around for a long time.

UNIX kernel. A component of the UNIX operating system that ensures consistency in the implementation of UNIX by all users.

Macintosh Operating System

Unlike earlier operating systems that were procedural in nature, the Apple Macintosh operating system used an object-oriented language. By using icons on the screen that represent tasks, a mouse may be used to quickly select an activity. For example, a file folder icon is used to represent opening a file and is selected by pointing to it with a mouse and pressing a button.

The advantage of using icons for an operating system interface is that the system is easy to use, often requiring little or no training for its user. Rather than needing to know specific commands such as DIR, or ERASE, the user simply needs to recognize a few common symbols.

An offshoot of using icons in the operating system has been application programs that take the same approach. Using icons in a word processor or spreadsheet makes it easier to learn and the user becomes productive very quickly. Macintosh's success in using the object-oriented approach is evident in the way that OS/2, Windows, and even DOS are implementing similar features first developed by Apple.

Because the Macintosh was designed along with the operating system, the two have been more closely integrated than other systems. As a result the graphical user interface (GUI) can take full advantage of the hardware. Networking with other Macs has been a feature of this computer from the beginning. The Macintosh operating system has evolved to the point where it now supports multiple languages, multitasking, TrueType fonts, and a hierarchical file management system.

Graphical user interface (GUI). A system that uses icons for the selection of specific tasks rather than menus or commands.

Microsoft Windows. A graphical user interface software platform that works with DOS to provide the ability to work with more than one application at a time.

WINDOWS

Microsoft Windows is the dominant GUI program for the MS-DOS environment. Unlike DOS or OS/2, Windows is a software platform rather than an operating system. Although it is the operating environment that the user sees and uses, Windows requires DOS to be present for it to function.

Windows Basics

A **window** is a rectangular area of the screen that appears on a background called the **desktop**. Windows may be overlapped or changed in size or location as applications are run. Windows uses icons to present the user with operational choices (Figure 6-12) on the desktop that are selected with a mouse. An **icon** is a graphic image that represents an activity or operation. Icons may be present for desktop maintenance, file management, and applications such as a word processor, spreadsheet, or database.

When the Windows program is activated, the first window that appears is the **Program Manager** (Figure 6-13), which runs as long as you are using Windows. The Program Manager displays the **Main** group, which contains icons for applications available for your use. Other icons may display for other groups such as Applications, Games, Accessories, or StartUp. When a group icon is activated, a window for that group is opened and icons showing the available activities are displayed.

By double clicking on an icon, that operation or program is begun in a window. With a simple keystroke or mouse operation, Windows can switch from one application program to another without losing your place in the program. When the program is ended, the window shrinks back to an icon.

Windows and Non-Windows Applications

Microsoft Windows can run both Windows applications or non-Windows application programs. A **Windows application** is a program that conforms to Windows standards for the types of window, style of menus, use of the

FIGURE 6-12
Microsoft Windows uses windows to display a variety of applications and options available to the computer user. (Courtesy Microsoft.)

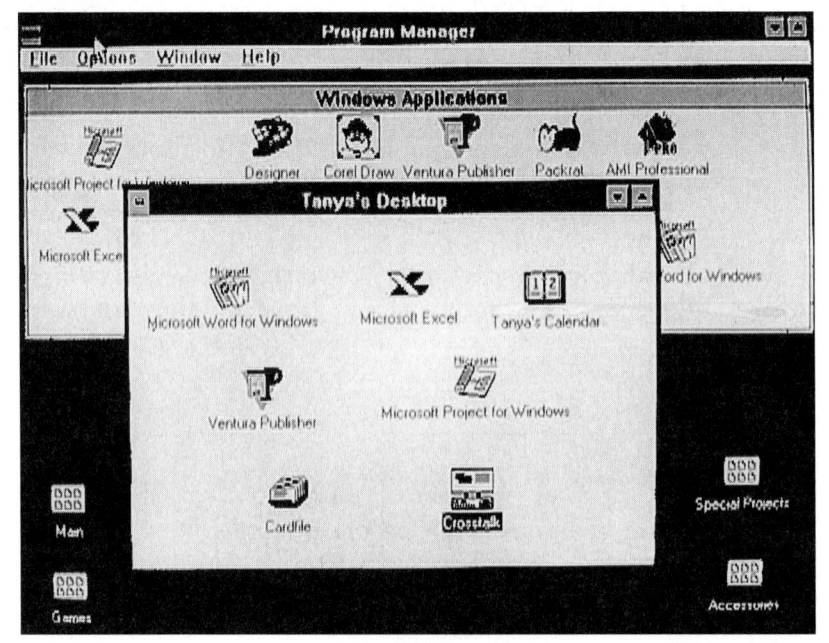

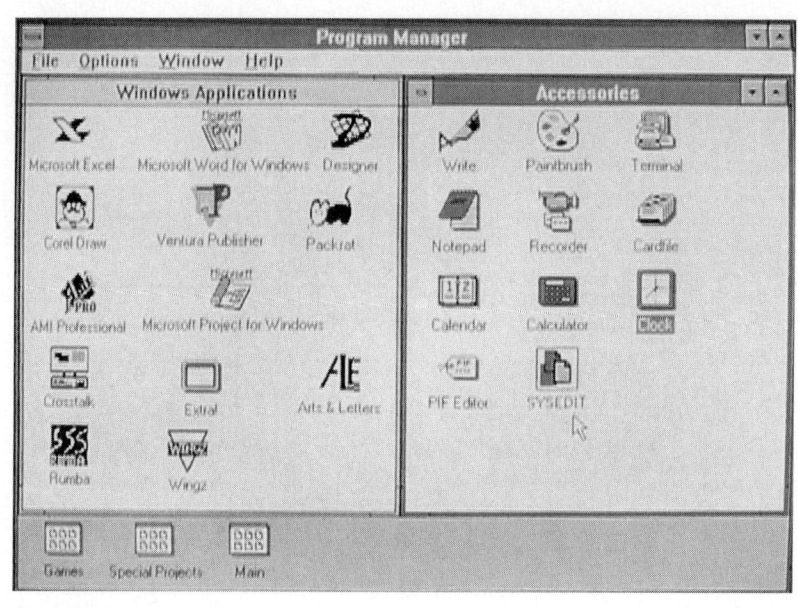

FIGURE 6-13
The Windows Program Manager displays icons that are used to select applications to be run. (Courtesy Microsoft.)

mouse or keyboard, and graphics-based screen display. Many existing programs are being released under the new Windows standards, including WordPerfect for Windows, Lotus 1–2–3 for Windows, and Harvard Graphics for Windows.

Non-Windows applications are those that do not follow the standards for Windows software. This includes most popular DOS-based software such as WordPerfect 6.0, Lotus 1–2–3, and dBASE IV. Although this software does not take advantage of many Windows features, many users find they run effectively in the new environment.

Object Linking and Embedding (OLE)

Windows-based programs may be run in separate windows and the data they create may be shared between them. With **object embedding** you can create an object, such as a drawing or graphic, and embed (insert) it in another document. If the object is changed, only the copy is changed where it is used. Other uses of the object are not affected by the change. **Object linking** uses the same information in several documents. The object, such as a drawing, is created separately and then linked to as many documents as necessary, thus requiring only one copy of the drawing and saving disk space. If a change is made to a linked object, the change takes effect everywhere the object is used.

Using OLE, a business proposal can be created in a word processor such as AmiPro or WordPerfect for Windows using a variety of objects to complete the document (Figure 6-14). A graph created in Excel 4.0 can be brought into the proposal showing financial data graphically. An illustration could be included from CorelDraw to put the final touches on the doc-

Object linking and embedding (OLE). A method of transferring and sharing data between applications.

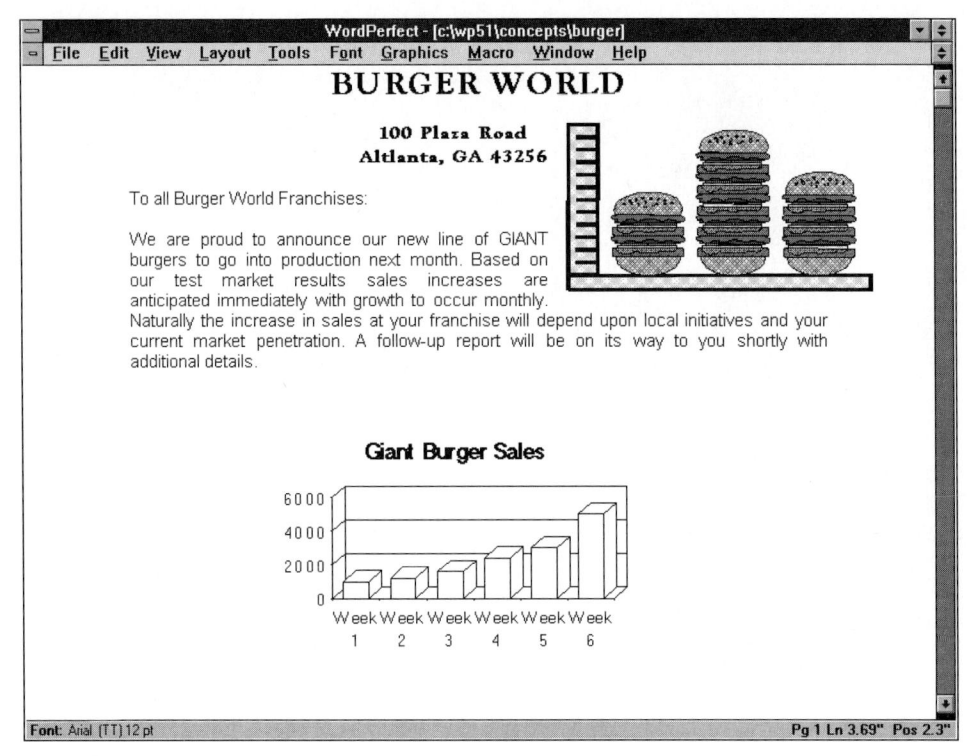

FIGURE 6-14
Using Object Linking and Embedding in a WordPerfect for Windows document.

▶ WINDOWS NT

Windows NT is Microsoft's answer to OS/2. It is a 32-bit operating system that is aimed at the top 10 percent of PC users. Windows NT (for "New Technology") addresses up to 4 gigabytes of RAM, has built-in networking, and multitasking.

When applications are run under NT they are isolated from each other so that programs cannot crash the system or overwrite each other's memory. Windows NT claims to support Windows, OS/2, and UNIX software to give it broad appeal and compatibility, although some specific software packages may not run because of inherent design differences.

Networking is one of NT's significant strengths. Offices that use networked computers may find NT to be especially appropriate. Provided in the software are server capabilities that include security, auditing, and file sharing. Every station on the network can act as a client or as a server. Clients access other disk drives and printers, while servers provide services such as access to databases or software to other users on the network.

Onscreen, Windows NT looks very much like Windows 3.1, thus making the switch relatively painless for existing Windows users. One difference is that in NT the user will need to sign on each time with a password. NT also provides some new tools such as a backup utility and an upgraded Media Player. Because NT requires a 486 computer with 16MB of RAM and up to 60MB of free space on the hard disk, it may not be quickly adopted by home or small business users of Windows; however, power users with a high-end computer may find that it significantly improves the performance over using DOS and Windows.

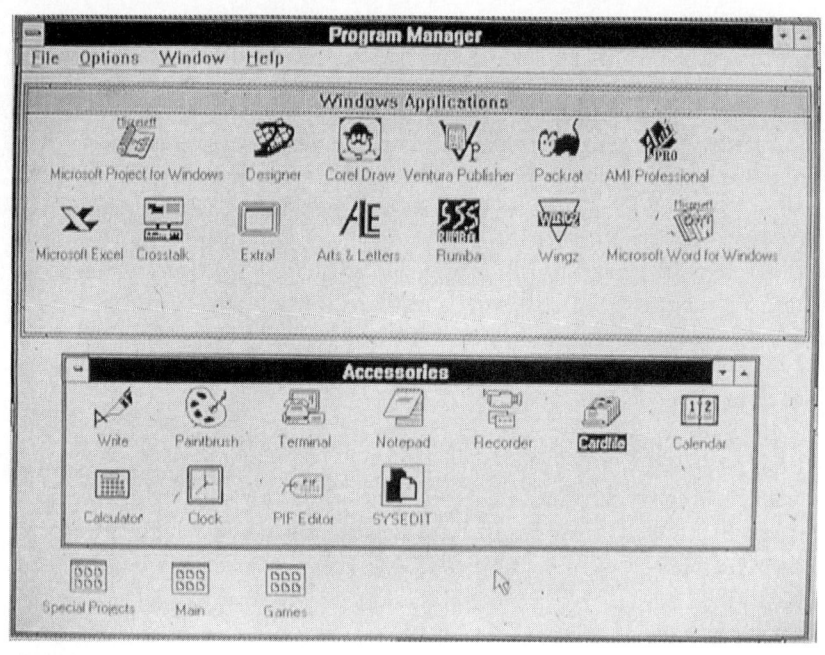

FIGURE 6-15
The Accessories Window provides a variety of standardized applications for Windows users. (Courtesy Microsoft.)

ument. When you double click on one of the objects, not only is the object selected but the program used to create it is activated. Thus, if you select the graph object, a window is opened with Excel ready to edit the graph. Changes are then reflected immediately in the document. Clearly, OLE is a powerful new way of thinking about using software and has enormous implications for the future development and use of operating systems and platforms.

Windows Applications

Windows 3.1 comes with a variety of built-in applications called Accessories (Figure 6-15). Among the applications are a basic word processor, a paintbrush program for creating drawings, a communications program, notepad, calendar, clock, and card file. By standardizing the commands and windows layout, each application is similar in operation. Once you know the primary commands in one program for File operations, printing, and other common activities, you know them for all programs. This standardization extends to other programs written for Windows such as WordPerfect or Word.

Microsoft Windows provides an extensive list of features well beyond the space available here to discuss them. Millions of users have already adopted the Windows standard for their operating environment. The widespread success of this system suggests that Windows will be with us for a long time.

OPERATING SYSTEMS TODAY

We have seen that operating systems for personal computers have developed new and more powerful features since the early versions of these programs were released. As PCs have grown in power and capacity they have begun to adopt features formerly available in the mainframe computer. The ability to do multitasking and to serve multiusers originated with the mainframe, but these features are now available on personal computers with operating systems such as OS/2. Newer platforms such as Windows have gained widespread use, although they continue to rely on DOS for their operation.

CHAPTER SUMMARY

1. The **operating system** is a program that manages all activity in the computer and its components.
2. **Booting** is the term used to describe when the operating system is loaded into memory from disk.
3. **Input/output (I/O) management** takes care of the flow of data to and from the various devices attached to the computer.
4. **Memory management** is a component of the operating system that controls where programs are located in memory and whether there is room for application and resident programs and the loading of main and overlay programs.
5. The **command processor** handles commands such as for file copying, or erasing, and directory listing, that are entered by the computer user.
6. **Utility programs** are another component of operating systems that can be run to perform disk maintenance activities such as formatting a new disk.
7. **Single tasking** operating systems work on one task at a time, **multitasking** systems perform two or more tasks simultaneously in foreground and background, and **multiuser** systems permit more than one user to have access to a single computer from separate terminals.
8. The **MS-DOS Shell** is a graphical interface that provides users with menus to select a variety of DOS operations.
9. **Internal** commands are contained in the COMMAND.COM program, which is loaded into memory when DOS is booted. **External** commands are contained on disk as separate DOS files.
10. **DOS commands** are typed at the DOS prompt, which is usually A> for a floppy disk or C> for hard disk. When using DOS from the Shell, commands are selected from a menu using either the keyboard or a mouse.
11. A **directory listing** of files may be displayed by most programs or by using a DOS command prior to running the program.
12. DOS actions will take place on **default disk drive** unless otherwise requested in the command.
13. **Directory** organization on the hard disk can be thought of as an upside down tree structure. The trunk is the **root** or **parent** directory, which can contain other directories.

CHAPTER 6 Operating Systems and Software Platforms

14. **OS/2** is a multitasking, single-user operating system that incorporates windowing and a graphical Workplace Shell Desktop which uses icons for the user interface.
15. An **icon** is a graphic image that represents an activity or operation.
16. The OS/2 Workplace Shell is object-oriented. **Objects** are items such as icons, folders for system information, applications, and files. **Object-oriented** means that the user concentrates on the task to be done and not on the commands needed to do the job by using icons on the screen that represent tasks.
17. **UNIX** is a multiuser multitasking operating system developed for personal computers, minis, and mainframes.
18. The **Shell** is the part of UNIX that communicates with the user.
19. The **kernel** is the part of the UNIX that ensures consistency between all versions of UNIX.
20. The **Macintosh operating system** uses an object-oriented user interface with icons used to represent tasks.
21. **Microsoft Windows** is the dominant graphical user interface (GUI) program for the MS-DOS environment.
22. A **window** is a rectangular area of the screen that appears on a background called the **desktop**.
23. A **Windows application** is a program that conforms to Windows standards for the types of window, style of menus, use of the mouse or keyboard, and graphics-based screen display.
24. **Object linking and embedding (OLE)** is a method of transferring and sharing data between Windows applications.

IMPORTANT TERMS AND CONCEPTS

Background
Booting
Cold start
Commands
Default disk drive
Directory
Disk operating system (DOS)
External commands
Foreground
Hierarchical directory
Icon
Input/output management
Internal commands
Kernel
Memory management
MicroSoft Disk Operating System (MS-DOS)
Microsoft Windows
Multitasking
Multiuser
Objects
Object-oriented
Object Linking and Embedding (OLE)
Operating system
Personal Computer Disk Operating System (PC-DOS)
Root Directory
Shell
Single tasking
UNIX
Utilities
Warm start
Window
Windows Application

SELF-TESTING QUESTIONS

Fill-In

1. The term DOS is an abbreviation for _____ _____ _____.
2. The _____ _____ component of the operating system takes care of the flow of data to and from the various devices.
3. Programs called _____ are supplied with an operating system to perform disk maintenance and other activities.
4. A _____ operating system permits two or more tasks to function at the same time.
5. The MS-DOS _____ is a graphical interface that provides users with menus for a variety of DOS operations.
6. Hard disks may be organized into _____ to help organize hundreds of files into meaningful groups.
7. The _____ disk drive is the disk that DOS will operate on unless instructed otherwise.
8. In OS/2 _____ are items such as icons, folders for system information, applications, and files.
9. In Microsoft Windows a _____ is a rectangular area of the screen that appears on a background called the desktop.
10. With object _____ you can create an object, such as a drawing or graphic, and embed (insert) it in another document.

True/False

1. PC-DOS and MS-DOS are in the class of operating systems that permits more than one task at a time.
2. A utility program, such as FORMAT, that is used to perform disk maintenance activities must be purchased at additional cost from a third-party software company.
3. The DOS Shell is a sophisticated program that lets computer users link with other computers on the network.
4. A directory is used on disk to help manage the many files that may be stored on the disk.
5. UNIX is a multitasking, multiuser operating system used primarily on minicomputers.
6. A graphical user interface (GUI) means the computer must have a CD-ROM with graphics to function.
7. Windows is a software platform under DOS that provides a graphical user interface and permits the use of more than one application at a time.
8. An icon is a graphic image that represents an activity or operation.

ANSWERS

Fill-In: 1. Disk Operating System, 2. input/output management, 3. utilities, 4. multitasking, 5. shell, 6. directories, 7. default, 8. objects, 9. window, 10. embedding

True/False: 1. F, 2. F, 3. F, 4. T, 5. T, 6. F, 7. T, 8. T

Questions for Critical Thinking

1. Some industry observers have suggested that operating systems should be stored in ROM and made a permanent part of the hardware rather than residing on disk. What implications would this have for computer users? for software publishers?

2. Because Microsoft has both Windows and MS-DOS, the most popular operating system for PCs, they have an uncontested market share of the operating platform software industry. Some observers feel that Microsoft is too dominant and should be broken up to allow for fairer competition. What do you think?

3. Some computer companies are bundling Microsoft Windows with their computers, creating an automatic market for the software. As a result buyers may not even consider the alternatives. Is this a fair market practice or should computer manufacturers be restrained from using this strategy?

CHAPTER

7

APPLICATION SOFTWARE

A VIEW OF THE CHAPTER AHEAD

After reading this chapter you will understand

- ▶ how application software is used on a personal computer.
- ▶ how the keyboard and mouse are used.
- ▶ the different types of user interfaces used by computer programs.
- ▶ why it is necessary to install software before it can be used to its full capacity.

INTRODUCTION

Early computer users were required to memorize commands or use a reference manual to find them and then type the command into the computer for execution. Commands could be complicated and require a knowledge of syntax as well as the use of certain keywords. No wonder only trained users or computer junkies bothered to use the computer while most other people were awed by them. By contrast, software of the 90s uses pull-down menus, dialog boxes, and icons that let you point and click for many operations (see Figure 7-1), but commands are still used for some of the more demanding operations. This chapter discusses the ways of using software and the basic skills required to begin the process of learning a variety of software packages.

We saw in Chapter 6 that the disk operating system (DOS) controls the input and output activity from active programs in the computer. Before a program is run it is important that DOS first be **resident** in the computer's memory. Then the application software is loaded into the computer by typing the program's name at the DOS prompt, by selecting it from a menu, or clicking on an icon.

The rules for using a specific software package are unique to that program. Rules of use that have been learned for one program may not necessarily apply to another. Even some simple things such as the use of a key on the keyboard may take on different meanings. So in this chapter we will discuss general principles for using application software.

> **Application software.** A program that performs a specific function such as a spreadsheet or word processor.

APPLICATION SOFTWARE PACKAGES

What the majority of users see when using the computer is the application software. Much of the work of computer training companies goes into teaching the user an application package and then how to become produc-

FIGURE 7-1
Icons used in Windows for starting a variety of application software.

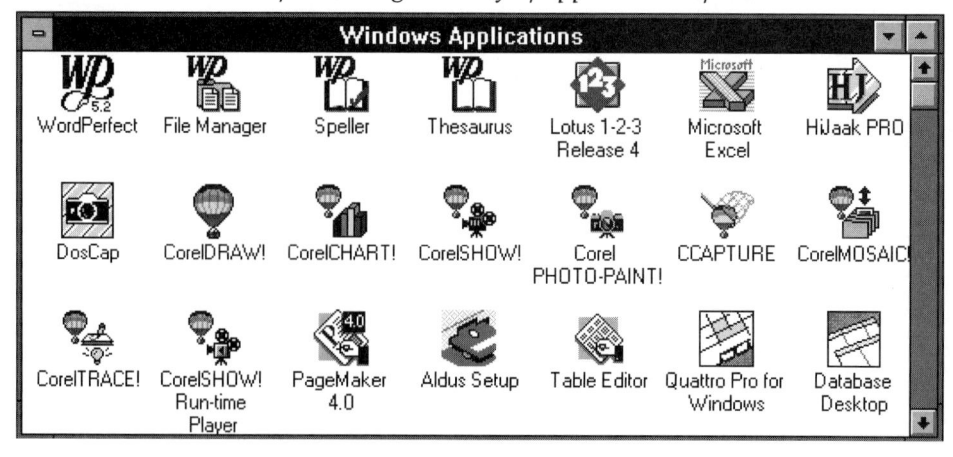

tive with it. Application packages include hundreds of programs in several different major groups (see Figure 7-2) but most users need to learn only a handful of programs to function effectively. Some of the most well known of these are the spreadsheets Lotus 1–2–3 or Quattro Pro, database software dBASE IV or Paradox, and word processors such as WordPerfect and Microsoft Word. Of course there are many more programs available in each of these categories, and you may well have some favorites that are not mentioned here.

Software Packages

Application software consists of more than just the disk that the software resides on. As Figure 7-3 shows, a software package often comes in a neatly packaged carton (thus the origin of the name software package) suitable for storing the material supplied for easy reference.

A complete software package makes it easier to install the program on your computer and to learn how to use the software. Packages typically include the following components.

- **Diskettes.** Included with the package are one or more diskettes containing the program and other necessary data. Typical packages contain 5 or 6 disks; some have many more. If $3\frac{1}{2}$-inch disks are provided then only half as many disks are needed. It is common to compress disk files to reduce the number of disks required in the package. In addition to the main program, diskettes may also include help information, an on-screen tutorial to demonstrate the use of the program, an install program to install the software on your unique computer system, printer drivers, and conversion programs to convert data prepared by other software.
- **Manuals.** Most important is the instruction manual that explains the use of the software. Some of the better packages also include a separate installation manual, and an overview manual or lesson that quickly and easily introduces the owner to the more commonly used features of the program without getting into all of its complexities. A few of the more complex packages may also have a separate manual that explains the advanced features of the software.
- **Keyboard Template.** Much of today's software makes use of the function keys provided on the computer's keyboard. The plastic template fits over the function keys and lists all of the function key commands for easy reference at the keyboard.
- **Quick Reference Guide.** This is a handy reference to all of the commands in the software. Once the contents of the reference manual have been mastered, most users find a reference card to be an easier way to look up instructions.
- **Warranty Card.** This card is similar to one you might get with a new stereo or camera which is filled out and mailed to the manufacturer. Registering your software gives coverage in the event that a failure occurs with the software or its disk. This does not necessarily cover bugs in the program, but may entitle you to free or low-cost updates if a revised program is made available in the near future.

Software Category	Specific Applications	
Productivity	Graphics Spreadsheet Word processing Presentation graphics Integrated software Desktop publishing	
Business systems	Accounting Payroll Decision support systems Industry specific	
Data base management	Flat file databases Relational databases	
Communications	Local area networks Online services Micro-mainframe link	
Artificial intelligence	Knowledge-based systems Robotics	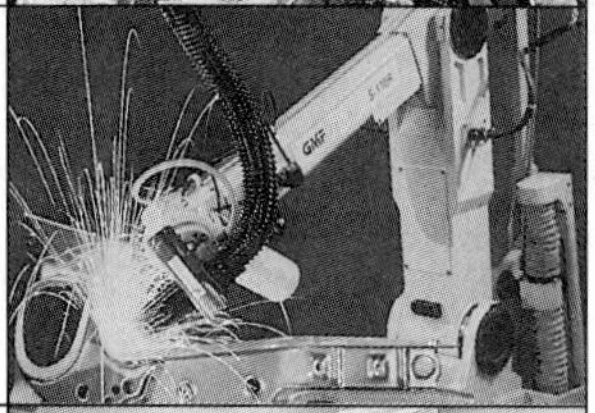
Education	Tutorial Administration Languages	
Home Systems	Entertainment Record keeping	

FIGURE 7-2
The seven major categories of application software. (Courtesy of IBM; Apple Computer, Inc.; IBM; Home Shopping Network; GNF Robotics; Apple Computer, Inc.; Apple Computer, Inc.)

FIGURE 7-3
A complete software package includes diskettes, one or more instruction manuals, a quick reference guide, a keyboard template, and a warranty card. (Courtesy WordPerfect.)

Main and Overlay Programs

Complex application software such as database, spreadsheet, or word processing programs contain a considerable amount of program code. For example, the code for dBASE IV contains a total of over 4 million bytes on disk not including some of the special features. If all of this code were required to reside in RAM at one time, a 640K or even a 2MB computer could not handle it. With DOS present, a 5MB computer could barely fit all this code in its memory with little room left for data.

To solve this problem, software is often developed in parts: the main program and one or more overlay programs (Figure 7-4). The main part is the controlling program called the .EXE (pronounced exec) for an executable program. For dBASE this consists of 92,320 bytes of code. The rest of the program is stored in an overlay file on disk, and parts of this program are called into memory as they are required. dBASE has a large overlay file called DBASE.OVL as shown in the directory. As certain features of the program are required, the code for executing those features is temporarily brought into the overlay area of RAM. When a new program feature is required, it replaces the code formerly in the overlay area thus minimizing the amount of memory required to run the program.

Other program overlays are also handled in this manner. Overlays for help files, messages, and menus are also provided and brought into memory only as they are needed.

```
Directory of dBASE IV on disk

Directory of C:/DBASE

.                    <DIR>
..                   <DIR>
DBASE     .EXE       92,320      04-17-92   12:56p   ← dBASE IV Program
DBASE     .OVL    2,027,440      03-10-92   01:50a   ← Overlay Program
DBASE1    .HLP      436,335      03-10-92   01:50a
DBASE1    .RES       81,738      03-10-92   01:50a
DBASE2    .HLP       79,958      03-10-92   01:50a   ← Help File
DBASE2    .RES      102,497      03-10-92   01:50a
DBASE3    .RES        8,377      03-10-92   01:50a
DBSETUP   .EXE      200,698      03-10-92   01:50a   ← Setup Program
DBSETUP   .ICO        1,086      03-10-92   01:50a
DBSETUP   .PIF          545      03-10-92   01:50a
DBSETUP   .PRD        9,631      03-10-92   01:50a   ← Setup Files
DBSETUP   .RES       44,279      03-10-92   01:50a
```

RAM

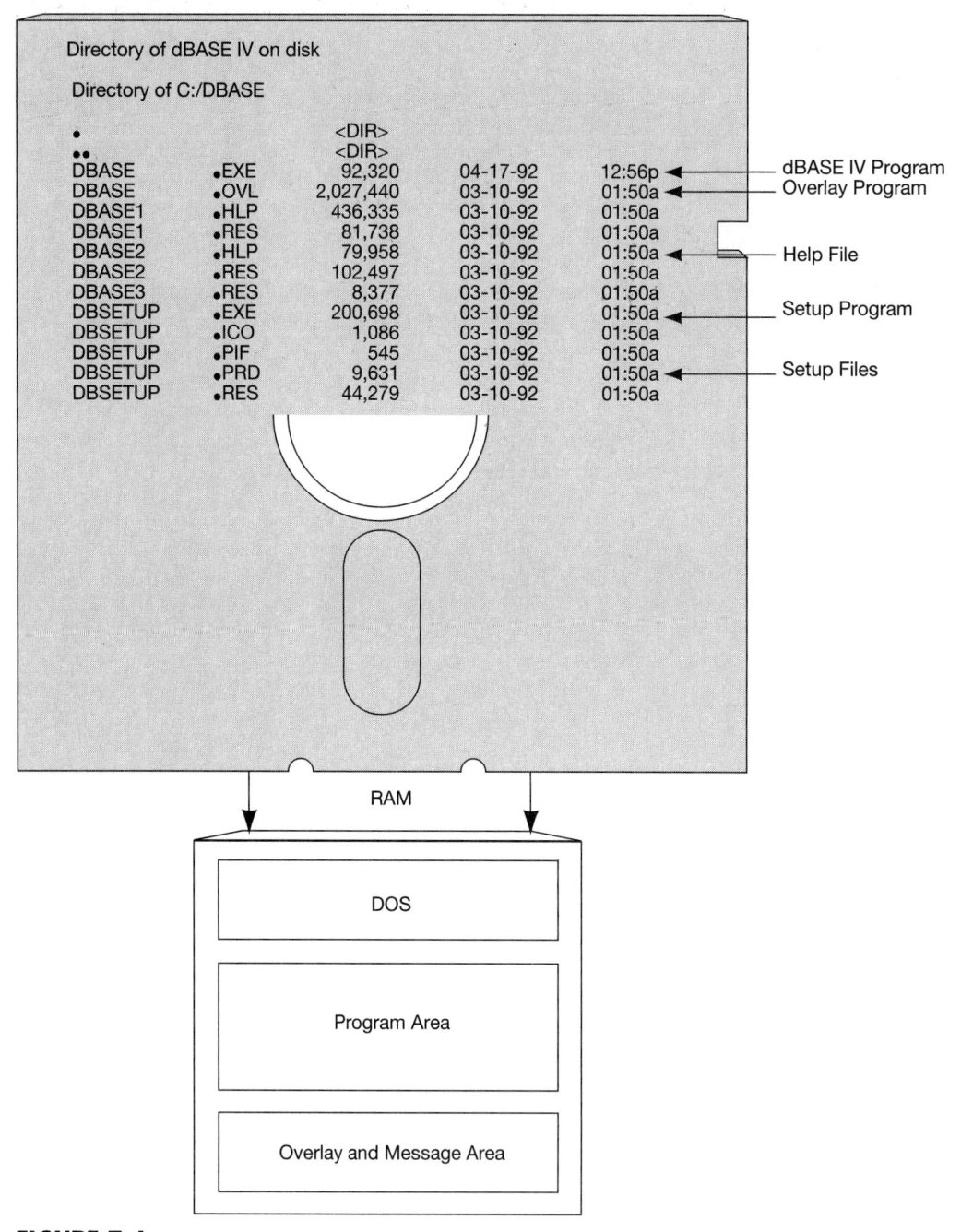

- DOS
- Program Area
- Overlay and Message Area

FIGURE 7-4
Using overlays in RAM to reduce the total memory requirements for an application program.

To Program or Use Application Software?

Pioneers in computing were required to write a program for each application that was needed on the computer. But, during the four generations of computer use, an abundance of software has accumulated for an almost un-

▶ PROGRAMMING LANGUAGES FOR PCS

Assembler	Forth
BASIC	Fortran
C	Pascal
COBOL	Prolog

limited variety of applications. Does this widespread availability mean that it is no longer necessary to write programs? Or even to learn a programming language?

For many computer users writing a program will be unnecessary, and even learning to program might be a questionable activity although some programming skills may help you to use some of the application software's advanced features. Before deciding to write a program you need to ask a few pointed questions.

1. Is there a program available that will do the task required? Will it run on my computer?
2. Would it be less costly to purchase the program than to write an equivalent one?
3. Can an existing program be adapted to my needs? Will it take less time and money than writing a completely new program?
4. Can the application be implemented with spreadsheet or database software instead of using a traditional programming language?

Many applications have already been developed and can be used as is. Most programs for personal computers cost a few hundred dollars, some cost considerably less. Writing a complex program can require hundreds of hours, which far exceeds the cost of buying a program. In other cases, some changes will need to be made to an existing program, but this is much easier and less costly than writing a completely new program.

Sometimes, the only option is to write a program that will do your unique job. If this is necessary, following an orderly, well-planned approach is vital to successful program development. Hacking together a "quick and dirty" program is rarely a satisfactory solution.

Another approach that is becoming more and more popular is to implement the solution to a business problem using a spreadsheet or database software package. Because these are general-purpose packages, a wide variety of applications can be developed with them. Using a spreadsheet or other general-purpose package can speed up application development many times over using a programming language. And, because they are not programming languages, almost anyone can master their use.

However, learning to program does have its advantages. To use software, such as a spreadsheet like Lotus 1–2–3, or a database such as dBASE IV, to its greatest advantage requires the use of programming-like tools. Thus, having some programming knowledge can pay dividends when developing applications on many different types of software packages.

Writing a program from scratch can also be useful if the user requirements are not suited to application packages. Although packages are generally flexible, they do have some limitations that can often be easily overcome with a program in Assembler, BASIC, Pascal, or C language. Writing your own program, or having a professional write it, offers the most flexibility if you are prepared to wait and to pay the price for a custom job.

USING THE KEYBOARD

Using any software requires that you have an understanding of the keyboard. In this section we will discuss the primary keys and their use for most software packages. The insert "Using the PC Keyboard" explains the purpose of the keys for commonly used keyboards. If you are using some other keyboard on a PC or compatible, there will likely be some differences but they will be few. Regardless of the keyboard you are using, there are three basic categories of operation that it provides to the computer user. These are

1. Entry or changing of characters
2. Cursor movement
3. Entry of program commands

While much of the use of the keyboard is common between application programs, there are differences. Categories one and two are often quite similar from one software package to another, while category three can be

---

▶ USING THE PC KEYBOARD

The most widely used keyboard is the Enhanced keyboard shown in the picture. Other keyboards may be used and will likely differ only slightly from this one. So if you master this one, then adapting to another keyboard will be quite easy. Most keys are auto-repeat, meaning that if you hold them down the character or action will be repeated until the key is released.

IBM Personal System/2 Keyboard. (Courtesy IBM.)

CHAPTER 7 Application Software

Function Keys

The function keys are assigned for special duties in each software package. In Lotus 1–2–3, F1 is used for help information while F10 is used to draw a graph. Many programs use only keys F1 to F10.

F1 to F12

Main Keyboard

The Escape key is used to escape from an operation before it is completed.

The Tab key is used to move the cursor to preset tab stops across the screen. Reverse Tab is used with the Shift key to move to a previous tab stop.

The Ctrl (control) key is used with another key (usually a letter) to issue a command to the software. Holding down Ctrl and pressing the S key will stop scrolling in DOS.

The shift keys are used to select uppercase letters or to type the character found at the top of a key such as the $ above the 4.

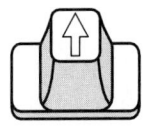

The Alt (alternate) key is used like Ctrl with another key. In WordPerfect, holding down Alt and pressing F2 starts the search and replace operation.

Backspace is used to delete the character to the left of the cursor position.

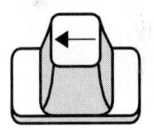

The Return or Enter key is used to complete an entry. In DOS, after typing the name of a program, Enter is pressed to enter the command and load the program into memory.

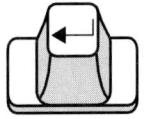

Print screen can be used to print the entire contents of the screen on your printer.

When pressed, all alphabetic keys will type capital letters. Press again to return to lowercase.

Ins (insert) is used to turn insert mode on or off. In a word processor this mode will let you insert letters or words in existing text.

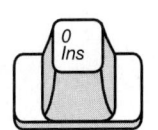

The Del (delete) key is used to delete a character at the cursor position.

Numeric Key Pad

Pressing Num Lock causes the numeric keypad to go into number mode. Keys pressed will enter numbers. Pressing Num Lock again will return to cursor mode.

In some software, such as Lotus 1-2-3, pressing Scroll Lock will permit lines on the screen to move but not the cursor.

Moves the cursor to the top left corner of the screen. Has a special function in some software.

Moves the cursor to the bottom of the screen. Has a special function in some software.

Moves the screen contents up one page to the previous page.

Moves the screen contents down one page to the following page.

Cursor up moves the cursor up one line.

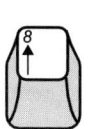

Cursor down moves the cursor down one line.

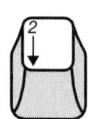

Cursor left moves the cursor left one character.

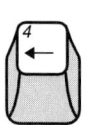

Cursor right moves the cursor right one character.

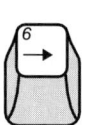

In most software this key enters a minus sign.

In most software this key enters a plus sign.

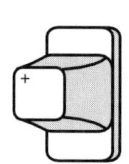

FIGURE 7-5
A color-coded function key template used in WordPerfect for DOS. Entries in black use the function key by itself. Red entries require the Ctrl key, green uses the Shift key, and blue the Alt key for a total of 40 different function key combinations. (Courtesy WordPerfect.)

totally different, although the same keys are used but for different purposes.

Keyboard Templates

Because application software packages each have different uses for the function keys, a method is needed to easily reference the use of these keys. Many software packages, such as Lotus 1-2-3 and WordPerfect, provide a plastic keyboard template that fits directly over the function keys on the keyboard (Figure 7-5). Each key's function is clearly identified on the template, and by pressing that key the specific action will occur.

In WordPerfect for DOS, 40 different functions are provided by combining the Crtl, Shift, and Alt keys with the functions keys. Ten functions are available with the function keys alone, ten with the Ctrl and function keys, ten more with Shift, and another ten with Alt. Some functions are duplicated on keys F11 and F12.

Remembering 40 different functions is no mean feat, so WordPerfect provides a color-coded template with all of the functions on it. Pressing the appropriate combination of keys activates the required function. For example, pressing F3 by itself calls up the help screen. Pressing Ctrl and F2 activates the spelling checker.

Keyboard template. A plastic device that fits over the function keys to define their use by a specific program.

USING A MOUSE

Many programs support the use of a mouse in addition to the keyboard. If your computer has a mouse and the mouse software is loaded, then a mouse pointer appears on the screen. The pointer moves on the screen as you move the mouse on the desk. Usually the mouse is used for making selections from a menu or GUI instead of the keyboard. The following list describes several activities that are unique to a mouse.

Mouse. An input device attached to the serial port that is used to move a pointer on the screen and select options by pressing a button.

Activity	Action
Point	Roll the mouse to move the pointer to a screen location.
Click	Quickly press and release the left mouse button.
Double click	Quickly press and release the left mouse button twice.
Drag	Press the left button and hold it down while you move the mouse pointer. Release the button when you are finished.

When software has been effectively designed for the use of a mouse, operations will be faster and easier to perform than with a keyboard. However, the mouse cannot replace the keyboard, because of the need for typing data into most programs.

USING SOFTWARE

Application software often begins by displaying an opening screen that presents copyright information and an agreement for use. Most programs will clear this information from the screen after a few seconds, but others, such as dBASE III Plus, ask you to press the Enter key to assent to the agreement. Occasionally software may ask you to insert a key disk at this point, if you are running from a hard disk drive.

Following these preliminaries, the program presents the first screen which you will need to understand to use the program. What is presented at this time varies considerably from one program to another and depends to a large extent on the way the user interface to the program was designed. A **user interface** is the method provided by the program for the user's interaction with the computer. Several types of interfaces are used and many programs use a variety of them. Some of the most common interfaces are the following:

User interface. A method provided by the program for interaction with the user.

1. Menus
2. Function keys
3. Prompts
4. Commands
5. Form filling
6. Graphical user interface (GUI)

User Interfaces

Menus. You are certainly familiar with menus, at least those you might find in a restaurant where you make a choice of several appetizing alternatives. It is much the same with a software menu. A list of choices is presented on the screen (Figure 7-6) and the user makes a selection from this list.

Menu. A list of choices presented by the program from which the user makes a selection.

A *menu*, such as that used by WordPerfect, requires that you type a letter or number which identifies the selection. Typing the letter will immediately activate the command. For example, pressing the letter R will cause a docu-

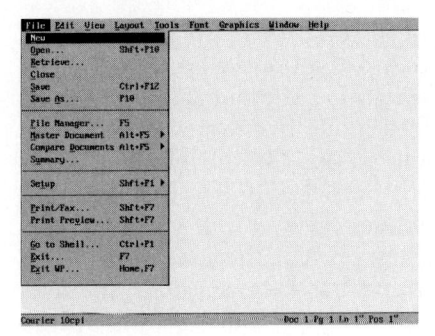

FIGURE 7-6
A menu screen displayed from WordPerfect 6.0. Typing a single letter from the menu activates the related operation.

ment to be retrieved. When a letter describes the operation, such as R for Retrieve, P for Print, and S for Save, then the command is called **mnemonic**.

Some menu systems require that the Enter key be pressed after the selection is made. The advantage with this method is you can change your mind if you want a different option or if a typing error was made.

Cursor Pointing. While menus have been around since the first microcomputers, the next enhancement led to the use of cursor pointing to make a selection. This concept was made popular by Lotus 1–2–3 with its menus displayed on the top line, called a command line, of the screen (Figure 7-7). The menu is displayed by first pressing the slash (/) key. Then, pressing the right or left cursor keys causes the highlighted bar, called a pointer, to move from one option to another. When the pointer is resting on the required option, say the Print option, the Enter key is pressed to make the selection.

To make the software even easier to use, the first letter of any option in the menu may be pressed instead of moving the pointer. Simply pressing /P causes the Print option to be chosen. By a clever choice of names, each option begins with a different letter and therefore also has a mnemonic meaning.

FIGURE 7-7
Menus in Lotus 1–2–3 use cursor keys to move the cell pointer to the option required in the menu.

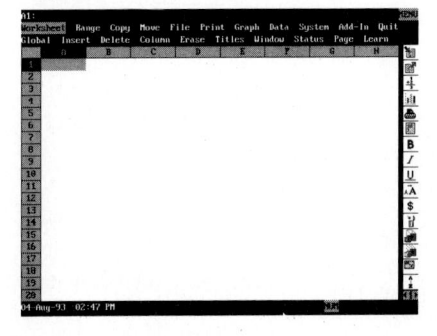

Multilevel Menus. Many application software programs use several levels of menus for their operation. Both Lotus 1–2–3 (Figure 7-8) and WordPerfect (Figure 7-9) use multilevel menus, although in different ways. A multilevel menu means that once a choice has been made from one menu, it can lead to further choices on a second menu and so on. Multilevel menus generally begin with a single main menu, which branches out to one or more subsidiary levels where further choices are made.

The benefit of multilevel menus is that they present the user with fewer options at any one time. Then, when an option has been selected, the user is presented with further choices that pertain only to the previous option chosen. This greatly simplifies the use of the software and helps to make it user-friendly. For more detail on using menus of this type refer to the tutorial modules on Lotus 1–2–3, WordPerfect, and other software.

Pull-down menu. A menu that pulls down from a horizontal menu at the top of the screen.

Pull-down and Pop-up Menus. These menus are an alternate method of presenting a multilevel menu where several entries need to be made to take a specific action. Pull-down menus frequently require fewer keystrokes than multilevel menus. As a choice is made from a menu at the top of the screen, a submenu drops down to show the lower level choices to be made. These are selected by pointing with the cursor keys or typing the first letter of the choice.

An example of a pull-down menu is shown for dBASE IV in Figure 7-10. When Layout at the top of the screen is selected, the pull-down menu shows the choices that may be made. By pointing to any one of these with the cursor key and then pressing Enter, the choice is made.

Pop-up menu. A menu that appears in the middle of the screen.

A pop-up menu is one that appears somewhere in the middle of the screen. This menu is activated by some predefined keystroke on the keyboard. Figure 7-11 shows a pop-up menu, called a dialog box, that appears in DOS 5 when the Change Attributes selection is made from the File pull-down menu. Selections in this box are made by using the cursor keys and pressing Enter or by pointing and clicking with the mouse.

FIGURE 7-8
The use of multilevel menus in Lotus 1–2–3. A choice of Print at the top level menu leads to a choice of Printer, File, Encoded, or Background at the second level. Selecting Printer gives a third level menu with a number of choices. Choosing Options at this level gives a further list of activities relating to printing.

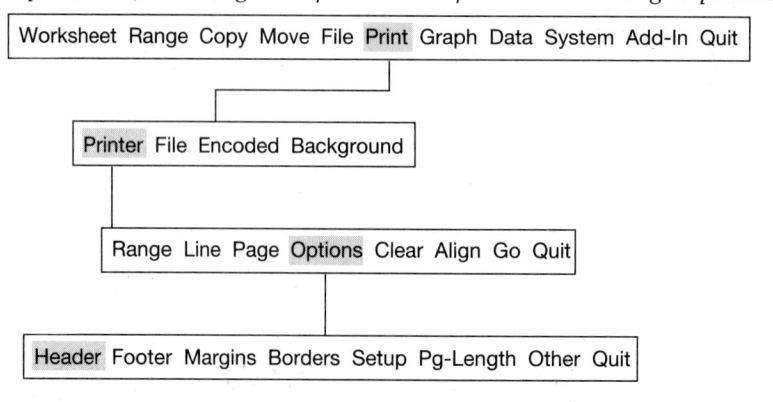

Worksheet Range Copy Move File Print Graph Data System Add-In Quit

Printer File Encoded Background

Range Line Page Options Clear Align Go Quit

Header Footer Margins Borders Setup Pg-Length Other Quit

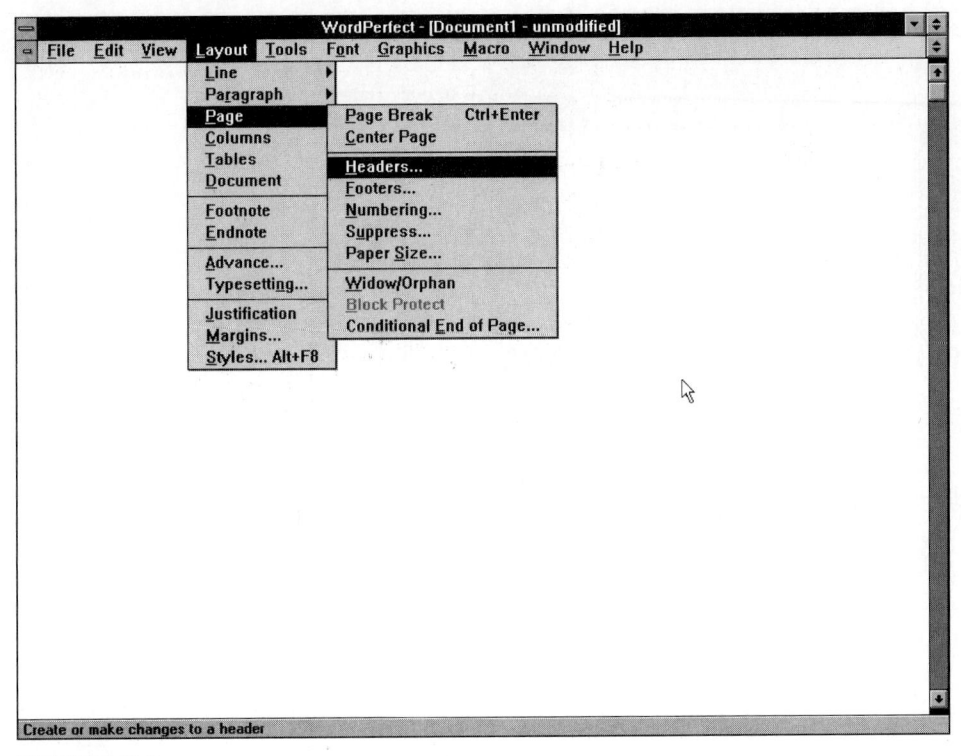

FIGURE 7-9
Multilevel menus used in WordPerfect 5.2 for Windows. Here Layout has been selected from the first menu at the top of the screen. Then Page was selected from the Layout menu, causing another menu of choices to be presented where Header is highlighted for selection.

Function Keys. With the trend to using general-purpose personal computers in the office, function keys also became general purpose, thus the numbering from F1 to F12. (Some keyboards are numbered F1 to F10.) Many software designers have recognized the wisdom of providing the commands for the program on the function keys. As we saw earlier, function keys are given specific duties for the particular software that is used, and they will be different from one program to another.

Prompts. Prompts are used by programs to query the user about an operation to be done by the program. Usually one prompt is issued at a time and the user responds to it by typing Y or N for Yes or No, entering a number such as the position of the right margin, or the name of a file to be saved. Single character responses often do not need to be followed by the Enter key, but entering several characters such as the name of a file requires the Enter key to be pressed after the name has been typed (Figure 7-12).

Prompt. A question or statement from the program to which the user types a response.

Prompts are considered a useful form of user interaction because a specific question is asked of the user. Unlike menus, which are usually short entries, the prompt can be self-explanatory. On the down side, prompts take more time to read and the response often takes longer to enter.

Commands. Command-driven programs require that the user know exactly what operation is to be done and the command required to invoke the

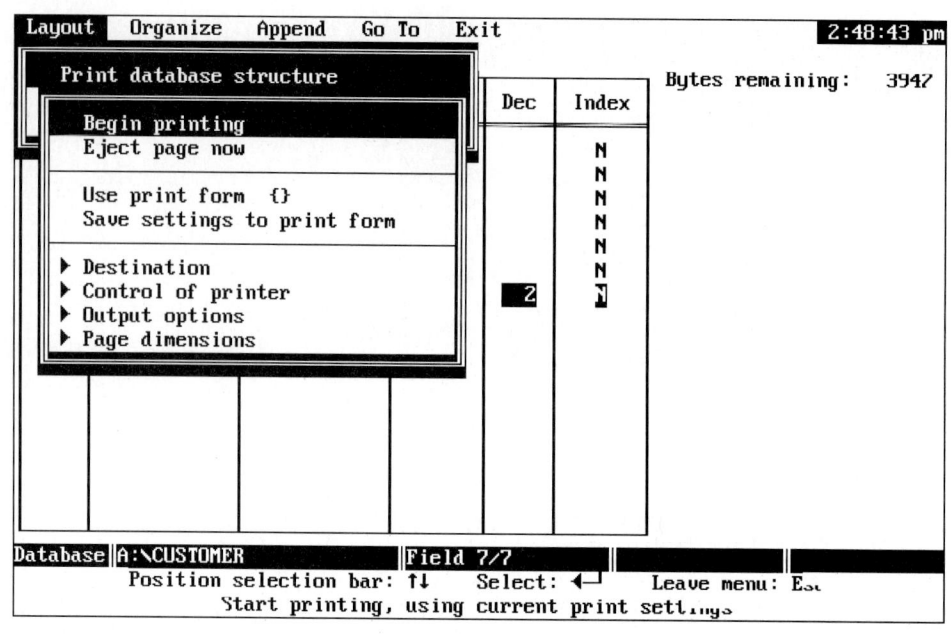

FIGURE 7-10
Pull-down menus are used in dBASE IV for selecting program options. As each option in the menu at the top of the screen is highlighted, a new pull-down menu will appear below it.

FIGURE 7-11
DOS 5 uses a pop-up menu that appears over the existing activity on the screen. When the desired choice has been selected, the menu disappears and the screen returns to its previous activity.

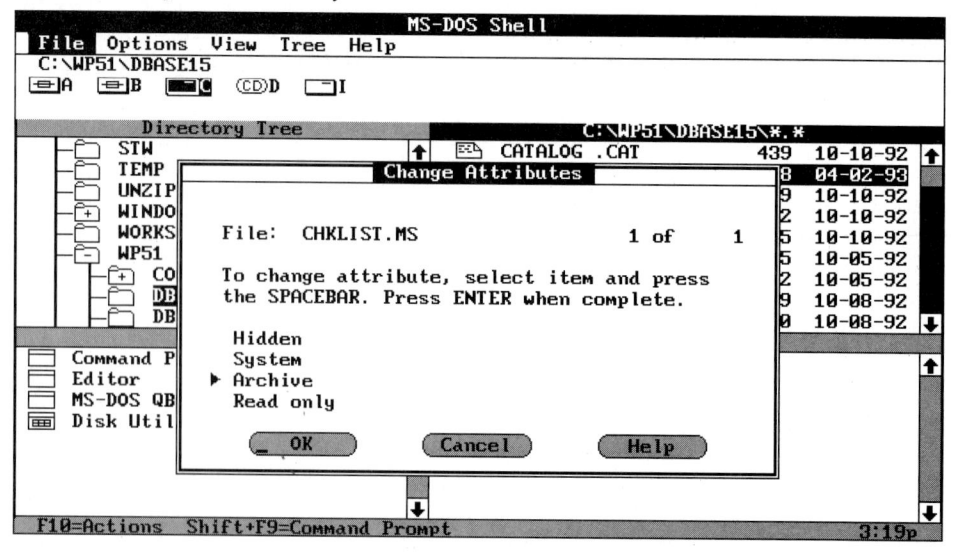

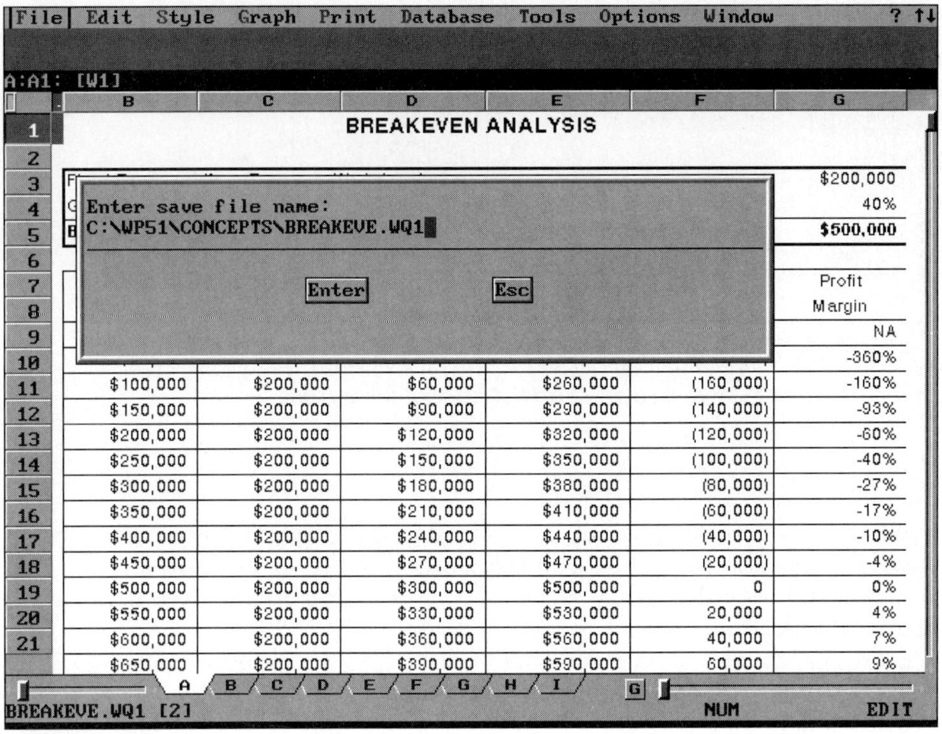

FIGURE 7-12
A prompt in Quattro Pro asks the user for the name of the file to be saved.

action. DOS is an example of a command-driven program. Figure 7-13 shows a screen where the DOS prompt is all that the user sees. To cause any action to occur the user must know the command and its precise format. There is often no help, prompting, or list of choices presented on the screen.

The second screen in the figure shows a command entered by the user for copying a file from drive A to drive B. The user must know the name of the command (copy) and the format of the entries for the source file (a:expenses) and the drive to receive the copy (b:).

Command-driven programs are more difficult to learn to use but are considered to be more direct and faster to use once the commands are known. Because of the longer learning time, few programs today are command driven. Even MS-DOS 5 and OS/2 are menu driven, but they can also be operated in command mode. Other programs, such as dBASE IV, offer menus for the new user and a command mode for the experienced user.

Form Filling. You have no doubt filled out a form as an application for college or to apply for a driver's license. Software form filling is a type of user interface where a screen is presented with empty spaces and used something like a blank paper form. Each space may have some identifying label so that the user will know what data is to be entered on the form. As data is entered, the cursor, under program control, moves from field to field in the form indicating what is to be entered next.

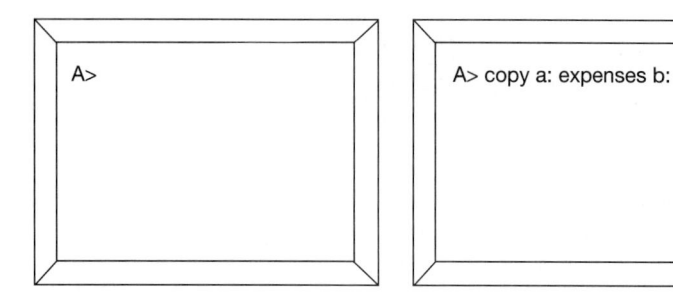

```
                                    Some DOS Commands
    A>          A> copy a: expenses b:    dir a:
                                    date
                                    diskcopy a: b:
                                    erase b:memos5.bak
                                    rename sample trial
```

FIGURE 7-13
PC-DOS is an example of a command-driven program. On the left is the screen with the DOS prompt waiting for a command to be entered. The screen on the right shows the copy command that has been given to copy the file expenses from the A to the B disk.

Business software for accounting or payroll frequently uses this type of interface for data entry. Some software also uses it for user interaction. Figure 7-14 shows a dBASE IV screen that is used for defining the fields when creating a file.

FIGURE 7-14
A form filling screen used in dBASE IV to create a database file. At each entry line in the form a field name, type, width, and number of decimal positions is entered. When a field is complete the program automatically moves the pointer to the next empty field in the form.

```
Layout    Organize   Append    Go To    Exit              11:58:29 am

                                                  Bytes remaining:  3985
 Num | Field Name | Field Type | Width | Dec | Index

  1    ORDER_NO    Numeric       3       0     N
  2    ITEM_NO     Character     2             N
  3    CUST_NO     Numeric       2       0     N
  4    QUANTITY    Numeric       2       0     N
  5    UNIT_COST   Numeric       6       2     N
  6                Character                   N

Database C:\dbase\ORDERS         Field 6/6
            Enter the field name. Insert/Delete field:Ctrl-N/Ctrl-U
Field names begin with a letter and may contain letters, digits and underscores
```

Graphical User Interface (GUI).

The use of icons on the screen for user interfacing was made popular by the Apple Macintosh computer and is now used on other systems, especially in Windows applications. An **icon** is a graphic image on the screen that represents a file, notepad, disk, printer, or other object used in a process or activity in the software.

MicroSoft Windows provides access to many programs written for the PC varying from database to desktop publishing and expert systems to CAD. Windows also provides some basic functions and uses icons to show a word processor, calculator, notepad, clock, and other features. Icons work best with a mouse. An option is selected by pointing the mouse to the icon and clicking the button to make the selection.

Many new software packages are being introduced with GUI as their main mode of user interaction. Other software, such as WordPerfect for Windows (Figure 7-15) has been rewritten using the Windows standard for the user interface.

Graphical user interface (GUI). The use of icons for user interaction with the program.

Icon. A graphic image used to represent an activity or process.

Multi-interface Programs

Most software today makes use of several types of user interfaces and not just one exclusively. Although a program such as dBASE IV may primarily use pull-down menus, it also uses prompting, cursor pointing, function keys, and command-driven interfaces. Each of these methods is appropriate at different times during the use of the program, and the switch from one to the other occurs quite naturally when a program is well designed.

FIGURE 7-15
Microsoft Excel for Windows uses a Graphical User Interface (GUI) to simplify user interaction with the program.

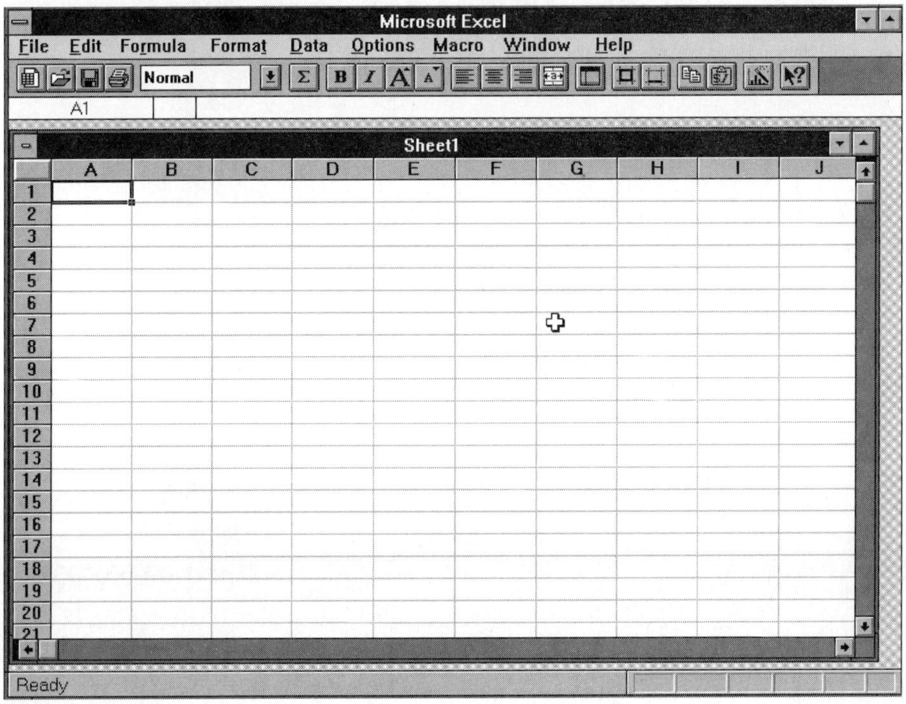

Many of the leading programs for word processing, spreadsheets, and databases will use several types of interfaces and not depend on just one for their operation. Although GUI systems may depend less on other forms of interaction, they too will use more than one approach for user interfacing.

Help Screens

What do you do when using a software package and you can't remember how a command works? One solution is to find the manual, look up the command in the index, and then read the instructions on its use. A faster solution is to use the Help system built into the software. By pressing a key you can access a screen of information about the use of the program.

There are basically two types of help systems. One is general in nature and requires multiple keystrokes to get to the information you require. This type of help is used in WordPerfect. To get help in WordPerfect you first press the Help key (F3), and then press the key for the command you require help on.

Context sensitive. A system that responds with help for the specific activity engaged by the user.

The second type of help system is called **context sensitive**. Context-sensitive help systems take a look at what you are doing in the program and then give you help on that specific type of operation. Lotus 1-2-3 is an example of this system, as Figure 7-16 shows. Help on this screen was requested when using the graph command.

FIGURE 7-16
A context-sensitive help screen for the Graph Options command in Lotus 1-2-3.

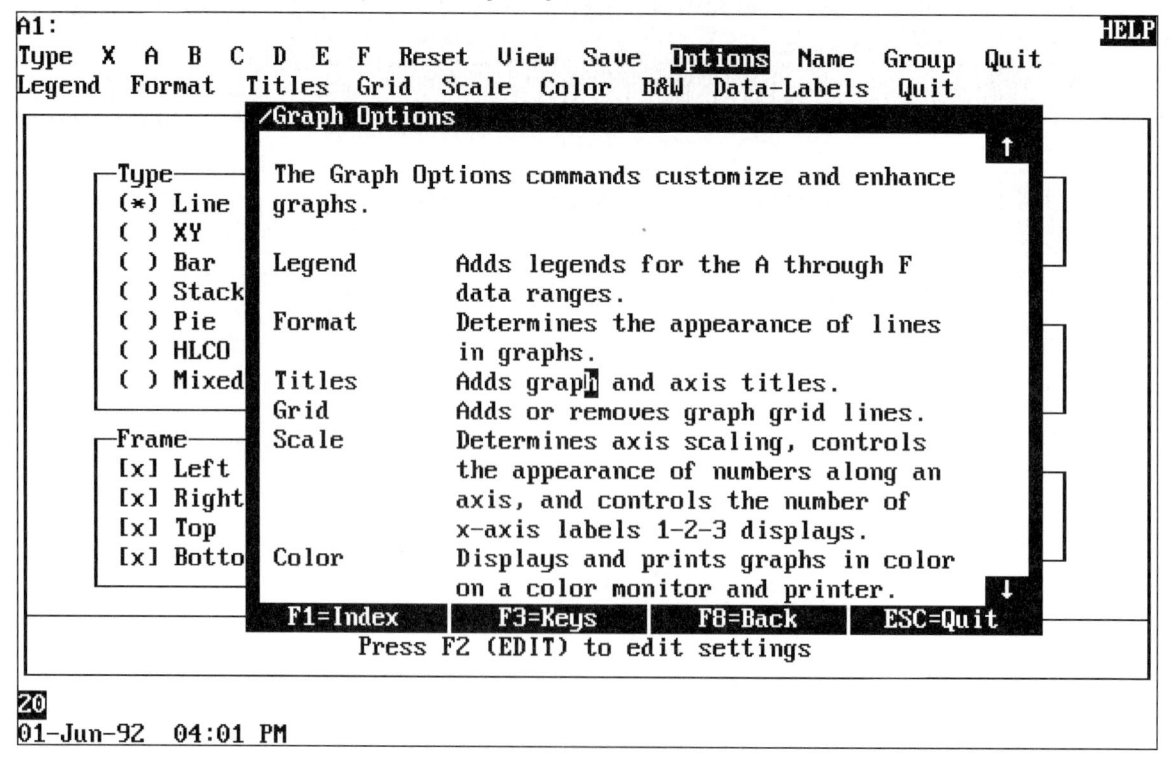

```
A1:                                                                    HELP
Type  X  A  B  C  D  E  F  Reset  View  Save  Options  Name  Group  Quit
Legend  Format  Titles  Grid  Scale  Color  B&W  Data-Labels  Quit
                        ╔═/Graph Options══════════════════════════╗
                        ║                                       ↑ ║
          ┌─Type──────  ║  The Graph Options commands customize and enhance
          │ (*) Line    ║  graphs.
          │ ( ) XY      ║
          │ ( ) Bar     ║  Legend      Adds legends for the A through F
          │ ( ) Stack   ║              data ranges.
          │ ( ) Pie     ║  Format      Determines the appearance of lines
          │ ( ) HLCO    ║              in graphs.
          │ ( ) Mixed   ║  Titles      Adds graph and axis titles.
          └─────────    ║  Grid        Adds or removes graph grid lines.
          ┌─Frame─────  ║  Scale       Determines axis scaling, controls
          │ [x] Left    ║              the appearance of numbers along an
          │ [x] Right   ║              axis, and controls the number of
          │ [x] Top     ║              x-axis labels 1-2-3 displays.
          │ [x] Botto   ║  Color       Displays and prints graphs in color
                        ║              on a color monitor and printer. ↓ ║
                        ╠═══F1=Index═══╦══F3=Keys═══╦══F8=Back══╦══ESC=Quit╣
                            Press F2 (EDIT) to edit settings
20
01-Jun-92  04:01 PM
```

▶ WINDOWS INTERFACES

If the variety of user interfaces for application software seems confusing, it's understandable. This may be an important reason why Microsoft Windows and Windows applications have gained a large following. One of the basic premises of Windows is to provide a standard interface for all Windows applications so that users who become familiar with one program will find that other Windows programs use similar interfaces.

Windows programs are launched by double clicking on an icon in the Program Manager screen. When a program, such as Microsoft Excel, is run the user sees a screen layout that has similarities to other Windows software. Although each program will have unique characteristics and operations, there are many components that are the same in each program.

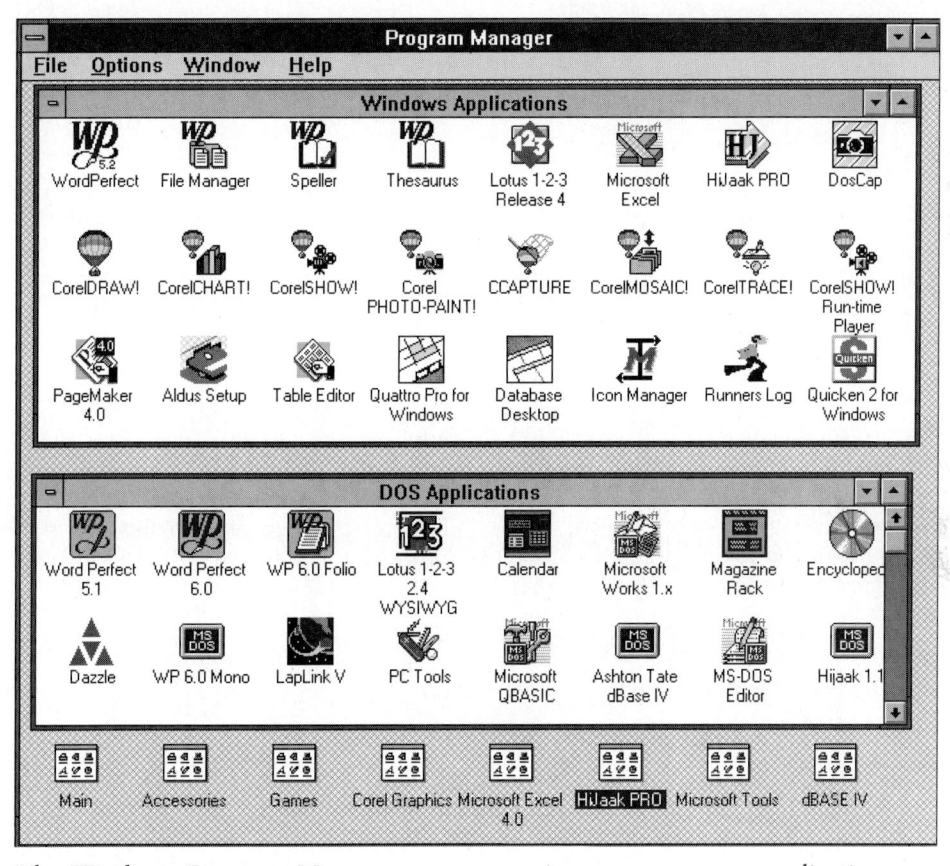

The Windows Program Manager screen uses icons to represent application programs. Double clicking on an icon launches the application.

Menus are activated in the same way in every Windows application. The menu bar is located near the top of the screen and a selection is made by clicking on a name such as File, Edit, or Window. Alternately the menu choice may be made by pressing Alt and the underlined letter in the menu name. For example, pressing Alt+F activates the File menu. Using either method causes a pull-down menu to appear.

When the File menu is activated, common input/output activities are identified which are standard in all Windows applications. Entries such as New, Open, Close are common to most programs. So are Save, Print, and Exit. Some

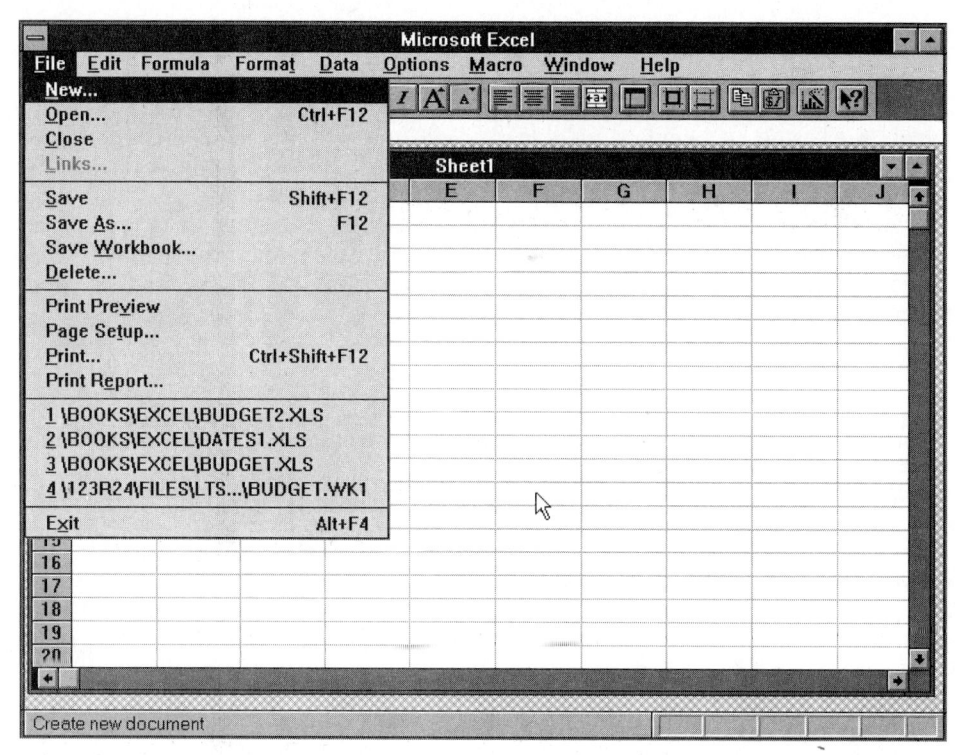

The File menu in Excel is similar to File menus in all Windows applications.

menu options are followed by an ellipsis (. . .) which means that this menu choice will lead to another menu or a dialog box.

A menu choice such as Open . . . leads to a dialog box. A dialog box is another standard Windows interface that is common to Windows applications. Operations such as Save As, Open, and Print all lead to similar dialog boxes that are unique to the operation yet have standard features for their use. Dialog boxes contain one or more of the following components:

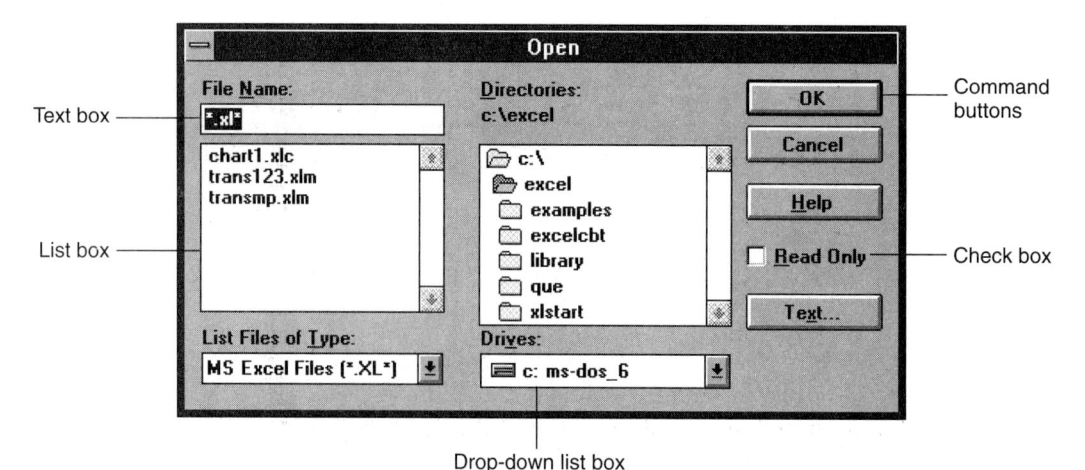

Text box is used for typing text such as a filename.

List box contains a list of items, such as a list of filenames, from which you make a choice.

Drop-down list box is a list that uses limited space in the dialog box. When you click on the downward pointing arrow the list box drops down, revealing the choices you can make.

Command buttons are clicked on to tell the program to take a specific action. Typical actions are OK, to proceed with the operation; Cancel, to cancel the use of the dialog box; and Help, to give help on the use of this box.

Check box is checked to select a software feature.

Option buttons are used to choose a program option. They are similar to a check box except that only one option may be made, whereas multiple check boxes may be selected.

Windows menus are a common interface in each program. A menu choice is made by clicking on an option such as Contents in this Help menu. Alternately the user can use the cursor keys to move the highlight bar to the choice and press Enter. Choices also contain an underlined letter which may be typed to make the menu choice.

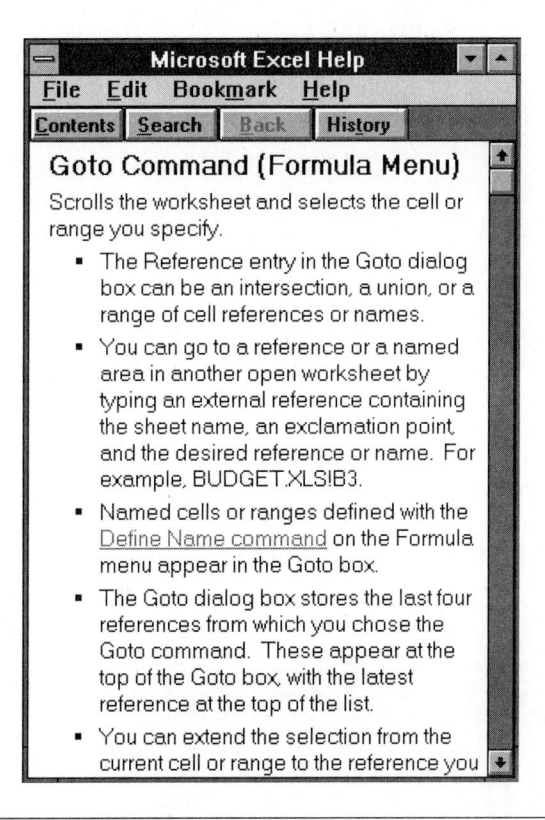

In this example, an Excel Help box is displayed. Again the Help system used in Windows applications is standardized to ease the transition from one program to another. Features such as a list of help contents, a menu bar for choosing other information, and a button bar for doing a word search or looking at a history of your Help choices are common to Windows applications.

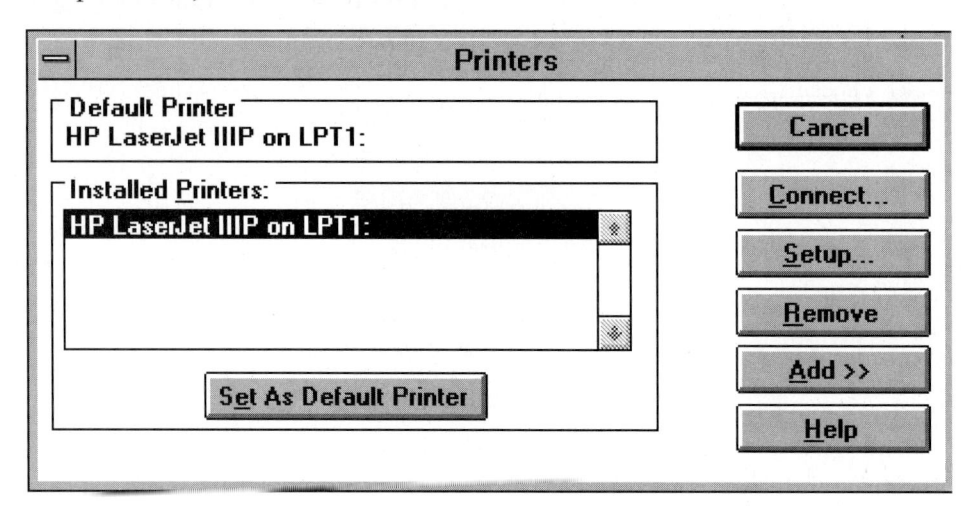

A common activity in most programs is printing. Again, this is an area where Windows offers standardization. The Printer Setup box is common to all applications because Windows uses a Print Manager program that manages printing from every program in the system.

By using common interfaces in each Windows program the learning curve for using new software is decreased once the computer user has learned to use a single Windows application. Features such as menus, dialog boxes, and setup boxes function in the same way, so once you know how to use them in one program you understand their use in every program.

INSTALLING SOFTWARE

Software meant for the PC should run on all computers without any user modification. True or False? In many instances, this statement is false because the software needs to be **installed** on a specific computer system configuration before it can be used. Software often depends on the memory size of the computer, the type of screen whether monochrome or color, low or high resolution, whether a mouse will be used for interaction, and the type of printer to be used for reports or graphs. Until the program has been installed, many of these features will either not work or will function incorrectly.

Install program. A program that assists in installing and customizing software to the specific needs of the user.

INSTALL PROGRAMS

Many software packages come with an **install program** that helps the user to identify the unique features of his or her computer. By typing the com-

CHAPTER 7 Application Software

mand INSTALL, or some similar name, the procedure for installing the software on your computer is begun. Figure 7-17 shows a screen from Lotus 1–2–3's install program. Programs such as this one take the user step by step through the installation procedure. The better written install programs require very little technical knowledge on the part of the user, and many are able to detect the type of hardware used on the system where the program is installed. For special features the install program will use prompts or menus so the user merely needs to select the options that apply to the computer in use or their preferences for using the program.

Device Drivers

Some input or output devices are so different from one another that software companies must provide a **device driver** with the install disk to give information about the device. To some extent screens have this problem. There are both monochrome and color screens, and a variety of resolutions in each category and different graphic adaptor boards may be used for these screens. Thus, a device driver is needed to provide all of the data required by the program to correctly display information on the screen.

Printers are especially notorious for having differences. With the widespread capabilities for draft or letter quality, enhanced or compressed print-

Device driver. Software that supplies the information needed to use a specific device, such as a printer, with the application program.

FIGURE 7-17
An install screen for use when installing Lotus 1–2–3 on a personal computer. This screen provides options for first time installation and for updating the program if the computer's configuration has been changed.

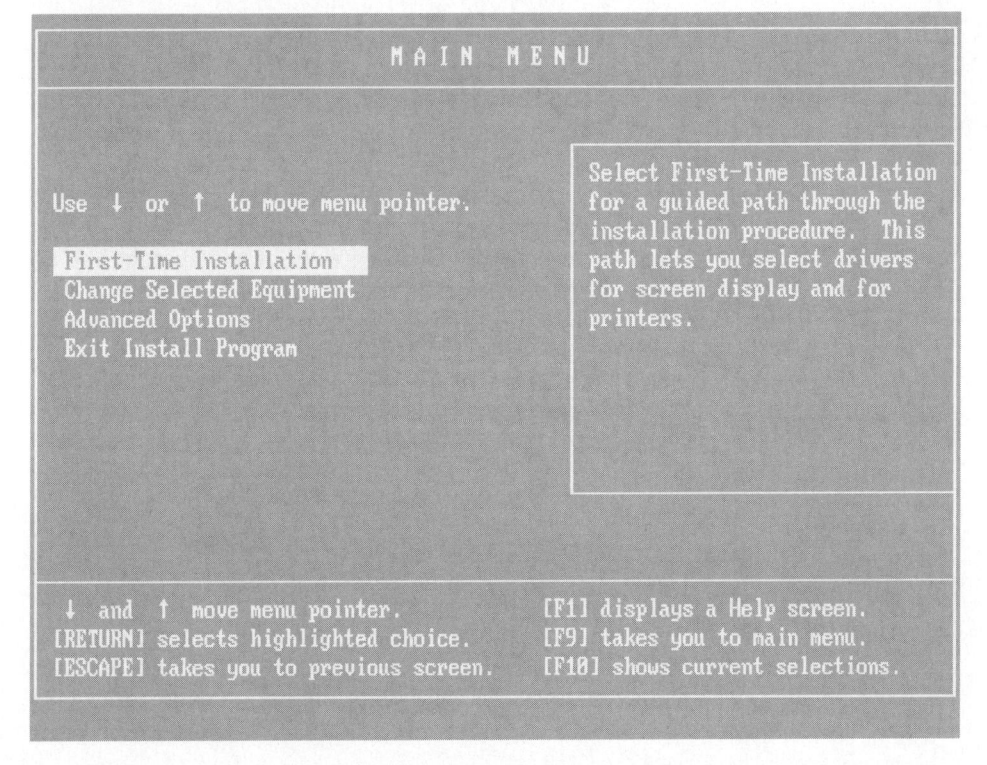

```
                        MAIN MENU


  Use ↓ or ↑ to move menu pointer.    Select First-Time Installation
                                      for a guided path through the
  ┌─────────────────────────┐         installation procedure. This
  │ First-Time Installation │         path lets you select drivers
  └─────────────────────────┘         for screen display and for
    Change Selected Equipment         printers.
    Advanced Options
    Exit Install Program






  ↓ and ↑ move menu pointer.        [F1] displays a Help screen.
  [RETURN] selects highlighted choice.  [F9] takes you to main menu.
  [ESCAPE] takes you to previous screen.  [F10] shows current selections.
```

ing, italics, graphics, super- and subscripts, line drawing, and so on, printers must be precisely defined in the program. To make matters worse, printers often use different commands from one another to activate the same feature. Recently there has been some standardization such as the Epson standard and the IBM standard, but even these companies don't follow their own standards absolutely.

Default Settings

Sometimes a software publisher will supply the software with the programs preset for a certain set of specifications. It may for example assume that the program will be run on a computer with a monochrome screen, use two floppy disk drives, and have an Epson compatible printer. These **default settings** may permit the software to be used immediately without the need to go through a special installation procedure unless your computer system differs from this norm.

A second meaning for default settings refers to features inside the software. For example, a word processor may have defaults for line spacing, margin settings, line justification, and so on. If the user wants different settings, then a command in the program will need to be entered at the time the setting is to be changed. Changing defaults such as these allows users to customize the software to their own needs.

Default. A normal state in the program that is used by the software unless changed by the user.

APPLICATION SOFTWARE AND YOU

We have seen that to run application software you must first load the operating system and then an application program may be loaded for your specific needs. Using a program requires that you know the specific commands or procedures for that package. These commands may be found in the documentation that comes with the software, by the use of menus, function keys, icons, or other form of user interface, or through the program's Help system. Because each computer has a different mix of components, software must first be installed to match the specifications of the system and to adapt it to user requirements. In the next chapter we will look at some of the specific details of application software used with personal computers.

CHAPTER SUMMARY

1. DOS is a **resident** program that occupies memory while another program is running on the computer.
2. Seven major software categories are: productivity software, business systems, database management, communications software, artificial intelligence, educational, and home systems.
3. **Software packages** typically include one or more of the following: diskettes, manuals, keyboard template, quick reference guide, and a warranty card.

4. A large program often exists in several parts. There is the main program and one or more overlay programs. There may also be overlays for help files, messages, and menus.
5. Using an application program can be considerably less costly and less time consuming compared to writing your own. Spreadsheet or database packages can also be a better way of implementing a solution rather than using a traditional programming language.
6. A keyboard **template** fits over the function keys to tell the user of a software package how each function is used. Functions may also be available with the Ctrl, Shift, and Alt keys.
7. A **mouse** may be used with some software for making selections from a menu or GUI instead of the keyboard.
8. A **menu** offers a list of choices on the screen from which the user makes a selection by typing a number or character. A mnemonic character has built-in meaning such as P for Print.
9. **Cursor pointing,** in software such as Lotus 1–2–3, is used to make a selection from a menu.
10. **Multilevel menus** are used to narrow the number of choices and to group them into meaningful categories.
11. **Pull-down menus** come down from the top of the screen and **pop-up menus** appear in the middle of the screen. Their use can require fewer keystrokes to make a choice.
12. **Function keys** are used by some software as a primary means for making program selections.
13. **Prompts** are used to query the user about an operation and often require a yes or no response or an entry such as a file name.
14. **Commands** require the user to know and enter the command needed for a specific action. There is no help, prompting, or list of choices presented. Command-driven applications are harder to learn but can be faster to use after the commands are known.
15. **Form filling** is a technique that presents a screen looking like a form where empty spaces are filled with data. As data are entered the cursor moves from field to field to prompt for the next entry.
16. A **graphical user interface (GUI)** uses icons to present a graphic image on the screen that represents a file, notepad, disk, printer, or an action that will be taken when selecting that icon. Icon software works best with a mouse.
17. **Help** screens may be accessed by one or more keystrokes to get information about a program feature. **Context sensitive help** gives information directly about the operation you are working on at the time that help is requested.
18. An **install program** is run to identify the unique features of a user's computer and to adapt the software to the screen, printer, and other user needs.
19. **Device drivers** are files that provide information during installation about specific screens, printers, and plotters.
20. **Default settings** refer to options that will ordinarily be used when software is run. For example, defaults may be used for single spacing or right justification unless the user requests otherwise.

IMPORTANT TERMS AND CONCEPTS

Application package
Command
Context sensitive
Default setting
Device driver
DOS prompt
Form filling
Function keys
Graphical User Interface (GUI)
Help system
Icon
Install program
Keyboard template
Main program

Manual
Menu
Mnemonic
Multilevel menus
Overlay program
Pop-up menu
Programming language
Prompt
Pull-down menu
Quick reference guide
Resident
Software package
Warranty card

SELF-TESTING QUESTIONS

Fill-In

1. It is necessary to _____ DOS before application software can be run on the computer.
2. A software _____ is usually supplied with a manual, disks, reference card, a warranty, and a keyboard template.
3. To select an icon with the mouse you point to the icon and _____ the left mouse button.
4. _____ provide a list of options from which a selection is made.
5. Software such as Lotus 1–2–3 lets you use either the _____ key to point at a specific choice or to type the first letter of the entry.
6. A _____ menu, such as in dBASE IV, shows two levels of choices: a main menu at the top of the screen and one that drops down to show a submenu.
7. Software that uses _____ keys often supplies a template to show the options available on the keyboard.
8. A _____ shows an icon representing the selection to be made from the software.
9. Running an _____ program is often necessary to have access to the full features of a program and to customize it for your computer's screen, printer, and other devices.
10. A device _____ is often needed to match the software to the specific printer or screen used on your computer.

True/False

1. Writing a program is usually a reasonable alternative to buying a software package.

2. Keyboard commands typically vary from one software package to another.
3. A mouse is used in software that cannot access the keyboard for input.
4. A menu is a message or query that asks the user for a response or a specific command.
5. An icon is a symbol used on the screen to select certain features of the program.
6. A keyboard template is only required when the mouse is provided as an alternative to keyboard use.
7. Context sensitive help is a new technique that is only available to users of Windows application software.
8. Default settings in a program can help to get the program up and running faster than if you need to create your own settings.

ANSWERS

Fill-In: 1. boot, 2. package, 3. click, 4. Menus, 5. cursor, 6. pull-down, 7. function, 8. Graphical User Interface, 9. install, 10. driver

True/False: 1. F, 2. T, 3. F, 4. F, 5. T, 6. F, 7. F, 8. T

Questions for Critical Thinking

1. Software such as WordPerfect, dBASE IV, and Lotus 1–2–3 use different commands and user interfaces. Discuss how this might affect users when using a variety of software packages.
2. Recent software has incorporated both menus and icons for the user interface. Discuss the pros and cons of each interface and give an opinion on which one you think would be easier and more productive to use.
3. Discuss which should come first in a computer purchase decision: the hardware, the operating system, or the application software.
4. Whether you are buying a word processor, spreadsheet, or database, there are many different packages to choose from. Develop a list of general principles that might be suitable to follow when choosing any software package.

CHAPTER 8
WORD PROCESSING AND DESKTOP PUBLISHING

A VIEW OF THE CHAPTER AHEAD

After reading this chapter you will understand

- ▶ the concepts and uses of word processing.
- ▶ the stages of word processing from text entry to printing a document.
- ▶ the basic features available in word processing software packages.
- ▶ the features provided by Windows-based word processors.
- ▶ the concepts and uses of desktop publishing.

INTRODUCTION

Money Concepts is a company that provides financial advice, personal financial planning, retirement planning, and investment vehicles for its clients across the United States, Canada, Australia, New Zealand, and the United Kingdom. As a franchise organization, the Money Concepts Canadian head office in Mississauga, Ontario supports the activities of franchises across Canada. Naturally, a company of this kind processes a lot of paperwork and, to assist in the operation, personal computers are used extensively. For the preparation of letters, memos, legal documents, and contracts, WordPerfect is the word processor of choice in the head office. For other documents requiring special fonts and graphics, such as business proposals, AmiPro for Windows is used. Money Concepts also publishes a newsletter for its franchisees and for this application Ventura Publisher, a desktop publishing program, is the primary software package used.

One of the first applications for which a computer is used in the office is word processing, which as a result is the number one category of software used on personal computers and is frequently the application that prompts the purchase of a first computer. While the typewriter has not totally met its demise in many offices, the PC, with word processing software, is fast becoming the productivity tool of choice in today's modern businesses such as Money Concepts.

THE BENEFITS OF WORD PROCESSING

Word processor. A computer program that aids in the typing, editing, and formatting of text ranging from memos to book length manuscripts.

Unlike the typewriter, when a word processing package is used, a draft copy of a document can easily be made, corrections and changes noted on the page (Figure 8-1), and then the changes are made in the original by using the word processor again. A new copy of the document is then printed by the computer without the need to retype words or lines that were originally correct. The time saving over using a typewriter can be dramatic.

Beyond the editing of a document, which is a relatively simple procedure, word processors can be used for a variety of applications such as preparing camera-ready copy for publishing, newsletters, or announcements. By using advanced features such as graphics, line drawing, and multiple columns, sophisticated documents can be prepared and printed right on the PC. The resulting text is then duplicated for use directly in a publication without the need for typesetting, which can be time consuming and costly.

STAGES OF WORD PROCESSING

The user of a word processing system soon recognizes a pattern of activities or a cycle that is followed. These stages are essentially the same for every word processor, although the specific actions taken may differ and they may not proceed in an orderly fashion. The stages (Figure 8-2) are entering

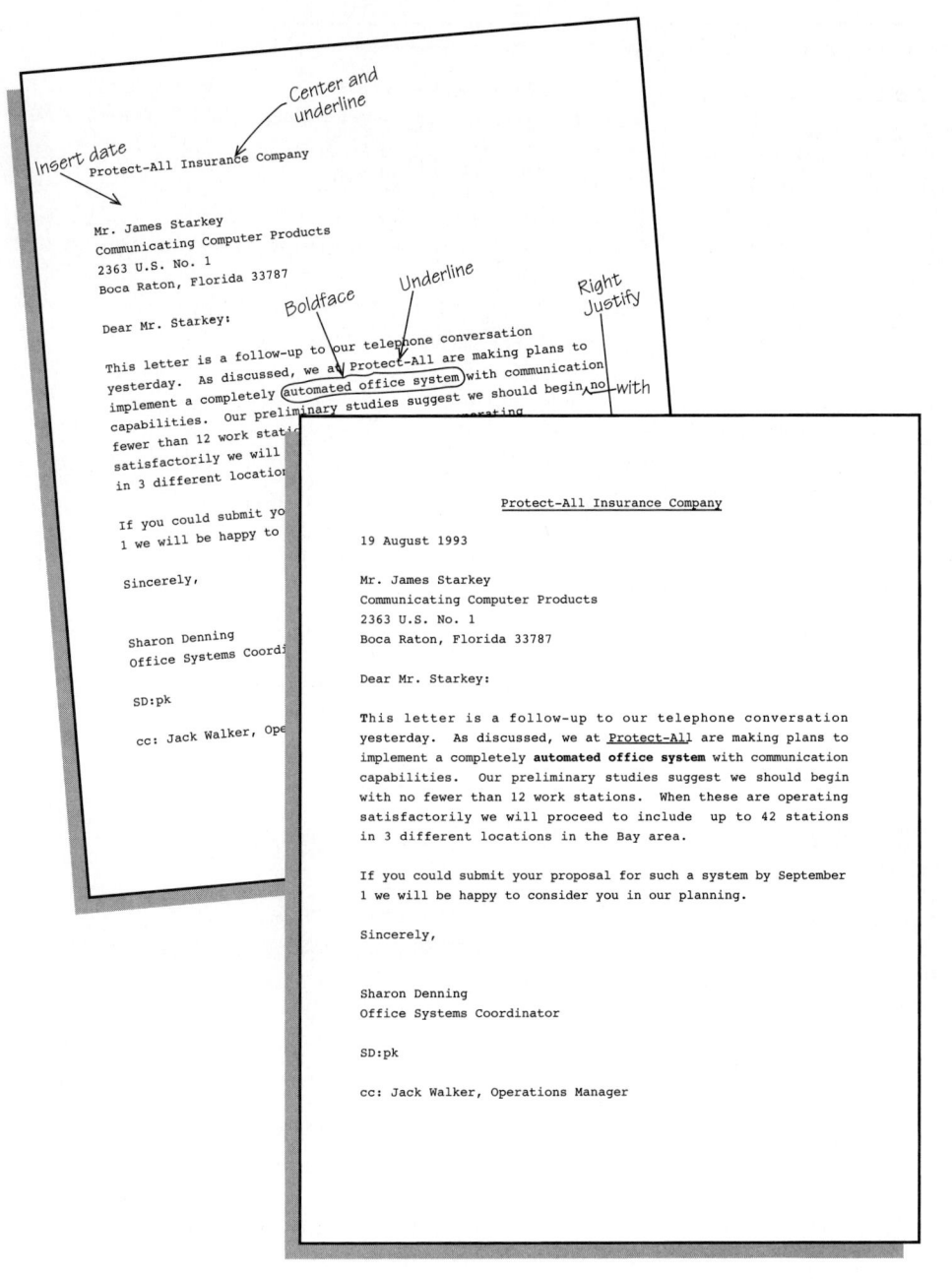

FIGURE 8-1
A draft copy of a document is printed from the word processor. Changes are noted in writing on the document and then keyed into the word processor. Correct text does not need to be reentered, only the changes need to be typed. Finally the computer prints a copy of the new version of the document.

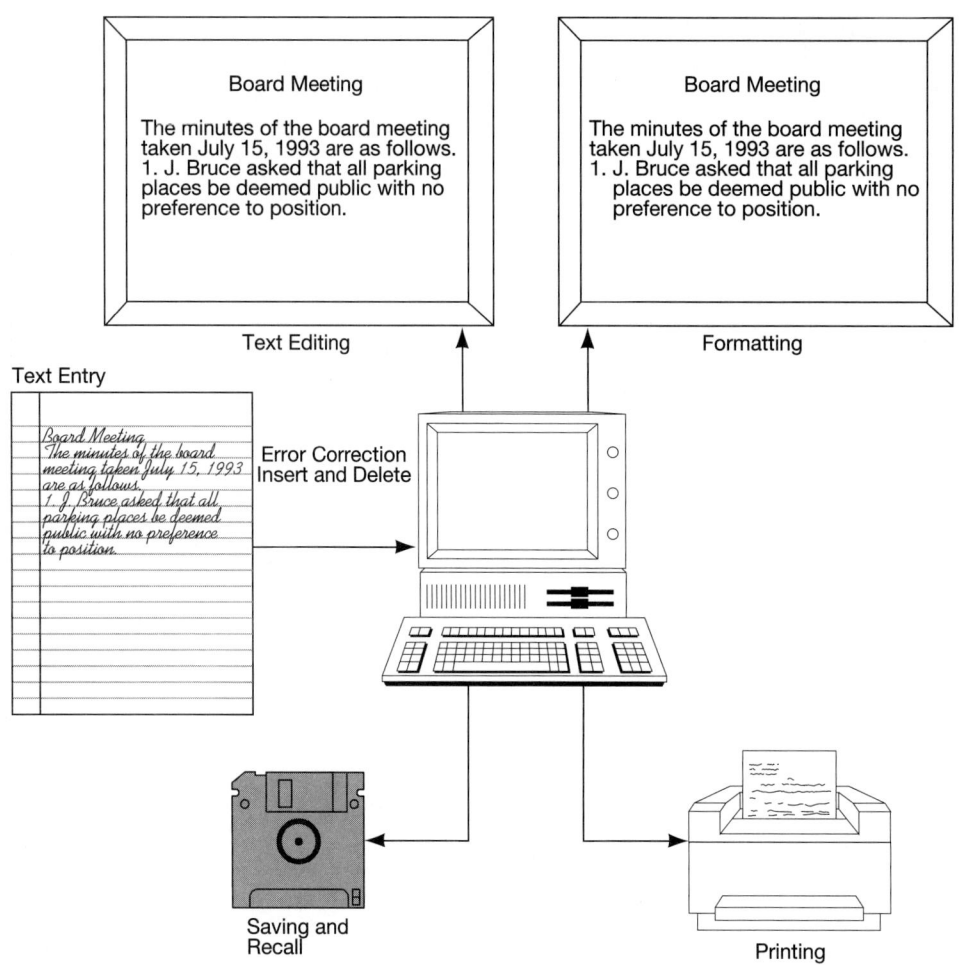

FIGURE 8-2
The stages of word processing from original text entry to the final printing of the document.

text, editing, print formatting, printing, and saving or recalling the text to or from disk.

- **Text entry.** The first stage in the process is to enter the text of the document into the word processor. This is usually done by typing the contents on the keyboard making minor corrections as you go.
- **Editing.** The next stage is to edit the document until it is in the final form desired. To edit the document you may rewrite parts of the text, **delete** sections that are no longer required, or **insert** new words, sentences, or paragraphs. A good word processor will save text you delete in a buffer so it can be easily restored if the deletion was done by mistake or you have a change of heart.

Cut and paste. The process of removing text from one location in a document and inserting it in a new location.

Most word processors will also permit you to **move** or **cut and paste** text from one location to another in the document. Similar to the move is the ability to **copy** text. This editing operation can save a lot of typing if the same material is required several places in the text. Using the **search and replace** feature automates the replacement of many occurrences of the same word, such as replacing all uses of the word "document" with the word "manuscript."

- **Print formatting.** Print formatting is preparing the text for printing and affects how the document will look when it is printed. The main features are line spacing and margin settings. You can also select from a ragged right margin (letter style) or right margin justification (book style). Some word processors will also provide for **proportional** spacing, where each letter occupies a different width similar to that in a typeset document. Formatting typically provides for **underlining** and **boldface** of characters and different typefaces such as **condensed** or **expanded** print. Many word processors now provide for access to laser printers with a variety of type **fonts**. Another feature is the ability to include **header** and **footer** lines automatically on each page, as well as automatic page numbering.
- **Printing.** When the document has been developed to the satisfaction of the user, it is ready for printing. Usually this is a simple command that activates the printing operation. Many users like to print a **draft** copy (sometimes using the high-speed draft mode of a dot matrix printer) before all formatting is complete. The draft copy is then marked with changes, which are made in the word processor prior to printing the final copy.
- **Saving or retrieving text.** When the document has been typed, then it is usually saved on disk so it may be retrieved at a later time for reference or changes. Saving a document is simply a matter of entering the save command, which is usually one or two keystrokes, and then giving the document a file name that will identify it on the disk. At a later time the document may be recalled from disk by entering the retrieve command. You are then prompted to type the name of the file or to point at it from a list of file names. The document is retrieved from disk and presented on the screen where additional editing, formatting, or printing may be done before it is once again saved on disk.

THE LANGUAGE OF WORD PROCESSING

Part of the task of learning to use a word processor effectively is to become familiar with its language. This is true of any skill, isn't it? Even learning to drive a car requires us to know the meaning of terms like yield, caution, one way, and so on. These are familiar terms to most people and we often understand them intuitively because of our constant exposure to them.

Some terms in word processing are likewise familiar, but many are unique to word processing software and need to be understood to use the package successfully. In this section we will discuss the concepts by using WordPerfect, one of the leading word processors today. Once we know the terminology and gain some experience in one word processor, it is fairly easy to learn a second or other word processing language.

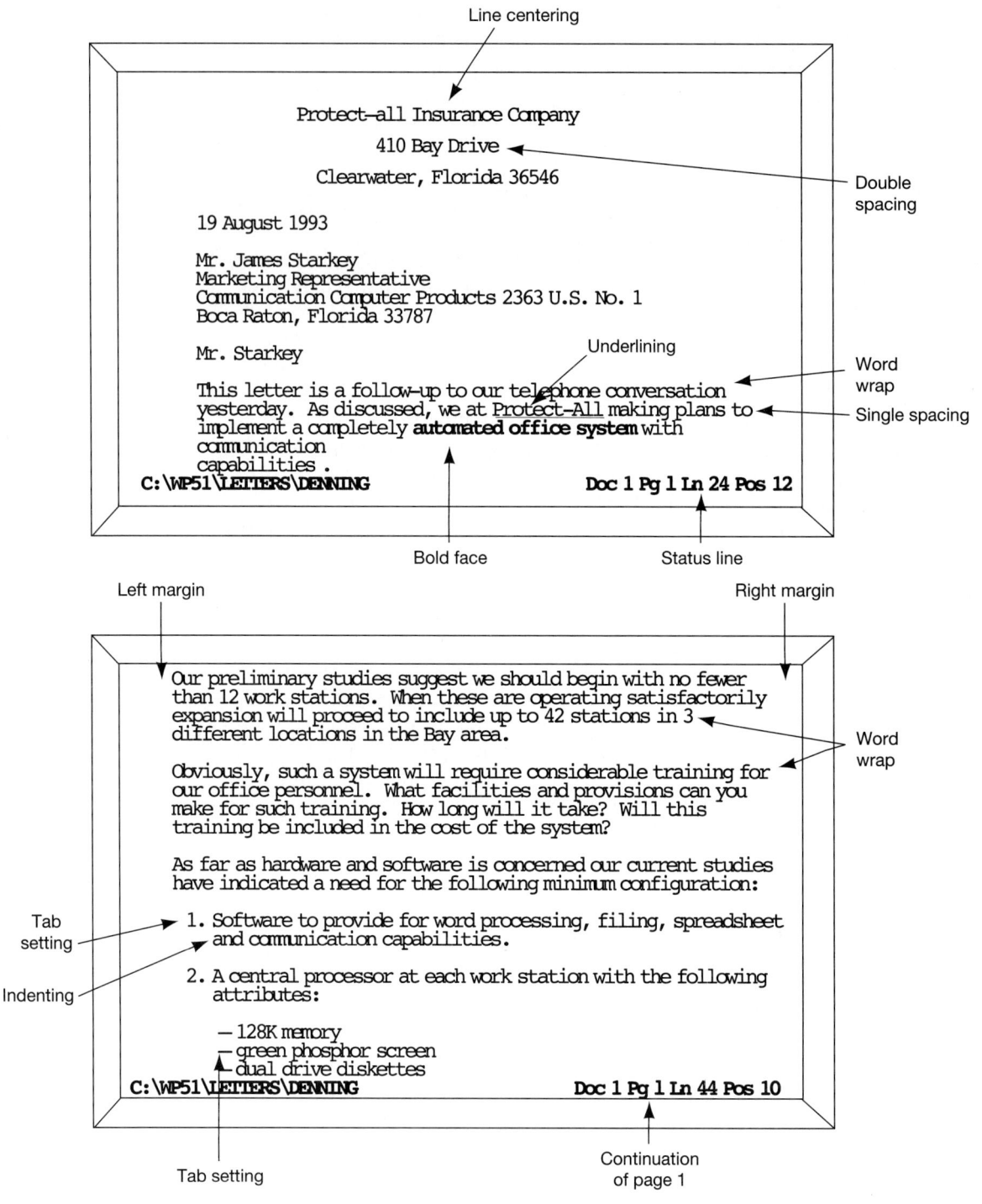

FIGURE 8-3
Screens showing parts of a letter as it appears in WordPerfect. This screen shows some of the basic elements of a text created with a word processor. (Software WordPerfect 5.1 courtesy of WordPerfect Corporation.)

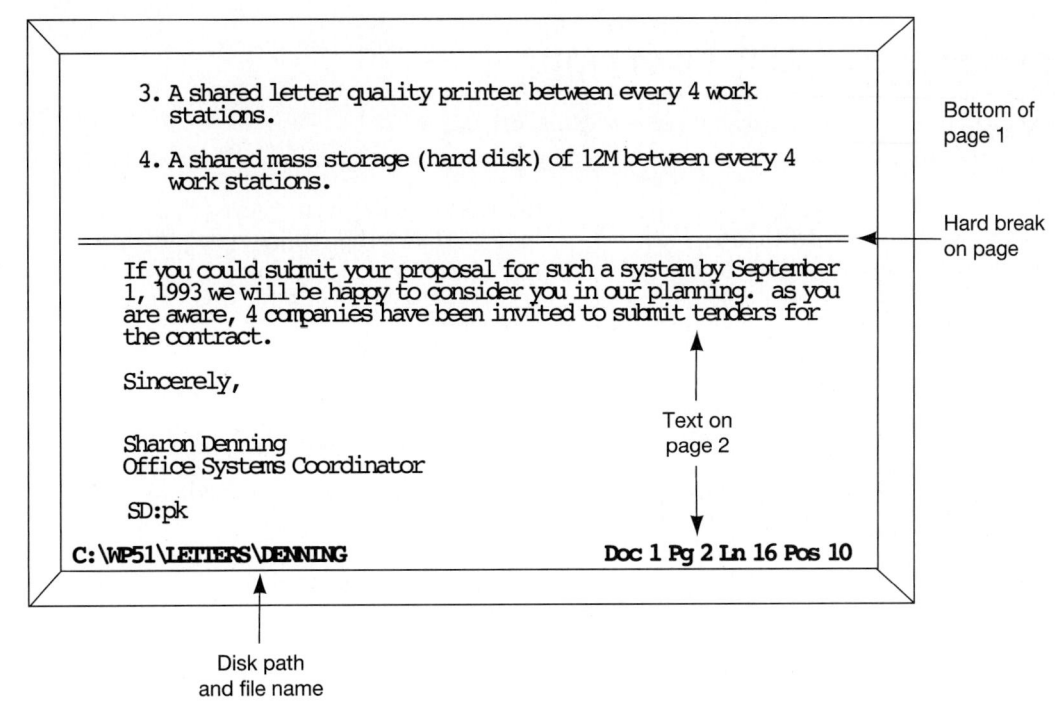

```
          3. A shared letter quality printer between every 4 work       Bottom of
             stations.                                                  page 1
          4. A shared mass storage (hard disk) of 12M between every 4
             work stations.
     ═══════════════════════════════════════════════════════════  ◄──   Hard break
                                                                        on page
       If you could submit your proposal for such a system by September
       1, 1993 we will be happy to consider you in our planning.  as you
       are aware, 4 companies have been invited to submit tenders for
       the contract.

       Sincerely,
                                                            Text on
       Sharon Denning                                       page 2
       Office Systems Coordinator

       SD:pk

       C:\WP51\LETTERS\DENNING                 Doc 1 Pg 2 Ln 16 Pos 10
                 ▲
                 │
              Disk path
           and file name
```

FIGURE 8-3 (Cont.)

The screen displays in Figure 8-3 show a letter that has been typed using WordPerfect. This letter occupies three screens but when it prints will require only one full page and part of a second. Because computer screens generally show only 25 lines or less, even one page of printout will require two or more screens to display the document.

These screens show a number of features used in word processing. First is the difference between **single spacing**, which is useful for letters, and **double spacing**, which can also be used in letters but more often is used for reports or manuscripts. **Word wrap** is an automatic feature of most word processors. As a paragraph is typed, the cursor will automatically move to the next line as soon as the current line is filled. A word that may have started on the previous line, but is too long to fit, will automatically be brought (wrapped) to the next line. **Line centering** is used to automatically center a heading on the line as it is typed.

At the bottom of the screen is a **status line**, which shows the name of the document being edited, the document number (for split screen use), page number, line, and cursor position. Some word processors show a status line at the top of the screen, while others display a menu that includes status information.

The double line across the screen represents a **hard page break** meaning that the user forced the page break to occur at a specific line. If a hard break is not requested, the word processor will create a **soft page break** automatically when a page is full. In WordPerfect a soft break is shown by displaying a single line across the screen.

Left and **right** margins in WordPerfect 5.1 are set automatically to 1

▶ WORD PROCESSING FEATURES

Ragged Right Margin

Traveler's checks were devised by the American Express Company in 1891 to protect travelers who might otherwise carry large amounts of cash that could be lost or stolen.

Justified Right Margin

Traveler's checks were devised by the American Express Company in 1891 to protect travelers who might otherwise carry large amounts of cash that could be lost or stolen.

Using a Tab

1. Traveler's checks are accepted as payment almost everywhere in the world; they can also be converted into cash and are redeemable in foreign currencies according to the prevailing rate of exchange.

Using an Indent

    Traveler's checks are accepted as payment almost everywhere in the world; they can also be converted into cash and are redeemable in foreign currencies according to the prevailing rate of exchange.

Bold Font - 12 Point

Traveler's checks are accepted as payment almost everywhere in the world.

Single Spacing

Traveler's checks were devised by the American Express Company in 1891 to protect travelers who might otherwise carry large amounts of cash that could be lost or stolen.

Double Spacing

Traveler's checks were devised by the American Express Company in 1891 to protect travelers who might otherwise carry large amounts of cash that could be lost or stolen.

Bold Font - 18 Point

Traveler's checks are accepted as payment almost everywhere in the world.

Subscript and Superscript

Subscript$_1$ and Superscript^2

▶ PHOTO ESSAY—WORDPERFECT FOR WINDOWS

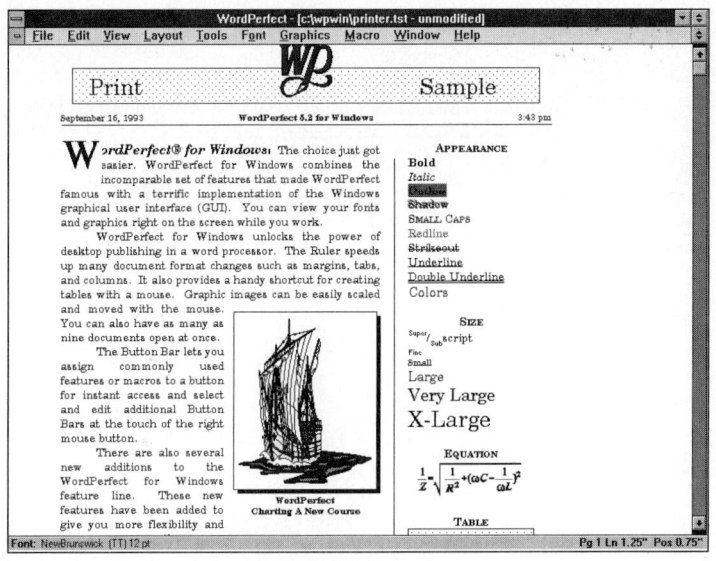

WordPerfect for Windows displays text, graphics, different fonts, and other features on screen as you work.

Combining text and graphics with the standard user interfaces offered by Windows, several leading word processor publishers are offering a new breed of word processor. One of these is Wordperfect for Windows which displays text with a variety of fonts, graphics, lines, multiple columns, and equations all in the same document.

As you write with WordPerfect for Windows the screen display will closely match the way the text will appear when it is printed. As shown here in the sample document WordPerfect uses for printer testing, all of these special features display in the edit screen.

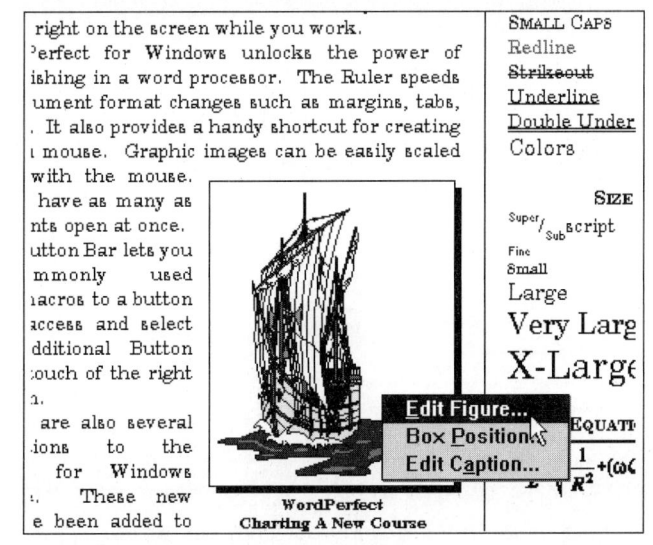

Click the right mouse button to edit a graphic image.

Graphics may be easily inserted anywhere in the text and the result immediately displays on the screen. Graphics may be moved or sized by dragging a corner or edge of the image with the mouse pointer. Clicking on the graphic with the right mouse button brings up a menu where the user can choose to edit the figure, change the box position, or edit the caption.

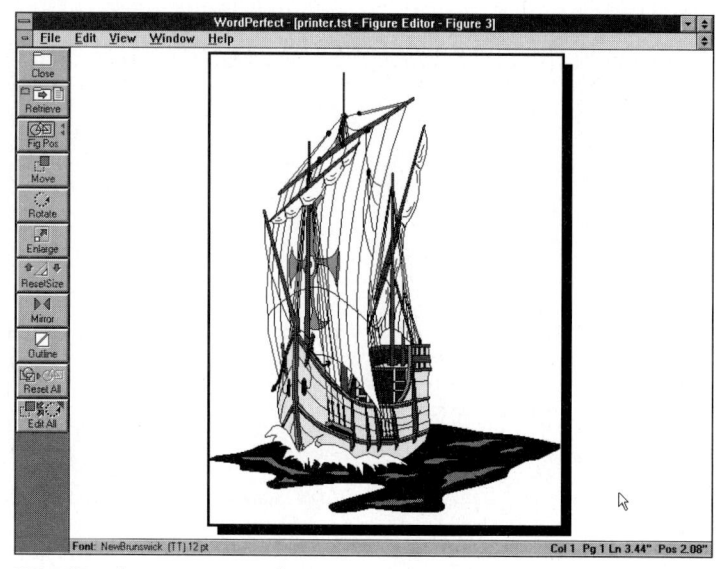

WordPerfect's Figure Editor.

Choosing the Figure Editor provides a screen that retrieves a graphic from a disk file and displays the entire graphic for further processing. A graphic may be sized, rotated, moved, changed to black and white, a caption may be added, and other display options selected.

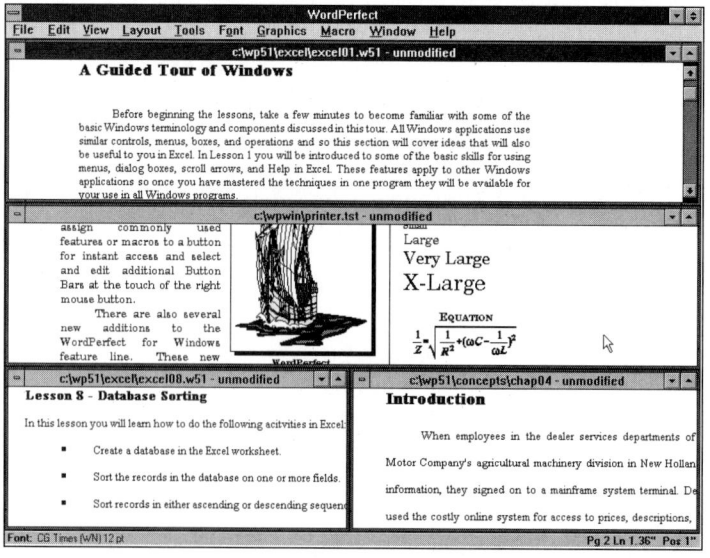

Using tiled windows to display the contents of two different documents.

CHAPTER 8 Word Processing and Desktop Publishing

In WordPerfect you can open as many as nine document windows to show different documents or different parts of the same document. Windows can be cascaded one behind the other or tiled as shown in this figure. Information can be selected in one document and cut and pasted or copied to another document in one easy process. WordPerfect for Windows also supports object linking and embedding (OLE) to link objects from other applications to your document.

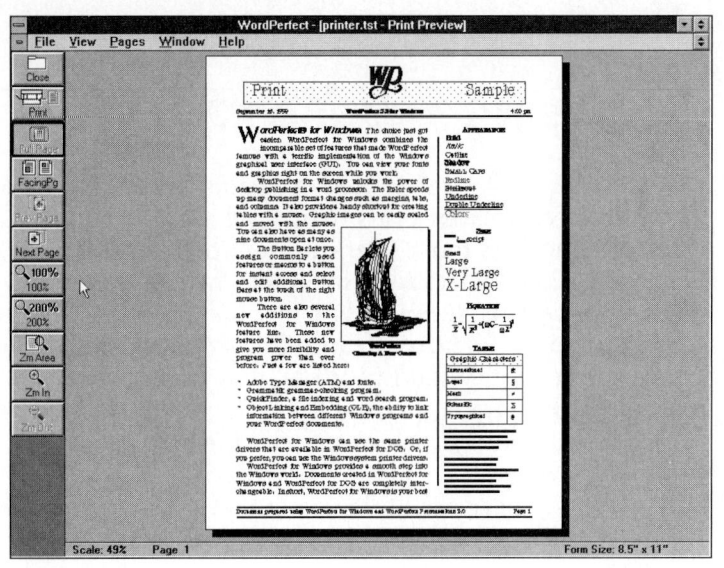

Displaying a full page in WordPerfect for Windows' print preview screen.

Before printing a document, the Print Preview screen can be used to show how the final result will appear. The button bar lets you select a full page, half a page (100%), or an even smaller portion for a close-up look (200%) at the results. Zoom buttons let you select a specific portion of the screen to look at in the very finest of detail. Other buttons are used to display the next or previous page of the document or to print the final result.

Frequently used operations in WordPerfect can be added to a button bar at the top of the screen. Instead of selecting the File menu to save a document, the procedure is reduced to simply clicking on the Save button. Similar activities such as Printing a document or Opening a file are also included. The WordPerfect user may also add her own special features that are used frequently to the button bar.

inch, leaving room for blank margins on both sides of the paper. These settings can be changed at will to either narrower or wider settings.

Some text, such as the list of four points beginning on the second screen, looks better if indented. **Indenting** is a feature on a word processor where the text word wraps to the indent position which is normally defined several columns past the starting position of the first line.

Tab settings are preset on most word processors to every five columns.

Tabs are like the tab setting on a typewriter and use the tab key to quickly move to a preset tab stop. Tab settings may be removed or reset by entering a few keystrokes.

These features, or others similar to them, are provided by most word processors, but many go well beyond these basic features, providing a higher level of productivity for the user. However, a longer training time is then needed to learn to use the software.

CHOOSING A WORD PROCESSOR

The DOS-based word processor against which most others are compared is WordPerfect because of its many and varied features as well as its excellent performance for most operations. When choosing a word processor there are several considerations including features, performance, and price. For some, price will be important because it can vary from less than $50 to $500 or more for a full-featured system. Executive word processors, such as LetterPerfect, Windows Write, and Lotus Write, are often a good choice for someone who is a casual user. These have limited features, are generally easy to use, and are low priced. Professional word processors, such as AmiPro, Word for Windows, and WordPerfect, are full-featured word processors. These are more costly and take longer to learn but offer extensive capability for the most sophisticated users.

Early word processors were either **function key driven**, such as WordPerfect, or **menu driven**, such as WordStar. More recently, word processors have combined the advantages of both types of user interfaces. WordPerfect can be used with function keys or with pull-down menus as can WordStar. Windows word processors use a **graphic user interface (GUI)** with icons that represent many of their commands.

When choosing a word processor, major attention should be given to the features that you require. Some features, such as merging form letters, may be nice, but will form letters be an important activity for you? On-screen display of page formatting (WYSIWYG) is also nice, but do you need to spend the extra hundred dollars for this feature? Of course the answers might be yes to these and many other questions, but asking them will help to rule out some word processors and include others.

Another basis for your decision is to know who developed and markets the software. This will have some bearing on the amount of support you can receive from the company should you run into difficulty. Some of the lesser known and usually inexpensive programs will not come with much in the way of manufacturer support, although some are well supported. In contrast, the larger companies typically provide toll-free lines with personnel who can answer most of your questions when you run into difficulty.

Finally, a decision for an office or company should consider compatibility with other word processors that may already exist in the company. If you intend to share files and documents with other employees, then either the same word processors should be used or ones that have utility programs to convert from one word processor to another. Similar concerns apply if electronic mail is used, if documents are to be uploaded or downloaded to

WYSIWYG. What you see is what you get. A characteristic of a word processor where the document on screen is displayed as it appears when printed.

► SOME OF THE MANY WORD PROCESSORS FOR THE PERSONAL COMPUTER

Ami Pro	Multimate	StarWriter Plus
Displaywrite	Nota Bene	Textra
Easy Extra	OfficeWriter	Webster New World Writer
Einstein Writer	Paperback Writer	WordPerfect
Final Word II	PC-Write	WordPerfect Executive
Leading Edge Word	Perfect Writer	WordPerfect for Windows
Letter Perfect	Professional Write	WordStar
Lotus Manuscript	Q&A Write	WordStar Professional
MacWrite	R Word Plus	WordStar 2000
Microsoft Word	Samna Plus IV	Write Plus for Windows
Microsoft Word for Windows	Signature	Wywrite

► WHAT TO LOOK FOR IN A WORD PROCESSOR

Word processors are available with many different strengths indicated by the type of features they contain. Some features, such as a spelling checker or mail merge, will help to determine if the program contains everything that is required of a word processor for your needs. Others, such as page or document orientation, are a matter of personal preference and operating style. This list is not meant to be absolutely complete, but to give a flavor of the features that you can find in full-featured word processors.

(Courtesy Lotus Development Corporation.)

(Courtesy WordPerfect.)

(Courtesy Microsoft.)

(Courtesy MicroPro.)

Basic Features
Cursor control
Insert—character, word, sentence, line, paragraph
Delete—character, word, sentence, line, paragraph
Block move
Block copy
Word wrap

Margin settings
Tab settings
Margin justification
Page or document orientation

Print Enhancement
Boldface
Underlining
Subscript

Superscript	Automatic figure numbering
Overprint	Graphics
Pitch change	Spelling checker
Italics	Thesaurus
Alternate fonts	Table of contents
	Mailmerge
Advanced Text Handling	Indexing
Search	Line and box drawing
Search and replace	Word processor conversion
Go to page number	Importing from spreadsheets or databases
Headers and footers	
Automatic paragraph reform	
Macros	**Windows Word Processors**
Math	Graphical User Interface (GUI)
Column blocks	Object Linking and Embedding (OLE)
	Graphics and text
Other Features	True type fonts
Outliner	Multiple file processing
Footnotes	

or from a mainframe computer, or if data from spreadsheets or databases are to be used in the word processor.

OTHER FEATURES

Many word processors provide other more advanced features that generally render them more useful to a broader range of needs. Generally, the lower priced word processors contain fewer of these capabilities than the higher priced software. However, price is not always a good indication of the variety of features that a program may have. The following material discusses some of these features.

Spelling Checkers

Spelling checker. A word processor feature that checks the accuracy of spelling in a document and suggests corrections.

A **spelling checker** is considered virtually a necessity on today's word processors. Most of the leading word processing programs include a spelling check feature as part of the package. For others, the spell check is an option or can be purchased separately from software publishers, such as Webster's New World Spelling Checker, which specializes in word processor utilities. Spelling checkers usually consist of a dictionary disk containing 80,000 to over 100,000 words. Most will allow the user to either add words to the existing dictionary or to create a personal dictionary of additional words (Figure 8-4). Some even adapt the spelling to the country where the checker is sold, so that the U.S., Canadian, or British user will get the correct spelling for the appropriate country. In many cases a special-

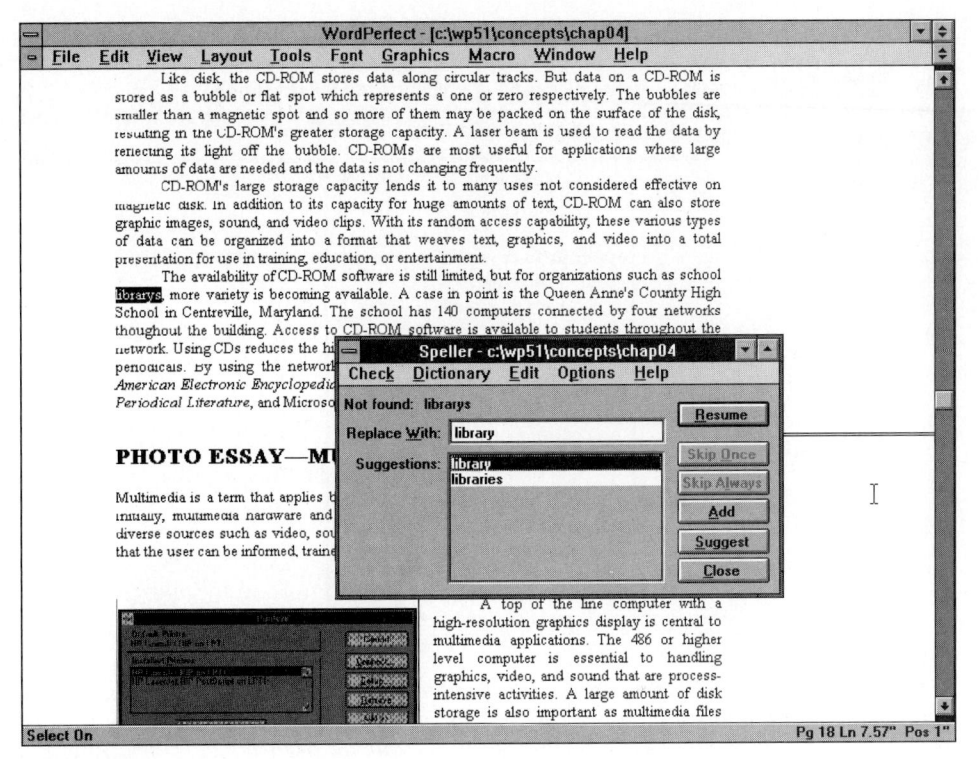

FIGURE 8-4
WordPerfect for Windows' spelling checker finds the word "librarys" is misspelled and offers a number of suggestions for the correct spelling. To select the correct spelling of "libraries" the user simply clicks on the accepted spelling and then on Replace and the word in the text is replaced with the correct one.

ized dictionary is available containing legal, medical, or other terms relating to a specific profession.

Thesaurus

A **thesaurus** is a program that provides synonyms for words in the text. The most popular of these in printed form is Roget's Thesaurus, which is used by most college students. When a thesaurus is provided for a word processor it typically contains over 100,000 synonyms. Some also contain antonyms. For word processors that do not contain a thesaurus, an add-on one may be installed from several suppliers. Some of these are Random House's Reference Set, Microlytics' Word Finder, and Webster's New World On-Line Thesaurus from Simon and Schuster, which has 20,000 root words and 120,000 synonyms.

Using a thesaurus is easy. If you have a word in the text that you would prefer to replace with one that has a similar meaning, the command to activate the thesaurus is entered when the cursor is resting on the word you want to change. The program then presents a list of words that have a simi-

Thesaurus. A word processor feature that supplies a choice of synonyms for selected words in a document.

```
the spelling to the country where the checker is sold so that the
U.S., Canadian, or British user will get the correct spelling for
the appropriate country. In many cases a specialized dictionary is
available containing legal, medical, or other terms relating to a
specific profession.
┌appropriate=(a)──────────────────────────────┐
│ 1 A ·correct              ·seize            │
│   B ·fitting              ·snatch           │
│   C ·proper                                 │
│   D ·seemly         appropriate-(ant)────── │
│   E ·suitable         5  ·improper          │
│                          ·irrelevant        │
│ 2 F ·germane                                │
│   G ·pertinent        6  ·give              │
│   H ·relevant            ·relinquish        │
│appropriate-(v)──────                        │
│ 3 I ·allocate                               │
│   J ·allot                                  │
│   K  apportion                              │
│   L ·assign                                 │
│                                             │
│ 4 M ·commandeer                             │
│   N ·grab                                   │
│1 Replace Word; 2 View Doc; 3 Look Up Word; 4 Clear Column: 0
```

FIGURE 8-5
When WordPerfect 5.1's Thesaurus is activated the word at the cursor position is checked for synonyms, which are then displayed in the first column on the screen. If there are more synonyms a second column will be used if necessary. A word from the first list, such as "relevant," may also be looked up, as shown here in the second column. The process may be repeated until a suitable word is found.

Form letter. A standard letter sent to a number of clients or customers. In word processing the form letter is the primary file and the names and addresses are the secondary file. A merge operation combines the two to create individualized letters.

Outline generator. A program that assists in creating and updating an outline prior to writing a report or lengthy document.

lar meaning, as shown in Figure 8-5. The user then selects the new word, which replaces the original in the text.

Mail Merge

The business that frequently requires a form letter to be sent to its clients can benefit immensely from the mail merge feature of some word processors. First, the text of the letter to be sent to each client is prepared as the primary file (Figure 8-6) in the word processor. A secondary file of names and addresses is also typed.

To create the form letters the merge feature of the word processor is used which automatically combines the text of the letter from the primary file and the names and addresses from the secondary file, thus producing a personalized letter for each client. Only one original letter needs to be typed and the computer does the rest of the work, thus saving many hours of laborious typing by the office staff.

Outliners

While an **outline generator** may not be very useful to an office secretary, it can be an immense aid to writers who use the computer for developing ideas and writing about them or to anyone who writes reports. An outline feature permits the writer to create a general outline of the material to be

The Primary Form Letter File

```
{FIELD}1~
{FIELD}2~
{FIELD}3~

Dear {FIELD}4~:

     We at Protect-All are making plan to implement a completely
automated office system with communication capabilities.  Our
preliminary studies suggest we should begin with no fewer than 12
work stations.  When these are operating satisfactorily we will
proceed to include up to 42 stations in 3 different
locations in the Bay area.

If you could submit your proposal for such a system by September
1 we will be happy to consider you in our planning.

Sincerely,


Sharon Denning
Office Systems Coordinator

SD: pk
cc: Jack Walker, Operations Manager
```

The Secondary Merge File

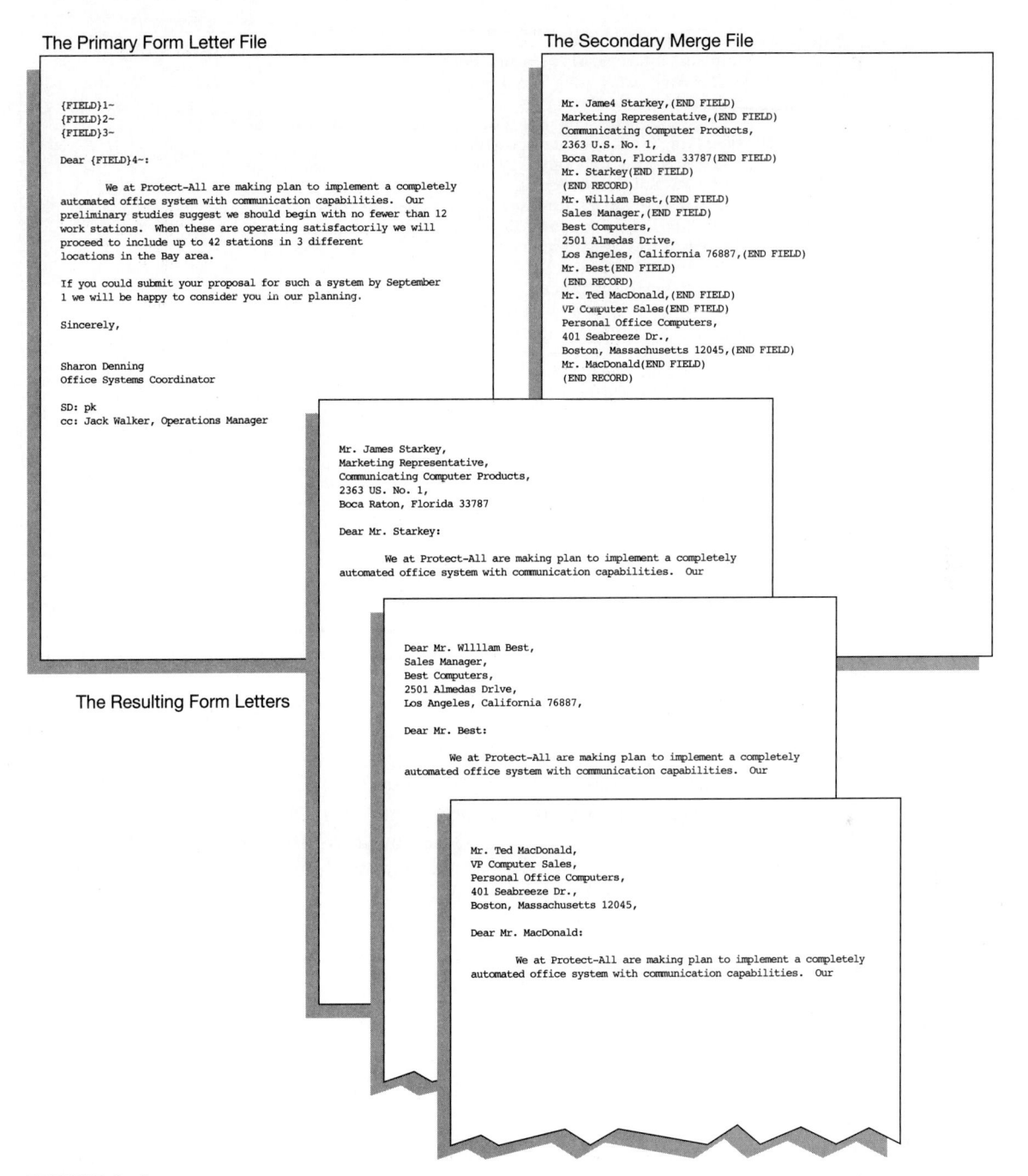

```
Mr. Jame4 Starkey,(END FIELD)
Marketing Representative,(END FIELD)
Communicating Computer Products,
2363 U.S. No. 1,
Boca Raton, Florida 33787(END FIELD)
Mr. Starkey(END FIELD)
(END RECORD)
Mr. William Best,(END FIELD)
Sales Manager,(END FIELD)
Best Computers,
2501 Almedas Drive,
Los Angeles, California 76887,(END FIELD)
Mr. Best(END FIELD)
(END RECORD)
Mr. Ted MacDonald,(END FIELD)
VP Computer Sales(END FIELD)
Personal Office Computers,
401 Seabreeze Dr.,
Boston, Massachusetts 12045,(END FIELD)
Mr. MacDonald(END FIELD)
(END RECORD)
```

The Resulting Form Letters

```
Mr. James Starkey,
Marketing Representative,
Communicating Computer Products,
2363 US. No. 1,
Boca Raton, Florida 33787

Dear Mr. Starkey:

     We at Protect-All are making plan to implement a completely
automated office system with communication capabilities.  Our
```

```
Dear Mr. Wllliam Best,
Sales Manager,
Best Computers,
2501 Almedas Drlve,
Los Angeles, California 76887,

Dear Mr. Best:

     We at Protect-All are making plan to implement a completely
automated office system with communication capabilities.  Our
```

```
Mr. Ted MacDonald,
VP Computer Sales,
Personal Office Computers,
401 Seabreeze Dr.,
Boston, Massachusetts 12045,

Dear Mr. MacDonald:

     We at Protect-All are making plan to implement a completely
automated office system with communication capabilities.  Our
```

FIGURE 8-6
Text is created in a primary file so that form letters may be printed easily from the word processor. A secondary file containing names and addresses is merged with the form letter to automatically produce the letters.

```
I. Application Development
    A. Conventional Applications Development
        1. Work Load and Overload
        2. Labor Cost
        3. Time Requirements for Applications Development
    B. User Applications Development
        1. Systems Concepts
        2. PC Software Tools
        3. Query Languages and Report Generators
        4. Decision Support Systems
    C. Information Centers
        1. User Training
        2. User Assistance
        3. Standards Administration
II. System Acquisition
    A. Proposal
    B. Management Evaluation
    C. Needs Allocation
III.




Outline                                      Doc 2 Pg 1 Ln 4" Pos 1.4"
```

FIGURE 8-7
An outline created using WordPerfect's Outline feature. Level numbers are generated automatically as new entries are made in the outline. If an entry is deleted or a new one inserted, the outline feature automatically updates the level numbers to maintain the sequence.

written. This is a process that most writers use in order to collect their thoughts and to create a plan for their work. After the general outline has been developed (Figure 8-7) more detail may be added, steps may be deleted, moved, or expanded. As these revisions are made the outliner automatically updates the numbering system with new numbers or subcategories as necessary to keep the outline in order.

▶ GRAMMAR CHECKERS

Most word processors now provide a spell check capability and many also make a thesaurus available to help with your writing. But how often have you found a sentence that was badly constructed or grammar that just did not seem to be correct? A grammar checker is a software product for computer users who need assistance with the presentation of their letters, memos, or reports. Grammar checkers such as RightWriter and Grammatik are usually programs that are separate from the word processor but operate on word processing documents.

Grammatik is one writing aid that helps you create strong, clear documents. It examines the text and analyzes it for problems with spelling, grammar, style, word usage, and punctuation. Checking is done interactively and you can respond to each problem by accepting Grammatik's suggestions, making your own changes, or leaving things the way they are. Statistics are included at the end to provide a word use profile, a rating of the text's readability, and a comparison of readability to a standard document.

The program does not generate the same results as a human. It will not find certain subtleties in the use of language or in the exercise of literary license. Grammatik cannot find all errors and in some cases may point out an error that is a correct use of the language.

But Grammatik can identify words or phrases that should be replaced by simpler or more common words. It can also identify sentences that are too long which may be potentially confusing. It also flags the use of the passive voice where a stronger sentence or phrase could be used for more effective writing.

Grammatik is meant to be an aid for all types of writers. There are 10 different writing styles supported including Business Letters, Memos, Technical, Journalism, and Fiction. Its 58 rule classes (similar to rules used in expert systems) are based on mistakes commonly made by writers. And if your style of writing is different from these, you can change the rules that Grammatik uses to correspond to your type of writing.

Grammatik is an example of the new and interesting software packages that are making the computer a truly helpful device. With software developments such as this the computer is going beyond the level of a productivity tool and becoming an electronic assistant to those who communicate with words.

Original document.

> There is a problem of a severe nature in widget production.
> It is clear that our current system will not cut the mustard.
> We may possibly need to move on this reasonably quickly. To
> start, it would be advantageous to see if a new design is doable.
> (This should be looked into at once.

Grammatik identifies a problem in the document, explains what the concern is, and offers a suggested solution.

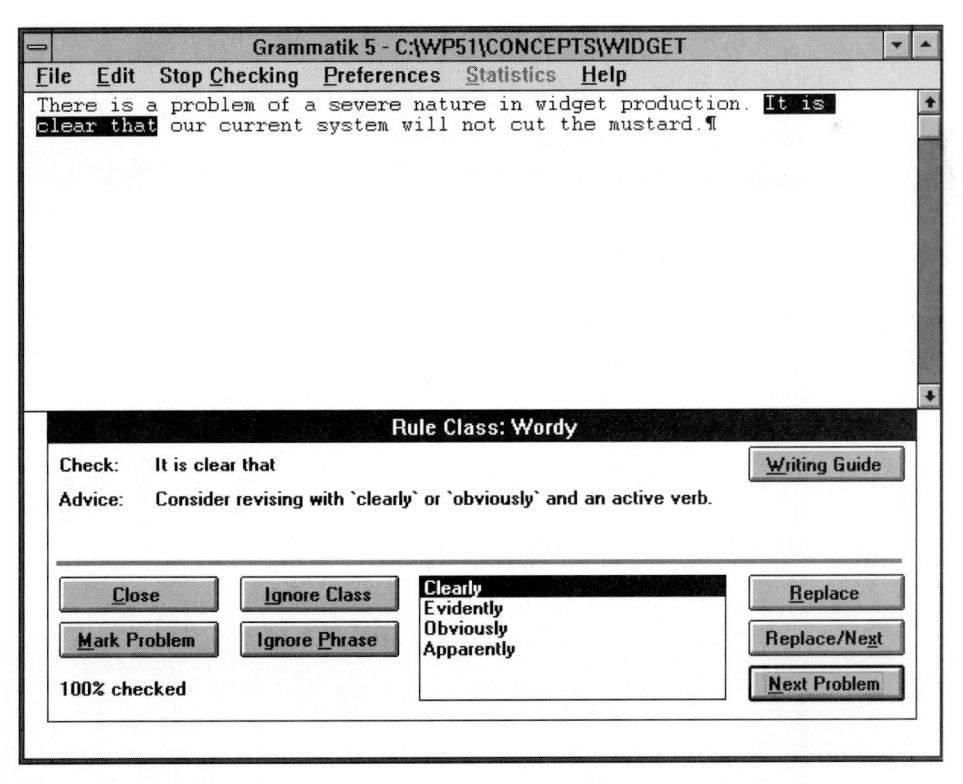

WINDOWS WORD PROCESSORS

One complaint users of DOS-based word processors have is that they are not "what you see is what you get" (WYSIWYG) displays. Some of them have print preview screens that display an image similar to the printed output, but as you edit text or other information, the screen does not represent exactly how the printed document will appear.

With the advent of Windows-based word processors, the WYSIWYG problem has all but disappeared. Word processors, such as Word for Windows, WordPerfect for Windows, and Ami Pro, display text, graphics, and fonts on the screen as they will appear when printed (Figure 8-8).

Windows-based word processors also take advantage of the standards inherent in Microsoft Windows. They use a graphical user interface (GUI) for user interaction with the program. Some of these word processors also use object linking and embedding (OLE) so that data may be shared between other programs in the system. Many can display a fully formatted screen or a view for editing. Using the edit view saves space on the screen, makes the program work faster, and makes the user more productive. High-end processors also permit the use of multiple files, and provide for sophisticated typography and graphics handling.

It may seem that a Windows word processor will be the ultimate solution for text and graphic-oriented processing. But Windows word processors are slower than DOS-based systems especially when a lower speed processor, such as a 386SX, is used. They do add further complications to

FIGURE 8-8
Ami Pro is a Windows-based word processor that displays text on screen as it will appear when printed. (Courtesy Microsoft.)

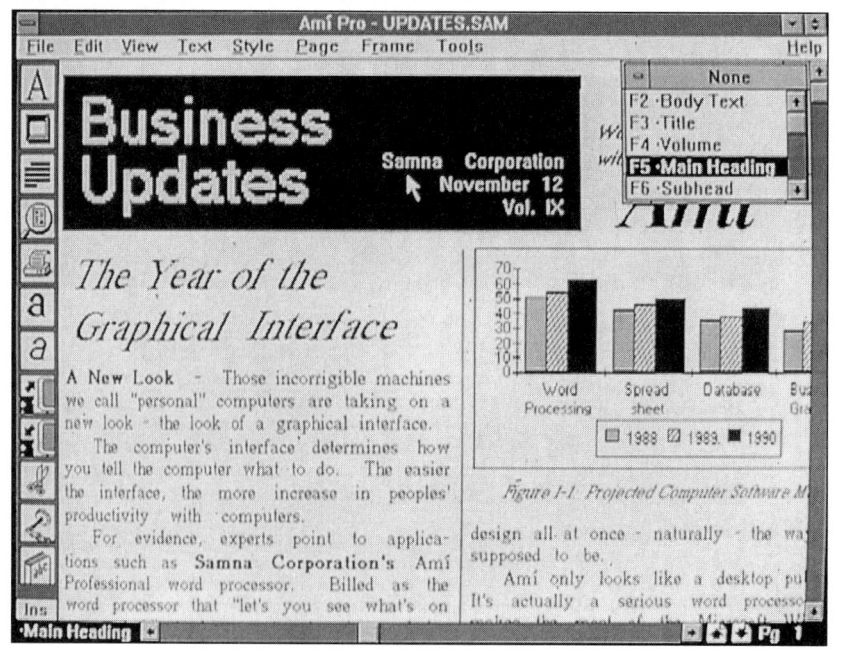

the software, but some, such as WordPerfect for Windows, let you use the commands from the DOS-based program. With more and more users moving to Windows, it is likely that this will continue to be a growth area for word processors.

DESKTOP PUBLISHING

With the advent of more powerful computers, laser printers, and sophisticated software, desktop publishing has became a natural step up from word processing. **Desktop publishing** takes the concept of WYSIWYG to its limit by providing the software that can display a page on the screen in exactly the format it will be printed. Desktop software can display different fonts and graphics integrated together on the same document as they will be printed (Figure 8-9). In addition, the software provides for minute control over formatting, and provides for line, circle, and box drawing.

Using desktop publishing is a definite advantage for the small business. By eliminating typesetting costs and artist fees, publications can be created for considerably less expense than with previous methods. A desktop publishing program can be used to produce newsletters, letterheads, brochures, and even books or manuals.

For successful desktop publishing a system requires 5 or 6 main components: page composition software, a personal computer, a high resolution

Desktop Publishing. Software that is used to integrate text with a variety of fonts, graphics, and clip art to produce a complete, professional-quality document.

FIGURE 8-9
Desktop publishing software, such as the Ventura Package from Xerox Corporation, integrates text and graphics to display the document as it will be printed. (Courtesy Ventura Software Inc.)

display, a keyboard and a mouse, and a suitable printer. In the following sections we will look at each of these requirements for desktop publishing.

Page Composition Software

Page composition software is the heart of the system. This name refers to the desktop publishing software that is used to create pages of text. The software, such as Aldus Pagemaker or Xerox's Ventura Publisher, is the program that brings graphics and text together on the screen. Page composition software provides the tools to format the text and lay out the content, with columns, boxes, lines, headings, and so on.

Software for the PC generally runs in the $200–$500 range or at the top end of the word processor market. Formerly, comparatively expensive systems for minicomputers were used by typesetting professionals and offered considerably more power and features than the PC software. But as micros have grown in capability, this software is being redesigned for the PC.

Frequently, a word processor such as Microsoft Word or WordPerfect is used with the page composition software to aid in the creation of text. Because of this marriage of the two software packages, compatibility is an important concern when choosing software for desktop publishing. Choosing the right packages can reduce training time and enhance operator efficiency.

Ideally the page composition software should show on screen exactly what will be printed (WYSIWYG). Because most screens are less than a full page in length, scrolling is usually necessary to see all of the page. Many packages will also show a reduced text view so that you can see all of the page at once on the screen. This technique will result in some loss of legibility, and in some cases the software does not show actual words but just illegible symbols to represent the words.

The Computer

Many of the page composition packages that are available for the personal computer will require at minimum a 386SX with 2MB or memory and a hard disk to operate effectively. The need for a fast processor and large memory is dictated by both the size of the program used for page composition and also the use of bit-mapped graphics for the display. Because text and graphics are displayed together, bit mapping is required to create the display.

The Screen

Because users of desktop publishing systems need to see on the screen what will be printed, a high resolution display is required. The IBM Enhanced Graphics Adaptor (EGA) is a minimum level of resolution acceptable for page composition, but most recommend VGA or SuperVGA (see Chapter 3 for an explanation of EGA and VGA). The screen can be monochrome, although some desktop software now supports color so a color monitor may be in order. Monitors that display a full page, such as one from the Princeton Graphics System (Figure 8-10), are available and give a true WYSIWYG (what you see is what you get) format.

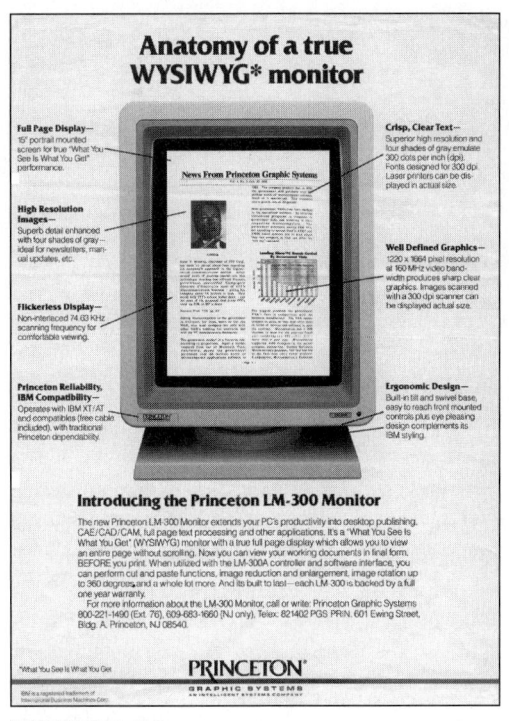

FIGURE 8-10
Fullpage displays such as that shown here make desktop publishing easier by presenting the entire contents of a page at one time on the screen without resorting to a reduced size required by some displays. (Courtesy Princeton Graphic Systems.)

The Input

The primary input device for desktop publishing is, of course, the keyboard. Much of the input will be text and is often entered through a full-featured word processor which also uses the keyboard. But for formatting text, entering graphics, choosing options from the page composition software, and so on, a mouse (Figure 8-11) can sometimes function more effectively than the keyboard. Some software supports both a mouse and keyboard for all functions, but users find that when a mouse is used to enhance the keyboard's function, the software is much more effective.

Clip Art Software

For graphics applications, users generally do not create their own art because that is too time consuming. Instead, so-called clip art software is available that provides a library of graphic images for use in page composition software. Required images are extracted from the clip art software and inserted into the document as it is prepared using the desktop publishing program. Clip art use is no longer limited to desktop publishing. Many word processors and spreadsheets can include clip art images into their documents or files, and the applications are quickly becoming more widespread as new software is released.

Clip art. Graphics files that provide prepared images for use in graphical-oriented software packages.

FIGURE 8-11
A mouse is an effective input device for working with a page composition software package. Using a mouse simplifies the selection of options in the software, formatting the document, and even for creating your own graphics. (Courtesy Sun Micro Systems.)

The Printer

Effective desktop publishing requires the use of a laser printer. The laser offers a higher resolution for good quality printing; a variety of type fonts are also available to satisfy the needs of a diversity of publishing requirements. Although laser printers do not match the quality results available from professional typesetting and graphic artists, the results are suitable for all but the most demanding applications.

Dot matrix printers can also be used for desktop publishing, but they present a compromise on quality. Although a matrix printer can create the images developed with page composition software, it cannot produce the higher resolution of the laser printer. Serious users will need to consider an investment in a laser printer for an effective desktop publishing system.

Is Desktop Publishing for Everyone?

Desktop publishing may seem to be the solution for many business problems. No longer is it necessary to send out manuscripts to a typesetter and printer, which can be time consuming and costly. Even the graphic artist is not required because graphics can be developed along with the text, again saving time and money.

An argument against desktop publishing is that the results are generally lower in quality than that produced by graphic artists. Because desktop publishing is a new field, the software and the hardware are only beginning to evolve to the point where quality results are comparable to that produced by graphic arts professionals.

Usually these professionals can produce results that are superior to desktop publishing. However, for some applications, such as an internal company newsletter, professional results may not be worth the cost, whereas desktop publishing may be the solution that keeps the newsletter alive. As software and hardware improve and users become more knowledgeable, there is no doubt that desktop publishing is going to have a major impact on the printing business.

CHAPTER SUMMARY

1. **Word processing** is considered to be the leading use of personal computers and is frequently the main application that prompts the purchase of a first computer.
2. With word processing a **draft copy** of a document can be made, corrections and changes noted on the page, and then the changes are made using the word processor without the need for retyping the document.
3. The **stages of word processing** are entering text, editing, print formatting, printing, and saving or recalling the text to or from disk.
4. **Formatting** features include line spacing, margin settings, right margin justification, and tab settings. In addition a choice of printer fonts, printers, settings for headers and footers, and the insertion of page numbers may be available.
5. Word processors use a variety of terms to describe their operation. Users should be familiar with the terms word wrap, line spacing, line centering, underlining, and boldface. The status line gives information about the page and the word processor operation. Other terms used are left and right margins, soft and hard page breaks, indenting and tab settings.
6. **Search and replace** finds a word or phrase and replaces it with another. A wildcard may be used in the search string so that a range of words may satisfy the search.
7. Word processor **advanced features** may include a spelling checker, thesaurus, mail merge, and an outliner.
8. **Form letters** are produced easily with a word processor by creating the letter in a primary file and names and addresses in a secondary file. A merge program combines the contents of these files, producing the letters.
9. **Windows-based word processors** use WYSIWYG to display text, graphics, and fonts on the screen as they will appear when printed. Using the standards inherent in Microsoft Windows they use a graphical user interface (GUI) and object linking and embedding (OLE) to share data between other programs in the system.
10. **Desktop publishing** takes the concept of WYSIWYG to its limit by providing software that can display a page on the screen in exactly the format it will be printed including different text fonts and graphics.
11. **Page composition software** is the desktop software that is used to create the pages of text.
12. Desktop hardware will include a higher end PC, a keyboard and mouse, and a laser printer.
13. **Clip art software** may be useful for providing graphic images in desktop applications.

IMPORTANT TERMS AND CONCEPTS

Clip art software
Copy
Cut and paste
Desktop publishing
Editing
Formatting
Form letter
Function key driven
Grammar checker
Graphical user interface (GUI)
Mail merge
Menu-oriented
Move

Outline generator
Page composition software
Print formatting
Printing
Recalling text
Saving text
Screen preview
Search and replace
Spelling checker
Thesaurus
Windows word processor
Word wrap

SELF-TESTING QUESTIONS

Fill-In

1. The process of _____ is used for making changes such as inserting or deleting text in the document.
2. _____ _____ occurs when typing a line of text and a word that will not fit at the end of the current line is moved automatically to the next line.
3. Text that is aligned on the right margin is called _____ _____.
4. Using an _____ causes text to wrap to a new margin or tab setting.
5. Using the _____ checker will help to find typing and spelling errors in the text.
6. The _____ and _____ command is used to look for a word that has been used in the text and change it to another word.
7. A _____ and _____ operation would be used to move a paragraph from one location in the document to another.
8. Using the _____ _____ feature can be an efficient method for creating form letters.
9. A _____ based word processor uses a graphical user interface (GUI) for user interaction with the program.
10. Using _____ _____ software is one way to combine text, graphics, and line drawing into the same document.

True/False

1. Proportional spacing uses characters that vary in width depending on the need of the character.
2. Printing a draft copy of a document is done only when using a laser printer.
3. A hard page break is created by the user while a soft page break occurs automatically when the page is filled with text.

4. A 12-point font will be larger and occupy more space on the line than an 18-point font.
5. Search and replace is used to change margins or line spacing in a document.
6. A thesaurus is a popular feature used by word processors for grammar checking.
7. Windows-based word processors usually provide WYSIWYG display of the document, while most DOS-based word processors don't have this provision.
8. Clip art includes graphic images that have been prepared for use in desktop publishing and other software packages.

ANSWERS

Fill-In: 1. editing, 2. word wrap, 3. justified, 4. indent, 5. spelling, 6. search and replace, 7. cut and paste, 8. mail merge, 9. Windows, 10. desktop publishing

True/False: 1. T, 2. F, 3. T, 4. F, 5. F, 6. F, 7. T, 8. T

Questions for Critical Thinking

1. Will using a spell check, thesaurus, or grammar checker improve or inhibit good writing skills?
2. A decision to use desktop publishing or Windows word processing applications may have a significant effect on the hardware configuration. Discuss.
3. Because computer and word processing skills are becoming so widespread, the traditional idea of a manager with a secretary who does the typing may be approaching extinction. Consider the effect on the office environment when most business people have these computer skills.

CHAPTER 9

SPREADSHEET SOFTWARE

A VIEW OF THE CHAPTER AHEAD

After reading this chapter you will understand

- ▶ the use of spreadsheets in business and their strengths when asking "what if?" questions.
- ▶ the basic components of a spreadsheet such as cells, values, labels, and formulas.
- ▶ some of the basic operations of a spreadsheet such as the use of functions, formatting, ranges, and graphing.

INTRODUCTION

Not only are spreadsheets the second most widely used software on personal computers, after word processing, but they have also spawned a whole industry of support software. When you think of spreadsheets, the image might be of a department manager using a spreadsheet to administer the department budget. And for thousands of users that is an accurate picture. But spreadsheet software is capable of much more sophisticated applications than creating a budget.

In California, Palo Alto Software provides a set of spreadsheet templates to businesses or individuals who want to simplify the process of creating a business plan. The templates are available for Excel or Lotus 1-2-3, and they reduce the complex mathematics often required to develop a successful business plan to a spreadsheet that any business person can manage. By contrast, Dairy Production Medicine Software is a software package that contains over 30 Lotus 1-2-3 spreadsheets aimed at dairy farm management to analyze the health, nutrition, economics, and productivity of dairy cows.

These examples represent two extremes in the hundreds of applications of a computer wth spreadsheet software. In the first example, the spreadsheet is used as a general-purpose tool that can be applied to the development of a business plan for any type of business. The second example shows the use of a spreadsheet in a very specific application, the management of the health of dairy herds. These examples demonstrate the flexibility that spreadsheets have for a variety of uses.

Spreadsheets are relative newcomers to the computer software club. The first spreadsheet, VisiCalc, was released in 1979 for the Apple computer and represented a new way of thinking about computing that had not previously been considered. The concept was so revolutionary that it was claimed to have sold users on purchasing a microcomputer on the strength of the software alone.

Spreadsheet. A program that stores data in rows and columns for use in numerical calculations.

▶ THE FIRST SPREADSHEET

In the information processing time frame, spreadsheets are a recent development. In 1978, a college student named Dan Bricklin was sitting in class at Harvard Business School watching his professor create a model budget on the blackboard. As the professor changed a value in one column of the model, it was necessary to recalculate related numbers in the other columns. This is typical of an operation done when creating a budget, where values are adjusted, some increased, and others decreased to try and stay within the financial limits available.

Bricklin was puzzling over the need for constant recalculations and suddenly realized that a computer could do all of the recalculations if the data could be represented in rows and columns. He discussed this concept with a friend, Robert Frankston, who was an experienced computer programmer. Together they realized that even if they could create such a program it would need to be marketed, so they took the project to Dan Fylstra, a fledgling software publisher. Between them, the program VisiCalc was developed, which became an instant hit in the marketplace.

SPREADSHEETS

Soon other companies created their own versions of the spreadsheet, including Lotus 1–2–3, Borland's Quattro and Quattro Pro, and Microsoft's Excel. Of these, Lotus 1–2–3 has become the uncontested leader (Figure 9-1) by virtue of its ease of use and wide range of features, but mostly because it was one of the first full-featured spreadsheets available for the IBM personal computer.

Typical Spreadsheet Applications

Spreadsheets are frequently used as a convenient method for recording numerical data, taking advantage of the automatic calculations that can be done efficiently with a spreadsheet program. Users of spreadsheets find them useful for hundreds of applications, some of them quite widely used, such as the following:

- Preparing and analyzing financial statements to show the assets and liabilities of the company.
- Forecasting sales by analyzing previous trends and projecting future growth based on trends and sales objectives.
- Controlling inventory and updating the data when shipments are made or items are received.

FIGURE 9-1
The clear leader in the spreadsheet software industry is Lotus 1–2–3. Lotus has done much to legitimize the personal computer market and is a software package used by the majority of spreadsheet users. (Courtesy Lotus Development Corporation.)

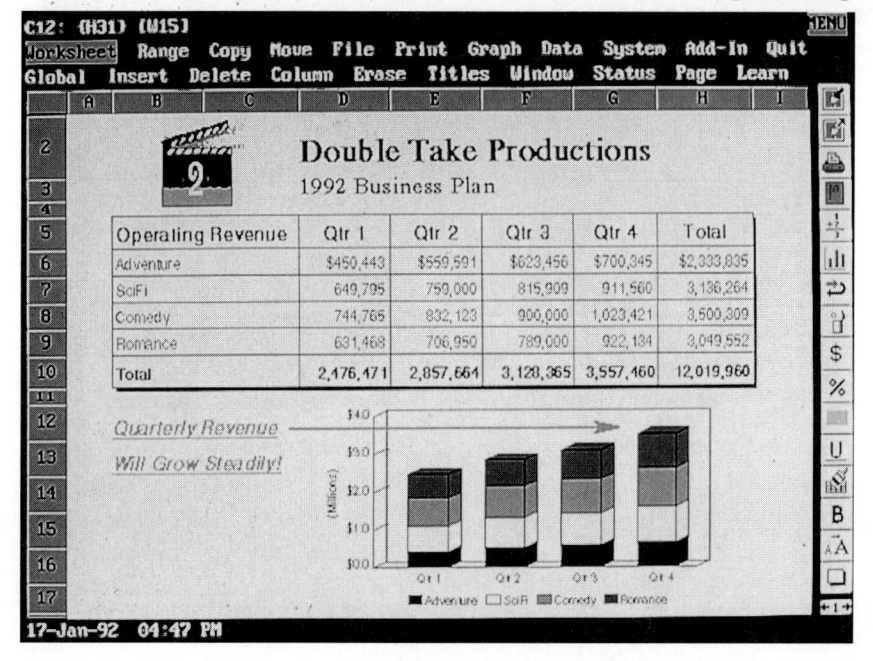

- Pricing goods based on purchase cost, cost of storage, the cost of processing an order, and other factors unique to the product.
- Analyzing product performance on factors such as cost of production, amount of sales, and customer satisfaction.
- Creating graphics for easier spreadsheet analysis and presentation of business data.
- Other applications such as investment alternatives, cash flow projections, and rate structure analysis.

"What If" Questions

What if question. A procedure that tries different values in the spreadsheet to automatically recalculate results or produce forecasts.

Spreadsheets today generally provide three major areas of capability: spreadsheet, graphics, and database. The fundamental component of these three is the spreadsheet, which is used for creating a **model** and asking "what if?" questions. Some of the discussion in this chapter will concern the use of a spreadsheet to create a model (Figure 9-2) and ask questions about what happens if certain values are changed.

The bottom of the model shows a net loss of $4,880. The question "what if we spend less for travel?" can be asked by changing the travel expense of $40,000.00 in the first quarter (or any other quarter) to some other value such as $35,000.00. The spreadsheet will then automatically re-

FIGURE 9-2
A budget planning model is built into a spreadsheet to show expenses by quarter in five different categories.

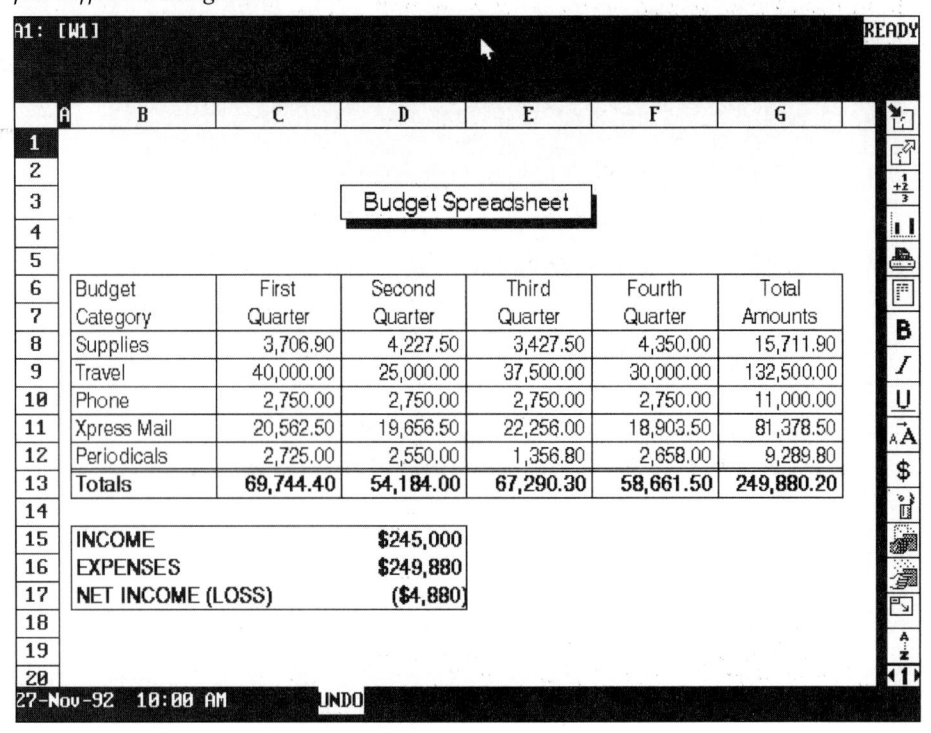

Budget Category	First Quarter	Second Quarter	Third Quarter	Fourth Quarter	Total Amounts
Supplies	3,706.90	4,227.50	3,427.50	4,350.00	15,711.90
Travel	40,000.00	25,000.00	37,500.00	30,000.00	132,500.00
Phone	2,750.00	2,750.00	2,750.00	2,750.00	11,000.00
Xpress Mail	20,562.50	19,656.50	22,256.00	18,903.50	81,378.50
Periodicals	2,725.00	2,550.00	1,356.80	2,658.00	9,289.80
Totals	69,744.40	54,184.00	67,290.30	58,661.50	249,880.20

INCOME	$245,000
EXPENSES	$249,880
NET INCOME (LOSS)	($4,880)

calculate the totals for travel, in the first quarter totals, and in the total expenses and the net income.

There are many alternatives that the manager could seek an answer for. It is also possible to make several changes and view the results. So within a few minutes many possible combinations of budget values can be considered and the results seen immediately on the screen.

Spreadsheet Components

Spreadsheets, like the one in Figure 9-3, consist of a number of cells arranged in rows and columns. This organization is similar to the ledger pad used by accountants to assist in recording and calculating all of the values needed for financial planning. In a computer spreadsheet a value, label, or formula can be stored in each cell.

The number of rows and columns depends on the spreadsheet used and even on the version of the spreadsheet. For example, Lotus 1–2–3 Version 2 has 256 columns and 8,192 rows for a total of 2,097,152 cells. While the number of cells provided may seem extravagant, they were provided at the demand of spreadsheet users who found earlier versions of the software to be too restrictive for their applications. Whether or not a computer can use all of this space depends on the amount of memory installed. In some cases special memory expansion boards are required to take advantage of the extensive capability of a spreadsheet program.

FIGURE 9-3
A spreadsheet display with the major components identified.

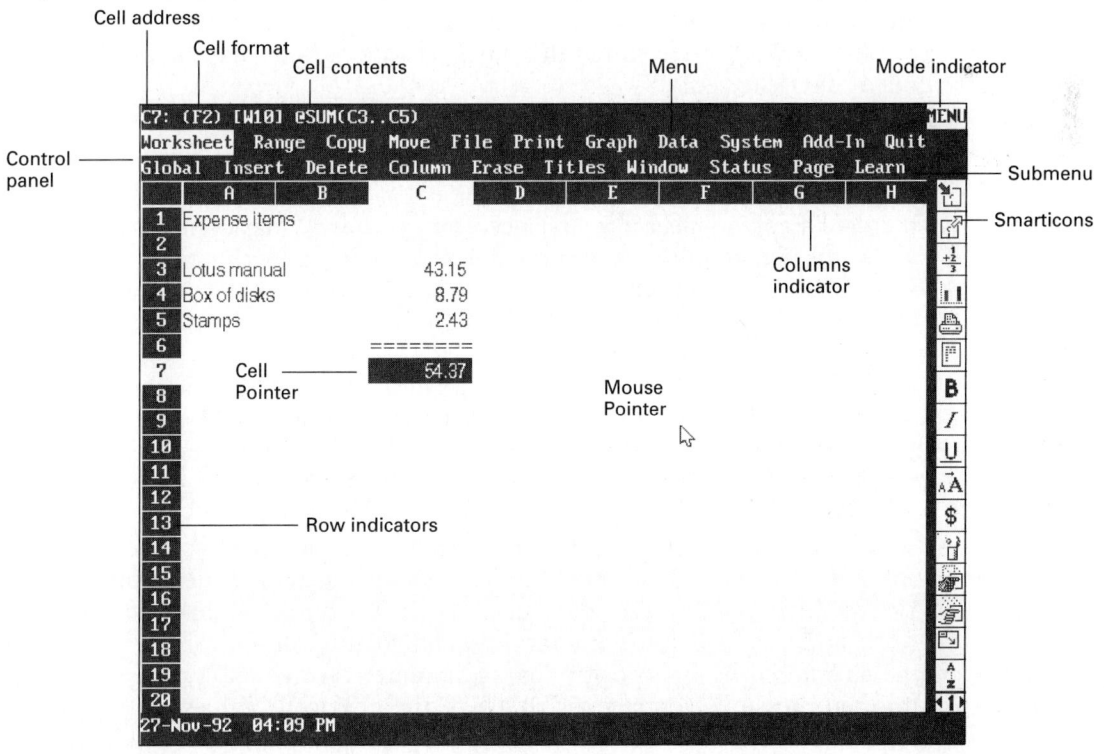

Cell. The intersection of a row and column where a label, value, or formula is located.

Cell address. A reference such as A1 or CB23 that is used in a formula or function to refer to the contents of a cell.

Label. Descriptive cell contents such as a name or address.

Value. A numeric amount that may be used in a formula or function.

Cells and Addressing. A **cell** is located where a row and column meet on the screen. At the intersection of column A and row 1 is a cell where a value may be placed in the spreadsheet. The address of this cell is composed of the column and row number, and for this cell is address A1. Cell A1 is also called the **Home** address. Moving one cell to the right is cell B1 and so on. A spreadsheet like Lotus 1–2–3 goes all the way out to column IV for a cell address of IV1.

Moving down from the Home address is cell A2, then A3 and so on. Lotus 1–2–3 Version 2 goes all the way down to address A8192.

The Control Panel. Spreadsheet programs use a **control panel** or **status line** to communicate with the user. One or more lines are used to display menus, prompts, cell contents, current cell address, and mode. Not all of this information will display at one time, as it depends on the operation being done.

The **cell pointer** is the highlighted bar that points to the current cell where a value or formula may be entered or edited. The **cell address** refers to the cell where the pointer is currently positioned. The **cell contents** are shown in the control panel.

The **menu line** appears when the slash (/) key is pressed or the area is clicked with a mouse. The menu displays a list of options that may be selected. A **submenu** shows additional options when the bar is positioned on the menu line. A **mouse pointer** and several **icons** appear on some spreadsheets to indicate that a mouse is an alternate to the keyboard for entering commands. Some spreadsheets, such as Quattro Pro 4.0, display a **speedbar** across the top. This bar displays common activities such as summing a column of numbers, and provides a quick way to get a total.

The **mode indicator** identifies the current mode or status that the program is in. Modes determine the types of actions that may be taken or the type of data entered.

Creating a Spreadsheet

To create a spreadsheet it is first necessary to have a basic understanding of the results we require. A mental image or even a rough paper image of what the spreadsheet will look like is a good planning step. Ideas for rows and columns, where the labels will go and what cells will contain values or formulas, are necessary first steps in our planning.

Assume that we are planning a spreadsheet for first quarter expenses, but a reasonable guess would suggest that eventually there will also be second, third, and fourth quarter values. So a good analyst would lay out the cells so that additional quarters can be easily added. Figure 9-4 shows how we want the spreadsheet to appear when it is finished.

Four types of entries can be made on most spreadsheets: labels, values, formulas, and functions. **Labels** are entries such as names, descriptions, and titles. **Values** are numeric data such as quantity, costs, and percentages. Labels and values may be entered interchangeably on the spreadsheet. Each label is entered by first positioning the pointer on the cell, typing the entry, and then pressing a cursor key to get to the next cell. Values are entered in the same manner and include decimal points or minus signs if needed.

CHAPTER 9 Spreadsheet Software   239

	A	B	C	D	E	F	G
1							
2			Budget Spreadsheet				
3	Budget	First					
4	Category	Quarter					
5							
6	Supplies	37.69					
7	Travel	300					
8	Phone	75					
9	Xpress Mail	106.25					
10	Periodicals	72.5					
11							
12		591.44					
13							

FIGURE 9-4
A spreadsheet plan prior to making the initial entries. Developing a plan saves time and ensures that entries made will represent the model effectively.

A **formula** is an arithmetic expression or formula that does a calculation using values on the spreadsheet. The calculation of a value such as the sum of all budget values requires the use of a formula in cell B12. The formula +B6+B7+B8+B9+B10 finds the sum of the values in all five cells. A **function** provides a shortcut for writing a formula and often provides for calculations that could not otherwise be done. In Figure 9-5, a function, @SUM(B6..B10), is used which defines the range of the cell that are summed for the total. Because the values we want to add are cells B6 to B10, the formula

@SUM(B6..B10)

is used to create the total. A function is often simpler than writing a formula.

A result of typing a formula or function is that the result of calculating

FIGURE 9-5
The entry of labels, values, and a function on the spreadsheet. When a function is entered into cell B12 the result of calculating the function is displayed in the cell. The function itself will display on the control panel when the pointer is positioned on cell B12.

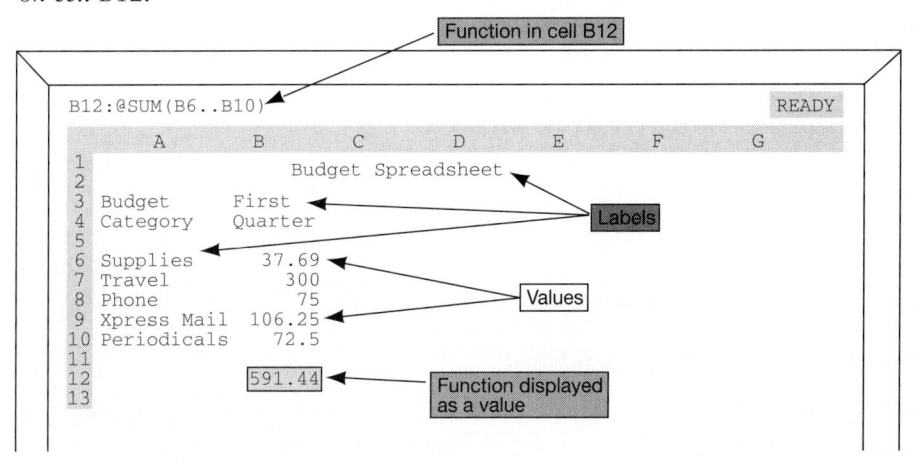

```
B12:@SUM(B6..B10)                                            READY
         A          B          C          D          E          F          G
 1
 2                       Budget Spreadsheet
 3  Budget     First
 4  Category   Quarter
 5
 6  Supplies      37.69
 7  Travel          300
 8  Phone            75
 9  Xpress Mail  106.25
10  Periodicals    72.5
11
12              591.44
13
```

Function in cell B12
Labels
Values
Function displayed as a value

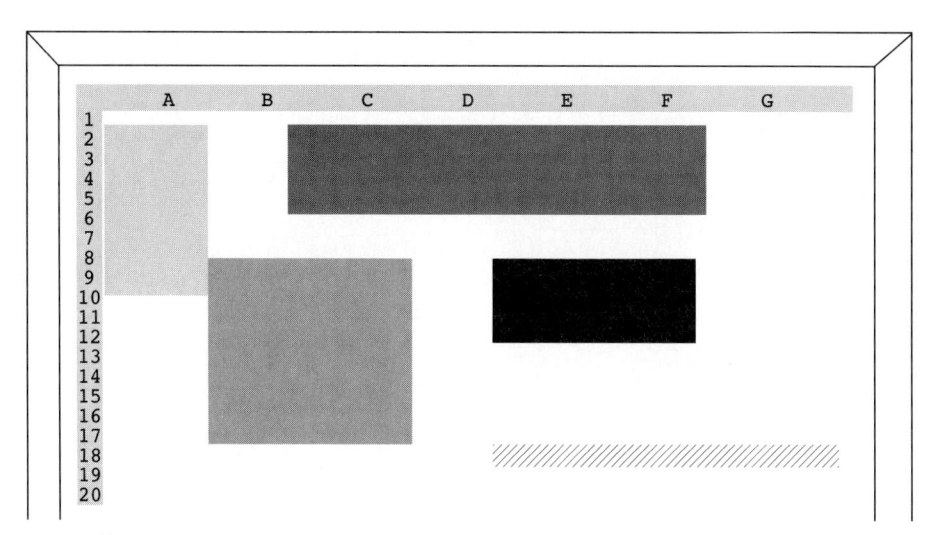

FIGURE 9-6
Several ways in which a range may be defined in a spreadsheet. A range is always identified by the first and last cell in the range, such as A1..A10, which includes all cells in column A from row 1 to row 10.

the formula appears in the cell. Thus, cell B12 will display the sum of cells B6 to B10 and not the formula that was typed. By placing the pointer on the cell containing the formula, the contents of that cell will appear in the control panel at the top of the screen.

Ranges

Range. A square or rectangular block of cells used in a spreadsheet operation and referred to by the upper left and lower right addresses.

To simplify entries, such as those used in formulas, spreadsheets provide a **range** definition that includes one or more cells in a simple expression. Figure 9-6 shows different ways in which cells can be included as a range. A range (some spreadsheets use the name block) is a square or rectangular shape and is identified by the first and last cell address in the range. A range may be a single cell or many cells. The range B6..B10 refers to cells B6, B7, B8, B9, and B10. The range D3..F5 refers to cells enclosed in a rectangle with these upper left and lower right coordinates. In most spreadsheets ranges must be contiguous cells, but in some, such as Microsoft Excel, noncontiguous cells may belong to a range.

Using Ranges in the Spreadsheet

Ranges are used in two basic ways in a spreadsheet. One use is in a formula that requires a range of cells such as finding the sum of a column of numbers. The other use of a range is when giving a spreadsheet command (slash command) that requires a range of cells for the operation such as when copying formulas or values from one range of cells to another.

Formatting the Spreadsheet

As a variety of data is entered on a spreadsheet, the appearance of the values may not be exactly as desired. This is especially true when formulas

CHAPTER 9 Spreadsheet Software

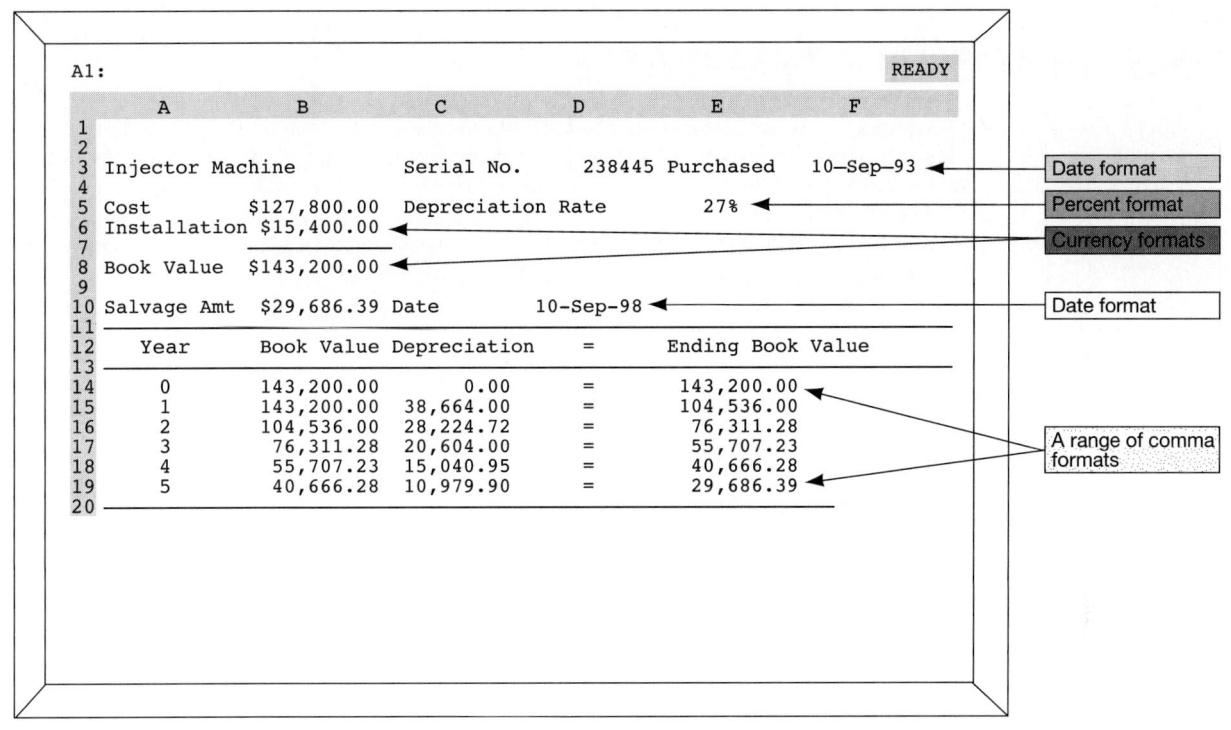

```
A1:                                                            READY
       A          B           C           D          E          F
 1
 2
 3  Injector Machine       Serial No.    238445 Purchased  10-Sep-93    ← Date format
 4
 5  Cost        $127,800.00 Depreciation Rate         27%               ← Percent format
 6  Installation $15,400.00                                             ← Currency formats
 7  ─────────────────────
 8  Book Value  $143,200.00
 9
10  Salvage Amt  $29,686.39 Date           10-Sep-98                    ← Date format
11  ────────────────────────────────────────────────────
12      Year      Book Value Depreciation    =    Ending Book Value
13  ────────────────────────────────────────────────────
14       0        143,200.00       0.00     =        143,200.00
15       1        143,200.00   38,664.00     =        104,536.00
16       2        104,536.00   28,224.72     =         76,311.28        ← A range of comma
17       3         76,311.28   20,604.00     =         55,707.23          formats
18       4         55,707.23   15,040.95     =         40,666.28
19       5         40,666.28   10,979.90     =         29,686.39
20  ────────────────────────────────────────────────────
```

FIGURE 9-7
A variety of formats used in a depreciation spreadsheet developed in Lotus 1–2–3.

have been used to develop some values and the results go into several decimal places. In such a case, values may have differing decimal positions and will not align in the column.

Other times there may be large numbers that could benefit from the use of commas to set off the thousands position. Dollar values sometimes look better with a dollar sign. A percentage such as 0.25 would be more readable if it were displayed as 25%.

The appearance of one or more cells may be changed by using a **format** command. Figure 9-7 shows a depreciation spreadsheet where currency, date, comma, and interest formats have been used. Both single cells and a range of cells are formatted in this spreadsheet, indicating the variety of formatting needs in a business application.

In addition to formatting, spreadsheet programs such as Lotus 1–2–3 Releases 2.4 and 3.4, Quattro Pro, and Excel permit the use of different fonts, boldface, and underlining to enhance text and values on the spreadsheet. Line and box drawing and the use of shading are also used. These presentation quality features are becoming a required feature on spreadsheets and are standard on Windows-based spreadsheets.

Addressing in Formulas

Figure 9-8 shows a formula used in a stock investment spreadsheet that uses relative addressing. A **relative address** is used when the row number or

Formatting. A technique for displaying the contents of a cell using certain specifications such as the number of decimal positions or the use of a dollar sign or comma.

Relative address. An address such as B5 whose row or column reference is adjusted when the formula is copied to a new cell.

▶ SPREADSHEET TEMPLATES

Applications, such as invoices, use a common format for the spreadsheet while the data entered will be different for each order. Instead of recreating the spreadsheet for each new invoice, a template is prepared and saved on disk until it is needed. The empty template is then read into memory and filled with the data unique to the customer's order. The filled template then becomes a permanent record of the order which can be printed, saved on disk, and used for follow-up with the customer. The next order begins with the empty template and the process is repeated.

```
     A      B      C     D        E         F        G          H
 1                            INVOICE                 #       10004
 2
 3                      McVEY POOL SUPPLIES
 4                   36 ARLINGTON DR. DOWLING, ON
 5                          (705) 855-3171
 6
 7  Customer Name    :
 8  Customer Address:                          Phone :
 9
10  Date     05/30/93
11
12             Item Number Description     Price   Quantity     Cost
13
14
15
16
17
18
19
20
```

An empty template used for a customer invoice.

```
     A      B      C     D        E         F        G          H
 1                            INVOICE                 #       10004
 2
 3                      McVEY POOL SUPPLIES
 4                   36 ARLINGTON DR. DOWLING, ON
 5                          (705) 855-3171
 6
 7  Customer Name    :S. Todd
 8  Customer Address:23 SW4th St.              Phone :865-3594
 9                   Dowling, ON
10  Date     05/30/93
11
12             Item Number Description     Price   Quantity     Cost
13
14              111        Chlorine st 8kg  65.10       5       325.50
15              122        Super Tabs 8kg   72.30       1        72.30
16              116        Shock .5kg        6.20       7        43.40
17              118        PH Down 4kg      34.30       3       102.90
18              119        Chlor Pucks 8kg  76.43       4       305.72
19
20
```

The invoice template filled with data.

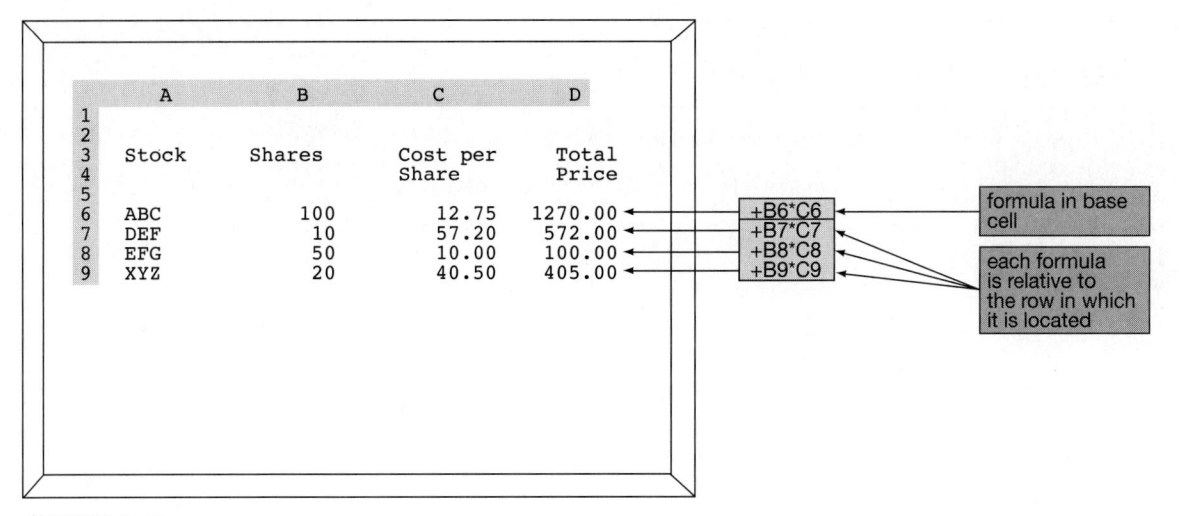

```
        A          B           C           D
1
2
3    Stock      Shares     Cost per      Total
4                           Share        Price
5
6    ABC         100         12.75      1270.00   ←   +B6*C6       formula in base cell
7    DEF          10         57.20       572.00   ←   +B7*C7
8    EFG          50         10.00       100.00   ←   +B8*C8       each formula is relative to
9    XYZ          20         40.50       405.00   ←   +B9*C9       the row in which it is located
```

FIGURE 9-8
Relative addressing causes the formula in each cell to be addressed relative to the position it occupies in the spreadsheet.

column letter is adjusted in the formula when it is copied to another cell. When the formula in cell D6 is copied to the second cell (D7), its addresses are adjusted so that the correct row and column will be referenced. Thus, the relative address B6 becomes B7 in the next cell, and so on. The figure shows how this affects each row number in subsequent cells affected by the copy.

When an **absolute address** is used, an address in the formula is not to be adjusted when a formula is copied. Let's take another look at the depreciation spreadsheet in Figure 9-9, which uses a depreciation rate in cell E5. Every time this rate is used, it must be taken from cell E5. Therefore, when a formula is copied that uses the address E5, it must be treated as absolute and the row or column may not be adjusted.

To use a cell as an absolute address it is necessary to enter it with dollar signs. Cell E5 would be entered as E5 to be treated as an absolute address. Either the row or column can be treated as absolute by entering a dollar sign in front of just the row or the column.

A third form of addressing is a **mixed address.** This address is used in a formula when either the row or the column portion (but not both) of the formula is to be absolute. An address such as $A5 has the column A as absolute but the row is relative. If this formula is copied, the column will not change but the row will if the formula is copied to a different row. Similarly, the address A$5 specifies that the column is relative but the row 5 is absolute because it contains the dollar sign. Thus, the column reference can change during copying but the row will not change.

Absolute address. An address such as B5 whose row or column reference is not adjusted when the formula is copied to a new cell.

Graphs

When data is shown on the spreadsheet, it is sometimes difficult to understand the meaning of the numbers and their relationship to each other. By

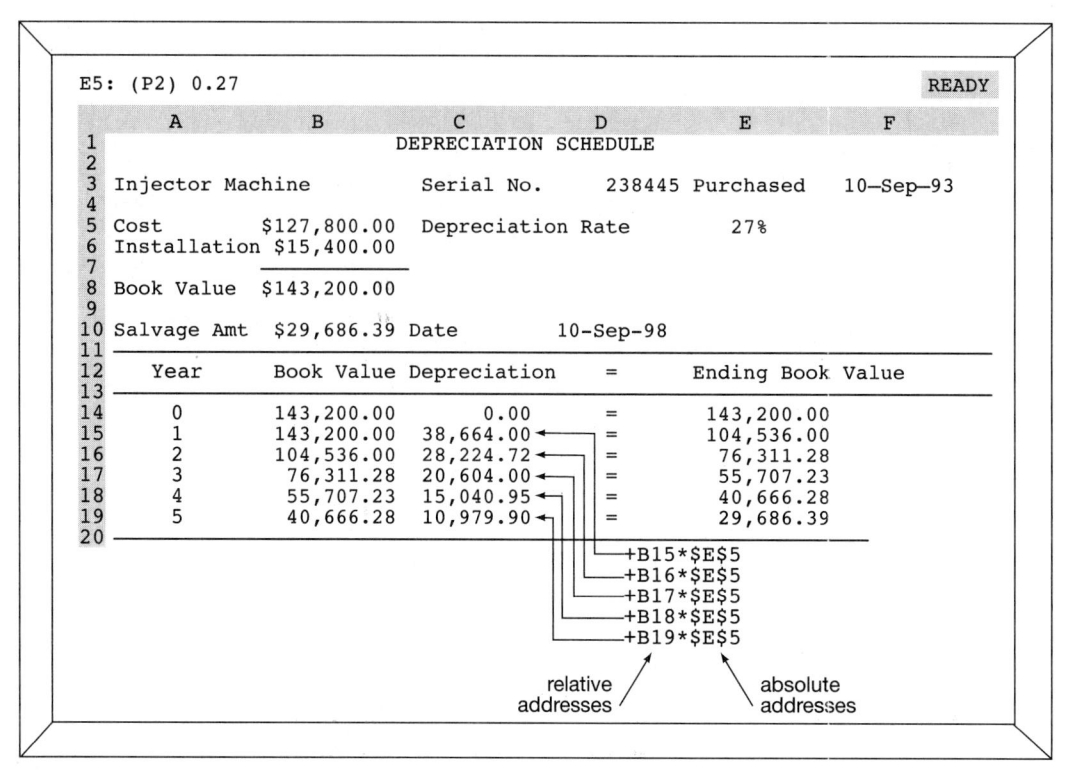

```
E5: (P2) 0.27                                                    READY
            A              B             C           D          E           F
     1                         DEPRECIATION SCHEDULE
     2
     3  Injector Machine            Serial No.    238445  Purchased   10-Sep-93
     4
     5  Cost           $127,800.00  Depreciation Rate             27%
     6  Installation   $15,400.00
     7                 _____
     8  Book Value     $143,200.00
     9
    10  Salvage Amt    $29,686.39   Date         10-Sep-98
    11  _____
    12      Year       Book Value   Depreciation    =     Ending Book Value
    13  _____
    14       0         143,200.00        0.00       =        143,200.00
    15       1         143,200.00    38,664.00 ←─┐  =        104,536.00
    16       2         104,536.00    28,224.72 ←┐│  =         76,311.28
    17       3          76,311.28    20,604.00 ←┼┤  =         55,707.23
    18       4          55,707.23    15,040.95 ←┤│  =         40,666.28
    19       5          40,666.28    10,979.90 ←┘│  =         29,686.39
    20  _____
                                       ┌─────────+B15*$E$5
                                       ├─────────+B16*$E$5
                                       ├─────────+B17*$E$5
                                       ├─────────+B18*$E$5
                                       └─────────+B19*$E$5

                                   relative            absolute
                                   addresses           addresses
```

FIGURE 9-9
The use of absolute addressing in a formula where the depreciation rate is taken from a single cell.

doing arithmetic or other operations on the data, we can sometimes produce helpful results, which can greatly enhance our understanding of the data. All of this is well and good, but there are many times when a graph or chart can convey significantly more meaning and in a more concise form.

Business reports frequently include bar charts, pie charts, or line graphs to present information in a pictorial form, rather than as raw data. These graphs, when used appropriately, can have a much greater impact on the reader than mere numbers alone. By using graphs, the manager or business person can make immediate observations, such as salaries that represent well in excess of half the budget, or that sales in region 3 have been steadily declining over the past three years.

Types of Graphs. Most spreadsheet software will produce a variety of graphs, some with more types than others. Figure 9-10 shows a variety of graphs produced in Lotus 1-2-3 Release 2.4. These graph types are selected by the user of the software depending on the type of data to be represented. The major graph types available in most spreadsheet software are:

1. **Line graph.** This graph plots points on a grid and connects them with a line. This is a suitable graph for representing a frequency distribution of a set of values. A line graph can also be used for comparing several sets of values, such as the trend of different stocks over a period of time.

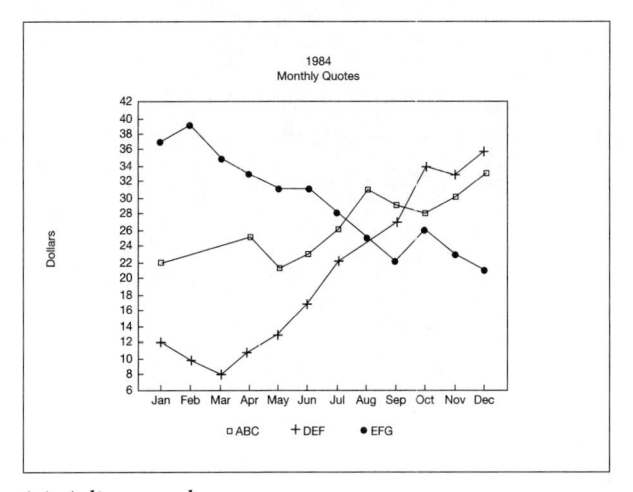

CHAPTER 9 Spreadsheet Software   245

(a) A line graph

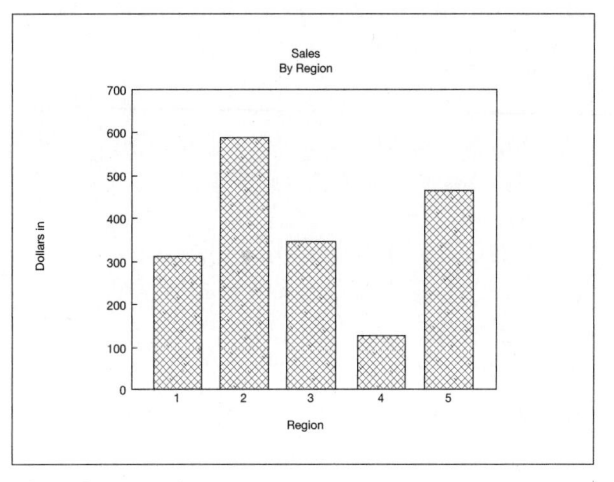

(b) A bar graph

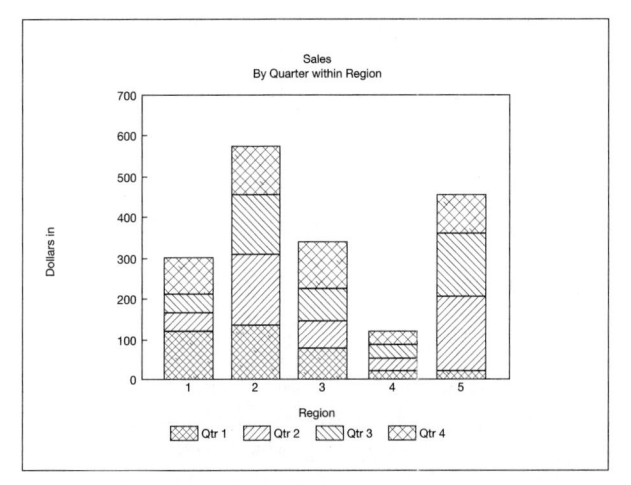

(c) A stacked-bar graph

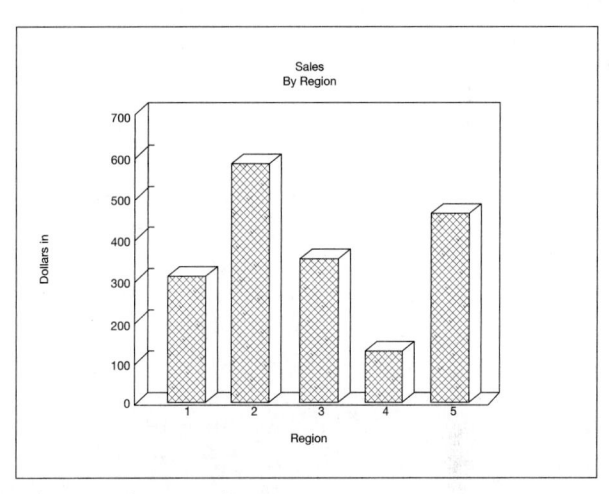

(d) A 3D bar graph

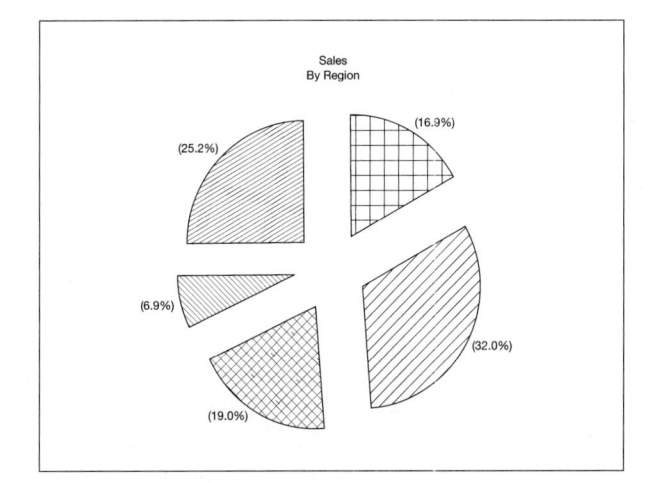

(e) A pie graph

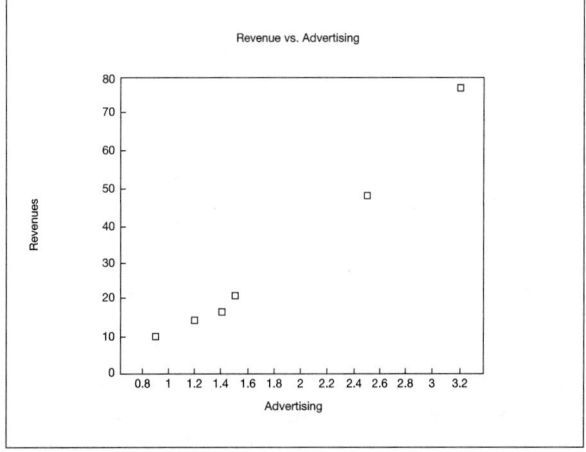

(f) An XY graph

FIGURE 9-10

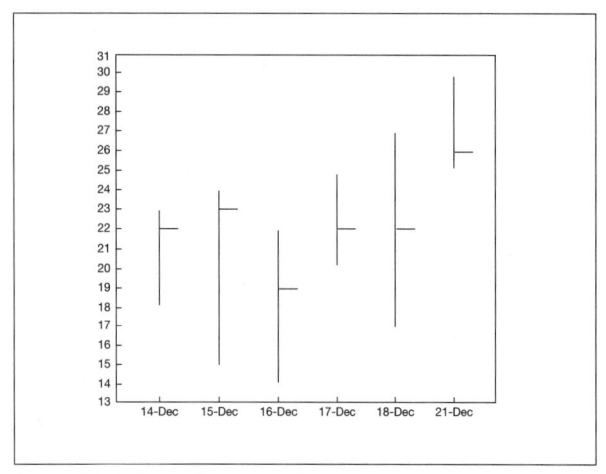

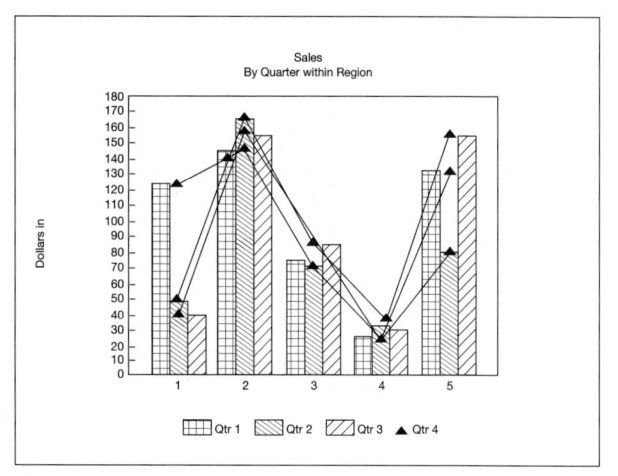

(g) *A high-low-close graph* (h) *A mixed graph*

FIGURE 9-10 (Cont.)

2. **Bar graph.** This graph represents values in bar form. Values, such as individual sales amounts for five different regions, will each be represented by a single bar.
3. **XY graph.** The XY graph is similar to the line graph, except that the data are represented by both X and Y coordinates. This is useful for charting one value against another, such as revenue against advertising costs. It can also be used for mathematical graphs, such as for plotting sine waves.
4. **Stacked-bar graph.** This is similar to the bar graph except each bar shows an accumulation of values. For example, sales for four quarters within a region would be shown on a single bar to show accumulated sales for the year.
5. **Pie graph.** The fifth form of graph is the pie chart. Using a pie chart automatically represents the data in terms of percentages. For example, if the data for sales in five regions were displayed as a pie instead of a bar chart, then each region would represent a wedge of the pie. Each wedge would show the sales for the region as a percentage of total sales.

Some spreadsheet software also provides **high-low** graphs for plotting the opening and closing values of stocks, **mixed** graphs that show data with different plotting such as bar and line together, and **3D** graphs that portray data in a three-dimensional grid.

Macros

Macro. A technique for storing frequently used keystrokes to automate their use in the program.

Advanced spreadsheets provide a macro facility to help automate the use of the spreadsheet. Macros can be written at two levels. The first simply records the keystrokes used to operate the spreadsheet. This can include operations such as saving or retrieving a file, displaying a graph, accepting data, or issuing a recalculation of the spreadsheet. All of these steps can be done manually but they require some knowledge of the use of the spread-

▶ CHOOSING A DOS- OR WINDOWS-BASED SPREADSHEET

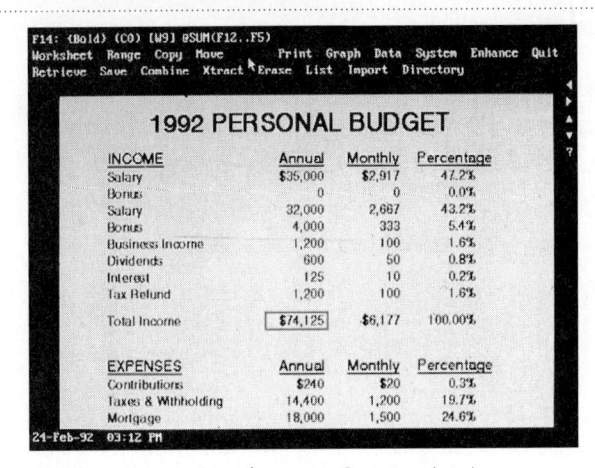

(Courtesy Lotus Development Corporation.)

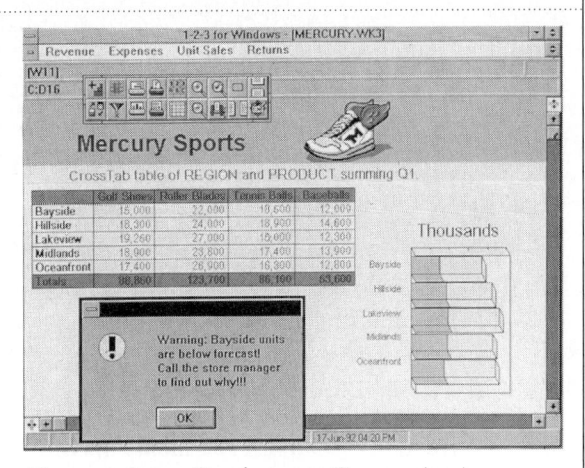

(Courtesy Lotus Development Corporation.)

With new spreadsheets, such as 1-2-3 for Windows, Quattro Pro for Windows, or Excel 4.0 for Windows, why should anyone want to use a DOS-based product? There are indeed many new features available on the Windows-based products, but the DOS spreadsheets still offer a great deal for the informed user.

DOS-based spreadsheets, such as Lotus 1-2-3 Release 2.4, and Quattro Pro 5.0, are sophisticated spreadsheets with many powerful features. They can use text mode for faster operation, but they have a graphics mode for presentation features and a WYSIWYG display. The top line DOS-based spreadsheets have extensive macro writing capability so that complex spreadsheets can be automated for anyone to use. Hundreds of add-in programs are available for these spreadsheets, especially for Lotus 1-2-3, that provide features not available in the original program.

By contrast, Windows-based spreadsheets are new on the market, so many add-ins are not yet available for them. They are not often compatible with spreadsheet applications developed for DOS, especially those using macros. In Windows, spreadsheets are generally slower than a comparable DOS-based product. But, the Windows-based spreadsheet offers important advantages to the user. They are easier learn and to use because of the graphical user interface (GUI) that is compatible with other Windows applications. Icons provide powerful alternatives to operations that were time consuming in a DOS spreadsheet. For example, in 1-2-3 for Windows you can click a calendar icon to place a date in the spreadsheet instead of using the @DATE function.

Windows spreadsheets support dynamic data exchange (DDE) which provides a hotlink from the spreadsheet to another document in a Windows-based program. You can use this feature to include a table created in 1-2-3 in a WordPerfect report. If values in the table are changed by the spreadsheet, the table in the report automatically changes as well. Most Windows spreadsheet publishers are promising to provide object linking and embedding (OLE) in new releases of their programs. So Windows-based spreadsheets seem to be the wave of the future, but for many users the DOS programs provide all the features they need.

sheet commands. By automating the commands, a simple keystroke can activate them, letting the user concentrate on the data.

The second form of macro lets the spreadsheet developer create applications with spreadsheet-like commands. Using the Lotus 1-2-3 command

```
            J                K              L              M
 1                      MACROS
 2
 3    \0                {GOTO}S1~
 4    \z                {MENUBRANCH MENU1}
 5
 6
 7    MENU1             Expenses         Car              Office
 8                      Daily Expenses   Maintenance Costs Office Expenses
 9                      {BRANCH EXPENSES} {BRANCH CAR}    {BRANCH OFFICE}
10
11    EXPENSES          {GOTO}A142~{DOWN}/wth{END}{DOWN}{DOWN}
12    REPEATEX          @today{edit}{calc}~{right}
13                      {MENUBRANCH TYPE}
14
15    TYPE              Supplies         Meals            Postage
16                      Press Enter      Press Enter      Press Enter
17                      Supplies~        Meals~           Postage~
18                      {RIGHT}{?}~      {RIGHT}{?}~      {RIGHT}{?}~
19                      {RIGHT}{?}~      {RIGHT}{?}~      {RIGHT}{?}~
20                      {RIGHT}{?}~      {RIGHT}{?}~      {RIGHT}{?}~
```

FIGURE 9-11

Part of a macro using Lotus 1–2–3's command language. Lines such as MENU1 and TYPE define menus that are displayed and used in the same manner as Lotus commands. Other commands, such as {GOTO}A142~ and {RIGHT}{?}~, represent keyboard macros that automate the use of the spreadsheet.

language (Figure 9-11) a program is written that creates its own menus. These menus are used in the same manner as Lotus 1–2–3 menus but they are specifically developed for the application. Thus, choices such as Expenses, Car, and Office are made available. With a command language the user only needs to know the application and is relieved from the need to know spreadsheet commands.

Three-Dimensional Spreadsheets

Traditional spreadsheets display data in two dimensions using rows and columns. Now software such as Lotus 1–2–3 Release 3 and QuattroPro for Windows (Figure 9-12) offers spreadsheet programs with three-dimensional capability. This does not mean that the spreadsheet displays with a 3D image on the screen, but rather that there is a third dimension to the spreadsheet. In QuattroPro this dimension is treated as a notebook with a tab at the bottom of the screen to select the sheet you require. In the example screen, different dimensions or notebooks are used to provide the pricing information of several different exotic automobiles. Because QuattroPro supports graphics, clip art is used to present a picture of the car alongside the costs. The first screen shown presents a menu of choices. Then by clicking on the appropriate choice, the notebook for that car is displayed on the front window. Windows can also be tiled so that several car's data can appear at the same time.

When using a two-dimensional spreadsheet, a budget might be displayed with budget items down the first column with additional columns side by side showing amounts for each month of the year. A three-dimensional spreadsheet can show the items and amounts for one month on the screen as the first page. A second page (behind the first) with a similar format is

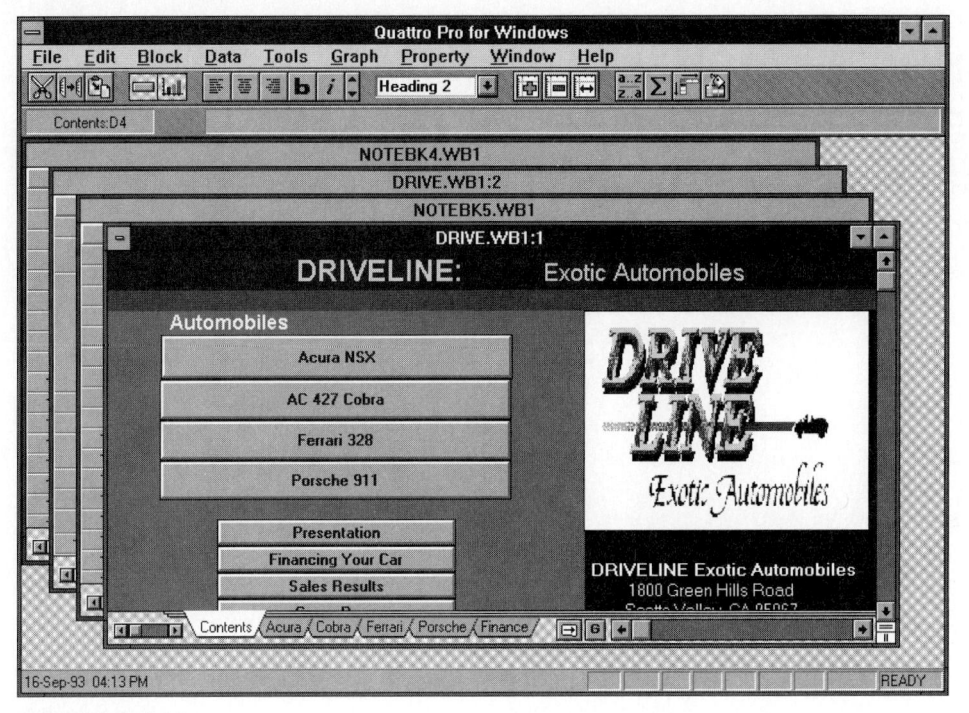

FIGURE 9-12
Quattro Pro for Windows uses the concept of notebooks to provide three-dimensional capabilities to its spreadsheet. To select a dimension click on the tab for that component of the worksheet. As shown in this screen, different notebooks can be cascaded to provide quick reference to any data. (Courtesy Borland International.)

used for the next month. A total of 12 pages would be used for an annual budget. Only one page is visible at a time, so the 3D spreadsheet appears similar to a two-dimensional one.

Three-dimensional spreadsheets tend to display data in a simpler fashion because less data needs to be visible at any one time. This makes for less crowded displays and easier design. True three-dimensional applications can be developed more easily, whereas a two-dimensional spreadsheet requires some ingenuity. For example, a sales application with sales for each product by region and month is awkward to manipulate on a two-dimensional spreadsheet but is quite natural on a three-dimensional one.

While 3D spreadsheets may seem to be a natural evolution for spreadsheet programs, they had not received a great deal of attention until Windows spreadsheets came on the market. One reason may be that spreadsheets, like Lotus 1–2–3 Release 2, provided more capability than many users need and so for them, there is little reason to use a three-dimensional spreadsheet. But some Windows spreadsheets are now providing three-dimensional capability as a standard feature and in a form that is easier to learn than older 3D products.

An alternative to three dimensions is to use **file linking**, which allows many separate files to be linked to a single spreadsheet. Each spreadsheet resides on disk as a separate file. Formulas in the spreadsheet not only refer

▶ SPREADSHEET FEATURES

Spreadsheet programs come with a wide range of features. Some, such as functions, are absolutely required for effective use while others, such as file linking, may be dispensable for some users. This list provides a general sense of features you might consider when choosing a spreadsheet, but for a complete list you should reference the documentation of the program in question.

Basic Features
Labels
Values
Formulas
Functions
Copy command
Column width setting
Formatting
Automatic recalculation
Printing
Headers and footers
Page numbering

Spreadsheet Features
Split screens
Titles, freezing
Undo
File import and export
Extract partial spreadsheet
Combine partial spreadsheet
WYSIWYG
Hidden columns
Hidden cells
Mouse support
Uses expanded/extended memory
Lotus 1–2–3 compatibility
Three dimensions
File linking
Drag and Drop

Functions
Database
Date and time
Financial
Logical
Mathematical
String
Statistical
Matrix operations
Regression analysis
What if tables

Graphs
Bar
Stacked-bar
3D bar
Pie
Hi-Lo
XY
Line
Area

Presentation Features
WYSIWYG preview
Combine text and graphs
Fonts
Line and box drawing
Shading
Landscape printing
Voice annotation

to different cell addresses but also to other spreadsheets on disk. With linked files, an update link operation is often necessary to ensure that each spreadsheet that is linked contains current information. Some spreadsheets, such as Borland's Quattro Pro for Windows, provides both three-dimensional and file linking features.

SPREADSHEET PRESENTATION FEATURES

Spreadsheets are not limited to the recording and calculating of numerical data. Many spreadsheet programs provide a variety of tools to turn the

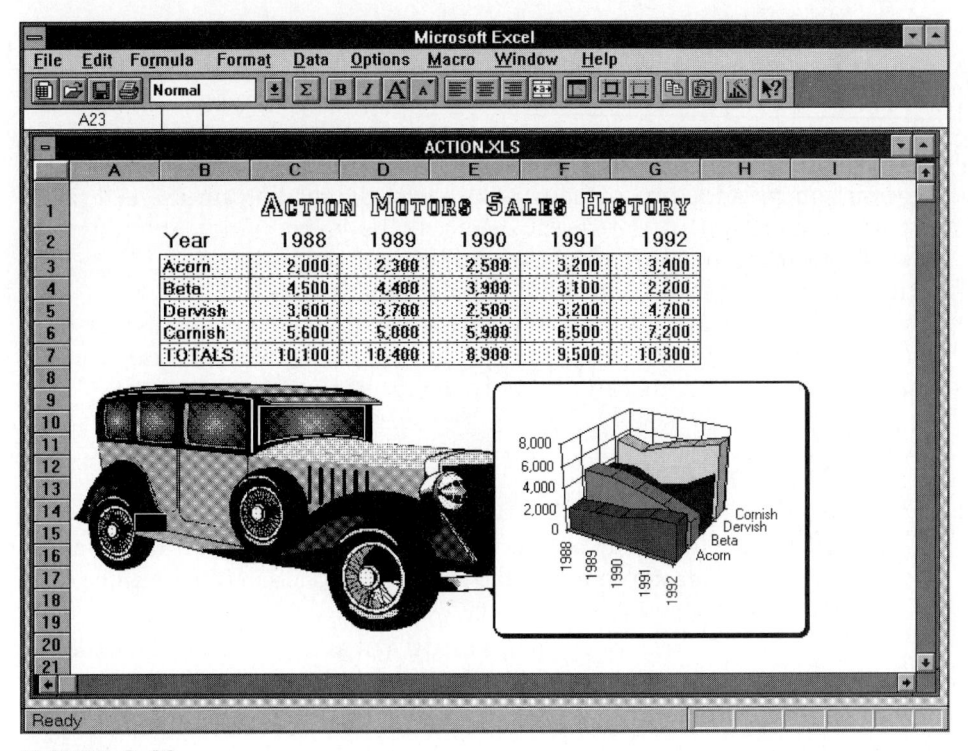

FIGURE 9-13
This spreadsheet, created in Microsoft Excel, includes different fonts, boldface, line drawing, and shading to enhance the spreadsheet data. A 3D chart inside a shadow box provides a visual interpretation of the spreadsheet data, and clip art imported from Corel Draw adds interest to the presentation.

spreadsheet into a vehicle (see Figure 9-13) that combines numbers, text, fonts, lines, charts, and graphics to be used for business presentations. Some, such as Microsoft Excel and Quattro Pro for Windows, let you create a slide show from the components of the spreadsheet. Powerful spreadsheet programs such as these go beyond the spreadsheet to provide a whole array of features that formerly required several different software packages.

A simple enhancement to any spreadsheet can be created by using several different fonts to emphasize headings, labels, or important values. Fonts can be selected from a variety of styles and can be applied in different point sizes. Usually boldface and underlining are available in addition to the standard font, and some programs provide color options. However, choosing too many different fonts can detract from the presentation rather than enhance it.

Another presentation feature is the use of line drawing to create lines, boxes, or outlines. Often the box or outline is used to make an important component of the spreadsheet stand out and draw the reader's attention to this element of the presentation. Using a shadow around the box or shading inside it can further enhance the appearance.

Most spreadsheets let you create a graph from the data in the spreadsheet, but only recent ones have been able to display the graph on the same screen and print it with the spreadsheet. Enhancement tools can be used to size and rotate the graph, add text to it, or even draw lines, arrows, ovals, or other objects to the spreadsheet. Then for the ultimate in pizzazz add a graphic from a clip art file to the spreadsheet.

Imagine hearing a verbal explanation of a complex part of a spreadsheet. With the addition of a sound board and the appropriate software, voice annotation can be added to some spreadsheets. By clicking on the cell or an icon an explanation of the spreadsheet can be given. Voice annotation is quickly spreading to other applications beyond spreadsheets, so expect to see it soon in word processor and database applications.

Many of the features discussed here that can enhance a spreadsheet have their origin in presentation graphics programs. In the next chapter we will examine some of these features in more depth.

CHAPTER SUMMARY

1. **Spreadsheets** are frequently used as a convenient method for recording numerical data and taking advantage of the automatic calculations that can be done efficiently with a spreadsheet program.
2. The spreadsheet is used for creating a **model** and asking "what if?" questions.
3. Spreadsheets consist of a number of cells arranged in rows and columns. In a computer spreadsheet a value, label, formula, or function can be stored in each cell.
4. A **cell** is located where a row and column meet on the screen. The **address** A1 is the intersection of column A and row 1 is a cell where a value may be placed in the spreadsheet.
5. Spreadsheet programs use a **control panel** or **status line** to communicate with the user. One or more lines are used to display menus, prompts, cell contents, current cell address, and mode.
6. The **menu line** appears when the slash (/) key is pressed or the area is clicked with a mouse.
7. The **mode indicator** identifies the current mode or status that the program is in.
8. A **formula** is an arithmetic expression or formula, such as +A1+A2+A3, that does a calculation using values on the spreadsheet. A **function,** such as @SUM(A1..A3), provides a shortcut for writing a formula and often provides for calculations that could not otherwise be done.
9. A **range** is a rectangular or square grouping of cells. Ranges are identified by the upper left and lower right cell addresses of the range.
10. A **format** may be used to set values to display in different ways. Some formats display dollar signs, commas, dates, or interest rates.
11. A **relative address,** such as D5, is used when the row number or column letter is adjusted in the formula when it is copied to another cell.
12. An **absolute address,** such as D5, is used when an address in the formula is not to be adjusted when a formula is copied.
13. **Graphs** are used in business reports that frequently include bar charts, pie charts, or line graphs to present information in a pictorial form, rather than as raw data.

CHAPTER 9 Spreadsheet Software

14. Most spreadsheet software will produce a variety of graphs, some with more types than others. Five common types of graphs are line, bar, XY, stacked-bar, and pie.
15. Advanced spreadsheets provide a **macro** facility to help automate the use of the spreadsheet.
16. **Three-dimensional spreadsheets** are used to manipulate data in three dimensions—row, column, and page. Data on the 3D spreadsheet often tends to be simpler and easier to manipulate than on a two-dimensional spreadsheet.
17. Many spreadsheet programs provide a variety of presentation tools that combine numbers, text, fonts, lines, charts, and clip art graphics to prepare the spreadsheet for an effective business presentation.

IMPORTANT TERMS AND CONCEPTS

Absolute address	Model
Address	Mouse pointer
Cell	Pointer
Column	Presentation tools
Control panel	Range
Format	Relative address
Formula	Row
Function	Speedbar
Graph	Spreadsheet
Label	Template
Macro	Three-dimensional spreadsheet
Menu	Value
Mode indicator	"What if" question

SELF-TESTING QUESTIONS

Fill-In

1. A budget planning _____ can be built into a spreadsheet showing total expenses per year using a number of different categories.
2. A _____ is the area found at the intersection of a column and a row.
3. A _____ question is used to ask what happens to the model if certain values are changed.
4. The _____ _____ is the highlighted bar that points to the current cell where a value or formula may be entered or edited.
5. An entry on the spreadsheet such as +B6+B7+B8+B9+B10 is called a _____.
6. An entry such as @SUM(B6..B10) is called a _____.
7. A _____, such as A1..A10, refers to a group of cells specified by the address of the first and last cell in the group.
8. When a formula is copied into a new cell the _____ will be adjusted to correspond to the new location.
9. A graph called a _____ chart represents spreadsheet data in percentages.

10. Spreadsheet _____ features include items such as line drawing, boxes, shading, different fonts, and clip art graphics.

True/False

1. Word wrap is used when a formula is too large for the width of a cell.
2. The process of giving a cell a fixed, currency, or percent notation is called copying.
3. A template is a spreadsheet containing blank entries where data is to be entered.
4. A range refers to a group of adjacent cells that may be formatted, copied, or moved.
5. A label is used in a cell where a calculation is required.
6. A speedbar on some spreadsheets identifies common activities such as summing a column of numbers.
7. A relative address in a formula is adjusted during copying while an absolute address is not.
8. Macros are tools that provide a way to link data in a spreadsheet to your favorite word processor.

ANSWERS

Fill-In: **1.** model, **2.** cell, **3.** "what if," **4.** cell pointer, **5.** formula, **6.** function, **7.** range, **8.** address, **9.** pie, **10.** presentation

True/False: **1.** F, **2.** F, **3.** T, **4.** T, **5.** F, **6.** T, **7.** T, **8.** F

Questions for Critical Thinking

1. Because of the spreadsheet's ease of working with numbers it will soon make your bank book obsolete.
2. Just as pocket calculators replaced the adding machine, the spreadsheet will soon become the method of choice for working with numbers in a pocket calculator. Discuss.
3. Some personal computers are being supplied with a spreadsheet program preinstalled, thus eliminating the need for the owner to buy the program separately. What are the pros and cons of this practice? To the purchaser? To the computer and/or software company?

CHAPTER 10
INTEGRATED, GRAPHICS, AND OTHER SOFTWARE

A VIEW OF THE CHAPTER AHEAD

After reading this chapter you will understand

- ▶ the advantages of integrated software over separate packages.
- ▶ the function and use of presentation graphics software.
- ▶ why graphics software packages are becoming widespread.
- ▶ specialized software such as project management software and CAD/CAM.

INTRODUCTION

While word processing, spreadsheet, and database software represent the lion's share of software sold for the PC, there are other types of software that are gaining attention by users everywhere. People who frequently do business presentations, or nonbusiness for that matter, are finding that presentation software packages provide a great deal more power and flexibility than most word processors. Others who create documents, newsletters, flyers, or other productions that are graphical in nature find that graphics software supplements, and in some cases replaces, their desktop publishing software. Then there are the engineers and technical designers who use specialized software (CAD/CAM) to assist in the design and production of mechanical and electrical devices. So we see that computer software has cut a wide swath in the field of computer users everywhere. But first we will look at an alternative to standalone software—the integrated software package.

INTEGRATED SOFTWARE

Integrated software. A program that contains several major features such as word processing, spreadsheet, database, graphics, and communications in a single package.

Integrated software such as Microsoft Works, First Choice, Enable, and Lotus Works generally provides a combination of spreadsheet, database, word processing, graphics, and communications in a single package. Instead of buying three or four separate programs, a single integrated program may be purchased, often for the price of one application. For example, Microsoft Works for Windows (Figure 10-1) generally costs less than Word for Windows or WordPerfect for Windows. Yet Works contains the features of the four major program groups mentioned above, granted that many integrated programs are limited versions of a single application software package.

Integrated programs try to provide a smooth transition from one application to another on the computer with a minimum of change in the mode of operation. In a certain sense Lotus 1–2–3 achieves the spirit of integration by providing spreadsheet, graphics, and database capabilities in a single environment. The command structure for each component of the package is the same; they even use the same data organization.

This is the essence of integration: several applications are combined into one software package and each is used in a similar manner within the software. While 1–2–3 might be considered integrated, it is not; it is mostly an excellent spreadsheet program. Its graphic or database components do not compare to the features available on a stand-alone graphics package, such as Harvard Presentation Graphics, or compared to a full-featured database, such as dBASE IV. Neither does 1–2–3 offer word processing or data communication that integrated software generally provides.

Benefits of Using Integrated Software

There are several reasons why computer users are attracted to integrated packages. Although different packages may offer an assortment of features,

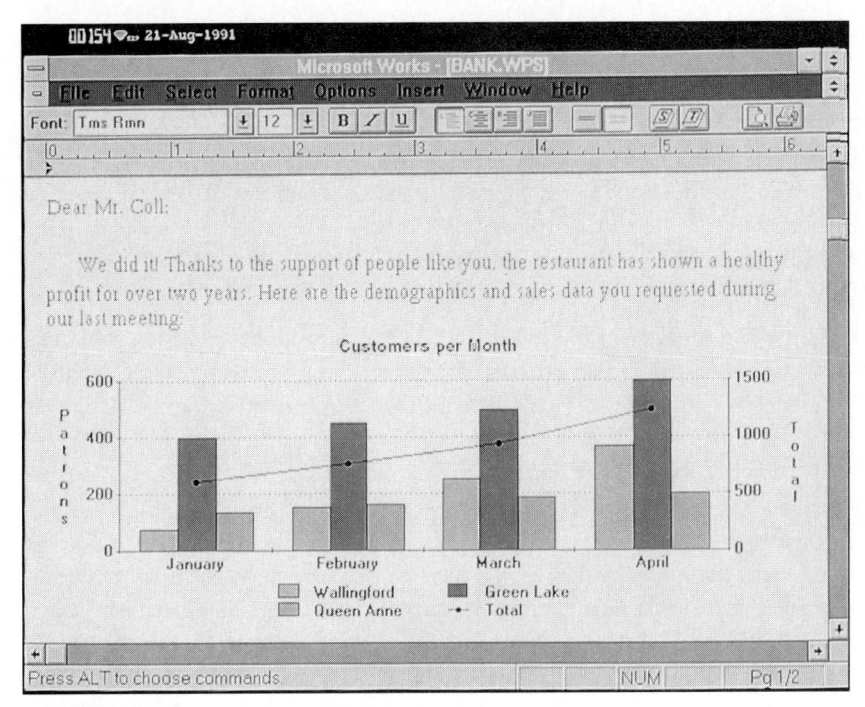

CHAPTER 10 Integrated, Graphics, and Other Software

FIGURE 10-1
An integrated software package such as Microsoft Works offers the user a choice of modes. Word processing, spreadsheet, graphics, data management, and data communications are all components of the software. Data can be readily transferred between windows as needed by different parts of the application. (Courtesy Microsoft.)

there are some common reasons stated for choosing an integrated software package. Some of these reasons are:

1. They reduce the number of software packages that the user needs to learn.
2. They are less costly than buying many separate programs.
3. It is easier to switch from one mode to another.
4. Data can be readily transferred between applications.

Let's look at each of these benefits of integrated packages in more detail.

Reducing the Number of Packages to Learn. A computer user who requires a variety of software such as a spreadsheet, database, word processor, and communications will typically buy four different programs. After buying this software, the next step is to learn each package, which no doubt will take some time. It may take several weeks to have a good command of one program.

This user will also soon realize that each program is quite different from the other. So once the spreadsheet has been mastered, the learning process starts over again with the database package. Few software packages adopt their commands from other software unless they are doing the same thing.

So a package such as Lotus 1–2–3 may have many similarities to Quattro Pro (another spreadsheet) but will have no similarity to dBASE IV (a database program).

An integrated program can help to reduce the time it takes to learn the capabilities of the software. A well-designed integrated program will use a similar command structure for all of its features. So once you know how to use the spreadsheet, learning the word processor will not be so difficult or time consuming. Naturally, some integrated packages have succeeded at incorporating this similarity among its features better than others.

Reducing the Cost of Software. Another benefit of using an integrated package is cost. It is simply less expensive to buy one integrated program than three or four or more separate ones. A good integrated software package can generally be purchased for under two hundred dollars, considerably less than buying four major packages.

Changing Environments. Because an integrated package offers several modes of operation, a keystroke is usually all that is necessary to change from one mode to another. If the user is in the database environment, a simple command can switch instantly to the spreadsheet or word processor environment. Thus, a user can create a form letter in the word processor and switch to the database to get the names and addresses.

Compared to separate programs, this speed of change is attractive to users who require a frequent change of software environment to do their work. With stand-alone packages the user must first save the current file in the database, exit from the program to DOS, then load the spreadsheet program. Finally, a file would be retrieved in the spreadsheet. All this might take a minute or more, a long time in computer terms.

Data Transfer. Integrated packages generally store their data in a common format. Thus, data from the database can be read by the spreadsheet or the word processor or even transmitted to another computer over the telephone. With separate packages, this data transfer process can range from quite simple in some cases to extremely difficult or virtually impossible in other situations.

Exporting data from a dBASE IV database and **importing** it into a Lotus 1–2–3 spreadsheet is possible but requires some technical knowledge on the part of the user or the use of a separate program to translate from one form to the other. However, an Enable user can easily transfer data from an Enable database environment to the Enable spreadsheet with a few keystrokes.

Thus, PC users who have the need to move data from one environment to another on a frequent basis will find that an integrated package will handle this operation with little difficulty.

Problems with Integrated Packages

While it might seem that integrated packages are the answer to all the needs of most users, they are not without limitations. By trying to cover all of the bases by offering uniformity among its features, there are obvious drawbacks. A command structure that works well for a spreadsheet may not be as appropriate for the word processor.

The way data is stored in an integrated package may not always be suitable for the different components. A spreadsheet with rows and columns and cells with formulas does not lend itself well to a word processing document or to a database with fields and records. Thus, the concept of data transfer between the applications may not always work so simply in real life. Finally, integrated packages seldom offer the full range of features seen in single application programs. If you want all the "bells and whistles," then separate programs are one solution.

Windows Software

Another alternative to consider is Windows applications. There are integrated packages for Windows, but Windows software generally provides many of the features previously available only if an integrated package was used. Although Windows programs are not integrated in the sense we have discussed, they do offer a common user interface (GUI) and techniques (OLE and DDE) for sharing data between applications. If you have the necessary hardware configuration, then several programs may be opened in different windows and data shared between them. For some users, Windows software may provide a powerful new solution to an old problem.

Presentation Software

Part of any business requirement is the need for effective communication. Whether the manager is presenting the plans for a new operation or reviewing the results of past accomplishments, effective communication tools are needed to make the presentation both interesting and informative. Presentation graphics computer software, from under $100 to over $500, is available to help to prepare and present quality graphics.

Using a software package, such as Harvard Presentation Graphics (Figure 10-2), Freelance Graphics for Windows, or Corel Draw (see Photo Essay), tables, charts, or graphs can be prepared on the computer for use in a business presentation. A chart is something that contains text while a graph contains analytical data presented as a pie, bar, line, or other form of graph. Either of these can be prepared as masters for an overhead transparency or as color slides. Graphics packages can also be used to display the charts or graphs on a screen using a projector system attached to the computer.

A presentation graphics program is also used to design a slide using a variety of images, graphs, clip art, or symbols. Text can be added that uses a variety of fonts. Large type can be used to emphasize important points or topics and smaller type for the finer details. Different type styles, shading, or outlines also contribute to the effectiveness of the chart. Most software permits italics, boldface, underlining, or even color for extra emphasis.

Presentation graphics programs can also produce graphics from data that is either entered into the program itself or data that is imported from a spreadsheet. Many graphic programs accept data from Lotus 1–2–3, Excel, or other spreadsheet software, thus eliminating the need to retype data that is already available on the computer.

Presentation graphics. Software that is used in the preparation and presentation of charts or graphs and other items used for presentations.

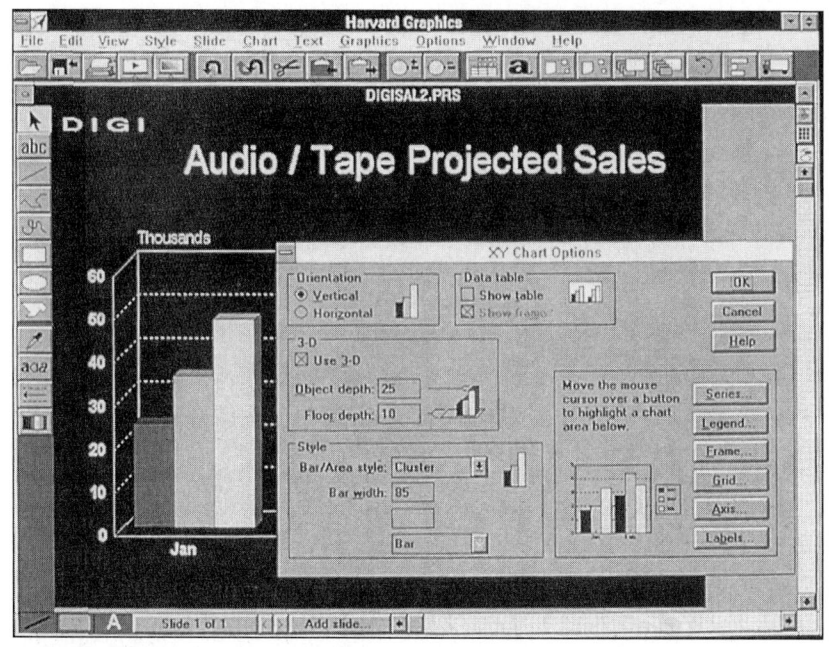

FIGURE 10-2
Harvard Graphics for Windows is a graphics package that provides numerous chart options, importing from popular spreadsheets, line drawing with a variety of lines styles and fill options, color selection, 500 clip art images, and scalable type faces. The program also imports images from other graphic sources and provides some multimedia support. (Courtesy Software Publishing Corp.)

Importing of graphic files from other programs is an important feature if the program does not supply all of the graphic images you need. Typical presentation software will provide a clip art library, but the better programs will allow you to import images from other sources.

Output from a graphics program is initially on a color monitor. Once the slide has been prepared it can be printed on a graphics printer such as a laser or color printer. Alternatively, a plotter can be used to create high-quality drawings of the chart or graph using color as required for exceptional results.

Some presentation graphics packages provide for film output. Using a special interface, a device such as the Polaroid Palette or MAGICorp slide service can be used to produce color slides from the program. This form of output gives the highest quality results, but the camera device is an expensive attachment. A less costly alternative is to use a service company to produce the slides from your files.

But most presentation software users prepare and present their show directly on the computer. The slides are created using the software and then organized into a show which consists of a series of slides. By connecting a notebook computer to an LCD display the show can be presented from the computer using the presentation software as a slide projector.

As presentation graphics software becomes more sophisticated, additional features are becoming available. Not only do these newer packages create good graphs or charts, but they can now do animation. Corel Draw is a good example of this class of software. It combines a paint program, a graphics package, and an image editor for manipulating the images. Animated shows are displayed on the screen as a series of slides and are useful for exciting business presentations.

GRAPHICS SOFTWARE

Sophisticated software for word processing, spreadsheets, database, and presentation all provide for the use of graphics in the application. In many cases more than one type of graphic can be used. Graphics not only make a report or other document more interesting, but they can add meaning that is not easily represented by words or numbers. Some programs create their own graphics, such as when a spreadsheet creates a graph, but many rely on clip art or other graphics programs such as Adobe Illustrator and CorelDRAW at the top end, or Windows PaintBrush at the low end.

All graphics programs provide for drawing and editing of graphics, but the high-end programs have sophisticated tools for creating complex graphics. In the accompanying box are some of the tools that are available in Corel PhotoPaint, a subset program of CorelDRAW. Several categories of tools are provided including control of the display of the graphic, selecting portions of the graphic for processing, and tools for drawing, painting, erasing, coloring, spraying, and adding text to the graphic. Other tools for drawing arcs, circles, ellipses, boxes, and irregular shapes are available in

Graphics software, such as Zenographics, can be used to enhance presentations by providing images, clip art, and graphs. (Courtesy Zenographics.)

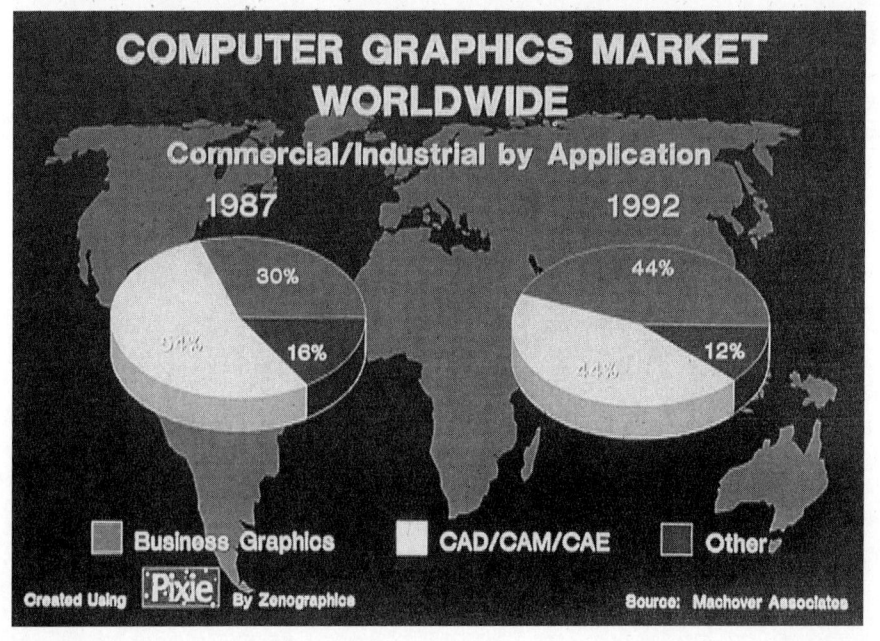

Selection Tools:

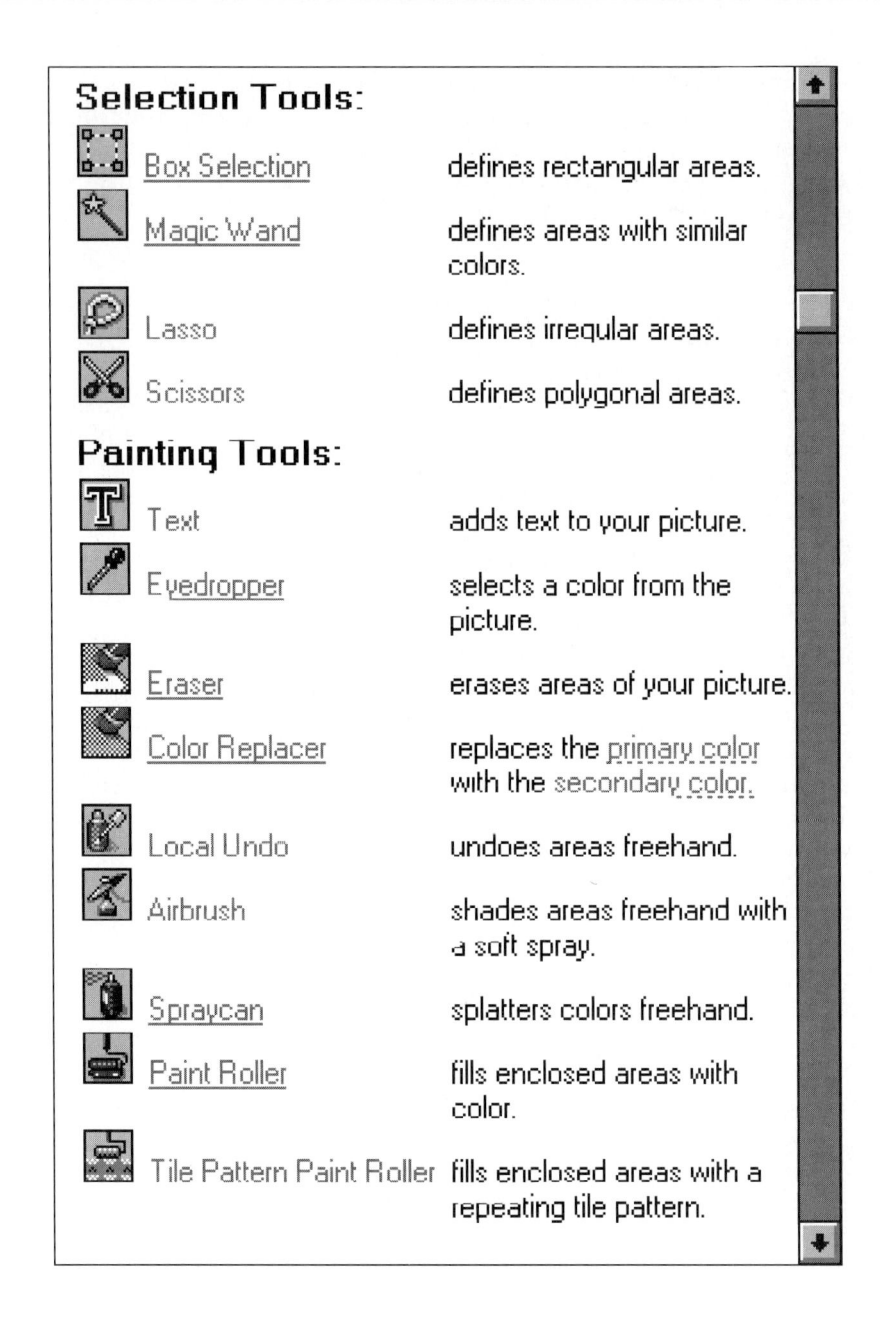

	Box Selection	defines rectangular areas.
	Magic Wand	defines areas with similar colors.
	Lasso	defines irregular areas.
	Scissors	defines polygonal areas.

Painting Tools:

	Text	adds text to your picture.
	Eyedropper	selects a color from the picture.
	Eraser	erases areas of your picture.
	Color Replacer	replaces the primary color with the secondary color.
	Local Undo	undoes areas freehand.
	Airbrush	shades areas freehand with a soft spray.
	Spraycan	splatters colors freehand.
	Paint Roller	fills enclosed areas with color.
	Tile Pattern Paint Roller	fills enclosed areas with a repeating tile pattern.

most programs. Advanced programs provide functions to align images, blend, extrude, and change perspective.

Learning the basic features of such programs is fairly easy, but mastering all of the advanced tools is a demanding task that takes time, training, and practice. Most important, using a graphics program does not turn everyone into a graphic artist. Having some basic artistic talent is useful for getting the best out of these programs.

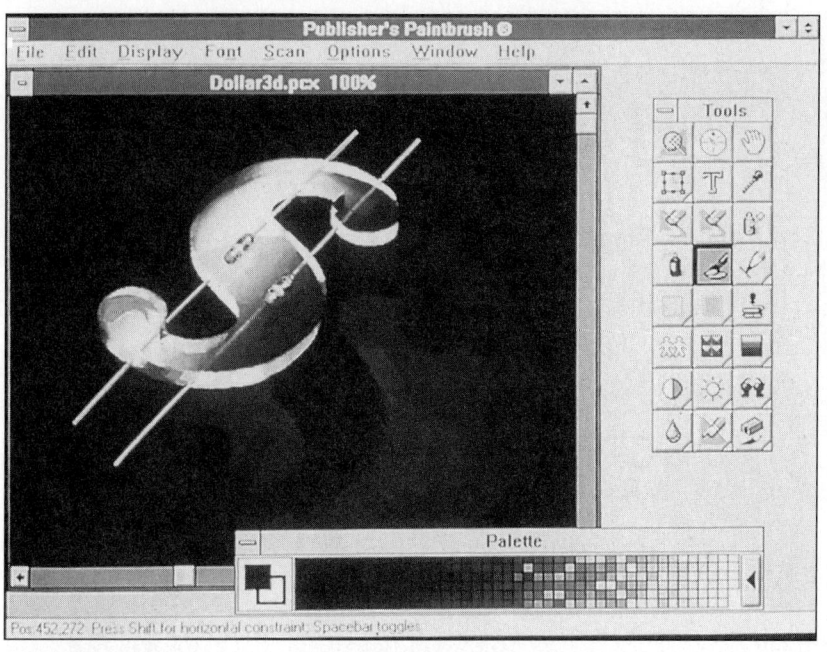

FIGURE 10-3
A bitmapped graphic is created in a paint program such as Publishers Paintbrush. Individual pixels are turned on or off to create the picture. (Courtesy Z-Soft Corporation.)

Graphic Types

Graphics generally are stored as either bitmapped or vector graphics. Some of the simpler programs can only use bitmapped graphics, but the more complex ones can use either type. **Bitmapped** graphics are composed of a series of pixels that form an image (Figure 10-3). Individual pixels are turned on or off in a pattern that creates an image. Pixels may also be assigned shades of gray or color to enhance the graphics. Bitmapped graphics are also known by the name **raster graphics,** which is based on the display technology used to show the image on the screen. Paint programs typically create bitmapped graphics. Many clip art graphics are composed of bitmapped images. Programs such as WordPerfect, Word, Excel, and Paradox for Windows can all incorporate bitmapped graphics in their applications.

A second type of graphic is **vector graphics,** which creates a drawing by connecting points or vectors with lines (Figure 10-4). Vectors use mathematical formulas to form images such as lines, circles, rectangles, and other more complex shapes. Using vectors for an image makes resizing the image efficient with no loss of information. Draw programs such as CorelDRAW use vector graphic techniques for creating images, but can also use bitmapped images as the application demands. Other programs such as Lotus 1–2–3 create graphs using vectors.

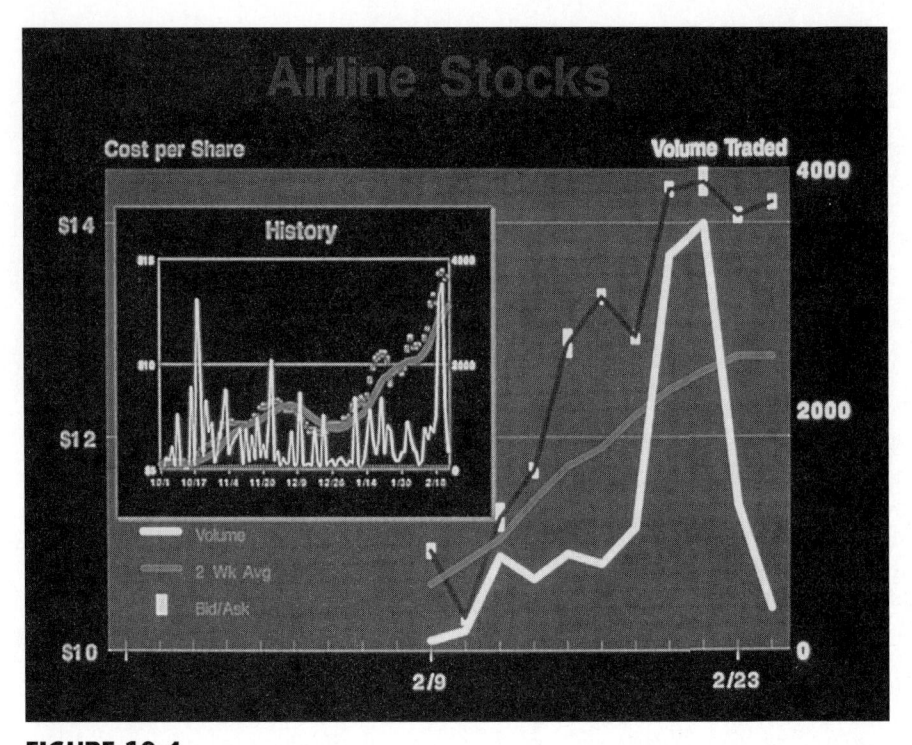

FIGURE 10-4
This image is a vector graphic created in Harvard Graphics. (Courtesy Software Publishing Corp.)

OTHER SOFTWARE PACKAGES

Personal Information Managers

Personal information managers (PIMs) are programs that replace traditional office tools with an electronic equivalent. Some of the items that may be found in a desktop program are:

- Appointment book
- Calendar
- Clock
- Note pad
- Phone book and dialer
- Calculator
- Text editor
- Electronic mail links

Depending on the program, more or less of these features will be found. Borland's SideKick Plus, Lotus Organizer, and Microsoft Windows Acces-

▶ PHOTO ESSAY CORELDRAW

CorelDRAW is a complete graphics package that includes components to create illustrations, make charts and graphs, do bitmap editing, and produce presentations with slides and animation. The package can be used to create anything from simple graphics to complete page layouts, ads, posters, technical illustrations, and business presentations.[1] CorelDRAW is a complete graphic package that consists of program disks, manuals, a CD-ROM containing over 12,000 clip art images and symbols, and over 250 TrueType fonts. It even contains a video tape to help you get started.

CorelDRAW

The primary component of the package is CorelDRAW, which is a vector illustration program. It provides precise drawing power, easy text handling, libraries of fonts and symbols, clip art, and full color.

CorelDRAW has text handling capabilities that rival the best anywhere. It gives precision type control, hundreds of fonts, and dazzling special effects. Images may be created with layering effects, 3D objects that can be manipulated in three dimensions, and editing in full color or wire frame mode. And OLE support is provided so CorelDRAW can interface with other software packages.

CorelDRAW 3.0

CorelCHART

CorelCHART is a program that turns data into meaningful charts. Using data that is keyed into the program or imported from a spreadsheet or database, CorelCHART creates stunning graphs ranging from 3D bars to pies or area charts.

CorelCHART goes beyond the features in even the most sophisticated spreadsheets to create charts that are vertical or horizontal bar, line, or area charts, pies with single or multiple ranges, scatter graphs, spectral graphs, histograms, and true 3D bar, ribbon, or surface charts. You can even use clip art to create a pictograph where the clip art forms the bar in the chart.

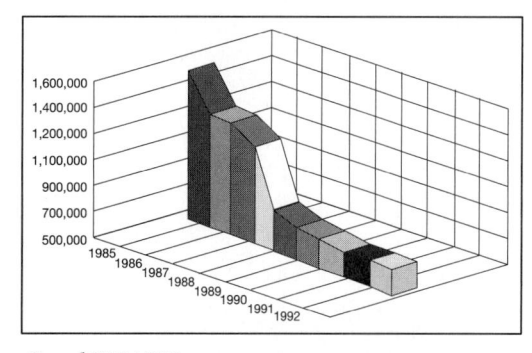

CorelCHART

---

[1] Images and information courtesy of Corel Corporation.

Data can be entered in three different ways: by typing it directly, by using DDE links to other software such as Lotus 1–2–3 or Excel, or data may be imported directly from Excel, Lotus 1–2–3, Harvard Graphics, or dBASE.

CorelSHOW

When you have created a series of charts or illustrations, the next step may be to organize them into a slide show. That's when Corel-SHOW is used to organize and present elements from CorelDRAW, CorelCHART, and CorelPHOTO-PAINT. A show can contain all of these images plus backgrounds from a library of files. To add some excitement to the production, add animation with Autodesk Animator or 3D Studio. The program can also produce slides, overhead transparencies, and paper handouts for the participants.

CorelPHOTO-PAINT

CorelPHOTO-PAINT is a bitmapped program used for photo editing. Using a toolset of soft brushes, fountain pen, and spraycan, create special effects like emboss, motion blur, tile and mosaic patterns. Other tools are used to sharpen, blend, smudge, smear, tint, clone, and brighten images. Nationwide Kodak Photo CD centers will even put your photos on a CD to use in CorelPHOTO-PAINT.

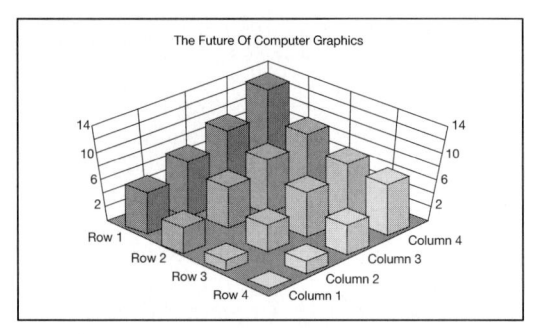

CorelCHART

CorelSHOW

CorelPHOTO-PAINT

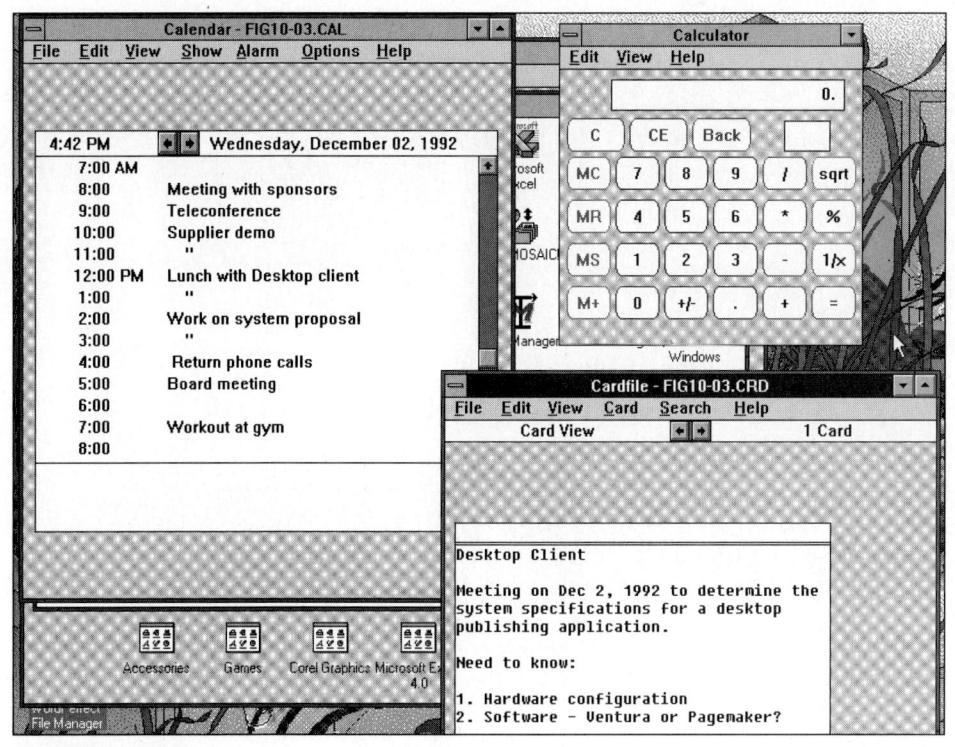

FIGURE 10-5
Using the Calendar, Calculator, and Card File features in Windows Accessories.

sories (Figure 10-5) are examples of programs that contain a collection of these features.

Project Management

An important function of management is planning: planning new projects, scheduling the necessary activities, and doing follow-up to keep everything on schedule. Computer age managers are beginning to use computer software (Figure 10-6) to aid in the management of ongoing projects.

Project management software typically produces a chart that helps the user to manage the project effectively. One type of chart is the **PERT** chart (Program Evaluation and Review Technique) which shows the relationships between tasks. It uses a critical path method to show the order in which tasks must be done and identifies those tasks that are critical to the timing of the project. These tasks must be completed in a given time frame to ensure that other dependent tasks are completed on schedule. Other noncritical tasks may be done at any time without an untoward effect on the project.

Another type of chart is a **Gantt** chart, which shows the timing of each task. By comparing the timing on the Gantt chart to the current status of each task, it is possible to determine if a task is on schedule.

Project management. Software that assists in the organization and management of projects and tasks.

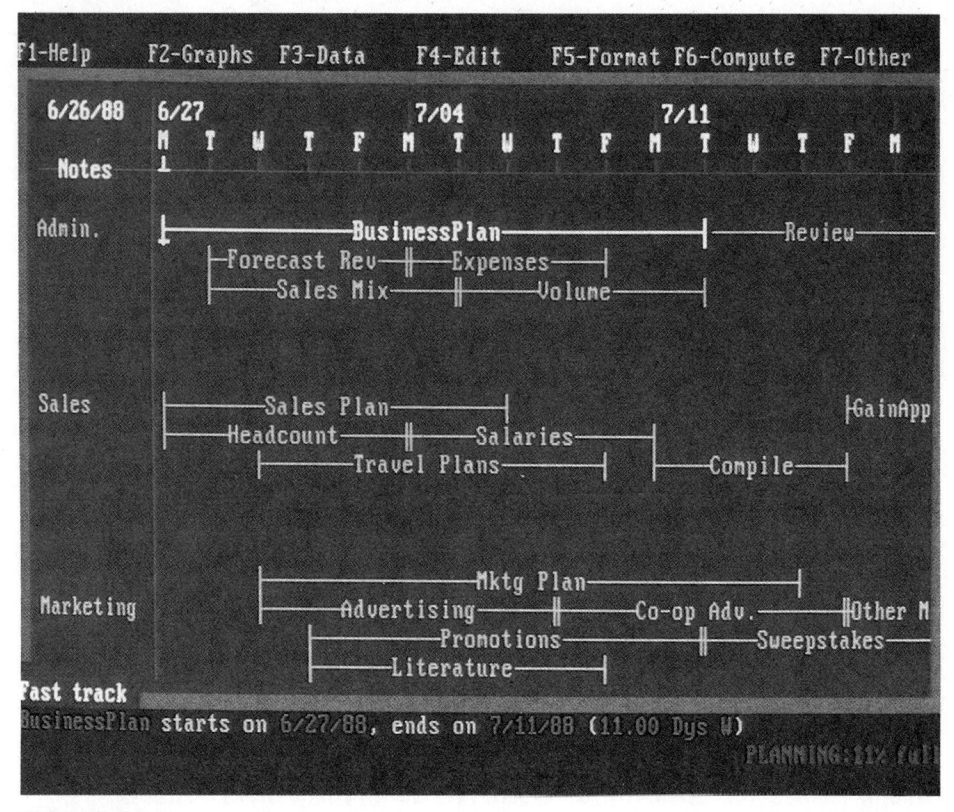

FIGURE 10-6
This output from the Harvard Total Project Manager shows how software is used for project management. Software can identify critical tasks and show dates when specific tasks must be completed.

MULTIMEDIA SOFTWARE

One of the fastest growing areas of computer technology is multimedia. The best known component of multimedia is the CD-ROM, but the term encompasses text, graphics, sound, and animation. Perhaps the most popular use of CD-ROM is for electronic encyclopedias such as The New Grolier Electronic Encyclopedia and Compton's Family Encyclopedia. Other popular products are National Geographic Society's Mammals, Microsoft Bookshelf, and Software Toolworks Reference Library.

Most of these products make use of a range of multimedia features, and to get the most out of them a CD-ROM drive with multimedia extensions such as a sound board are necessary. For example, the Software Toolworks Multimedia Encyclopedia contains the 21–volume text of the Grolier Academic America Encyclopedia with some 33,000 articles, 250 maps, over 50 video clips, and over 30 minutes of sound. Searches can be done by topic, words, or groups of words. Not only can you find John F. Kennedy's inauguration speech, but you can see and hear it from a video on the CD-ROM, or watch Neil Armstrong's first step on the moon.

While a CD-ROM based encyclopedia may have an appeal for the home,

CD-ROM software can provide over 650 million bytes of text and pictures, video, and sound on a single CD. (Courtesy Microsoft.)

other works such as Computer Select or Magazine rack are useful for libraries and businesses that need current data from a variety of publications. Computer Select is a subscription-based CD-ROM that provides monthly updates. The CD-ROM contains 12 months of articles from over 160 leading computer publications such as *PC Magazine*, *PC Week*, and *MacUser*. It also contains specifications for over 75,000 hardware, software, and communications products and profiles, addresses, and phone numbers for over 13,000 computer companies. Typical users are college libraries, and companies that use computers extensively or have frequent contact with computer organizations.

Other uses of multimedia go beyond the already traditional text and graphics orientation. Add-ons such as the NEC Multimedia Upgrade Kit provide a CD-ROM drive, audio board, amplifier and speakers, stereo headphones, and a microphone and supporting software. Using this configuration will not only let your imagination run wild but will implement your ideas by combining graphics, animation, and sound. Other configurations support MIDI sound synthesizers, or how about combining video from a movie with your sound and graphics. A practical application of multimedia is for training medical personnel in recognizing and diagnosing illness or injuries. Live action can be shown from a laser disk and then the computer can ask questions to which the trainee responds. Immediate feedback lets the student know if the patient will recover and if the treatment prescribed was correct. Clearly, multimedia is at the cutting edge of a new revolution in computer technology which has great potential for interesting and exciting new projects.

CAD/CAM

The twins CAD and CAM are acronyms for Computer-Aided Design (CAD) and Computer-Aided Manufacturing (CAM). CAD usually refers to software run on a personal or larger computer system that is used for drawing designs for new products ranging from chairs to airplanes. CAD is the computer age equivalent of the drafting board and is to images what word

Computer-Aided Design (CAD). Software used instead of the drafting board for drawing the designs for new products.

processing is to words. CAM normally refers to using a computer to run machine tools that shape parts on the shop floor.

A CAD image on the computer screen typically consists of lines, arcs, or circles that represent the design of a product. The leading software for CAD is AutoCAD (Figure 10-7) with competitors AutoDesk Auto CAD, VersaCAD, and CAD-plan. These are expensive programs—AutoCAD costs over $3000—but less costly software, such as DesignCAD or EasyCAD, are available for $1,000 and less.

CAD software is attractive to engineers and designers because of the productivity gains it offers over manual systems. It is particularly productive when repetitive tasks are done, but speed isn't the only reason for using CAD. Because the program can store drawings on disk, output them when required, and edit the contents, a quality gain is an important consideration.

Because drawing is an important component of CAD software, the programs interface with a mouse or digitizer pad. Keyboard entries are used to access functions or to type descriptions on the drawing. A VGA resolution screen or better is used to give the high level of resolution needed for drafting. Hard copy output is often on a plotter, although a laser printer may also be used.

Computer Aided Manufacturing (CAM). Software and hardware that is used to assist in the automated manufacturing of products.

Until recently, drawings that were produced on a CAD system would be re-entered on a CAM system for manufacturing. Because the two systems were not compatible, the specifications for manufacturing would be entered into the shop floor computer as a separate operation. Now newer CAD/CAM systems, such as Rocketdyne's linkcd with Allen Bradley's automation control, allows CAD data to be linked directly with the CAM computer for manufacturing of the product. Systems of this type are of the minicomputer variety, but will soon be possible with PC-level systems.

Many new software packages continue to appear on the market that will date a chapter like this early in its life. New software products and upgrades to existing ones are appearing regularly, and the user needs to know what is available and which package will best meet his or her needs. Interested users should subscribe to a computer magazine or other publications to keep informed of these latest products.

FIGURE 10-7

AutoCAD is the leading Computer-Aided Design software for use on personal computers. (Courtesy AutoDesk, Inc.)

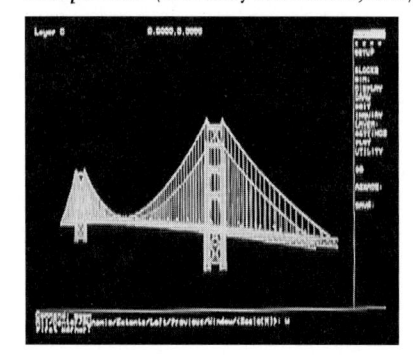

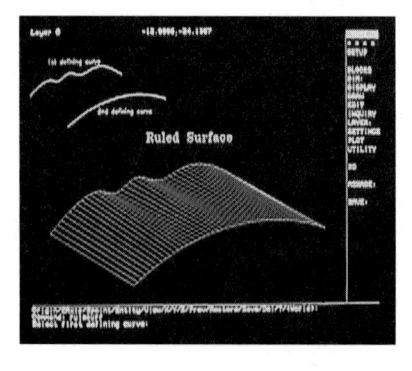

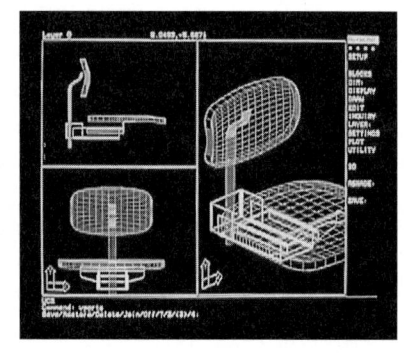

CHAPTER SUMMARY

1. **Integrated software** combines several applications such as spreadsheet, word processing, database, and communications into a single software package.
2. Integration reduces the number of software packages that a user needs to learn and is less costly than purchasing separate programs.
3. Switching from one mode to another, such as from word processing to spreadsheet, is easier to do in an integrated package. Data stored in one form, such as a database, in an integrated package can readily be transferred to another, such as a word processor.
4. Integrated packages may not have the same power that a single program has. Thus, a word processor may have greater capabilities than the word processing component of the integrated package.
5. **Presentation software** assists in the preparation of charts or graphs for use in a business presentation. These charts can be printed, plotted, or recorded on film in black and white or color.
6. **Graphics programs** generally provide drawing, text handling, font control, clip art, and the ability to combine a series of slides into a slide show to be presented directly from the computer.
7. **Bitmapped** graphics are composed of a series of pixels that form an image.
8. **Vector graphics** creates a drawing by connecting points or vectors with lines using a mathematical formula.
9. **Personal information managers (PIMs)** are programs that include a range of features such as an appointment book, calendar, clock, note pad, phone book and dialer, and text editor.
10. **Project management software** produces a PERT chart or a Gantt chart to aid in the development and management of projects. The **PERT** chart provides critical path analysis of the tasks to be completed, while a **Gantt** chart shows task timing to determine if tasks are completed on schedule.
11. **Computer-Aided Design (CAD)** and **Computer-Aided Manufacturing (CAM)** are used by engineers for the design and manufacturing of a wide variety of products. **CAD** usually refers to software run on a personal or larger computer system that is used for drawing designs for new products. **CAM** normally refers to using a computer to run machine tools that shape parts on the shop floor.

IMPORTANT TERMS AND CONCEPTS

Bitmapped graphics
Computer-Aided Design (CAD)
Computer-Aided Manufacturing (CAM)
Exporting
Gantt chart
Importing
Integrated software
Personal information manager (PIM)
PERT chart
Presentation software
Project management
Vector graphics

SELF-TESTING QUESTIONS

Fill-In

1. _____ software provides a word processor, spreadsheet, database, graphics, and communications in a single program.
2. The process of _____ data is sending it from the program currently in use to another program.
3. The category of _____ software is used for preparing overhead transparencies, color slides, and even for doing a slide show.
4. A program that contains a calendar, note pad, phone book, calculator, and an electronic mail link is called a _____ _____ _____.
5. A _____ chart is used in project management to show the relationship between tasks.
6. _____ software combines the technologies of sound, graphics, and animation on the computer.
7. A _____ _____ _____ program is used to draw designs for new products and is the computer equivalent of the drafting board.
8. CAM is an acronym for _____ _____ _____.

True/False

1. It is generally easier to learn to use integrated software than separate software packages.
2. Because of its complexity, an integrated package is usually more expensive than single-use separate software packages.
3. The term PIM means Project Integrated Management.
4. CD-ROM is a system that provides the basis for multimedia applications on the personal computer.
5. CD-ROM, while fascinating, is mainly a tool for use in business and large organizations such as schools.
6. CAM is a special-purpose computer that is used in meat processing.

ANSWERS

Fill-In: 1. Integrated, 2. exporting, 3. presentation, 4. personal information manager, 5. PERT, 6. Multimedia, 7. computer-aided design, 8. computer-aided manufacturing

True/False: 1. T, 2. F, 3. F, 4. T, 5. F, 6. F

Questions for Critical Thinking

1. Software such as WordPerfect, dBASE IV, and Lotus 1–2–3 store their data in different formats. Discuss how this might affect the way users need to function when using a variety of software packages. What solution might you offer?

2. Research several types of presentation graphics software packages and develop a chart that would be useful for comparing their features.
3. What type of hardware is needed for effective use of graphics software? Would hardware used mainly for DOS word processing be effective?

CHAPTER 11

DATABASE SYSTEMS

A VIEW OF THE CHAPTER AHEAD

After reading this chapter you will understand

- ▶ the concept of a database and know why it is more effective than a sequential file for data storage.
- ▶ the differences between a flat file database and a Database Management System.
- ▶ some of the methods for creating and using a database.
- ▶ the unique problems with a local area network that uses a database.

INTRODUCTION

Databases represent a broad range of complexity from a record of video tapes in your local video store, to the inventory of products in a superstore, to a public information service such as CompuServe which has over 1,500 databases linked together in one system. When applications like these are computerized, data storage from a few thousand records to complex interrelated data requiring billions of characters is necessary. For databases, a different storage and retrieval method is required if data is to be accessed quickly and effectively.

Applications such as word processing and spreadsheets use sequential disk files to store documents and data that require the reading of all data in the file from beginning to end. Sequential processing is necessary for such applications and provides a fast and efficient means for reading data. However, sequential files are only useful when data has a high level of activity; otherwise, excessive time is spent reading data that is not required by the application. You can imagine waiting to check out a video tape while the computer reads all of the data for 5,000 tapes in the store.

Database software provides a means of recording and recalling data without the need to process every record in the file each time. This method is beneficial when applications such as inventory records or customer orders are processed and only a few of the records on file need to be accessed. The database can then find only the records that are required and ignore all of the others for much faster data retrieval. Databases are useful when data has a low level of activity because only active records need to be accessed.

Because of their flexibility, today's databases can also be used effectively

FIGURE 11-1
As orders are received by phone in a mail order business they are entered on the computer, where a database both provides customer and product information and is updated by the order. (Courtesy FPG International.)

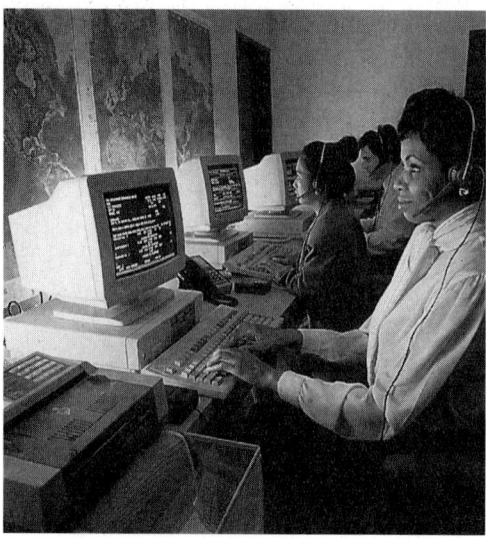

CHAPTER 11 Database Systems

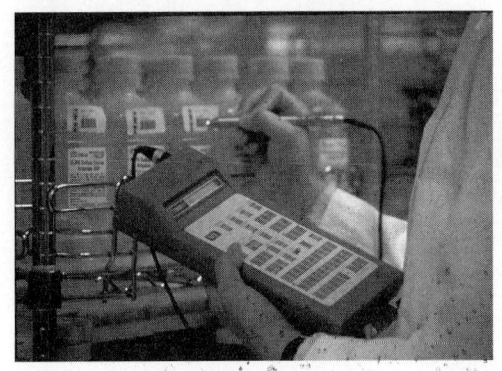

Data entry in supermarkets is done on this hand-held device as the operator reviews the shelf contents. After data entry is complete the portable unit is attached to the store's main computer, where the database is updated with current information. (Courtesy Intermec.)

for files with a high level of activity. This access would occur when a report is generated that contains most or all of the records in the database.

Fields and Records

Figure 11-1 shows a data entry screen for entering customer invoice data. Descriptions on the screen indicate the type of data that is to be entered and the order in which it is entered. These spaces where the data will be entered are called fields. A **field** is one or more bytes containing a unit of data such as an invoice number, client, or description. All of the data on the screen in this example forms a record. A **record** consists of all information that relates to a single transaction, such as the customer invoice data in this example.

Field. A unit of data consisting of one or more bytes.

Record. Data relating to a single transaction contained in one or more fields.

WHAT IS A DATABASE?

A **database** is a collection of logically related files used for a variety of purposes. A customer order database (Figure 11-2) may have a file of customer records containing data about the customer's name, address, date of last order, and so on. The database may also contain a file showing the items that each customer has ordered. Thus, the two files are related due to common information between them, which might be the customer number. A third file may contain unique data about the items ordered by the customer such as the item's description and quantity in stock. This file is accessed by the item number.

Databases vary from simple packages called **file managers** to the more complex and sophisticated ones known as **Database Management Systems (DBMS)**. File managers generally work with only one file at a time. A DBMS can work with several files at once for more intricate applications.

A database has many uses. Customer records, order entry, inventory con-

Database. A collection of related files that may be used for a variety of applications.

File manager. A database program that operates with one file at a time.

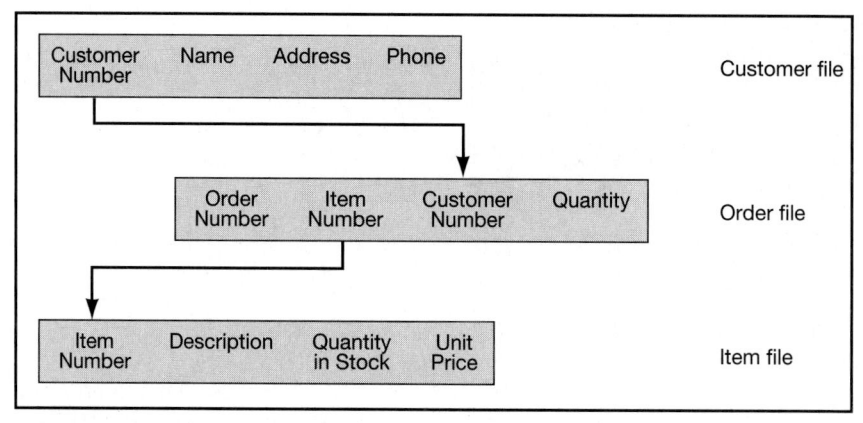

FIGURE 11-2
A database consisting of customer, order, and item files. Using separate files reduces data redundancy, simplifies updating, and provides faster access to the data needed.

Database Management System (DBMS). A program that can work with data from several files at one time.

trol, mailing lists, data analysis, and accounting are a few of the ways a database can be used.

Database software packages are used to create and maintain a database. PC database software usually costs a few hundred dollars for a complete package. File managers, such as PFS:file, are simple to learn and require very little training or experience to use, while DBMS packages, such as dBASE IV, are more complex and can require a course or training session with an expert user or instructor.

Once the database has been created, many kinds of activities can be done with it. There is the usual updating of records, such as changing the customer's address or phone number, and adding new records or deleting old ones. Reports can be generated, bills printed, and reminders sent. But the database can also be used to do searches for specific data, such as who ordered the disk controller card, or queries, such as how many customers live in Detroit. Database records can also be sorted, extracted, or combined with other records.

FILE MANAGERS AND DBMS

A file manager is a program that can only work with one file at a time. This is a useful program for applications such as keeping a mailing list or an inventory of items such as a record or book collection. This type of file organization is acceptable for storing data and permits some useful analysis or reporting from the data. It can be used to create mailing lists, envelope labels, a customer listing, and some can be used to generate form letters.

The main problem with the file manager is its restriction to a single file. A customer order system would be difficult to implement and inefficient to operate with a single file system. However, a DBMS could keep the customer data in one file and the order data in another as discussed previously.

Moving from a file manager software package to a DBMS helps to mini-

▶ THE BIRTH AND DEVELOPMENT OF dBASE

In 1978 Wayne Ratliff, an engineer with Martin Marietta working on NASA's Viking space program, created a database program in his spare time that he called Vulcan. By late 1979 he was marketing the software through *Byte* magazine and received an encouraging response of 60 sales over a 9-month period.

To concentrate on software development Ratliff joined forces with George Tate of Ashton-Tate who took over the marketing responsibilities. The first major change suggested by Tate was the name. Vulcan became known as dBASE II, implying an upgrade to the program. In less than three years dBASE II had sold more than 140,000 copies.

dBASE II, the first programmable relational database, was introduced in late 1980, offering a wide range of features which caused it to quickly become the leading database package. dBASE II was originally written for 8-bit CP/M-based microcomputers and was limited to 64K of RAM. This memory limitation continued to apply even when used on the much larger IBM PC. When competing packages, such as MDBS' KnowledgeMan and MicroRim's R:BASE 4000, came on the market, dBASE began to decline in market share and was thus ready for a new release with major improvements.

dBASE III represented a complete rewrite of the software to take advantage of the 16-bit computer generation. Ashton-Tate used the C language when developing dBASE III to improve the speed and efficiency of the new program. Using C also eased the conversion of dBASE to other operating systems such as UNIX-based computers.

By early 1986 another release, dBASE III Plus, offered further enhancements. The ASSIST menus provided pull-down menus for easy selection of program features, thus improving the user interface. Support for Local Area Networks and file locking opened the door to a broader use of LANs with dBASE III Plus applications. Originally, dBASE was a software package tailored for the single user environment. With dBASE III Plus, files created for single users can be used in a network with little trouble.

dBASE's most powerful feature was its extensive programming language. It was easily as complete as many popular programming languages and was a favorite of software developers and PC consultants. Programming in dBASE has been available from the beginning and no doubt was a major factor in pushing this product to the top of the database software market.

dBASE III Plus handles up to 1 billion records per file. However, the total file length must not exceed 2 billion characters. Records can consist of a maximum of 128 fields or 4,000 characters. And dBASE can work with up to 10 files simultaneously. With these capabilities dBASE III Plus was able to handle all but the most demanding tasks.

(Courtesy Borland International.)

In 1988 Ashton-Tate announced a much improved database called dBASE IV. A major upgrade, Version 1.5 was released in 1992, 2.0 in 1993, and Ashton-Tate was purchased by Borland International. This software supported both OS/2 and MS/DOS systems with improved interfaces for program development. The dBASE IV Control Center made user interaction for accessing and managing data easier than earlier releases. Design tools were provided to help the user create database tables, data entry forms, reports, labels, and queries. A new applications generator is included to make applications development easier for programmers and nonprogrammers alike. dBASE IV includes improved networking capability over III Plus and a new dBASE/SQL language which combines IBM's Structured Query Language used on mainframes with dBASE's query capabilities. dBASE IV is another example of a successful product that has gone through another release to continue to meet or exceed the competition's software products and user requirements.

mize several problem areas that are a concern with the file manager. The following are a few of the major problems that DBMS can help to eliminate.

1. **Data redundancy.** File managers tend to store a lot of duplicate data among different files. A customer's name and number might be stored in the customer file and in the order file and again in the accounting file. Because a file manager does not have ready access to these files at one time, some duplication is necessary.
2. **Data dependence.** When the same data is stored in several different files, any updating on this data must be done on each file when a change occurs. A DBMS can store the data in a common file and thus reduce dependence by updating only the one file.
3. **Excessive manual operations.** A DBMS can usually be programmed so that frequently used activities in the database can be automated. This avoids the need for a user to be trained in the technical aspects of the database because the program does all of the difficult parts. Many file managers do not have programming capabilities and therefore the user must learn the command language of the software package and do these operations manually.
4. **Security.** A DBMS offers improved control over who has access to the database, what data can be seen, and what data can be altered by the user.

DESIGNING A DATABASE

To design a relational database we need to first collect the type of data that will be needed in the database. Figure 11-3 shows an example of the data needed in a Customer file which will become part of a database. Other files such as an order file and an item file may also be included as development of the database progresses.

When designing the database we need to consider the kinds of questions it will be used to ask and the kinds of reports that it will generate. Some of the questions our database could be called on to answer are:

- Which customers do not have credit with the company?
- What is Andy Bow's phone number?
- Which customers have a credit limit of $500.00 or more?

In choosing the data to be included in a database, it is necessary to consider the kinds of questions that might be asked. Leaving out this step could result in a database that cannot provide important information. For example, the customer database shown could not be used to ask the question: Which customers have a zip code of 33540? because the code is not part of the record.

Customer Number	Surname	First Name	Address	Phone	Credit	Credit Limit
12	Bow	Andy	15 Maple St.	452-6745	Y	500.00
13	Down	Charlotte	18th Avenue	451-7457	N	0.00
14	Holt	Edward	12 Wade St.	551-6346	Y	1299.99

FIGURE 11-3
A preliminary design of a customer database. The credit field signifies whether credit is granted the customer or not. In the design only three sample customers are shown, but the actual file will contain more.

CHARACTERISTICS OF THE DATABASE

A PC DBMS is usually based on a **relational** data structure. This structure is organized in rows and columns similar to a spreadsheet (Figure 11-4). Each **row** represents a record that contains facts about one customer. A **column** is equivalent to a field and contains the same type of data for each customer. The first column contains the customer number and, although, it is a different number for each customer, the value in the column is always a customer number.

In the relational database the customer file is searched to get address information about the customer. The relation, customer number, is used to search the item file to find out which items the customer ordered.

To help organize and control a complex database environment, a **data dictionary** may be used to document and maintain the data definition. Among other details, the data dictionary records the types of data and their relationships within the database.

A **database administrator (DBA)** is a position in the organization responsible for the control of the database. In large corporations one or more people may have this function. The DBA establishes data definitions, defines the database standards for the company, and maintains the integrity of the data relationships.

Relational database. A database design where data in one file is related to data in another file based on common information such as a customer number.

FIGURE 11-4
A PC database uses a relational structure. Data is organized into rows containing one customer record and columns that contain the same type of data for each customer.

Column ↓

Customer Number	Surname	First Name	Address	Phone	Credit	Credit Limit
12	Bow	Andy	15 Maple St.	452-6745	Y	500.00
13	Down	Charlotte	18th Avenue	451-7457	N	0.00
14	Holt	Edward	12 Wade St.	551-6346	Y	1299.99

Row →

▶ DATABASE FIELD TYPES

Database software permits a variety of field types to satisfy the needs of different applications. Depending on the software used for the DBMS, the field types may vary slightly or the terminology may be different. The field types discussed here refer to some of those available in dBASE IV.

J. Jones SL-3189 CD System (519) 858-2301	**Character** fields are fields that store text, including letters, numbers, special characters, and spaces. This type of field is often used for names, addresses, zip and postal codes, descriptions, and even phone numbers.
2139.75 35 −79.89 .015	**Numeric** fields are those that store numbers. Numbers may be either integer or decimal and may be positive or negative. Numeric fields are generally those used in calculations and include quantities, costs, and rates. Sometimes a numeric field is not used for calculations such as those used for customer numbers or account numbers.
.T. .F.	**Logical** fields are fields that can be either true (T) or false (F) indicating two alternatives. A field such as sex could use T to represent male and F for female. A customer with a credit account would be coded as T but one without credit would be F.
10/25/92	**Date** fields store a date. Date is usually in the form of mm/dd/yy representing month, day, and year.
Learning dBASE IV in Ten Easy Lessons	**Memo** fields are like character fields except they may contain substantially more data. Memo fields are stored separate from the database.

CREATING A DATABASE

A database file is initially set up by selecting the appropriate options from menus and pull-down menus presented on screen by the software. Figure 11-5 shows the entries made in dBASE IV to create a database for the customer file.

Defining the File

First the option to create a database is selected from a menu. Then a name is given to the file that will be used throughout its life as a database. The last step is to define each field in the database. Each field must have a name that uniquely identifies the field.

The type of field is also specified, as is the width of the field and the number of decimal positions it contains if it is a numeric field. Decisions about field sizes and types must be taken seriously at this stage of the implementation because changes are not easily made once the database is created.

CHAPTER 11 Database Systems

```
 Layout   Organize   Append   Go To   Exit                    7:23:37 pm
                                            Bytes remaining:     3947
```

Num	Field Name	Field Type	Width	Dec	Index
1	CUST_NO	Character	2		N
2	SURNAME	Character	10		N
3	FIRST_NAME	Character	10		N
4	ADDRESS	Character	15		N
5	PHONE	Character	8		N
6	CREDIT	Logical	1		N
7	LIMIT	Numeric	7	2	N
8		Character			

```
Database  A:\CUSTOMER           Field 8/8                          Ins
         Enter the field name. Insert/Delete field:Ctrl-N/Ctrl-U
Field names begin with a letter and may contain letters, digits and underscores
```

FIGURE 11-5
When the file name has been entered, dBASE IV presents this screen. On it, each field in the database is defined with a field name, type of field, its width, and the number of decimal positions where applicable.

A data entry screen used to enter data into a database file. The screen is designed to simplify the entry of data so that a data entry operator can enter the data efficiently and accurately. (Courtesy of Hewlett-Packard.)

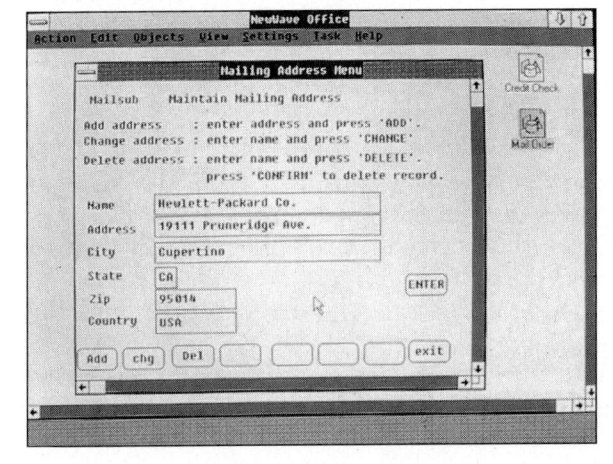

				INTERSTATE Distributing Company 9841 Cavell Ave. Bloomington, MN 55403				INVOICE No.2222	INVOICE No.2222

JDC

SOLD TO: Sports Unlimited, 12 North 15th Ave., Minneapolis, MN 55406

SHIP TO: Sports Unlimited Warehouse, 33 Exchange St., Mechanicsville, VA 02939

Sports Unlimited

DATE	SALESP.	ORDER NO	ORDER DATE	SHIPPED VIA	TERMS	INVOICE NO.	INVOICE DATE	INVOICE NO.
06/08/9X	WNG	1111	1111	UPS	1.0%/ 10	2222	06/06/9X	2222

ORDERED	QUANTITY SHIPPED	BACKORDERED	ITEM NUMBER	DESCRIPTION	UNIT	UNIT PRICE	AMOUNT
10	7	3	333	Tennis Racquet Mod 1	EA	30.00	210.00
4	4	0	777	Bicycle ZT200	EA	125.00	500.00

JDC

PLEASE RETURN THIS PORTION OF THE INVOICE WITH YOUR PAYMENT

NON-TAXABLE	TAXABLE	SALES TAX	FREIGHT	MISCELLANEOUS	INVOICE TOTAL		INVOICE TOTAL
.00	710.00	28.40	25.00	.00		763.40	763.40

An invoice such as this one is often the source document for providing data to create a database. After the structure of the database has been defined, the data is supplied for entry from the form. (Courtesy D.G. Dologite and R.J. Mockler, *Using Computers*, 2nd ed. (Englewood Cliffs, N.J.: Prentice Hall, 1989), p. 335. Reprinted by permission of Prentice-Hall, Inc., Englewood Cliffs, N.J.)

SORTING THE DATABASE FILE

As records are appended and deleted over a period of time, the file that might have originally been in customer number sequence may now be in a more or less random order. One solution to this problem is to sort the file. A **sort** reorders the records in the database into a specific sequence based on the contents of one or more fields and creates a new database with the records in the new sequence.

Although sorting may seem to be a useful operation, it is time consuming and requires double the disk space for storing the new sorted file. The larger the database file becomes, the less efficient sorting will be. As a result

CHAPTER 11 Database Systems

▶ UPDATE ACTIVITIES IN A DATABASE

One of the strengths of a DBMS is the ability to apply updating to the contents of the database. All database software provide updating capabilities, but some have more features than others. Using dBASE terminology, some of the commonly provided update features are:

- **Append** adds a new record to the end of the current database file. After appending new records, it is sometimes necessary to sort the file to maintain a required sequence of records, such as customer number sequence.
- **Edit** presents the contents of record so that changes may be made to it. Fields may be revised or deleted in edit mode.
- **Display** provides a means for showing the contents of the current record on the screen.
- **Browse** lets you look at records in the database. Several records will appear on the screen together and cursor keys are used to move through the database file. In Browse records may be revised, deleted, or appended to the file.
- **Replace** is a powerful operation that can change the contents of a given field throughout the database file.
- **Delete** is used to delete the current record from the database. The name is a misnomer because the record is only flagged for deletion and needs a Pack operation to finally remove it from the database.
- **Recall** restores a record to active status that has been marked for removal by the Delete command.
- **Pack** removes all records from the database file that have been marked for deletion by the Delete command. Recall cannot restore a deleted record after the database has been packed.

---

another technique, called indexing, is used that is more effective than using a sort.

USING AN INDEX

Because sorting takes a lot of time and requires disk space for the sorted file in addition to the original unsorted file, indexing is an often used alternative. **Indexing** is an operation that creates a second file called an index file. The index file stores only the key field that identifies the database file sequence and a record number that is used as a link to the original record in the database, thus saving considerable space over sorting the database.

Figure 11-6 shows the customer file as it might appear as an unsorted file. There is no sequence on the desired field customer number. By creating an index file as shown, the database can be treated as if it were in customer number sequence. The index file contains the customer number, which is the key field. The index also contains the record number of the record in the database. Because the index retains the data in customer number sequence, the database can be accessed in that order by reading each record according to the record number in the index file.

Indexing a database is also more useful than sorting because a database file can have several indexes describing different sequences. One may index

Update. An activity that results in a change to the contents of a database.

Indexing. An efficient process where an index file is used to present records from the database in a specified order.

Customer File – Actual Sequence

Record #	CUST_NO	NAME	ADDRESS	PHONE	CREDIT	LIMIT
1	12	Bow	15 Maple St.	452-6745	.T.	500.00
2	23	Jade	101 Crescent Blvd.	452-3301	.F.	0.00
3	13	Down	18th Avenue	451-7457	.F.	0.00
4	14	Holt	12 Wade St.	551-6346	.T.	1299.99
5	19	Voney	1 Yonge St.	744-6011	.T.	500.00
6	22	Brent	33 Main St.	551-6347	.T.	1299.00
7	18	Trent	93 Mission Rd.	555-2323	.F.	0.00
8	24	Lau	85 Wade St.	551-6632	.F.	0.00
9	16	Able	21 Knoop St.15	921-8833	.T.	1000.00

Index File

Record number link to customer file

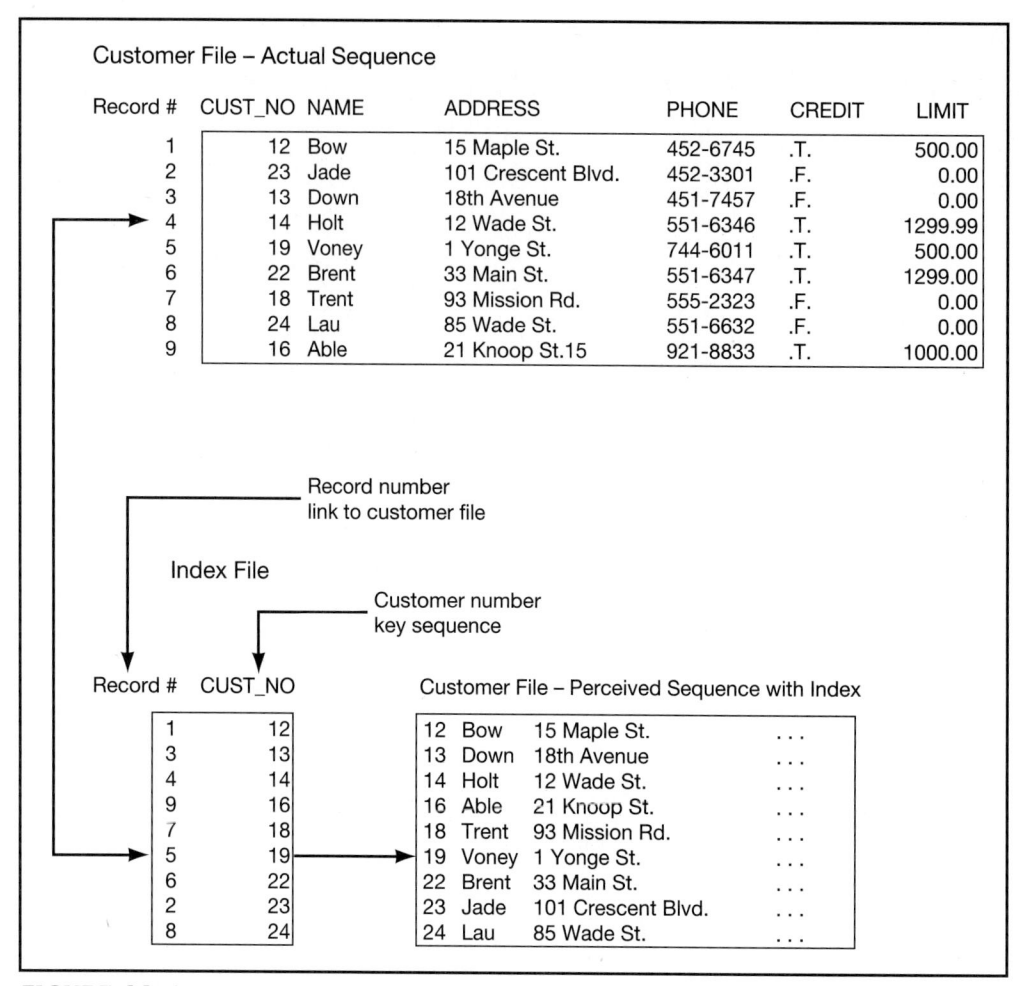

Customer number key sequence

Record #	CUST_NO
1	12
3	13
4	14
9	16
7	18
5	19
6	22
2	23
8	24

Customer File – Perceived Sequence with Index

12	Bow	15 Maple St.	...
13	Down	18th Avenue	...
14	Holt	12 Wade St.	...
16	Able	21 Knoop St.	...
18	Trent	93 Mission Rd.	...
19	Voney	1 Yonge St.	...
22	Brent	33 Main St.	...
23	Jade	101 Crescent Blvd.	...
24	Lau	85 Wade St.	...

FIGURE 11-6
An index file is used to access the database file in customer number sequence. Rather than sorting the entire database file, only the index is sorted on the key field and the record numbers are used as a link to the database file.

on the customer number, another may be in name sequence, and yet another by address. Thus, a database may be easily accessed in any number of sequences depending on the needs of processing in a given application.

DATABASE QUERIES

Query. The process of using a specified criteria to examine the database and present only records that match the query.

A **query** is a request for information or an inquiry into the contents of a database. One of the benefits of having a database is that inquiries can easily be made of it. Companies using a database may want to ask questions such as "What orders do we have from customer number 19?" or, "We have a problem with reliability on item number 27, so identify all orders in the database for item 27."

Menu-Driven Queries

Software such as dBASE IV provides a series of menus (Query by example) for the user to identify the conditions of the query. When asking a question about the orders for customer 19, a sequence of menus and submenus are presented on the screen where a search condition is built to access records that meet the requirements of the inquiry.

Figure 11-7 shows the menus used to display all orders for a customer. Prior to this time the database file must be accessed and then a Query operation begun. A search condition is built which asks for records with a Customer Number equal to 19. Finally, the records that meet the conditions are displayed.

Menus, in this setting, have the advantage of directing the user through each step of building a condition. If the next step is uncertain, the menu always presents the choices to follow. Very little experience is needed to work through the menus and develop a successful query. Although menus may take a little time because of all the choices, they are easy to use and all the information needed is presented on the screen.

Query by example (QBE). A query that is defined by typing an example of the kind of data required in the results.

Query Languages

Complex queries frequently require several conditions or relations to be satisfied in a search of the database. A query such as "List all orders for item number 27 with a quantity greater than 5" requires two conditions. The accompanying box shows the relational operators that can be used in stating a condition. In addition to these operators, the .AND. and .OR. operators can be used to combine two or more conditions.

Figure 11-8 shows a condition in dBASE IV command mode which asks for a list of item number 27 that have a quantity ordered greater than 5. dBASE can use this type of command, which is called a nonprocedural query language. dBASE IV also supports SQL, which is a nonprocedural language based on IBM's mainframe database systems. Other languages, such as COBOL or BASIC, would require a complete program or procedure to be written to accomplish the same result and are therefore called procedural languages.

Some database software permits a conversational style of making inquiries. Thus, a natural language query such as "Tell me the customers who

▶ RELATIONAL OPERATORS

Operator	Meaning
=	Equal To
<=	Less Than or Equal To
<	Less Than
>	Greater Than
>=	Greater Than or Equal To
<>	Not Equal To

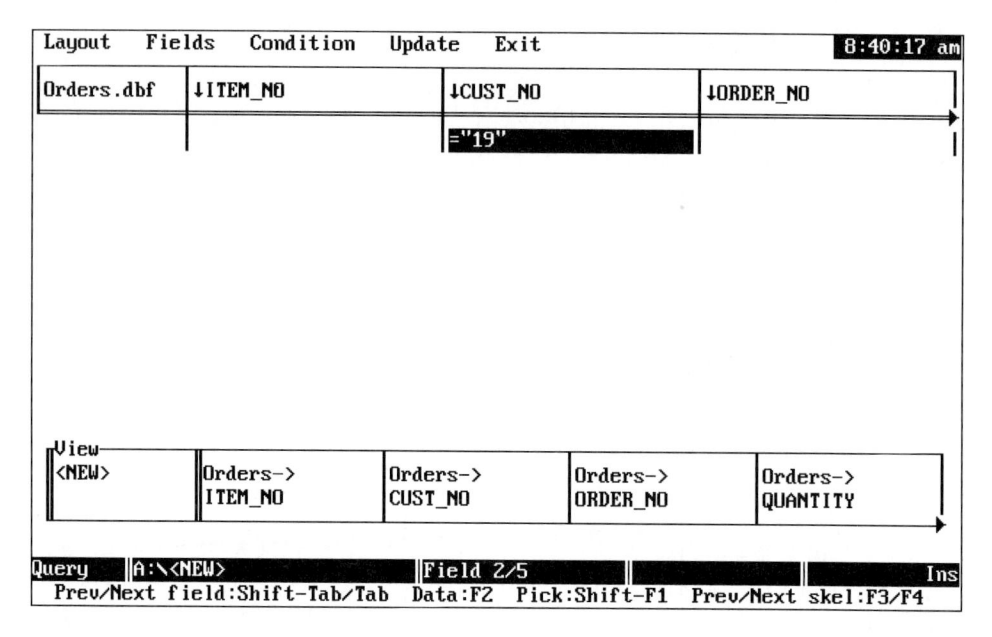

```
Layout    Fields    Condition   Update    Exit                           8:40:17 am
Orders.dbf  |↓ITEM_NO         |↓CUST_NO         |↓ORDER_NO
                              |="19"
┌View─────────────────────────────────────────────────────────────────────
│<NEW>   ║Orders->  ║Orders->   ║Orders->   ║Orders->
│        ║ITEM_NO   ║CUST_NO    ║ORDER_NO   ║QUANTITY
Query   |A:\<NEW>          |Field 2/5                                 Ins
Prev/Next field:Shift-Tab/Tab   Data:F2   Pick:Shift-F1   Prev/Next skel:F3/F4
```

```
Records    Fields    Go To    Exit                                 8:41:40 am
ITEM_NO | CUST_NO | ORDER_NO | QUANTITY
  11      19        157                                                20
  13      19        157                                                 2
  32      19        157                                                 4




Browse  |A:\<NEW>          |Rec 10/15    |View                         Ins
                         View and edit fields
```

FIGURE 11-7
A query to display all orders for customer number 19 is built. The first screen shows the query definition to select CUST_NO = 19. When the user asks for the data, records for customer 19 are displayed as shown on the second screen.

ordered more than 5 of item 27" could be used and understood by the software.

Natural language interfaces require a dictionary of words that are used to understand the use of common words. Thus, the words "Tell me" could mean "List," which translates it to the nonprocedural form before the command is processed. Natural language is becoming a more widely used tool

```
.LIST FOR ITEM_NO = '27' .AND. QUANTITY > 5
Record#  ORDER_NO  ITEM_NO  CUST_NO  QUANTITY  UNIT_COST
     2      123       27       12        17       5.75
     8      156       27       16        10       5.75
```

FIGURE 11-8
Using a nonprocedural query language in dBASE IV simplifies making an inquiry.

in computer software and will no doubt become the language in favor by new users of sophisticated computer systems.

MULTIPLE FILE DBMS

Database management systems such as dBASE IV and Paradox permit the use of more than one file in the database. This offers much greater flexibility in the applications of the software and provides for greater efficiency in data storage and retrieval. Multiple files provide for the linking of data between different applications so that activity in one may influence the other.

The application used throughout this chapter of the customer and order files demonstrates this principle. When a customer places an order, information about the customer such as the name, address, or credit rating can be retrieved from the customer file. At the same time the database application can access the order file to record information about the order, such as the item number and quantity ordered. Queries can also use data from both files in a multiple file database application.

Normalizing Files

When a multiple file database is designed, the process of normalizing is essential if efficient operation is to result. **Normalizing** is the process of eliminating redundant or duplicate data from each file. Including the customer's name in both the customer file and the order file would be an example of redundancy and is an inefficient use of storage space. Redundant data also contributes to the need for updating data in two or more different locations, which results in slower processing.

An order file might contain a unit cost field for an item that is ordered. However, if an item file was designed for the database, then the unit cost would be stored there and would be redundant if it also appeared in the order file. Effective design ensures that the files used in the database are normalized before filling them with data.

Redundant data. Data that is repeated in more than one file in the database.

Relations

A relational multiple file database is designed with fields that are used to establish a linkage between the files. The customer file in Figure 11-9 uses the customer number to form a relation between it and the order file. An order is always made for a given customer, so the order file contains a customer

Relation. A common item of data that establishes a link between two or more files in a database.

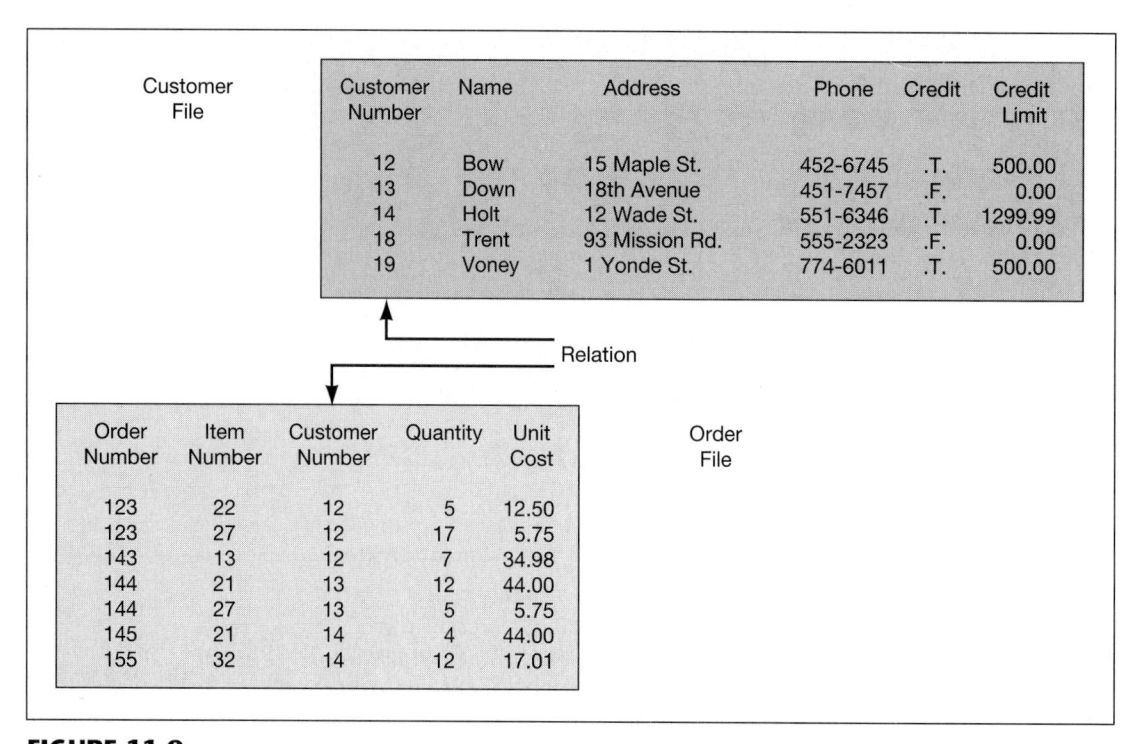

```
Customer          Customer   Name    Address         Phone      Credit   Credit
File              Number                                                 Limit

                  12         Bow     15 Maple St.    452-6745   .T.      500.00
                  13         Down    18th Avenue     451-7457   .F.        0.00
                  14         Holt    12 Wade St.     551-6346   .T.     1299.99
                  18         Trent   93 Mission Rd.  555-2323   .F.        0.00
                  19         Voney   1 Yonde St.     774-6011   .T.      500.00
                                          ↑
                                          │── Relation

Order   Item     Customer  Quantity  Unit      Order
Number  Number   Number              Cost      File

123     22       12        5         12.50
123     27       12        17         5.75
143     13       12        7         34.98
144     21       13        12        44.00
144     27       13        5          5.75
145     21       14        4         44.00
155     32       14        12        17.01
```

FIGURE 11-9
A relation is established on the customer number field between the customer file and the order file.

number field that establishes a relation between it and the customer file. Without a field forming a relation between files in a database, the file would operate in isolation, which is essentially how a single file database operates.

When more than two files are established in the database, the third file will require a relation to be established with only one of the other two files. Thus, an item file could establish a relation with the order file through the item number. The item file does not require a customer number because it can access the customer number in the order file. Obviously large database applications can become very complex and require considerable planning to design and implement.

Joining Files

Data from two or more database files may be joined to create a composite file or report. Figure 11-10 shows a join operation using the customer and order files. First, a relation is set between the customer numbers. In this example the application requires a list of orders for customer number 12.

The record for customer 12 is joined with the records in the order file that match the customer. Specific fields in each file are accessed to create the joined file. Not all fields are needed so in this application only the customer number, name, and address are extracted from the customer file. The order file provides the order number, item, quantity, and unit cost. Although the

CHAPTER 11 Database Systems

Customer File

Customer Number	Name	Address	Phone	Credit	Credit Limit
12	A. Bow	15 Maple St.	452-6745	.T.	500.00
13	C. Down	18th Avenue	451-7457	.F.	0.00
14	E. Holt	12 Wade St.	551-6346	.T.	1299.99
18	R. Trent	93 Mission Rd.	555-2323	.F.	0.00
19	K. Voney	1 Yonde St.	774-6011	.T.	500.00

- select 1
- use customer
- select 2
- user order
- Join with customer to custorder for cust_no=customer–>cust_no

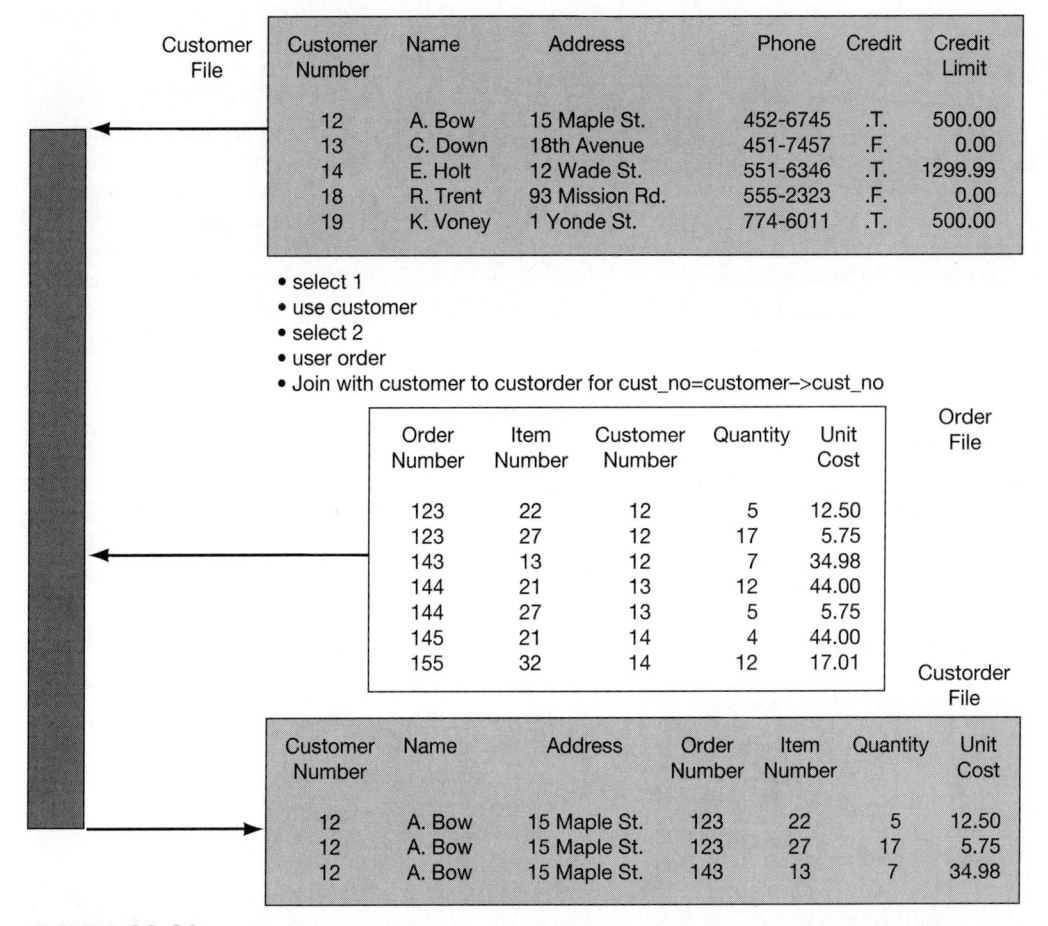

Order File

Order Number	Item Number	Customer Number	Quantity	Unit Cost
123	22	12	5	12.50
123	27	12	17	5.75
143	13	12	7	34.98
144	21	13	12	44.00
144	27	13	5	5.75
145	21	14	4	44.00
155	32	14	12	17.01

Custorder File

Customer Number	Name	Address	Order Number	Item Number	Quantity	Unit Cost
12	A. Bow	15 Maple St.	123	22	5	12.50
12	A. Bow	15 Maple St.	123	27	17	5.75
12	A. Bow	15 Maple St.	143	13	7	34.98

FIGURE 11-10
Data from two database files are combined in a Join operation. A Join defines the relation on which the operation occurs, such as in this case for customer number 12. The join also defines the fields from each file that are to be included in the resulting file.

result of the join is shown for only one customer, it could be done for any number or even all customers in the file.

DBMS PROGRAMMING

Full-featured database software such as dBASE IV and Paradox provide a programming capability for more advanced users. Programming of database software is also frequently done by microcomputer consultants and application software developers. dBASE IV in its several releases since 1980 has become the favorite software package for developing database application programs and is in widespread use in the industry.

Programming a database is done for two fundamental reasons.

▶ VISUAL DATABASES

Databases have always been text oriented in their design and operation, but with the graphical orientation of Windows a new breed of database software is emerging. These database packages use the Windows environment to develop complex applications with little or no programming by offering powerful graphical tools. Visual databases incorporate icons and drag and drop techniques without sacrificing the powerful tools, such as SQL or programming features, needed for major applications.

One of these new databases is Borland's Paradox for Windows. Creating a database (called a table) is as easy as listing the field names, types, sizes, and descriptions. You can even use file formats recognized by other databases such as Paradox 3.5 or dBASE IV.

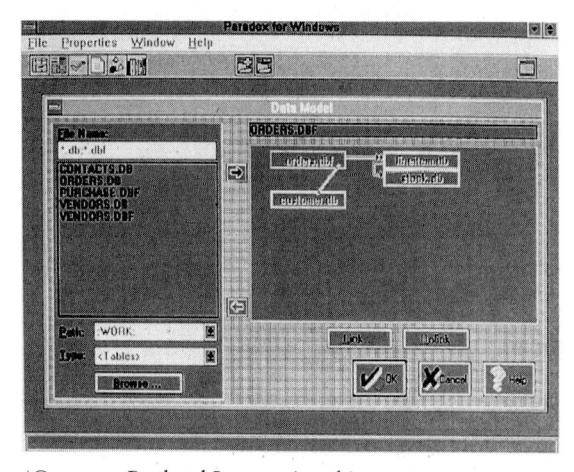

(Courtesy Borland International.)

Data may be entered directly into the table or into a data entry form. If you don't have a form, just click a single icon and Paradox will create a Quick Form for you. Other tools are available to create more complex forms or reports. For reports, a layout screen lets you choose from field or columnar orientation, single or multiple records output, and page layout. Paradox uses a property inspector to make changes to tables, forms, or reports. By right clicking the mouse button on the object to be changed, the Property Inspector appears. For example, on a report the inspector can be used to change fonts, alignment, color, or pattern.

To work with databases you open a data model window. Here you choose the databases to work on and the relationships between them. Rather than typing commands to form the field relations, you simply use visual tools to connect the databases. Query by example (QBE) is a graphical process using check boxes to indicate the fields to include in the query.

Microsoft Access is another visual database that simplifies the development of complex database applications. Access uses a window to list all of the tables, reports, forms, queries, and programs that comprise the application. To create a form you click on the Form Wizard icon which gives you a variety of form choices. Click on the style and orientation of the form you want and Form Wizard creates the form for the active database. Like Paradox for Windows, Microsoft Access lets you work on databases using graphical techniques of point and click and drag and drop. Linking databases and doing queries all use visual techniques to simplify database operations.

Graphical databases are an important new trend in DBMS systems. Some users may prefer to stay with the character-based systems because of their faster operating speed, but the new systems do make development of a DBMS easier and they are generally faster to implement than using DOS-based programs.

1. A _____ program provides a way of storing frequently used command sequences so that they do not need to be typed on the keyboard each time.
2. A _____ program permits the development of complex applications in the database making use of a wide variety of features not readily available with the menus.

> ## ▶ THE ETHICS OF ACCESS TO PRIVATE DATA
>
> Users of database systems frequently have access to data that is of a private or confidential nature. Whether the data relates to health records, consumer credit, sales information, or financial data, this is data that requires security of access. Most databases use a password system to prohibit access to unauthorized users and limit access to authorized users to the need to know.
>
> But what about those who have legitimate access to the data? Is it acceptable for them to discuss the health record or financial status of a client with their co-workers? Maybe there is a need for this part of the time, but not always. What about telling their spouse or a friend about someone's record? Where does the right to privacy end and what are the ethics involved? Clearly this is not a black and white issue, but many companies are using an internal code of ethics that their employees must agree to follow when their job requires them to have access to private data.

Programs themselves may also call other programs. Thus, a program can be developed that consists of many modules, each of which concentrates on doing a single task such as updating a record or adding a new record to the database.

NETWORKS AND DATABASE SYSTEMS

Using a database on a local area network (LAN) presents some unique problems that do not occur on stand-alone systems. A LAN permits many PC stations on the network to communicate with each other. Database files and commonly used software are often situated on the file server so that access may be had by all users in the system (Figure 11-11). Other devices such as printers, plotters, or modems may also be shared by stations on the local area network. Most full-featured DBMS software packages have network versions that address the unique problems of this environment.

File Locking

One of the problems on a network occurs when two or more stations attempt to access the same database, or worse, the same record. For example, an order system may receive an order at one station for 25 lamps. The system may show 25 in stock so the order is placed. Simultaneously, a second station receives an order for 20 lamps. If the station looks at the stock record before the first station has recorded the order, then the record will continue to show 25 in stock. Thus, unknown to both stations, orders will be placed for a quantity that exceeds the stock.

To get around this problem, networked database software uses a file locking technique. File locking is a feature of database software that will not let a second station access the database while it is in use by another station. There will be a slight delay at the second station until the first has fin-

FIGURE 11-11
A DBMS uses a local area network permitting several users access to the same files. (Courtesy Xerox Corp.)

ished with the database, but this avoids the problem outlined above. Some database software also provides for record locking. With record locking only access to the record is denied if it is already in use.

File Security

As more users have access to data on a network, there is an increased possibility of unauthorized access to data. LAN-based database software provides for several types of data security. The most common is the use of passwords to ensure that only authorized users will have access to specified databases. Changing passwords on a regular basis helps to maintain continued security over time.

Another level of security gives users either read-only or write capability. Some users will be able to only view the contents of a database (read-only) while others will have a security code that permits both reading and updating (write) of the database contents.

Networks, PCs, and Mainframe Systems

Large organizations typically began using computers when only mainframes were available. Over the years smaller systems, such as the minicomputer, and more recently the PC, have all made an impact on various departments in the organization. Today, users of the PC also need access to data on the mainframe. And mainframe users often need access to information that only exists on the PC. Much development is being done by companies like Borland and Microsoft in the PC arena and DEC and IBM in the mainframe scene to tie together these diverse uses of the computer.

Networks are being installed with gateways to the mainframe to provide a communication path between both systems. Other networks, such as Token-Ring, provide for a minicomputer system as a part of the personal computer network. With these developments a given user will often be unaware whether he or she is accessing another PC, a minicomputer, or a mainframe. So for the larger organization the computer system might be thought of as a utility not unlike the telephone or electrical utility, except that instead of electricity or voice, information is the service provided to the user.

CHAPTER SUMMARY

1. Database software provides a means of recording and recalling data without the need to process every record in the file each time.
2. A **database** is a collection of one or more logically related files. Using separate files reduces data redundancy, simplifies updating, and provides faster access to the data needed.
3. Software varies from simple packages called file managers to the more complex and sophisticated ones known as Database Management Systems (DBMS).
4. A **file manager** can only work with one file at a time. This is a useful form of database for applications such as keeping a mailing list or an inventory of items such as a record or book collection.
5. A **DBMS** provides for the processing of more than one file by using a relational operation. A DBMS can reduce redundancy and data dependence in a database system.
6. **Data redundancy** refers to duplicate data stored among different files.
7. **Data dependence** occurs when the same data is stored in several different files requiring updating on each file when a change occurs.
8. Database software provides for update activities such as **append,** which adds records to the end of the database; **edit,** which provides a screen to change the contents of a record; **display,** to show the contents of a record on screen; **browse,** which displays a series of records and permits changes to them; **replace,** which provides a means for changing field contents in a group of records with a single command. **Delete** permits the temporary deletion of a record, recall can make it active again, while **pack** makes the delete permanent.
9. **Sorting** a database creates a new database file that has been ordered into the sequence requested.
10. **Indexing** is an operation that creates a second file called an index file. The index file requires only a key field that identifies the database file sequence and a record number that is used as a link to the original record in the database.
11. A **query** is a request for information or an inquiry into the contents of a database.

12. **Query languages** are generally nonprocedural, as in dBASE IV. Some DBMS packages can use a natural language interface for the query.
13. A multiple file DBMS provides for the linking of data between different applications so that activity in one may influence the other.
14. **Programming** a database management system provides a means of storing frequently used commands in a file to be used as needed without the need to type them each time. A DBMS program also permits the development of complex applications making available more powerful features of the software.
15. Using a database on a **local area network (LAN)** presents some unique problems that do not occur on stand-alone systems. If several users try to access the database simultaneously, the database software uses a file locking technique to permit only one access.
16. **Security** of access is maintained by the use of passwords to ensure that only authorized users will have access to specified databases.
17. Some users will be able to only view the contents of a database (read-only), while others will have a security code that permits both reading and updating (write) of the database contents.

IMPORTANT TERMS AND CONCEPTS

Append
Browse
Database
Database administrator (DBA)
Database Management Systems (DBMS)
Data dependence
Data dictionary
Data redundancy
Edit
File locking
File manager
Indexing

Join
Natural language queries
Nonprocedural query language
Normalizing
Passwords
Programming
Query
Read-only files
Relational
Replace
Security
Sort

SELF-TESTING QUESTIONS

Fill-In

1. A database is a collection of _____ related records.
2. A _____ _____ is a database program that handles only one file at a time.
3. DBMS is an acronym for _____ _____ _____.
4. Using separate files in a database helps to eliminate data _____ or duplication of the data.

CHAPTER 11 Database Systems

5. In a _____ data structure data is stored in the form of tables with relations established between each item.
6. A _____ field type in a database stores data such as quantities, costs, and rates.
7. Using a data _____ can help to document and maintain the data definition.
8. When changes are necessary against a database, such as changing an address or phone number, an _____ operation is done to make the modifications.
9. The _____ command places new records at the end of the database.
10. A _____ might be done to find all orders for customer 19 rather than looking through all of the other customers.

True/False

1. A DBMS is a collection of fields, records, and files relating to a specific application.
2. A browse operation lets you look at the data in a database and if necessary make revisions to the records.
3. Sorting is a desirable technique that efficiently provides access to the database in a variety of sequences.
4. An index is a special type file that is used to reference the records in a database in a specific order. Each database may have more than one index.
5. QBE means Query By Example when used in a database context.
6. Normalizing is the procedure of removing changes to a database and returning the contents to normal.
7. File locking is a technique used to lock out users from accessing sensitive data when they do not have the appropriate authorization or password.
8. Some users may be able to read data from the database but not make changes to it.

ANSWERS

Fill-In: 1. logically, 2. file manager, 3. database management system, 4. redundancy, 5. relational, 6. numeric, 7. dictionary, 8. edit, 9. append, 10. query

True/False: 1. T, 2. T, 3. F, 4. T, 5. T, 6. F, 7. F, 8. T

Questions for Critical Thinking

1. Consider the different types of data that would be required in a database for a college registration system using your college as a model.
2. Design an input screen for use in the student registration system. Compare screen designs with other students and discuss items that should have been added, deleted, or changed.
3. An organization has decided to eliminate the mainframe computer and replace

it with networked personal computers. Each computer has a hard disk and also has access to a file server with disk storage capability. What are some of the problems that might be encountered when changing from a mainframe to networked PCs?

4. Draft a code of ethics to be followed by employees whose job requires them to have access to private health data. The code should define when it is acceptable to discuss the data with another person and under what circumstances.

CHAPTER 12

PROGRAMMING CONCEPTS

A VIEW OF THE CHAPTER AHEAD

After reading this chapter you will understand

- what a program is and why it is necessary.
- the importance of program specifications.
- the use of structure charts, flowcharts, and pseudocode for structured program design.
- the importance of good style and structure when coding a program.
- the difference between procedural and fourth-generation languages.
- the importance of object-oriented languages.

INTRODUCTION

Many of today's widely known programs represent major success stories for their original creator. You read the stories earlier in the book about Wayne Ratliffe, the creator of dBASE, and Dan Bricklin, the originator of VisiCalc—the forerunner of Lotus 1-2-3. Maybe you have also seen or heard of the program called PC Globe that was originated in 1987. PC Globe displays maps, demographic, health, agricultural, industrial, and economic data for over 177 countries. It also provides information from its extensive database on major cities, including their time zones, populations, and tourist attractions.

The author of PC Globe, Roy Kessler, studied comparative literature at Princeton and later earned an MBA from Columbia. While working at Renault in Paris, France, he found himself consulting reference books to locate information on various countries that related to the worldwide operation of the company. He realized that this information could be computerized and become a central resource for people and companies who needed this type of data. The outcome was PC Globe, a PC program that reached $7 million in sales by 1990. It seems that software success stories by individual programmers are still possible.

WHAT IS PROGRAMMING?

One thing that all computers have in common is that they all require a program to operate. And systems that use computers must then use computer programs. We know that programs may be either purchased, if one exists for the application, or developed, if the application is unique. In this chapter we want to look at how a computer program is developed and at some of the languages used for writing computer programs.

Program. A set of instructions written in a language for computer use.

Or we might also ask: What is a program? A **program** is a series of instructions that define how the computer is to process data. It follows that **programming** is the activity of creating or writing a computer program. But programming is more that simply writing a series of instructions for the computer to follow. Because programs for realistic applications tend to become large and complex, a programmer needs to learn a discipline of creating computer programs.

There are five steps that are followed when creating a computer program. These steps are:

- Program specifications
- Input and output definition
- Program design
- Program coding
- Debugging and testing

Only the fourth step, program coding, requires the writing of instructions known as program code. The previous three steps are all part of planning a successful program, and the last step ensures that the program was written correctly.

PROGRAM SPECIFICATIONS

Before a program is written, it needs to be defined. Are we writing a payroll program? Accounting? Sales analysis or a mailing list? The **specifications** define the problem. Not only is the type of program defined, but detailed requirements are identified, such as where the data originates, what process steps are to be applied to the data, and what output is to be produced as a result of running the program.

If we are to have complete and accurate programs, careful definition is required prior to writing the program. Otherwise we are likely to get something other than the results required. Developing program specifications also helps to clarify exactly what we expect the program to achieve.

Figure 12-1 shows a sample program specification for a simplified payroll program. It defines the name of the program, gives a description of it, identifies input and output, and defines the processing requirements as a se-

Specifications. A definition of the requirements of the program including input, processing steps, and output.

The program specifications define the requirements of the program. Included are input, output, and process needs, which are identified during system design by the user, systems analyst, and the programmer. (Courtesy Uniphoto.)

PROGRAM SPECIFICATIONS

PROGRAM NAME: Payroll   **PROGRAM ID:** PAY

PREPARED BY: Don Cassel   **DATE:** January 15, 1993

Program Description:

    The payroll program produces a basic pay statement from an input of hours worked and rate of pay.

Input File(s): Keyboard provides hours and rate.

Output Files(s): Screen.

Program Requirements:

1. Accept as input the hours worked and rate per hour for an employee.
2. Calculate gross pay by multiplying hours worked by rate per hour.
3. Calculate a basic tax deduction of 15 percent.
4. Determine the net pay by subtracting the tax from the gross.
5. Display all values on the screen.

FIGURE 12-1
Program specifications are developed prior to writing the payroll program.

ries of steps. Usually the specifications are developed as a team effort by the programmer, systems analyst, and the user all taking part. Once the general specifications are ready, detailed input and output requirements can be developed.

INPUT AND OUTPUT

The three main components of a program's activity are input, process, and output. Input to a program is the data that the program reads from a keyboard or other device. The input provided to the program determines what data the program has available for processing. Data that is provided as input can be either numeric, alphanumeric, or alphabetic. Table 12-1 shows some types of input data in each category with an example of how the data might look.

    In addition to this information about the data, some programming languages may require a length which defines the number of characters or digits in the field. Numeric fields may also require the number of decimal positions in the number to be specified. Many of the specific rules that are

CHAPTER 12 Programming Concepts

TABLE 12-1 Three types of data that are commonly used as input to a computer program. Some languages, such as dBASE IV, group alphanumeric and alphabetic together in one category called character data. A code, such as Credit, might also be defined as a unique field type called logical data.

Type of Data	*Example*	*Value in Field*
Numeric	Account No.	34522
	Quantity	25
	Cost	47.29
Alphanumeric	Address	37 Main Street
	Date	6/12/93
	Phone	853–233–0189
Alphabetic	Name	John Wilson
	Description	Compact Disk
	Credit	Y

required for input definition depend on the language used and can vary widely.

Output defines the results of processing the input data. Your first program usually displays output on the computer's screen to be read visually directly after it is displayed. Output can also be printed if a permanent hard copy is required. Disk output is frequently used when data needs to be stored for processing at a later time.

Figure 12-2 shows how input is supplied to the program from the keyboard. The program processes this input data and then displays the results on the screen. Output may also have field definitions such as numeric, or alphabetic. Specific definitions depend on the programming language and the type of output device being used by the program.

FIGURE 12-2
Input provided from the keyboard is processed by the program. Following processing the results are displayed as output on the screen.

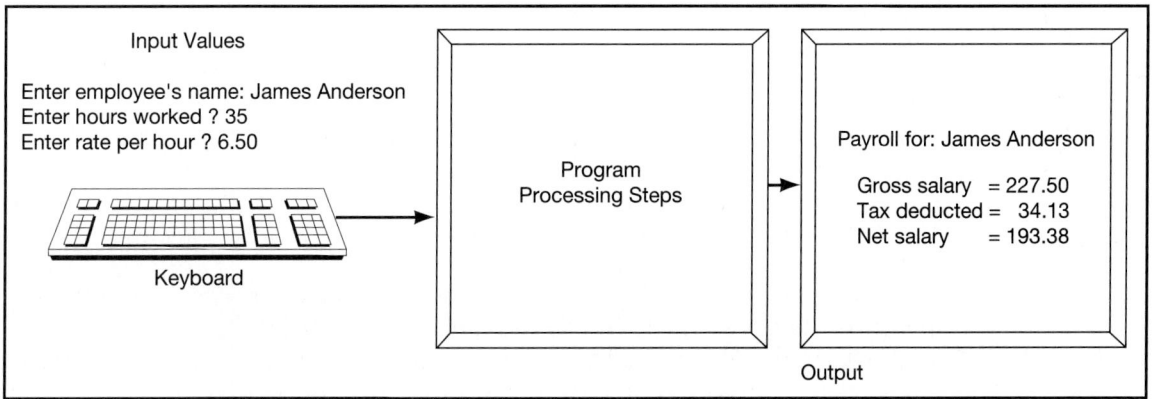

Input Values

Enter employee's name: James Anderson
Enter hours worked ? 35
Enter rate per hour ? 6.50

Keyboard

Program Processing Steps

Payroll for: James Anderson

Gross salary = 227.50
Tax deducted = 34.13
Net salary   = 193.38

Output

THE TOOLS OF PROGRAM DESIGN

Simple programs, such as one for the payroll problem in the previous section, can often be written directly from the specifications. But programs are frequently more complex than this one. Other factors such as employee pension, government social security, unemployment insurance, overtime pay, and so on need to be considered in a real payroll application. To design programs such as these effectively, tools such as structure charts, flowcharts, and pseudocode are both helpful and necessary.

Structure Charts

Structure chart. A chart that is used to develop the solution to a problem in hierarchical fashion. Also called a top-down chart or a hierarchy chart.

A **structure chart** shows the solution to a problem in a hierarchical fashion from the top level to the bottom. At the top of the chart is a general statement about the problem. The next level shows more detail, which may be expanded to a third level as required until the solution is completely defined. Each box is a **module** that represents a **task**. A lower level box is a sub-task that further defines the module.

Figure 12-3 shows a general structure chart pattern that may be used to help think about organizing the solution to a problem. As with any general solution, it may need to be adapted to the needs of a specific problem. In this case the problem is defined in terms of input, processing, and output requirements. Since most programs require all three of these components, this is often a useful way to begin.

A structure chart for the payroll problem is shown in Figure 12-4. It follows the input, process, output pattern, but this time specific references are made to the problem. When a structure chart such as this one is developed, the programmer should begin by thinking about the general solution to the problem and record this as the top level of the structure chart. Then each box is expanded further as more details to the solution to the problem are considered. In this way only small parts of the solution are designed at one time, keeping complexity to a minimum.

FIGURE 12-3
The fundamental parts of a structure chart.

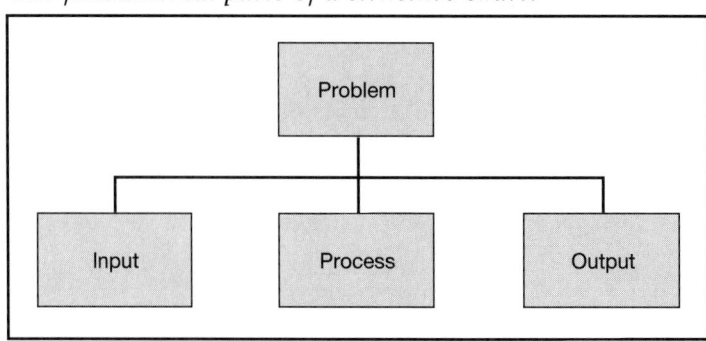

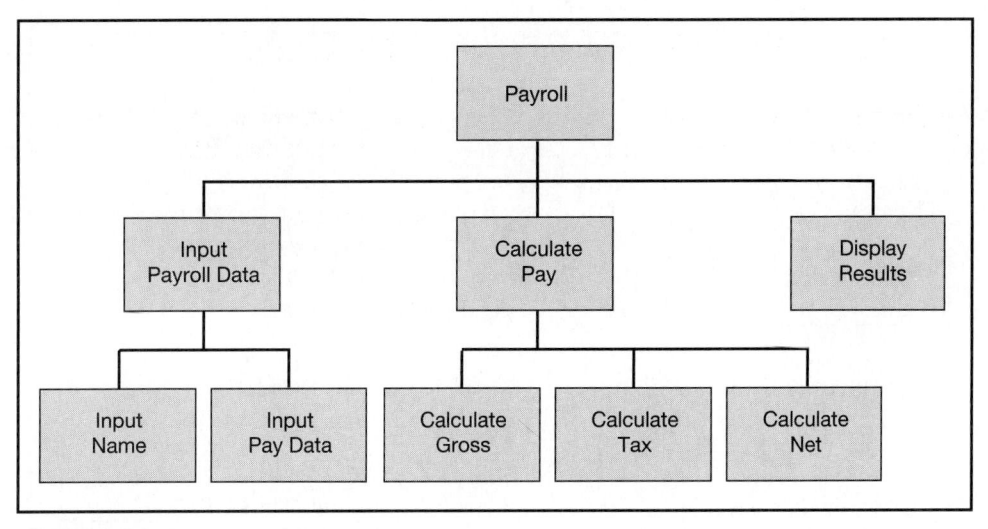

FIGURE 12-4
The structure chart presents a top-down solution to the payroll problem. The top level of the chart is general, with more specific details shown as lower levels of the solution are developed.

Pseudocode

Writing pseudocode may be thought of as a dry run at writing the program. **Pseudocode** uses programlike statements without the detailed and sometime more complex syntax required of a programming language. Pseudocode also uses the concept of top-down design used for developing the structure chart. Often, writing pseudocode is the next step in program design after the structure chart has been created.

Pseudocode represents the logic of the program by showing each step taken, decisions that need to be made in the program, and looping or repetition of program code.

Figure 12-5 shows the pseudocode for the payroll problem. The solution

Pseudocode. Programlike statements that are written as an aid to structured program logic development.

FIGURE 12-5
Pseudocode for the payroll program. Each line in the pseudocode represents a line of program code, but in a simplified form.

```
Program: Payroll

    DOWHILE another employee
        INPUT employee's name
        INPUT hours and rate
        Compute gross
        Compute tax at 15% of gross
        Compute net
        PRINT results
    ENDDO
```

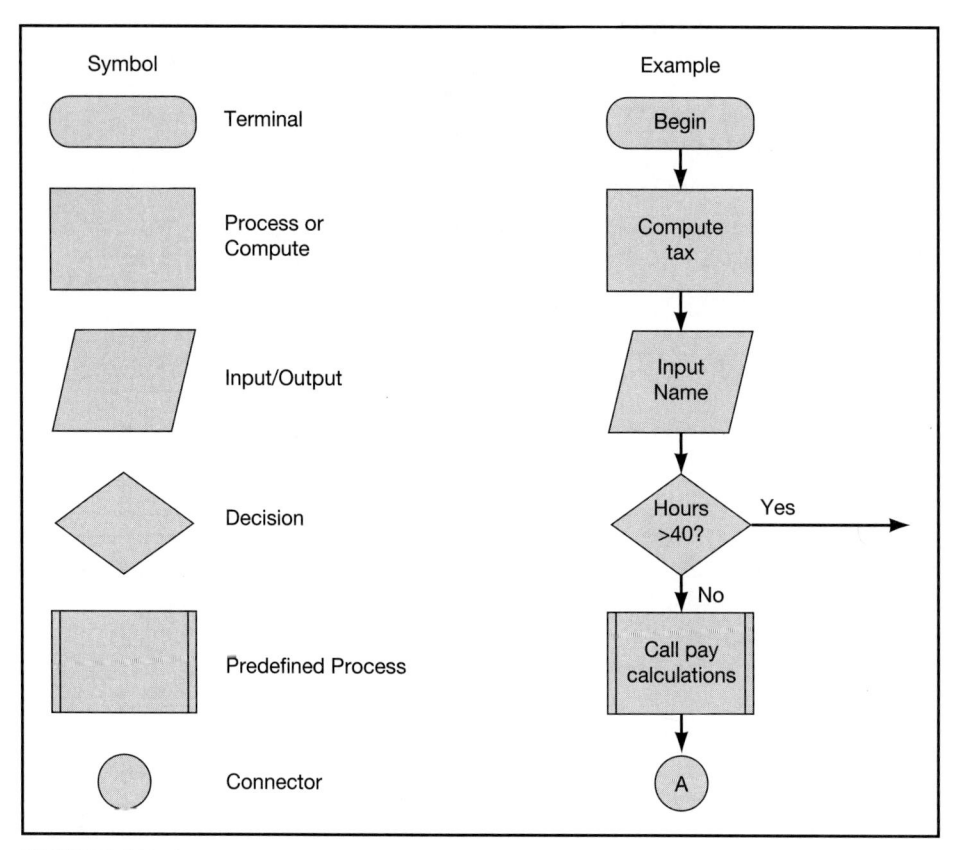

FIGURE 12-6
Symbols used for creating program flowcharts.

at this level includes the possibility of more than one employee and so the "DOWHILE another employee" entry is included. This entry defines a loop that causes the code to be repeated until there are no more employees to be processed.

Program Flowcharts

Flowchart. A chart used to assist in the development of program logic.

While pseudocode uses programlike statements to develop program logic, a **flowchart** uses a diagram to develop program logic. Pseudocode is a series of statements written in point form, while flowcharts are a graphic representation of the logic. Although both methods have the same purpose, some programmers have a preference of one over the other.

Program flowcharts use the symbols from Figure 12-6 that can represent all program logic. In a flowchart the symbols are connected by lines and arrows to represent the flow of logic in the program. When creating a flowchart the flow should normally go from the top to the bottom or to the right in the flowchart. Other directions are permitted, such as when branching left from a decision symbol, but should occur less often. Connectors are used when remote parts of the flowchart need to be connected.

Figure 12-7 shows a flowchart solution for the payroll problem. This

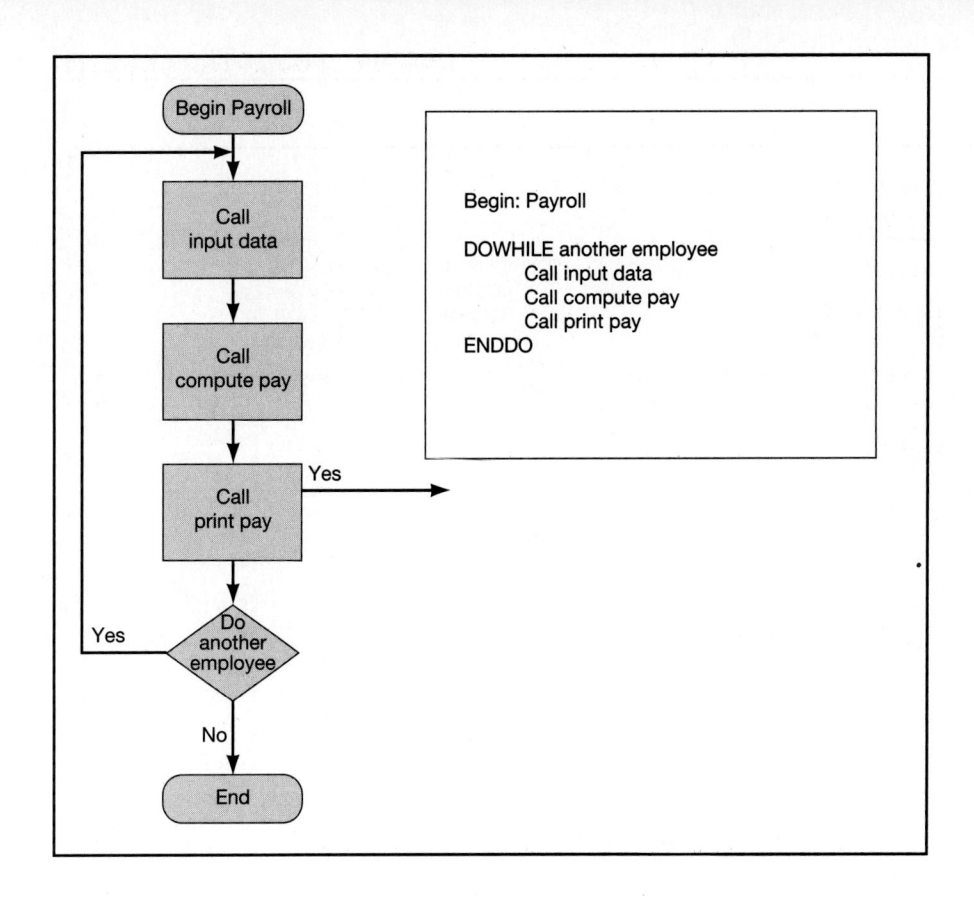

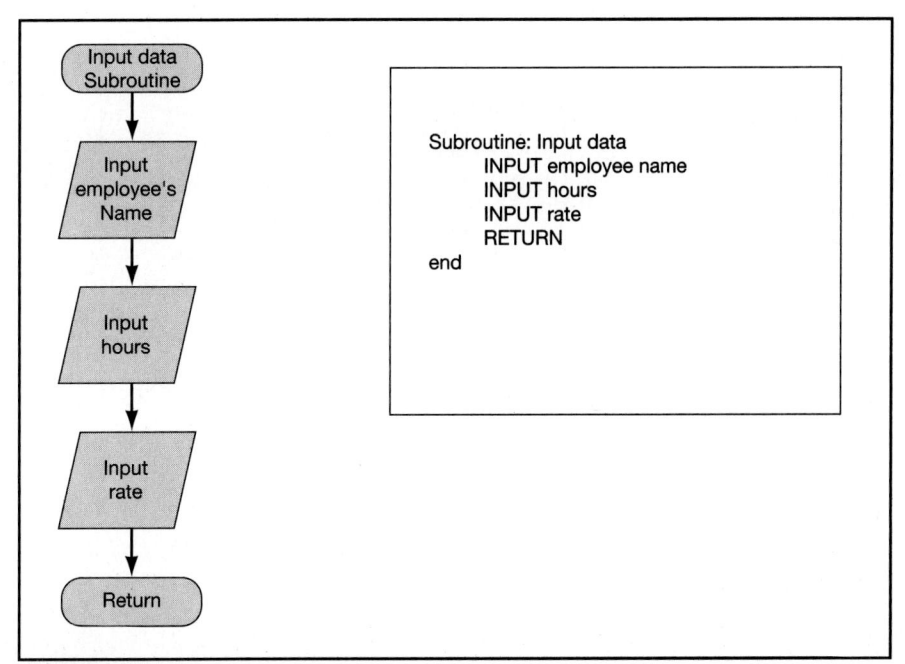

FIGURE 12-7
Flowchart and pseudocode for the payroll problem. The mainline chart (Begin Payroll) provides the calls to access subroutines for reading data, doing the payroll calculations, and printing the results. The mainline also provides a loop so that additional employees may be processed if required. Then each subroutine does the input, processing, and output in that order.

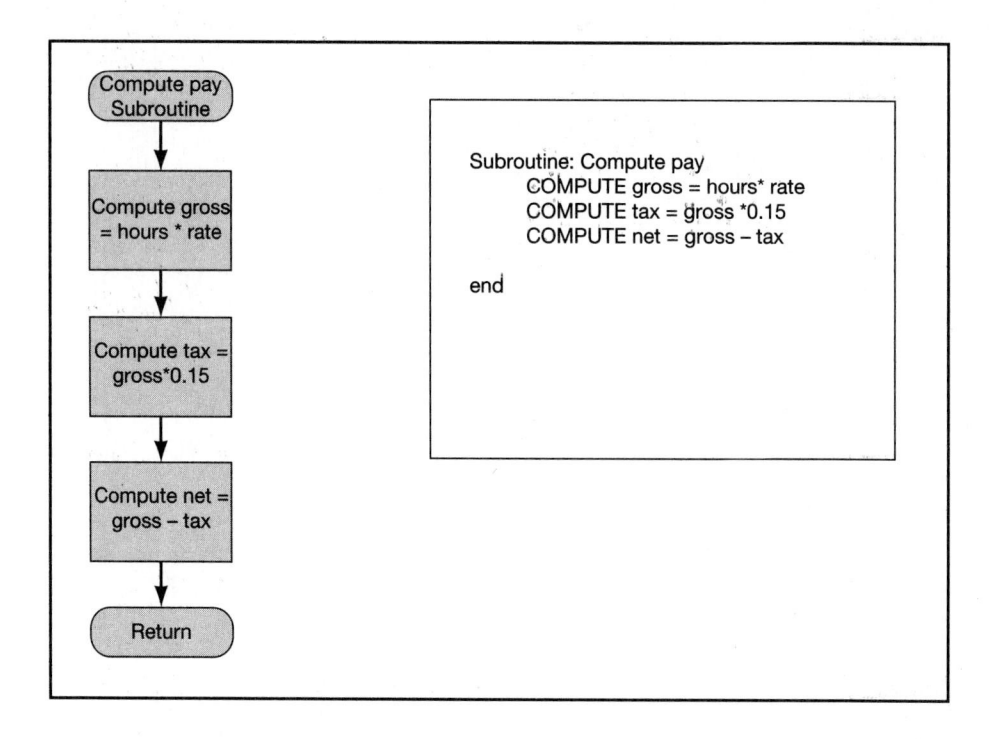

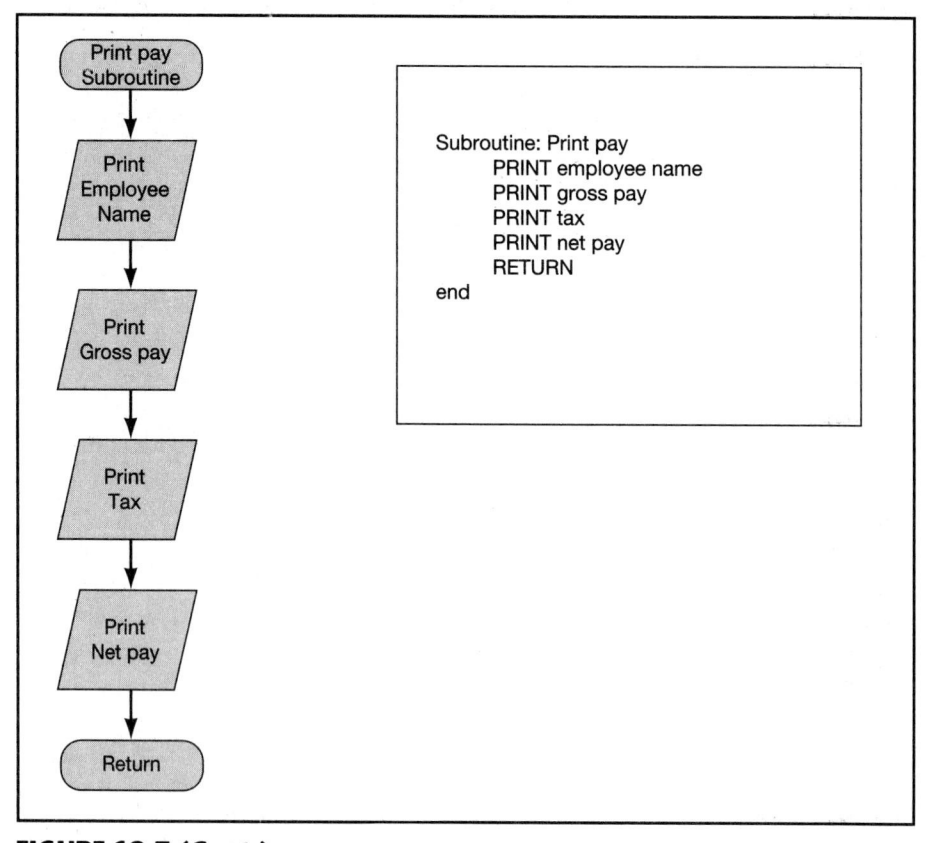

```
Subroutine: Compute pay
        COMPUTE gross = hours* rate
        COMPUTE tax = gross *0.15
        COMPUTE net = gross – tax

end
```

```
Subroutine: Print pay
        PRINT employee name
        PRINT gross pay
        PRINT tax
        PRINT net pay
        RETURN
end
```

FIGURE 12-7 (Cont.)

flowchart is organized into modules or subroutines that each provide the solution for one part of the problem. Using such an approach is called a structured flowchart and is consistent with the method used earlier for developing the top-down solution with a structure chart.

The flowchart begins with a **mainline** section, sometimes called a **driver module.** This module controls the activity of the program and calls other subroutines as they are required. After each subroutine completes its task it returns control to the driver module, which determines the next activity. Pseudocode is also provided with the flowchart for comparison purposes.

STRUCTURED PROGRAMMING

A **structured program** is one that is based on the use of three kinds of program structures called control structures. Early programmers frequently produced programs that were not well organized and used frequent branching or looping. These programs were hard to follow and sometimes were known as "spaghetti code" because of their unorganized structure (or lack of structure). Using the program structures defined here is a method of creating a structured program without unnecessary complexity of logic. The three types of structures are defined as follows:

1. Sequence structure
2. Selection structure
3. Repetition or loop structure

These structures apply not only to programs, but also to pseudocode and flowcharts. They are really quite simple and can be thought of in the following ways.

Sequence Structure

The sequence structure refers to a simple sequence of activities such as reading, printing, calculating, or calling a subroutine. The sequence structure is fundamental to all programming. It does not make decisions or loop but simply proceeds from one statement to the next. Here is an example of three pseudocode statements that are a sequence structure. To the right is a flowchart which graphically portrays the same structure.

Sequence. A series of program statements that execute one after the other.

Selection Structure

The selection structure represents decision making in the flowchart or pseudocode and ultimately in the program. A decision has a condition that is evaluated. If the condition is determined to be true, one action is selected to be done. If the condition was determined to be false, the other action is selected. Notice that only one action or the other is selected; never both.

Selection. A program structure that makes a decision and chooses from two alternatives.

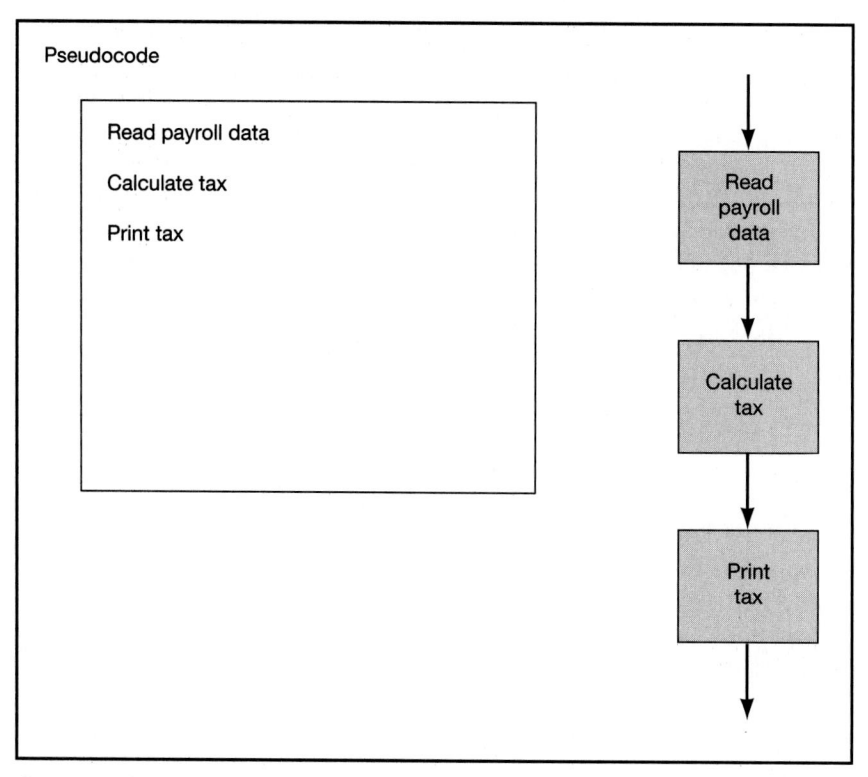

Pseudocode

    Read payroll data
    Calculate tax
    Print tax

Sequence Structure.

Repetition. A program structure that repeats one or more instructions until a given condition occurs.

Repetition Structure

The repetition or loop structure also contains a decision, but the difference lies in the use of repetition. In this structure the decision determines if the action is to be repeated or if the program is to leave the structure.

Selection Structure.

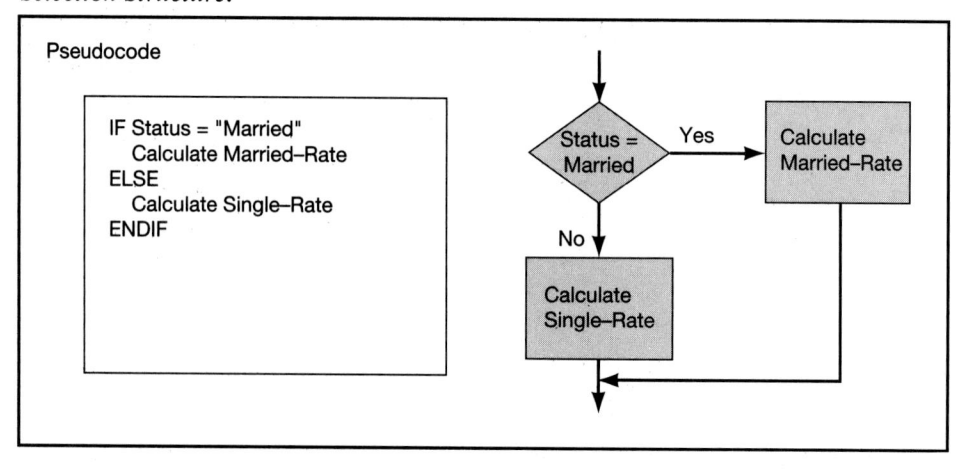

Pseudocode

    IF Status = "Married"
        Calculate Married–Rate
    ELSE
        Calculate Single–Rate
    ENDIF

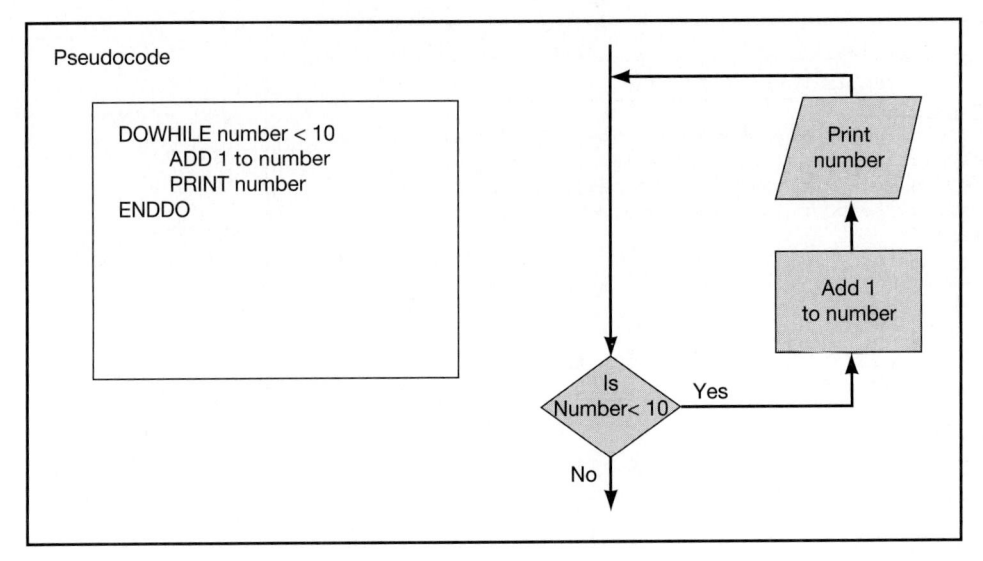

```
Pseudocode

    DOWHILE number < 10
        ADD 1 to number
        PRINT number
    ENDDO
```

Repetition Structure.

PROGRAM CODING

When the program has been designed using the tools of program design, then the **program code** is written. Figure 12-8 shows a program written in the BASIC language for the payroll application developed in this section. The program code follows the logic developed in the pseudocode and flowchart but now uses BASIC language coding to implement the solution.

Programming requires not only that the program code be written to implement the solution but also that code is written clearly. The programmer should be able to easily read the code and understand how it works. Clear programming style is necessary so that the program can be tested and debugged with a minimum of confusion. Good style also makes it easier to change the program when the needs of the application change.

The payroll program uses good style by including several standards for program coding. These standards are:

1. Begin the program with comments including the name of the program, a description, and the name of the programmer.
2. Begin each subroutine with a remark that identifies the purpose of the subroutine.
3. Use descriptive variables names such as HOURS rather than a single letter variable. If necessary use a descriptive abbreviation such as EMP$ for an employee name.
4. When nested code is used, such as in a WHILE loop, indent code within the loop a common number of columns to make the nesting obvious.
5. Use spaces around operators such as +, −, /, *, and = to improve readability.

Program coding. The process of writing a solution to the problem in a programming language.

```
100  REM ****************************************************************
110  REM *                  Sample Payroll Program                      *
120  REM * Description:                                                 *
130  REM *   This program reads hours and pay rate data for an employee *
140  REM *   and calculates a gross salary. A 15% tax deduction is      *
150  REM *   computed and the net salary to be paid. After the results  *
160  REM *   are printed the user is allowed to repeat the process.     *
170  REM * Programmer:                                                  *
180  REM * Don Cassel                                                   *
190  REM ****************************************************************
200  Y$ = "yes"
210  WHILE Y$ = "yes"
215      CLS
220      GOSUB 1000
230      GOSUB 2000
240      GOSUB 3000
250      INPUT "Input another employee (yes/no";Y$
260  WEND
270  END
1000 REM ****************************************************************
1010 REM *                 Input Payroll Data Subroutine                *
1020 REM ****************************************************************
1030 REM
1040 INPUT "Enter employee's name ",EMP$
1050 INPUT "Enter hours worked ";HOURS
1060 INPUT "Enter rate per hour ";RATE
1070 PRINT
1080 RETURN
2000 REM ****************************************************************
2010 REM *                     Compute Pay Subroutine                   *
2020 REM ****************************************************************
2030 REM
2040 GROSS = HOURS * RATE
2050 TAX = GROSS * .15
2060 NET = GROSS - TAX
2070 RETURN
3000 REM ****************************************************************
3010 REM *                    Print Payroll Subroutine                  *
3020 REM ****************************************************************
3030 REM
3040 PRINT "Payroll for: ";EMP$
3050 PRINT
3060 PRINT "Gross salary = ";GROSS
3070 PRINT "Tax deducted = ";TAX
3080 PRINT "Net salary = ";NET
3090 PRINT
3100 RETURN
```

FIGURE 12-8

A BASIC program using good techniques of style to implement the payroll application.

Figure 12-9 shows a sample screen from the payroll program. The first three lines of the screen display show the input data requested by the program and the values entered. The remaining lines are the results created as output from the program. In this example some of the calculated values have from one to three decimal places, depending on the results of the cal-

```
Enter employee's name James Anderson
Enter hours worked ? 35
Enter rate per hour ? 6.50

Payroll for: James Anderson

Gross salary = 227.5
Tax deducted = 34.125
Net salary = 193.375

Input another employee (yes/no)?
```

FIGURE 12-9
A screen display from the payroll program.

▶ DESK CHECKING

Programming often involves more than simply designing and writing the program. After the program is written, the programmer needs to review the program code and check it against the specifications to ensure that nothing was overlooked and to catch any errors. Doing a review of this type is sometimes called a walkthrough. But since the beginning of programming this process has been called desk checking because it occurred at the programmer's desk. Much of this work is done today at a terminal or PC.

▶ DEBUGGING AND TESTING

When a program has been written, it needs to be **tested** by running it on the computer to ensure that it runs correctly and satisfies the requirements of the program specifications. No matter how careful a programmer may be, programs are seldom written correctly the first time. Therefore, the programmer needs to check the results by reviewing the output and looking for errors. This process of finding errors in a program and correcting them is called **debugging**.

culations. This is a common characteristic of BASIC and can be modified by more extensive programming.

PROGRAMMING LANGUAGES

Coding is the process of writing the computer program in a language such as BASIC. Programmers often write the program on paper before entering it on the computer, although some prefer to type it as the program is developed. In either case, constant reference to the design documents is necessary to ensure a correct program.

Interpreter. A program that reads each statement in a source program and translates it for computer execution.

Compiler. A program that translates a source language program and creates a machine language program called an object program.

Source program. The original program written in a high-level language prior to compiling or interpreting.

Object program. A machine language program produced as a result of compiling a source program.

After the program has been written, it is run on the computer to be tested to ensure that it contains no errors. Because the program is written in a language such as BASIC or C, it must first be interpreted into a computer language which at the lowest level consists of ones and zeros. Several methods of interpretation are used, depending on the language or computer.

An **interpreter** is a program that reads each statement in the BASIC program (or other language) and interprets it for the computer. This process is something like a human interpreter who listens to your English and after each sentence you speak interprets it into French for a listener who only understands the French language.

A **compiler** performs a similar function to an interpreter but in a different manner. When a compiler translates the program, it creates an entirely new program that is in the computer language. You might compare this process to a human interpreter who interprets an English language book and creates a French book from it. A compiled program will run much faster than an interpreted one and is desired on systems where lack of speed can be a problem.

When a program is compiled, the original program is called the **source program** and the compiled version is the **object program**.

A program that is compiled or interpreted may contain errors such as statements that are coded incorrectly. Maybe a comma is missing or a parenthesis is used in the wrong place. In such cases a diagnostic error mes-

Where did a term such as debugging originate? Allegedly, in 1945 a problem occurred in the Mark I computer. Grace Hopper, a computer pioneer of the day, was asked to find the problem. Eventually, a moth was found in the relays and the term "bug" was associated with an error in computer hardware and software. (Courtesy Naval Surface Weapons Center.)

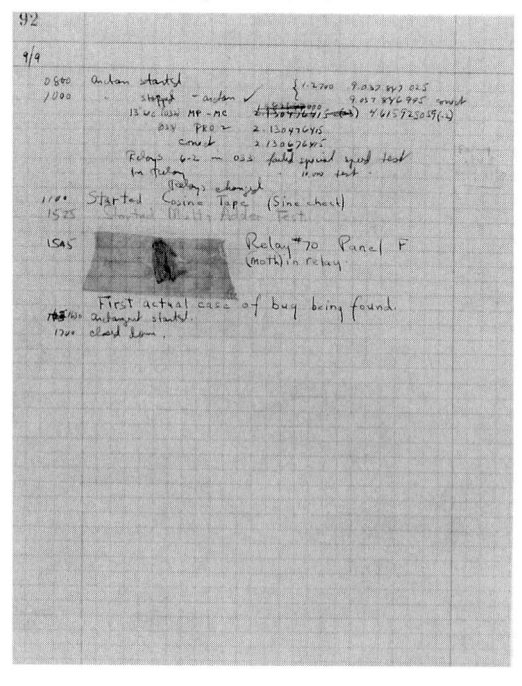

sage is produced, and the programmer must find the error and correct it. The procedure is known as **debugging** the program and is a necessary process for every program.

Finally, program **testing** is done when data is entered and the results are checked to ensure the program is operating correctly. Good testing procedures will also attempt to use data that is in error to see if the program will reject it rather than attempt to process incorrect data. Testing can be as much of an art (and some science) as programming and is a time-consuming but essential task for the producers of business or other software.

In Appendix A you will see the difference between four generations of languages and the development of programming from machine language, through symbolic, to high-level languages and now fourth generation. The main difference between the last two generations is that high-level languages are procedural, while fourth-generation frequently are nonprocedural. These are the two categories of programming languages used on personal computers today.

Procedural Languages

Languages such as BASIC, C, COBOL, FORTRAN, and Pascal are called procedural languages because they are coded and written as sequentially ordered statements. Decision making and looping are an essential part of procedure-oriented languages, and the language structure provides statements to accommodate this need.

Procedural languages are in widespread use on both mainframe and personal computers and have developed into dependable and competent languages.

BASIC. The name BASIC means Beginners All-Purpose Symbolic Instruction Code. BASIC was developed at Dartmouth College for use on a mainframe computer in a time-sharing environment. But when personal computers came on the scene, BASIC was adopted as their primary programming language. Computers such as the Apple, Commodore PET, and eventually the IBM PC all provided BASIC as a standard language.

BASIC was ideal for the PC because of its interactive nature. Keyboard input and screen output are easy to use and form the basis for many PC applications. BASIC is considered an easy language to learn, but there are many variations of it on different computer systems. Although BASIC is often a first language that a programmer learns, it does have many limitations which results in the programmer moving to more recently developed and sophisticated languages such as C or Pascal.

COBOL. The name COBOL means COmmon Business-Oriented Language and was developed primarily for business applications. COBOL was developed in 1959 and gained prominence during the 1960s as the leading mainframe computer language. Its foothold in the industry is so strong that the majority of mainframe applications today continue to use COBOL.

COBOL's main strength is its file handling ability. It was designed to process a variety of file types and can handle sequential, relative, and VSAM files equally well. However, it is not particularly well suited to interactive applications using the screen and keyboard. If applications require

Procedural Languages. Languages that are coded and written as sequentially ordered statements including decision making and looping.

heavy interaction, other software is used with COBOL to provide the link with the user.

With personal computers exceeding the memory size and capacity of mainframes of only a few years ago, COBOL is now able to run on many PCs. Although the applications are few, some companies are using COBOL

```
IDENTIFICATION DIVISION.
PROGRAM-ID.
    EXP01.
*REMARKS.
*    PRINTS DEPARTMENTAL EXPENSE REPORT.

ENVIRONMENT DIVISION.
CONFIGURATION SECTION.
SOURCE-COMPUTER.
    IBM-370-138.
OBJECT-COMPUTER.
    IBM-370-138.
SPECIAL-NAMES.
    C01 IS TO-NEW-PAGE.

INPUT-OUTPUT SECTION.
FILE-CONTROL.
    SELECT EXP-IN ASSIGN TO SYS004-UR-2501-S.
    SELECT EXP-RPT ASSIGN TO SYS005-UR-1403-S.

DATA DIVISION.

FILE SECTION.
FD    EXP-IN
      RECORD CONTAINS 80 CHARACTERS
      LABEL RECORDS ARE OMITTED
      DATA RECORD IS IN-REC.
01 IN-REC.
      05 IN-DEPT      PIC 9(03).
      05 IN-DATE      PIC X(08).
      05 IN-TYPE      PIC X(13).
      05 IN-AMOUNT    PIC 9999V99.
      05 FILLER       PIC X(50).

FD EXP-RPT
      RECORD CONTAINS 133 CHARACTERS
      LABEL RECORDS ARE OMITTED
      DATA RECORD IS OUT-REC
01 OUT-REC
      05 FILLER PIC X(133).

WORKING-STORAGE SECTION.
01 WORK-AREA.
      05 EOF-FLAG    PIC 9       VALUE ZERO.
      05 WORK-TOTAL  PIC 9(5)V99 VALUE ZERO.

01 OUT-HEAD-1.
05 FILLER          PIC X(015)  VALUE SPACES.
05 FILLER          PIC X(118)
                   VALUE 'DEPARTMENTAL EXPENSE REPORT'.
```

FIGURE 12-10
A sample COBOL program.

```
01 OUT-HEAD-2.
   05 FILLER        PIC X(030)
                    VALUE '    DEPARTMENT          DATE         '.
   05 FILLER        PIC X(103)
                    VALUE 'TYPE OF EXPENSE        AMOUNT'.
01 OUT-DETAIL.
   05 FILLER        PIC X(004) VALUE SPACES.
   05 OUT-DEPT      PIC 9(003).
   05 FILLER        PIC X(010) VALUE SPACES.
   05 OUT-DATE      PIC X(008).
   05 FILLER        PIC X(005) VALUE SPACES.
   05 OUT-TYPE      PIC X(013).
   05 FILLER        PIC X(006) VALUE SPACES.
   05 OUT-AMOUNT    PIC 9999.99.
01 OUT-FOOTER.
   05 FILLER        PIC X(049) VALUE SPACES.
   05 OUT-TOTAL     PIC 9(4).99.

PROCEDURE DIVISION.

000-HOUSE-KEEPING.
   OPEN INPUT EXP-IN.
   OPEN OUTPUT EXP-RPT.
   PERFORM 150-PRINT-HEADINGS.

100-MAINLINE.
   PERFORM 200-READ-ROUTINE.
   PERFORM 300-PROCESS-DATA
       UNTIL EOF-FLAG = 1.
   PERFORM 400-TOTAL.
   CLOSE EXP-IN.
   CLOSE EXP-RPT.
   STOP RUN.

150-PRINT-HEADINGS.
   MOVE OUT-HEAD-1 TO OUT-REC.
   WRITE OUT-REC
       AFTER ADVANCING TO-NEW-PAGE.
   MOVE OUT-HEAD-2 TO OUT-REC.
WRITE OUT-REC
       AFTER ADVANCING 2 LINES.
   MOVE SPACES TO OUT-REC.
   WRITE OUT-REC
       AFTER ADVANCING 1 LINES.

200-READ-ROUTINE.
   READ EXP-IN
       AT END MOVE 1 TO EOF-FLAG.
```

FIGURE 12-10 (*Cont.*)

```
300-PROCESS-DATA.
    ADD IN-AMOUNT     TO    WORK-TOTAL.
    MOVE IN-DEPT      TO    OUT-DEPT.
    MOVE IN-DATE      TO    OUT-DATE.
    MOVE IN-TYPE      TO    OUT-TYPE.
    MOVE IN-AMOUNT    TO    OUT-AMOUNT.
    MOVE OUT-DETAIL   TO    OUT-REC.
    WRITE OUT-REC
        AFTER ADVANCING 1 LINES.
    PERFORM 200-READ-ROUTINE.

400-TOTAL.
    MOVE WORK-TOTAL TO    OUT-TOTAL.
    MOVE OUT-FOOTER TO    OUT-REC.
    WRITE OUT-REC
        AFTER ADVANCING 2 LINES.
```

FIGURE 12-10 (*Cont.*)

programs originally developed for the mainframe on personal computers. Thus the application can be taken to where the user needs it.

Figure 12-10 shows a sample COBOL program that prints a simple expense report. The example demonstrates both a major strength and a major weakness of COBOL. The strength is COBOL's readability. Even someone who sees a COBOL program for the first time can make some sense of it. A weakness is COBOL's wordiness. Even the most elementary program requires many lines of code, whereas only a few lines can produce a useful BASIC program.

FORTRAN. FORTRAN has been a widely used programming language in the engineering, mathematical, and scientific communities for many years. The name FORTRAN is taken from FORmula TRANslation, which implies correctly that the main use of the language is for programming mathematical formulas. Although many other languages are taking its place, it endures as a popular language when the applications are of a mathematical nature (Figure 12-11).

The language was first developed by IBM and released in 1957. As one of the first high-level languages, it made computer power more readily available, and its use became widespread. During the 1960s FORTRAN became available on most computers of the period and is still widely available from PCs to mainframes today.

Because of its orientation to solving mathematical problems, FORTRAN was not suited to the business community. Programs that create reports or do file processing are not as easily developed in FORTRAN as in other languages such as COBOL. More advanced business applications using indexed files or interactive user operations are best done using a language oriented to these operations, leaving FORTRAN for the engineers and scientists.

Pascal. Pascal is a language that was developed by Nicklaus Wirth, a widely recognized computer scientist. Wirth intended Pascal to be independent of the computer on which it was run so that a program written on one

CHAPTER 12 Programming Concepts

```
C         SUM OF A SERIES 1 TO 100
          INTEGER COUNT, SUM
          SUM = O
          DO 20 COUNT = 1, 100
              SUM = SUM + COUNT
20        CONTINUE PRINT 30, 'THE SUM OF 1 TO 100 IS ', SUM
30        FORMAT (' ', A23, I6)
          STOP
          END
```

FIGURE 12-11
A FORTRAN program for finding the sum of the series of integers 1 + 2 + 3 + ... + 100.

make of computer could run equally well on a different make without the need for program changes. Pascal was one of the first languages to provide for the language structures needed for effective structured programming (Figure 12-12).

Pascal is easy to learn, although perhaps not as easy as BASIC, and is taught as a primary language in many computer science courses. Pascal is also useful for software development and has been used to develop many software packages for business. It is frequently used on personal computers, thanks to the well-known Turbo Pascal which made the language affordable for the micro.

Modula-2. Ten years after Nicklaus Wirth developed Pascal he set a goal to improve on the language. The result was Modula-2 (Figure 12-13). The new language was created to help programmers avoid some kinds of errors that were easily created in Pascal and to simplify advanced programming applications. Many computer science courses are now making the switch from Pascal to Modula-2. Changing to the new langauge is relatively easy because much of the language structure is identical to Pascal.

C Language. The C language was developed by Bell Laboratories in the early 1970s and used on UNIX-based operating systems for software development. C creates object code that is comparable to an assembly language

FIGURE 12-12
An example of a structured Pascal program. Statements enclosed in braces {} are comments.

```
program interest(input, output);
     var Balance, Interest, Principal: real;
         Period: integer;
     begin
     {Read initial values}
     read(Principal, Interest, Period);
     {Calculate balance with interest}
     Balance := Principal*(1 + Period*Interest)
     writeln('The new balance is',Balance);
end.
```

```
MODULE Sampleprogram;
FROM InOut IMPORT
     Writestring, WriteLn;
BEGIN
     WriteString ('Sample Lines of Modula-2 Output');
     WriteLn;
     WriteLn;
     WriteString ('These are sample lines of printed output');
     WriteString ('from a Modula-2 program.');
     WriteLn;
END Sampleprogram.
```

FIGURE 12-13
Modula-2 is a language derived from the Pascal language. Both languages were developed by Nicklaus Wirth.

in efficiency, while using high-level language features for programming. Structured programs are easily written in C (Figure 12-14) owing to its language structure, which promotes top-down coding.

Like Pascal, C is independent of the computer on which the program is written. This feature, as well as its efficiency, have caused it to be adopted by many software developers for the PC. The latest version is called C++, an object-oriented programming language. Using C++ programmers can develop applications in Windows using Object Linking and Embedding (OLE), Dynamic Data Exchange (DDE), and even multimedia.

Although C is considered to be a relatively difficult language to master, C language programmers are in great demand.

Fourth-Generation Languages

What attracted early users to the personal computer was its natural productivity. Instead of submitting requests to a mainframe computer and then

FIGURE 12-14
A C language program that finds the sum of integers from 1 to a number entered by the user of the program.

```
/*       Sample C language program          /*
/*  Finds the sum of integers from 1 to number */
main()
{     int counter = 0; number; sum = 0;
      printf("This program finds the sum of integers from 1 to");
      printf("a number that you enter. Enter the number and ");
      printf("press the return key");
      scanf("%d",&number);
      while (counter < number)
         {
             counter + + ;
             sum = sum + counter
         }
      printf("The sum of the numbers is %F" ,sum);
}
```

User-friendly software made computers available to users from many disciplines. No longer is it necessary to be a computer programmer to develop applications for the PC. Using nonprocedural languages, users can develop some of their own applications without the need for writing a computer program. (Courtesy IBM Corporation.)

waiting days or weeks for a result, they could spend a few hours at a PC and get the information needed for their job. Because of its apparent simplicity, demonstrated by its user-friendly nature, the PC was available to many more users than the mainframe.

Early PC users had to write their own programs in a procedural language, usually in BASIC. But with software such as Lotus 1–2–3 and dBASE IV, fewer programming skills were needed and the user could concentrate on the application rather than on using a procedural language.

More software for the PC is becoming available on a continuing basis that is nonprocedural in its use. These packages, such as PC/FOCUS, provide nonprocedural commands for easy access to data and for data analysis. A number of fourth-generation languages (4GL) were first developed for use on mainframe computers and have now filtered down to personal computers. Frequently, applications developed on the PC can be run on the mainframe and vice versa.

Users can learn to use 4GL tools very quickly without a lot of prior training, thus reducing the load on programmers for new application development. 4GLs can both speed up and simplify the process of developing a new application. Coding and testing the system can be done by the user by using easy-to-understand nonprocedural, English-type statements. Prototyping, which is the development of a sample of how the system will function, can be more readily developed with 4GLs.

4GLs offer facilities for doing queries in a database, generating reports, and updating files. For programmers, 4GLs can be used for automatic code

Nonprocedural language. A solution-oriented language that defines the task to be done rather than the method for accomplishing the task.

generation, which permits faster program development than writing program code directly. By using these tools the professional can reduce the backlog of applications waiting to be developed and improve the time needed for software maintenance.

The mechanism that is fast becoming a standard for communicating between a 4GL and a database is IBM's Structured Query Language (SQL). SQL is a language used for submitting queries to a database. Originally developed for mainframe application, SQL is now appearing in PC software products, such as Borland's dBASE IV. Users write queries in SQL as part of a 4GL to extract information from their database.

Using 4GLs in the corporation is leading to a new phenomenon in the way systems are developed and maintained. Formerly, systems design used a linear methodology, as we will discuss in the chapter on systems analysis. The sequence of events was analysis, design, test, and implementation. With 4GLs a more circular systems methodology is beginning to be apparent: analysis, prototyping, user review, prototype enhancement. Testing is done at various levels of the development instead of near the end. Best of all is the more complete user involvement at all levels of systems development.

OBJECT-ORIENTED PROGRAMMING

Programming in procedural languages such as C or COBOL is a time-consuming, labor-intensive activity. No wonder fourth-generation languages are becoming popular alternatives to traditional programming. Another trend that merits serious attention is object-oriented programming (OOP) which has received much attention from the programming community since the early 1990s. Languages such as Apple's HyperCard, Borland's C++ (Figure 12-15), and Turbo Pascal are examples of programming environments that have adopted the OOP philosophy and promise to provide a way of coping with the increasing complexity of the next generation of software. Much of the software being developed for the ill-fated NeXT computer and now sold as software for other systems is based on object-oriented techniques. When traditional approaches to software development are used, a huge monolith of program code is developed. As the program expands with new features it becomes more difficult to manage the development process because of the increasing complexity. Object-oriented programming offers a way out of this complexity by providing a fundamentally new approach.

What Do You Mean Object-Oriented?

Using object-oriented programming, programmers create **objects** that combine program code and data. In traditional programming, programs and data are kept separate, requiring a redefinition of the data each time a program is written and often complex linkages between modules of program code exist. When OOP is used, the instructions, called **methods,** define how

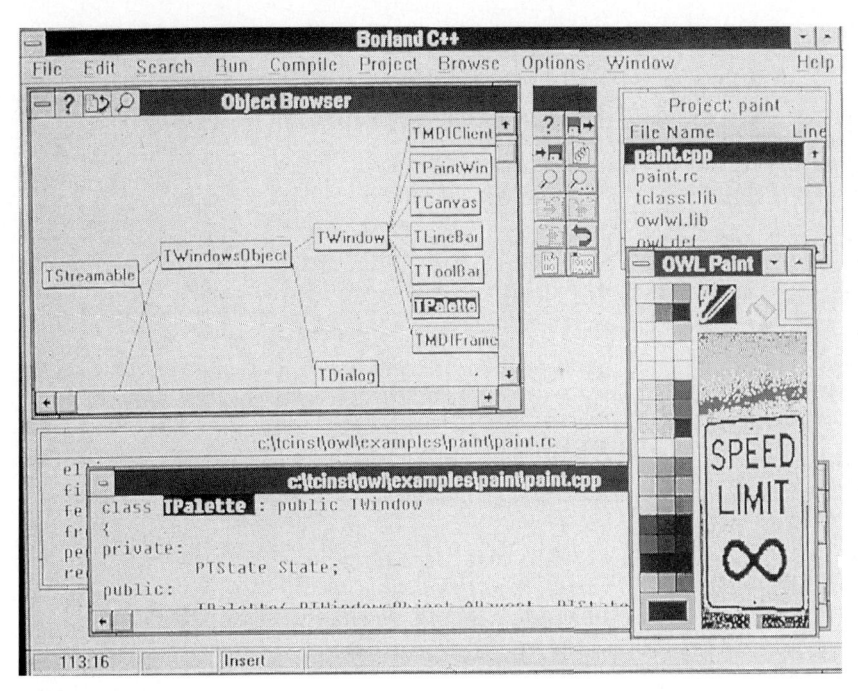

FIGURE 12-15
C++ is a popular object-oriented programming language. By combining OOP technology with the widely used C language, Borland has eased the transition for programmers moving to object-oriented techniques. (Courtesy Borland International.)

the object acts when it is used by a program. So when an object-oriented program accesses a customer's object, the data definition and the rules for acting on the data are already present. If the customer object is used by a print invoice object, then the print invoice object **inherits** the properties from the customer object (Figure 12-16). The programmer doesn't need to reprogram the data definition and program instructions each time the customer object is used.

The print invoice object may also require the use of inventory information to successfully print a customer order. Thus, the print invoice object also inherits the properties of an inventory object. In a complete application objects will frequently be composed of smaller identities that can be used more widely in a variety of application scenarios. Objects are reusable components that can be used by any programmer, thus reducing the time to develop new applications and to update old ones.

Objects used in this context are **event-driven** because they respond to a specific user action. When the user clicks on the print invoice icon, this action is an event which drives the activity that will print the invoice. The customer object is then driven by the print invoice object and in turn supplies data needed for the invoice. Writing object-oriented programs is different from the process of procedural programming, which is more linear because each object is independent of the other and is activated when needed.

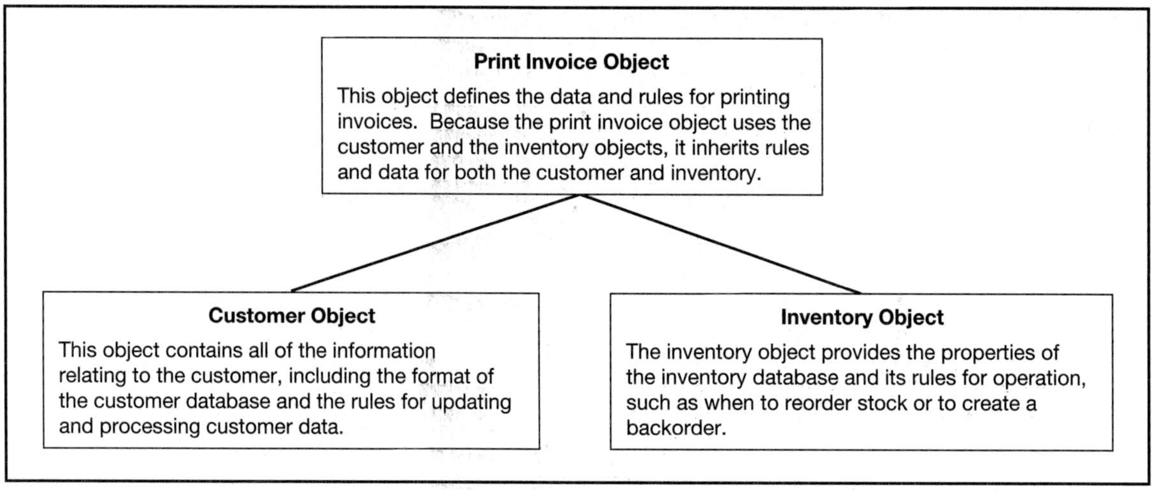

```
┌─────────────────────────────────────────────────────────────┐
│                    Print Invoice Object                     │
│         This object defines the data and rules for printing │
│         invoices. Because the print invoice object uses the │
│         customer and the inventory objects, it inherits rules│
│         and data for both the customer and inventory.       │
│                                                             │
│                              ╱╲                             │
│                             ╱  ╲                            │
│                            ╱    ╲                           │
│   ┌──────────────────────┐        ┌──────────────────────┐  │
│   │   Customer Object    │        │   Inventory Object   │  │
│   │ This object contains │        │ The inventory object │  │
│   │ all of the information│        │ provides the properties│ │
│   │ relating to the customer,│    │ of the inventory database│ │
│   │ including the format of│      │ and its rules for operation,│
│   │ the customer database │        │ such as when to reorder │  │
│   │ and the rules for updating│   │ stock or to create a  │  │
│   │ and processing customer data.│ │ backorder.            │  │
│   └──────────────────────┘        └──────────────────────┘  │
└─────────────────────────────────────────────────────────────┘
```

FIGURE 12-16

Object-oriented programming defines applications as objects that contain both data definition and the rules for processing the data. If an icon to print an invoice is clicked, the print invoice object knows to access both customer and inventory objects to get the data it needs. These objects each know the rules for providing either customer or inventory data.

The Benefits of OOP

Languages that have implemented object-oriented programming techniques such as C++ and Turbo Pascal 6.0 bring many new benefits to the programming occupation. First, they permit programmers who are familiar with traditional programming methods to mix the old and the new technology. This approach helps ease the transition to the newer method of programming. Using objects also hides the overall complexity of an application by reducing it to many smaller and thus less complex components. Using object-oriented techniques is said to result in quicker application development, and less time is spent doing program maintenance.

OOP languages have come into their own since Windows became a platform of choice for so many applications. Thus, OOP often uses GUI for improved user interaction. Other new Windows techniques such as object linking and embedding (OLE) and dynamic data interchange (DDE) are also in use. These languages make it easier to build menus, GUIs, dialog boxes, clipboards, and windows into applications, thus giving a more Windows-like appearance and also contributing to greater user satisfaction. OOP is a fast developing programming technology with more changes to come.

CHAPTER SUMMARY

1. A **program** is a series of instructions that define how the computer is to process data.

2. **Programming** is the activity of creating or writing a computer program.
3. **Program specifications** define where the data originates, what process steps are to be applied to the data, and what output is to be produced as a result of running the program.
4. **Input** to a program is the data that the program reads from a keyboard or other device.
5. **Output** defines the results of processing the input data and may be a screen display or data written on a file.
6. To design programs effectively, tools such as structure charts, flowcharts, and pseudocode are used.
7. A **structure chart** shows the solution to a problem in a hierarchical fashion from the top level to the bottom, from general to specific. Each box in a structure chart is a module that represents a task.
8. **Pseudocode** is a dry run at writing a program that uses programlike statements without the detailed and sometime more complex syntax required of a programming language.
9. **Flowcharts** use a diagram of connected symbols to represent program logic. A flowchart begins with a mainline section, sometimes called a driver module, and calls subroutines as they are required by the problem.
10. A **structured program** is one that is based on the use of three kinds of program structures: sequence, selection, and repetition.
11. **Coding** is the process of writing the computer program in a language such as BASIC. The program code follows the logic developed in the pseudocode and flowchart.
12. **Programming** requires not only that the program code be written to implement the solution but also that code is written clearly, using good style, so that it is easy to read and understand.
13. An **interpreter** is a program that reads each statement in the BASIC program (or other source language) and interprets it for the computer.
14. A **compiler** translates the program and creates an object program which is in the computer language.
15. **Debugging** is the process of finding coding errors from diagnostic messages and correcting them in the program.
16. **Testing** is the process of running the program with test data to discover if it works according to the specifications.
17. Languages such as BASIC, COBOL, Pascal, and C are called **procedural languages** because they are coded and written as sequentially ordered statements. Decision making and looping are an essential part of procedure-oriented languages.
18. **Nonprocedural languages** require fewer programming skills and let the user concentrate on the application rather than on using a procedural language.
19. Object-oriented programs use **objects** that combine program code and data. When one object uses another, it inherits the **properties** of that object, reducing the need for redundant programming.

IMPORTANT TERMS AND CONCEPTS

BASIC	Object program
C language	Output
COBOL	Pascal
Compiler	Procedural language
Computer generations	Program
Control structures	Programming
Debugging	Pseudocode
Flowcharts	Repetition structure
Input	Selection structure
Interpreter	Sequence structure
Mainline	Source program
Modula-2	Specifications
Module	Structure chart
Nonprocedural	Style
Object	Task
Object-oriented	Testing

SELF-TESTING QUESTIONS

Fill-In

1. A _____ is a series of instructions that define how the computer is to process data.
2. The _____ chart is a tool to show the solution to a problem in a hierarchical fashion from top to the bottom level.
3. _____ is a dry run at writing the program using programlike statements to represent program logic.
4. The _____ control structure represents decision making in the flowchart or pseudocode.
5. The original program that is compiled is called the _____ program, while the compiled version is the object program.
6. Program _____ ensures that the program contains no errors.
7. A _____ is a program that takes a source program and produces a machine language or object program.
8. Languages such as C, BASIC, COBOL, FORTRAN, and Pascal are called _____ languages because they are coded and written as sequentially ordered statements.
9. The _____ language was developed by Bell Laboratories based on the UNIX operating system.
10. C++ is a language that provides _____-_____ capabilities for developing Windows applications.

True/False

1. A nonprocedural language is used initially to define the requirements of the program including the input, process, and output needs.

CHAPTER 12 Programming Concepts

2. Debugging is the process of correcting errors such as a missing comma or a misplaced parenthesis in a program.
3. Desk checking is used to ensure that the program runs correctly and produces the expected output.
4. A nonprocedural language concentrates on solving a problem rather than on the method for the solution.
5. Program coding is the act of creating or writing a computer program.
6. A compiler is a program that reads each statement in the program and acts on it rather than creating a new machine language program.
7. All programming languages are essentially the same. Choosing one should be on a lowest cost basis.
8. SQL is a language originally developed for mainframe computers and is used for submitting queries to a database.

ANSWERS

Fill-In: 1. program, 2. structure, 3. Pseudocode, 4. selection, 5. source, 6. debugging, 7. compiler, 8. procedural, 9. C, 10. object-oriented

True/False: 1. F, 2. T, 3. F, 4. T, 5. T, 6. F, 7. F, 8. T

Questions for Critical Thinking

1. Software development is a very expensive process. Discuss why companies might develop a program rather than buying only prepackaged software.
2. Consider the different skills and training involved in developing a spreadsheet application compared to developing and writing a program in a procedural language.
3. Although more powerful programming languages have been developed and many prepackaged software applications are available, there does not seem to be a decline in the numbers of programmers required by industry. Is this statement true? Give your reasons for accepting or rejecting it.

CHAPTER 13
SYSTEMS ANALYSIS AND DESIGN

A VIEW OF THE CHAPTER AHEAD

After reading this chapter you will understand

- ▶ the importance of information to the operation of today's business.
- ▶ the concept of a business system.
- ▶ each of the components of the information system's life cycle.
- ▶ the processes required for developing and implementing a system.

INTRODUCTION

Information is an integral part of all business systems, and understanding it is a vital part of the process of systems analysis and design. Whether you are developing a new system or automating an old one, information is an important key to knowing how the system functions.

THE IMPORTANCE OF INFORMATION

Whether it is a clerical worker who processes orders from customers or a sales manager who directs the marketing staff, information is vital to the operation and productivity of a company. The order clerk may require access to current inventory so that orders taken will be processed quickly to maintain customer satisfaction. Information about the customer's credit

This order system provides immediate information to the order clerk when an order is received. Information such as the available inventory of an item and the customer's credit status is quickly available from the system by making a simple query. (Courtesy Superstock.)

status with the company may also be needed to ensure that orders can be sent without requiring advance payment.

Information for the daily operation of the company can be made available from printed reports or by direct inquiry from a computer screen. The benefit of the computer is its ability to provide timely and accurate information, while printed reports can become outdated rather quickly. In either case an information system is needed to collect, process, and distribute this information when it is needed.

TO PURCHASE OR DEVELOP A SYSTEM?

An information system can be either purchased or developed by the company. Because there are many PC-based systems available for accounting, inventory, and order processing applications, many companies purchase this software rather than develop their own. There are three major advantages to purchasing a packaged system:

- The system can be implemented in a relatively short period of time. By getting the system up and running, the company can receive immediate benefits from its use.
- A packaged system generally costs less to purchase and install compared to the cost of developing a new system.
- A packaged system has usually been in use by other clients and therefore has a track record. Because of this experience the system is more likely to be trouble-free than a new system that has yet to be proven.

Packaged systems also have a significant disadvantage. They are developed based on the needs of the average company. An accounting package will provide for the needs of the usual business operations but often do not consider special needs that are peculiar to a specific industry. So companies with special requirements must either adapt the package to their needs, adapt their operation to the package, or, if these alternatives are not feasible, develop their own system.

If a system is to be developed from the beginning by the company, a complete cycle of systems development is necessary to complete the task. Even packaged systems were originally developed by going through the process of system development. But this does not mean that buying a packaged system will eliminate the need for systems development. On the contrary, usually a packaged system is only part of the overall information systems operation of the company. Therefore, it is important that the package fit in with other system requirements so that the entire operation will function as a complete information system.

CHAPTER 13 Systems Analysis and Design

WHAT IS A SYSTEM?

System. A set of organized and related procedures used to accomplish a specific task.

We have been using the word system rather informally until now, but what is the real meaning of system? A **system** is a set of organized and related procedures used to accomplish a specific task. We are quite familiar with the term system when it is related to natural phenomenon such as the solar system with the sun and its collection of planets, moons, and asteroids. Although the solar system does not have a set of procedures, as a business system might have, it does follow certain laws of physics such as the law of gravity.

Business system. A set of procedures designed for the purpose of collecting and analyzing business information.

A **business system** is a set of procedures that are followed to ensure that the business and the people in it perform the necessary functions to meet the company objectives. For example, an accounting system processes transactions each day against its accounts. On the 30th day of the month a billing cycle is completed and current bills are sent to the accounts outstanding. If payment is not received within 15 days, a follow-up letter is sent to remind the customer that payment is past due. This is one example of a business system that operates on a cycle which is performed repetitively over a period of time.

Computer system. A computer and its various peripheral units including software for the processing and storage of data.

A **computer system** is a system that uses a computer as one of its components. Today most business systems use a computer to help automate their procedures and improve productivity and accuracy of the information that is processed. Part of the design of a system frequently requires a computer program in its solution.

Systems analyst. A person who analyzes the needs of a system and designs and implements a new system to meet those needs.

The **systems analyst** is the person who analyzes an existing system, determines the needs of the user, and designs a new system to meet those needs. A systems analyst must be familiar with the way the company operates and know how to use or adapt existing procedures or design new ones. The analyst needs to understand how a computer can be used in the solution and be knowledgeable about packaged computer software as well as the development of new software.

INFORMATION SYSTEMS LIFE CYCLE

Feasibility
Analysis
Design
Development
Implementation
Maintenance

Developing an information system involves a cycle of five phases. These steps are always followed when a system is being developed, and after implementation the cycle repeats itself as changes and new requirements are built into the system. The six phases of the systems life cycle are:

1. **Feasibility study.** This stage determines whether the system should be developed and if the necessary resources are available.
2. **System Analysis.** In this phase the existing system is analyzed to develop an understanding of it and to establish system requirements.

3. **System Design.** The new system is designed based on the needs determined during the feasibility and analysis phases.
4. **Program Development.** During this phase computer software is acquired or programs are written and tested to meet the needs of the system.
5. **Implementation.** Old files are converted to the new system, users are trained in the use of the new system, and it is placed into operation.
6. **Maintenance.** Problems with the system are corrected as experience is gained with its use. New requirements can also be implemented such as the need to address changing tax laws.

These six phases outline the topics that we will discuss in the remainder of the chapter. As we will see, each phase has unique characteristics and forms an important part in the process of developing and using a system. As a system is developed, each phase of the cycle will contribute to the understanding of the system or provide tools for its development.

FEASIBILITY STUDY

When a new information system is proposed by management, the first stage in the systems process is to do a feasibility study. The **feasibility study** determines if the proposed information system is economically, operationally, and technically possible. **Economic feasibility** is used to determine whether the system can be developed within the cost restrictions defined by management.

Operational feasibility is part of the study that determines whether the operation of the system is practical, or even possible. **Technical feasibility** decides if the hardware and software components are available or can be developed if necessary to complete the system. The feasibility study is an essential part of systems analysis because it determines the need, practicality, and economics of designing and implementing a new system.

The systems analyst, who conducts the study, will be a central figure in all stages of system development and implementation. A major responsibility of the analyst is to involve individuals in the company who either understand the current system or will be affected by the new one. To aid in this work, the organization chart (Figure 13-1) will prove valuable for identifying the formal reporting structure of management within the company.

System Definition

In the first part of the feasibility study the system must be defined so that it is clear exactly what the system is intended to accomplish. The definition should identify the nature of the problem to be resolved by designing a new system. Early in the cycle we must be sure that the new system will indeed resolve the problem before too much time and effort has been expended on a solution that will not really do the job.

Feasibility study. A study that determines if a system should be developed and if the necessary resources are available.

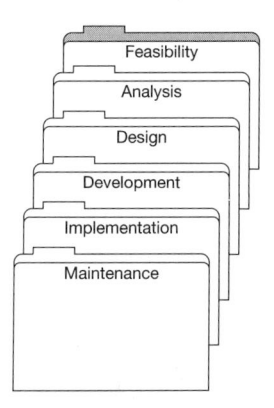

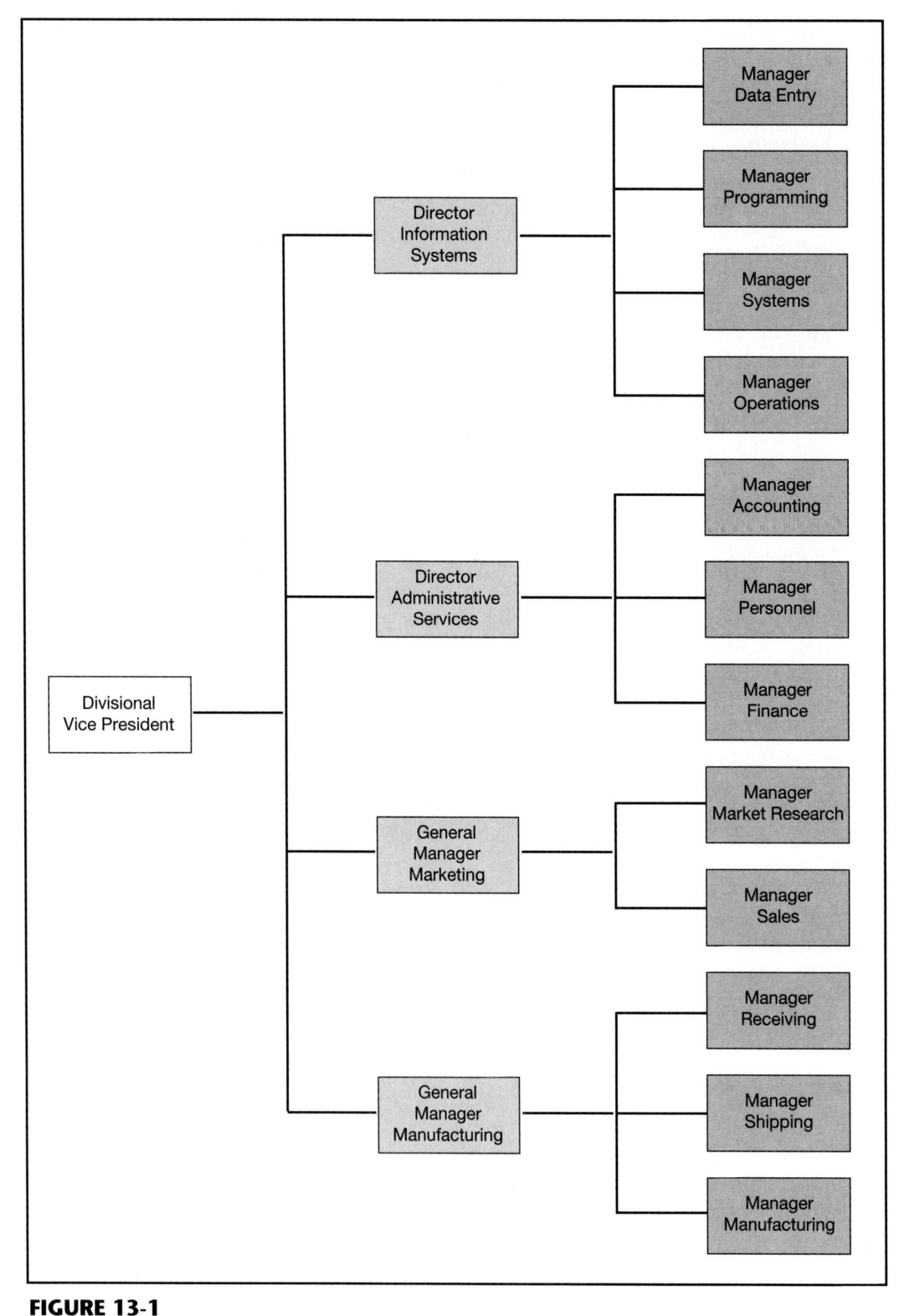

FIGURE 13-1
The organization chart identifies the formal reporting structure of management within a company. This chart shows the lines of responsibility for management under a Divisional Vice President.

> ## ▶ OUTSOURCING
>
> Medium- to large-sized corporations may be spending millions of dollars a year on information systems. With budgets of this magnitude it sometimes makes good management and economic sense to turn to outsourcing for some of their needs.
>
> **Outsourcing** is the practice of relying on outside sources for software development, data entry, and even computer processing. Instead of hiring or training experts in every area, a company can call on the expertise of other organizations that specialize in IS services of one form or another.
>
> Using outsourcing, the corporation can transform some of the fixed internal costs into variable costs that are paid on an as needed basis. Not only are costs reduced, but the company can take advantage of efficiencies and expertise offered by the supplier.

The study must also determine the effect of the system on the company and define the limits of its impact. Systems have a tendency to reach out to all areas of an organization, and unless some limits are imposed on the new system its development may be an unending process. While the overall impact may expect to be far reaching, it is best to limit the scope of the system both organizationally and within a clearly defined time frame.

Economics

A new system will have a cost to implement including the cost of personnel and other resources in the company. Computer costs for the system generally encompass both hardware and software unless existing resources can be used without further upgrading. The total cost of developing the system is then compared to the economic benefits derived from having the system in operation.

Economic benefits are not strictly limited to cost savings associated with increased productivity, reduced work force, or increased sales. These are tangible benefits that are important to the company and can be readily measured. A new system may also provide management with intangible benefits such as providing information that was not readily available from the old system, and improving user or customer satisfaction. Both tangible and intangible benefits need to be evaluated against the cost of developing the new system.

Feasibility Report

The final step in the feasibility study is to prepare a feasibility report that outlines the results of the system definition and the economic benefits. The report defines a proposed solution in general form and suggests a time table for the design and implementation of the project. At this point only general timing can be considered. More specific times will be formally established early in the design phase of the system.

System objectives will also be specified in the feasibility report. These objectives identify the user's needs and how they can be met by the new system. Getting the report and the system approved will require the support of both management and the user group. By specifying complete objectives, these parties can see how the new system will help to solve some of their problems.

When the proposed system has been approved, the next stage of development is the systems analysis phase, which begins getting into the specific details of the new system.

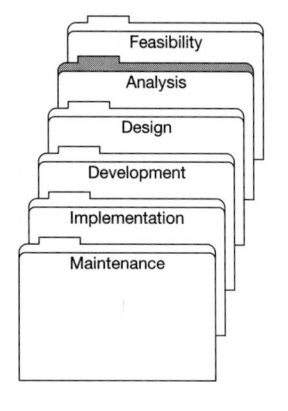

SYSTEM ANALYSIS

Providing management has given the "go ahead," the next stage in developing a new system is the analysis phase. In analysis, complete details of how the system operates is collected in a form that can be used for supporting the design of the new system. Analysis is the process that gives the systems analyst a complete and thorough understanding of the system, which is a necessary prerequisite before proceeding to the design stage. The first step in analysis is the process of data gathering.

Data Gathering

Data gathering is the procedure for collecting information about the system. Some information obtained during the feasibility study is available,

System analysis. The process of analyzing a system to develop an understanding of it and to establish system requirements.

Part of the function of systems analysis is data gathering. One method of collecting data about the existing system is by observing the system in action. (Courtesy IBM Corporation.)

but this was more general in nature. In the data gathering process, detailed data is accumulated in preparation for in-depth analysis. Some of the following sources may be used in the data gathering process.

- Observing existing procedures
- Interviews
- Questionnaires
- Data collection

Observing Existing Procedures. One approach to data gathering is for the analyst to spend some time observing how the task is currently being done. One advantage of this approach is that the independent observer is often better at understanding a process than the person doing it. A trained analyst is frequently able to identify important components of an operation that the operator cannot readily verbalize. Usually the analyst will take notes to create a record of the observation period.

Another component of observation is to collect documents, such as procedure manuals, that describe the operation. The procedure manual can be a great aid to the analyst in becoming familiar with any special terminology or technical jargon used in the job. Unfortunately the procedure manual (if

The interview is one method used for data gathering. In the interview the analyst asks questions about the current system and collects information from the user's viewpoint on how the system operates. Such information becomes an important resource when designing the new system. (Courtesy IBM Corporation.)

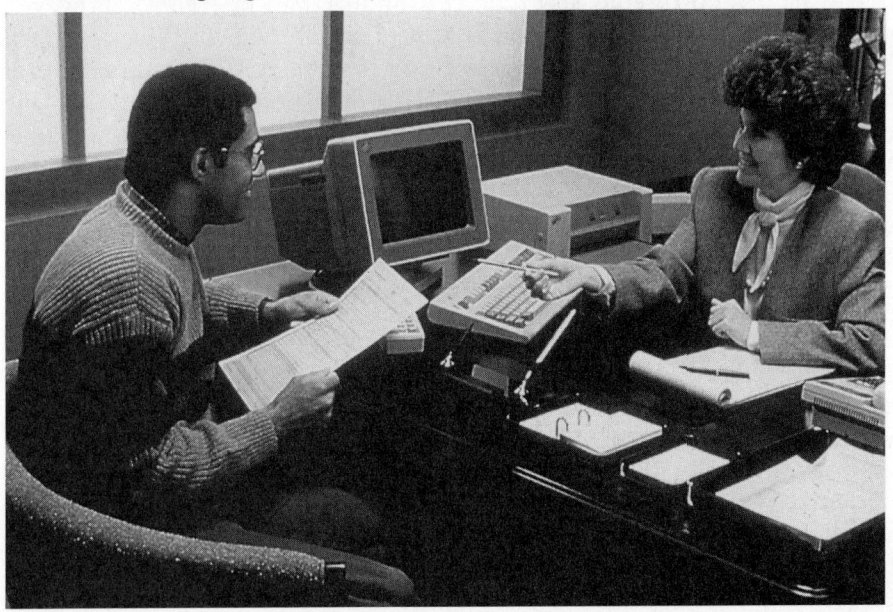

one exists) may not reflect the job as it is currently being done but rather how it was originally defined.

Interviews. Because informal changes to procedures are common, the second technique for data gathering is the interview. Through the interview, the analyst becomes familiar with the realities of the day-to-day operation and involves the user in the early stages of systems analysis. The user is also made to feel a part of the new system by being placed in a position of providing input for its design.

Interviews take place with a user representation who is knowledgeable about the system rather than attempting to talk to all potential users, which can be very time consuming. An interview can be either structured or unstructured, depending on the objectives to be met by the analyst.

Structured interviews are based on a detailed set of questions that the analyst has developed beforehand. In a structured interview, the questions are asked without deviation and no informal questioning is done. Structured interviews are useful if adherence to government regulations or laws are required or if consistent responses are sought.

Unstructured interviews are frequently more useful to the analyst than structured ones. In the unstructured interview, the analyst may also begin with a list of questions to give a pattern to the interview. But, as answers are received informal questions may arise that can be pursued immediately. The benefit of an unstructured interview is that it permits the user to contribute information believed to be important and may open up areas that were not previously considered in the data gathering phase.

Questionnaires. When large groups of users are involved, data gathering can be done effectively by the use of questionnaires. Using a questionnaire can be less costly and less time consuming than interviews; however, they do lack the personal touch that is part of an interview.

Questionnaires should be easy to use and to tabulate the results. Several formats are possible, such as requiring a yes or no response, selecting one of several possible answers by checking a box, or responding with a range of agreement between the values of 1 to 10. There is also the open-ended questionnaire, which lets the respondent write in a response. This last approach is not usually a good one because results from it are difficult to tabulate. The format used by the analyst depends on the type of information to be collected and the kind of results that are expected.

Data Collection. Current systems contain a wealth of data that can be useful to the systems analyst. Procedure manuals, mentioned earlier, are one source of data that describe the operation of the system. Other data that may prove useful are forms such as invoices, reports, form letters, and other documentation that is used in the system. If the current system is computerized, then copies of files, databases, inputs and outputs will all be essential. These data are useful resources for understanding the current system and will also become an important ingredient of the implementation when converting from the old system to the new one.

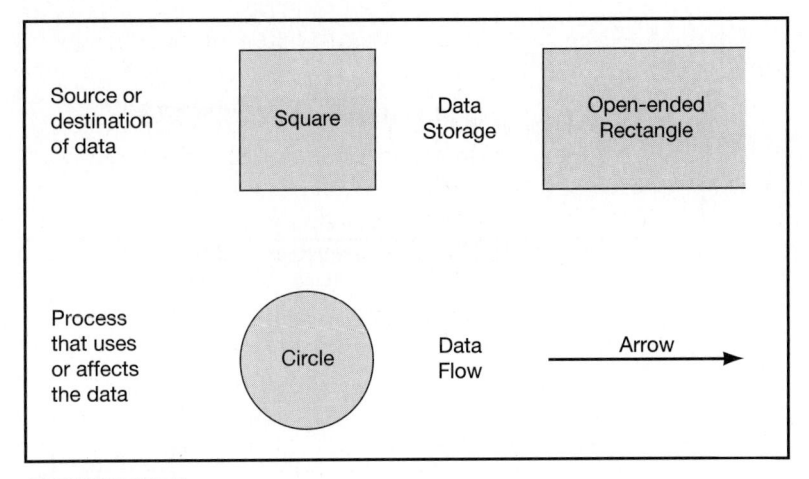

FIGURE 13-2
Four symbols used in creating data flow diagrams.

Charting the System

When all data about the system has been collected, the next step is to organize it into some coherent pattern. Data gathering tends to produce a lot of unconnected data that needs to take on an organized pattern if a solution to the problem in the form of a new system is to be the end result. To this end, a number of charting tools are available to the analyst that not only organize the data but help it to be understood in preparation for the system design phase.

Data Flow Diagrams. Understanding the operation of a system in large part requires a knowledge of how data moves or flows from one area to another. The **data flow** diagram is a chart used by systems analysts to document the flow of data within the company. The diagram is a model that shows where data originates, how it moves from one location to another, and where it is stored when not being used. In other words, the data flow diagram shows on paper how data moves in the real world of the system.

Data flow diagram. A chart used to document the flow of data within the system.

To create a data flow diagram the analyst first relies on the data gathered from various sources in the company. Then, by using the symbols in Figure 13-2, a diagram can be constructed to show the flow of data. There are four symbols used in data flow diagrams.

- The square symbol represents either the source of the data or its destination.
- A circle identifies a process where the data is handled in some manner such as validation or order preparation.
- Open-ended rectangles are used to show where data is stored such as in a file. The file can be a physical file or one on a computer system.

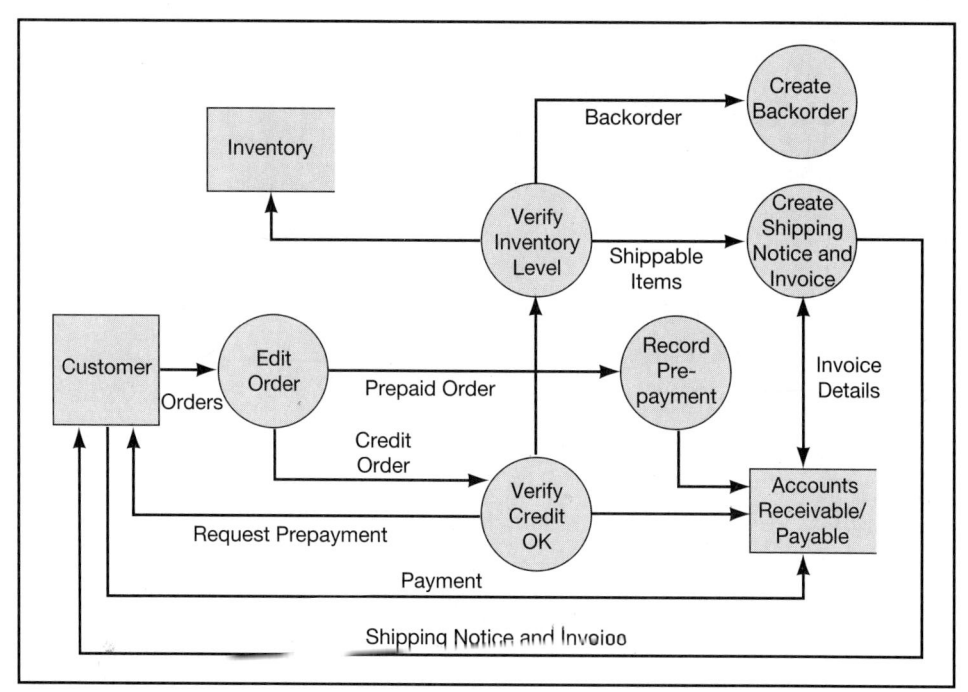

FIGURE 13-3
A data flow diagram for an order entry and processing system. In structured systems analysis, each process in this high-level diagram is decomposed into detailed data flow diagrams to give a complete diagram of each component of the system.

- Lines in the data flow diagram show the direction of data flow—where it begins and where it ends.

Figure 13-3 shows a data flow diagram for an order entry system that links inventory, shipping, and accounting. The system flow begins with the customer placing an order, which is represented by the source symbol at the left of the data flow diagram. The order then flows through the system where it is edited, and credit is verified if it is a credit order. Prepaid orders immediately update the accounts file to show that payment has already been received.

The order also goes to the inventory process, where the item ordered is picked from inventory or if there is not sufficient quantity, a back order is placed. The order then goes to shipping where a shipping notice and invoice are produced and the item is shipped. A copy of the invoice goes to accounting for follow-up if the bill is not paid.

Another input to the system is the customer payment, which originates at the customer source. When a payment is received it is sent to accounts receivable/payable where the file is updated to show that payment has been made.

It should be made clear that the data flow diagram shown here for processing orders is a general one. In **structured systems analysis** a decomposition method is used to progressively show the finer details of the system. Structured systems analysis uses a data flow diagram to provide an overview of the system. Then each process, represented by a circle, is decomposed to show the details of a specific operation. In our diagram, the circle representing the editing of the order would become a separate data flow diagram that shows all of the steps required for doing the editing. This diagram may also have several processes, flow lines, and data storage as required for the operation.

System Flowcharts. Another type of chart used for showing the flow of data in a system is the **system flowchart**. This chart goes back to the early years of computer system design and is still used by some analysts today, although the data flow diagram is gaining popularity because of its structured approach. Figure 13-4 shows some of the symbols used for system flowcharting. These symbols are based on an American National Standards Institute (ANSI) standard for systems flowcharts and are widely recognized by the computer industry.

A system flowchart is shown in Figure 13-5. In it, a computer program is used to process inventory requests from a keyboard. The display shows the status of inventory items accessed from the disk file by the program. When items are in short supply, a back order is created and written on the back-order file, which also resides on the disk.

The activity report is a printed report that is first separated into individual pages (burst) and then analyzed for unusual activity against inventory. Such a report can help to identify items that have unexpectedly high sales and may require special attention.

System flowcharts have the disadvantage of being nonstructured and thus more difficult to design. Attempts to do decomposition of the system using a system flowchart are more of a problem because of its fundamental unstructured properties. For this reason, data flow diagrams are becoming more widely used by analysts who favor the structured approach to system analysis and design.

Decision Tables. A decision table is used for expressing a logical solution to a problem in the form of a table. Decision tables are useful where related decisions are to be made and a variety of actions need to be selected. Unlike data flow diagrams or system flowcharts, they do not portray the flow of data but rather express the logic needed for decision making in the system. Decision tables are particularly well suited to developing some types of programming logic.

Figure 13-6 shows an example of its use for an order system. The decision table lists all of the decisions to be made in the left quadrant. Columns on the right contain a set of rules. Each rule identifies a combination of conditions using true and false indicators. Below the rules are actions that are to be followed if a particular rule is true.

For example, the order system has one rule that is in effect when there is "sufficient quantity in stock" for the order. In that case the actions to be

> **System flowchart.** A chart used to represent the flow of data in a system.

> **Decision table.** A table representing the logical solution to a problem by showing decisions and related actions.

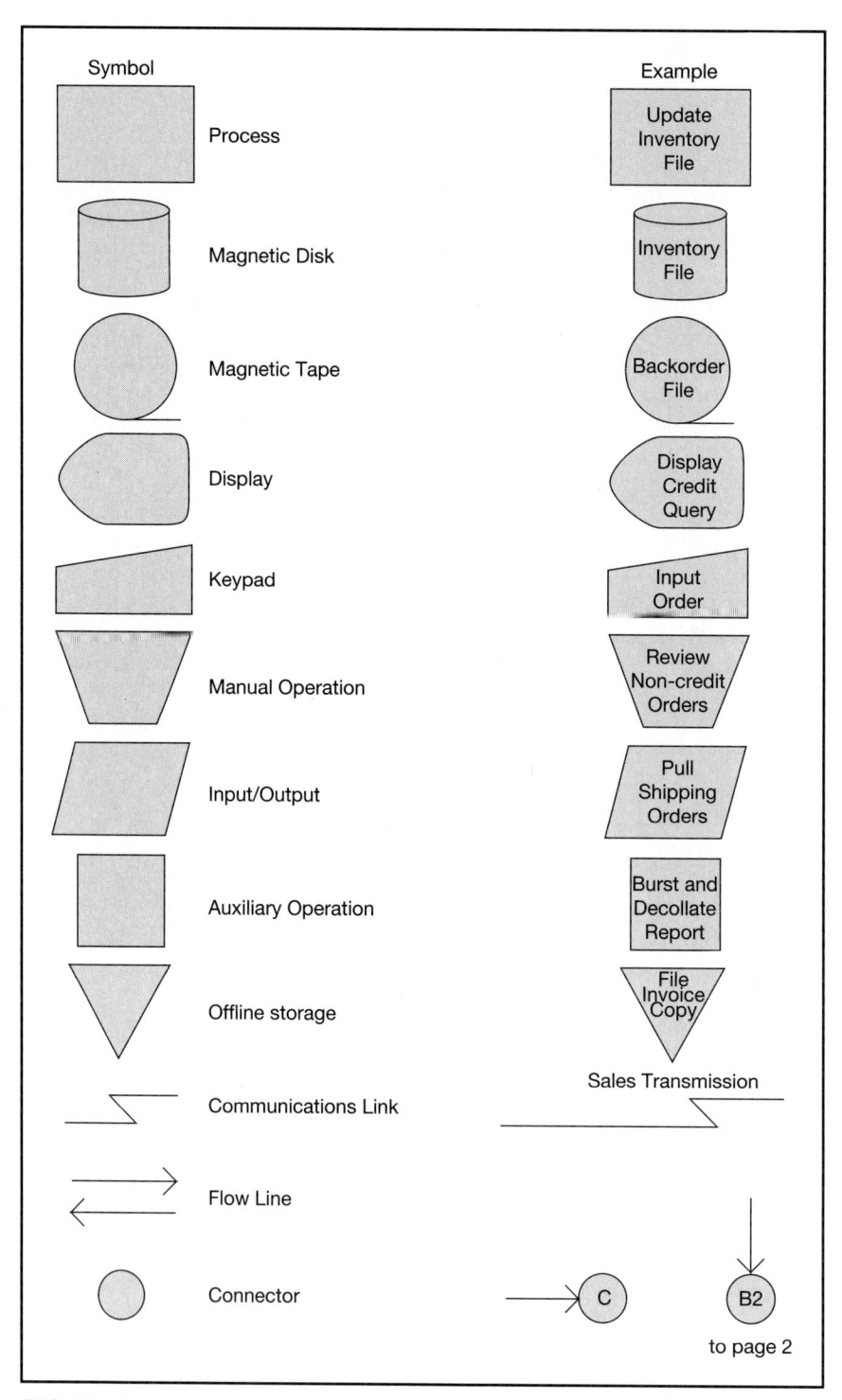

FIGURE 13-4
Symbols used for systems flowcharts approved by American National Standards Institute (ANSI).

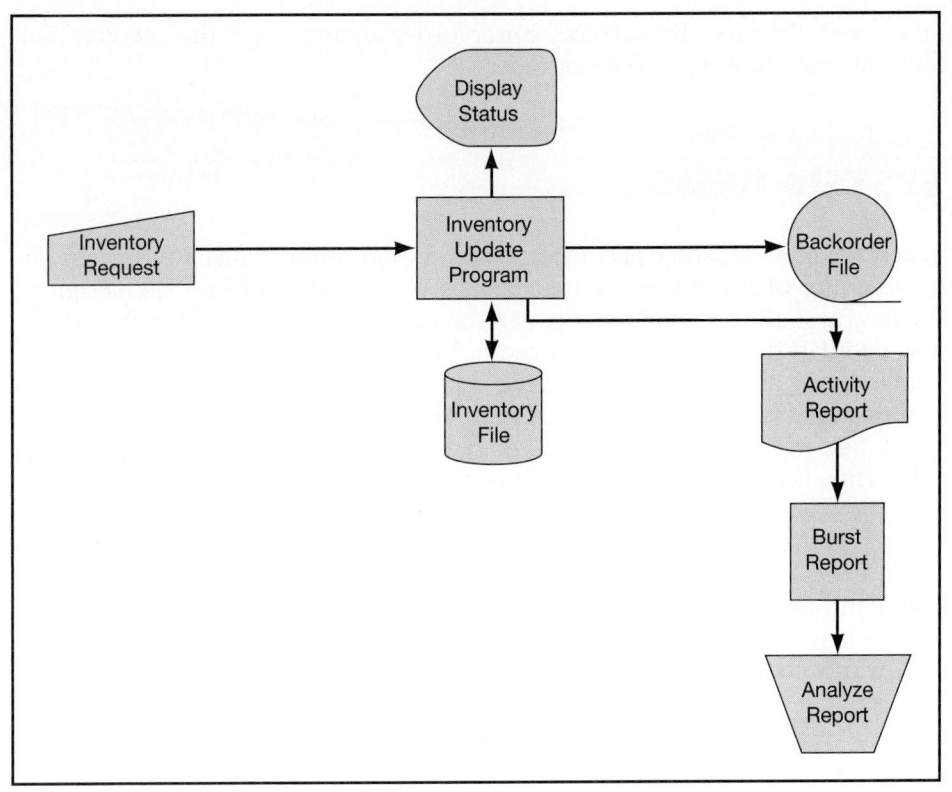

FIGURE 13-5
A system flowchart shows the flow of data between components of the system.

FIGURE 13-6
A decision table for processing an order. If there are enough items in stock an invoice is prepared for the order quantity and shipped to the customer. If the item is in stock but there is not enough to fill the order, then the stock quantity is placed on the invoice so the customer will receive a partial order. The difference between the order and stock quantity is back ordered. Lastly, if the item is out of stock the total quantity of the order is back ordered.

Order System	Rules				
	1	2	3	4	5
Sufficient Stock Quantity	Y	N	N		
Partial Quantity in Stock		Y	N		
Out of Stock			Y		
Prepare Invoice	X	X			
Enter Order Qty on Invoice	X				
Enter Stock Qty on Invoice		X			
Ship Invoice Qty to Customer	X	X			
Order — Stock on Backorder		X			
Order Quantity on Backorder			X		

taken are: Prepare the invoice; Enter order quantity on the invoice; and Ship invoice quantity to the customer.

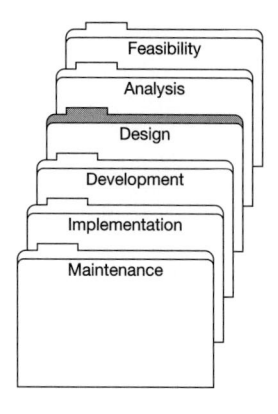

SYSTEM DESIGN

When the analysis stage is complete, the systems analyst has a thorough understanding of the present system and is now ready to begin the design of the new system. By now management has given the go-ahead for the system and detailed design begins in earnest. Many of the tools used for systems analysis may also be used during the design phase. Data flow diagrams, system flowcharts, or decision tables may all be used at different times during the design process. However, one of the first things to be done is to establish a time table for completing the system.

Project Scheduling

Users and management who will benefit from a new system are the first to ask "when will it be finished?" And, because time is money, management also wants to know how much time will be required to complete the project. A well-known tool used for graphing a project schedule is a Gantt chart.

Gantt chart. A chart used for scheduling the different phases of systems design and implementation.

The **Gantt chart** (Figure 13-7) identifies major areas of work to be done before the system is installed. Each area is represented by a horizontal bar that shows the amount of time required to complete the task. Because some tasks are done concurrently with others, there is an overlap of some bars on the chart. Using a Gantt chart also helps to determine if the project is on schedule at any point in time by comparing what has been completed to data with the plan represented by the chart.

Output Design

A major part of designing a system involves the outputs that the system is to produce. Outputs can be in the form of reports, screen displays, files, or databases. Each of these outputs has different features and many of them may be interdependent. Reports are generated from data present in a database, while the database depends on data that has been entered as input through a screen display. Each output may contain similar data but in different forms. Output is also dependent on input of data, which is another component of the design process.

Reports and screen displays have many features in common. They both have headings and labels to identify the data. Data itself is shown with decimal points and possible commas, dollar signs, and minus signs or parentheses for negative numbers. Figure 13-8 shows how a report appears after it has been printed by a computer program. This report is known as a two-up report because there are two columns of data, which has the effect of re-

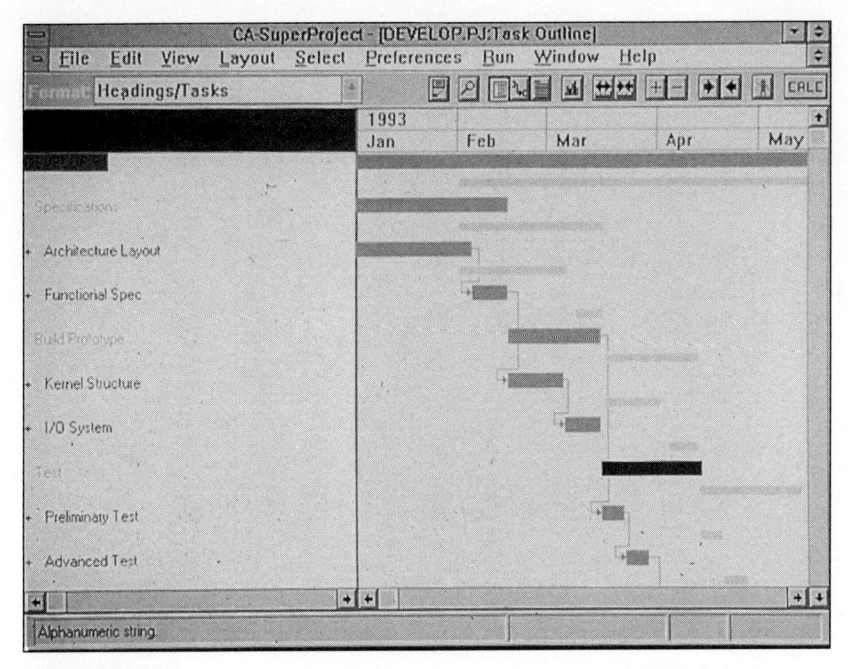

CHAPTER 13 Systems Analysis and Design

FIGURE 13-7
A Gantt chart for scheduling the many phases of a project. Each bar shows the number of days or weeks allocated to a task. The beginning and end of a task is shown by its position on the horizontal axis. (Computer Associates.)

ducing the length of the report and at the same time places more data within the user's view at one time.

Reports can become somewhat complex because of the amount of data contained in them and as a result of the totals and formatting required. Although display screens can be thought of as a report that displays on a screen, there is more to it than titles, numbers, and formatting, as the screen in Figure 13-9 seems to indicate.

In addition to the layout considerations, a screen is often used for input as well as output. This means that the analyst must decide which fields are output values to be displayed and which are input to be entered by the user. And, because screens are part of an interactive terminal, certain inputs, such as a query, will result in an output that will be defined as a screen layout in the design stage.

Screen design frequently requires the use of boldface or highlighting and often uses color to emphasize specific areas of the output. Some displayed data is in the form of graphics or charts. All of these needs are identified by the analyst and become part of the output design for the screen display.

Input Design

Data to be entered into a computer must be defined as input. Input design depends on the source of the data and the type of device used for input.

BUDGET ANALYSIS
BY
COUNTRY/DIVISION/DEPARTMENT

COUNTRY	DIVISION	DEPT	ACCOUNT	BUDGET	ACTUAL	DIFFERENCE	COUNTRY	DIVISION	DEPT	ACCOUNT	BUDGET	ACTUAL	DIFFERENCE
1	1	10	123	10,000	10,000	0	2	1	10	123	10,000	10,000	10,000
1	1	10	124	15,000	15,000	5,000	2	1	10	126	15,000	120,000	120,000
1	1	10	126	120,000	100,000	20,000	2	1	10	130	120,000	45,000	50,000
1	1	10	130	45,000	40,000	5,000	2	1	10	123	45,000	3,000	2,050
		DEPARTMENT	TOTALS	190,000	160,000	30,000			DEPARTMENT	TOTALS	178,000	182,050	(4,050)
1	1	11	123	3,000	3,500	(500)	2	1	13	126	5,905	1,600	4,305
1	1	11	126	5,900	6,000	(100)	2	1	13	127	120,000	130,000	(10,000)
1	1	11	127	120,000	100,000	20,000			DEPARTMENT	TOTALS	303,905	313,650	(9,745)
		DEPARTMENT	TOTALS	128,900	109,500	19,400			DIVISION	TOTALS	481,905	495,700	(13,795)
1	1	14	126	115,000	107,550	7,450	2	2	12	126	5,905	6,000	(95)
1	1	14	130	45,000	45,500	(500)	2	2	12	127	120,000	111,100	9000
1	1	14	123	3,000	3,500	(500)	2	2	12	126	120,000	130,000	(10,000)
1	1	14	126	5,905	6,000	(95)			DEPARTMENT	TOTALS	245,905	247,000	(1095)
1	1	14	127	120,000	119,000	1,000	2	2	15	130	45,000	50,000	(5,000)
		DEPARTMENT	TOTALS	173,905	174,000	(95)	2	2	15	123	3,000	30,500	(27,500)
		DIVISION	TOTALS	492,805	443,500	49,305	2	2	15	226	5,905	5,600	305
1	2	11	126	5,905	5,600	305			DEPARTMENT	TOTALS	245,905	247,000	(1,905)
1	2	11	127	120,000	130,000	(10,000)	2	2	15	130	45,000	50,000	(5,000)
		DEPARTMENT	TOTALS	618,710	579,100	39,610	2	2	15	123	3,000	30,500	(27,500)
1	2	12	126	115,000	117,500	(2,500)	2	2	15	226	5,905	5,600	305
1	2	12	330	45,000	42,000	3,000			DEPARTMENT	TOTALS	53,905	86,100	(32,195)
1	2	12	126	110,000	110,000	10,000			DIVISION	TOTALS	299,810	333,100	3,000
1	2	12	130	50,000	50,000	(5,000)							(33,290)
1	2	12	123	2,800	2,800	200			COUNTRY	TOTALS	781,715	828,800	(47,085)
1	2	12	226	5,600	5,600	305			COMPANY	TOTALS	2,067,135	2,019,800	47,335
		DEPARTMENT	TOTALS	173,905	168,400	5,505							
		DIVISION	TOTALS	792,615	168,400	5,505							
		COUNTRY	TOTALS	1,285,420	1,191,000	94,420							

FIGURE 13-8

A report that lists detailed budget figures for an international corporation. Totals for each department, division, and country for the company are printed at the end of the relevant group. Budget or accounting software is designed to produce reports such as this one.

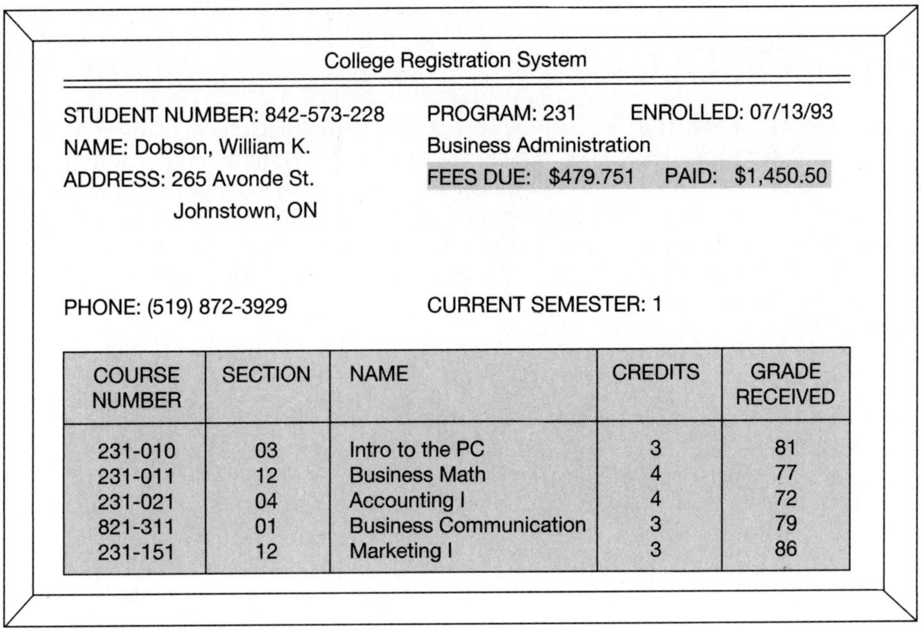

```
                College Registration System
        ═══════════════════════════════════════════

STUDENT NUMBER: 842-573-228    PROGRAM: 231    ENROLLED: 07/13/93
NAME: Dobson, William K.       Business Administration
ADDRESS: 265 Avonde St.        FEES DUE:  $479.751   PAID:  $1,450.50
         Johnstown, ON


PHONE: (519) 872-3929          CURRENT SEMESTER: 1
```

COURSE NUMBER	SECTION	NAME	CREDITS	GRADE RECEIVED
231-010	03	Intro to the PC	3	81
231-011	12	Business Math	4	77
231-021	04	Accounting I	4	72
821-311	01	Business Communication	3	79
231-151	12	Marketing I	3	86

FIGURE 13-9
A screen display format design for a college registration and grade reporting system.

Personal computers mostly use the keyboard for data entry, and its input design goes together with the screen definition as discussed in the previous section. Input may also be entered from a modem, and in some cases from a document reader, or even voice input.

When designing the input, control over the type of data entered is often an essential part of the design process. Correct data is imperative to successful system operation and depends on a validation procedure that will accept only correctly entered data. Validation considers detecting some of the following errors made during data entry.

- Nonnumeric data exists where numeric should be entered. Values such as dollar amounts, account numbers, and quantities should always be numeric.
- Numeric values should normally be entered as positive values without the need for a sign.
- Values such as amounts or quantities might need to be tested for being within a given range. Rate paid per hour in a payroll system should not likely exceed $100.00 or even a value much less than one hundred. Some items may require a minimum quantity to be ordered.
- Missing data needs to be detected. When an input requires a name, address, or other data, then the design should provide a test to ensure that it is entered during the input operation.

> ## ▶ CIRCULAR METHODOLOGY
>
> Using 4GLs and other productivity enhancing software in the corporation is leading to a new phenomenon in the way systems are developed and maintained. Formal systems design uses a linear methodology as discussed in this chapter on systems analysis. The sequence of events is analysis, design, test, and implementation. With 4GLs and personal computer software such as sophisticated database packages and spreadsheets, a more circular systems methodology is beginning to emerge: analysis, prototyping, user review, prototype enhancement. Testing is done at various levels of the development instead of near the end. Best of all is the more complete user involvement at all levels of systems development.

Much of input design depends on the output requirements of the system. Once the output is thoroughly understood, then the input can be properly designed. Although input comes first in the system's operation, its design follows the design of the output because the output design reflects the user needs that are identified early in the system design process.

File and Database Design

Most computer-based systems make use of files or databases in their operation. Designing these files is part of the input and output design process. However, a file or database is generally used as both input and output depending on the operation being done at the time, so one design will serve both purposes.

On personal computers the file design is often inherent in the input design for data entry. This is true for database packages such as dBASE IV where the input format is a function of the database and can serve for both data entry and the database file itself. However, dBASE does provide for input design that is separate from the database format for easier data entry (Figure 13-10).

Other software, such as Lotus 1–2–3, uses files but does not require the analyst to design its format. However, spreadsheet layout can be an important part of the design and is part of the design phase.

Prototyping

Prototype. A model of a real system that is developed to demonstrate its operation and features.

Prototyping is building a miniature model of the real system to demonstrate its operation. A prototype is a limited working system that has the major attributes of the system under design. In a short period of time the model is built, including display screen formats, databases, and query capabilities. Using the prototype gives the user a feel for the system and results in immediate feedback if the results are not satisfactory.

A prototype has many limitations which separates it from the real system. First, it will not have the full range of edit checks normally provided in

CHAPTER 13 Systems Analysis and Design

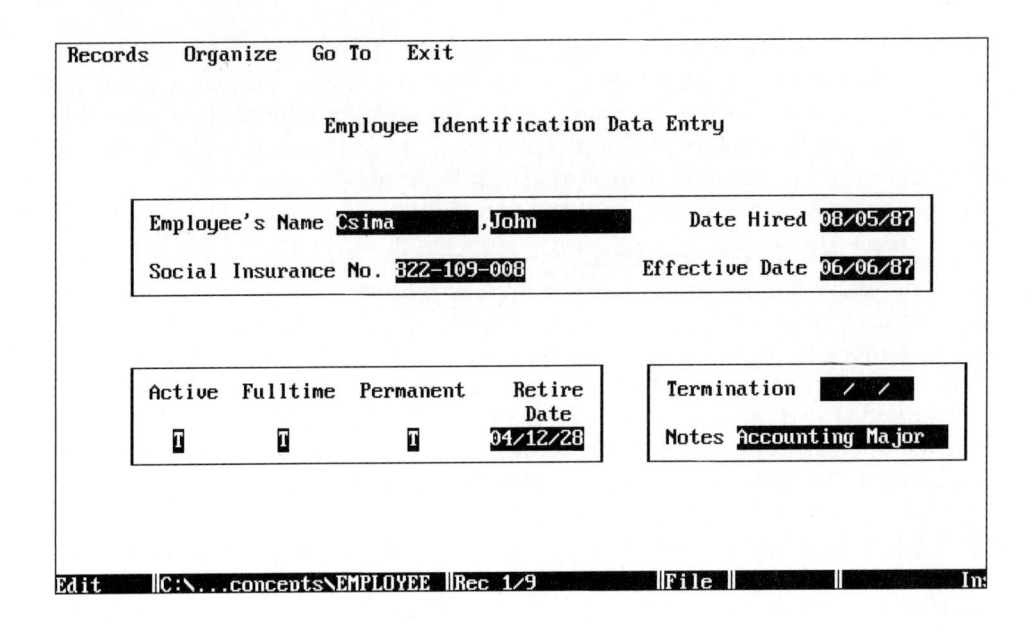

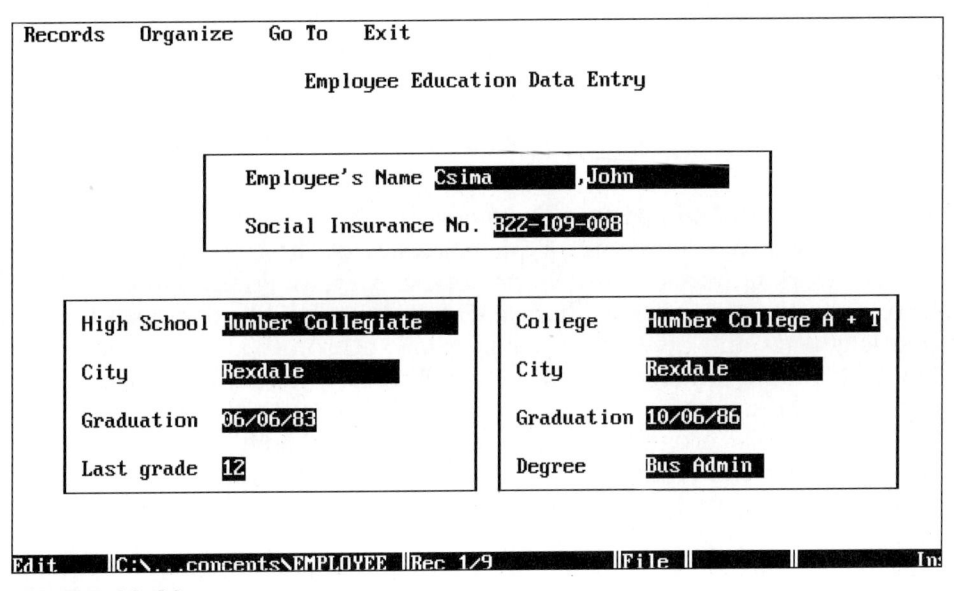

```
Records    Organize    Go To    Exit

                    Employee Identification Data Entry

        Employee's Name  Csima         ,John         Date Hired    08/05/87
        Social Insurance No.  322-109-008            Effective Date 06/06/87


        Active  Fulltime  Permanent   Retire          Termination    /  /
                                      Date            Notes  Accounting Major
          T       T          T        04/12/28

Edit    C:\...concepts\EMPLOYEE   Rec 1/9      File                        In:
```

```
Records    Organize    Go To    Exit
                    Employee Education Data Entry

              Employee's Name  Csima         ,John
              Social Insurance No.  322-109-008


     High School  Humber Collegiate        College    Humber College A + T
     City         Rexdale                  City       Rexdale
     Graduation   06/06/83                 Graduation 10/06/86
     Last grade   12                       Degree     Bus Admin

Edit    C:\...concepts\EMPLOYEE   Rec 1/9      File                        In:
```

FIGURE 13-10
Two data entry and updating screen designs for use in dBASE IV for a personnel application. Highlighted fields are supplied for entering the data while other fields supply information to the user.

a complete system. Although users may have access to a database, they must ensure that data they enter is valid because these controls are not included in the prototype. There may be a limited amount of data available for access by the prototype, and security to the system may be minimal. Reports may be incomplete and totals and summaries may not be fully accurate, but only representative of the real thing.

Benefits of Prototyping. By getting immediate user feedback the systems team can act on revising system requirements before too much investment of time and money has been made. Ordinarily, a new system may require months of development before the user is able to use it, which delays useful feedback on potential design problems. A prototype can often be developed in a matter of a few days. Thus, immediate feedback from the use of the prototype can actually reduce the amount of time for systems development by reducing the time committed to making revisions to the system.

A prototype can also be used as a tool for selling the user on the benefits of the new system. By using the prototype, the user can see more readily the advantages of the system over previous methods of operation.

Although a prototype is usually built once and then discarded, it can become the foundation for the final system. When a prototype is developed using productivity tools such as fourth-generation languages, it can become a forerunner of the real system. As the prototype is produced, it is massaged based on user feedback and the evolving understanding of the system requirements. Changes are made to the prototype until the complete system emerges from the process.

Tools for Prototyping. Third-generation software technology only occasionally gave rise to prototyping because of the time required to develop a working model. Usually prototypes were only developed for very large and complex systems. Today, with the availability of fourth-generation languages and other productivity tools, a prototype can be built in a few days which formerly might have taken weeks or months of work.

Besides the use of 4GL, there are application generator software tools that are used for program development. Display screen generators, report generators, natural language query systems, and database management systems can all be used for developing a prototype and ultimately the final system.

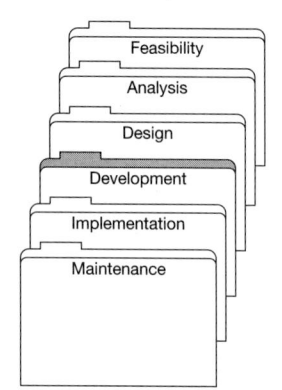

PROGRAM DEVELOPMENT

Designing the system's input and output is only a preliminary step toward creating an operational system. The computer-based components of the system now require detailed development, programming, and testing to create functional application programs. In some cases existing software is adapted to the needs of the new system. This section considers the specific requirement of developing new computer programs to implement components of the system design.

The Steps of Program Development

Most people consider writing a program to be the main occupation of a computer programmer. Although programming may be the most visible and best understood part of developing computer programs, there are really several layers of activity that go into the development of a successful computer program. Briefly, these activities are as follows.

- Developing program specifications.
- Designing input and output.
- Designing the program.
- Writing program code.
- Debugging and testing the program.

Table 13-1 elaborates on these steps, discussing some of the activities that occur at each level of the program development process. It is clear that programming can be as complex a task as systems analysis and design is intricate. The programmer also has tools for the design process, such as structure charts and pseudocode, just as the systems analyst does, although the specific tools vary somewhat.

Some of the work done by the systems analyst may reduce or eliminate some of the steps taken in program development. For example, the system design process often creates the design for inputs to and outputs from the system. If these designs are done accurately, then the programmer will not need to duplicate this effort. In some systems, developing program specifications is part of the systems analyst's duty and would not be included in the programmer's job description.

IMPLEMENTATION

The final stage of the information system development is the process of implementing the new system. This stage puts the newly designed and programmed system into operation. All of the new or revised procedures are implemented at this time and computer programs that receive or supply information to the system are installed and placed in operation.

Implementation is the time when all of the hard work and long hours reach their culmination. Finally, the payback of the investment into developing the system begins, and the company can now reap its reward. But the new system can also create new or unforeseen problems, so the process of implementation is as important as any other stage in the system.

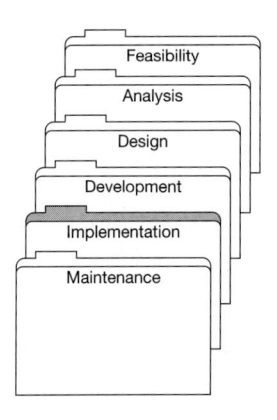

TABLE 13-1 The Basic Steps of Program Development

Function	Description
Program specifications	The specifications describe the program to be written, identify the files to be used, and outline the processing steps to be performed. This is an essential document needed for the program design stage.
Input and Output design	Designing the inputs and outputs may be part of the systems design phase in some applications. By this time in the development of the new system inputs and outputs need to be described in detail and the formats finalized. These designs are essential to the program design and coding stage of program development.
Program design	The program is designed using structure charts, pseudocode, or structured flowcharts. The structure chart shows a program design in a top-down or hierarchical manner as the programmer gets into progressively finer details of the design. Program logic is developed using pseudocode or structured flowcharts.
Program coding	The program is written based on the information presented in the design documents. Coding is done in a language such as BASIC, COBOL, Pascal, dBASE IV, C, etc., depending on the needs of the system.
Debugging the program	Debugging is the process of finding and correcting errors that were accidentally coded into the system.
Testing the program	Testing determines if the program works the way it was intended to work and if it satisfies user requirements. There is a fine line between debugging and testing and often the two are considered part of the same process.

Training

Users who will be working with the new system need to understand its operation and know what is expected from them. The user needs to understand the use of the system's software and the commands that are available for use. Documents and reports that are part of the system's operation must be understood by the user if the operation of the system is to be successful.

All of the components of the system's operation are brought together in the process of training the user. Training can begin before the system is completed and usually continues until the system begins operation. User training may be as simple as a few hours of instruction to many days or weeks of classroom and hands-on training depending on the complexity of the system.

Preparation for user training may require the development of documents

When several users will be using a new system, classroom training is often an effective method for presenting the concepts of the system. Classroom instruction is often followed by hands-on exercises to familiarize users with the operation of the system. (Courtesy Superstock.)

or manuals to be used in the instruction process. Hands-on experience on the new system is also an important part of training and may use files that have been especially prepared for the training process. After the training period the user is ready to begin using the actual system. Training should be scheduled so that it is completed close to the time when the user will begin operation on the new system; otherwise much of the newly learned material will be forgotten if there is a lengthy delay before the system is actually used.

Conversion

New systems are rarely implemented on their own merit. Rather, the new system is usually intended to replace an old one that no longer does the job effectively. Thus, implementation often involves the conversion from an existing system to the new one. There are two aspects to converting to the new system.

- **File conversion.** Existing files and data need to be changed to the format used by the new system. Old files may become part of a relational database in the new system and will need to be copied to the new format. Formerly manual files may need to be entered on the computer to create computer files. File conversion may require both computer programs to be written and data entry to be done to complete the conversion.
- **System conversion.** Users of the old system have been accustomed to operating in a given manner following older procedures that may no longer be valid with the new system. New forms and documents may also be used. System conversion requires the change of procedures, forms, and

documents to the new mode. Often, system conversion is integrated with the user training process.

Parallel Operation

When the new system is put into operation there may be a degree of uncertainty about whether it will do all that was intended. Less optimistic management may even be concerned about whether it will function correctly at all. To put these concerns aside and to prepare for the worst, if it occurs, good system planning demands that the old system should operate in parallel with the new for a short period of time until it is clear that the new system functions correctly.

Because of the cost and time required to operate in parallel, some systems use the old only as a backup in the event of an early failure of the new system. In the unlikely event that the new system "crashes," the user can quickly revert to the old until the problem has been corrected. When this is done, another conversion will be needed to get the new system back into operation.

MAINTENANCE

No matter how much time, effort, and planning has gone into the development of a new system, some errors or dissatisfaction with it is likely to occur. Programs, no matter how well tested, can have undetected bugs that appear only after the system is implemented. These bugs will need to be found and corrected. And the system's operation may look good, even to the user, during the design and implementation stages, but when it goes into operation with a full work load, some weaknesses are likely to appear. These defects need to be corrected to ensure both user satisfaction with the system and effective operation.

Most systems can benefit from ongoing improvements that become part of the maintenance stage. While improvements to the system early in its life may be implemented with little question, later changes are frequently implemented only if they will be cost effective or offer some other benefit for improved system operation. Eventually, this system will age and be less useful as the organization changes, and a new system will need to be designed. Thus, the system cycle will repeat itself once more.

CHAPTER SUMMARY

1. For the day-to-day operation of the company, it is necessary to collect, process, and distribute information when and where it is needed. The computer provides the ability to produce timely and accurate information.

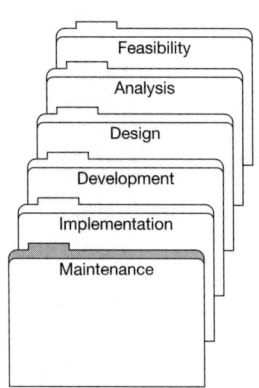

CHAPTER 13 Systems Analysis and Design

2. Information systems may either be developed from the ground up or an existing system may be purchased and adapted to the company's needs.
3. A **system** is a set of organized and related procedures used to accomplish a specific task.
4. A **business system** is a set of procedures that are followed to ensure that the business and the people in it perform the necessary functions to meet the company objectives.
5. A **computer system** is a system that uses a computer as one of its components.
6. The **systems analyst** is the person who analyzes an existing system, determines the needs of the user, and designs a new system to meet those needs.
7. The six phases of the **systems life cycle** are the feasibility study, systems analysis, system design, software development, implementation, and maintenance.
8. The **feasibility study** determines if the proposed information system is both economically and technically possible.
9. The **organization chart** identifies the formal reporting structure of management within a company.
10. **Systems analysis** is the phase that gives the systems analyst a complete and thorough understanding of the system, which is a necessary prerequisite before proceeding to the design stage.
11. **Data gathering** is a procedure for collecting information about the system. Methods used for data gathering are observing existing procedures, interviews, questionnaires, and data collection.
12. The **data flow diagram** is a chart used by systems analysts to document the flow of data within the company. In structured systems analysis a decomposition method is used to progressively show the finer details of the system.
13. The **systems flowchart** is another method for showing the flow of data in a system. It uses symbols based on the American National Standards Institute (ANSI) standard for systems flowcharting.
14. A **decision table** is used for expressing a logical solution to a problem in the form of a table. Unlike data flow diagrams or system flowcharts, they do not portray the flow of data but rather express the logic needed for decision making in the system.
15. **Systems design** uses many of the same tools used for systems analysis. Data flow diagrams, system flowcharts, or decision tables may all be used at different times during the design process.
16. The **Gantt chart** identifies major areas of work to be done before the system is installed. Each area is represented by a horizontal bar that shows the amount of time required to complete the task.
17. A major part of designing a system involves the outputs that the system is to produce. Outputs can be in the form of reports, screen displays, files, or databases.
18. Data to be entered into a computer must be defined as input. Input design depends on the source of the data and the type of device used for input.

19. The computer-based components of the system now require detailed development, programming, and testing to create functional application programs.
20. After the system has been designed and programs developed, the process of implementing the new system follows. **Implementation** may involve the areas of user training, file conversion, system conversion, and parallel operation of the old and new systems.
21. The systems life cycle is completed when **maintenance** begins on the system and changes and additions are made to it.

IMPORTANT TERMS AND CONCEPTS

Business system
Computer system
Data flow diagram
Decision table
Feasibility study
File conversion
Gantt chart
Implementation
Interview
Organization chart
Packaged system
Parallel operation

Program development
Project schedule
Questionnaire
Software development
Structured systems analysis
System
System analysis
System conversion
System design
System flowchart
Systems analyst
Systems life cycle

SELF-TESTING QUESTIONS

Fill-In

1. A _____ system is a set of procedures that are followed to ensure that the business and the people in it perform the necessary functions to meet the company objectives.
2. A _____ _____ is a person who analyzes an existing system to determine its needs and designs a new system to meet those needs.
3. The information systems _____ cycle are a series of steps that are followed when a system is being developed.
4. A _____ study determines whether a proposed system is economically, operationally, and technically justified.
5. The _____ chart identifies the formal reporting structure of management with a company.
6. A procedure for collecting information about the system is called _____ _____.

CHAPTER 13 Systems Analysis and Design

7. An _____ is a one-on-one technique for discussing system needs with the user.
8. A _____ _____ diagram is used to show how data moves from one location to another in the system.
9. Project scheduling frequently uses a _____ chart to identify and schedule major work areas of the project.
10. Program coding is part of the program _____ step of the systems development life cycle.

True/False

1. A system is a set of organized and related procedures used to accomplish a specific task.
2. Technical feasibility determines if the programmer has the necessary skills to complete the project.
3. A questionnaire is the preferred method of data collection when large groups of users are affected by the system.
4. A decision table is a set of organized and related procedures used to accomplish a specific task.
5. In structured systems analysis a decomposition method is used to progressively show the finer details of the system.
6. A data flow diagram is a chart that expresses a logical solution to a problem in the form of a table.
7. Prototyping is a method for developing a new system using only state-of-the-art software tools.
8. File conversion is necessary when files from an old system need to be adapted to the newly developed system.

ANSWERS

Fill-In: **1.** business, **2.** system analyst, **3.** life, **4.** feasibility, **5.** organization, **6.** data gathering, **7.** interview, **8.** data flow, **9.** Gantt, **10.** development

True/False: **1.** T, **2.** F, **3.** T, **4.** F, **5.** T, **6.** F, **7.** F, **8.** T

Questions for Critical Thinking

1. Discuss the implications for a company converting a manual system to a computerized database.
2. Consider the specific training needed for someone who is planning to develop and implement a system as opposed to using an ad hoc approach.

3. Large organizations generally have trained professional systems analysts who develop applications for the computer. Alternatively, they may hire consultants to do this work. Discuss the implications for small businesses who do not have full-time analysts yet are implementing personal computers within the company.

CHAPTER 14

MANAGEMENT SUPPORT SYSTEMS

A VIEW OF THE CHAPTER AHEAD

After reading this chapter you will understand:

- ▶ the purpose of management information systems.
- ▶ the need for decision support systems and how they are used for business decision making.
- ▶ how a spreadsheet can be an effective tool for developing a decision support system.
- ▶ the concept of expert systems and see how they can be used in a variety of business applications.

INTRODUCTION

Marketing News Magazine reports that marketers are increasingly turning to on-line databases for decision-making support. The use of electronic (computer)-based information has increased to the level where expenditures are expected to reach $2.8 billion by 1995. By using CD-ROM technology, on-line information searching is becoming easier and more productive. With international trade becoming the fastest growth area in today's companies, readily available information that is up-to-date and reliable is essential. And even for those companies that are not international, timely information is essential if they are to compete effectively in the marketplace. Businesses use several categories of systems to assist in their daily operation and to help in making business decisions. In this chapter you will begin by looking at the most common system in use—the management information system. Next comes the decision support system, and last a relative newcomer to the scene—the expert system.

MANAGEMENT INFORMATION SYSTEMS

Management Information System (MIS). A computer information system that is integrated with manual or automated methods of providing information for management decision making.

Managers of business operations require information about the operation of the business to assist in the day-to-day transaction of business. Usually this information is supplied through a management information system (MIS) which collects data and either presents it in the form of reports or makes it available in the form of queries to a database.

Defining an MIS

While all businesses have methods or procedures for providing information, they may not have a true MIS. A **management information system (MIS)** is a computer information system that is integrated with manual or automated methods of providing information for management decision making. The computer is used for collecting and storing data which is then processed and supplies the database for management information.

In a fast-food franchise, the computer may collect data on the sales of each item. The data collected may also include the cost of raw materials, salaries, and property. Processing this data can provide information on the profit margin of each product and help management make decisions on future pricing and promotion of their products. Other far-reaching decisions can be made from the information that may include closing unprofitable stores, expanding profitable ones, and opening new stores in areas where business has been exceptional.

MIS and Business Objectives

An MIS, such as the one described for the fast-food chain, needs to function with clearly defined objectives. Clearly, the types of information made available by the MIS are a result of using data collection and computer pro-

CHAPTER 14 Management Support Systems

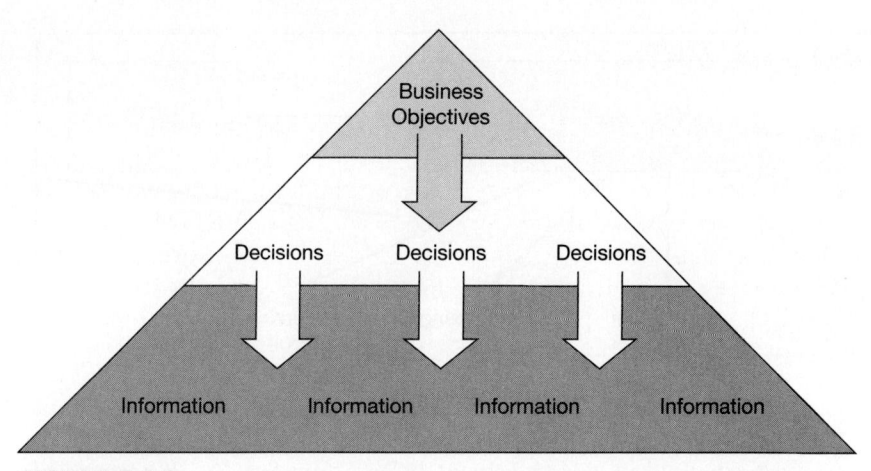

FIGURE 14-1
Information is used by management to help in making informed decisions. Good decision making contributes to effectiveness in implementing company objectives.

grams with a specific outcome in mind. A business objective of the company might be to promote a new product. To pursue this objective the MIS can produce reports showing how the product is doing, the pattern of sales, and the profits that result from the campaign. As these results are reviewed, decisions can be made about the promotion and its results.

Figure 14-1 shows the relationship between the objectives of the corporation, the decisions essential to its implementation, and the information required to carry out the decisions and track their results. None of these components can stand on their own merit. Rather, there is a flow of influence in both directions, because as objectives are defined and decisions made, the information gathered can be used for further decision making and developing new or modified objectives.

Information Reporting

The traditional method for reporting within the MIS is by printed reports. Many systems also provide on-line information, but reports on paper are still the preferred method because of their ease of use and portability—you can easily take a few pages into the board room. There are generally four types of reports (Figure 14-2) provided by an information system:

1. **Scheduled reports** are provided on a regular basis, whether daily, weekly, monthly, or some other interval.
2. **On-demand reports** are provided only on request. These reports often address a specific need or decision that is not made on a regular basis. With database query systems the demand report is becoming an on-line activity that is done at the keyboard.
3. **Forecasting reports** are used to make future projections. These reports play an important role in the decision-making process and help management to plan strategy for setting company objectives. Often spreadsheet

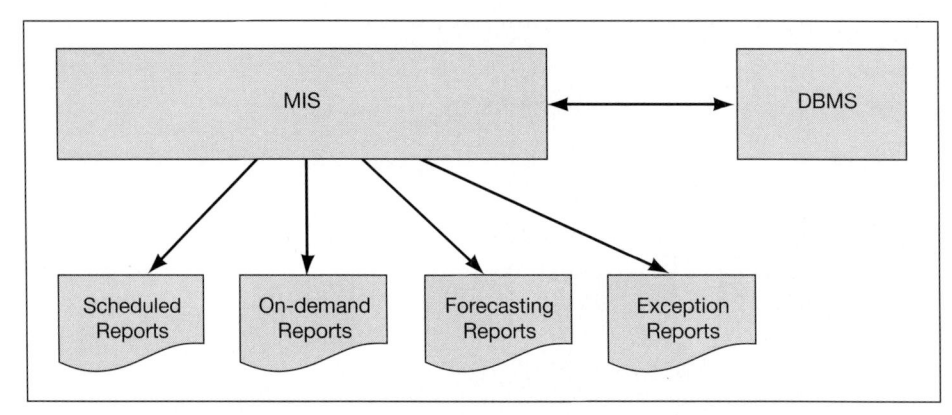

FIGURE 14-2
Four types of reports used in a Management Information System. Reports can be hard copy, as shown here, or they may be displayed on the computer's screen. Hard copy reports can get out of date rather quickly, while displayed reports make use of current data from the system's database (DBMS).

or other models are used and "what if" questions asked in what is called a decision support system.
4. **Exception reports** are created to identify abnormal situations such as low or out-of-stock inventory or customers who are behind in their payments. This information can be useful for planning corrective action and getting the system back on track.

Data for these reports comes from the database, which is an integral part of the MIS. Databases for all areas of the company from accounting to engineering and finance to production may all be needed to generate the necessary information for good decision making by management. Thus, a well-designed system is required—one that has been developed with careful and detailed planning with appropriate information links between each component of the system. Rarely does this occur without the techniques of systems design, which was discussed in the previous chapter.

The Organization of MIS

If a well-designed system is important to the functioning of the company, then the organization of MIS is also crucial. In small companies the MIS may be only a few people, such as the president and accountant, while in large organizations many individuals will be involved in decision making. Information systems in most large corporations come in two parts: MIS as seen in the corporate structure and the information systems department which services the MIS.

Corporate Structure. This is the group of managers who use information from the MIS and define its function. Figure 14-3 shows a typical corporate structure. Each of these positions in the company reports directly to the president and forms the corporate structure. The controller is the chief accounting officer who manages the firm's accounts payable and re-

Reading and acting on reports and other sources of information are an essential part of a manager's job. (Courtesy Four by Five.)

ceivable and payroll. This office is the source of the financial records that report on the well-being of the company.

Marketing manages the sales force and the promotion of the company's products or services. Production deals with the acquisition of materials and the manufacturing of a product, while engineering develops new or improved products. Each of these parts of the organization depends on MIS

FIGURE 14-3
The structure of management in a corporation. While all divisions require the services of information systems, it is also a separate division that reports to the company president or frequently to a vice-president.

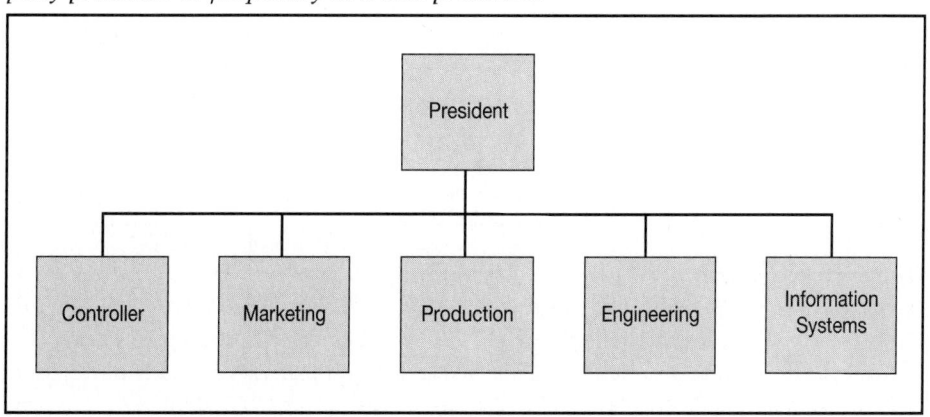

```
                    President
        ┌──────┬───────┼───────┬──────────┐
   Controller Marketing Production Engineering Information
                                              Systems
```

for their own operation and effective communication between each area of the company.

Information Systems Department. In Chapter 1 we saw the need for an information systems department in a large organization. When a large mainframe computer or networked personal computers are used in the MIS, a central body of professionals is required to design, implement, and operate the system. In organizations where personal computers are used, a central authority may also be required to ensure standards are defined and followed. In many companies today, both the mainframe and personal computer are important to the functioning of the MIS.

Figure 14-4 shows an organizational structure of the information systems department. These are the people who design systems, write programs, interact with the users, operate the mainframe computer, install software, and manage the database. Just as managers require specialized education for their position, so do the information systems personnel.

A successful MIS requires the cooperation of the management identified in the organizational structure and the personnel in the information systems department. These two groups make many of the decisions about the infor-

FIGURE 14-4
The organizational structure of a MIS department. Large organizations will have more levels than this, while a small company may only have a few positions. The MIS structure was a product of the influence of the large mainframe system on the operation of the company. As personal computers and interactive terminals came into widespread use in the organization a new position, the information center, arose to provide technical support to these users.

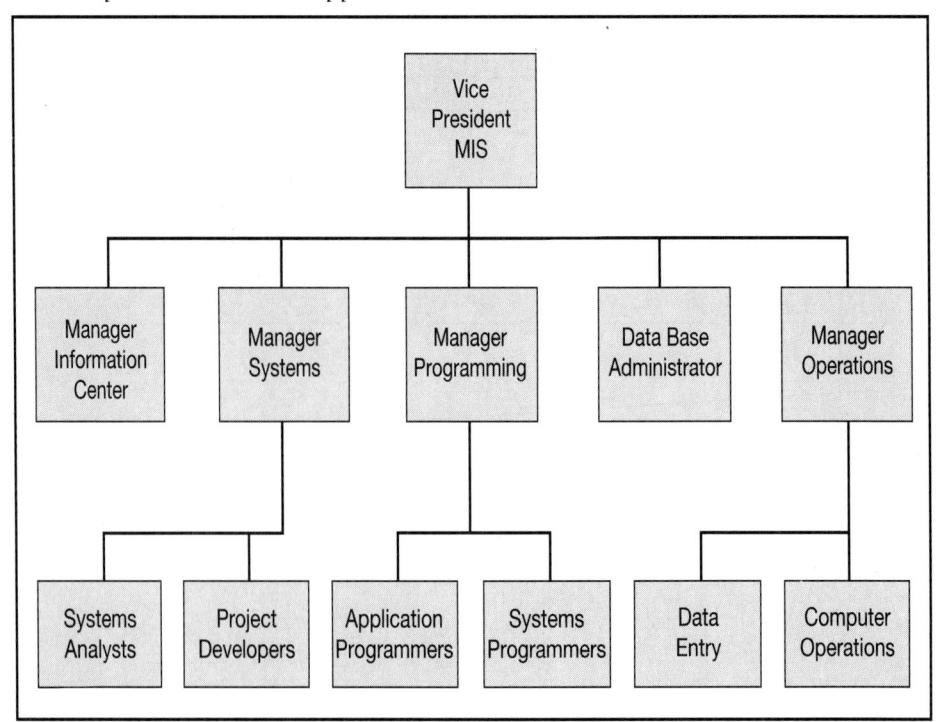

▶ PHOTO ESSAY—SOFTWARE FOR POWER USERS

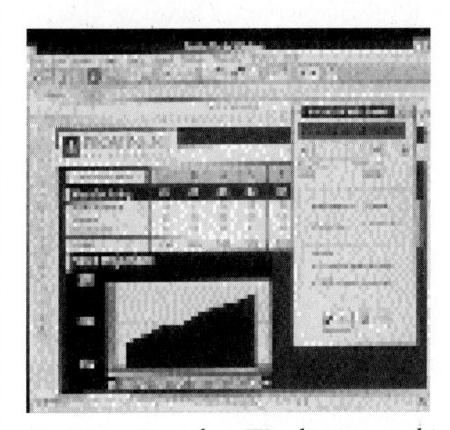

Quattro Pro for Windows combines spreadsheet, graphics, and publishing features for a power packed spreadsheet program. Using object linking data or graphics can be combined from other software in the Quattro Pro spreadsheet. (Courtesy Borland International.)

WordPerfect for Windows provides numerous features for the word processing power user. Here document windows are tiled to give a view of nine different files. (Courtesy WordPerfect.)

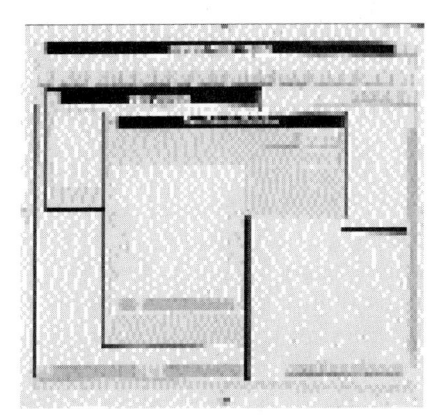

Microsoft Project for Windows provides the tools for project planning, scheduling and performance analysis. A Windows-based program it can link data from other popular Windows-based programs for use in project planning. (Courtesy Microsoft.)

CorelDraw is a many faceted graphics program that combines text, graphics, clip art, and photographs into a single graphic image. CorelDraw is the leading PC based graphics program and is the software of choice among graphics illustrators. (Courtesy Corel Corporation.)

mation and reports supplied by the system. Operational employees such as accountants, clerks, engineers, salespeople, and others provide the data for the MIS which is used by management for their planning and decision making.

While most companies have a management information system of some form, only some are moving into a new level of system. This new development in business planning by using advanced computer software is called a decision support system, which is our next topic.

DECISION SUPPORT SYSTEMS

Decision Support System (DSS). A system that provides management with information for making decisions that affect the future operation of the company.

A **decision support system (DSS)** may be thought of as going beyond the MIS to provide information for decisions about the future. Decisions that affect the future of the company such as what products to promote, how to meet the competition, or how to respond to government regulations must be considered. Making such decisions is much more difficult and challenging than the routine operational decisions made daily by management. These choices often require a different level of information than that provided by the MIS.

Decision support systems should provide more than just the operational data and thus require access to more or different information than an MIS. Historically, this separation between MIS and DSS was valid, but today there is a distinct blending of the two in practical operation of the business establishment. Although there is a tendency for the systems to overlap, there is a class of software that is presented as decision support software. Some of this software is specialized for DSS, a limited number of programs use expert system techniques, while others simply make use of general-purpose software such as a spreadsheet.

Models

Model. A mathematical representation of a real life system.

One of the early approaches to decision support systems was the use of a model. A **model** could mathematically represent a real life system by using a computer program. When models were first used in business, the manager would supply the data to a computer programmer who would then write a program or modify an existing one to simulate the activity.

Programs used input values called **independent variables** because they could be changed as necessary. These values would be represented by data such as the current sales dollars for a product or the expected growth of sales represented as a percentage. The output data from the model are called **dependent variables** because they depend on the values entered. Dependent data could be the dollar sales projected for next year because it would depend on the current sales and expected growth for the year.

One of the problems with early modeling applications was the time required to get the data back to the manager. By the time the request was submitted for programming, the programming done, and changes made to test the model, the results were frequently too late to do much good in the planning process. But with personal computers, this has all changed; now

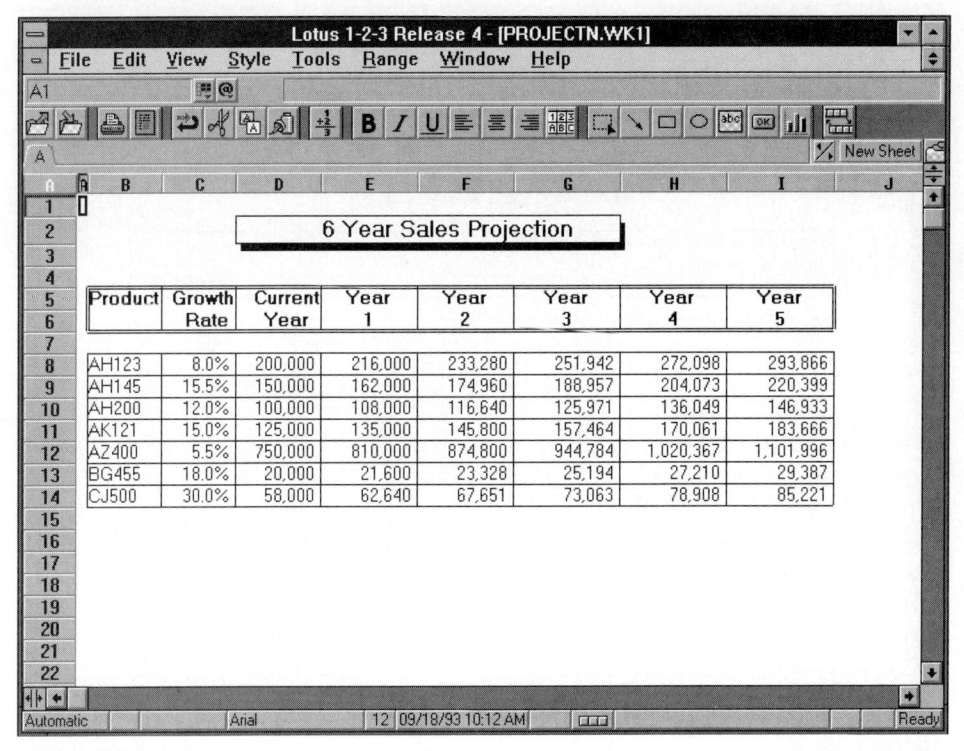

CHAPTER 14 Management Support Systems

[Screenshot of Lotus 1-2-3 Release 4 spreadsheet titled "6 Year Sales Projection"]

Product	Growth Rate	Current Year	Year 1	Year 2	Year 3	Year 4	Year 5
AH123	8.0%	200,000	216,000	233,280	251,942	272,098	293,866
AH145	15.5%	150,000	162,000	174,960	188,957	204,073	220,399
AH200	12.0%	100,000	108,000	116,640	125,971	136,049	146,933
AK121	15.0%	125,000	135,000	145,800	157,464	170,061	183,666
AZ400	5.5%	750,000	810,000	874,800	944,784	1,020,367	1,101,996
BG455	18.0%	20,000	21,600	23,328	25,194	27,210	29,387
CJ500	30.0%	58,000	62,640	67,651	73,063	78,908	85,221

FIGURE 14-5
A spreadsheet is a useful tool for developing models in a decision support system. By entering growth rates for each product, the model projects the sales for the product over a period of 5 years.

the manager can develop the model in a short time using software packages such as a spreadsheet.

Figure 14-5 shows a spreadsheet that presents a simplified model of a sales projection. With such a model the manager can quickly try different growth rates for each product and observe the results immediately on the screen. Instead of waiting weeks or months for the results, only a few minutes of time is needed for the decision support information to be provided.

"What If" Questions

Spreadsheets are particularly good for asking "what if" questions of the data. In the sales projection spreadsheet the question is asked "what if we can get an 8% growth in the sales of product AH123." Then the answer is that in 5 years sales will have reached almost $300,000.

When questions like this one are asked on the PC, the results are returned quickly so that effective management decisions can be made. The personal software used for decision support systems will also permit trying many values in quick succession. Thus, the planning manager can quickly suggest a variety of growth scenarios and immediately observe the results.

Using such software is an aid to effective management, but the user must still have management and planning skills that the software cannot replace.

"What if" question. A question asked by entering a value on the spreadsheet and observing the effect it has on other cells in the model.

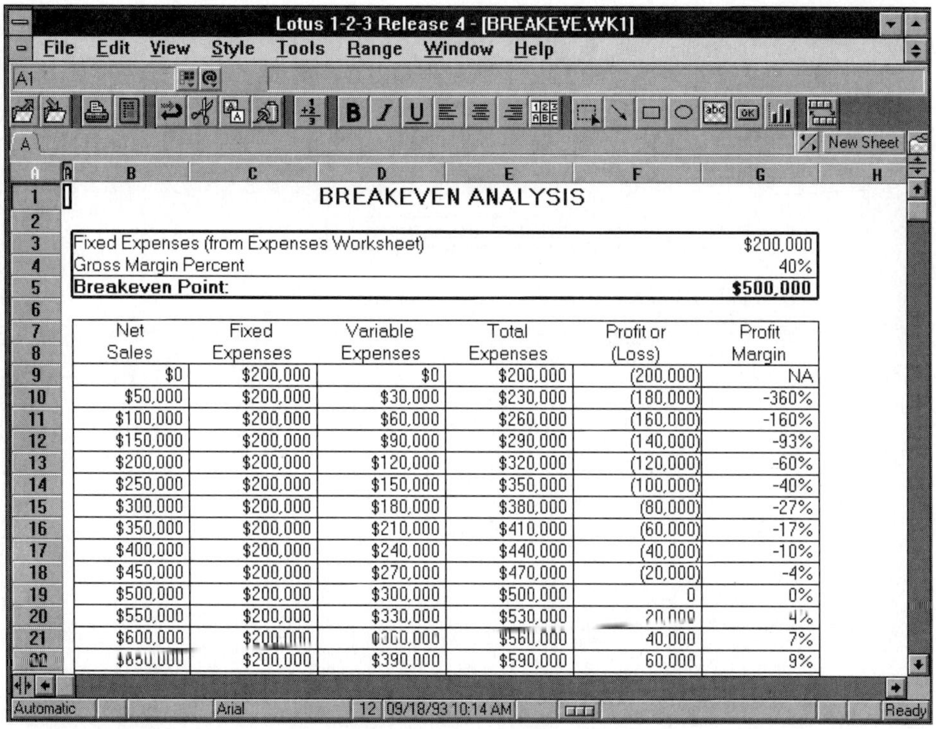

BREAKEVEN ANALYSIS

Fixed Expenses (from Expenses Worksheet)	$200,000
Gross Margin Percent	40%
Breakeven Point:	**$500,000**

Net Sales	Fixed Expenses	Variable Expenses	Total Expenses	Profit or (Loss)	Profit Margin
$0	$200,000	$0	$200,000	(200,000)	NA
$50,000	$200,000	$30,000	$230,000	(180,000)	-360%
$100,000	$200,000	$60,000	$260,000	(160,000)	-160%
$150,000	$200,000	$90,000	$290,000	(140,000)	-93%
$200,000	$200,000	$120,000	$320,000	(120,000)	-60%
$250,000	$200,000	$150,000	$350,000	(100,000)	-40%
$300,000	$200,000	$180,000	$380,000	(80,000)	-27%
$350,000	$200,000	$210,000	$410,000	(60,000)	-17%
$400,000	$200,000	$240,000	$440,000	(40,000)	-10%
$450,000	$200,000	$270,000	$470,000	(20,000)	-4%
$500,000	$200,000	$300,000	$500,000	0	0%
$550,000	$200,000	$330,000	$530,000	20,000	4%
$600,000	$200,000	$360,000	$560,000	40,000	7%
$650,000	$200,000	$390,000	$590,000	60,000	9%

FIGURE 14-6
This breakeven analysis spreadsheet is a tool used by financial planners to determine what sales are needed to break even if a given gross margin is used.[1]

It might look good on the computer to suggest that product AZ400 should have a growth rate of 30 percent per year but the corporate reality might be that it is an aging product with a limited lifespan. Thus, the growth rate of 5.5 percent might be more realistic and obtainable.

Figure 14-6 shows a breakeven analysis where the profit margin is found for a gross margin of 40% and fixed expenses of $200,000. Different values for expenses and margin can be used to analyze the effect these amounts have on the profit margin for the product.

Goal Seeking

Goal seeking. A technique used in models and spreadsheets for determining the necessary actions required to reach a specific goal.

Goal seeking is the opposite of the "what if" question. A "what if" question uses a spreadsheet to ask what happens "if" a specific value is entered on the spreadsheet. This is what happened on the breakeven spreadsheet where the question is asked "What if a profit margin of 40% is used?" and the result is shown as a breakeven point.

Instead of asking the question what happens if a given value is used, the

[1] Adapted from "*Preparing Your Business Plan with Lotus 1–2–3*," William R. Osgood and Dennis P. Curtin, Englewood Cliffs, N.J.: Prentice Hall, 1984.

CHAPTER 14 Management Support Systems 369

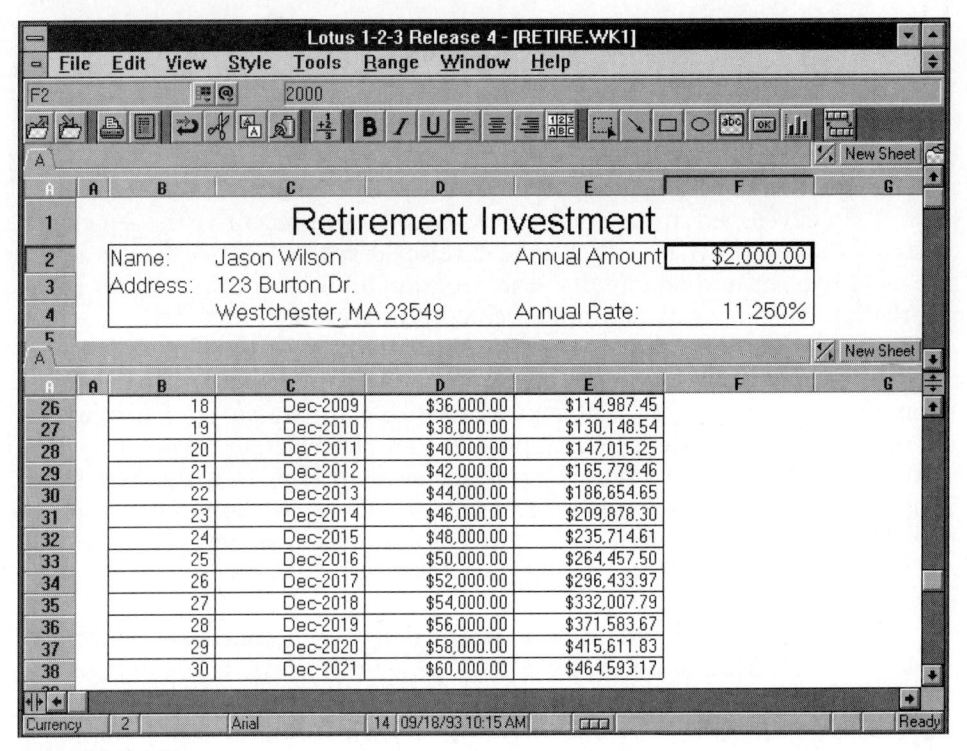

FIGURE 14-7
Using goal seeking in an investment spreadsheet with a split window so that investment values at the top and current values on the bottom line may be seen together. As the user enters trial values for the annual amount the goal cell will change in value until the amount needed to reach an investment goal of $1 million after 30 years is displayed.

goal seeker asks what it will take to reach a specific value or goal. This goal may be a complex one such as what changes need to be made in tax preparation to reduce the tax payable to a given amount. Changes to entries such as charitable contributions, investments, claim of deductible capital losses, and so on may all be part of the goal-seeking process.

Figure 14-7 shows an example of goal seeking in a financial planning spreadsheet for retirement investment. Assuming the investor has a goal of reaching $1 million in 30 years, then this bottom line in the spreadsheet may be found by trying various annual amounts. Alternatively, the goal-seeking process may take place by establishing a given annual amount but trying different interest rates until the goal of $1 million is reached.

Spreadsheets, such as Quattro Pro 4.0 and Lotus 1–2–3 Release 2.4, have a backsolver feature that may be employed in situations where goal seeking is needed. Using the backsolver in the model, the spreadsheet can automatically calculate the needed annual investment to reach a goal of $1 million. This feature eliminates the need for trial and error entries made by the user to reach the goal required.

EXPERT SYSTEMS

Introduction

Expert system. A computer-based system that is developed with a series of rules derived from human experts.

Expert systems are the leading edge of artificial intelligence (AI) tools that have been developed in the computer science labs in recent years. An **expert system** is a computer system that is developed with a series of rules based on the advice of human experts. The program advises or takes action based on the knowledge it has of human behavior in a similar situation.

An expert system is different from other programs that follow a strict set of rules or instructions. Instead, they are able to learn a set of rules and from them infer answers that may not be directly stated by the rules. As an expert system is used, it may pick up new knowledge about the application from the people who are using the system. However, expert systems emphasize the solution to structured problems as opposed to problems that require inventive or creative solutions. Problems that are well defined with clearly defined solutions are a good prospect for an expert system.

Knowledge-based system. A system that uses a collection of facts about an application to assist in the decision-making process.

A **knowledge-based system** is a system that uses a collection of facts to assist in the making of decisions. Often the terms knowledge-based and expert systems are used interchangeably. Expert systems, then, are knowledge-based systems because they have the knowledge of an expert built into them. For example, an expert system on financial planning is developed with the aid of an expert financial planner. The rules that are coded into the program are based on the knowledge that the expert planner has and how these rules are used for financial planning. For this reason the term knowledge-based system is often used to mean expert system.

Once the expert system has been given all of the rules for financial planning, it can simulate the actions of the human financial planner. Instead of going to a professional financial planner, who may be in short supply, you could do your own financial planning by using the program. The program would ask a number of questions about your objectives and financial status. Then based on the rules, it can advise you on handling your finances to meet your goals, much like the expert could do.

Expert System Applications

Many different expert systems have been developed in recent years. Systems in financial planning (Applied Expert Systems), sales (Sales Edge), insurance risk analysis (Syntelligence), locomotive diagnosis (General Electric), and medical diagnosis are a few of the systems already available. Revenue from expert system software was expected to grow to $900 million by the early 1990s.

Business. Although business is one of the biggest users of computers, it has been slow getting on the road to expert systems. But since the early 1980s more applications for business have been developed using knowledge-based systems. These applications range from financial planning to credit card charge analysis from direct mail to database queries. Most systems are currently mainframe-based, but, with software becoming available on the personal computer, more expert systems are being developed for a broad range of applications.

One such expert system was developed for American Express,[2] a leader in the credit card business. The American Express card is popular with businesspeople not only because of its recognized status but also due to its no preset spending limit.

But this policy, contrasted with a bank whose preset limit made analysis easy, created administrative headaches when determining when charges get too high. American Express uses a sophisticated network of authorizers who access up to 13 different databases when making authorization decisions. To help reduce this complexity, an expert system with about 800 rules was devised to look for charge and spending patterns of card holders.

When a merchant phones American Express to have a purchase approved, the expert system, developed by Inference in Los Angeles, looks for unusual spending patterns. If such a pattern is detected the authorizer gives the merchant and the customer a wait signal. Then further searches can be done to see if the customer is the true card holder and if the charge is likely to be paid.

Basically, the expert system implements the rules that an authorizer would use but in less time and with greater accuracy. Using such a system for credit card spending approval increases American Express' ability to reduce fraud and unpaid charges. The productivity of the authorizers has also been increased by 20 to 30 percent.

Another type of expert system developed for business is the Business Strategy Software series of programs published by Human Edge Software. One of these programs, the Sales Edge, is used by budding salespeople who need an edge in meeting with a prospect. The session on the computer begins with a series of about 100 questions about the user. Questions like "Job disappointments don't bother me for long," and "People usually have hidden motives when they negotiate," are asked. Then a second series of questions are asked about the sales prospect.

When all of the questions have been answered, the program generates a series of long and detailed reports on how to close the sale with this person or company. Also included with the software is a manual that is used to help interpret the report.

The problem with this type of software is that there are many assumptions made about the person filling in the form and about the way sales negotiations are conducted. Although an inexperienced salesperson might get some useful help from the program, some costly or embarrassing errors could also be made.

The danger with the current status of expert systems in areas that are not well defined is that it can persuade you it has expertise that it doesn't. In areas such as medicine, however, there are diagnostic skills that can be well defined and built into an expert system.

Medicine. Expert systems are a branch of artificial intelligence research that began in the mid–1960s. One of the early pioneers was Edward

---

[2]Dwight B. Davis, "Artificial Intelligence Goes to Work," *High Technology*, April 1987, 11–18.

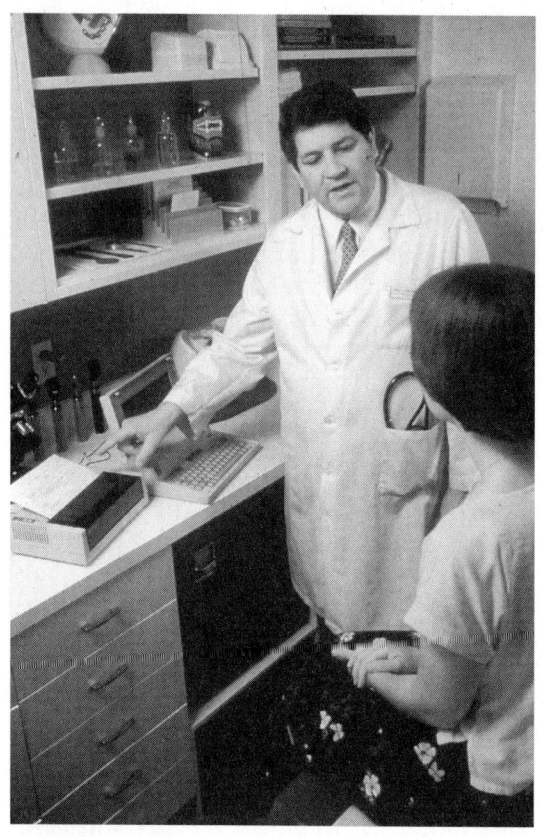

FIGURE 14-8
Expert systems are particularly useful for fields such as medicine where complex decisions are often made. Because there are no fixed equations for diagnosing a patient's disease, expert systems work well at capturing some of the complex processes of human reasoning and arriving at a solution. (Courtesy Hewlett Packard.)

Feigenbaum of Stanford University, who began work on computerizing the thought processes of scientists. One of his projects was automating medical diagnosis. This research was done in collaboration with Edward Shortliffe, a physician. The result was a program they called Mycin that was able to diagnose a narrow class of diseases.

Mycin was a landmark system in several ways. It was the first expert system to use the rule-based inference method that is commonplace in today's expert systems. And it was the first such system that could explain how it arrived at a given conclusion. Although it operated on a narrow class of medicine, its diagnosis was almost as good as physicians in the same discipline.

The program works by interviewing the patient's physician. By displaying questions on the screen (Figure 14-8) to which the physician responds, a profile is created of the problem. First, basic facts such as the patient's name, age, and sex are entered, followed by more detailed questions about the disease. When all of the data has been supplied, Mycin produces a ranked list of possible diagnoses.

CHAPTER 14 Management Support Systems

To make a diagnosis, Mycin has a knowledge base of about 500 rules that describe what medical experts know about diagnosing disease. The rules are expressed as a series of statements in the form of: IF some condition or conditions are true; THEN some conclusion is likely. Each rule has a value from 0 to 1 attached to it to signify its certainty, because not all rules are absolute.

Next, Mycin uses an inference engine (a computer program) that can interpret the rules in a meaningful way. Inference is an important component of expert systems which provides the reasoning ability that is used to derive a conclusion from the analysis of many different rules.

Although most doctors do not yet use expert systems for their diagnosis, the development of such systems as Mycin is an important step forward. Many physicians may hesitate to use such a system in their office, and yet this type of application may be a significant development for the third world and other nations where there are too few physicians for the populations they are attempting to serve.

Financial Planning. Financial planning is something that everyone should do, but few people are willing to pay for a professional financial planner's services. Expert systems make financial planning a good candidate for computerization. An expert system can learn a set of rules that a financial planner would follow and from these infer a plan that a nonexpert can follow. Some systems, such as PlanPower from Applied Expert Systems

FIGURE 14-9

PlanPower is an expert system used by financial planners. The system is sold as a complete unit with both hardware and software. (Courtesy Acumen International, Inc. Cambridge, MA.)

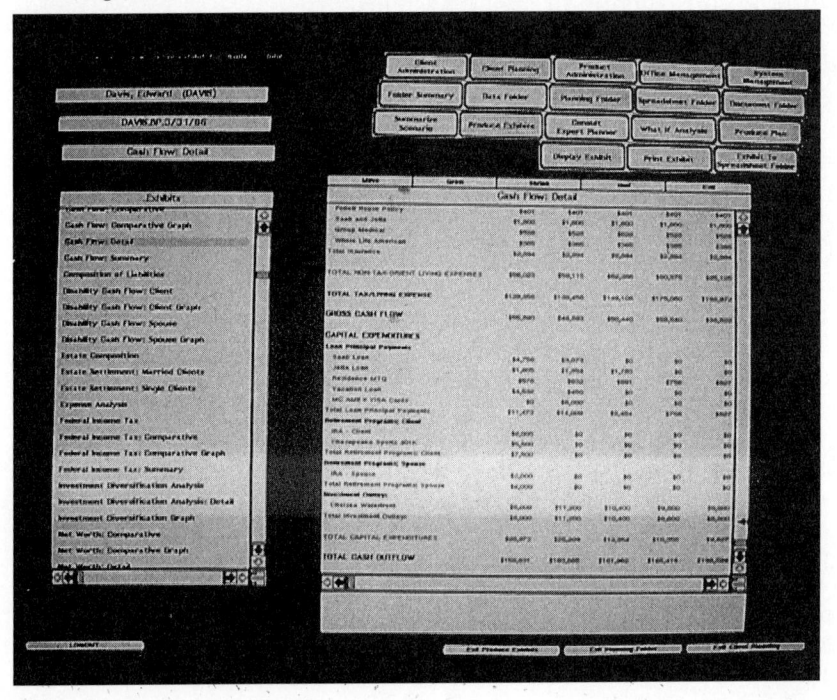

(Figure 14-9), are beginning to be used by accounting and legal firms. Most home systems have not yet used expert system techniques.

A financial planning expert system begins by asking you questions in plain English about a wide range of financial matters. The program then analyzes the input based on rules that have been designed into the system. The system can produce a report, including charts and graphs, in about a quarter of the time required for a human planner.

PlanPower's knowledge base includes some fundamentals such as interest rates and inflation rates. It also knows the tax laws and standard investment strategies that an experienced financial planner would use. After creating the financial plan the program can also explain why it made the choices it did. This can be an immense aid to the planner so that the reasons for certain investment strategies used by the expert system are known.

Because of the relatively high cost, $45,000 for PlanPower including the computer, software for financial planning is primarily used by professionals. Software for home use is often good software, but is not knowledge based and cannot be expected to draw inferences that the more costly systems can deliver. As further developments occur in this field we will likely be seeing expert systems that are affordable for the average consumer.

Knowledge Engineering

Knowledge engineering. The process of building a knowledge-based system.

The practice of building an expert system is called **knowledge engineering**. When an organization seeks to develop an expert system for medical diagnosis or financial planning, there are a number of professionals who must be involved in the process. One of these is the knowledge engineer, who is familiar with the construction of expert systems.

▶ THE TURING TEST

Suppose you sat down at your computer and it began to converse with you. As you type a statement on the keyboard it either answered your request or responded more or less intelligently to it. If your computer was linked to other computers on a network, how could you be sure that it was the computer talking to you (actually the software) or just someone else at another computer that you were communicating with?

In 1950 a British mathematician, Alan Turing, proposed a method to determine whether a computer possesses intelligence. This method came to be known as the Turing test and was similar to the scenario presented above. Turing's idea was to have a panel of judges who would pose questions on teletype machines which would be either attached to a computer or to another human on a similar teletype. If the panel could not tell which machine was attached to a computer and which to a human, then the computer could be considered to possess intelligence.

Today computers can do humanlike activities such as play chess, give expert advice, write poetry, or compose music, and in some of these activities it is difficult to tell the human result from the computer's. Turing, who died in 1954, never lived to see his dream come true of a computer that could pass for human.

CHAPTER 14 Management Support Systems

▶ A VARIETY OF EXPERT SYSTEMS

Expert System	Application
AUDITOR	An accounting system used to model the judgment of an auditor when analyzing a firm's allowance for bad debts.
PRICE	A knowledge-based simulation of management decision making used by business students to understand the maximizing of profit in a firm.
ZOG	A knowledge-based AI system used by the U.S. Air Force for price analysis and procurement.
GARI	An expert system that plans a series of processing steps for the machining of mechanical parts.
ISIS	A knowledge-based system that considers shop constraints when creating job schedules.
INNOVATOR	An expert system-based framework that uses analogies to draw inferences. One use is by NASA to emulate an inventor/engineer.

A knowledge engineer is a computer scientist or programmer who has specialized in the field of expert or knowledge-based systems. Because this is a young field, there are few experts who are educated in this discipline. In addition to the knowledge engineer, a professional from the task that is being developed into an expert system is needed. If the system is for medicine, then a skilled physician would be used; for financial planning, an expert financial planner. It is important when developing an expert system to use an expert from that field because the system is only as good as the person who supplies it with the knowledge base.

Knowledge engineer. A person with computer science or engineering background who has specialized in the field of expert or knowledge-based systems.

When Is an Expert System Useful?

An expert system may seem to be like an employee that is brilliant on the job, is always on time, and never gets tired or bored. But does this make any job a candidate for an expert system? The answer is a clear no as we will see. There are a few basic requirements for an expert system candidate.

1. The rules or procedures of the system must be clearly definable.
2. The system must normally require a trained expert or professional to function.
3. If there is a shortage of skilled people, then the system is a good candidate.

To be a good prospect for an expert system, an application must first be definable. Medicine is a good case for an expert system because much of diagnosis requires collecting the symptoms and comparing them to a pattern of disease. This is not as simple as it sounds because physicians rely on the accumulation of thousands of past cases and, by applying a few general principles, are able to abstract a diagnosis.

That brings us to a second consideration for a candidate for an expert system. Is the system complex enough to require a trained expert to solve problems? A task that may only require a few days or weeks of training is hardly a candidate for an expert system. But one that takes years of training and more years of experience would justify the time and expense of developing the knowledge base. Thus, medicine is one of many fields that presents an excellent opportunity for the development of expert systems.

A shortage of skilled professionals may also be a strong indicator that an expert system is a potential solution. When there is a shortage, workers with less training can often function well until a complex problem occurs that would normally require a specialist. That is where the expert system can step in. Instead of going to the specialist, who is in short supply and may not be easily available, the expert system provides the same level of support.

Developing an Expert System

Expert systems are developed by knowledge engineers by building a knowledge base while working with an acknowledged expert in the field. Questions are asked of the professional who provides the answers and explanations until a knowledge base is built based on a set of rules. These rules will be used to analyze questions that are presented to the system. When the expert system is used, the solution to a problem is a goal that is found by analyzing the rules that were originally entered during system development.

One such system was developed because there was a shortage of skilled people. When Aldo Cimino at Campbell's Soup Company in Camden, New Jersey, was nearing retirement he was considered to be irreplaceable. Mr. Cimino was the resident expert on "cookers" and no one had his talent for troubleshooting them. Because Campbell's had more than 90 of these cookers around the world, Cimino's expertise was critical to the continued success of the company (see Figure 14-10).

Working along with Michael Smith of Texas Instruments, Cimino began

FIGURE 14-10
An expert system is used at Campbell's Soup to assist in the maintenance of soup cookers. The knowledge of a human expert is built into the computer software, which can then be used at plants around the world. (Photo courtesy of Campbell Soup Company.)

CHAPTER 14 Management Support Systems

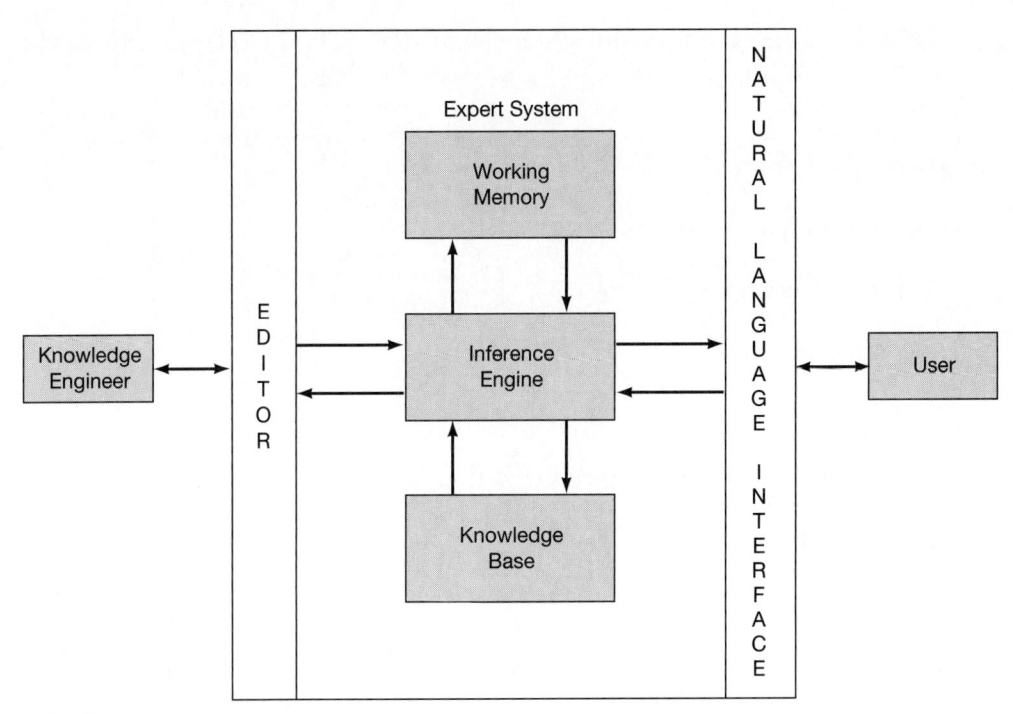

FIGURE 14-11
Expert system architecture consists of the knowledge engineer who defines the rules for the knowledge base. The user communicates with the system through a natural language interface. Input is analyzed by the inference engine based on the rules in the knowledge base and data in working memory. Working memory is used to analyze entries and to store the results of new knowledge.

to transfer his knowledge to an expert system. The system was eventually completed and contained more than 150 rules in the knowledge base. The system went into operation in eight plants in the United States, Canada, and Britain. When a problem arises that the technicians or maintenance managers can't solve they use the expert system, at least for 95 percent of the problems. It seems that a computer can't entirely replace Aldo Cimino.

Expert System Architecture. Expert systems are built with a knowledge base containing rules or facts about a specific application. This knowledge base is attached to a program called an inference engine (Figure 14-11). An **inference engine** applies the rules of the knowledge base to the queries entered by the user and attempts to infer a conclusion.

The inference engine begins its task when the user consults with the expert system. First, there is a **natural language interface** which lets the user consult with the expert system and engage in a question and answer period. The user may also question the expert system on the reasoning used for a given conclusion. The inference engine processes this activity by using a process called goal seeking, which is the specific value or answer it is looking for to solve the problem.

Inference engine. A computer program that applies the rules of the knowledge base to a query and infers a solution.

Rules. A rule in an expert system is an IF – THEN relationship of the form

IF condition
THEN action

A condition may be an expression such as

Money to invest > $1000

An action might be

Purchase Money Market Fund

The complete expression would be written as

IF Money to invest > $1000
THEN Purchase Money Market Fund

A sequence of rules may be connected to form a list as shown in Figure 14-12. If the first query is true, then the next is considered and so on. This process continues until a solution for investment is found for the amount that the investor has available. In a complete system more complex rules would be used to consider how the user prefers to invest. Some prefer more security in their investment, while others prefer to take greater risks with a chance of receiving greater returns.

FIGURE 14-12
A rule tree of IF – THEN relationships in an expert system.

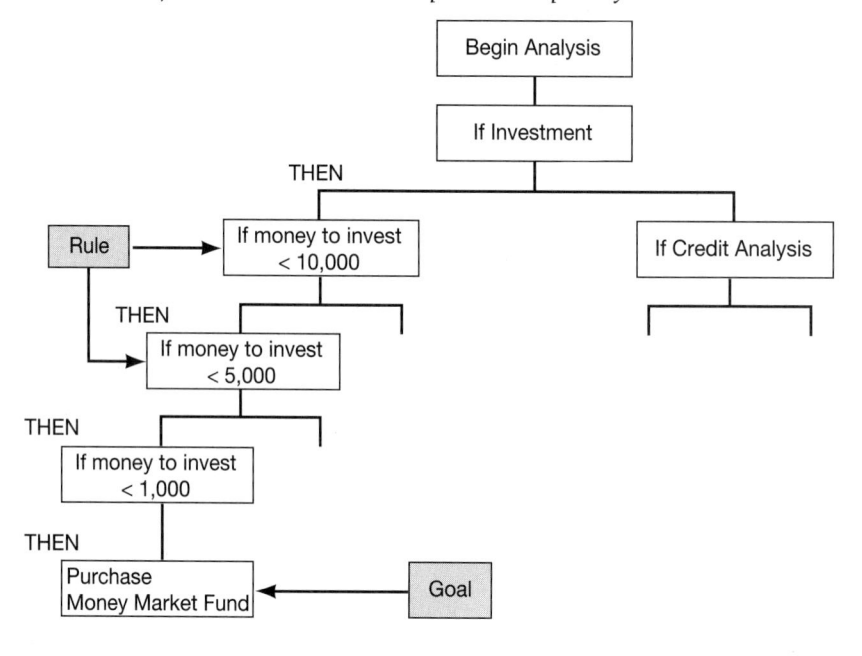

Languages for Expert Systems

Programming an inference engine requires specialized computer languages. One such language is LISP (LISt Processing) which was developed by John McCarthy at Massachusetts Institute of Technology in 1958. LISP is used for programming applications that do list processing, which is a fundamental part of artificial intelligence (AI). Some of today's expert systems also use LISP to formulate the rules in the inference engine and for coding the knowledge base. Some computers have been especially designed to work effectively with LISP.

Another language used for artificial intelligence and expert systems is PROLOG (PROgramming LOGic). It was developed by Alan Colmerauer at the University of Marseilles in 1972. PROLOG is a logic-based programming language that has seen widespread use in Japan for the development of artificial intelligence projects. In the 1980s, PROLOG was fast replacing LISP as the language of choice for AI applications.

Because developing an expert system from the ground up is a difficult and time-consuming task, many organizations adopt an expert system shell. An **expert shell** provides the supporting software for developing an expert system. Using a shell, the knowledge engineer only needs to be concerned with the application and the user expert. No knowledge of programming is required. The availability of expert shells is an important step forward in the growth and development of expert systems.

CHAPTER SUMMARY

1. A **decision support system (DSS)** may be thought of as going beyond MIS to provide information for decisions about the future.
2. One of the early approaches to decision support systems was the use of a model. A **model** mathematically represents a real life system by using a computer program.
3. Programs use input values called **independent variables** because they can be changed as necessary. The output data from the model are called **dependent variables** because they depend on the values entered.
4. **"What if"** questions are asked of the decision support system. The benefit of the personal computer for DSS is that the results are returned quickly so that effective management decisions can be made.
5. **Goal seeking** is the opposite of the "what if" question. Instead of asking the question "what happens if a given value is used," the goal seeker asks what it will take to reach a specific value or goal.
6. An **expert system** is a computer system that is developed with a series of rules based on the advice of human experts. The program advises or takes action based on the knowledge it has of human behavior in a similar situation.
7. A **knowledge-based system** is a system that uses a collection of facts to assist in the making of decisions.
8. Since the early 1980s, applications for business have been developed using knowledge-based systems. These applications range from financial planning to credit card charge analysis from direct mail to database queries.

9. **Knowledge engineering** is the practice of building an expert system. A **knowledge engineer** is a computer scientist or programmer who has specialized in the field of expert or knowledge-based systems.
10. To be a candidate for an expert system the rules of the system must be clearly definable. The system must normally require a trained expert or professional to function and it helps if there is a shortage of skilled people.
11. An expert system contains a knowledge base that is attached to a program called an inference engine. The **inference engine** applies the rules of the knowledge base to the queries entered by the user and attempts to infer a conclusion.
12. The system uses a **natural language interface** which lets the user consult with the expert system and engage in a question and answer period. The inference engine processes this activity by using a process called goal seeking which is the specific value or answer it is looking for to solve the problem.
13. A **rule** in an expert system is an IF – THEN relationship.
14. Two widely used programming languages for developing expert systems are LISP and PROLOG. Frequently they use an expert shell that provides the supporting software for developing an expert system.

IMPORTANT TERMS AND CONCEPTS

Decision support system (DSS)
Dependent variables
Expert shell
Expert system
Goal seeking
Independent variables
Inference engine
Knowledge base
Knowledge-based system

Knowledge engineering
LISP
Management information system (MIS)
Model
Natural language interface
PROLOG
Rule
"What if" question

SELF-TESTING QUESTIONS

Fill-In

1. A _____ _____ _____ is a computer information system that is integrated with manual or automated methods of providing information for management decision making.
2. _____ reports are provided on a regular basis such as daily, weekly, or monthly.
3. _____ reports are created to identify abnormal situations such as low or out-of-stock inventory or customers who are behind in their payments.
4. A _____ _____ _____ may be thought of as going beyond the MIS to provide information for decisions about the future.

CHAPTER 14 Management Support Systems

5. A _____ is used to mathematically represent a real life system by using a computer program.
6. Programs use input values called _____ variables because they can be changed as necessary.
7. _____ software are particularly good for asking "what if" questions of the data.
8. An _____ system is a computer system that is developed with a series of rules based on the advice of human experts.
9. The practice of building an expert system is called _____ engineering.
10. A knowledge-based system uses a _____ _____ interface which lets the user consult with the expert system and engage in a question and answer period.

True/False

1. An on-demand report is generated when a weekly or monthly system cycle is complete.
2. A rule represents an IF – THEN relationship in an expert system.
3. Goal seeking is the opposite of using "what if" questions and looks for a specific value.
4. A MIS is a manual or automated system for providing management with required information for making business decisions.
5. A knowledge-based system is a system that uses a data flow diagram to represent decisions made by the user.
6. Spreadsheets are not as good as database software for developing models in a decision support system.
7. An expert system is developed with a series of rules based on the advice of human experts.
8. Unlike a management information system, problems that are well defined are not good prospects for an expert system.

ANSWERS

Fill-In: 1. management information system, 2. Scheduled, 3. Exception, 4. decision support system, 5. model, 6. independent, 7. Spreadsheet, 8. expert, 9. knowledge, 10. natural language

True/False: 1. F, 2. T, 3. T, 4. T, 5. F, 6. F, 7. T, 8. F

Questions for Critical Thinking

1. Discuss the concept of a management information system. While this term originated with the mainframe computer in large corporations, consider the implications of MIS in organizations that use personal computers exclusively.

2. Discuss the concept of a decision support system and the role that models play in a DSS.
3. Consider the ethical implications of using the knowledge of a skilled worker to train an expert system when using the system reduces or eliminates the need for employees with that expertise.
4. What new careers might result from the introduction of expert systems into business and industry?

CHAPTER 15

ISSUES AND TRENDS

A VIEW OF THE CHAPTER AHEAD

After reading this chapter you will understand

- ▶ the types of fears and fantasies associated with computers.
- ▶ some methods used to thwart software piracy.
- ▶ the types of computer crime and some of the methods used to ensure computer security.
- ▶ the various career opportunities available in the computer profession.

INTRODUCTION

The computer has spawned a wide range of uses over its short life span. In this book you have examined many of these applications, but we have not directly looked at the social impact of the computer. For some, the computer represents an object to be feared, or at least used with much foreboding. For a few, it becomes a tool for crime. But for many people the computer offers, at the least, a powerful and useful tool, or, at the most, an exciting and rewarding career.

FEARS AND FANTASIES

When a machine as powerful and productive as the computer comes onto the human scene, there are likely to be certain fears associated with it as well as fantasies about its potential. To get these two extremes into balance, it's best to remember that the computer is just an electronic device, although a complex one. Because at times it may seem to exhibit some humanlike qualities, such as the ability to do mathematics much better, or at least much faster, than people do, the computer is often considered far more capable than it really is. This perception causes many potential computer users to approach the computer with an excessively high level of anxiety.

William James, a turn-of-the-century psychologist, was to have said that "the best way to get rid of your fears is to face them." While this may seem to be simplistic advice to us today, it does seem to help when encountering computer phobia. Those people who have a fear of using the computer usually find that after the first few sessions at the keyboard their fear has disappeared. There is virtually nothing that a computer user can do to hurt or damage the computer, so the only real problem is that of making a few mistakes. Fortunately, today's computers are designed to handle our errors, and thus as users there is little to fear from initial fumbling as we learn to make use of the computer.

Computer Errors

While users do not need to fear the occasional mistake when using the computer, programmers must be more concerned about their role. These professionals have a greater responsibility because every instruction that a computer follows must be supplied in the form of a program. Programs are written by computer programmers and the program code requires exacting detail. Because of the level of detail required in a program, it is quite possible for the programmer to introduce errors in the program writing stage. Some of these **program errors** are obvious and are corrected immediately, while others may remain hidden for months or years before they surface, maybe in the form of a telephone bill for $100,000 or a paycheck for $1,000,000.

Errors are usually made by the people who use computers and not by the computer itself. Appropriate training, operating procedures, and backup methods can help to minimize the result of errors. (Courtesy IBM.)

While these types of programming errors are rare, they do receive the most notice and often seem to suggest that computers are error prone. When an error does occur on the computer, it is most frequently due to human error as a result of either writing the program or entering data incorrectly.

By contrast, the computer itself has many error-checking circuits built into it so that computer-generated errors are quite rare. These **hardware errors** are totally different from programming errors. Usually they result from component failure but may sometimes be the result of a design problem with the circuitry. Hardware errors are very unusual and are normally self-correcting. In fact, many computers today will operate for several years before a hardware failure occurs.

Computers also depend on the data they are supplied with if the results produced are to be useful to the user. If inadequate or inaccurate data is supplied to the computer then the information the computer generates will either be in error or at least misleading. Thus, the term **garbage in-garbage out (GIGO)** is used, which clearly explains the effect of using incorrect data.

GIGO (garbage in-garbage out). A term used to indicate that the output from the computer is only as good as its input.

Unemployment

Unemployment is another fear associated with computer use. When computers were first used by business and industry, a significant concern was that the computer would put people out of work. Indeed there were some cases where this did happen. But, with the computer came many new job opportunities: programmers, systems analysts, computer operators, computer maintenance technicians, manufacturing, and sales were only some of the many new jobs that were created as a result of the computer. So the computer did result in a shift of employment. Significantly, the shift was often from the more menial and unfulfilling job to many jobs that represented excitement and challenge while the computer itself took on the drudgery.

Computers and the Solution to Your Problems

"Get a computer in your business and all your problems will be solved." That seemed to be the credo at one time and certainly represents a common fantasy, but the more realistic businessperson is aware that a computer can only do what it is told. And, unlike a human, it is not very good at making its own judgments. As a result, implementing a new computer will often create some problems of its own, which will take time and effort to correct.

Installing a computer will require training of the users, and some time will be needed to gain experience with the system before the computer can be used to its utmost potential. Most companies find that there is a learning curve required of their personnel when a computer is originally installed. At first, the new system may even operate a bit more slowly than the one that it replaced, but as experience with the system is acquired, the full benefits of the change will begin to take effect.

You Need to Be Good at Math or Be a Programmer to Use a Computer

This mistaken belief has led more than one person to abandon the quest for using a computer in his or her work. Contrary to popular notion, to use a computer successfully does not require a high level of mathematics. The average businessperson who understands the basic concepts of arithmetic needed to function effectively in business can also use a computer successfully.

Most computer users do not have or require programming skills and probably never will. While the computer professional certainly needs to be trained in programming, the business user of the computer needs no programming ability or training to use the computer effectively. However, training in the use of some computer software is usually important if you want to use the computer successfully. Ordinarily this training is of short duration, lasting only a few days, and does not normally include mathematics or programming. The tutorials that accompany this book provide some basic training in popular hardware and software use.

SOFTWARE PIRACY

The accompanying box tells a true story of a person who ran a business selling copied software. This story is an example of software piracy at its most obvious. **Software piracy** is the act of illegally copying software. Selling copied software is clearly illegal, as the story tells us, but the act can be illegal even if the copy is not for sale.

Copying a program is not automatically an illegal act. For example, many software packages come with instructions to copy the software onto new disks before using the program. This procedure ensures that if something goes wrong with the disks you are using to run the program, it is always possible to go back to the original. However, the same companies will

> ## ▶ SOFTWARE PIRATE GETS 5 MONTHS
>
> Randy Trent (not his real name), the owner of R/T Software, has been sentenced to five months in jail for the unauthorized copying and selling of copyrighted software.
>
> Trent was convicted on March 26, 1987 on three counts of fraud involving copied software. His company was in the business of copying commercial software for the questionable purpose of customer evaluation. Presumably customers who evaluated the software and found it suitable would then purchase the legitimate package. But many customers simply continued to use the copied software on their system and never purchased a legitimate copy from the software publisher.
>
> Complainants, including IBM, Ashton-Tate (the dBASE IV company), and Lotus, flew in expert witnesses from California and Texas to Toronto where the trial was held. The software industry watched the trial closely for a precedent to be set to help in their fight against software piracy.

often state that the program can only be used on one computer at a time, thus prohibiting the user from making copies for friends.

But what is to stop the person who purchases a program from running off any number of copies? In many cases there is nothing to stop the person other than his or her own code of ethics. In the case of corporations, making illegal copies can cost the software publisher millions of dollars. Such was the case when Lotus Corporation sued Rixon Corporation for $10 million for making illegal copies of 1–2–3. In late 1992, the U.S. Congress passed an amendment to Title 18, United States Code, instituting criminal penalties for copyright infringement of software. Penalties include fines of $2,500 to $250,000 and/or imprisonment up to 5 years.

SOFTWARE LICENSING

When you buy a piece of software it invariably comes with a **license agreement** (Figure 15-1). Often, simply by opening the package containing the diskettes, you agree to the conditions of the license. These conditions may include not making other copies (sometimes one copy is permitted for backup reasons), using the software on only one machine, and not using it on a network. You may also agree to the return of the package to the publisher upon request, although this is rarely, if ever, requested. Of course, the license also includes a warranty that protects the purchaser if something goes wrong with the original disk. It can usually be returned for replacement.

License agreement. A legal contract with a software publisher giving the user the rights to install and use the software on a computer or network.

Site license. A license agreement that permits the use of the same software on more than one computer at a single location.

Site Licensing

Licensing becomes a problem in sites where several computers use the same software. Naturally the purchaser would prefer to buy one package and run it on several computers in the company. This practice is illegal according to the license agreement of most software publishers.

Microsoft License Agreement

(SINGLE-USER PRODUCTS)

This is a legal agreement between you, the end user, and Microsoft Corporation. BY OPENING THIS SEALED DISK PACKAGE, YOU ARE AGREEING TO BE BOUND BY THE TERMS OF THIS AGREEMENT. IF YOU DO NOT AGREE TO THE TERMS OF THIS AGREEMENT, PROMPTLY RETURN THE UNOPENED DISK PACKAGE AND THE ACCOMPANYING ITEMS (including written materials and binders or other containers) TO THE PLACE YOU OBTAINED THEM FOR A FULL REFUND.

MICROSOFT SOFTWARE LICENSE

1. GRANT OF LICENSE. Microsoft grants to you the right to use one copy of the enclosed Microsoft software program (the "SOFTWARE") on a single terminal connected to a single computer (i.e., with a single CPU). You may not network the SOFTWARE or otherwise use it on more than one computer or computer terminal at the same time.

2. COPYRIGHT. The SOFTWARE is owned by Microsoft or its suppliers and is protected by United States copyright laws and international treaty provisions. Therefore, you must treat the SOFTWARE like any other copyrighted material (e.g., a book or musical recording) except that you may either (a) make one copy of the SOFTWARE solely for backup or archival purposes, or (b) transfer the SOFTWARE to a single hard disk provided you keep the original solely for backup or archival purposes. You may not copy the written materials accompanying the software.

3. OTHER RESTRICTIONS. You may not rent or lease the SOFTWARE, but you may transfer the SOFTWARE and accompanying written materials on a permanent basis provided you retain no copies and the recipient agrees to the terms of this Agreement. You may not reverse engineer, decompile, or disassemble the SOFTWARE.

4. DUAL MEDIA SOFTWARE. If the SOFTWARE package contains both $3^{1}/_{2}''$ and $5^{1}/_{4}''$ disks, then you may use only the disks appropriate for your single-user computer. You may not use the other disks on another computer or loan, rent, lease, or transfer them to another user except as part of the permanent transfer (as provided above) of all SOFTWARE and written materials.

5. LANGUAGE SOFTWARE. If the SOFTWARE is a Microsoft language product, then you have a royalty-free right to reproduce and distribute executable files created using the SOFTWARE. If the language product is a BASIC or COBOL product, then Microsoft grants to you a royalty-free right to reproduce and distribute the runtime modules of the SOFTWARE provided that you: (a) distribute the runtime modules only in conjunction with and as a part of your software product; (b) do not use Microsoft's name, logo, or trademarks to market your software product; (c) include Microsoft's copyright notice for the SOFTWARE on your product label and as part of the sign-on message for your software product; and (d) agree to indemnify, hold harmless, and defend Microsoft from and against any claims or lawsuits, including attorney's fees, that arise or result from the use or distribution of your software product. The "runtime modules" are those files in the SOFTWARE that are identified in the accompanying written materials as required during execution of your software program. The runtime modules are limited to runtime files, install files, and ISAM and REBUILT files.

LIMITED WARRANTY

LIMITED WARRANTY. Microsoft warrants that (a) the SOFTWARE will perform substantially in accordance with the accompanying written materials for a period of 90 days from the date of receipt; and (b) any hardware accompanying the SOFTWARE will be free from defects in materials and workmanship under normal use and service for a period of one year from the date of receipt. Any implied warranties on the SOFTWARE and hardware are limited to 90 days and one (1) year, respectively. Some states do not allow limitations on duration of an implied warranty, so the above limitation may not apply to you.

CUSTOMER REMEDIES. Microsoft's entire liability and your exclusive remedy shall be, at Microsoft's option, either (a) return of the price paid or (b) repair or replacement of the SOFTWARE or hardware that does not meet Microsoft's Limited Warranty and which is returned to Microsoft with a copy of your receipt. This Limited Warranty is void if failure of the SOFTWARE or hardware has resulted from accident, abuse, or misapplication. Any replacement SOFTWARE will be warranted for the remainder of the original warranty period or 30 days, whichever is longer.

NO OTHER WARRANTIES. MICROSOFT DISCLAIMS ALL OTHER WARRANTIES, EITHER EXPRESS OR IMPLIED, INCLUDING BUT NOT LIMITED TO IMPLIED WARRANTIES OF MERCHANTABILITY AND FITNESS FOR A PARTICULAR PURPOSE, WITH RESPECT TO THE SOFTWARE, THE ACCOMPANYING WRITTEN MATERIALS, AND ANY ACCOMPANYING HARDWARE. THIS LIMITED WARRANTY GIVES YOU SPECIFIC LEGAL RIGHTS. YOU MAY HAVE OTHERS, WHICH VARY FROM STATE TO STATE.

NO LIABILITY FOR CONSEQUENTIAL DAMAGES. IN NO EVENT SHALL MICROSOFT OR ITS SUPPLIERS BE LIABLE FOR ANY DAMAGES WHATSOEVER (INCLUDING, WITHOUT LIMITATION, DAMAGES FOR LOSS OF BUSINESS PROFITS, BUSINESS INTERRUPTION, LOSS OF BUSINESS INFORMATION, OR OTHER PECUNIARY LOSS) ARISING OUT OF THE USE OF OR INABILITY TO USE THIS MICROSOFT PRODUCT, EVEN IF MICROSOFT HAS BEEN ADVISED OF THE POSSIBILITY OF SUCH DAMAGE. BECAUSE SOME STATES DO NOT ALLOW THE EXCLUSION OR LIMITATION OF LIABILITY FOR CONSEQUENTIAL OR INCIDENTAL DAMAGES, THE ABOVE LIMITATION MAY NOT APPLY TO YOU.

U.S. GOVERNMENT RESTRICTED RIGHTS

The SOFTWARE and documentation are provided with RESTRICTED RIGHTS. Use, duplication, or disclosure by the Government is subject to restrictions as set forth in subdivision (b)(3)(ii) of The Rights in Technical Data and Computer Software clause at 252.277-7013. Contractor/manufacturer is Microsoft Corporation/16011 NE 36th Way/Box 97017/Redmond, WA 98073-9717.

This Agreement is governed by the laws of the State of Washington.
Should you have any questions concerning this Agreement, or if you desire to contact Microsoft for any reason, please write: Microsoft Customer Sales and Service/16011 NE 36th Way/Box 97017/Redmond, WA 98073-9717.

FIGURE 15-1
A software license agreement.

There are two legal approaches for solving this problem. One is to buy as many copies as you have computers that will be running it, which can be a very expensive solution. The other is to buy a **site license** which permits the use of multiple copies of the same software. Site licenses are frequently less costly than buying multiple copies and are of special importance to companies that have many PCs using the same software.

Network Licensing

A **network license** permits a single copy of a program to be used by several stations served by a network. When networks are used, frequently only one copy of the software is needed on the file server. All other computers on the network can download the software for use on their machine. But using a single licensed copy of the program is not acceptable to the software publisher in this situation. Users argue that only one copy of the software is used and that it is protected by the network from illegal pirating of the program. But the software publisher argues that each station on the network is using a copy (in memory) of the program and thus the company should purchase a network license.

Network license. A license that permits a single copy of a program to be installed on the network file server for use by multiple users on the network.

COMPUTER CRIME

A computer vandal broke into the computers of at least 21 different companies and destroyed the files of one of these companies. Thieves used a computer to break into the computer of a bank in Vancouver and transferred $2.8 million to a bank in Los Angeles. Employees of a company tapped into the company mainframe to use computer time for personal profit by running jobs for outside clients without their employer's knowledge or approval. An exporting company is buying computers in the United States and selling them illegally to countries in eastern Europe.

All of these true stories are examples of the ways that computer crime is being committed today. Crime, of course, is not unknown in any industry, but computers are unique in the sense that some of these crimes can be perpetrated at a distance. The person who commits the crime does not need to be at the scene but could operate from the comfort of home or from a remote computer in a school or business. The above examples identify different categories of crimes perpetrated with the use of computers, which will now be examined separately.

Unlawful Computer Entry

This category of crime is probably the most widespread misuse of computers. Unlawful entry involves the access to a computer system, usually from a remote computer by modem, for the purpose of accessing programs or data on the system. Gaining access usually means breaking a security system of some sort, stealing a password, or finding a weakness in the software that provides security against unlawful entry.

Most people who perform this crime are not intent on destroying data or files, although some do, but are more curious about looking at information that is not legally theirs to see. Although accessing a computer in this manner to satisfy one's curiosity may not seem to be a harmful act, it is an illegal act and like all computer crimes is a punishable offense. To guard against this activity, many systems now require several levels of passwords to access sensitive data. Some systems are designed to record your phone number, which is then checked against a list of approved numbers. If you are on the list, it then phones you back and connects you to the system.

Theft of Currency by Computer

Using a computer to transfer money from one bank to another is routine business today. The crime occurs when a computer user intentionally directs the computer to transfer money from another person's account to their own account. This is really no different from stealing money directly, but the computer is used as a part of the transaction. More sophisticated thieves have tried to accomplish similar thefts but by deducting only a few cents from many thousands of accounts, hoping that no one would notice. Advanced auditing techniques are being adopted by computer auditors to ensure that even methods such as this do not go undetected.

Theft of Computer Time

Using the company computer to run off your Christmas card list or to calculate your loan payments might be considered a theft of computer time. These are rather trivial incidents, but we are concerned here about the illegal use of computer time for personal gain. An employee who runs mailing lists which are sold to outside companies for personal profit is a more serious type of computer crime. Companies are within their rights to charge the employee with theft, but often simply terminate the employee rather than go to court.

Theft of Computer Hardware

Whether selling computers to foreign countries is a crime depends on the laws relating to that country. Certainly selling computers to many countries in the free world is not a crime and many companies do well financially in this marketplace. However, other countries cannot legally purchase computers from the United States. Thus, companies that surreptitiously buy computers and ship them via other countries for the purpose of selling to these communist countries are committing a computer crime.

PRIVACY AND SECURITY

Computers are exceptionally efficient machines for storing and disbursing information about all kinds of things. When data is collected about things such as products and sales, most people are indifferent, but when the data contains personal information, many become quite concerned about their

▶ THE AGE OF THE COMPUTER VIRUS

In November 1988 a computer virus spread across the United States, affecting the performance of thousands of computers. Included were computers in a nuclear weapons lab, the Pentagon, and several major universities. Very little information was lost but the virus inconvenienced many thousands of computer users. And who doesn't remember the Michelangelo virus scare in 1992 that had users around the world checking their computers for hidden effects.

A **computer virus** is a program that is hidden in other programs in the system. The virus is written by a programmer who intends to corrupt or interfere with users of computer systems. Usually the virus program is hidden on a network that many computer users access regularly.

After writing the virus program the malicious programmer hides it in a program that other computer users are likely to use. It might be a game or a more serious application or utility program. Frequently the virus copies itself to DOS' COMMAND.COM program which is necessary for the operation of most personal computers.

When a user accesses the program or the system containing the virus, things may seem to be normal for a while. But, after a given time period, or when a certain day occurs (such as Friday the 13th) the virus program is activated. It may simply display a harmless message, but the more sophisticated ones may do damage to files or programs on the user's system. Some have been known to wipe out the entire contents of a hard disk. The virus may also copy itself to other programs so that if the original program is erased from the disk the virus will still be present.

Hearing about virus programs often causes users to believe they have caught a virus on their system. It is relatively easy for some errors to occur on a system without a virus being at fault. Erasing a file or even an entire disk can result from simply using the wrong DOS command or using a command incorrectly. Power fluctuations, magnetic media wear, dust, or smoke particles can all cause data errors which have nothing to do with a virus. So be sure that when the problem is encountered it is not due to one of these factors.

However, there are several practices to follow that can help you to avoid being hit by a hidden virus. Floppy disks are the primary source of viruses. While floppy disks from software manufacturers can generally be relied on, indiscriminate use of floppies from unknown sources, especially those that require a system boot, can leave you vulnerable to a computer virus. First, don't load programs on your system from sources that are not known to be reliable. Frequent use of bulletin boards that are not strictly controlled can open up one's system to the potential of getting hit by the next virus. Reliable bulletin board systems will have virus checking programs in place to avoid the problem before it can spread to other systems. Using software from reliable sources, such as the major software companies, will also minimize the chances of being infected.

Last, there is the use of a virus checking program. Programs such as Central Point Anti-Virus and Norton AntiVirus look for the presence of a virus on a disk before it is used on the system. They can also check your hard disk for existing viruses. Unfortunately, no virus checking program is foolproof and a bright programmer intent on creating a virus can bypass the vaccine as well. Ultimately, the best solution to the computer virus is to know the source of your software and accept only proven programs for residence on your system.

privacy and the security of the information. Data about a person's credit rating, spending habits, education, employment history, subscriptions they hold, insurance policies, and so on is all on computer files somewhere. Mailing lists are often bought and sold as a commodity, and so by getting your name on one list you may soon appear on many other lists and receive offers to subscribe to a magazine, get a credit card, or purchase land in Florida.

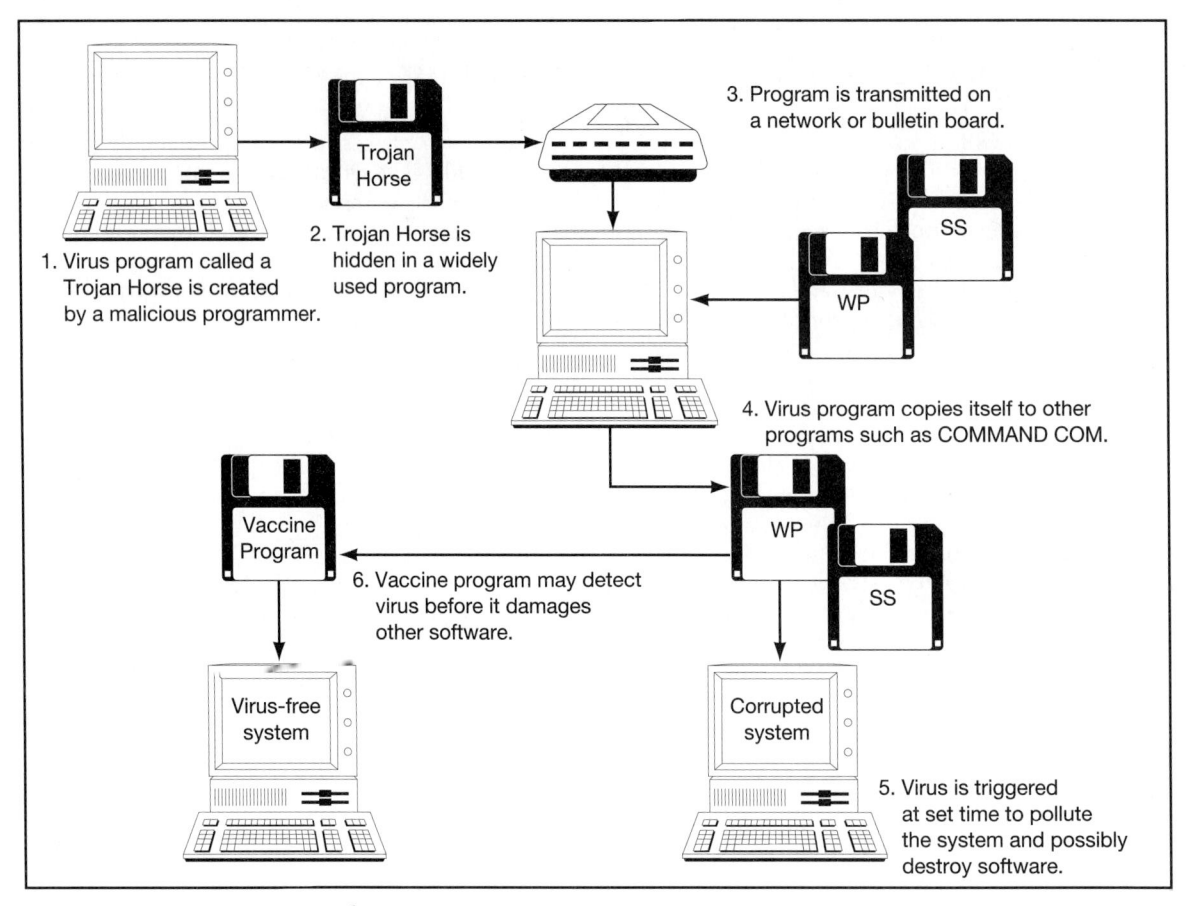

How a computer virus spreads.

A case in point is the widespread use of on-line bulletin boards for discussing software problems with the software publisher. Forums exist on services such as CompuServe for popular software like WordPerfect and dBASE for discussing problems and solutions with other users and technical people at the publisher. Normally when a problem is reported by phone or letter, the user's serial number is required so that the company can check whether you are an authorized user. But when a bulletin board is used, entering your serial number can make it public knowledge, which could then be used by other unauthorized people. Therefore, publishers warn against the use of identifying information when using a public network.

It is the ease with which information can be exchanged between computers that has raised the concern about security and privacy in the computer industry. **Privacy** is the issue about who has access to personal information and whether the information is complete and accurate. **Security** is the issue which concerns the organization that controls the data. Do only the right people or computers have access to information and is there sufficient protection to ensure that unauthorized individuals cannot gain access?

Government is only one organization that stores data on individuals, but it is by far the largest. The U.S. government has over 200 million records on more than 100 million people and data is traded regularly by as many as fifteen federal agencies. State and local governments also maintain computer records and exchange data about taxes, welfare recipients, crime, and student loans.

To ensure that individuals have a right to privacy, two major acts were placed into law in 1970. The Freedom of Information Act was passed to give everyone access to data collected about them by federal agencies. Second, the Fair Credit Reporting Act was also passed in 1970 to give persons access to information stored about them by credit agencies. As a result of these acts, everyone can have access to records kept about them. However, getting access to these records is not always automatic and may even require court action by the individual.

The Federal Privacy Act, legislated in 1974, stipulates that no secret personal files be permitted and that individuals must be permitted to see the contents of files that do exist and how the data about them contained in the file is used. The law applies to both government and private agencies that deal with the government. Agencies cannot simply ask for a certain type of information but must show just cause for receiving it.

Many critics of the act have shown that there is insufficient control over the exchange of information and that agencies have more freedom of access than the act provides. The lack of a government watchdog to ensure that information is not easily traded has reduced the effectiveness of the Privacy Act.

ETHICS

Crimes such as stealing a computer or the illegal transfer of funds to a personal account are obviously criminal acts. To perform crimes such as these is a calculated attempt to steal or commit fraud, which is clearly subject to prosecution by the legal authorities.

These acts obviously demonstrate a lack of ethics on the part of the person who commits the crime. But what about the person who makes a copy of a spreadsheet or word processing program to avoid the expense of buying the package? Or the student who uses the college computer to gain illegal access to the registrar's records or dials into a company's mainframe from a home computer?

Ethics refers to a moral code and relates to what one perceives as right or wrong. When someone copies a program to avoid the expense of purchase, several moral ideals are being broken. First, the person is obtaining a program that clearly has some value to him or her without paying the price for it. Breaking this moral code is more apparent when we are talking about taking a car or even a book. In the case of a program, the copying may seem to present a different situation from a car or book.

We can't easily copy a car, and although a book could be copied, the price of the copy is usually more than the original cost of the book, so no one bothers to take this approach. But copying software denies the software company, the programmer, and the distributor a rightful profit for creating the program and making it available to their clients. It's easy to say that a software company is wealthy and can afford it, but with a little thought we can see that if everyone had this attitude the software business would be out of business. The wealth of the company cannot justify taking an unethical position on the copying of software.

Another ethics issue is the illegal use of computer systems. Breaking into a computer by using an unauthorized password or by forcing entry through a weakness in the security system is not much different from physically breaking into an organization's office. Although one activity involves a physical act and the other an electronic one, the principle is essentially the same.

Gaining access to unauthorized files also demonstrates a lack of respect for the privacy of the individuals' records that are viewed by the computer hacker. The privacy act discussed earlier was passed for the very reason that the files of others should be respected. Hackers also may inadvertently cause damage to the files by not being totally familiar with the system operation and the organization of the files. Although this damage may be unintentional, it nevertheless is real and can result in serious consequences for both the company and the hacker.

To stress the importance of taking a position on the matter of ethics, several organizations that represent computing professionals have adopted a code of ethics that their members must adopt. Organizations such as the Data Processing Management Association (DPMA) and the Association for Computing Machinery (ACM) have a statement of ethics to which their members subscribe.

Ethics is not a concern that is limited to the computer profession. Management in many companies and organizations are concerned with the standards of conduct demonstrated by their people. Dr. Kenneth Blanchard and Dr. Norman Vincent Peale in their book *The Power of Ethical Management* provide an ethics check that goes as follows:

1. Is it legal? Will I be violating either civil law or company policy?
2. Is it balanced? Is it fair to all concerned in the short term as well as the long term? Does it promote win-win relationships?
3. How will it make me feel about myself? Will it make me proud? Would I feel good if my decision was published in the newspaper? Would I feel good if my family knew about it?

These are simple questions that can have a profound influence on the individual's decision-making process when ethics are involved. Ethics is not always a standard that begins with the passing of some law or determined by some authority figure, but it is something that each of us can and should develop as a personal standard of conduct.

COMPUTER CAREERS

In the 1970s, a career in computers was considered one of the most desirable directions a college student could take. Thousands of graduates descended on this employment market and found satisfying and financially rewarding careers as a result. After 20 years, computer-related careers have continued to persist and even expanded into many new venues. By the early 1990s, this career path has undergone many changes and will continue to do so into the twenty-first century.

Twenty years ago a computer career was primarily in the mainframe computer area. Programmers, operators, and systems analysts were in the mainstream of employment opportunities. Because of many changes and new developments in the mainframe computer and its use, and due to the extensive use of personal computers in business, the job market in computers has broadened considerably. But with the expansion, the number of positions has not increased accordingly but are of wider variety, which appeal to a greater range of aptitudes and interests.

We must not overlook the fact that other careers are being impacted by the widespread use of computers. College graduates in a variety of disciplines from business to technology need to be not only computer literate, but to have specific computer skills to find suitable employment in their own discipline. Thus, computer courses have sprung up in many educational and training programs that in themselves may not directly lead to a computer career.

CAREER OPPORTUNITIES

On the following pages we will look at several categories of jobs that are typical of the computer career (Figure 15-2). Some of these jobs are strictly mainframe, others are related to the personal computer, while some may require knowledge of both areas. The path one takes depends mainly on personal interest and the type of courses chosen at college. Programs are available that stress several different career paths, and one should choose a direction with personal priorities in mind.

Data Entry Operator

Data entry is the process of entering source data, usually by keyboard, into the computer. A **data entry operator** is a person who has typing or keying skills and has been trained in the use of the computer. Training is both application oriented and in the use of specific software required by the application. Data entry positions are available for all levels of computers from micros to mainframes, but are declining in numbers as more automated means of source data entry become available.

Data entry. The process of entering data into the computer for storage or processing.

Computer Operations

A **computer operator** is someone who runs the computer and is responsible for the monitoring, control, and operation of the computer hardware (Figure 15-3). This is a mainframe job and often has other supporting positions such as librarians, quality assurance, and management. An operator mounts tapes, disks, feeds paper into the printer, brings up programs, and solves operational problems.

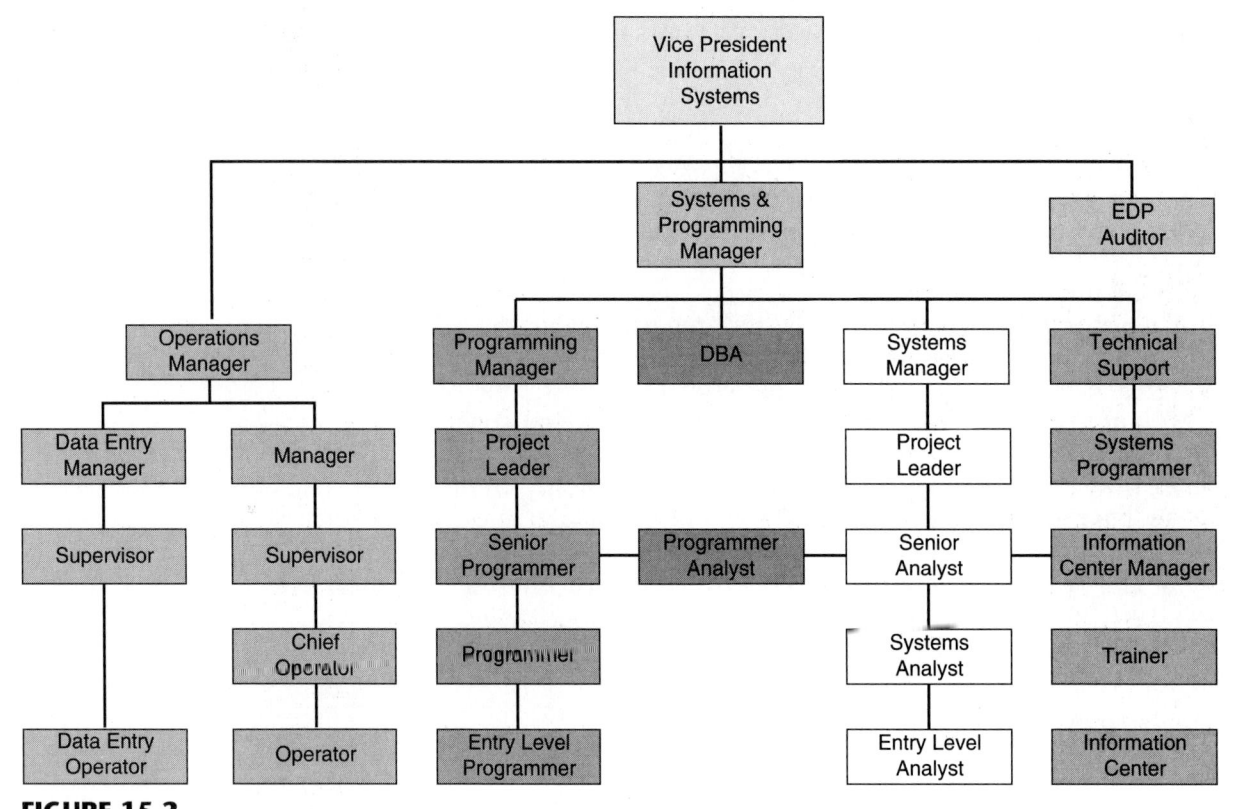

FIGURE 15-2
Computer-related career paths.

Data entry requires keyboard skills and training in the use of computer hardware and software. (Courtesy Stock Market.)

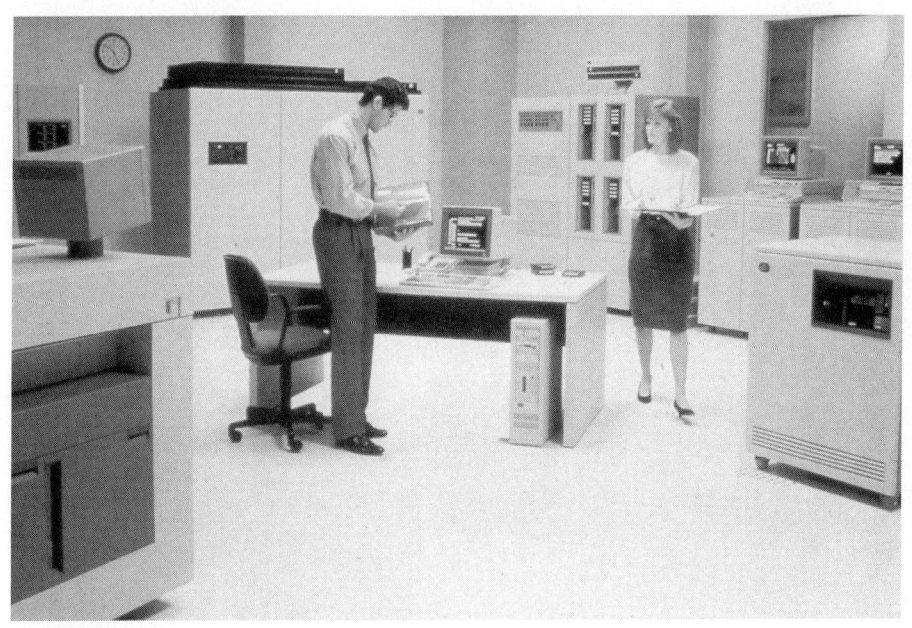

FIGURE 15-3
A computer operator runs the mainframe computer, mounts tapes, monitors the operation, and solves operational problems. (Courtesy IBM.)

Operators generally begin with a limited amount of responsibility, which is increased as their skill and maturity grows. An operator will frequently enter the job with college education for either operations or programming. Many companies consider operations to be entry level for future programmers and use the time in operations as a training period to acquaint the employee with the company's computer system.

Programmers

This term covers many areas of computer programming. In general, there are systems and applications programmers (Figure 15-4) and these jobs relate to both personal and mainframe computers.

Systems Programmer. A **systems programmer** works on systems software such as compilers, operating systems, macros, and other general use software. Usually this is a position for the technically oriented programmer who has had a few years of experience in the applications programming area. An education in computer science or similar discipline is a necessary background for this position.

Applications Programmer. The **applications programmer** designs, codes, tests, and debugs applications programs. Program maintenance of existing programs is becoming an important part of the applications programmer's job. Application programs include accounting, payroll, inventory control, education, insurance, and many other applications.

This is the most widely available position in computers today and continues to be one with a strong career potential. Entry level jobs are avail-

FIGURE 15-4
A computer programmer has the challenging task of designing, coding, testing, debugging, and maintaining computer programs. (Courtesy IBM.)

able for those who have completed a college program in data processing, information systems, or computer science. As the employee progresses in his or her career, other job levels from junior to senior programmer and programming management are available.

New directions are developing for the applications programmer including fourth-generation languages, database administration, and expert systems. The personal computer has also opened many new opportunities for the individual with knowledge and skills relating to the PC and its software.

Systems Analyst

The **systems analyst** is the person who designs and implements applications for the computer. Because applications involve people in the organization and their information needs, the analyst needs to be a people-oriented person. Someone who can talk the language of the application and yet communicate in a more technical way with the programmer is required for this position.

Often, the systems job is a promotion from programming and may be considered an alternate career path. Education in information systems is important, and a strong business and management component is helpful. Systems analysts spend much of their time with user departments in many areas of the company. As a result, they become intimately familiar with the internal operations of the corporation. This background is often an excellent basis for promotion into management.

Business Analyst

The **business analyst** position is similar to the systems analyst with a greater stress on knowledge of the business operation. A business analyst is frequently promoted from a career path in the company that was not information systems related. People from accounting, finance, marketing, and other disciplines who are well grounded in the operation of their area of expertise often make good business analysts after receiving some training in analysis and design methodology.

Database Administrator (DBA)

A **database administrator (DBA)** is a position in the information systems department responsible for the design, control, and administration of the company's databases. In large corporations, one or more people may have this function. In smaller organizations it may be combined with other functions. The DBA establishes data definitions, defines the database standards for the company, determines who has access to what information, and maintains the integrity of the data.

Information Center Staff

The **information center** is usually a small department in the company that assists users with day-to-day operational problems. They may assist with problems users have with computer use and even act as an interface between a user and the information systems department. When new software or systems are placed into operation, the information center frequently provides the training for the user departments. This is especially true when personal computers are used and training is needed in the use of PC software. Information center support usually encompasses both PC and mainframe systems.

Marketing

Strictly speaking, this is not a computer job but one in sales. Selling mainframe and mini-computers was a highly lucrative profession in the 1970s and is still one with great potential. Marketing of computers ranges from the large mainframe systems to the relatively small personal computer sold from the local computer store (Figure 15-5).

First, and foremost, an education in marketing is important to this career path. A business administration program with a minor in marketing is also well accepted as background for entry into computer marketing. Second to the marketing diploma is training in computers. Many colleges also offer this as part of the overall program, but the employer will often supplement this with training on the specific products the salesperson is selling. An individual with a strong business program and an interest in the computer field might consider computer marketing as a potential career.

FIGURE 15-5
Selling computers combines business training, marketing skills, and an interest in computers. (Courtesy Chemical New York Corp.)

CHAPTER SUMMARY

1. To get the two extremes of fear and fantasy into balance, it's best to remember that the computer is just an electronic device, although a complex one.
2. **Program errors** are introduced when writing a computer program. Some are obvious and are corrected immediately, while others may remain hidden for months or years before they surface.
3. **Hardware errors** usually result from component failure but may sometimes be the result of a design problem with the circuitry. Hardware errors are very unusual occurrences and are normally self-correcting.
4. **Installing** a computer will require training of the users and some time will be needed to get experience with the system before the computer can be used to its utmost potential.
5. Contrary to popular notion, to use a computer successfully does not require a high level of mathematics or programming ability.
6. **Software piracy** is the act of illegally copying software.
7. When you buy a piece of software it invariably comes with a **license agreement** which defines the conditions for making other copies, using the software on only one machine, and not using it on a network.
8. A **site license** is a license that permits the use of multiple copies of the same software by a corporation or agency.
9. A **network license** permits a single copy of a program to be used by several stations served by a network.

CHAPTER 15 Issues and Trends

10. **Computer crime** is unique from most other crimes in the sense that crime committed by computer can be perpetrated at a distance.
11. A **computer virus** is a program that is hidden in other programs in the system with the intent of creating malicious activity or damage in the system.
12. **Privacy** is the issue about who has access to personal information and whether the information is complete and accurate.
13. **Security** concerns the organization that controls the data and who has access to that data.
14. **Ethics** refers to a moral code and relates to what one perceives as right or wrong.
15. A **data entry operator** is a person who has typing or keying skills and has been trained in the use of the computer.
16. A **computer operator** is someone who runs the computer and is responsible for the monitoring, control, and operation of the computer hardware.
17. A **systems programmer** is one who works on systems software such as compilers, operating systems, macros, and other general use software.
18. The **applications programmer** is one who designs, codes, tests, and debugs applications programs such as accounting, payroll, inventory control, education, insurance, and many other applications.
19. The **systems analyst** is the person who designs and implements applications for the computer. This position requires someone who can talk the language of the application and yet communicate in a more technical way with the programmer.
20. The **business analyst** position is similar to the systems analyst with a greater stress on knowledge of the business operation, in areas such as accounting, finance, and marketing.
21. A **database administrator (DBA)** is a position in the information systems department responsible for the design, control, and administration of the company's databases.

IMPORTANT TERMS AND CONCEPTS

Applications programmer
Business analyst
Computer operator
Copy protection
Data entry operator
Database administrator (DBA)
Ethics
GIGO
Hardware errors
Information center
Key disk
License agreement

Network license
Privacy
Program errors
Security
Site license
Software piracy
Systems analyst
Systems programmer
Unemployment
Vaccine program
Virus

SELF-TESTING QUESTIONS

Fill-In

1. Computer errors generally exist in the _____ and not in the hardware.
2. Software _____ is the act of copying software without authorization from the software publisher.
3. A _____ agreement spells out the rights of the software publisher and the purchaser of the program.
4. A program that is hidden in another program on the computer with malicious intent is called a _____.
5. _____ is the issue about who has access to personal information stored on computer files.
6. A code of _____ is a statement about personal conduct and the difference between right and wrong actions of the individual.
7. The position of computer _____ refers to someone who runs the computer and monitors its operation
8. An applications _____ develops, codes, and maintains programs for applications such as accounting and payroll.
9. The _____ _____ is a person whose profession is designing and implementing applications for the computer.
10. Staff in the _____ _____ are responsible for the training of computer users and assisting with systems implementation.

True/False

1. Garbage in - garbage out refers to a computer virus that trashes input data.
2. To be a computer programmer it is essential to be an expert in mathematics.
3. Making a backup copy of software you have purchased for you own safety is not considered software piracy.
4. A license agreement is a contract supplied with a software package to which the purchaser agrees when the package has been opened.
5. Site licensing is usually necessary when a program is purchased for a desktop computer but not for a laptop.
6. Signing on to a remote computer and accessing data for which you have not been authorized is a criminal act.
7. Ethics is a moral code that one follows in making decisions on personal actions.
8. A computer virus can be avoided by using the best quality floppy disks on your system.

ANSWERS

Fill-In: **1.** program or software, **2.** piracy, **3.** license, **4.** virus, **5.** Privacy, **6.** ethics, **7.** operator, **8.** programmer, **9.** system analyst, **10.** information center

True/False: 1. F, 2. F, 3. T, 4. T, 5. F, 6. T, 7. T, 8. F

Questions for Critical Thinking

1. Discuss your opinions on the type of skills and training that you will require to be an effective computer user.
2. Students often need to have access to a variety of software packages to assist in their school work. Is it ever ethical to "borrow" a copy of the software for use on your own computer?
3. Some computer hackers get their "kicks" from signing on to unauthorized systems and looking at the data stored on the system. Although they don't cause any damage to data or software on the system, should they be prosecuted when they are caught by the authorities?

APPENDIX A

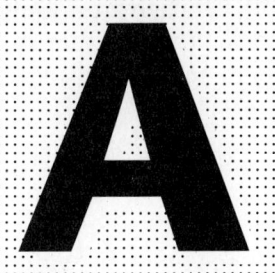

ORIGINS: A HISTORY OF COMPUTING AND INFORMATION SYSTEMS

You are probably familiar with the names APPLE, Commodore, and Atari and rightly associate them with home computers. But these are a recent event in the history of computers. Computers go as far back as the early 1940s when John W. Mauchly and J. Presper Eckert Jr. constructed ENIAC at the Moore School of Engineering at the University of Pennsylvania. But the origins of the concepts behind the computer go back much further in time. In this section we will look at a few of the highlights in the evolution of the computer.

ABACUS

Back around 2000 B.C. a device known to us as the abacus was in widespread use in China and the Far East for arithmetic calculations. By 1200 A.D. the abacus used consisted of a rectangular frame that could be easily held by hand. In the frame were several fixed rods strung with moveable beads. The beads were arranged in two groups separated by a fixed bar. The top group consisted of rows of two beads each, while the bottom group had five rows of beads. The beads on the rightmost rod represented the units position, the second rod the tens position, and so on. Each bead on the top bar represented a value of five and the beads on the lower rod had a unit value. By moving the beads toward the bar a number was recorded.

In parts of China and other Asian countries the abacus is still in use today. As primitive as it seems, it is still an effective device for numerical calculations. When adding a column of numbers, a skilled abacus operator can keep pace with the user of an electronic calculator, thus demonstrating its effectiveness. However, doing other arithmetic operations is considerably more difficult on the abacus, and the calculator is easily the superior device.

BLAISE PASCAL

Blaise Pascal was known as a genius for his work in many disciplines. Born in 1623, he was a French philosopher, scientist, and mathematician with

3000 B.C.
Abacus (Courtesy of IBM Archives.)

1642
Blaise Pascal (Courtesy of IBM Archives.)

works on projective geometry, the theory of the behavior of fluids, and a series of letters which influenced church reform. Between 1641 and 1647 he invented the first calculating machine. It used pinwheel gearing and numbered disks something similar to the wheels used for an odometer in today's cars.

His reason for inventing the calculator showed the dislike Pascal had for routine, menial types of work. It all began in 1638 when his father, who was a lawyer and mathematician, formed a protest against the policy of the government's treasury department. This kind of activity was not taken too lightly at that time and he was required to go into hiding to save his life. But he was soon to be pardoned and given the job of special tax commissioner in Normandy.

It was a difficult job and Blaise Pascal was conscripted into the work by his father. Young Pascal was more interested in abstract mathematics and had little interest or patience for the hard and boring work of calculating tax tables. In the interest of self-survival he invented the calculator to help in this work. The calculator operated on the decimal principle and could do addition and subtraction.

Pascal gave up the scientific life at the age of 27 to pursue a life of religious contemplation with the Jansenists, a religious order of that time. When he died at the early age of 39, mankind lost one of its greatest philosophers and mathematicians.

GEORGE BOOLE

The invention of calculating machines is not the only important development leading to today's computers. Systems of thought and computation also made an important contribution to the development of new techniques. Such was the work of George Boole (1815–1864), who was an English logician and mathematician. Boole was one of the developers of the algebra of logic which expresses and manipulates problems in logic by the use of mathematical symbols.

1642
Pascal Calculator (Courtesy of IBM Archives.)

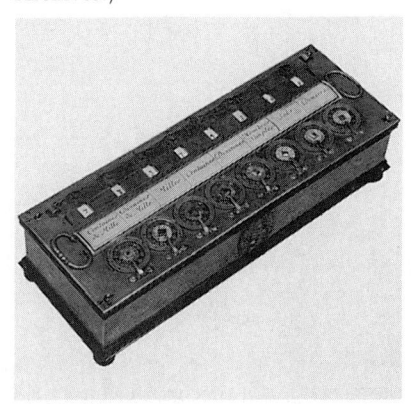

1827
George Boole (Courtesy of the Bettmann Archive.)

Boole defined an algebra in which all variables could take on only two states: True and False. By manipulating these variables according to his special algebra, he found that he could describe and investigate many real world problems. Boole's algebra became the perfect tool to design complex binary logic circuits of the computer, a century after he invented it. Fortunately, we can use computers today without needing a formal understanding of Boole's laws, which are often called Boolean Algebra.

CHARLES BABBAGE

Charles Babbage was another genius who conceived of a machine that would go beyond addition and subtraction. Born in 1792 in Devonshire, England, Babbage was a sickly child who spent much of his time with books and in deep thought (he called it childish reasonings). By the time he went to college he was astonished to discover that he knew more about calculus than his instructors.

One day he was sitting in the rooms of the Analytical Society daydreaming, as usual, over a book of logarithm tables. When asked by a friend what he was doing, he announced that he had been thinking it might be possible to calculate the logarithms by machinery. That was the idea that spurred him on to the development of the Difference Engine. The first model built could produce the tables mechanically with an accuracy of 20 digits. That model had 96 computing wheels mounted on 24 shafts. It required such precision to build that widescale manufacturing proved impossible.

No sooner had Babbage designed the Difference Engine than he had an idea for a new device called the Analytical Engine. Although it was also mechanical, it contained many of the concepts used in today's computers. It had memory, a control unit, an arithmetic unit, and input and output capabilities. Surprisingly it also had the ability to be programmed by punched cards. While this new machine represented a significant step forward in Babbage's thinking, the world was not yet ready for this development.

1833
Charles Babbage (Courtesy of the Bettmann Archive.)

1833
Difference Engine (Courtesy of IBM Archives.)

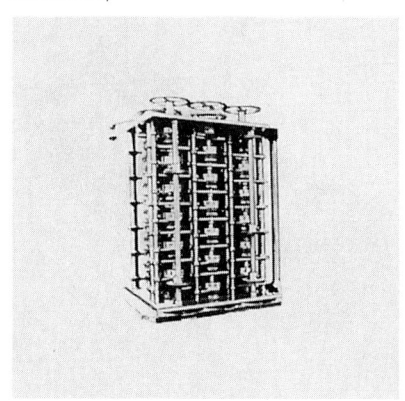

Then he met Ada, the Countess of Lovelace. She was the daughter of Lord Byron and a gifted mathematician, which was an unusual occupation for a woman in the nineteenth century. Ada took an interest in Babbage's work and was one of the first to fully appreciate and understand the designs of his machines. In 1842 she began to translate Babbage's notes into French, which helped considerably in making his work known around the scientific world.

One hundred and forty-one years later, in 1983, the U.S. Department of Defense adopted a single programming language for all of its computer applications. That language is called Ada, named after the world's first programmer, the Countess of Lovelace.

JAMES RITTY AND NCR

In 1878 James Ritty was an American restaurant owner and not a mathematician, unlike many of the other people we have discussed. During that year he took an ocean voyage to Europe and was captivated by the operation of a gauge that counted the number of revolutions of the propeller. Being interested in simplifying business operations, he decided that a similar device could be constructed that would record the transactions made each day in his business.

Following Ritty's arrival home, he and his brother John constructed a machine with two rows of keys and a large clocklike dial containing two rows of figures showing dollars and cents. This device was the forerunner of the cash register. Sales were recorded by punching holes in a roll of paper with a sharp pin. Ritty's cash register business did poorly and was eventually sold to Jacob H. Eckert for $1,000.

Eckert added a few more features such as the cash drawer and a bell to indicate a sale. But his register did not do much better and the business was sold to John H. Patterson. Patterson had a keen business sense and after calling the company the National Cash Register Company (NCR), sales be-

1842
Ada Lovelace (Courtesy of the Bettmann Archive.)

1842
Mark I computer (Courtesy of IBM Archives.)

1878
Ritty's cash register (Courtesy of NCR Corporation.)

gan to improve. His first factory employed 13 workers and built four or five cash registers a week. Today NCR is one of the largest producers of business machines, data terminals, and computers.

WILLIAM S. BURROUGHS

William Burroughs was born in 1857. His first job was in a bank where the adding and checking of columns of figures was more work and drudgery than he could handle. He soon left the bank and went to St. Louis where he began working in a machine shop.

Soon he became intrigued by the idea that a machine could be built not only to add figures but also record them in a column on paper with a running total so that by pressing a key the total could be printed at any time. He sought the help of Thomas Metcalf and with an initial investment of $700 began to build a machine based on his concepts.

The first machine didn't work properly unless Burroughs himself operated it. It seems that you had to pull a lever at just the right time or else the numbers printed were incorrect and only Burroughs had the right feel for the machine.

In 1886, Burroughs formed the American Arithmometer Company with Metcalf and several other backers. The first machine sold for $475 and gradually the company got off the ground and became a worldwide organization, Burroughs Corporation, well known in the computer field today.

HERMAN HOLLERITH

Herman Hollerith was born in Buffalo in 1860. In 1879 he got a job with the U.S. Census Bureau and by 1880 was deeply into the operation of the census for that year. Five years later, Hollerith and the Bureau were still struggling to compile the results from the 50 million citizens of the country.

1886
William Burroughs (Courtesy of UPI/Bettmann Newsphotos.)

1890
Herman Hollerith (Courtesy of IBM Archives.)

APPENDIX A Origins: A History of Computing and Information Systems

Hollerith saw the possibilities inherent in the problem of census recording and began work on a machine that would compile population and other statistics. One day he was watching a conductor punch tickets with a basic description of each passenger and was inspired to use a similar idea in his machine. To develop the idea further he left the Census Bureau for a job at MIT and then moved to the patent office in 1884.

His early work consisted of a machine using a roll of paper, but by the 1890 census he had devised a punched card that was the forerunner of the standard IBM card which was used for many years by data processors.

Hollerith's method was so successful that the 1890 census was tabulated in less than two months. In 1896 Hollerith formed the Tabulating Machine Company and began selling his equipment to railroads, to audit freight statistics, and insurance companies, where they were used for classifying risks. By 1911 the company had merged with the International Time Recording Company, the Dayton Scale Company, and Bundy Manufacturing to form the Computing-Tabulating-Recording Company (CTR). In 1924 CTR was renamed International Business Machines (IBM), which is today's largest computer company.

THOMAS WATSON AND IBM

Thomas Watson made his start in the business world in 1892 in a butcher shop in Elmira, New York. His job was bookkeeping, which like many of his predecessors he found to be drudgery. He promptly quit and got a job selling pianos, organs, and sewing machines. He found this more challenging and eventually moved to Buffalo, where he took a sales job with NCR.

At this time in NCR's history, other companies were being formed by enterprising individuals to repair used NCR equipment and then resell it, undercutting NCR's profits in the process. John Patterson, NCR's president, picked Thomas Watson, his star salesman, to head up a new organization to fight the competition and let NCR do their own repair. Watson was so good at the job that he soon became the third man from the top in NCR.

1890
Punched cards (Courtesy of IBM Archives.)

1937
Howard Aiken (Courtesy of IBM Archives.)

1914
Thomas Watson (Courtesy of IBM Archives.)

But this proved his undoing. He couldn't get along with the boss and was soon fired by Patterson. Watson soon joined forces with the Computing-Tabulating-Recording Company (CTR) which became IBM. For many years Thomas Watson was the driving force behind the spectacular growth of IBM, to be followed by his son Thomas Watson Jr.

PRESPER ECKERT, JOHN MAUCHLY, AND ENIAC

ENIAC is an acronym for Electronic Numerical Integrator and Computer. Developed by Mauchly and Eckert at the Moore School of Electrical Engineering at the University of Pennsylvania in the early 1940s, it was the first electronic general-purpose computer and consisted of 18,000 vacuum tubes. The tubes were so unreliable that maintenance men had to run around with spares and replace burnt out tubes while the computer operated. ENIAC could do 300 multiplications per second and was a great improvement over manual methods of calculation.

Eckert and Mauchly founded their own company in 1946 and developed a new computer that was to become known as UNIVAC I. At that time IBM was a fledgling accounting machine company and had not yet moved into the computer business. Beginning in 1951, UNIVAC I was successful in replacing some of IBM's punched card equipment at the census bureau and so IBM moved quickly to get into the computer business by releasing the 650 computer in 1954. Later UNIVAC was to merge with Sperry Corporation to become Sperry-Univac. In 1986, Burroughs Corporation and Sperry Corporation merged to form Unisys Corporation.

JOHN VON NEUMANN AND EDVAC

Further computer developments at the Moore School led to the Electronic Discrete Variable Automatic Computer or EDVAC. It was designed with

1941
John Mauchly (left) and Presper Eckert (Courtesy of Sperry Corporation.)

1946
ENIAC (Courtesy of Sperry Corporation.)

1946
UNIVAC (Courtesy of Sperry Corporation.)

APPENDIX A Origins: A History of Computing and Information Systems

1949
John von Neumann next to EDVAC
(Courtesy of IBM Archives.)

improved techniques over the ENIAC and only required 5,900 vacuum tubes. EDVAC also used the first solid state devices known in computer design; 12,000 diodes. EDVAC was completed in 1949 and was considerably faster than ENIAC and could add two numbers in 864 millionths of a second.

Mauchly and Eckert worked on the EDVAC but John von Neumann, from Budapest, Hungary would also become involved. von Neumann came to the Moore School as a consultant in 1944. He often conferred with Mauchly and Eckert on the design of the EDVAC computer and has frequently been named as the inventor of the stored program concept used in virtually all computers today. However, recent data suggests that the stored program concept was discussed prior to von Neumann's appearance at the Moore School and did not originate with him.[1]

COMPUTER GENERATIONS

First Generation (1951–1959)

The computers produced during the 1950s were to be known as **first-generation** computers. They were built with vacuum tube circuits and were usually used for scientific or mathematical applications. Programming these computers, by wiring the circuits, was a time-consuming task and required great skill and expertise. The physical computer was called the **hardware** and the programs that gave it its instructions were the **software**.

Data and programs were entered into the computer using punched cards, which were slow compared to tape and disk that were to follow in later generations. The computer's memory was often a magnetic drum and had slow access time because of the need to wait for the drum to revolve to the address the computer needed. Very few people had the training or skills to use first-generation computers, and so their use was not widespread.

---
[1] Joel Shurkin. *Engines of the Mind—A History of the Computer*. W. W. Norton & Company, 1984.

IBM 704 (Courtesy IBM Corporation.)

Second Generation (1960–1964)

In 1960, IBM announced a **second generation** of computers using solid state transistors instead of the vacuum tube. These computers were faster and more compact than the first generation. One of these computers was the IBM 1401, which became popular as a business computer. Other competing companies such as NCR, Sperry UNIVAC, Honeywell, and Burroughs also produced second-generation computers.

Both magnetic tape and disk began to be used as secondary storage for faster and easier storage of data and programs. Today's personal computers have disk drives that are faster and have greater capacity than disks used on second-generation mainframe computers.

A parallel development was the higher-level language, such as FORTRAN and COBOL. Symbolic and assembly languages were still the most popular and were easier to use than machine language. However, they still required a high level of training and competence to use. Second-generation computers were the first used largely by business and applications such as accounting, payroll, and corporate finance were gradually moved to the computer.

Third Generation (1964–1970)

By 1964, a **third generation** of computers was ushered in when IBM announced their System/360 series of computers. These led to the System/370 family in the 1970s, followed by the 4300 and 3000 series. These computers were characterized by increased use of miniaturization in their circuitry and **integrated chips** (ICs) became the new buzzword. Offering a family of

APPENDIX A Origins: A History of Computing and Information Systems　　　　　415

IBM 1401 (Courtesy IBM Corporation.)

computers provided the customer with upward compatibility. Programs written for one model of computer in the family would run on all other models without the need for change. By adopting such a computer, the user could begin with a lower level, and less costly, computer and then, as their need for increased computer power grew, a larger, faster computer from the same family could be installed.

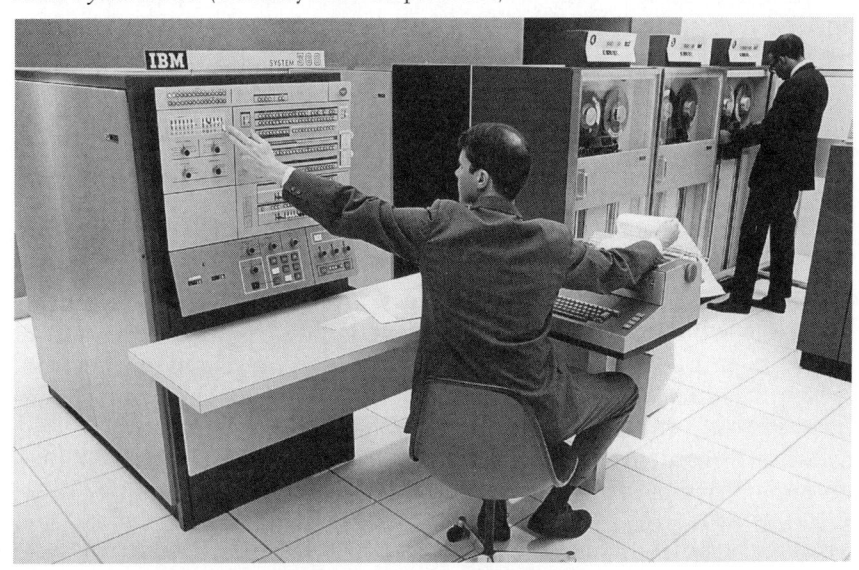

IBM System/360 (Courtesy IBM Corporation.)

High-level languages like BASIC and RPG (Report Program Generator) were developed and adopted for many needs because they improved the programmer's productivity. Third-generation computers are still in use today and most medium- to large-scale businesses make use of these computers for an extensive range of applications.

All of these computers were called **mainframe** systems, intended for centralized use and required computer professionals for their implementation and operation. The user rarely had direct access to the computer until the late 1970s, when remote terminals began to be used interactively at the user's site. The mainframe computer was located centrally and data was either transported physically or by electronic means to the computer for processing. Results were then delivered back to the user with resulting delays of days or even weeks.

During the third-generation time period, many smaller computers were developed by companies such as Digital Equipment Corporation (DEC) and Data General. These **minicomputers**, such as the DEC PDP-8 and PDP-11, were intended for the smaller company who could neither afford the larger mainframe nor had the need for a larger system.

COMPUTER LANGUAGES AND SOFTWARE

Computers are instructed in their operation by a program that is written using a specific programming language such as BASIC or COBOL. Languages for programming the computer have a history that is separate yet parallel to the development of the hardware. Early computers, like the Mark I, were wired to perform specific operations. If new operations were required, the computer would be rewired to the new specifications.

The next computer, UNIVAC I, could store its program in a memory device, thus UNIVAC used the first stored program and was the forerunner of today's computers which load their programs from a magnetic disk. Changing UNIVAC's program was as easy as reading the new requirements (the program) into the store or memory and the computer was then ready to solve a new problem.

Four computer generations are outlined here, showing the characteristic features of each generation.

First-Generation Computers

The first computer generation had a memory, usually a magnetic drum or magnetic core in which the program was stored. The program consisted of binary numbers in the form of 0's and 1's which represented the instructions. These programs were written in machine language. The symbolic instructions were only for the programmer to read, not the computer. The programs were difficult to write, and even more difficult to read. If they contained bugs (errors), which was inevitable, it was extremely difficult to find and correct the error.

Machine Language

Symbolic Language	Machine Language	Description
A A1,B3	011101011010	Add
M Z2,Z3	110100101011	Move
B START	10101001	Branch

Second-Generation Computers

As faster computers with greater capacity became available, the demand for computer languages that were easier to use and to debug also grew in demand. This demand resulted in true symbolic languages being developed where the programmer wrote the program code in the symbolic language and the computer translated it into machine code. Thus, the programmer did not need to understand the machine's language but just the symbolic language. Although this language was certainly easier, it was still no simple task to create a sophisticated program.

Languages such as FORTRAN and COBOL came on the scene at this time but did not come into widespread use until third-generation computers were available.

Symbolic Languages

Assembly Language	Description
A AMT,TOTAL	Add instruction
MVC NAME,PRINTA	Move instruction
B AGAIN	Branch

FORTRAN - 1954

```
    READ(5,110) XLEN,WID
    AREA=XLEN*WID
    WRITE(6,220) AREA
    STOP
110 FORMAT(2F5.1)
220 FORMAT(1X,I5)
    END
```

Third-Generation Computers

As computer languages became easier to use, they also required more of the computer's resources. So the next major development in languages had to wait for the increased power and lower cost of the third generation of computers. Although languages such as FORTRAN and COBOL had been around since second generation, most computers lacked the power to use them efficiently. Now faster computers with more memory opened new doors for computer applications in engineering, the sciences, business, and education. Other languages including PL/1, RPG, and Pascal were only the leading edge of many new programming languages introduced with third-generation computers.

High-Level Languages

COBOL - 1959

```
PROCEDURE DIVISION.
TOTAL-ROUTINE.
     ADD AMOUNT TO TOTAL.
     MOVE NAME TO PRINT-AREA.
     WRITE PRINT-LINE
          AFTER ADVANCING 1 LINE.
```

BASIC - 1964

```
100 T1 = T1 + A
110 PRINT A, T1, N$
120 GO TO 100
```

Computers and Fourth Generation

While the distinction between the first three generations of computers and their technology was clear, the fourth generation did not have as clear a definition. Certainly the personal computer was an important component of computer development. Perhaps the PC was the single new development that affected the most people.

But other developments in large-scale and supercomputers also had an impact on software development. The evolution of **fourth generation languages** such as Intellect and Focus was a significant step forward in the growth of user-oriented languages. On the personal computer the term **user-friendly** described the type of software that was coming to be expected by the user.

User Friendly Languages

Mainframe Language

```
INTELLECT
PRINT THE COMPANY NAME, 1989 SALES,
     1989 INCOME, SORTED BY COMPANY NAME.
```

PC Language

```
dBASE IV
SORT ON COMPANY_NAME TO NAME
DISPLAY ALL COMPANY_NAME, SALES_89, INCOME_89
```

THE FIRST PERSONAL COMPUTERS

In 1972, INTEL Corporation announced a new integrated chip called the 8000 series microprocessor. These small integrated circuits could do everything a large computer could do provided they were connected to a power

An integrated circuit chip contains as many as 1 million circuits engraved in less than a square inch (6.54 cm^2). ICs made possible the personal computer by offering computer power in a small space with low power requirements and at an affordable price. (Courtesy of Motorola, Inc.)

supply, keyboard, and display screen. One of these makeshift microcomputers was advertised in Popular Electronics magazine in 1975 and sold either as a kit (for $395) or completely assembled ($695). Few people saw the vision at that time and few of these computers were sold.

The Birth of Apple and the IBM PC

Soon after the INTEL computer was announced, two friends, Steve Jobs and Stephen Wozniak, decided to build their own microcomputer as a result of enthusiasm developed by their membership in the Homebrew Computer Club in the San Francisco Bay area. They built a small computer and demonstrated it to their friends at the club. Encouraged by the positive response, they decided to form a company and sold Job's Volkswagen, Wozniak's calculator, and borrowed $5,000 from a friend to get started. The first microcomputer, called the Apple I, cost $666.66. The term personal computer was to come into popular use a few years later. In 1977 they improved the microcomputer and produced the Apple II, which became a runaway bestseller. From 1977 to 1981, sales rocketed to over $300 million and Apple became the fastest growing company in America. Again two dreamers made computer history, but this time it was a personal computer that could be used by virtually anyone. Parallel developments came from Commodore and Radio Shack. The **personal computer** came to be understood as a computer that could be used by one person.

Not to be kept out of the picture, IBM developed the IBM Personal Computer (PC) which was released in 1981 and quickly became the standard for personal computing. Until IBM produced the PC, the microcomputer was not taken very seriously by computer professionals or by business. But once the leader of the computer industry took the plunge, the computer became a serious business tool and there has been no looking back.

The Apple II was the first runaway best-seller in the microcomputer market. Although other computers were previously available, including an Apple I, Steven Jobs' and Stephen Wozniak's Apple II opened the door to the micro market, and many other manufacturers soon flooded it with their own offerings. (Courtesy Apple Computer, Inc.)

Parallel developments in software made these computers easy to use. They required a minimum of training, whether used for business or personal applications from spreadsheets to financial planning, or accounting to computer graphics.

APPENDIX B
CHECKLIST FOR BUYING A COMPUTER

Buying a computer can at best be an exciting experience and at worst an intimidating one. Having come this far in the book, you should not be intimidated by the complexities of buying a computer, but rather be confident that your knowledge base is more than adequate to make informed choices. However, in this appendix we will attempt to focus on some of the crucial issues you may want to consider when buying a computer for your personal use. After reading the following material, fill out the chart at the end of the appendix and you will be ready to take the next step: buying your own computer system.

GETTING STARTED

To begin the process you might want to clip some advertisements from a local newspaper. This will give you some ideas about prices and features so you will be able to compare a variety of systems and components and to focus on the price range that fits your budget. Next, visit several stores to see some computers in action. If possible, try to see the same software run on each computer so you can compare display quality, speed, use of the keyboard and mouse, and the general aesthetics of the system.

BASIC CHOICES

You might want to make a general decision early on whether you are in the market for an IBM PC-compatible or an Apple Macintosh type of computer. The PC-compatible computers represent about 75 percent of the market while the Macintosh is about 10 percent. Although the Mac is considered easier to use, a PC with Windows offers a similar user-friendly approach. Although the Mac offers most mainstream software applications, there are many more choices of software available for the PC. However, you might find that the Mac has the look and feel that is comfortable for you and would best satisfy your needs. In business, an important consideration when selecting a computer is compatibility between other computers in the office. What others are using may strongly suggest that you should make a similar choice so that you can share data between computers. The following section describes some specific items you should consider when buying a computer.

SELECTING HARDWARE

When you are buying a computer you are really buying a computer system which consists of a number of components. How you select these components will have a total effect on how the system functions. Having 16 megabytes of RAM but a hard disk of only 40 MB does not usually result in an effective computer or a wise expenditure of your finances. Choosing

Tower case. *This mid-sized tower case for the PC is a good choice when you expect to add additional features to the computer.* (Courtesy Dell Computer Corp.)

capacity, speed, and quality are related to how you intend to use the computer and the software you will run on it. Many stores offer packaged systems which have matched components that create an effective system. Once you know the level of computer you need, buying a packaged system can be an effective choice.

System Unit

The system unit contains the processor, memory, display adaptor, and usually a hard disk and floppy disk drive. It may also contain other items such as a CD-ROM drive and built-in modem. We will consider each of these items separately in the sections that follow. One choice you will have at the system unit level is the case that contains the components. Do you want a desktop unit or a tower? If your desk space is at a premium, the tower may be a preferred choice because it can sit on the floor. Towers generally come in three sizes; mini, mid-size, and full-size. The larger the tower, the more room there is for optional features. If you expect to add a lot of features to your computer, then look at the mid- or full-size tower.

The Central Processor

Choosing a processor means selecting a 386, 486, or higher when using a PC or the 68020 or higher for the Macintosh. Within each family of processor are a variety of speeds. Thus the 386 can be found with 25 MHz, 33Mhz, or 40 MHz speeds. A 486 25MHz processor runs about twice as fast as the 386 25Mhz because of design differences. The more processing your applications will be doing, the higher the speed you will need for effective results. If you are using basic DOS-oriented word processing or spreadsheets, the lower end computer will work effectively for most applications. If you are running Windows and Windows application software, a higher speed computer will be necessary for efficient performance.

Memory

A basic 386 PC with a minimum of 4MB is becoming a popular configuration. This includes 640K of main memory and the remainder as extended memory. Many DOS programs cannot take advantage of the extra memory unless a memory manager is used, so expanding memory beyond this amount makes little sense. Windows users can take advantage of the expanded memory. Up to a limit (about 8MB), the more memory you have the more efficiently Windows and Windows applications will run.

Display

The display you choose must work with a display adaptor that is installed in an expansion slot in your computer. The minimum acceptable level of resolution today is the VGA screen and many new systems come with Super-VGA as the entry level. Either of these are suitable for DOS applications and Super-VGA is quite effective for most Windows applications. A 14″ screen is usually the minimum size, although some Macintosh models use 12″ screens effectively. If you are considering working extensively with graphics or desktop publishing, then a higher resolution such as 1024x768 or higher and a screen size larger than 14″ might be considered.

Video card. This video adaptor card is installed in an expansion slot to match the display screen characteristics to the computer. (Courtesy Plus Development Corp.)

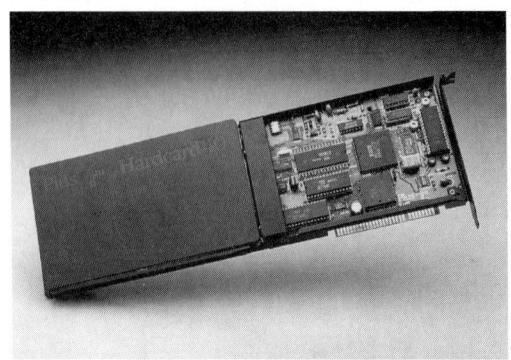

APPENDIX B Checklist for Buying a Computer

Display screen. *Choosing a high-quality display such as this SuperVGA screen will provide the greatest flexibility for use in graphics and text oriented applications.*

Color or Monochrome. Unless you are doing applications that are essentially black and white, such as desktop publishing or CAD/CAM, then color is probably the best choice you can make. When a wide variety of applications, such as word processing, graphics, spreadsheets, and presentation software are used, color is essential. Would you buy a black and white television today? The same consideration applies to a computer monitor. For specialized uses (CAD/CAM), a devoted computer with a black and

Specialized computer uses such as CAD/CAM may benefit from a high-resolution black and white screen. (Courtesy IBM Corporation.)

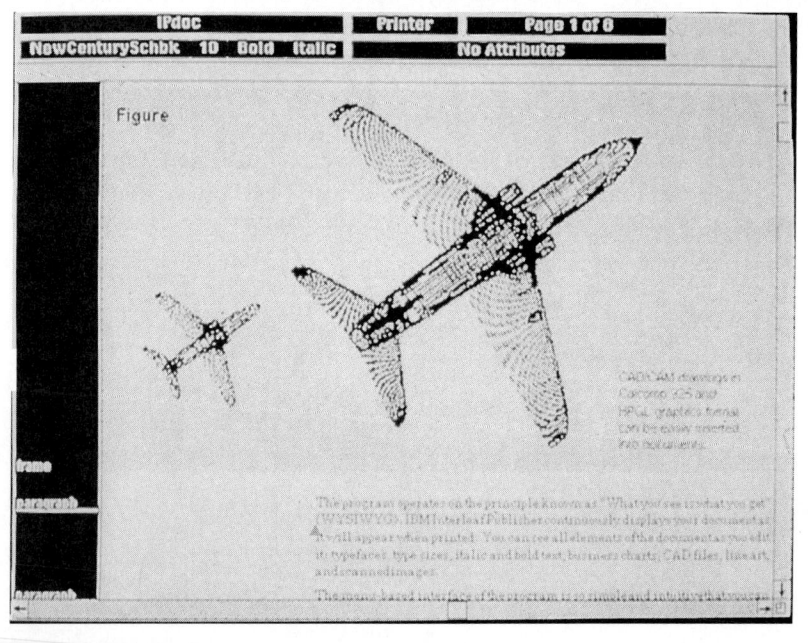

white monochrome screen would be a good choice if it is not used for other applications.

Screen Ergonomics. Before selecting a display, compare the display on several different models. A screen with a lower dot pitch will create a clearer image on the screen that is easier on the eyes. Try out the brightness and color controls to see if they have an acceptable range for your use. Some people need a wider range of brightness than others and only you can decide whether a screen offers a suitable range. Also look for flicker in the display, and don't accept a screen that has an obvious flicker. Look at the edges of the screen to ensure that characters and images retain their proper shape.

Another ergonomic consideration is the ability to position the screen. Tilt and swivel features can ease the stress of working on the computer if you spend long hours in front of the screen. Some screens have a swivel arm (which can also be purchased as an option) which allows movement of the screen closer or farther away from your eyes. For those with vision problems this feature may be an essential.

Keyboards

Often a computer system comes with a standard keyboard unless you ask about the alternatives. Most keyboards use the QWERTY layout and have function keys at the top with cursor and other keys in pads to the right of the main keyboard. This layout is known as the extended keyboard. Notebook and other small computers may use a different layout due to size restrictions. When optional keyboards are available, the primary difference is usually in the tactile feedback you get from the keys. You need to try typing on a few keyboards to feel the difference. If your work requires large volumes of typing, then a good quality keyboard is worth the minor additional cost.

The keyboard should have a built-in tilt feature so that it can be adjusted to your finger position. Adequate space above the function keys should be

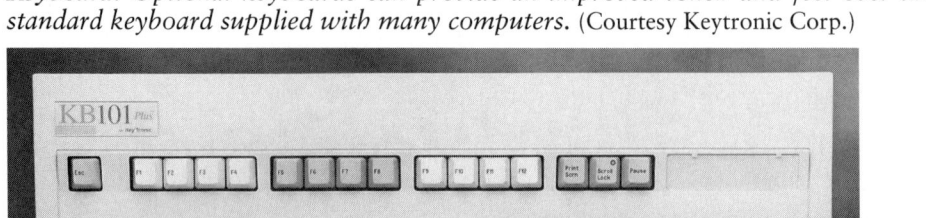

Keyboard. Optional keyboards can provide an improved touch and feel over the standard keyboard supplied with many computers. (Courtesy Keytronic Corp.)

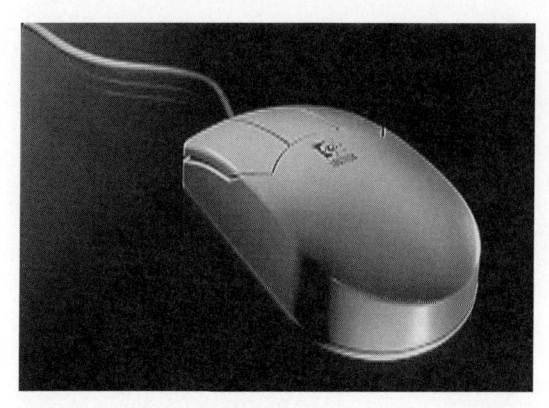

Mouse. Users of Windows, OS/2, and many application software packages can benefit from the use of a mouse. (Courtesy Logitech Inc.)

provided so that a template can be placed here for reference when working with software that uses function keys. The cord should be long enough so that it will reach from the port in the back of the computer to your desk; otherwise an extension may be required.

Mouse

Many computers today are being sold with a mouse as part of the package. If you intend to work with Windows, graphics, or desktop publishing then a mouse is a must. Many other software packages now provide mouse support and using the mouse can greatly increase your efficiency. Avoid inexpensive mouse imitators unless you will rarely use the mouse. Both right- and left-handed mice are available. Many software packages also provide a method to switch buttons for left handed users. A mouse pad is also a useful feature, especially when the desk surface makes mouse movement imprecise.

Disk Drives

Your computer will require at least two disk drives: a hard disk and a floppy disk drive. The hard disk will be used for storing data and software while the floppy is used for installing new software, backing up data from the hard disk, and transporting data from one computer to another.

Hard Disk. Consider that many software packages require 5MB or more of hard disk storage space, some considerably more. As a result many computer packages are now suggesting disk storage of 80MB or more as a minimum. Windows users with a variety of Windows software might start as high as 200MB. It is generally less expensive to start with disk storage capacity higher than you need than it is to upgrade to a higher capacity disk later on. Hard disk drives come with different speed ratings with the lower number, such as 15 ms, being the faster drive.

Floppy Disk. The $3\frac{1}{2}$" high density floppy disk drive is the standard today, with the $5\frac{1}{4}$" being the less common choice. If you will be trading

Hard disk drive. *Every computer requires a hard disk drive to store programs and data. The storage capacity should be chosen based on the software you expect to use.* (Courtesy Seagate.)

data with other users and they have the 5¼" drive, then you might consider installing both sizes of disk drives.

Printers

Eventually you will want to print out the results of your work. You have dot matrix, ink jet, and laser printers to choose from. Clearly your budget will be a major factor in deciding what printer to choose. An important consideration is what you will do with the printed output. If it is mainly for school reports, then an inexpensive dot matrix will be fine. If you are a budding entrepreneur, then a higher quality printer may be needed for those important documents that you will be creating for your clients. Within your budget constraints consider the speed, print quality, and potential service available for the printer. Because the printer is largely a mechanical device, it is more subject to breakdown than other computer components.

Other Devices

We have covered most of the components that a first-time computer buyer usually requires on the computer. But there are plenty of other devices that

Floppy disks. *Most new computer users will use the smaller 3½" disks for data storage and backup. For greater flexibility the 5¼" disk may also be useful.* (Courtesy BASF Corp. Information Systems.)

APPENDIX B Checklist for Buying a Computer 429

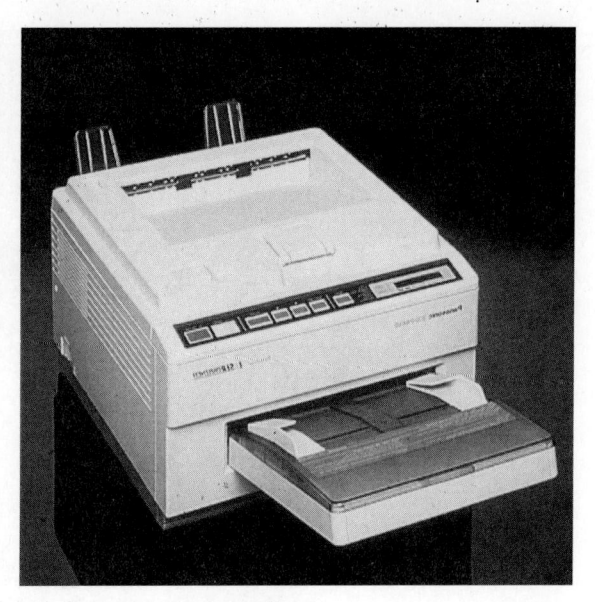

Dot matrix and laser printers are at the opposite ends of the price and quality spectrum. (Courtesy Panasonic Communications & Systems Company and Epson America, Inc.)

may be essentials for some users. First is the modem. If you plan to connect to a bulletin board or other communication service then a modem will be an essential. Choose one that will at least operate at 2400 bps and is Hayes compatible. An internal Fax-modem may be an alternative to the modem if you will be sending and receiving faxes.

Another device is a scanner. If you work with desktop publishing and need to convert images on paper to a computer graphic a scanner will do the job. Look for resolution and speed when making a selection. Lastly, a CD-ROM drive is becoming a useful tool for computer users that need access to large amounts of information. Again, speed is an important factor for effective use of the CD. Many drives now have multimedia capability and can be used for text, pictures, videos, and sound.

Modem. *A modem is a must for users who access bulletin boards or communication services.* (Courtesy Hayes Microcomputer.)

CD-ROM. *A CD-ROM drive is an affordable option that makes available large amounts of information directly on your computer.* (Courtesy Toshiba America Information Systems, Inc.)

SERVICE AND SUPPORT

Choosing a computer dealer can be as important as choosing a computer. Buying at the absolutely lowest price is not always the best choice, although price alone does not guarantee good support. Look for a dealer who has been in business for a few years. Chances are the company will still be

Dealer support. *The dealer you choose should provide both products and service.* (Courtesy Superstock.)

around a few years from now when you need service. Recommendations from others who have had good experiences with a computer dealer can provide helpful input. Check out the warranty before you buy. Does it cover parts and labor for a reasonable time period? You may also be able to purchase a maintenance contract that extends beyond the warranty period. If your business depends on your computer, you might want to buy from a dealer who will provide a loaner in the event that your computer is in for extended service.

SOFTWARE

Computer software is perhaps more personal a choice than hardware. Because there are literally thousands of programs available, you will never run out of options where software is concerned. Most computers come with an operating system installed. The PC usually has MS-DOS and many packages now provide Windows. For application software, you might want to begin with the basics: word processing, and a spreadsheet. Later you can add other programs as your needs grow. Beware, three or four software packages can cost as much or more than the hardware.

By going to a computer or software store, you may be able to see the software in action before you buy it. Ask for a demonstration and if possible try your hand at using the program. Be aware that many programs require an extensive learning period before you become skilled at its use, so don't be too quick to write off a package that doesn't seem to work as you expect. When you purchase the program, send in the registration card so that you will be on the publisher's mailing list for updates when revisions are available.

Computer Buyer's Checklist

Hardware	My Choice	Quotation A	Quotation B
CPU processor (386, 486, 68020, etc.) speed (25, 33, 40 MHz etc.)			
Desktop or tower case			
RAM (2, 4, 8 MB, etc.)			
Display (VGA, SuperVGA, 14″, color, monochrome, etc.)			
Video adaptor board			
Keyboard			
Mouse			
Hard disk drive, capacity (80, 105, 170MB etc.), speed (15ms)			
Floppy disk drive 3½″			
Floppy disk drive 5¼″			
Printer (dot matrix, ink jet, laser)			
Modem			
Fax/modem			
CD-ROM			
Scanner			
Software			
Operating System (MS-DOS, OS/2)			
Windows			
Word Processor			
Spreadsheet			
Database			
Communications			
Desktop Publishing			
Graphics			
Programming Language			
Total Price			

APPENDIX C

NUMBER SYSTEMS

All computers use numbers for their operation and certainly we depend on the computer to provide information in the form of numbers after processing is complete. While we are accustomed to using decimal numbers, and that is how the computer normally displays or prints them, internally things are different.

In RAM, a computer represents data in the form of bits which is based on the binary number system. **Binary numbers** consist of the digits 0 and 1, unlike decimal numbers which consist of digits 0 to 9. Binary is called a base two number system because it uses only two digits while decimal is base ten. Most humans use base ten numbering, which was developed in Egypt as far back as 3400 B.C., but there have been times and places when other systems were in use. The Papuan language tribes of the Torres Strait of Australia and parts of New Guinea use a base two number system. Some tribes in the Terra del Fuego used base 3 and 4 number systems and a South American language called Saraveca used a base 5 system.

Table C-1 shows a comparison of decimal numbers with equivalent values in binary, octal, and hexadecimal. Because hexadecimal numbers must count up to 15 the letters A to F are used to represent digit values 10 to 15. Base eight (octal) and base 16 (hexadecimal) have been widely used in computers over the years. Today binary and hexadecimal are the most common way of interpreting numbers in computer memory.

TABLE C-1 Comparison of Different Number Systems.

Decimal	Binary	Octal	Hexadecimal
0	0	0	0
1	1	1	1
2	10	2	2
3	11	3	3
4	100	4	4
5	101	5	5
6	110	6	6
7	111	7	7
8	1000	10	8
9	1001	11	9
10	1010	12	A
11	1011	13	B
12	1100	14	C
13	1101	15	D
14	1110	16	E
15	1111	17	F
16	10000	20	10

DECIMAL NUMBERS

0 1 2 3 4 5 6 7 8 9

Decimal or base ten numbers are those most commonly used in today's world for counting. Each of the ten digits in the number system has a specific value, but, when two or more digits are used in the number, then the value of the digit depends on its position in the number. We call this the place value.

For example, the number 545 may be understood as follows.

5	4	5
↑	↑	↑
5 Hundreds	4 Tens	5 Units
5×100 +	4×10 +	5×1

The 5 in the units position represents the digit value of 5. The 4 in the tens position represents the value 4 times 10 or 40, while the 5 in the hundreds position is 5 times 100, or 500. Although its digit value is still 5 its positional value is different than the 5 in the units position.

Counting to 16 in Decimal	*Powers of 10*
1	$10^0 = 1$
2	$10^1 = 10$
3	$10^2 = 100$
4	$10^3 = 1,000$
5	$10^4 = 10,000$
6	
7	
8	
9	
10	
11	
12	
13	
14	
15	
16	

All this may seem elementary and is intuitive to most of us. But the principle becomes important when we want to understand other number systems that we don't use every day.

The number 545 has a position notation that is used to represent all decimal numbers. The position notation is given as follows.

$$5 \times 10^2 + 4 \times 10^1 + 5 \times 10^0$$

The tens used in this expression are called the base. The values 0, 1, and 2 are the exponents or powers of ten. If we multiply these values and add each result we get the following.

$$5 \times 100 + 4 \times 10 + 5 \times 1 =$$
$$500 + 40 + 5 = 545$$

The sum of this expression gives 545 which is the original number.

Numbers used by computers are often referred to by their high order or low order digit. In a number such as 7034, the digit 7 is the high order, sometimes called the most significant digit, and 4 is the low order, or least significant digit.

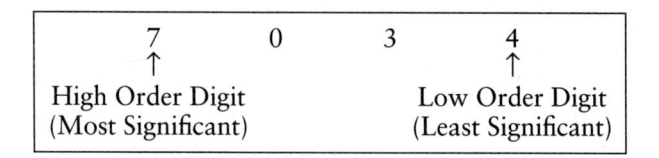

```
    7        0        3        4
    ↑                          ↑
High Order Digit        Low Order Digit
(Most Significant)      (Least Significant)
```

BINARY NUMBERS

$$0 \quad 1$$

Early in the development of computer technology it was discovered that binary numbers were better suited to computer usage because of the two state nature of electronic devices. Two states mean that only two values, on-off, true-false, or 0 and 1, may be represented.

Counting to 16 in Binary	Powers of 2
0	$2^0 = 1$
1	$2^1 = 2$
10	$2^2 = 4$
11	$2^3 = 8$
100	$2^4 = 16$
101	
110	
111	
1000	
1001	
1010	
1011	
1100	
1101	
1110	
1111	
10000	

A binary number such as 1101 may be understood by applying the rules of positional notation as used in the decimal number system. Instead of using the base of ten we use a base two which gives the following expression for the number 1101.

$$1 \times 2^3 + 1 \times 2^2 + 0 \times 2^1 + 1 \times 2^0$$

Simplifying the expression by first applying the powers of two and then calculating the values gives the following result.

$$1 \times 8 + 1 \times 4 + 0 \times 2 + 1 \times 1 =$$
$$8 + 4 + 0 + 1 = 13$$

In effect, by calculating the expression using the positional notation we have converted the binary number to decimal which is easier to understand.

APPENDIX C Number Systems

Another method for converting a binary number to its decimal equivalent is to sum the positional values. Using the following chart simplifies this method for finding the decimal value of 1101011.

| 64 | 32 | 16 | 8 | 4 | 2 | 1 | Positional values |
| 1 | 1 | 0 | 1 | 0 | 1 | 1 | Binary number |

To convert to decimal, simply add the positional values as follows.

$$64 + 32 + 8 + 2 + 1 = 107$$

HEXADECIMAL NUMBERS

0 1 2 3 4 5 6 7 8 9 A B C D E F

Although computers are designed based on the binary principle, we sometimes find it easier to work with other representations. One, of course, is decimal, but programmers often use hexadecimal because of the way memory and addressing is organized. Writing program code in an assembly language often requires the use of hexadecimal.

Hexadecimal is base sixteen meaning that each digit position has a positional value of 16. With sixteen digits it is necessary to use letters A to F to represent the digits 10 through 15 (see insert).

To understand how hexadecimal works let's take the number 1A5. To change this number to decimal write it using the positional notation method used for both decimal and binary but this time use the exponent 16 as follows.

$$1 \times 16^2 + 10 \times 16^1 + 5 \times 16^0$$

Notice that the letter A in the hexadecimal number is entered as 10 in the positional notation. Expanding this expression gives the following result.

$$1 \times 256 + 10 \times 16 + 5 \times 1 =$$
$$256 + 160 + 5 = 421$$

The number 421 is decimal equivalent to the hexadecimal number 1A5.

Counting to 16 in Hexadecimal	Powers of 16
1	$16^0 = 1$
2	$16^1 = 16$
3	$16^2 = 256$
4	$16^3 = 4,096$
5	$16^4 = 65,536$
6	
7	
8	
9	
A	
B	
C	
D	
E	
F	
10	

CONVERTING BETWEEN BINARY AND HEXADECIMAL

Converting between binary and hexadecimal is an easy process because four binary digits are equal to one hexadecimal digit. The reverse is also true. One hexadecimal digit converts to four binary digits. For example, the binary number 1011 can be converted as follows.

8	4	2	1	Positional value
1	0	1	1	Binary digits
		B		Hexadecimal value

We arrive at the hexadecimal value of B because the binary number 1011 is equivalent to 8 + 2 + 1 which is 11 in decimal. And 11 in decimal is expressed as B in hexadecimal.

A second example converts the hexadecimal number 1A5 to binary. Each hexadecimal digit converts to a group of four binary digits.

1	A	5	Hexadecimal digits
0 0 0 1	1 0 1 0	0 1 0 1	Binary digits
8 4 2 1	8 4 2 1	8 4 2 1	Positional values

The binary equivalent of 1A5 is 000110100101 or if we delete the leading zeros the number is 110100101. By using the groups of four binary digits for each hexadecimal digit the conversion is easily done.

CONVERTING DECIMAL TO OTHER BASES

Decimal numbers may be converted to binary or hexadecimal and other bases by the method of successive division. This is done by dividing the dec-

APPENDIX C Number Systems

imal number by the base of the number system to which you want to convert. To convert to binary divide by 2. To convert to hexadecimal divide by 16. Next record the remainder of this step. The quotient is then divided again and the remainder recorded. This process is repeated until a quotient of zero is reached.

For example, to convert the decimal value 13 to binary 1101 the following steps are taken.

$$
\begin{array}{r}
6 \\
2\overline{)13} \\
12 \\
1
\end{array}
$$

$$
\begin{array}{r}
3 \\
2\overline{)6} \\
6 \\
0
\end{array}
$$

$$
\begin{array}{r}
1 \\
2\overline{)3} \\
2 \\
1
\end{array}
$$

$$
\begin{array}{r}
0 \\
2\overline{)1} \\
0 \\
1
\end{array}
$$

$$1\ \ 1\ \ 0\ \ 1$$

To convert decimal 2620 to hexadecimal A3C the following steps are taken. Remainders between 10 and 15 are substituted with the letters A to F.

$$
\begin{array}{r}
163 \\
16\overline{)2620} \\
16 \\
102 \\
96 \\
60 \\
48 \\
12
\end{array}
$$

$$
\begin{array}{r}
10 \\
16\overline{)163} \\
16 \\
03 \\
0 \\
3
\end{array}
$$

$$
\begin{array}{r}
0 \\
16\overline{)10} \\
0 \\
10
\end{array}
$$

$$A\ \ 3\ \ C$$

GLOSSARY

Absolute addressing. Address formulas in a spreadsheet that do not adjust row and column references as the formula is copied or moved.

Access arm. The arm on which the disk's read/write head is mounted.

Access time. The time taken to access a record from disk. It includes the time to position the read/write head to the track or sector and to rotate the disk to the required record.

Accounts payable. A system or program that keeps track of the debts owed to a company by its suppliers.

Accounts receivable. A system or program that keeps track of the dollar amount that the company has credited the customer.

Acoustic coupler. A modem that attaches to a telephone by placing the handset onto rubber cups in the coupler.

Address bus. The path that carries memory addresses to all devices connected to the data bus.

ALU. See Arithmetic and Logic Unit.

American Standard Code for Information Interchange (ASCII). A 7-bit coding system used for representing characters in the computer.

Append. The process of adding a record to the end of a file or database.

Applications software. Software that is designed to perform a specific function such as accounting or inventory control.

Arithmetic and Logic Unit. The part of the processor that performs arithmetic and decision making in the computer.

ASCII. See American Standard Code for Information Interchange.

Assembler. A translation program that converts assembly language programs into machine language.

Assembly language. A second generation language that uses symbolic program code.

Asynchronous transmission. A mode of data transmission that uses start and stop bits to identify the beginning and ending of the data.

Auto-answer. Automatic answering by a modem of a call from another modem.

Auto-dial. Automatic calling from a modem to another modem.

Automatic recalculation. A process where formula values are computed after a change has been made to a spreadsheet.

Backup. A procedure for maintaining copies of crucial files on tape or disk in the event of a loss or failure of the primary file.

BASIC. A high-level programming language that is standard on most personal computers.

Basic Input Output System (BIOS). A program stored in ROM that assists in the process of starting up the computer and doing basic input/output operations.

Batch. A method where data is collected over a period of time and processed as a group.

Batch file. A disk file containing a series of DOS commands.

Binary. A two-state number system based on the values zero and one.

BIOS. See Basic Input Output System.

Bit. The smallest element or value represented in the computer. Derived from binary digit.

Bitmapped graphics. Graphics that are composed of a series of pixels that form an image.

Bit mapping. A method of displaying information on a screen by controlling individual pixels.

Bit rate. The rate at which data is transmitted on a communications line. Transmission speed is measured in bits per second.

Block. A group of text ranging from one or more characters or words to sentences, lines, or paragraphs that may be moved, copied, or deleted in a word processor.

Boilerplate. Commonly used text such as phrases or paragraphs.

Booting. The process of starting up the computer and loading the operating system.

Bus. An electronic circuit that sends data and messages between the various components of the computer system.

Business system. A set of procedures designed for the purpose of collecting and analyzing business information.

Byte. The basic unit of data in the computer. A byte is used to represent a character, digit, or symbol and is usually composed of eight bits.

CAD. See Computer-Aided Design.

C language. A high-level programming language developed by Bell Laboratories with assembly language efficiency.

CAM. See Computer-Aided Manufacturing.

CD-ROM. A form of compact disk that contains computer readable data. Storage capacity typically exceeds one billion bytes.

Cell. An element of a spreadsheet at the intersection of a row and column that contains a value, label, or formula.

Central processing unit (CPU). An electronic device made of one or more silicon chips consisting of memory, ALU, and control unit sections operating under the direction of the program.

Client/server. A technology that offers a common interface for PC and mainframe users so that much of the sign-on and operating procedures become transparent. Often a graphical user interface is provided.

Clock speed. A speed measured in megahertz (MHz) that identifies the speed at which the processor carries out its operations.

COBOL. A high-level computer language used mainly for developing business applications on mainframe computers.

Coding. The process of writing a computer program.

Cold Start. The process of booting the computer by turning on the power.

Command-driven. Programs that require the user to type each command. PC-DOS is one of the most common command-driven programs.

Communication medium. A line that links computers together for the purpose of data communication.

Compiler. A program that translates a source language program and creates a machine language program called an object program.

Compression. A disk utility program that takes the data on a disk and compresses it so it requires only half or less of its original space.

Computer-Aided Design (CAD). Using a computer graphics system to assist in the design of a product.

Computer-Aided Manufacturing (CAM). Using a computer system to assist in the manufacturing of a product.

Computer system. An electronic device that consists of several components that provide the capability of executing a stored program for input, output, and processing.

Concurrent processing. A software system that permits the user to switch between several tasks without leaving the current task.

Control unit. Decodes each program instruction and directs the activity of the CPU.

Control structures. The basic types of patterns used for controlling logic flow in a program. The three basic structures are sequence, selection, and iteration.

Copy protection. A hardware or software method that prohibits the user from making unauthorized copies of the software.

CP/M. Control Program for Microcomputers is an operating system developed by Digital Research Corporation for 8–bit microcomputers. CP/M–86 is the 16–bit version.

CPU. See Central Processing Unit.

CRT. See display screen.

Cursor. The flashing symbol on the display screen that shows where the next entry will be made.

Daisy wheel. An impact printer that creates a solid character by impacting the paper with the character contained on a spoked wheel. Used for letter quality printing.

Data. A collection of facts or raw material that are gathered and used for input to the computer.

Data Base Management System (DBMS). A software system for maintaining and accessing data on the computer for one or more related applications.

Database. A collection of files containing data relating to a given application with query and update capabilities.

Database administrator. A position in a company with the responsibility for designing, implementing, and maintaining the databases in a mainframe environment.

Data bus. The path through which data or instructions flow between the components of the computer.

Data dictionary. A definition of the contents of a database including file, record, and field definitions.

Data entry. The process of entering data into the computer for storage or processing.

Data flow diagram. A chart used by system analysts to document the flow of data within a system.

Data rate. The speed in bytes per second at which data is transferred to and from an I/O device.

DBMS. See Data Base Management System.

Debugging. The process of finding and correcting syntax and logic errors in a computer program.

Decision Support System (DSS). A system that provides management with information for making decisions that affect the future operation of the company.

Decision table. A table for representing the logical solution to a problem by showing decisions and related actions.

Desktop managers. A memory resident software package that provides services such as a calendar, calculator, clock, and phone dialing.

Desktop publishing. Software used to integrate text, with a variety of fonts, and graphics, including clip art, to produce a WYSIWYG document.

Device driver. Software that is used to interface an input or output device with a program. Drivers are fre-

Glossary

quently used to interface printers in word processing programs.

Directory. A list of the names of files contained on a disk. The list may also include the size, date, and time each file was created.

Diskette. See Floppy disk.

Disk Operating System (DOS). An operating system program that aids in the handling of disk and other input and output operations. See also Microsoft Disk Operating System.

Display screen. An output device composed of a cathode ray tube (CRT) that displays computer output.

DOS. See Disk Operating System.

Dot matrix. A type of impact printer that forms a character with a pattern of dots by pressing a set of wires against an ink ribbon to make the character on the page.

Downloading. The process of receiving data at the PC from a mainframe computer.

Downsizing. The process of replacing a larger computer, such as a mainframe, with a smaller computer.

EBCDIC. See Extended Binary Coded Decimal Interchange Code.

Electronic mail (E-mail). A computer network that provides for the transmission of mail electronically between subscribers to the service.

Electronic Private Branch Exchange. A private communication network that operates electronically.

EPBX. See Electronic Private Branch Exchange.

Expansion board. A circuit board that is plugged into an expansion slot to provide the computer with additional capabilities such as color graphics or the use of a mouse.

Expansion slot. Provide a space for expansion boards for adding extra features such as a mouse or modem to the computer.

Expert shell. The supporting software used for developing an expert system.

Expert system. A computer-based system that is developed with a series of rules derived from human experts.

Extended Binary Coded Decimal Interchange Code (EBCDIC). An 8-bit coding system for data representation used primarily in mainframe computer systems.

Feasibility study. A study that determines whether a system should be developed and if the necessary resources are available.

Field. An item of data such as a quantity or name. A component of a record.

File. A collection of records relating to a specific application.

File locking. A software control that prohibits a user from accessing a database when it is currently in use by another user.

File server. A central computer on a network that provides data storage and software for other computers on the network.

Fixed disk. An external storage device of large capacity consisting of a fixed magnetic platter that is rotated under a read/write head. Also called a hard disk.

Floppy disk. A removable mylar disk that stores data magnetically. Common sizes are $5\frac{1}{4}$" and $3\frac{1}{2}$".

Flowchart. A chart used to develop the logic of a computer program. See also System flowchart.

Fourth generation languages. A computer language for applications development that is essentially nonprocedural.

Function key driven. Software that primarily uses function keys to receive user commands.

Function keys. A set of ten or twelve keys, labeled F1 to F10 or F12 on the keyboard, that are assigned specific operations for the software in use.

Gantt chart. A chart used for scheduling the different phases of system design and implementation.

Garbage in–Garbage out (GIGO). An expression that suggests the output from a computer can only be as good as the input data provided.

General-purpose computers. A computer system that may be used for a variety of applications.

Goal seeking. A technique used in models and spreadsheets for determining the necessary actions required to reach a specific goal.

Graphical user interface (GUI). A system that uses icons for the selection of specific tasks rather than menus or commands.

Graphics. Software that assist in the preparation, editing, and presentation of graphic data.

Hard disk. See Fixed disk.

Hierarchical directory. See Subdirectory.

IC. See Integrated circuits.

Icon. A graphic image displayed on the screen to identify an action that may be selected by the user of the program.

Imaging. A computer-based technology that uses an image scanner to record data from forms, invoices, notes, and other documents including photographs.

Impact printer. A type of printer that forms a character by impacting an ink ribbon against the paper. Includes dot matrix, daisy wheel, and chain printers.

Indexed sequential access method (ISAM). A file access method that uses an index to provide access to any record in the file. The file may also be accessed sequentially.

Inference engine. A component of an expert system that applies the rules of the knowledge base to queries entered by the user.

Information. This is the data that has been processed and organized into a useful form.

Information system (IS). A system that collects and organizes data into a useful form.

Ink jet. A printer that forms characters by firing a jet of ink at the paper to form the character.

Input. Data that are supplied to the computer for processing or storage.

Input device. A peripheral device such as a keyboard, disk, or mouse that provides input data to the computer.

Install program. A program that is used to install software to customize it to the configuration of the computer on which it is used and to set defaults to user preferences.

Integrated circuits (IC). Silicon chips that contain a number of transistors on one chip. ICs are the foundation for microprocessor technology.

Integrated software. Software that provides a variety of applications usually including word processing, spreadsheet, database, graphics, and communications.

Interface. A port or device used to attach an input or output device to the computer.

Interpreter. A program that reads each statement in a BASIC or other source language program and translates it for computer execution.

ISAM. See Indexed sequential access method.

Job control language (JCL). Commands for use on mainframe operating systems.

Kernel. The core program in the UNIX operating system that is a common component of all implementations of the system.

Keyboard template. A plastic overlay for function keys that identifies the use of each key for a specific software package.

Knowledge-based system. A system that uses a collection of facts about an application to assist in the decision-making process. See also Expert system.

Knowledge engineer. A person with computer science or engineering background who has specialized in the field of expert or knowledge-based systems.

Knowledge engineering. The process of building a knowledge-based expert system.

LAN. See Local area network.

Laser printer. A nonimpact printer that uses laser technology to print computer output a page at a time.

License agreement. A legal contract with a software publisher giving the user the rights to install and use the software on a computer or network.

Life cycle. See Systems life cycle.

Light pen. A pen that detects light to make choices from the menu on the display screen.

Local area network (LAN). A network that links computers together for purposes of data and program sharing. Computers on a LAN are generally in close proximity to each other.

Machine language. A low-level language written in binary for direct computer execution.

Macro. A method of storing frequently used keystrokes or commands for use by a program.

Mainframe computer. A large-scale computer system capable of supporting many users with a variety of peripheral devices.

Management information system (MIS). A computer information system that is integrated with manual or automated methods of providing information for management decision making.

Megabyte. A measure of millions of bytes of storage.

Megahertz (MHz). The number of cycles per second at which the clock operates to control the speed of the computer.

Memory. A device that stores the program and the data being processed by the computer.

Memory-resident. A program that resides in memory (RAM) while other programs are active.

Menu. A list of options presented by a program from which the user makes a selection.

Menu-oriented. A software package that uses menus as the primary user interface.

Microcomputer. A small-scale computer based on the microprocessor chip. See also Personal computer.

Microprocessor. The integrated circuit or chip that contains the processor, arithmetic and logic unit, and control unit.

Microsoft Disk Operating System (MS-DOS). A disk operating system developed by Microsoft for use on microcomputers. A version is also known as PC-DOS.

Microsoft Windows. A graphical user interface software platform that works with DOS to provide the ability to work with more than one application at a time.

Minicomputer. A medium-scale computer system that usually supports multiple users.

MIS. See Management information system.

Model. A mathematical representation of a real life system.

Modem. An electronic device that converts a computer's digital signal to analog or the reverse for the purpose of data communication.

Monitor. See Display screen.

Monospace. A method of printing where each character occupies the same amount of space on the line.

Mouse. A device that moves a pointer on the screen in a direction that corresponds to the movements of the mouse on the desktop. Pressing a button on the mouse makes a selection.

MS-DOS. See Microsoft Disk Operating System.

Multimedia. Hardware and software used to present a variety of information from diverse sources such as video, sound, graphics, and text.

Multimedia system. A computer system that uses a mixture of audio and visual devices for sound, video, graphics, text, and animation.

Multiprocessing. A system that uses more than one processor to run several programs simultaneously.

Multiprogramming. A system with the ability to run more than one program concurrently.

Multitasking. An operating system that may do two or more tasks at the same time.

Multiuser. A system that permits many users to access the same database and share software resources on a central computer.

Natural language interface. A software interface that lets the user respond with English language queries.

Near-letter-quality (NLQ). A mode of operation for a dot matrix printer where printing quality approximates that of a letter quality printer.

Network. A communication system that provides for data transfer between the computers on the network.

Network topology. The type of physical organization of communication lines and devices used in a network. Three basic topologies are star, ring, and bus.

Nonimpact printer. A group of printers that forms a character without the need to impact the paper with a physical object. Includes laser and ink jet printers.

Nonprocedural language. A problem-oriented language that defines the task to be done rather than how to accomplish the task.

Object. An item such as an icon that is used to represent a task.

Object linking and embedding (OLE). A method of transferring and sharing data between applications.

Object-oriented programming. Uses objects that combine program code and data. When one object uses another, it inherits the properties of that object, reducing the need for redundant programming.

Object program. A machine language program produced as a result of compiling a source program.

On-line. A method where data is entered into the computer and processed as it is received.

Operating System. See Disk Operating System.

Organization chart. A chart that identifies the formal reporting structure of management in an organization.

OS/2. A multitasking operating system from IBM for 32–bit microprocessor-based computers.

Output. The information created as a result of computer processing.

Output device. A peripheral device such as a display screen, disk, or printer that records or shows output data from the computer.

Packet switching. A method of data communication that sends data in groups of characters called packets.

Page composition software. Software that is used in desktop publishing to compose the contents of a page by integrating text and graphics.

Parallel interface. An interface that transmits or receives one byte at a time. Printers generally use a parallel interface.

Path. A PC-DOS/MS-DOS expression that defines the subdirectory to be used in a disk operation.

PBX. See Private Branch Exchange.

PC-DOS. A version of MS-DOS used on the IBM personal computer.

Personal computer (PC). A desktop microcomputer for personal use.

Pixel. The smallest dot or point of light that can be displayed on the display screen.

Plotter. An output device that creates graphics or charts by drawing the image using a collection of colored pens.

Pop-up menu. A menu that appears somewhere in the middle of the screen.

Port. A plug or socket provided to attach input and output devices to the computer.

Presentation graphics. Software used to prepare material such as bar or line graphs, pie charts, or other information suitable for presentation as overhead transparencies, slides, or other form of figure.

Printer. An output device for producing printed output.

Private Branch Exchange (PBX). A communication system for private use within an organization.

Procedural language. Languages such as BASIC, COBOL, Pascal, and C that are coded and written as sequentially ordered statements that include decision making and looping. Procedural languages define how to accomplish a task as contrasted to nonprocedural languages.

Processor. See Central processing unit.

Productivity software. General-purpose software such as spreadsheets, word processing, database, and graphics that are suitable for a variety of applications.

Program. A set of instructions written in a language for computer use.

Program development. The process of designing, writing, debugging, testing, and implementing a computer program.

Programmer. A person who is trained in the design, coding, debugging, and testing of computer programs.

Programming. The process of writing a computer program.

Programming language. A language designed specifically for the purpose of writing computer programs.

Prompt. A question or statement from a program to which the user types a response. Can also be a symbol such as the DOS prompt (>) or the dot prompt in dBASE.

Proportional spacing. A method of printing where each character occupies a different width based on its size.

Pseudocode. Programlike statements that are written as an aid to structured program logic development.

Pull-down menus. A menu that comes down from the top of the screen.

Query. A process for making an inquiry and receiving a response from a database.

Query by example (QBE). A query that is defined by typing an example of the kind of data required in the results.

RAM disk. A part of RAM that is set aside to store data or programs from a disk file for faster access.

Random access memory (RAM). Volatile memory where a program resides during execution by the computer.

Raster graphics. See Bitmapped graphics.

Read only memory (ROM). A memory chip that stores information permanently in the computer.

Record. All of the data pertaining to a single transaction.

Relational. A data structure where the relations in the data are presented in logically related tables.

Relative addressing. A cell address in a spreadsheet such as D12 which automatically adjusts the row or column reference if the formula containing the address is moved or copied.

Relative file. A file access method that permits access to the record by its record number which corresponds to its position in the file.

Resolution. The number of pixels that can be displayed on the display screen that determines the clarity of characters or graphics on the screen.

RGB. A color display screen that receives three different signals for the red, green, and blue colors.

Rule. An IF–THEN relationship in an expert system.

Secondary storage. A storage device such as disk or tape that stores data external to the computer.

Sequential file. A file that stores its records in order from the first to the last records. Records must also be accessed in this order.

Serial interface. An interface that transmits or receives only one bit at a time. A modem generally uses a serial interface.

Shell. In general a shell is a program that passes control to other modules in a system and receives control when the module is finished. In UNIX, it is the part that communicates with the user.

Single tasking. An operating system that performs only one task at a time.

Software. A program that provides the instructions for the computer's operation.

Sort. The procedure of rearranging records or data into a predefined sequence.

Source program. The original program written in a high level language prior to compiling or interpreting.

Special-purpose computer. A computer that is designed for a specific application such as in a digital watch or microwave oven.

Spreadsheet. A program that permits the entry of data and formulas in rows and columns on the screen.

Stored program. See Program.

Structure chart. A chart that is used to develop the solution to a problem in hierarchical fashion.

Structured systems analysis. A decomposition method that analyzes the system from the general to the more detailed level of the system.

Subdirectory. A directory on fixed disk that has several branches, each of which contains files or programs.

Supercomputer. A large-scale, high-speed computer system used for scientific or other complex computing activities.

Synchronous transmission. A method of data transmission that synchronizes the data with a clock to establish the timing of sending and receiving data bits.

System. A set of organized and related procedures used to accomplish a given task.

System analysis. The process of analyzing a system to develop an understanding of it and to establish system requirements.

System analyst. A person who analyzes the needs of a system and designs and implements a new system to meet those needs.

System design. The process of designing the procedures and components of a new system.

System flowchart. A chart used to represent the flow of data in a system.

System life cycle. The five stages of development of an information system. These stages are feasibility study, system analysis, system design, program development, and implementation.

System software. General-purpose programs, such as DOS, that are used to make the computer and other software function effectively.

Terminal. An I/O device with a screen and keyboard that attaches to the computer.

Testing. Running a program with test data to ensure that it produces the correct results.

UNIX. A multiuser multitasking operating system developed by Bell Laboratories.

Uploading. The process of sending data from a PC to a mainframe computer.

User. A person who makes use of the computer hardware and software.

Utility. An operating system program that is used to perform disk maintenance or other frequently encountered activities.

Vector graphics. Creates a graphic drawing by connecting points or vectors with lines.

Video Display Terminal (VDT). See Terminal.

Virtual storage. A memory technique that uses both primary and secondary storage. Programs and data in primary storage are swapped to disk when they become inactive and are swapped back to memory when they are again needed.

Virtual Storage Access Method (VSAM). A disk access method used primarily on mainframe computers that uses an index system to both maintain and provide access to records either directly or sequentially.

Voice recognition. A computer input device that converts the human voice into equivalent digital code.

Warm start. Booting the computer by using a keystroke combination and without turning off the power.

What if question. A question asked by entering a value on the spreadsheet and observing the effect it has on other cells in the model.

Winchester disk. See Fixed disk.

Window. A window is used in a spreadsheet or other software so the user can see two or more parts of the same file or data from two or more files.

Windowing software. Software that provides the user with the ability to display several interrelated items of information in separate areas on the screen.

Word. A measure of storage consisting of a number of bits or characters.

Word processing. A program that aids in the typing, editing, and formatting of text ranging from short memos to long manuscripts.

Worksheet. See Spreadsheet.

WORM. An optical disk storage device that can be written once but read many times. Useful for backup applications.

WYSIWYG. An acronym for "what you see is what you get."

INDEX

4GL (*see* Fourth generation language)

Abacus, 406
Absolute addressing, 243
Accelerator board, 70, 74
Access arm, 96
Access methods, 111–14
Access time, 98, 102, 109
Acoustic coupler, 142
Ada, 409
Address, 42, 47, 238, 241–43
Address bus, 42
American Express, 371
American standard code for information interchange (ASCII), 38, 43, 51, 96
Ami Pro, 22, 167, 224
Analog, 140
Apple computer, 419
Apple Macintosh, 39, 47, 165, 193
Application program, 397–98
Application software, 21, 176–200
Applications programmer, 397
Arithmetic and logic unit (ALU), 16
Artificial Intelligence (AI), 178, 379
Association for Computing Professionals (ACM), 394
AT&T's StarLAN, 123, 126
AutoCAD, 269
Automated teller machine (ATM), 86–87

Babbage, Charles, 408–409
Background, 155

Backup, 102, 110
Bar code, 85, 87
Bar graph, 246
Base, 434
BASIC, 312, 315, 417
Bibliographic retrieval, 133
Binary, 37, 436–37
Bit, 37, 39
Bit mapping, 73, 263
Bit rate, 142
Bits per second (BPS), 142
Boldface, 71, 209
Boole, George, 407–408
Booting DOS, 150
Bug, 314
Bulletin Board Service (BBS), 137
Burroughs, William S., 410
Bus, 18, 42
Bus network, 124, 128–29
Business analyst, 399
Business system, 178, 332
Byte, 38, 39

Cache, 48, 104
CAD/CAM, 77, 269, 425
Campbell's Soup, 476–77
Careers, 394–400
CD-ROM, 20, 28, 94, 103–105, 268, 360, 429
Cell, 237–38
Centralized system, 10–11
Central processing unit (CPU), 16, 40
Checklist, choosing a printer, 84

Checklist, choosing a screen, 76
Circular methodology, 348
C language, 319, 322
Client/Server, 139
Clip art software, 227, 252, 260
Clock, 42, 48
CMOS RAM, 46
COBOL, 315, 414
Coding, 311–313
Cold start, 150
Color display, 68
Color graphics adapter (CGA), 69
Column, 237
Command, 189
Command processing, 152
COMMAND.COM, 152, 158
Commands (*see* DOS commands)
Communication line, 121
Communications, 27–28, 118, 133, 140, 178
Compact disk (CD) (*see* CD-ROM)
Compatible, 49–51
Compiler, 314
Composite display, 68
Compression, 104
CompuServe, 133, 135
Computer:
  buying, 422, 432
  careers, 394–400
  crime, 389–90
  defined, 6–7
  errors, 384–85
  fears, 384
  generations, 413–15
  languages, 415–18
  marketing, 399
  monitoring, 129
  operator, 395
  portable, 52
  programmer, 386, 397–98
  system, 13, 332
  use, factors to consider, 12–13
  virus, 391
Computer-aided design (CAD), 77, 269
Computer-aided manufacturing (CAM), 77, 269
Concurrent processing, 156
Context sensitive, 194
Control panel, 238
Control structures, 309
Control unit, 18
Conversion, 353–54

COPY, 153, 158
CorelDRAW, 26, 167, 260–65, 365
CPU (*see* Central Processing Unit)
Cray computer, 16
Cursor, 71, 187
Cursor keys, 182, 184
Cut and paste, 208
Cylinder, 109

Data, 8, 302, 344
Database, 24, 112, 133, 276–94
  creating, 282
  data entry, 27
  data redundancy, 289
  dBASE III Plus, 279
  dBASE IV, 179, 277, 287, 289
  DBMS, 277, 278, 289
  definition, 277
  design, 280, 348
  field types, 282
  file, 277, 293
  file locking, 293
  file manager, 277, 278
  file security, 294
  index, 285
  joining, 290
  networks, 293
  network software, 293
  normalizing, 289
  Paradox, 289, 292
  programming, 291
  query, 286–88, 292
  record, 277
  relational, 280–81, 289
  sorting, 284
  SQL, 279, 288, 292
  updating, 284
  visual database, 292
Database administrator, 281, 399
Database management system (DBMS), 24–25, 178, 277
Database design, 280, 348
Data bus, 42
Data collection, 338
Data compression, 104
Data entry, 8, 119, 277, 395
Data entry operator, 395
Data flow diagram, 339–41
Data gathering, 336–38

Index

Data Processing Management Association (DPMA), 394
Data rate, 98, 109
Data redundancy, 277, 279
Data sharing, 118, 132
dBASE III Plus, 279
dBASE IV, 25, 179, 188, 192, 277, 303
Debugging, 313
Decentralization, 12
Decimal, 434–36
Decision support system (DSS), 9, 11, 366
Decision table, 341–43
Default disk drive, 159
Default setting, 200
DEL (*see* ERASE)
Delete, 208
Demodulation, 141
Density, 99
Dependent variables, 366
Desk checking, 313
Desktop, 166
Desktop computer (*see* Personal computer)
Desktop publishing, 225–29
Device driver, 81, 199
Dialog box, 196
Difference engine, 408
Digital, 140
Digital transmission, 121
DIR, 153, 158
Direct-connect modem, 142
Directory, 159–62
Disk, 19, 95–103, 427
   access arm, 96
   access time, 98
   backup, 102
   data rate, 98
   directory, 159, 161
   fixed, 19, 99–101, 159, 427
   floppy, 19, 95, 97, 177, 427
   hard (*see* Disk, fixed)
   read/write head, 96
   rotational delay, 98
   sectors, 96
   subdirectory, 161
   tracks, 96
DISKCOMP, 158
DISKCOPY, 158
Disk Operating System (DOS), 21, 150, 176, 192
Disk Operating System/Virtual Storage (DOS/VS), 156

Display screen, 19, 67–78, 199, 227, 303, 424
Document imaging, 108
DOS commands:
   COPY, 153, 158
   DIR, 153, 158
   DISKCOPY, 158
   ERASE, 153, 158
   FORMAT, 153, 158
   RENAME, 153, 158
   TYPE, 158
   VER, 153, 158
DOS (*see* Disk operating system)
DOS prompt, 152, 158, 159
DOSSHELL, 154, 157
Dot matrix, 79–81
Dot pitch, 70
Double spacing, 212
Dow Jones News/Retrieval, 133
Downloading, 139
Downsizing, 55
Draft, 207, 209
Draw programs, 263
Driver, 81
Dynamic data exchange (DDE), 259, 320, 324

Email (*see* **Electronic mail**)
Eckert, Presper, 412–13
Economic feasibility, 333–35
Editing, 208
EDVAC, 412–13
Electronic funds transfer (EFT), 87
Electronic mail, 133, 136–37, 138
Enable, 27, 256
Enhanced graphics adaptor (EGA), 69
ENIAC, 412
Enter key, 183
ERASE, 153
Ergonomics, 426
Errors, 384
Ethernet, 123
Ethics, 21, 87, 129, 291, 393–94
Event driven, 323
Excel (*see* Microsoft Excel)
Exception report, 362
Expansion boards, 49
Expansion slots, 18
Expert shell, 379
Expert system, 370–79
   American Express, 371

Expert system (*continued*):
   applications, 370–74
   architecture, 377–78
   business, 370
   candidates for, 375
   developing an, 376
   financial planning, 373
   health related professions, 371
   languages, 379
   Mycin, 372–73
   PlanPower, 373–74
   rules, 370, 378
   Sales Edge, 371
Exporting, 258
Extended binary coded decimal interchange code (EBCDIC), 43
External commands, 158

Fax/modem, 141
Feasibility study, 332, 333–36
Field, 112, 277, 282, 302
File, 111
   conversion, 353–54
   design, 352
   locking, 293
   manager, 277–78
   security, 294
   server, 125
File allocation table (FAT), 159
File Manager, 154
File server, 125
First generation, 413, 416
Fixed disk, 19, 95, 99–101, 159, 161
Flat display, 74
Floppy disk, 19, 95, 97, 161, 177
Flowcharts, 306–309, 341
Fonts, 165, 209, 212
Footprint, 52
Forecasting report, 361
Foreground, 155
Form filling, 191
Form letter, 220
FORMAT, 153–54, 158
Formatting, 240–41
Formula, 239
FORTRAN, 318, 414
Fourth generation language (4GL), 320–22, 418
Freedom of information act, 393
Full page display, 73, 227

Function key driven software, 216
Function keys, 183, 185, 189

Gantt chart, 267, 344
Garbage in, garbage out (GIGO), 385
GEnie, 135
Gigabyte, 38
Goal seeking, 368–69, 377
Grammar checker, 222–23
Graph, 243–46
Graphical user interface (GUI), 64, 139, 165, 185, 193, 216, 259, 324
Graphics, 20, 25–26, 73–76, 213, 227
Graphics accelerator, 70, 74

Hard copy, 20, 78
Hard disk, 19, 95, 99–101, 159, 161
Hard page break, 211
Hardware, 16, 22, 413, 422
Hardware errors, 385
Harvard Presentation Graphics, 26, 167, 259
Hayes Smartmodem, 143
Help screens, 194, 198
Hexadecimal, 437–38
Hierarchical directory, 161
Hierarchy chart (*see* Structure chart)
Hollerith, Herman, 410–11
Host computer, 125

IBM, 411–12
IBM PC, 3, 39
IBM PC Net, 130
IBM PS/2, 3, 39
IBM Token Ring Network, 126, 131
Icon, 163, 165–66, 176, 193
Imaging, 108
Impact printers, 79
Implementation, 333
Importing, 258
Independent variables, 366
Index, 285
Indexed file, 285
Inference engine, 377
Information, 9, 330, 361–62
Information center, 399
Information system (IS), 9, 11, 331
   life cycle, 332–33
   department, 9, 11, 364–66

Inheritance, 323
Ink jet, 83
Input, 7
Input design, 302–303, 345–48, 352
Input device, 18–20, 62–66
Input/output management, 152
Inquiry, 118
Insert, 208
Install program, 198
Installing software, 198–200
Integrated circuits (IC), 43–45, 414
Integrated software, 26–27, 256–58
Intel, 48, 162, 418
Interface, 49, 51
Interface, user, 186
Internal commands, 158
Internet, 136
Interpreter, 314
Interview, 338
Italics, 71

JANET, 126
Join, 290

Kernel, 165
Keyboard, 19, 63, 426
Keyboard, using, 182–85
Keyboard template, 177, 185
Kilobyte, 38
Knowledge-based system, 370
Knowledge engineering, 374–75
Knowledge Worker, 6

Label, 238
LAN, 129–33, 163
Languages:
   BASIC, 312, 315, 417
   C language, 319, 322
   COBOL, 315, 414
   FORTRAN, 318, 414
   Modula-2, 319
   nonprocedural, 320–22
   Pascal, 318–19
   procedural language, 315–20
Laptop computer, 52
Laser disk, 107
Laser printer, 81–83, 228

License agreement, 387–89
Life cycle, 332
Light pen, 78
Line graph, 244
Liquid crystal display (LCD), 74
List box, 196
LISP, 379
Local area network (LAN), 28, 123, 129–33, 157, 168, 293
   bus network, 129
   cost, 130
   Ethernet, 123
   file locking, 293
   JANET, 126
   network license, 389
   Novell, 123
   passwords, 128
   PC Net, 130
   performance, 130
   reliability, 130
   security, 130, 294
   star network, 124
   StarLAN, 123
   Token Ring Network, 126, 131
   topology, 123
Local bus video, 70, 74
Lotus 1-2-3, 21, 23, 26, 187, 194, 234, 300
Lotus 1-2-3 for Windows, 167, 247
Lotus Freelance, 26, 259
Lotus Works, 256

Machine language, 416
Macintosh operating system, 156, 165
Macro, 246
Magnetic ink character reader (MICR), 89
Magnetic tape, 20, 110
Main program, 179
Mainframe computer, 10, 13, 53–55, 139, 415
Maintenance, 333, 354
Management information system (MIS), 9, 11, 139, 359–82
   business objectives, 360–61
   corporate structure, 362–63
   and decision support system, 366
   defining, 360
   information systems department, 364–66
   organization, 362
Manual, 177
Margins, 211

Marketing, 399
Mark sensing, 88
Mauchly, John, 412–13
MCI Mail, 138
Medium-scale integration (MSI), 45
Megabyte, 38
Megahertz (MHz), 42, 48
Memory, 41, 45, 53, 237, 424
   addressing, 47
   management, 152
   size, 39
Menu, 186–88, 196–97, 238
Merge, 220
Microcomputer (*see* Personal computer)
Microprocessor, 40, 43
Microsecond, 54
MicroSoft Disk Operating System (MS-DOS), 150, 155, 157–59
Microsoft Excel, 23, 167, 193, 247, 251
Microsoft Project, 365
Microsoft Windows, 21, 29, 64, 152, 165–69, 176, 195, 320
Microsoft Word, 22, 169
Microsoft Works, 27, 256
Millions of instructions per second (MIPS), 53
Millisecond, 54
Minicomputer, 13, 415
Mixed address, 243
Model, 236, 366–67
Modem, 19, 121, 141, 429
Modula-2, 319
Modulation, 141
Module, 304
Monochrome display, 67
Mouse, 19, 64, 185–86, 213, 427
MS-DOS, 150, 155, 157–59
Multi-level menus, 188
Multimedia, 28–29, 106–107, 268, 429
Multisync, 70
Multitasking, 155, 162, 164
Multiuser, 156, 164
Mycin, 372–373

Nanosecond, 54
Natural language interface, 377
NCR, 409–10
Network, 123–33 (*see also* Local area network)
Network license, 389

Network topology, 123
Node, 125
Non-impact printers, 81
Nonprocedural language, 288, 320–22
Nonprocedural query language, 321
Nonsequential file, 113
Normalizing, 289
Notebook, 52
Novell, 123
Number system conversion, 438–39
Number systems, 434–39

Object, 163
Object linking and embedding (OLE), 27, 167, 259, 320, 324
Object oriented, 163, 165
Object-oriented programming (OOP), 322–24
Object program, 314
On-line communications services, 133
On-demand report, 361
Online, 133
Operating System, 150
   classes of, 155
   command processing, 152
   functions, 151
   input/output management, 152
   memory management, 152
   multitasking, 155, 162, 164
   multiuser, 156, 164
   single tasking, 155
   utilities, 153
Operating System/2 (OS/2), 21, 48, 151, 156, 162–64
Operating System/Multiprogramming Virtual Storage (OS/MVS), 156
Operational feasibility, 333
Operator, 395–97
Optical character recognition (OCR), 87–89
Optical storage, 108
Order system, 330
Organization chart, 334
Organization structure, 364
Outline generator, 220
Output, 7
   design, 302–303, 344–45, 352
   device, 18–20, 303
Outsourcing, 335
Overlay program, 179

Page composition software, 226
Palmtop, 52
Paradox, 289, 292
Parallel operation, 354
Parallel port, 51, 78
Parent, 161
Pascal, 318–19
Pascal, Blaise, 406–407
Passwords, 128
PC Globe, 300
PC Net, 130
PC (*see* Personal computer)
PCDOS, 150, 157
   commands (*see* DOS commands)
   version, 156
Pen-based computer, 66
Pentium, 39, 48
Personal computer (PC), 3, 4, 13, 39, 50, 55–56, 139
Personal information manager (PIM), 264
Personal System/2 (PS/2), 3, 151
PERT chart, 267
PFS File, 277
Picosecond, 54
Pie graph, 246
Piracy, 386
Pixel, 67, 70, 74
PL/1, 417
PlanPower, 373–74
Plotter, 19, 83
Point of sale (POS), 85–86
Pop-up menu, 188
Port, 18, 49
Portable computers, 52
Positional notation, 435
PostScript, 82
Presentation features, 250
Presentation software, 259–60
Primary storage, 53
Primary storage section, 16
Printer, 19, 78–83, 199, 228, 428
Printing, 208–209, 215
Privacy, 390–93
Procedural language, 315–20
Process, 7
Processor, 16, 424
Prodigy, 133, 135
Productivity software, 178
Program, 20, 300 (*see also* Software)
   BASIC, 312, 315
   bug, 313
   C language, 319
   COBOL, 315
   coding, 300, 311–13, 352
   compiler, 314
   control structures, 309
   copying, 393
   debugging, 300, 313, 352
   design, 300, 304–309, 352
   development, 333, 350–51
   errors, 384
   flowcharts, 306–309
   FORTRAN, 318
   fourth generation, 320–22
   Modula-2, 319
   nonprocedural, 321
   object, 314
   object oriented, 322–24
   Pascal, 318–19
   procedural language, 315
   source, 314
   specifications, 300, 301–302, 352
   structured programs, 309
   testing, 300, 313, 352
Program Manager, 166, 195
Programmer, 20, 300, 386, 397–98
Programming, 180–82, 292, 300
Programming language, 181, 315
Project management, 267
Project schedule, 344
PROLOG, 379
Prompt, 189
Proportional spacing, 209
Prototype, 348–50
Pseudocode, 305
Pull-down menus, 188

Quattro Pro, 23, 247, 249, 365
Query, 286–88
Query by example (QBE), 287, 292
Questionnaire, 338
Quick Reference Guide, 177

Random access memory (RAM), 16, 36, 45–46, 94, 179
Range, 240
Raster graphics, 263
Read only memory (ROM), 46

Read/write head, 96
Recalling text, 208
Record, 112, 277
Reduced instruction set computer (RISC), 47–48
Redundant data, 289
Relational database, 280–81, 289
Relative addressing, 243
Relative file, 113
Removable disk, 97
RENAME, 153
Repetition structure, 310
Report design, 344
Reporting, 361–62
Reports, 344, 361–62
Resident, 176
Resolution, 70, 74
Return key, 183
Reverse video, 71
RGB, 68
Ring network, 124, 126–28
RISC computer, 47–48
Ritty, James, 409–410
Root directory, 161
Rotational delay, 98, 109
Row, 237
Rule, expert system, 370, 378

Sales Edge, 371
Saving text, 208
Scanner, 66–67
Scheduled report, 361
Screen (*see* Display screen)
Screen design, 345
Scrolling, 71
Search and replace, 209
Secondary storage, 20, 94
Second generation, 414, 417
Sector, 96
Security, 279, 390–93
Selection structure, 309
Sequence field, 112
Sequence structure, 309
Sequential file, 111
Serial port, 51, 78, 142
Shell, 154, 157, 162, 165
Single spacing, 212
Single tasking, 155
Site license, 387
Slide show, 260

Small-scale integration (SSI), 45
Smart modem, 143
Soft copy, 20
Soft page break, 211
Software, 20, 54, 186–200, 256, 413, 431
Software package, 177
Software piracy, 386–87
Software platform, 165
Sort, 284
Source program, 314
Specifications, 301
Spelling checker, 218
Spreadsheet, 22–23, 234–52, 367
   addressing, 238, 241–43
   applications, 235
   cell, 237
   choosing, 247
   features, 250
   file linking, 249
   format, 240–41
   formula, 239
   graph, 243–46
   label, 238
   Lotus 1-2-3, 23, 187, 234, 247, 300
   macros, 246
   menu, 238
   Microsoft Excel, 23
   model, 236
   range, 240
   template, 243
   three dimensional, 248
   value, 238
   voice annotation, 252
   what if questions, 236, 362, 367–68
   Windows, 23, 167, 247
Stacked bar graph, 246
StarLAN, 123, 126
Star network, 124–26
Status line, 211, 238
Storage, 94
Stored program, 412
Structure chart, 304
Structured programming, 309–11
Structured Query Language (SQL), 288, 292, 322
Structured systems analysis, 341
Subdirectory, 161
Supercomputer, 16
Superlarge-scale integration (SLSI), 45
SuperVGA, 70, 72, 74, 226
Symbolic language, 416

Index

System, 11, 330, 332–358
   analysis, 332, 336–44
   analyst, 332, 398
   business system, 332
   computer system, 332
   conversion, 353–54
   definition, 333–35
   design, 333, 344–50
   economic feasibility, 333
   feasibility, 332–36
   flowchart, 341
   implementation, 333
   life cycle, 332
   maintenance, 333
   outsourcing, 335
   packaged, 331
   programmer, 397
   prototype, 348–50
   software, 21
   structured systems, 341
System unit, 423–24

Tab setting, 212, 215
Tape (*see* Magnetic tape)
Tape backup system, 110
Technical feasibility, 333
Telecommunications, 140–143 (*see also* Communications)
Template, 177, 185, 242
Terabyte, 38
Terminal, 62
Testing, 313
Text box, 196
Text entry, 208
Thesaurus, 219
Third generation, 414, 417
Three-dimensional spreadsheets, 248–50
Token passing, 131
Token Ring Network, 126, 131, 294
Topology (*see* Network topology)
Touch screen, 76
Track, 96
Training, 352–53
True type fonts, 165
Turing test, 374

Undelete, 157
Underlining, 71, 209

Unemployment, 385
Unformat, 157
UNIVAC, 412, 416
Universal product code (UPC), 86
UNIX, 155, 164–65, 319
Updating, 284
Uploading, 139
User friendly, 321, 418
User interface, 186
Utilities, 153

Vaccine program, 391
Validation, 347
Value, 238
Vector graphics, 263
Ventura, 225
VER, 153, 158
Very large scale integration (VLSI), 45
Video display terminal (VDT), 156
Video graphics adaptor (VGA), 69, 72, 226
Videotext, 133
Virus, 391
VisiCalc, 234, 300
Visual database, 292
Voice annotation, 252
Voice reader, 20
Voice recognition, 20, 65
Volatile RAM, 46
von Neumann, John, 412

Wand reader, 86
Warm start, 150
Warranty Card, 177
Watson, Thomas, 411–12
"What if" questions, 236–37, 362, 367–68
Wide area network (WAN), 130, 132
Window, 166, 214, 248
Windows (*see* Microsoft Windows)
Windows applications, 166–67, 169
Windows interfaces, 195–98
Windows/NT, 48, 151, 156, 168
Word, 40
Word processing, 22, 206–29
   Ami Pro, 22, 167, 224
   choosing, 216
   cut and paste, 208
   editing, 208
   features, 212, 217

Word processing (*continued*):
  grammar checker, 222
  language, 209–16
  merge, 220
  Microsoft Word, 22, 169
  outliner, 220
  print formatting, 209
  printing, 208–209
  saving and recalling, 208
  spelling checker, 218
  stages, 206–209
  text entry, 208
  thesaurus, 219
  Windows, 213, 218, 224–25
  WordPerfect, 211
  WYSIWYG, 22, 216, 224–25
Word wrap, 211
WordPerfect, 22, 81, 159, 186, 211, 216
WordPerfect for Windows, 167, 193, 213–15, 365
Write-protect, 97
WYSIWYG, 22, 216, 224–25

XY graph, 246